SRA Real Math

Stephen S. Willoughby
•
Carl Bereiter
•
Peter Hilton
•
Joseph H. Rubinstein
•
Joan Moss
•
Jean Pedersen

SRA

Columbus, OH

The McGraw-Hill Companies

Authors

Stephen S. Willoughby
Professor Emeritus of Mathematics
University of Arizona
Tucson, AZ

Carl Bereiter
Professor Emeritus
Centre for Applied Cognitive Science
Ontario Institute for Studies in Education
University of Toronto, Canada

Peter Hilton
Distinguished Professor of
Mathematics Emeritus
State University of New York
Binghamton, NY

Joseph H. Rubinstein
Professor of Education
Coker College, SC
Hartsville, SC

Joan Moss
Assistant Professor, Department of Human
Development and Applied Psychology
Ontario Institute for Studies in Education
University of Toronto, Canada

Jean Pedersen
Professor, Department of
Mathematics and Computer Science
Santa Clara University, Santa Clara, CA

PreKindergarten and Building Blocks Authors

Douglas H. Clements
Professor of Early Childhood and Mathematics Education
University at Buffalo
State University of New York, NY

Julie Sarama
Associate Professor of Mathematics Education
University at Buffalo
State University of New York, NY

Contributing Authors

Hortensia Soto-Johnson
Assistant Professor of Mathematics
University of Northern Colorado, CO

Erika Walker
Assistant Professor of Mathematics and Education
Teachers College, Columbia University, NY

Research Consultants

Jeremy Kilpatrick
Regents Professor of Mathematics Education
University of Georgia, GA

Alfinio Flores
Professor of Mathematics Education
Arizona State University, AZ

Gilbert J. Cuevas
Professor of Mathematics Education
University of Miami, Coral Gables, FL

Contributing Writers

Holly MacLean, Ed.D., Supervisor Principal, Treasure Valley Mathematics and Science Center, Boise, ID
Edward Manfre, Mathematics Education Consultant, Albuquerque, NM
Elizabeth Jimenez, English Language Learner Consultant, Pomona, CA
Kim L. Pettig, Ed.D., Instructional Challenge Coordinator Pittsford Central School District, Pittsford, NY
Rosemary Tolliver, M.Ed., Gifted Coordinator/Curriculum Director, Columbus, OH

National Advisory Board

Justin Anderson, Teacher, Robey Elementary School, Indianapolis, IN
David S. Bradley, Administrator, Granite, UT
Donna M. Bradley, Head of the Lower School, St. Marks Episcopal Palm Beach Gardens, FL
Grace Dublin, Teacher, Laurelhurst Elementary, Seattle, WA
Leisha W. Fordham, Teacher, Bolton Academy, Atlanta, GA
Ebony Frierson, Teacher, Eastminister Day School, Columbia, SC
Flavia Gunter, Teacher, Morningside Elementary School, Atlanta, GA
Audrey Marie Jacobs, Teacher, Lewis & Clark Elementary, St. Louis, MO
Florencetine Jasmin, Elementary Math Curriculum Specialist, Baltimore, MD
Kim Leitzke, Teacher, Clara Barton Elementary School, Milwaukee, WI
Nick Restivo, Principal, Long Beach High School, Long Island, NY

SRAonline.com

Mc Graw Hill SRA

Printed in the United States of America.

Send all inquiries to:
SRA/McGraw-Hill
8787 Orion Place
Columbus, OH 43240-4027

ISBN 0-07-602999-9

2 3 4 5 6 7 8 9 VHJ 12 11 10 09 08 07 06

The McGraw·Hill Companies

Number Concepts

CHAPTER 1

Exploring Problem Solving Theme: Teamwork—Doing Things Together

CHAPTER 2

Multidigit Addition and Subtraction

Exploring Problem Solving Theme: Tree Houses

Measuring and Graphing

CHAPTER 3

Exploring Problem Solving Theme: Urban Gardens

CHAPTER 4

Multiplication Concepts

Multiplication and Division Facts

CHAPTER 5

Exploring Problem Solving Theme: Arts and Crafts

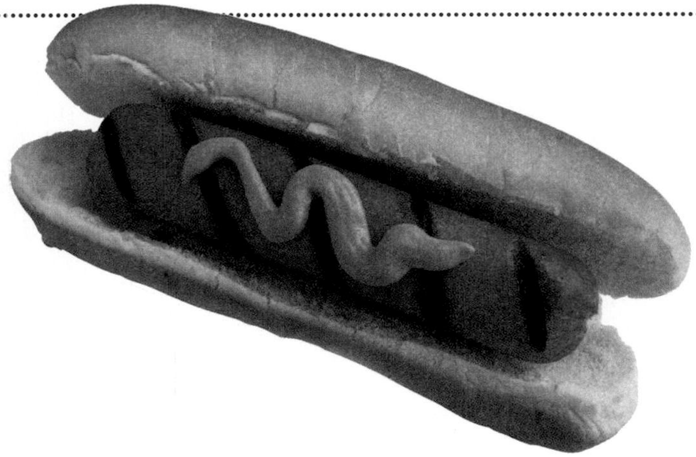

CHAPTER 6

Functions

Exploring Problem Solving Theme: Playgrounds— Real and Imaginary

Multidigit Multiplication and Division

CHAPTER 7

Exploring Problem Solving Theme: Banks and Money Machines

CHAPTER 8

Fractions

Exploring Problem Solving Theme: Advertising

Measurement

CHAPTER 9

CHAPTER 10 Decimals

Exploring Problem Solving Theme: Totem Poles and Other Monuments

Exploring Problem Solving Theme: Homes

CHAPTER 12 Data Analysis and Probability

Exploring Problem Solving Theme: Farms

Dear Student,

You will find a lot of things in this ***Real Math*** book.

You will find games that will give you a chance to practice and put to use many of the skills you will be learning.

You will find stories and examples that will show you how mathematics can help you solve problems and cut down the amount of work you have to do.

You will be reading and talking about many of the pages with your classmates. That is because mathematics is something people often learn together and do together.

Of course, this book is not all fun and games. Learning should be enjoyable, but it also takes time and effort. Most of all, it takes thinking.

We hope you enjoy this book. We hope you learn a lot. And we hope you think a lot.

The Authors of ***Real Math***

CHAPTER 1

Number Concepts

In This Chapter You Will Learn

- how to count, estimate, round, add, and subtract numbers.
- how to compare numbers using relation signs.
- how to use function machines.

Problem Solving

Try to find all the numbers in the picture. List each number you find and write where you found it.

Use the picture to talk about these questions.

1. Where do you see numbers in the picture?
2. What does each number tell you?
3. How do you know you found all the numbers?

LESSON 1.1 Counting and Estimating

Key Ideas

When you count objects, you determine an exact number.

When you estimate, you determine a number that is not exact. Sometimes an exact number is important. At other times an estimate can be used.

Find **the numbers that are written twice, and write them on your paper. Notice that the numbers are not written in order.**

1. Start counting from 8.
   8 12 10 11 9 16 14 18 11 13 15 17 13
2. Start counting from 47.
   49 51 47 52 56 55 50 53 57 48 50 52 54
3. Start counting from 96.
   105 97 102 96 101 106 99 103 100 104 99 106 98
4. Start counting from 379.
   387 381 388 382 386 379 383 385 380 383 382 384
5. Start counting from 212.
   212 216 214 215 213 220 218 222 215 217 219 221 218
6. Start counting from 77.
   79 81 77 82 86 85 80 83 87 78 80 82 84
7. Start counting from 32.
   35 43 32 40 33 38 34 41 38 36 39 42 37 35
8. Jana was saving 3 pennies a day in a glass jar. On September 5, she had 297 pennies. How many will she have on September 12?

This is a very crowded aquarium. Estimate how many fish are in it. Then count the fish in the aquarium.

9 My estimate is that there are about ▢ fish in the aquarium.

10 The actual number of fish in the aquarium is ▢.

Writing + Math **Journal**

Explain the strategy you used to estimate and to count the number of fish in the aquarium.

LESSON 1.2 Review of Addition and Subtraction Facts

Key Ideas

If you know one addition fact, you should know three other related facts. If you know $5 + 3 = 8$, then you also know the addition fact $3 + 5 = 8$, and the two subtraction facts $8 - 3 = 5$ and $8 - 5 = 3$.

These four statements form a fact family.

$5 + 3 = 8$ $\quad 3 + 5 = 8$ $\quad 8 - 3 = 5$ $\quad 8 - 5 = 3$

Give the sums and differences.

1. $7 + 6 = \square$
   $6 + 7 = \square$
   $13 - 7 = \square$
   $13 - 6 = \square$
2. $6 + 2 = \square$
   $8 - 6 = \square$
   $8 - 2 = \square$
   $2 + 6 = \square$
3. $15 - 7 = \square$
   $7 + 8 = \square$
   $15 - 8 = \square$
   $8 + 7 = \square$
4. $18 - 10 = \square$
   $10 + 8 = \square$
   $8 + 10 = \square$
   $18 - 8 = \square$

Copy each addition or subtraction fact, and complete each fact family. Then give the sums and differences.

5. $7 + 5 = \square$
   $5 + 7 = \square$
6. $13 - 8 = \square$
7. $5 + 6 = \square$
8. $18 - 9 = \square$ Be careful.

Addition and Strategies Practice

Roll a 15 Game

Players: Two or three

Materials: ***Number Cubes:*** two 0–5, two 5–10

Object: To get the sum closer to 15

Math Focus: Addition, mathematical reasoning, and probability

HOW TO PLAY

1. Roll one ***Number Cube*** at a time.
2. Add the numbers as you roll.
3. Stop after one, two, three, or four rolls.
4. The score closest to 15, either greater than or less than 15, wins.

If you rolled	The sum would be
7 and 1 and 4 and 7	19
8 and 5	13
4 and 4 and 8	16
9 and 3 and 3	15
5 and 10	15

Writing + Math **Journal**

Imagine that you have rolled a 9 and a 4. Tell what you would do on your next turn. Would you roll a cube? If so, which cube would you roll and why?

LESSON 1.3 Basic Facts and Missing Terms

Key Ideas

Knowing addition and subtraction facts helps you solve missing-term problems.

Keisha knows that Audrey has a 3 on her back. Keisha doesn't know what number is on her own back, but she knows that the sum of both numbers is 8. Keisha thinks

$3 + \square = 8$ and

$3 + 5 = 8.$

So Keisha knows she has a 5 on her back.

Find the missing terms. **Algebra**

1. $4 + \square = 9$
2. $14 - \square = 4$
3. $\square + 5 = 9$
4. $\square - 3 = 10$
5. $8 + \square = 15$
6. $18 - \square = 8$
7. $9 + \square = 15$
8. $\square - 7 = 6$
9. $4 + \square = 11$
10. $\square + 8 = 11$
11. $\square - 4 = 4$
12. $7 - \square = 3$

13. Judy rode her bicycle 8 miles from home to Irvin's house. Then she rode 3 miles toward home. How far is she from home?

14. Mark had \$13. He spent some of his money. Now he has \$5 left. How much did Mark spend?

eTextbook This lesson is available in the ***eTextbook.***

Match **each word problem with a correct math sentence. Then solve the problem.**

15. Before his birthday Indigo had 7 video games. After his birthday he had 12. How many video games did Indigo get for his birthday?

16. There were 19 toy horses on Iris's shelf in her bedroom. After giving her cousin all of the white horses, she has 10 horses left. How many horses did Iris give her cousin?

17. Kymani found 5¢ under her bed. She found 9¢ in the bottom of her dresser drawer. How much money did Kymani find altogether?

18. Tristan took 12 plastic dragons to the park. When he got home, he counted only 8. How many dragons did Tristan leave at the park?

19. Sachi has lost all 13 of her favorite pens. When cleaning her bedroom, Sachi found 3 of these pens. How many more of these pens must Sachi try to find?

20. On Deandre's desk there are 5 math books. Stephanie has 1 more math book on her desk than Deandre has. How many math books are on Stephanie's desk?

a. $5 - 1 = \square$	**b.** $19 + 10 = \square$	**c.** $13 + 3 = \square$	**d.** $7 + \square = 12$
e. $5 + 9 = \square$	**f.** $3 + \square = 13$	**g.** $19 - \square = 10$	**h.** $12 - \square = 8$
i. $9 - 5 = \square$	**j.** $5 + 1 = \square$	**k.** $7 + 12 = \square$	**l.** $12 + 8 = \square$

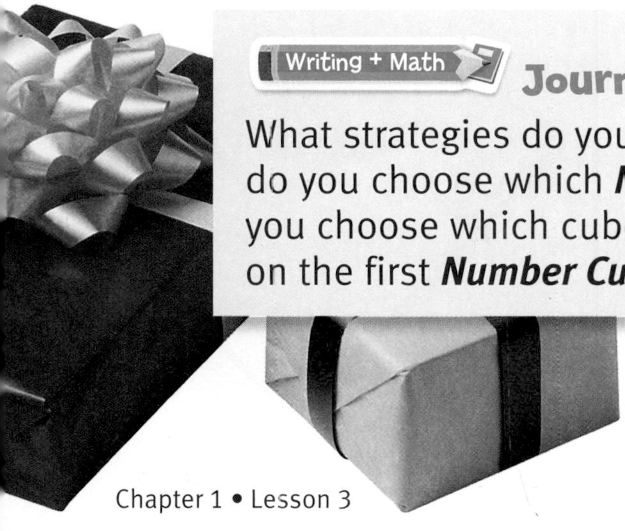

Writing + Math

Journal

What strategies do you use for the **Roll a 15 Game?** How do you choose which ***Number Cube*** to roll first? How do you choose which cube to roll second? Does the number on the first ***Number Cube*** influence your second choice?

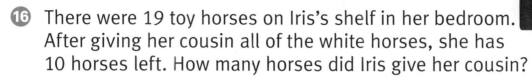

LESSON 1.4 Equalities and Inequalities

Key Ideas

The symbols <, =, and > can be used to show the relationship between two numbers.

The symbol < means "is less than."

To show that 27 is less than 30, write 27 < 30.

The symbol = means "is equal to."

To show that 27 + 3 is equal to 20 + 10, write 27 + 3 = 20 + 10.

The symbol > means "is greater than."

To show that 30 is greater than 27, write 30 > 27.

Write each statement with the correct sign. Use <, =, or >.

1. 8 ☐ 11
2. 752 ☐ 752
3. 612 ☐ 613
4. 2,001 ☐ 2,010
5. 5,738 ☐ 5,738
6. 830 ☐ 803
7. 483 ☐ 438
8. 5,341 ☐ 2,376
9. 1,000 ☐ 100
10. 345 ☐ 543
11. 8,209 ☐ 8,209
12. 222 ☐ 1,110
13. 1,764 ☐ 1,734
14. 921 ☐ 899
15. 6,015 ☐ 6,020
16. 696 ☐ 701

You can approximate a sum or a difference. You do this without actually adding or subtracting.

Which sign shows the relationship between the following expressions?

377 + 50 □ 376 + 45

Because 377 is greater than 376 and 50 is greater than 45, the sum on the left must be greater.

377 + 50 > 376 + 45

Use <, =, or > to make the statement correct.

17. 246 + 40 □ 546 + 140
18. 3 + 82 □ 2 + 83
19. 3,000 + 2,000 □ 3,001 + 2,001
20. 12 − 3 □ 14 − 1
21. 102 + 86 □ 586 + 240
22. 8 + 43 □ 43 + 8
23. 100 − 7 □ 200 − 7
24. 21 − 8 □ 28 − 1
25. 43 − 0 □ 53 − 10
26. 157 + 861 □ 57 + 61
27. 7 + 43 □ 43 + 72
28. 1,000 − 2 □ 1,000 − 43
29. 18 − 9 □ 19 − 10
30. 156 − 56 □ 166 − 66
31. 126 − 100 □ 126 − 10
32. 34 + 27 □ 27 + 34
33. 720 − 39 □ 720 − 49
34. 4,259 + 675 □ 4,259 + 575
35. 116 + 49 □ 47 + 116
36. 1,085 + 200 □ 1,085 + 202

Writing + Math **Journal**

Write two problems like the ones on this page, and then explain how you can insert the correct sign without actually doing the arithmetic.

LESSON 1.5 Simple Function Machines

Key Ideas

A function machine carries out the same operation on every number put into it.

You can use a function machine to show how things are related.
Example: John is 4 years older than his brother Zack.
When Zack was 2, John was 6.
When Zack was 3, John was 7.
When Zack is 6, John will be 10.

in → +4 → out

in	out
3	7
6	10
2	6
7	11

Copy each table. Find the *in values* or the *out values*. **Algebra**

1. in → +5 → out

in	out
3	8
4	■
5	10
6	■
7	■

2. in → −2 → out

in	out
6	4
7	■
10	■
4	2
2	■

3. in → +6 → out

in	out
3	■
■	6
5	■
■	10
4	■

4. in → +7 → out

in	out
■	8
■	10
■	12
■	14
■	16

5. in → −4 → out

in	out
5	■
10	■
16	■
■	10
■	16

6. in → +2 → out

in	out
3	5
■	11
5	7
7	■
■	15

eTextbook This lesson is available in the *eTextbook.*

Find the *in values,* the *out values,* or the *rule.*

7 in —(−6)→ out

in	out
10	▢
9	▢
8	▢
7	▢
6	▢

8 in —(+7)→ out

in	out
6	▢
7	▢
8	▢
9	▢
10	▢

9 in —(−10)→ out

in	out
20	▢
19	▢
18	▢
17	▢
16	▢

10 in —(◯)→ out

in	out
5	13
7	▢
10	▢
▢	12
7	15

11 in —(◯)→ out

in	out
1	10
3	▢
5	▢
9	18
▢	19

12 in —(◯)→ out

in	out
▢	7
▢	6
▢	5
7	4
6	3

13 in —(◯)→ out

in	out
18	9
17	8
▢	7
▢	6
▢	5

14 in —(−5)→ out

in	out
6	▢
▢	7
8	▢
▢	9
10	▢

15 in —(◯)→ out

in	out
2	5
4	7
6	▢
8	▢
10	▢

Writing + Math 📝 **Journal**

Draw two function tables without the rule, and then challenge your classmates to find the function rules.

Object: Work as a team to get your robot back to the spaceship.

1. Each player draws a card and will have to move the robot forward or backward the number of spaces shown on the card.
2. Players decide together how each of them should move so the robot ends up on the spaceship.

How can the team get the robot back to the spaceship on this turn?

Lisa's group is using a model and making a table to solve the problem.

Moves	Does robot land on spaceship?
→5 →8 →3 →4	No
→5 →8 →3 ←4	No
→5 →8 ←3 ←4	

1. What are the students in Lisa's group doing?
2. What do the arrows stand for in the table?
3. How would Lisa show a move of backward 5?
4. What are the students recording in each column of the table?
5. What will Lisa write next?
6. Do you think this strategy will work? Why or why not?

Raphael's group is breaking the problem into smaller parts to solve it.

7. What did Raphael's group realize about everyone moving forward?
8. How is Raphael's group going to break up the problem?
9. Why do you think Raphael's group is using this strategy?
10. Work with your group to solve the problem. Use any strategy you like.

Cumulative Review

Odds and Evens **Grade 2 Lesson 1.2**

Write whether the number is even or odd. Write how many sticks would be in each pile if split evenly.

1. 15   2. 10   3. 4   4. 9   5. 25

Using Multiple Addends **Grade 2 Lesson 2.7**

Add.

6. $2 + 0 + 8 = \square$
7. $4 + 4 + 4 = \square$
8. $3 + 0 + 9 + 5 = \square$
9. $7 + 5 + 6 = \square$
10. $1 + 3 + 4 + 6 = \square$

Applications of Addition and Subtraction **Grade 2 Lesson 3.6**

Solve.

Extended Response Jordan had \$20. He bought a music CD and now has \$8.

11. How much did the CD cost?
12. Could he have a \$5 bill? Explain.
13. Could he have a \$10 bill? Explain.

Simple Function Machines **Lesson 1.5**

Find the *in values* or the *out values.*

14.

in	−8 → *out*
16	8
14	▢
12	4
10	▢
8	▢

15.

in	+10 → *out*
▢	20
▢	35
▢	30
▢	35
▢	40

Missing Addends and Subtraction **Grade 2 Lesson 3.1**

Solve for each missing term.

16. $6 + \square = 12$
17. $\square + 6 = 8$
18. $8 + \square = 11$
19. $6 - \square = 2$

Vertical Bar Graphs **Grade 2 Lesson 4.10**

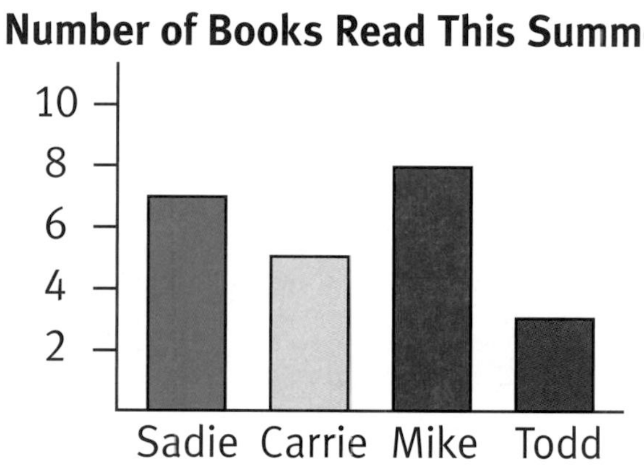

Use the bar graph above to answer these questions.

20. Who has read the most books? How many?
21. How many books has Carrie read?
22. How many more books did Sadie read than Todd?
23. How many more books did Mike read than Todd?
24. How many books did Sadie, Carrie, Mike, and Todd read altogether?

LESSON 1.6

Place Value

Key Ideas

Place value refers to the value of a digit based on where it is located in a number.

The table shows the number of hundred thousands, ten thousands, one thousands, hundreds, tens, and ones in each number. **Write** each number on your paper.

	Hundred thousands	Ten thousands	One thousands	Hundreds	Tens	Ones
1	0	7	5	4	5	3
2	0	0	4	0	4	7
3	9	6	5	4	0	3
4	0	0	0	1	0	0
5	0	4	1	2	3	4
6	1	0	0	0	0	1

7. In the number 1,234, what does the 2 stand for? What does the 3 stand for? Which of the digits, 1, 2, 3, or 4, stands for the greatest number?

8. In the number 14,498, how many ten thousands are there? How many thousands are there? How many hundreds are there? How many tens are there? How many ones are there?

9. In the number 2,001, what do the 0s stand for?

10. In the number 201,001, what does the 2 stand for? In which number does the 2 stand for a greater number, 20,001, or 2,100?

11. In the number 444,444, which digit in which place stands for the least number?

eTextbook This lesson is available in the ***eTextbook***.

Write each number in expanded form. The first one has been done for you.

12. 48,901 = 40,000 + 8,000 + 900 + 0 + 1
13. 34,585
14. 675,024
15. 987,110
16. 210,020

Solve.

17. Use the digits 2, 4, and 6 once. What is the greatest number you can make?
18. Use the digits 2, 4, and 6 once. What is the least number you can make?
19. Are there any other three-digit numbers you can make using 2, 4, and 6 once? How many can you make altogether? Write them all on your paper. Include the numbers you showed for Questions 17 and 18.
20. How many four-digit numbers can you make using each of the digits 9, 8, 7, and 6 once? Write them. Which is greatest? Which is least?

Writing + Math **Journal**

When writing the number 302, why do we need the digit 0? Could we just leave the tens column blank?

LESSON 1.7 Numbers to 10,000

Key Ideas

Our base-ten system makes counting and writing numbers easy.

2,141 =

One way to read this number is to say *two thousands, one hundred, four tens, and one.*

A shorter way to read it is to say *two thousand one hundred forty-one.*

If you counted on from 2,141, you would write 2,142; 2,143; 2,144; 2,145; and so on.

If you counted back from 2,141, you would write 2,140; 2,139; 2,138; 2,137; and so on.

Fill in the missing numbers.

Count on.

1. 454, 455, ___, ___, 458, 459, ___, 461
2. 7,364; ___; 7,366; ___; 7,368; ___; ___; 7,371
3. ___; 8,000; ___; 8,002; 8,003; ___; ___; 8,006
4. 4,567; ___; ___; 4,570; 4,571; ___; ___; 4,574

Count back.

5. 7,865; 7,864; ___; 7,862; ___; ___; 7,859; 7,858
6. 5,643; ___; ___; 5,640; 5,639; ___; ___; 5,636
7. 7,001 ___; ___; 6,998; ___; ___; ___; 6,994
8. 8,701; ___; ___; ___; 8,697; ___; ___; 8,694

Savannah, Diego, Andie, Maggie, Bryce, and Ling wanted to find out who could run the farthest in 15 minutes. They ran on a track that was 1,000 meters around. Each meter was marked on the track so they could tell how far they had run.

9 Savannah ran around the track 4 times plus another 535 meters. How far was that?

Copy and complete the table to show how far each student ran.

	Student	Distance (in meters)
	Savannah	4,535
10	Diego	■
11	Andie	■
12	Maggie	■
13	Bryce	■
14	Ling	■

- Diego ran around the track 3 times and another 987 meters.
- Andie ran around the track 5 times and another 48 meters.
- Maggie ran around the track 4 times and another 535 meters.
- Bryce ran around the track 4 times and another 378 meters.
- Ling ran around the track 4 times and another 783 meters.

15 Who ran the longest distance?

16 Who ran the shortest distance?

17 Did any runners run the same distance? If so, who?

18 Which relation sign shows the relationship between these two numbers?
4,378 ■ 4,783

19 **Extended Response** How can you recognize an even number?

20 **Extended Response** Can you express an odd number as a sum of two equal whole numbers?

LESSON 1.8 Rounding

Key Ideas

Sometimes an estimate is more appropriate than an exact answer.

At those times a procedure called rounding may be of some help.

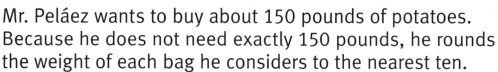

Mr. Peláez wants to buy about 150 pounds of potatoes. Because he does not need exactly 150 pounds, he rounds the weight of each bag he considers to the nearest ten.

- 29 is closer to 30 than to 20, so he rounds up to 30, or 3 tens.
- 37 is closer to 40 than to 30, so he rounds up to 40.
- 42 is closer to 40 than to 50, so he rounds down to 40.
- 43 is closer to 40 than to 50, so he rounds down to 40.
- 46 is closer to 50 than to 40, so he rounds up to 50.

Mr. Peláez chooses to buy three of the bags that weigh about 40 pounds and the bag that weighs about 30 pounds because $40 + 40 + 40 + 30 = 150$.

Mr. García owns the potato market. He wishes to charge Mr. Peláez 10¢ for each pound of potatoes he has bought. So Mr. García needs to know the exact weight of the potatoes.

He adds the following numbers:

29 + 37 + 42 + 43 = 151

So Mr. García charges for 151 pounds of potatoes.

Round **to the nearest ten.**

1. 36
2. 38
3. 73
4. 61
5. 87

When working with greater numbers, we sometimes wish to round to the nearest hundred.

Thus, 360 would round to 400, but 330 would round to 300.

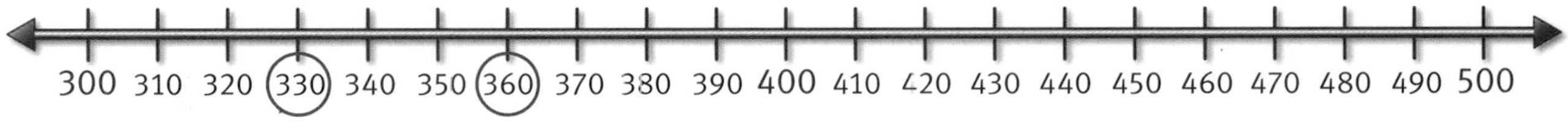

Round **to the nearest ten. Then round to the nearest hundred from the original number.**

6. 346
7. 751
8. 923
9. 118
10. 687

When working with very large numbers, we sometimes wish to round to the nearest thousand.

Thus, 3,650 would round to 4,000, but 3,350 would round to 3,000.

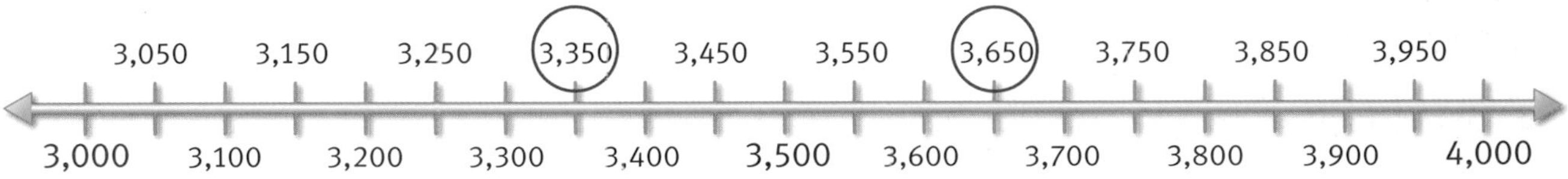

Round **to the nearest thousand.**

11. 2,440
12. 6,660
13. 9,459
14. 1,781
15. 8,555

16. **Extended Response** Jackson has $10. He wants to buy an action figure for $7.19 and a birthday card for $2.95. The tax that will be added to his purchase is 70¢. Explain how Jackson can round numbers to find out if he has enough money to make the purchase.

LESSON 1.9

Counting Beyond One Million

Key Ideas

No matter how great or small a number is, our base-ten system allows us to write it and understand it.

In the 2000 census, the population of the United States was 281,421,906. We read this number as *two hundred eighty-one million four hundred twenty-one thousand nine hundred six.* SOCIAL STUDIES

1. **Extended Response** Do you think the population was actually 281,421,906 when the census was taken? Why or why not?

The numbers below are given in standard form. Write each number in expanded form. Then write how to read the number. The first one has been done for you.

2. 622 = 600 + 20 + 2; six hundred twenty-two
3. 87
4. 1,681
5. 43,760
6. 245,977
7. 1,110,751
8. 6,538,200

e Textbook This lesson is available in the ***eTextbook.***

In Centimeter City all distances are measured and reported in centimeters. Use the map of Centimeter City to answer the questions.

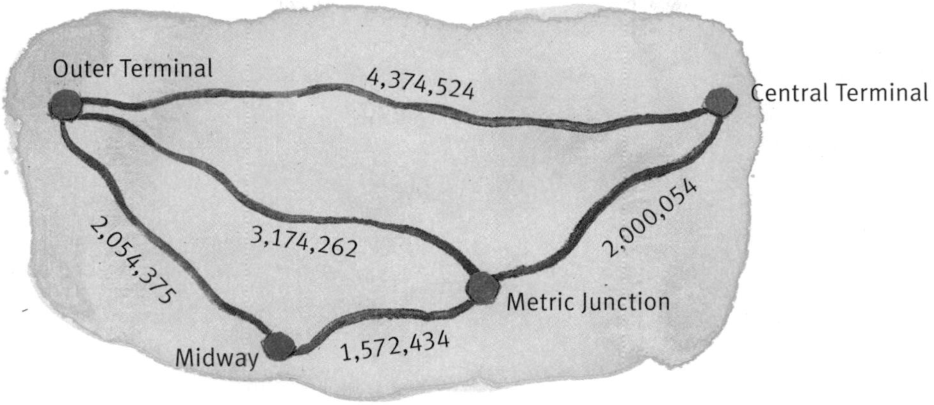

For each trip in Centimeter City, three distances are given. Pick the distance that is closest to the actual distance.

9. Outer Terminal to Metric Junction to Central Terminal
   - **a.** 5,000,000 centimeters
   - **b.** 5,500,000 centimeters
   - **c.** 6,000,000 centimeters

10. Midway to Metric Junction to Central Terminal
    - **a.** 3,000,000 centimeters
    - **b.** 3,500,000 centimeters
    - **c.** 4,000,000 centimeters

11. Outer Terminal to Midway and return to Outer Terminal
    - **a.** 3,000,000 centimeters
    - **b.** 3,500,000 centimeters
    - **c.** 4,000,000 centimeters

12. Midway to Metric Junction to Outer Terminal to Central Terminal
    - **a.** 90,000 centimeters
    - **b.** 9,000,000 centimeters
    - **c.** 7,000,000 centimeters

Writing + Math **Journal**

The mayor of Centimeter City suggested changing the name to Kilometer City. Why might he have suggested that?

Read and think about the problem.

The students at Golden Eagle Elementary School wanted to work together to raise money for a charity. They decided to collect one million pennies. The custodian said they could keep the pennies in an empty storage room if the pennies will fit.

Will one million pennies fit in the room?

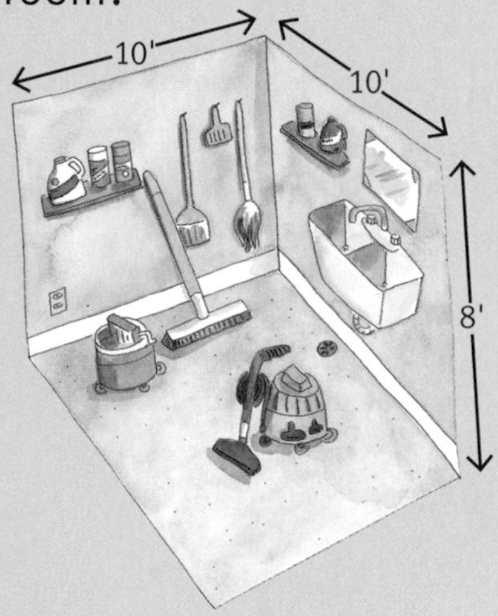

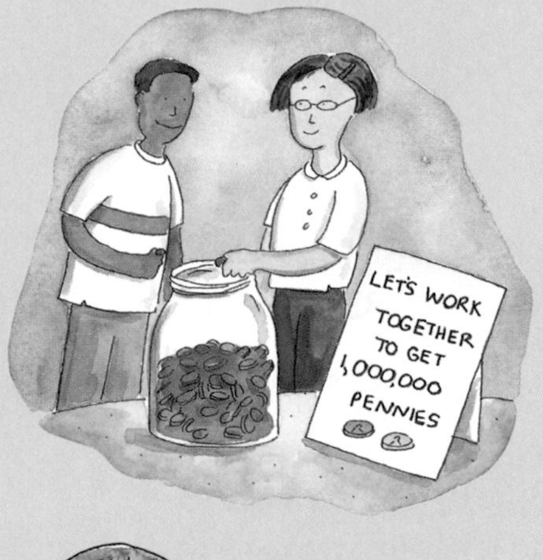

LET'S WORK TOGETHER TO GET 1,000,000 PENNIES

Think about and discuss the following questions.

1. How can you arrange the pennies to make them easier to count?
2. How will you know when you have one million?
3. How can you estimate how much space one million pennies will take up?
4. Is the storage room larger or smaller than our classroom?

Work in groups to decide if one million pennies will fit in the storage room. Show how you know.

Cumulative Review

Place Value **Lesson 1.6**

Identify the place value of each digit.

1. In 562
   How many hundreds? ▢
   How many tens? ▢
   How many ones? ▢

2. In 5,217
   How many thousands? ▢
   How many hundreds? ▢
   How many tens? ▢
   How many ones? ▢

3. In 10,784
   How many ten thousands? ▢
   How many thousands? ▢
   How many hundreds? ▢
   How many tens? ▢
   How many ones? ▢

4. In 951,320
   How many hundred thousands? ▢
   How many ten thousands? ▢
   How many thousands? ▢
   How many hundreds? ▢
   How many tens? ▢
   How many ones? ▢

Equalities and Inequalities **Lesson 1.4**

Use the sign $<$, $=$, or $>$ to make each statement correct.

5. 468 ▢ 486
6. 129 ▢ 126
7. 19 ▢ 21
8. 350 − 50 ▢ 450 − 50
9. 326 + 25 ▢ 226 + 150
10. 1,825 + 1,800 ▢ 1,825 + 1,900
11. 406 + 32 ▢ 23 + 406
12. 436 − 100 ▢ 436 − 10
13. 7,222 ▢ 7,722
14. 120 − 20 ▢ 110 − 10
15. 38 − 19 ▢ 48 − 29

Cumulative Review

Multiplication and Arrays **Grade 2 Lesson 11.3**

Use these pictures to solve the problems.

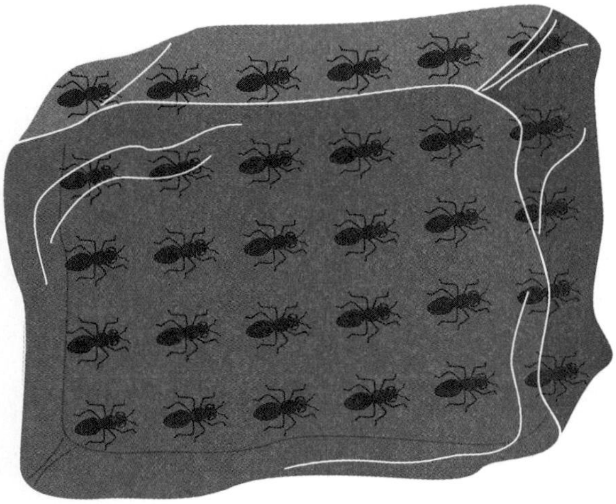

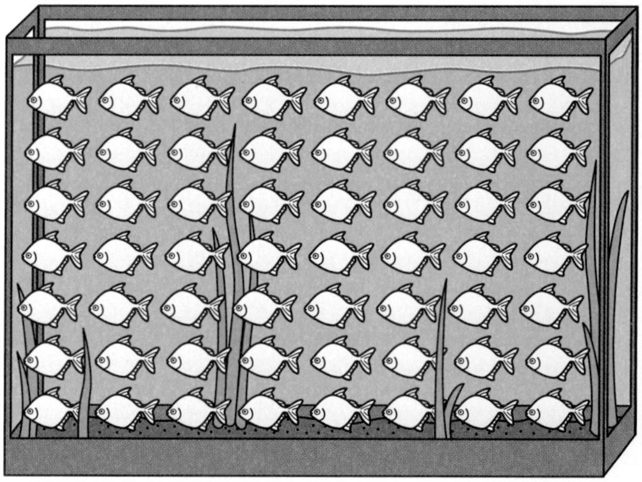

16 $6 + 6 + 6 + 6 + 6 =$ ■

17 $8 + 8 + 8 + 8 + 8 + 8 + 8 =$ ■

Halves, Fourths, and Thirds **Grade 2 Lesson 7.3**

Copy each figure. Then color each figure to show the fraction.

18 Color $\frac{1}{3}$ of the figure.

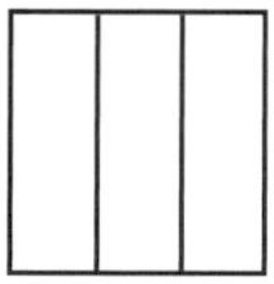

19 Color $\frac{1}{2}$ of the figure.

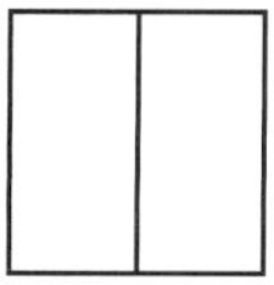

20 Color $\frac{2}{3}$ of the figure.

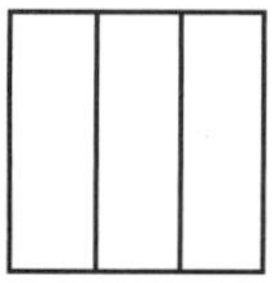

21 Color $\frac{3}{4}$ of the figure.

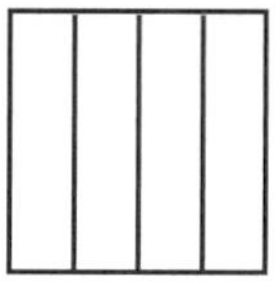

22 Color $\frac{2}{4}$ of the figure.

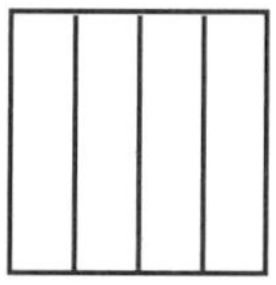

CHAPTER 1

Key Ideas Review

In this chapter you explored our base-ten number system, including numbers beyond one million.

You reviewed basic addition and subtraction facts.

You learned how to say and write very large numbers and how to identify place value in those numbers.

You learned how to round numbers up to 10,000 and how to know when an estimate is more useful than an exact answer.

Find the missing terms.

1. $\begin{array}{r} 8 \\ + \square \\ \hline 12 \end{array}$

2. $\begin{array}{r} 16 \\ - \square \\ \hline 9 \end{array}$

3. $\begin{array}{r} \square \\ + 6 \\ \hline 11 \end{array}$

4. $\begin{array}{r} \square \\ - 2 \\ \hline 8 \end{array}$

Answer each question.

5. What numbers complete the pattern?
8,892; ■; 8,896; ■; ■; 8,902

6. How do we round 77,660 to the nearest thousand? How do we round 77,660 to the nearest ten thousand?

7. What is the place value for each underlined digit?
$2\underline{6}8,4\underline{3}9,7\underline{7}1$

Extended Response **Provide** a detailed answer for the following exercise.

8. Douglas wants to buy 3 cans of fish food for \$3.79 each. He has one \$10 bill and three \$1 bills. How can he estimate the total amount of money he will have to spend? Does he have enough money to buy the fish food?

Chapter Review

Lesson 1.2 **Complete** each fact family.

1. $9 + ▢ = 12$
   $3 + ▢ = ▢$
   $12 - ▢ = 9$
   $12 - ▢ = ▢$

2. $▢ + 9 = 15$
   $▢ + ▢ = ▢$
   $15 - ▢ = 6$
   $15 - ▢ = ▢$

Lesson 1.3 **Find** the missing terms.

3. $18 - ▢ = 9$
4. $8 + ▢ = 16$
5. $15 - ▢ = 7$
6. $▢ + 8 = 14$

Solve the problem.

7. Before the softball season Andrea had 6 softball awards. At the end of the season she had 10 awards. How many awards did Andrea win this season?

Lesson 1.4 **Use** $<$, $=$, or $>$ to make each statement correct.

8. 676 ▢ 667
9. 1,010 ▢ 1,100
10. 43,809 ▢ 43,908
11. 22 + 8 ▢ 21 + 9

Lesson 1.5 **Find** the *in values* or the *out values*.

12.

in	−2 *out*
14	
	10
	8
	6
6	

13.

in	+4 *out*
	6
	9
	11
1	
0	

Lesson 1.6

14 What is the place value for each underlined digit?

$2\underline{2},\underline{3}41,\underline{2}31$

Write each number in expanded form.

15 590,989

16 151,370

Lesson 1.7

17 **Extended Response** Is 27 an odd number or an even number? Explain how you could use sticks to find the answer.

Lesson 1.8

Round to the nearest ten.

18 24

19 89

Round to the nearest hundred.

20 187

21 133

Round to the nearest thousand.

22 4,599

23 8,430

Lesson 1.9

Count on. Write the missing numbers.

24 372,418; □; □; □; 372,422

25 1,439,998; □; 1,440,000; □; 1,440,002; 1,440,003; □

Count back. Write the missing numbers.

26 2,340,201; □; □; 2,340,198; □

CHAPTER 1 Practice Test

Write the missing numbers. Count on or count back.

1. 398, ___, ___, 401, ___, 403
2. 201, ___, ___, 198, ___, 196
3. 1,099; ___; ___; ___; 1,103
4. 4,539; ___; 4,541; ___; ___; 4,544

Write the sum or the difference. Then write three statements that complete the fact family.

5. 8 + 9 = ___

   ___

   ___

   ___

6. 14 − 9 = ___

   ___

   ___

   ___

Use <, =, or > to make each statement correct.

7. 35 + 75 ___ 25 + 65
8. 11 + 101 ___ 101 + 11
9. 788 + 99 ___ 787 + 200
10. 1,020 + 2 ___ 1,000 + 2

Find the *in values,* the *out values,* or the *rule.*

11.

in (+10)	*out*
10	
8	
6	
4	
2	

12.

in ( )	*out*
8	1
9	
15	
	0
11	4

Answer each question.

13. What does the number 4 represent in 4,326?

Ⓐ 4 hundreds

Ⓑ 4 thousands

Ⓒ 4 tens

Ⓓ 4 ones

14. What does the number 5 represent in 514,672?

Ⓐ 5 hundred thousands

Ⓑ 5 thousands

Ⓒ 5 ten thousands

Ⓓ 5 millions

15. What is 391,508 in expanded form?

Ⓐ 300,000 + 90,000 + 1,000 + 500 + 80 + 0

Ⓑ 30,000 + 9,000 + 500 + 0 + 8

Ⓒ 300,000 + 90,000 + 1,000 + 500 + 0 + 8

Ⓓ 300,000 + 9,000 + 100 + 0 + 8

16. Caroline bought 3 pencils for 49¢ each and 2 notepads for 52¢ each. About how much did she spend?

Ⓐ about $2.50

Ⓑ about $2.00

Ⓒ about $1.80

Ⓓ about $1.10

17. Sasha's classmates are having a bake sale to raise money for a field trip. Sasha's mother baked 63 cookies. George's father baked 104 cookies. Alfredo's father baked 76 cookies. About how many cookies did the three students bring in for the bake sale?

Ⓐ about 400 cookies

Ⓑ about 350 cookies

Ⓒ about 300 cookies

Ⓓ about 240 cookies

18. Misha is 2 years younger than Mihal. Kim is 3 years younger than Misha. How many years younger is Kim than Mihal?

Ⓐ can't tell

Ⓑ 3 years

Ⓒ 5 years

Ⓓ 6 years

CHAPTER 1

Practice Test

Answer each question.

19. Andie rode her bike 11 blocks to her friend Gerry's house. They rode their bikes 9 blocks to the school. Then they rode 7 blocks to the park. How many blocks did Andie ride her bike altogether?

Ⓐ 27 blocks

Ⓑ 24 blocks

Ⓒ 18 blocks

Ⓓ 11 blocks

20. Lewis wants to buy 8 muffins at 95¢ each. What is the estimated cost of the muffins?

Ⓐ a little less than $4

Ⓑ a little more than $5

Ⓒ a little less than $8

Ⓓ a little more than $8

21. Mikala has one $5 bill and six $1 bills. Which items can she buy with the money she has?

Ⓐ two CDs for $6.95 each

Ⓑ one CD for $6.95 and one book for $7.99

Ⓒ one CD for $6.95 and one bottle of water for $1.99

Ⓓ two books for $7.99 each

Tell whether the sum is odd or even.

22. 23 + 25 = ▢

Ⓐ even

Ⓑ odd

23. 32 + 27 = ▢

Ⓐ even

Ⓑ odd

Add.

24. 9 + 6 + 7 = ▢

Ⓐ 13 Ⓑ 16

Ⓒ 22 Ⓓ 32

25. 8 + 5 + 6 = ▢

Ⓐ 11 Ⓑ 19

Ⓒ 22 Ⓓ 29

26. 20 + 11 + 9 = ▢

Ⓐ 32 Ⓑ 39

Ⓒ 40 Ⓓ 49

27. 13 + 9 + 7 = ▢

Ⓐ 29 Ⓑ 39

Ⓒ 22 Ⓓ 27

28. 10 + 9 + 10 + 8 = ▢

Ⓐ 39 Ⓑ 37

Ⓒ 40 Ⓓ 45

eTextbook This lesson is available in the *eTextbook.*

Extended Response **Solve.**

29. The third-grade students at Bowman School are having a read-a-thon. Every week the students in each third-grade class keep track of how many books they have read. The table shows the information for the first five weeks.

Class	Week 1	Week 2	Week 3	Week 4	Week 5
Ms. Brown	20	18	17	20	18
Mr. Tolland	17	16	14	16	17
Mr. Heiss	10	12	13	14	15
Ms. White	22	20	23	20	22

a. Whose class read the most books? Explain how you can find the answer without adding the numbers for each class.

b. Whose class read the fewest books? Explain how you know.

c. An award is given to the class that increases its total every week. Which class should receive this reward? Explain your answer.

30. There are about 20 cubes in the first box. About how many cubes are in the second box?

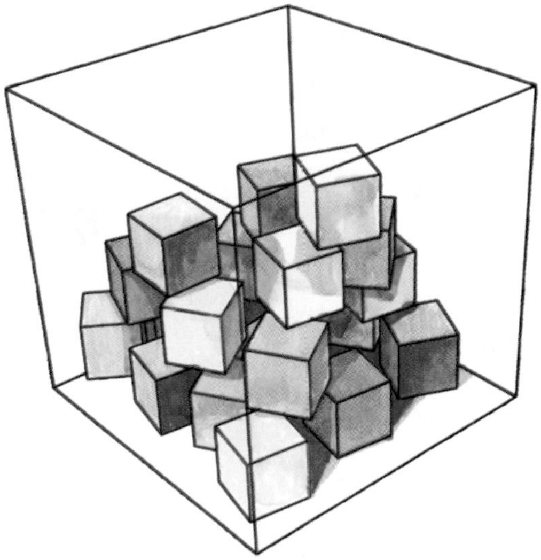

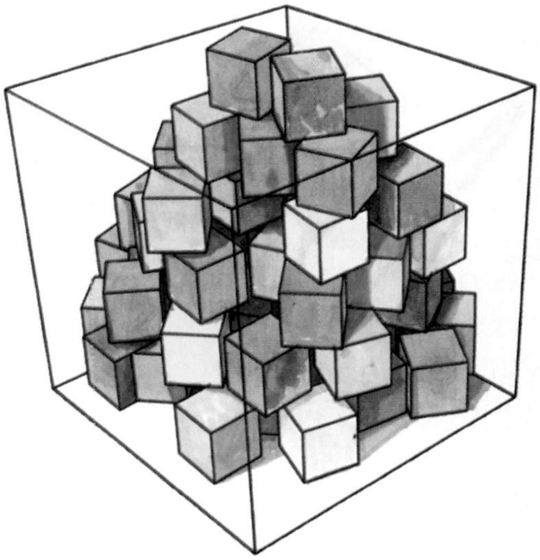

Thinking Story

Lemonade Incorporated

"What in the world are you up to now?" asked Cousin Trixie.

Ferdie had put a table out by the sidewalk and was busy painting some letters on a piece of cardboard. He had already painted the letters *L-E-M-O.*

What do you think Ferdie is doing?

"I'm setting up a lemonade stand," said Ferdie. "I do this every year when the weather is hot, and I make a little money selling lemonade to people who come past. Lots of other kids do the same thing."

"I've noticed that," said Trixie. "On the way over here I must have passed six other lemonade stands. They obviously don't know how to run a business! Every one has a messy handmade sign, and half the kids don't know how to spell *lemonade* right, or they get the cent sign backward. And they use just any old cups and pitchers, and nobody wears a uniform. Who would ever want to buy lemonade at places like that?"

"How would you do it?" Ferdie asked. He was interested, because he knew that Cousin Trixie was very good at earning money for herself.

"I'd organize a company," she said. "I'd get together with the other lemonade sellers, and we'd have booths that looked alike, we'd have signs printed by a printer, and we'd wear snappy uniforms. We might even have commercials on TV, telling people to buy our lemonade."

Do you see anything wrong with those ideas?

"Wouldn't all that cost a lot of money?" Ferdie asked.

"You don't understand how big business works," said Trixie. "We'd all put our money together and get things cheaper. We'd buy big cans of lemonade, which would be cheaper too, and we'd sell so much that we'd make piles of money."

Ferdie liked the idea so much that he ran off to tell all his friends who were selling lemonade.

Do you think Cousin Trixie's ideas will work?

Why or why not?

That afternoon the children met in a park, and Trixie explained the plan to them. Everyone agreed to join the company—everyone, that is, except Willy. He said he wanted to run his lemonade stand the way he always did.

"But you always make less money than anyone else," said Ferdie.

"I don't care," said Willy. "I like to do things my own way."

"You'll be sorry," Ferdie said.

Why do you think Willy doesn't want to join the company?

After Willy left, Trixie said, "Now the first thing we need is a president of the company. That will be me, of course. For every cup of lemonade you sell, you give me 1¢."

"You mean if we sell 50 cups of lemonade, we give you 50¢?" asked Manolita.

"That's right, but I expect you to sell much more than 50 cups. Five hundred cups a day will be more like it."

If Manolita sells 500 cups of lemonade, how many cents will she have to give Cousin Trixie?

How many dollars is that?

"If I sell 500 cups of lemonade, I'll have to give you 500¢. That's $5!" Manolita said.

"But you get to keep all the rest," said Trixie. "After expenses, I mean."

"Expenses?" asked Marcus.

"Of course," said Trixie. "You have to give me money to buy the lemonade, the cups, the pitchers, the signs, the uniforms, and things like that. So, to start with, I'd like each of you to give me $10 to buy the supplies."

None of the children had $10, which made Cousin Trixie angry. But she took whatever money they had and told them to pay her the rest from the money they earned selling lemonade.

Do you think the children will make a lot of money now that they are part of a company?

The next day Trixie brought each of the children some red and white paint to paint their lemonade stands. She also gave each of them a little red and white cap and a red and white sign that said *Lemonade Incorporated, Trixie Jones, President. Lemonade, 10¢ a Cup.*

By the end of the day, Ferdie had sold 10 cups of lemonade. Cousin Trixie came around to collect her money.

How much money did Ferdie earn altogether from selling 10 cups of lemonade?

How much money will he need to give Cousin Trixie?

How do you know?

"I sold 10 cups of lemonade," said Ferdie, "so you get 10¢—1¢ a cup."

"That's 10¢ for my share," said Cousin Trixie, "but I need all the rest of your money for expenses."

Ferdie groaned as he gave Trixie the whole dollar he had earned that day. "I wish you'd take back the red and white cap and let me keep some of the money," he said.

The next day business was better. Ferdie sold 24 cups of lemonade.

"I thought I was supposed to make a lot of money," Ferdie complained to his cousin, "but I don't sell any more lemonade than I used to, and I have to give all the money to you."

"That's the trouble," said Cousin Trixie. "You don't sell enough lemonade. If you sold 1,000 cups a day, then you'd have money left over after paying expenses."

"But how can I sell 1,000 cups a day?" Ferdie asked. "I have trouble selling 20."

"We'll have to start running ads in the newspaper to get people to buy more lemonade," Trixie said.

"Oh, no!" Ferdie groaned.

Why would Ferdie groan at that idea?

"That will cost more money," Ferdie said, "and I'll have to pay for it from the money I get."

"You have to spend money to make money," said Trixie.

One day while Ferdie was working at his lemonade stand, Willy came riding past on his bicycle. "I thought your bicycle was broken," Ferdie said.

"I took it to a repair shop and had it fixed," Willy said.

"Where did you get the money to have it fixed?" Ferdie asked.

Where could Willy have gotten the money to fix his bicycle?

"I earned the money selling lemonade," Willy said. "I sold more lemonade this year than I ever did before."

"But don't you have to spend all the money for expenses?" Ferdie asked.

"Expenses? What are expenses?" asked Willy.

"You know, money you spend for pitchers and cups."

"I use my mother's."

"What about money for lemonade?"

"It costs about 5¢ a cup," said Willy. "I sell it for 10¢ a cup."

How much money does Willy make on each cup of lemonade he sells?

"So I make about 5¢ on each cup of lemonade I sell," Willy explained. "How much do you make on each cup of lemonade?"

How much does Ferdie make?

"I don't make any money on a cup of lemonade," Ferdie said bitterly, "but Trixie does."

"You mean that Trixie makes money on every cup that everyone else in the company sells?" Willy asked. "She must be getting rich!"

"I told you she was good at earning money for herself," Ferdie said.

The End

CHAPTER 2

Multidigit Addition and Subtraction

In This Chapter You Will Learn

- how to regroup numbers for addition and subtraction.
- how to add and subtract numbers with two or more digits.
- approximation.
- Roman numerals.

Problem Solving

Austin and Charity are building a tree house. They want to put a window in the middle of one of the walls. The window will be 30 inches high and 24 inches wide.

They want the spaces above and below the window to be equal. They also want the spaces on the left side and the right side to be equal.

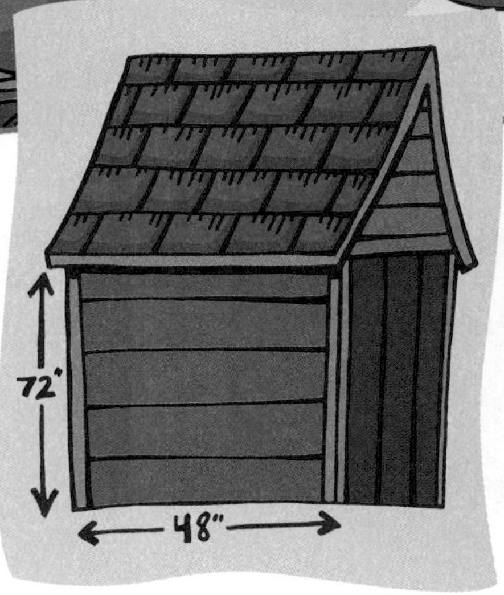

1. What are the dimensions of the wall?
2. What are the dimensions of the window?
3. How many inches will there be above the window and below the window?
4. How many inches will there be on each side of the window?

LESSON 2.1

Regrouping for Addition

Key Ideas

Knowing how to regroup tens and hundreds makes adding multidigit numbers easier. Numbers can be written in standard form, such as 25, and nonstandard form, such as 2 tens and 5.

You can regroup 2 tens and 15 as 3 tens and 5. The standard name for this number is 35.

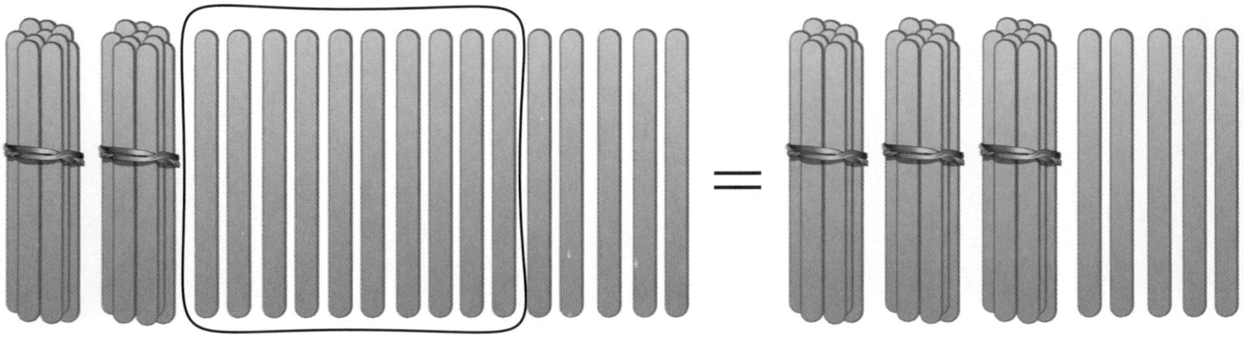

In the same way, you can regroup 2 hundreds and 15 tens as 3 hundreds and 5 tens. The standard name for this number is 350.

Write the standard name for each of these. You may use craft sticks or play money to help. The first one is done for you.

1. 2 tens and 8 = 28
2. 2 hundreds and 8 tens = ■
3. 5 tens and 12 = ■
4. 5 hundreds and 12 tens = ■
5. 6 tens and 15 = ■
6. 6 hundreds and 15 tens = ■
7. 4 tens and 0 = ■
8. 4 hundreds and 0 tens = ■
9. 7 tens and 16 = ■
10. 7 hundreds and 16 tens = ■

Write the standard name for each of these.

11. 0 tens and 14 =
12. 0 hundreds and 14 tens =
13. 8 tens and 3 =
14. 8 hundreds and 3 tens =
15. 8 tens and 13 =

21. 1 ten and 11 =
22. 1 hundred and 11 tens =
23. 1 ten and 12 =
24. 1 hundred and 12 tens =
25. 9 tens =

---

16. 8 hundreds and 13 tens =
17. 4 tens and 10 =
18. 4 hundreds and 10 tens =
19. 13 tens =
20. 13 hundreds =

26. 9 hundreds =
27. 2 tens and 11 =
28. 2 hundreds and 11 tens =
29. 0 tens and 11 =
30. 0 hundreds and 11 tens =

Solve.

31. **Extended Response** Lynn has five \$10 bills and seventeen \$1 bills. How can she regroup the money to get one more \$10 bill? How many tens and ones will she have?

32. **Extended Response** Corey has two \$100 bills and fourteen \$10 bills. How can he regroup the money to get one more \$100 bill? How many hundreds and tens will he have?

Adding Two-Digit Numbers

Key Ideas

When you add two-digit numbers, it may be easier if you start with the ones column. You might need to regroup to get the answer.

25 + 47 = ?

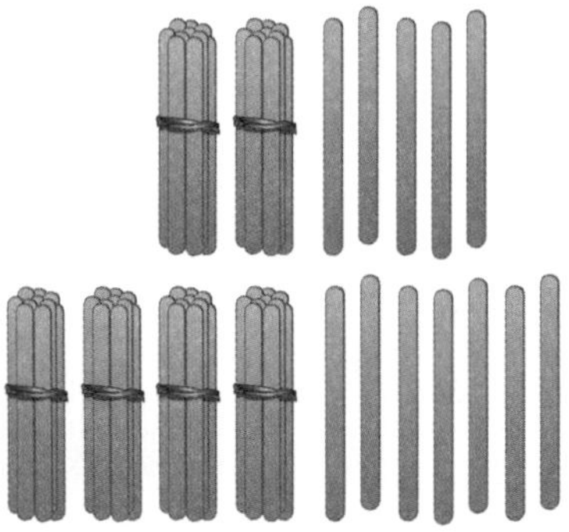

$$\begin{array}{r} \text{2 tens and 5} \\ +\ \text{4 tens and 7} \\ \hline \end{array} \qquad \begin{array}{r} 25 \\ +\ 47 \\ \hline \end{array}$$

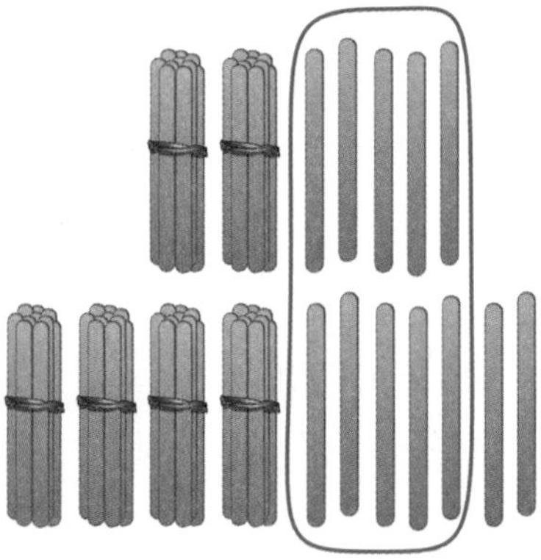

$$\begin{array}{r} \text{1 ten} \\ \text{2 tens and 5} \\ +\ \text{4 tens and 7} \\ \hline 2 \end{array} \qquad \begin{array}{r} 1 \\ 25 \\ +\ 47 \\ \hline 2 \end{array}$$

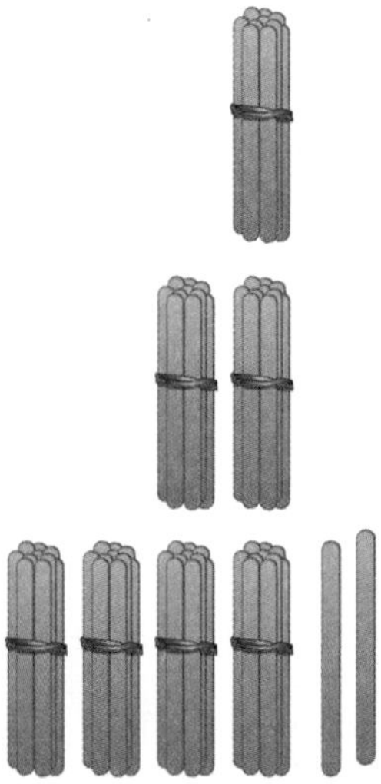

$$\begin{array}{r} \text{1 ten} \\ \text{2 tens and 5} \\ +\ \text{4 tens and 7} \\ \hline \text{7 tens and 2} \end{array} \qquad \begin{array}{r} 1 \\ 25 \\ +\ 47 \\ \hline 72 \end{array}$$

Add. You can use craft sticks or other materials to help.

1. $\begin{array}{r} 45 \\ +\ 26 \\ \hline \end{array}$	2. $\begin{array}{r} 51 \\ +\ 39 \\ \hline \end{array}$	3. $\begin{array}{r} 29 \\ +\ 39 \\ \hline \end{array}$	4. $\begin{array}{r} 27 \\ +\ 54 \\ \hline \end{array}$
5. $\begin{array}{r} 43 \\ +\ 28 \\ \hline \end{array}$	6. $\begin{array}{r} 57 \\ +\ 29 \\ \hline \end{array}$	7. $\begin{array}{r} 36 \\ +\ 51 \\ \hline \end{array}$	8. $\begin{array}{r} 36 \\ +\ 54 \\ \hline \end{array}$
9. $\begin{array}{r} 19 \\ +\ 38 \\ \hline \end{array}$	10. $\begin{array}{r} 25 \\ +\ 25 \\ \hline \end{array}$	11. $\begin{array}{r} 43 \\ +\ 20 \\ \hline \end{array}$	12. $\begin{array}{r} 43 \\ +\ 30 \\ \hline \end{array}$
13. $\begin{array}{r} 40 \\ +\ 40 \\ \hline \end{array}$	14. $\begin{array}{r} 39 \\ +\ 41 \\ \hline \end{array}$	15. $\begin{array}{r} 38 \\ +\ 42 \\ \hline \end{array}$	16. $\begin{array}{r} 37 \\ +\ 43 \\ \hline \end{array}$
17. $\begin{array}{r} 36 \\ +\ 44 \\ \hline \end{array}$	18. $\begin{array}{r} 35 \\ +\ 45 \\ \hline \end{array}$	19. $\begin{array}{r} 34 \\ +\ 45 \\ \hline \end{array}$	20. $\begin{array}{r} 76 \\ +\ \ 6 \\ \hline \end{array}$
21. $\begin{array}{r} 32 \\ +\ 42 \\ \hline \end{array}$	22. $\begin{array}{r} 29 \\ +\ 41 \\ \hline \end{array}$	23. $\begin{array}{r} 18 \\ +\ 18 \\ \hline \end{array}$	24. $\begin{array}{r} 19 \\ +\ 19 \\ \hline \end{array}$

Solve.

Tiffany has 23 trading cards. Seth has 34 trading cards. Makenzi has 17 trading cards. Craig has 18 trading cards.

25. Who has the most trading cards?
26. Who has the fewest trading cards?
27. If Tiffany and Seth put their trading cards together, how many will they have?
28. If Craig and Tiffany put their trading cards together, how many will they have?
29. If Craig and Makenzi put their trading cards together, how many will they have?
30. If Tiffany, Seth, Makenzi, and Craig put their trading cards together, how many will they have?
31. If Tiffany and Makenzi put their trading cards together and Seth and Craig put their trading cards together, which pair would have more trading cards?
32. If Makenzi and Craig put their trading cards together, how many more trading cards would they have than Seth?

Writing + Math **Journal**

How could you find the answer to Problem 31 without adding all of the numbers?

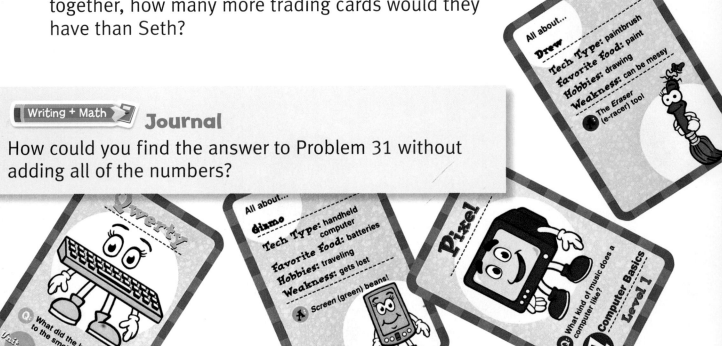

Game

Addition and Strategies Practice

Roll a Problem Game

Players: Two or more

Materials: ***Number Cube:*** one 5–10

Object: To get the greatest sum

HOW TO PLAY

1. Use blanks to outline an addition exercise on your paper, such as this:

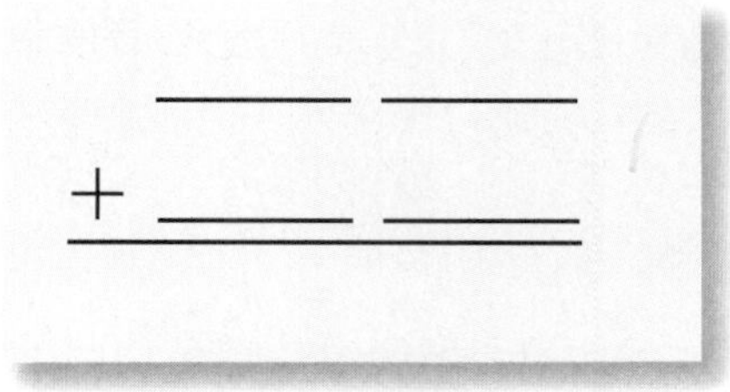

2. One player rolls the ***Number Cube*** four times.
3. Each time the ***Number Cube*** is rolled, write that number in one of the blanks in your outline. If a 10 is rolled, don't count it, and roll again. Once a number is placed, it cannot be moved.
4. When all the blanks have been filled in, determine the greatest sum. The player with the greatest sum is the winner.

LESSON 2.3

Regrouping for Subtraction

Key Ideas

Regrouping may make subtraction easier.

42 = 3 tens and 12

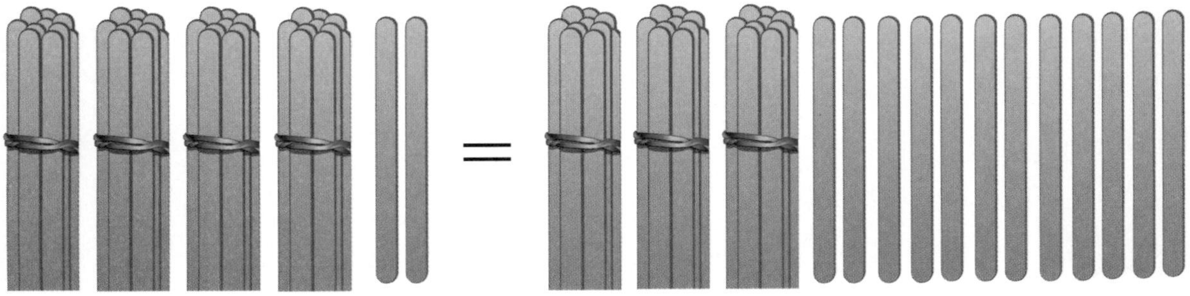

Rewrite each number to show at least 10 ones and no more than 19 ones.

1. 27 = ☐ tens and ☐
2. 80 = ☐ tens and ☐
3. 68 = ☐ tens and ☐
4. 70 = ☐ tens and ☐
5. 21 = ☐ tens and ☐
6. 51 = ☐ tens and ☐
7. 52 = ☐ tens and ☐
8. 62 = ☐ tens and ☐
9. 16 = ☐ tens and ☐
10. 12 = ☐ tens and ☐

Solve.

Jessica has four $10 bills and three $1 bills. She must pay Mr. Gómez $8.

11. How much money does Jessica have?
12. How can Jessica pay $8?
13. How much will Jessica have left after paying Mr. Gómez?

You can regroup hundreds and tens.

230 = 2 hundreds and 3 tens = 1 hundred and 13 tens

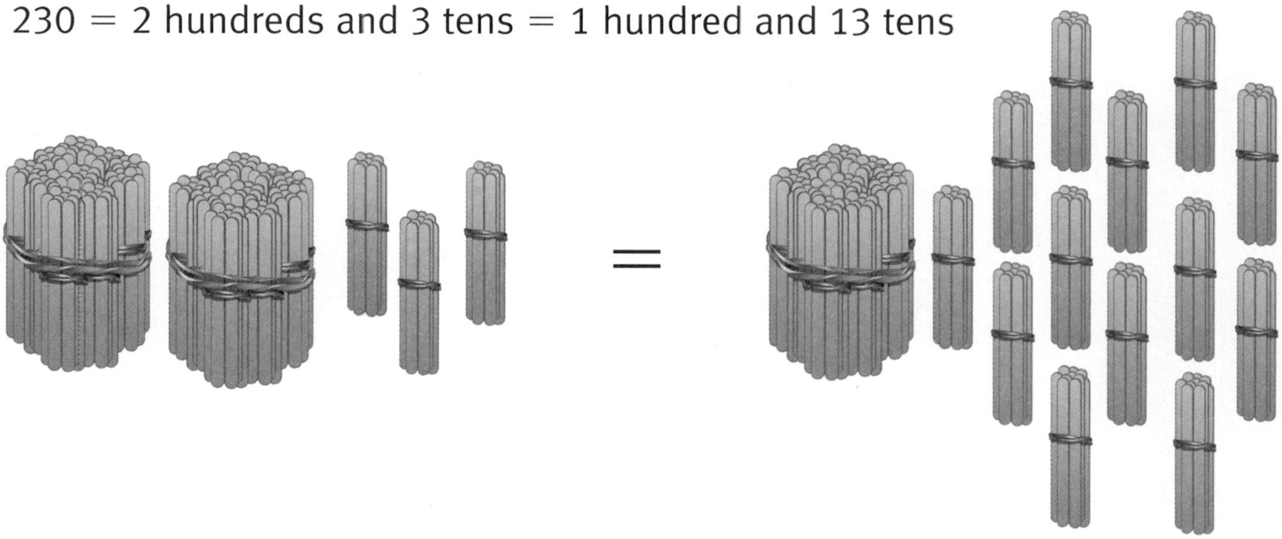

Rewrite **each number to show at least 10 tens and no more than 19 tens.**

14. 420 = ___ hundreds and ___ tens
15. 700 = ___ hundreds and ___ tens
16. 760 = ___ hundreds and ___ tens
17. 160 = ___ hundreds and ___ tens
18. 240 = ___ hundreds and ___ tens
19. 980 = ___ hundreds and ___ tens
20. 120 = ___ hundreds and ___ tens
21. 390 = ___ hundreds and ___ tens
22. 470 = ___ hundreds and ___ tens
23. 600 = ___ hundreds and ___ tens

Solve.

Mr. Taylor has one $100 bill and two $10 bills. He must pay Ms. Kwan $30.

24. How can Mr. Taylor pay $30?
25. How much money will he have left?

Here is another example of how numbers can be regrouped.

205 = 20 tens and 5 = 19 tens and 15

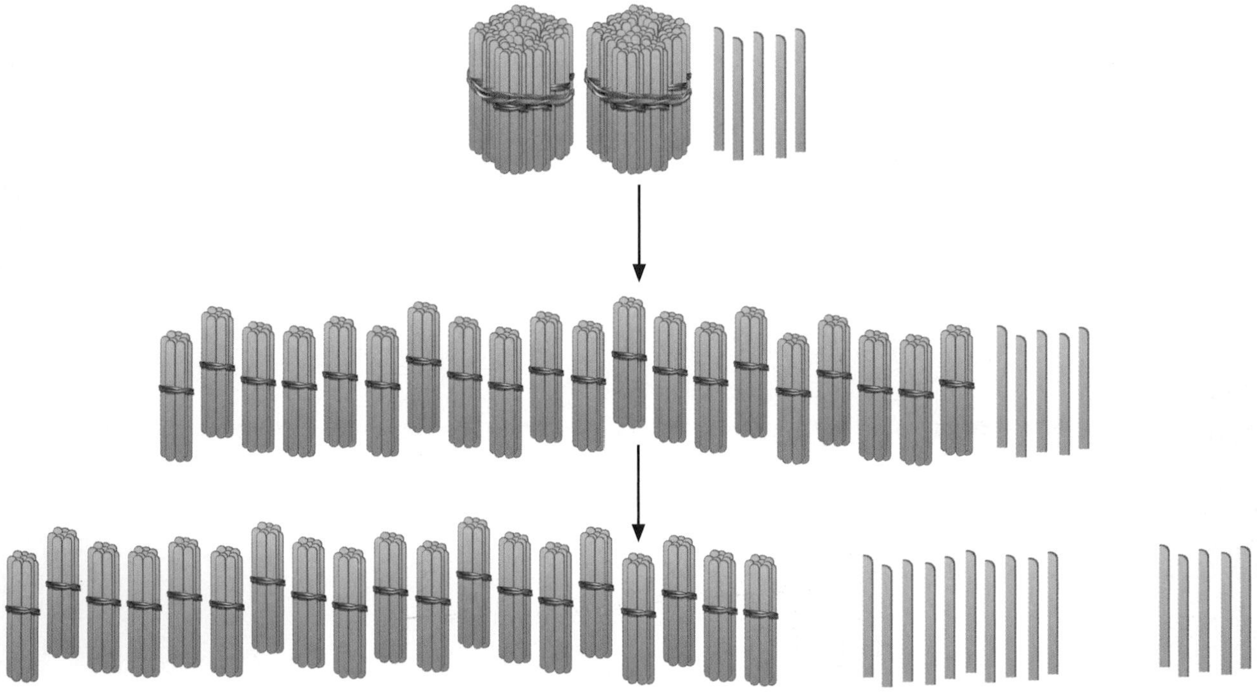

Regroup hundreds to get tens, and rewrite each number. Then regroup tens and ones, and rewrite each number again to show at least 10 ones and no more than 19 ones.

26. 307 = 30 tens and 7 = 29 tens and ____
27. 600 = ____ tens = ____ tens and 10
28. 604 = ____ tens and ____ = ____ tens and ____
29. 809 = ____ tens and ____ = ____ tens and ____
30. 700 = ____ tens = ____ tens and ____
31. 707 = ____ tens and ____ = ____ tens and ____

Solve the problems. You may use play money to help you. Use \$1, \$5, \$10, and \$20 bills only.

32. If you have a \$1 bill, a \$5 bill, a \$10 bill, and a \$20 bill, how much money do you have?

33. **Extended Response** Can Mary have four bills worth a total of \$17? If so, how?

34. **Extended Response** Can Nigel have eight bills worth a total of \$17? If so, how?

Writing + Math **Journal**

Show ten ways to make \$20 with \$1 bills, \$5 bills, \$10 bills, and \$20 bills.

a. What is the least number of bills you can use?

b. What is the greatest number of bills you can use?

c. Show all the ways.

LESSON 2.4

Subtracting Two-Digit Numbers

Key Ideas

When subtracting two-digit numbers, you often need to regroup tens and ones. Look at the example below.

31 − 14 = ?

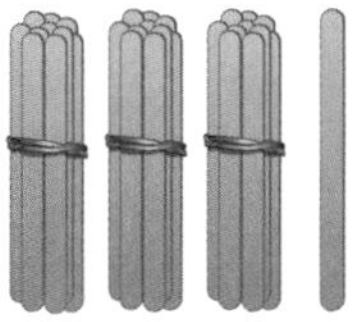

```
  3 tens and 1        31
− 1 ten  and 4      − 14
```

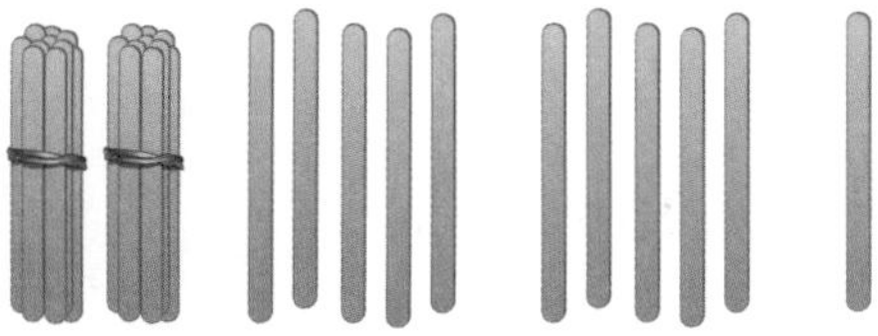

```
  2         11       2 11
  ~~3~~ tens and ~~1~~        ~~3~~~~1~~
− 1 ten  and 4      − 14
```

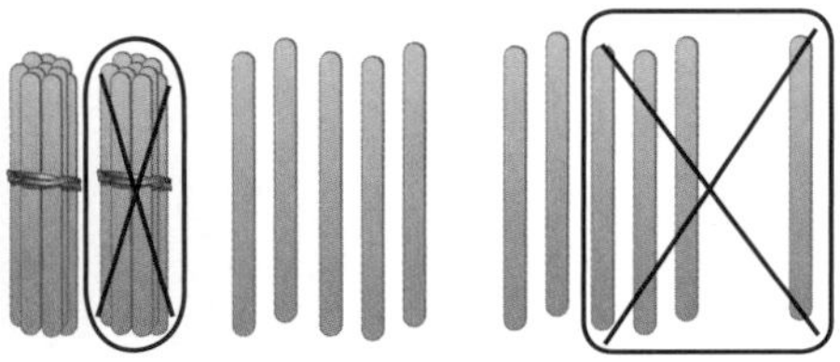

```
  2         11       2 11
  ~~3~~ tens and ~~1~~        ~~3~~~~1~~
− 1 ten  and 4      − 14
  1 ten  and 7        17
```

You can subtract the ones and then the tens, or you can subtract the tens and then the ones.

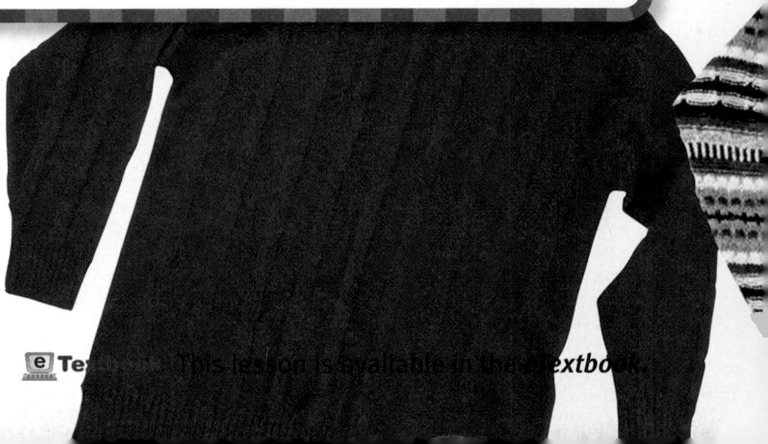

eTextbook This lesson is available in the eTextbook.

Subtract. Use shortcuts if you can.

1. $\begin{array}{r} 43 \\ -\ 29 \\ \hline \end{array}$	2. $\begin{array}{r} 87 \\ -\ 37 \\ \hline \end{array}$	3. $\begin{array}{r} 86 \\ -\ 37 \\ \hline \end{array}$	4. $\begin{array}{r} 28 \\ -\ 19 \\ \hline \end{array}$
5. $\begin{array}{r} 38 \\ -\ 19 \\ \hline \end{array}$	6. $\begin{array}{r} 50 \\ -\ 25 \\ \hline \end{array}$	7. $\begin{array}{r} 75 \\ -\ 50 \\ \hline \end{array}$	8. $\begin{array}{r} 75 \\ -\ 25 \\ \hline \end{array}$
9. $\begin{array}{r} 83 \\ -\ 19 \\ \hline \end{array}$	10. $\begin{array}{r} 83 \\ -\ 18 \\ \hline \end{array}$	11. $\begin{array}{r} 83 \\ -\ 17 \\ \hline \end{array}$	12. $\begin{array}{r} 83 \\ -\ 16 \\ \hline \end{array}$
13. $\begin{array}{r} 61 \\ -\ 47 \\ \hline \end{array}$	14. $\begin{array}{r} 94 \\ -\ 46 \\ \hline \end{array}$	15. $\begin{array}{r} 90 \\ -\ 45 \\ \hline \end{array}$	16. $\begin{array}{r} 80 \\ -\ 45 \\ \hline \end{array}$

Solve.

17. There were 60 sweaters on the shelves in Mrs. Dunlap's store. She sold some, and now she has 25 left. How many did she sell?

18. Mr. Downes had 54 pencils in a can. He gave out some. Now he has 27. How many did he give out?

19. Hana is 8 years old, and she has 37 sports cards. Her brother, Ling, is younger. How many sports cards does he have?

Janelle has $37.
Jay has $28.
Greg has $73.
Jermaine has $54.

20. Who has the most money?

21. How much more money does Jermaine have than Jay?

22. How much money do Janelle and Jay have altogether?

23. How much more money does Greg have than Jay?

24. How much more money does Greg have than Jermaine?

25. How much money do the four of them have altogether?

26. If they put all their money into one container and decide to share it equally, how much money will each of them get?

Writing + Math **Journal**

Make up ten subtraction exercises that you can use shortcuts to find the answers to. Then explain how to use the shortcuts.

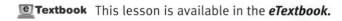

Subtraction and Strategies Practice

Roll a Problem Game

Players: Two or more

Materials: ***Number Cube:*** one 5–10

Object: To get the smallest difference

HOW TO PLAY

1. Use blanks to outline a subtraction exercise on your paper, such as this:

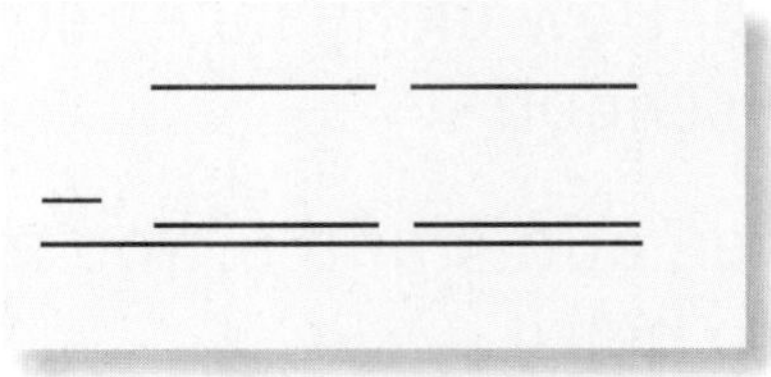

2. The first player rolls the ***Number Cube*** four times.
3. Each time the ***Number Cube*** is rolled, write that number in one of the blanks in your outline.
4. When all the blanks have been filled in, find the difference between the pair of two-digit numbers.
5. The player with the smallest difference that is zero or greater than zero is the winner.

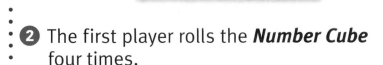

LESSON 2.5

Applications of Addition and Subtraction

Key Ideas

Addition and subtraction help to solve some problems.

Jameesa rides the bus home from school. Starting at the school, the bus travels south for 5 miles to the first bus stop. Then it travels 6 more miles south to Jameesa's house. How many miles south is Jameesa's house from the school?

To get the answer, add 5 and 6. You might also draw a picture to help.

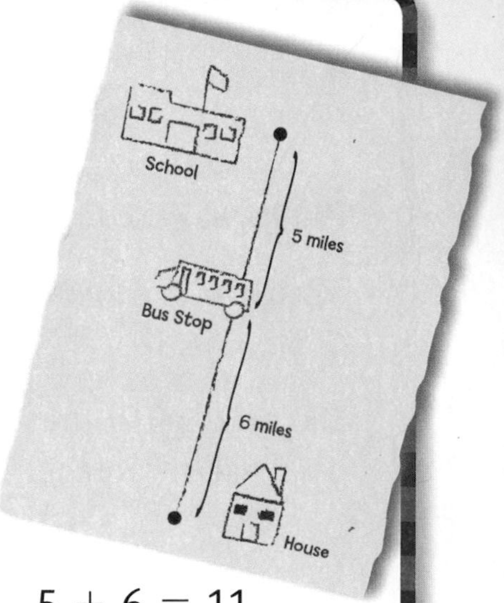

$5 + 6 = 11$

Jameesa's house is 11 miles south from the school.

Solve.

Alice and Emma started at home. Alice is 5 years older than Emma. They drove 32 miles east. Later they turned around and drove 17 miles west.

1. How far are Alice and Emma from home?
2. How far have they driven?

Mr. Cheng started at home. He drove 32 miles east. Then he drove 41 more miles east.

3. How far is Mr. Cheng from home?
4. How far has he driven?

Mr. Cheng and Mr. Smith started at the same location and drove in opposite directions. Mr. Cheng drove 63 miles. Mr. Smith drove 51 miles.

5. Who drove farther?
6. How much farther?
7. How far apart are they now?

Fruit for Sale	
Apples	35¢ each
Pears	42¢ each
Bananas	37¢ each
Oranges	25¢ each

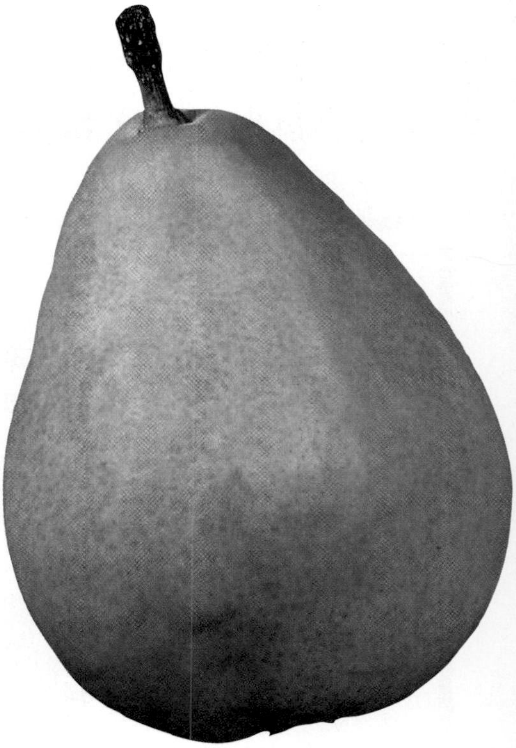

Solve.

8. How much do 1 apple and 1 pear cost?
9. How much do 2 apples cost?
10. Laura has $1 and wants to buy 4 pieces of fruit. What can she buy?
11. Brandon has 50¢.
    - **a.** Can he buy a banana and an orange?
    - **b.** How much more money will Brandon need to buy both pieces of fruit?
12. Juanita has $1 and wants to buy 3 different kinds of fruit.
    - **a.** Can one of the fruits be a pear?
    - **b.** Can one of the fruits be a banana?
    - **c.** What fruits can Juanita buy?
    - **d.** How much change will Juanita get?
13. Raulito wants to buy 2 apples, some pears, and 4 oranges. How much will he have to pay?
14. **Extended Response** Sarita wants to package 4 fruits in one box.
    - **a.** What will the least expensive box contain?
    - **b.** What will the most expensive box contain?
    - **c.** Suppose she wanted to package 10 fruits in a box. Would your method of finding the most expensive and least expensive boxes be the same or different? Explain.

LESSON 2.6

Applications with Money

Key Ideas

No matter which bills and coins are used to form an amount of money, the amount is written the same way.

= $5.25

= $5.25

Write how much. Use play money if you need to.

1. 2 one-dollar bills
   3 dimes
   2 pennies

2. 1 five-dollar bill
   6 dimes
   3 pennies

3. 5 one-dollar bills
   1 quarter
   3 dimes
   1 nickel
   3 pennies

4. 2 five-dollar bills
   1 one-dollar bill
   4 dimes
   1 nickel
   3 pennies

5. 1 ten-dollar bill
   1 five-dollar bill
   1 one-dollar bill
   3 pennies

6. 3 one-dollar bills
   7 dimes

7. 1 twenty-dollar bill
   1 ten-dollar bill
   3 one-dollar bills
   2 quarters
   1 nickel

8. 1 ten-dollar bill
   4 five-dollar bills
   2 one-dollar bills
   6 quarters
   1 nickel

Use the picture to solve the problems.

9 **Extended Response** Brittany and Jackson have saved $55.00.

a. Can they afford to buy 2 baseball caps together if the tax is $3.58? Explain your answer.

b. Can they afford to buy 1 baseball bat and 1 baseball glove together if the tax is $4.20? Can you use a shortcut to find the answer?

10 **Extended Response** If Jackson buys a soccer ball and a basketball, how many baseballs can he afford if he doesn't have to pay sales tax? Explain how you found your answer.

Writing + Math **Journal**

Use the picture to make up a problem involving addition or subtraction.

Austin and Charity are finishing their tree house. They have 9 pieces of paneling to cover one of the walls inside the house. Each piece is 2 feet wide. The wall is 6 feet wide. The children want to make as few cuts as possible.

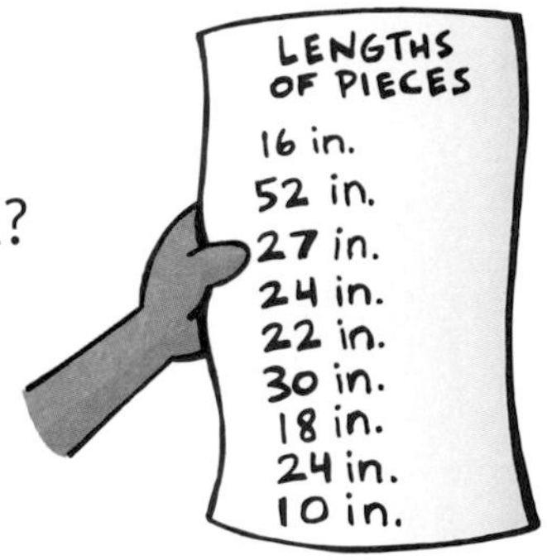

- How can they put the pieces together to cover the wall?
- Can they cover the wall by making only 2 cuts?

Maggie is making a physical model to try to solve the problem.

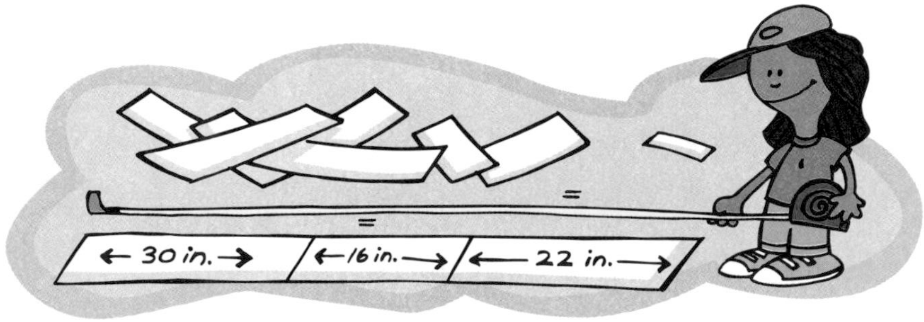

Think about Maggie's strategy. Answer the following questions.

1. In Maggie's model, what do the strips of paper stand for?
2. How do you think Maggie decided how long to make the strips?
3. Why is Maggie measuring three of the strips?
4. What can she do if they are less than 72 inches long?
5. What can she do if they are more than 72 inches long?
6. Do you think Maggie's strategy will work? Why or why not?

Bradley is using guess, check, and revise to solve the problem.

7. Why is Bradley looking for lengths that add up to 72 or a little more?

8. Why did Bradley cross out the first guess without finding the sum?

9. How is Bradley's second guess different from his first guess?

10. Do you have to use three pieces of paneling in each section?

11. If you were using Bradley's strategy, what would you do next?

12. Finish solving the problem using Maggie's strategy, Bradley's strategy, or one of your own. What strategy did you use? Why?

Cumulative Review

Place Value through 10,000 **Grade 2 Lesson 9.1**

Mark a point on the number line where you think each number belongs, and label it.

1. 3, 82, 20, 40

2. 700, 600, 300, 200

Basic Facts and Missing Terms **Lesson 1.3**

Find the missing terms.

3. $8 + \square = 15$
4. $12 - \square = 4$
5. $\square + 5 = 17$
6. $14 - \square = 6$
7. $10 + \square = 13$
8. $\square - 3 = 6$
9. $13 + \square = 21$
10. $\square - 7 = 4$
11. $9 + \square = 18$
12. $\square - 5 = 10$

Reading a Thermometer **Grade 2 Lesson 10.1**

Write the temperature.

13. 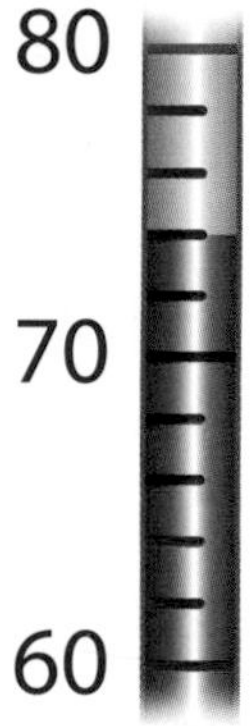

14. 

15. 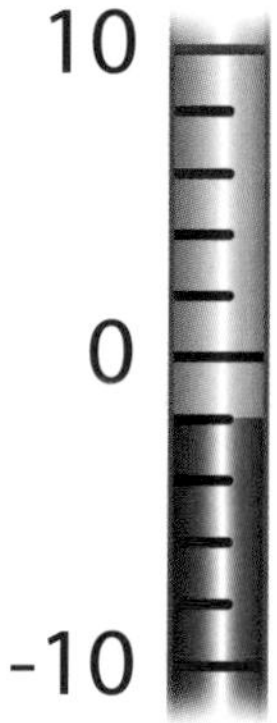

16. 

eTextbook This lesson is available in the *eTextbook*.

Counting and Estimating **Lesson 1.1**

Solve.

17 Sarah's class is making a three's chart. They put 3 new stars on it every day. This afternoon they put on today's stars, and now there are 132 stars on the chart.

a. How many stars were on the chart this morning?

b. How many stars will be on the chart when they leave school tomorrow?

Equivalent Fractions **Grade 2 Lesson 7.7**

Answer using pictures and words.

18 Which is bigger— $\frac{1}{2}$ of the tree trunk or $\frac{5}{8}$ of the tree trunk?

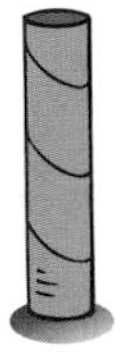

19 Which is larger— $\frac{1}{4}$ of the cardboard tube or $\frac{1}{6}$ of the cardboard tube?

20 Which is smaller— $\frac{3}{4}$ of the orange or $\frac{1}{2}$ of the orange?

Regrouping for Addition **Lesson 2.1**

Write the standard name for each of these.

21 5 tens and 4 = ☐

22 3 hundreds and 16 tens = ☐

23 8 tens and 18 = ☐

24 8 hundreds and 0 tens = ☐

25 7 tens and 11 = ☐

26 5 hundreds and 18 tens = ☐

27 9 tens and 0 = ☐

28 2 hundreds and 2 tens = ☐

29 8 tens and 15 = ☐

30 4 hundreds and 14 tens = ☐

LESSON 2.7 Adding Three-Digit Numbers

Key Ideas

Adding three-digit numbers is just like adding two-digit numbers. The procedure below can be used to add two three-digit numbers. For some problems, you can do the addition in your head and you don't have to use this procedure.

$436 + 287 = ?$

$$\begin{array}{r} 436 \\ +\ 287 \\ \hline ? \end{array}$$

Start at the right.
Add the ones.
$6 + 7 = 13$

$$\begin{array}{r} {\scriptstyle 1} \\ 436 \\ +\ 287 \\ \hline 3 \end{array}$$

$13 = 1$ ten and 3 ones

$$\begin{array}{r} {\scriptstyle 1} \\ 436 \\ +\ 287 \\ \hline 3 \end{array}$$

Add the tens.
$1 + 3 + 8 = 12$
There are 12 tens.

$$\begin{array}{r} {\scriptstyle 1\,1} \\ 436 \\ +\ 287 \\ \hline 23 \end{array}$$

12 tens = 1 hundred and 2 tens

$$\begin{array}{r} {\scriptstyle 1\,1} \\ 436 \\ +\ 287 \\ \hline 723 \end{array}$$

Add the hundreds.
$1 + 4 + 2 = 7$
There are 7 hundreds.

$436 + 287 = 723$

Add. Use shortcuts if you can.

1. 435 + 256
2. 379 + 182
3. 607 + 284
4. 200 + 200
5. 250 + 250
6. 251 + 250
7. 252 + 250
8. 249 + 251
9. 874 + 129
10. 325 + 492
11. 621 + 300
12. 621 + 299

Solve.

13. Clara's group collected 275 pounds of aluminum cans. Amelia's group collected 385 pounds. How many pounds did they collect altogether?
14. Paco drove 475 miles last week and 236 miles this week. How many miles did he drive in the two weeks?

LESSON 2.8

Subtracting Three-Digit Numbers

Key Ideas

Subtracting three-digit numbers is like subtracting two-digit numbers. The procedure below can be used to subtract three-digit numbers. For some problems, you can do the subtraction in your head and you don't have to use this procedure.

745 − 179 = ?

$$\begin{array}{r} 745 \\ -\ 179 \\ \hline ? \end{array}$$

Start at the right.
Subtract the ones.
You cannot subtract 9 from 5.

$$\begin{array}{r} {\scriptstyle 3\,15} \\ 7\not{4}\not{5} \\ -\ 179 \\ \hline \end{array}$$

Regroup the 4 tens and 5.
4 tens and 5 = 3 tens and 15

$$\begin{array}{r} {\scriptstyle 3\,15} \\ 7\not{4}\not{5} \\ -\ 179 \\ \hline 6 \end{array}$$

Subtract the ones.
15 – 9 = 6

$$\begin{array}{r} {\scriptstyle 13} \\ {\scriptstyle 6\,\not{3}\,15} \\ \not{7}\not{4}\not{5} \\ -\ 179 \\ \hline 6 \end{array}$$

Subtract the tens.
You cannot subtract 7 tens from 3 tens.
Regroup the 7 hundreds and 3 tens.
7 hundreds and 3 tens = 6 hundreds and 13 tens

$$\begin{array}{r} {\scriptstyle 13} \\ {\scriptstyle 6\,\not{3}\,15} \\ \not{7}\not{4}\not{5} \\ -\ 179 \\ \hline 566 \end{array}$$

Subtract the tens.
13 tens − 7 tens = 6 tens
There are 6 tens.
Subtract the hundreds.
6 hundreds − 1 hundred = 5 hundreds
There are 5 hundreds.

745 − 179 = 566

$506 - 148 = ?$

Here's how.

$$\begin{array}{r} 506 \\ -\ 148 \\ \hline \end{array}$$

Start at the right.
Subtract the ones.
You cannot subtract 8 from 6.
You cannot regroup 0 tens and 6.

$$\begin{array}{r} {\scriptstyle 4\,9\,16} \\ \not{5}\not{0}\not{6} \\ -\ 148 \\ \hline \end{array}$$

5 hundreds is the same as 50 tens.
Regroup 50 tens and 6.
50 tens and 6 = 49 tens and 16.
49 tens and 16 = 4 hundreds 9 tens and 16.

$$\begin{array}{r} {\scriptstyle 4\,9\,16} \\ \not{5}\not{0}\not{6} \\ -\ 148 \\ \hline 358 \end{array}$$

Subtract the ones. 16 − 8 = 8.
Subtract the tens. 9 tens − 4 tens = 5 tens.
Subtract the hundreds. 4 hundreds − 1 hundred = 3 hundreds.

$506 - 148 = 358$

Subtract.

1. $\begin{array}{r} 961 \\ -\ 309 \\ \hline \end{array}$

2. $\begin{array}{r} 401 \\ -\ 266 \\ \hline \end{array}$

3. $\begin{array}{r} 181 \\ -\ 175 \\ \hline \end{array}$

4. $\begin{array}{r} 791 \\ -\ 432 \\ \hline \end{array}$

5. $\begin{array}{r} 874 \\ -\ 362 \\ \hline \end{array}$

6. $\begin{array}{r} 402 \\ -\ 176 \\ \hline \end{array}$

Solve.

7. Last year Cara counted 533 pennies in her bank. This year she counted 491 pennies. How many more pennies were in her bank last year?

Subtract. Use shortcuts if you can.

8. $\begin{array}{r} 382 \\ -\ 179 \\ \hline \end{array}$

9. $\begin{array}{r} 464 \\ -\ 175 \\ \hline \end{array}$

10. $\begin{array}{r} 809 \\ -\ 275 \\ \hline \end{array}$

11. $\begin{array}{r} 875 \\ -\ 200 \\ \hline \end{array}$

12. $\begin{array}{r} 875 \\ -\ 199 \\ \hline \end{array}$

13. $\begin{array}{r} 875 \\ -\ 198 \\ \hline \end{array}$

14. $\begin{array}{r} 364 \\ -\ 37 \\ \hline \end{array}$

15. $\begin{array}{r} 504 \\ -\ 371 \\ \hline \end{array}$

16. $\begin{array}{r} 829 \\ -\ 199 \\ \hline \end{array}$

Add or subtract. Watch the signs. Use shortcuts if you can.

17. $\begin{array}{r} 426 \\ +\ 345 \\ \hline \end{array}$

18. $\begin{array}{r} 721 \\ -\ 356 \\ \hline \end{array}$

19. $\begin{array}{r} 305 \\ -\ 198 \\ \hline \end{array}$

20. $\begin{array}{r} 764 \\ +\ 219 \\ \hline \end{array}$

21. $\begin{array}{r} 812 \\ -\ 199 \\ \hline \end{array}$

22. $\begin{array}{r} 812 \\ -\ 198 \\ \hline \end{array}$

Solve.

23. There were 324 parking spaces in the parking lot. Then some trees were planted. Now there are only 255 parking spaces. How many more parking spaces were there before the trees were planted?

Ink has been spilled on this page.
One answer is correct in each case.

Decide which answer is correct.

24. $\begin{array}{r} 65 \\ +\ 2[illegible] \\ \hline \end{array}$
    a. 111
    b. 85
    c. 275

25. $\begin{array}{r} 82[illegible] \\ -\ 1[illegible] \\ \hline \end{array}$
    a. 921
    b. 688
    c. 835

26. $\begin{array}{r} 3[illegible]1 \\ +\ [illegible]6 \\ \hline \end{array}$
    a. 425
    b. 426
    c. 427

27. $\begin{array}{r} 32[illegible] \\ +\ 6[illegible]5 \\ \hline \end{array}$
    a. 974
    b. 839
    c. 1,025

28. $\begin{array}{r} 3[illegible]1 \\ -\ 3[illegible]9 \\ \hline \end{array}$
    a. 122
    b. 32
    c. 33

29. $\begin{array}{r} 63[illegible] \\ -\ 1[illegible]0 \\ \hline \end{array}$
    a. 572
    b. 429
    c. 539

Use <, >, or = to make the statement correct.

30. 336 + 60 ▢ 446 + 70
31. 800 − 67 ▢ 700 − 67
32. 97 − 0 ▢ 87 − 10
33. 6,000 + 2,000 ▢ 5,999 + 2,001
34. 11 + 34 ▢ 12 + 40
35. 1,402 + 76 ▢ 1,204 + 76

LESSON 2.9

Approximation

Key Ideas

When you approximate the answer to an addition or a subtraction exercise, you come close to finding the exact answer.

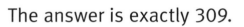

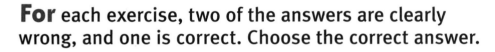

Approximate Answer

245 + 64 =

The answer is about 300 because

240 + 60 = 300.

Exact Answer

$$245 + 64 = \begin{array}{r} {}^{1}\\ 245 \\ +\ 64 \\ \hline 309 \end{array}$$

The answer is exactly 309.

For each exercise, two of the answers are clearly wrong, and one is correct. Choose the correct answer.

1. 48 + 27 =
   a. 45
   b. 25
   c. 75

2. 371 + 629 =
   a. 900
   b. 1,000
   c. 10,000

3. 276 + 28 =
   a. 304
   b. 84
   c. 204

4. 712 + 162 =
   a. 874
   b. 974
   c. 1,074

5. 206 + 259 =
   a. 285
   b. 465
   c. 315

6. 663 + 119 =
   a. 950
   b. 700
   c. 782

7. 329 + 329 =
   a. 458
   b. 558
   c. 658

8. 328 + 367 =
   a. 695
   b. 505
   c. 6,015

9. 612 + 398 =
   a. 810
   b. 1,010
   c. 9,010

10. 99 + 986 =
    a. 4,995
    b. 995
    c. 1,085

For each exercise, two of the answers are clearly wrong, and one is correct. Choose the correct answer.

11 687 − 614 =
- **a.** 103
- **b.** 73
- **c.** 13

12 823 − 77 =
- **a.** 246
- **b.** 746
- **c.** 46

13 299 + 515 =
- **a.** 644
- **b.** 814
- **c.** 1,004

14 999 − 299 =
- **a.** 510
- **b.** 700
- **c.** 300

15 417 + 583 =
- **a.** 780
- **b.** 860
- **c.** 1,000

16 17 + 675 =
- **a.** 805
- **b.** 692
- **c.** 725

17 590 − 248 =
- **a.** 92
- **b.** 112
- **c.** 342

18 864 − 468 =
- **a.** 396
- **b.** 196
- **c.** 96

19 152 + 245 =
- **a.** 397
- **b.** 290
- **c.** 507

20 306 + 694 =
- **a.** 1,500
- **b.** 1,000
- **c.** 1,150

Writing + Math **Journal**

Explain how you used approximation to choose the correct answer for two of the exercises on these pages.

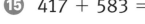

LESSON 2.10

Adding with Three or More Addends

Key Ideas

Several numbers can be added without finding the sum of any pair of them.

When adding several numbers, start at the right in the ones column. Then add the tens column. Add the hundreds column last. Regroup whenever necessary.

The third-grade classrooms at Springer School are setting up a lending library. They need to know how many books each third-grade teacher has in his or her classroom.

	22
Ms. Allen's classroom has 152 books.	152
Mr. Long's classroom has 114 books.	114
Ms. Vincent's classroom has 287 books.	287
Mr. Mancino's classroom has 199 books.	+ 199
There will be 752 books in the lending library.	752

Add. Use shortcuts if you can.

1. $\begin{array}{r} 76 \\ 13 \\ +\ 4 \\ \hline \end{array}$
2. $\begin{array}{r} 38 \\ 25 \\ +\ 25 \\ \hline \end{array}$
3. $\begin{array}{r} 25 \\ 25 \\ +\ 25 \\ \hline \end{array}$
4. $\begin{array}{r} 277 \\ 263 \\ +\ 491 \\ \hline \end{array}$
5. $\begin{array}{r} 278 \\ 264 \\ +\ 492 \\ \hline \end{array}$
6. $\begin{array}{r} 279 \\ 265 \\ +\ 493 \\ \hline \end{array}$
7. $\begin{array}{r} 314 \\ 262 \\ +\ 195 \\ \hline \end{array}$
8. $\begin{array}{r} 245 \\ 312 \\ 289 \\ +\ 128 \\ \hline \end{array}$
9. $\begin{array}{r} 250 \\ 250 \\ 250 \\ +\ 250 \\ \hline \end{array}$
10. $\begin{array}{r} 249 \\ 249 \\ 249 \\ +\ 249 \\ \hline \end{array}$

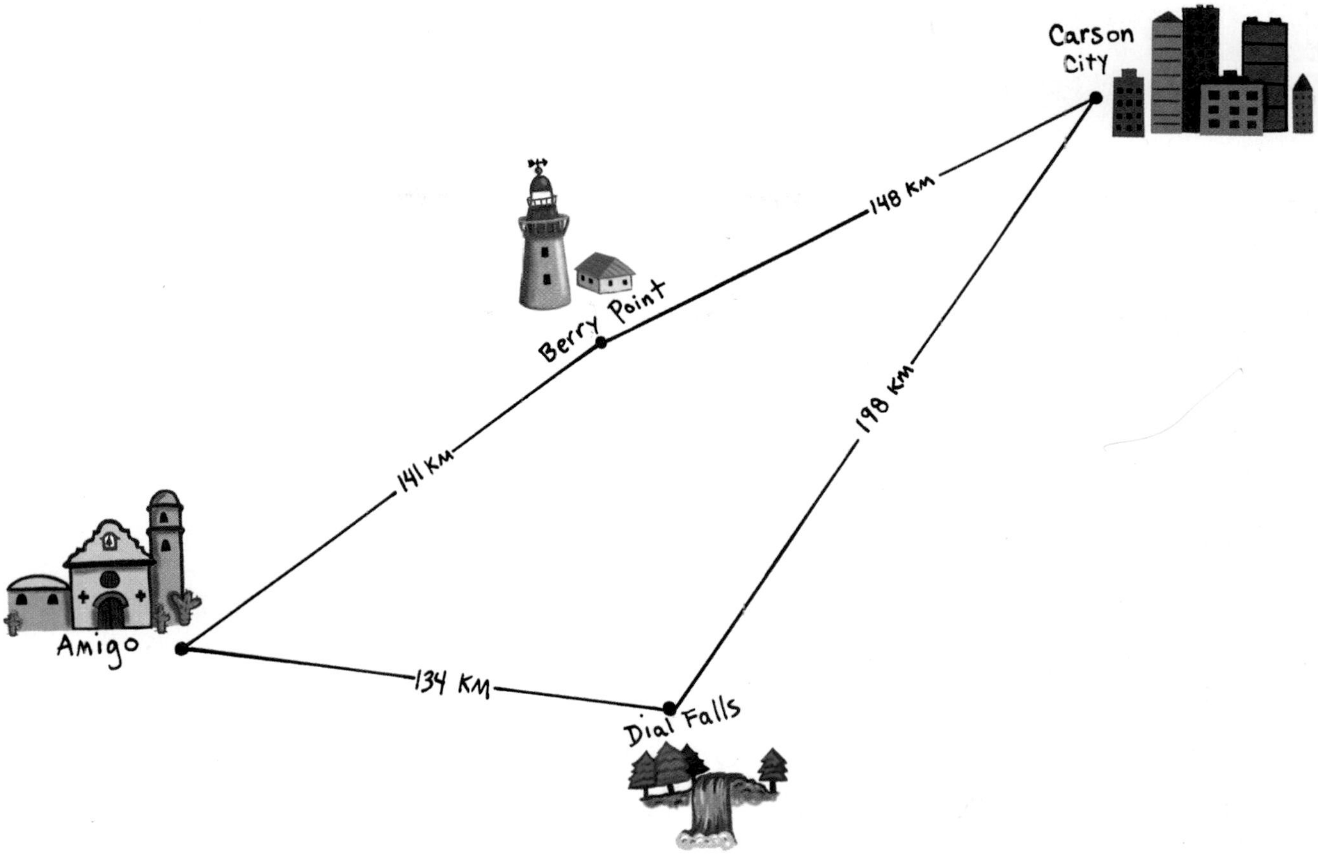

11. Miss Nakamura must drive from Amigo to Berry Point to Carson City to Dial Falls and back to Amigo. How far is that?

12. Mr. Ryan drives from Amigo to Dial Falls to Carson City to Berry Point to Amigo. How far is that?

13. Mr. Wolf lives in Carson City. He wants to visit his brother in Amigo. What is the shortest route that Mr. Wolf can take?

14. The Andersons are planning a trip from their home near Dial Falls to Berry Point. What is the shortest route they can take?

15. **Extended Response** If the Andersons could fly directly from Dial Falls to Berry Point, about how many kilometers would they fly? Explain how you found your answer.

LESSON 2.11

Adding and Subtracting Four-Digit Numbers

Key Ideas

If you can add or subtract three-digit numbers, you can work with numbers of any size.

To add or subtract four-digit numbers, start at the right with the ones column. Then move left, column by column. Remember to regroup when necessary.

$$\begin{array}{r} {\scriptstyle 1\;1\;\;} \\ 3254 \\ +\ 1762 \\ \hline 5{,}016 \end{array} \qquad \begin{array}{r} {\scriptstyle 2\;11\;15\;} \\ \not{3}\not{2}\not{5}4 \\ -\ 1762 \\ \hline 1{,}492 \end{array}$$

Find the answers. Watch the signs.
Use shortcuts if you can.

1. $\begin{array}{r} 4761 \\ -\ 2819 \\ \hline \end{array}$
2. $\begin{array}{r} 1000 \\ -\ 750 \\ \hline \end{array}$
3. $\begin{array}{r} 750 \\ +\ 250 \\ \hline \end{array}$
4. $\begin{array}{r} 1750 \\ +\ 1250 \\ \hline \end{array}$
5. $\begin{array}{r} 6133 \\ -\ 2533 \\ \hline \end{array}$
6. $\begin{array}{r} 3600 \\ +\ 2533 \\ \hline \end{array}$
7. $\begin{array}{r} 3600 \\ +\ 2534 \\ \hline \end{array}$
8. $\begin{array}{r} 3610 \\ +\ 2534 \\ \hline \end{array}$
9. $\begin{array}{r} 750 \\ 250 \\ +\ 350 \\ \hline \end{array}$
10. $\begin{array}{r} 29 \\ 35 \\ 62 \\ +\ 47 \\ \hline \end{array}$
11. $\begin{array}{r} 315 \\ 708 \\ 95 \\ +\ 116 \\ \hline \end{array}$
12. $\begin{array}{r} 480 \\ 565 \\ 249 \\ +\ 197 \\ \hline \end{array}$

13. $4083 + 2196$
14. $5000 - 1234$
15. $4893 - 962$
16. $584 + 1208$

Complete the table. Show how many years ago these famous people were born.

Name	Year of Birth	Born This Many Years Ago
Joan of Arc	1412	17
Hans Christian Andersen	1805	18
Gerónimo	1829	19
Lise Meitner	1878	20
Albert Einstein	1879	21
Pablo Picasso	1881	22
Eleanor Roosevelt	1884	23
Jackie Robinson	1919	24
Tsung-Dao Lee	1926	25
Martin Luther King Jr.	1929	26

27 Martin Luther King Jr. was born on January 15, 1929. He delivered his famous "I Have a Dream" speech at the Lincoln Memorial in Washington, D.C., in August 1963. How old was he when he gave his speech?

28 Tsung-Dao Lee was born in China on November 24, 1926, and later moved to the United States. He received the Nobel Prize in Physics in 1957. How old was he when he won this prize?

LESSON 2.12 Adding and Subtracting Very Large Numbers

Key Ideas

Adding or subtracting very large numbers is just like adding or subtracting two-, three-, or four-digit numbers. Start at the right with the ones column. Then move left, column by column.

You might add to find the total population of the United States and Mexico, or you might subtract to find how many more people live in the United States than in Mexico.

As of 2005, the population of the United States was 295,734,134, and the population of Mexico was 106,202,903.

So the total population of the United States and Mexico as of 2005 was 401, 937, 037, and 189,531,231 more people lived in the United States than in Mexico.

$$\begin{array}{r} {}^{1\,1}\quad{}^{1}\quad\; \\ 295734134 \\ +\ 106202903 \\ \hline 401937037 \end{array} \qquad \begin{array}{r} {}^{8\,15}\quad{}^{3\,11}\quad \\ 2\not{9}\not{5}73\not{4}\not{1}34 \\ -\ 106202903 \\ \hline 189531231 \end{array}$$

Add.

1. $\begin{array}{r} 375476239 \\ +\ 249627472 \\ \hline \end{array}$
2. $\begin{array}{r} 924376419 \\ +\ 237464528 \\ \hline \end{array}$
3. $\begin{array}{r} 802362148 \\ +\ 199278972 \\ \hline \end{array}$

Subtract.

4. $\begin{array}{r} 624397260 \\ -\ 570269371 \\ \hline \end{array}$
5. $\begin{array}{r} 875269314 \\ -\ 286319215 \\ \hline \end{array}$
6. $\begin{array}{r} 20000000 \\ -\ 19999999 \\ \hline \end{array}$

eTextbook This lesson is available in the ***eTextbook.***

D. R. Kaprekar, a mathematician from India, lived from 1905 to 1988. He found this interesting pattern.

Choose a three-digit number in which not all digits are the same.
For example, use 587.

Write the digits in order, from largest to smallest and from smallest to largest, as follows:
875, 578

Then subtract, as follows:
$875 - 578 = 297$

Repeat with the result, as follows:
$972 - 279 = 693$

Repeat for 693 and so on. You will know when to stop!

If you get a difference of 99 when you subtract two numbers, think of 99 as 099, and then write the digits in order from smallest to largest this way:

$990 - 99 = 891$

Compare your results with those of your classmates. Write what you have learned in your journal.

Repeat the process for four-digit numbers. Do you find a similar pattern?

Writing + Math **Journal**

Write about what you have learned from studying Kaprekar's patterns.

LESSON 2.13 Solving Problems

Key Ideas

An even number of items can be divided into two equal sets, but an odd number of items *cannot* be divided into two equal sets.

Ten is an even number.

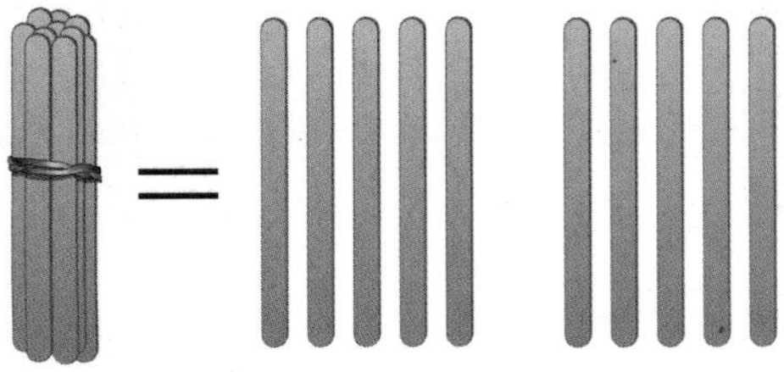

Eleven is an odd number.

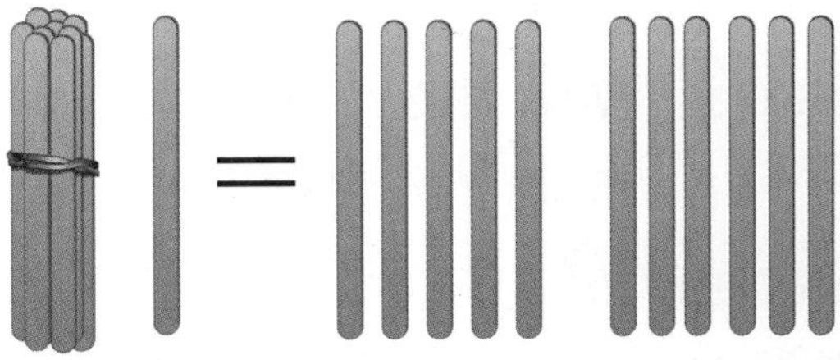

The Hill School has 342 students. The Valley School has 419 students. Think about odd and even numbers as you solve the following problems.

1. How many students are there in the two schools altogether?
2. How many more students does the Valley School have?
3. Today, 58 students are absent from the Hill School. How many students are at the school?
4. Which of the two school buildings is larger?

Next month 35 students are moving from the Valley School to the Hill School.

5. Which school will have more students next month if there are no other additions or removals from either school?
6. How many more students will there be in the school that has more students next month?
7. **Extended Response** How many more students would need to move from the Valley School to the Hill School for both schools to have the same number of students? Explain how you found your answer.

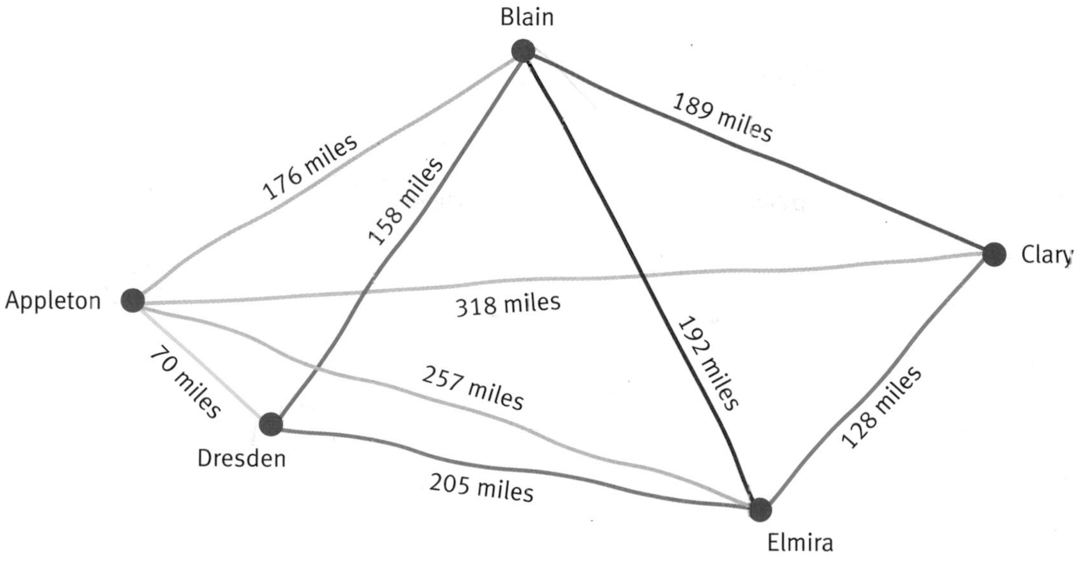

Use the map above to solve the problems. Find the most direct route.

8. How far is it from Appleton to Elmira?
9. How much farther is it from Appleton to Elmira than from Appleton to Dresden?
10. If you travel from Appleton to Blain, and then from Blain to Clary, how far will you go?
11. If you travel from Appleton to Dresden to Elmira, how far will you go? How much shorter would it be to go directly from Appleton to Elmira?
12. How far is it to go from Appleton to Clary, and then back to Appleton?
13. How far is it to travel from Dresden to Blain to Elmira? How much shorter would it be to go directly from Dresden to Elmira?

Mr. Cardona can drive about 500 miles in one day.

14. Can he drive from Blain to Elmira and back in one day? Explain.
15. Can he drive from Appleton to Clary and back in one day? Explain.
16. **Extended Response** If you took a direct flight from Dresden to Clary, about how many miles would you fly? Explain how you found your answer.

LESSON 2.14 Roman Numerals

Key Ideas

Roman numerals formed a number system that ancient Romans and other ancient Europeans used. We still use them in some situations today. Roman numerals are formed using letters. Some of those letters and the Arabic numbers they stand for are shown below.

C = 100
L = 50
X = 10
V = 5
I = 1

Write the Arabic numeral for each Roman numeral. Show how to add numbers as you read the Roman numeral. The first two have been done for you.

1. III = 1 + 1 + 1 = 3
2. VI = 5 + 1 = 6
3. VIII = ▢ + ▢ + ▢ + ▢ = ▢
4. XII = ▢ + ▢ + ▢ = ▢
5. XV = ▢ + ▢ = ▢
6. XXV = ▢ + ▢ + ▢ = ▢
7. LV = ▢ + ▢ = ▢
8. CL = ▢ + ▢ = ▢
9. CCLVI = ▢ + ▢ + ▢ + ▢ + ▢ = ▢

If a letter that stands for a smaller value is placed before a letter of greater value, subtract to read the Roman numeral.

IV = 5 − 1 = 4
IX = 10 − 1 = 9

Sometimes you have to add *and* subtract to read a Roman numeral, as in the following example:

XIV = 10 + 5 − 1 = 14

Try to find the output value for each input value. The rule for the function machine is "change the Roman numeral to the Arabic numeral." The first one has been done for you.

In	*Out*
XIV	14
XIX	
LIV	
LXIX	
CLIV	
CXIX	
CXXIV	
CLXXIX	

In	*Out*
XX	
XXVI	
LXXV	
LIX	
CLX	
CCX	
CCIX	
XXXVIII	

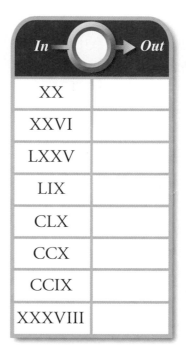

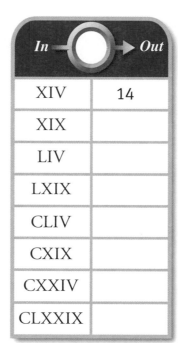

Exploring Problem Solving

Austin and Charity enjoyed their tree house, but they got tired of having to go up and down the ladder. They saw a picture in a book that gave them an idea. Their mom is going to take them to the hardware store on Saturday to buy the rope they will need for their personal food delivery system.

Answer these questions to help Austin and Charity.

1. How will the delivery system work?
2. What will be the path of the rope?
3. How much rope should Austin and Charity buy?
4. Can you figure out how many feet of rope Austin and Charity should buy?

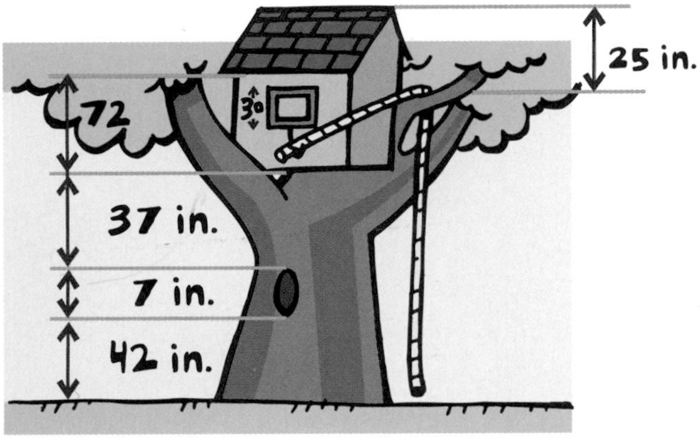

Cumulative Review

Place Value Lesson 1.6

Write each number in expanded form.

1. 222,781
2. 98,513
3. 54,783
4. 947,363
5. 826,753

Fractions of Numbers Grade 2 Lesson 7.8

Find the answers.

6. $\frac{1}{2}$ of 10 = ▢
7. $\frac{2}{2}$ of 200 = ▢
8. $\frac{1}{4}$ of 40 = ▢
9. $\frac{3}{4}$ of 80 = ▢
10. $\frac{2}{2}$ of 90 = ▢

Numbers to 10,000 Lesson 1.7

Fill in the missing numbers. Count on or count back.

11. 1,005; ▢; ▢; 1,002; 1,001; ▢; ▢; 998
12. 2,899 ▢; ▢; 2,902; ▢; ▢; ▢; 2,906
13. 4,876; 4,875; 4,874; ▢; 4,872; ▢; ▢; 4,869; 4,868; 4,867
14. 373, 374, ▢, 376, ▢, 378, 379, ▢, 381
15. 5,111; ▢; 5,113; ▢; 5,115; ▢; ▢; 5,118

Subtraction Grade 2 Lesson 6.5

Solve.

16. **Extended Response** Abdul has \$43. Alia has \$39. Do they have enough money to buy a present for their mom?
17. Lilly had \$54. She earned \$13. Now she has ▢.

Cumulative Review

Comparing Two-Digit Subtraction Expressions **Grade 2 Lesson 6.9**

Solve the following chain calculations.

18. $31 + 8 + 4 = \square$
19. $86 - 16 + 2 = \square$
20. $33 + 19 - 10 = \square$
21. $36 - 25 + 17 = \square$
22. $27 + 3 + 10 = \square$

Modeling Numbers through 1,000 **Grade 2 Lesson 9.2**

Write the following numbers in words.

23. 899
24. 412
25. 88
26. 567
27. 324

Missing Factors **Grade 2 Lesson 11.7**

Answer the questions. There are 7 days in 1 week.

28. How many weeks are there in 14 days?
29. How many weeks are there in 21 days?
30. How many weeks are there in 42 days?
31. How many weeks are there in 365 days?
32. How many weeks are there in 70 days?

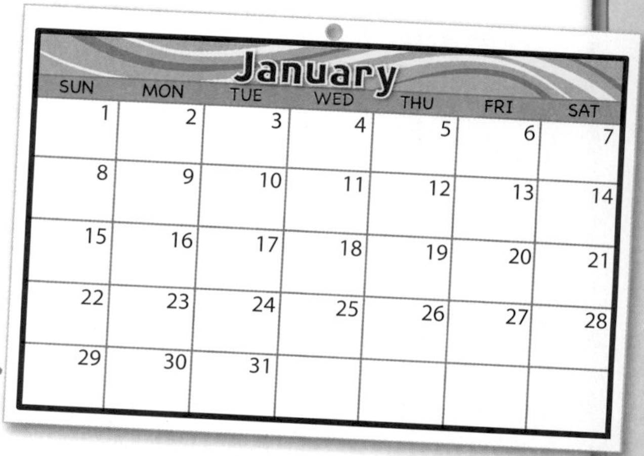

January
SUN MON TUE WED THU FRI SAT
1 2 3 4 5 6 7
8 9 10 11 12 13 14
15 16 17 18 19 20 21
22 23 24 25 26 27 28
29 30 31

Adding Two-Digit Numbers **Lesson 2.2**

Solve.

Sienna has 18 comic books. Abdul has 51 comic books. Moni has 29 comic books. Jenna has 33 comic books.

33. If Moni, Abdul, and Sienna put their comic books together, how many will they have altogether?
34. If Sienna and Abdul put their comic books together, and Moni and Jenna put their comic books together, which pair would have more comic books? Explain your answer.
35. If Sienna and Jenna put their comic books together, how many more comic books would they have than Moni?

eTextbook This lesson is available in the ***eTextbook.***

CHAPTER 2

Key Ideas Review

In this chapter you learned how to add and subtract numbers that have two or more digits.

You learned how to regroup tens and hundreds to make it easier to add and subtract multidigit numbers.

You learned how to approximate answers to addition and subtraction exercises.

Solve each problem.

1. Ana has 125 pennies. Her sister Lourdes has 57 pennies. How many pennies do they have altogether? How can they write that amount of money in dollars and cents?

2. Mrs. Jentes made 50 "First in Line to Lunch" award cards for her class. Last week she gave out 11 of the cards. This week she gave out 13 more. How many cards does she have left?

Write how much.

3. 3 five-dollar bills, 6 one-dollar bills, 5 dimes

4. 1 twenty-dollar bill, 1 five-dollar bill, 7 one-dollar bills, 4 nickels, 7 pennies

Extended Response **Provide** a detailed answer for the following exercises.

5. Ben has $5. He wants to buy 8 zucchini for 55¢ each. Does he have enough money to buy the zucchini? How could he approximate the total cost of the zucchini?

6. Mangoes cost 89¢ each. Without doing paper and pencil computation, Ben knows he cannot buy 8 mangoes with $5. How does he know this? Explain your answer.

CHAPTER 2 Chapter Review

Lesson 2.1 **Write** the standard name for each of these.

1. 8 tens and 5 = ■
2. 3 tens and 13 = ■
3. 5 hundreds and 11 tens = ■
4. 8 hundreds and 14 tens = ■

Lesson 2.2 **Add.**

5. $\begin{array}{r} 36 \\ +\ 18 \\ \hline \blacksquare \end{array}$

6. $\begin{array}{r} 64 \\ +\ 27 \\ \hline \blacksquare \end{array}$

Lesson 2.4 **Subtract.**

7. $\begin{array}{r} 75 \\ -\ 32 \\ \hline \blacksquare \end{array}$

8. $\begin{array}{r} 34 \\ -\ 29 \\ \hline \blacksquare \end{array}$

Lesson 2.5 **Solve** each problem.

9. Jon is 76 inches tall, and Austin is 63 inches tall. How many inches taller than Austin is Jon?

10. If Cindy is 25 inches shorter than Austin, who is 63 inches tall, how tall is Cindy?

Lesson 2.6 **Write** how much.

11. 1 five-dollar bill ■
9 one-dollar bills
7 dimes
2 nickels
4 pennies

12. 1 ten-dollar bill ■
2 five-dollar bills
8 one-dollar bills
9 dimes
10 pennies

Lesson 2.7

Add.

13. $\begin{array}{r} 308 \\ +\ 251 \\ \hline \blacksquare \end{array}$

14. $\begin{array}{r} 576 \\ +\ 238 \\ \hline \blacksquare \end{array}$

15. $\begin{array}{r} 690 \\ +\ 450 \\ \hline \blacksquare \end{array}$

16. $\begin{array}{r} 593 \\ +\ 212 \\ \hline \blacksquare \end{array}$

Lesson 2.8

Subtract.

17. $\begin{array}{r} 682 \\ -\ 211 \\ \hline \blacksquare \end{array}$

18. $\begin{array}{r} 347 \\ -\ 107 \\ \hline \blacksquare \end{array}$

19. $\begin{array}{r} 486 \\ -\ 318 \\ \hline \blacksquare \end{array}$

20. $\begin{array}{r} 563 \\ -\ 479 \\ \hline \blacksquare \end{array}$

Lesson 2.9

Extended Response **Choose** the correct answer. Explain why your answers make sense.

21. $414 + 189 =$
   a. 603
   b. 850
   c. 333

22. $588 - 279 =$
   a. 309
   b. 499
   c. 80

Lessons 2.11 and 2.12

Add or subtract.

23. $\begin{array}{r} 5096 \\ +\ 1142 \\ \hline \blacksquare \end{array}$

24. $\begin{array}{r} 8558 \\ -\ 7557 \\ \hline \blacksquare \end{array}$

25. $\begin{array}{r} 690854637 \\ +\ 191919191 \\ \hline \blacksquare \end{array}$

26. $\begin{array}{r} 684730124 \\ -\ 574730123 \\ \hline \blacksquare \end{array}$

Lesson 2.14

Write the Roman numeral for each Arabic numeral.

27. 7

28. 17

29. 54

30. 154

Practice Test

Write the standard name for each of these.

1. 12 tens = ▢
2. 12 hundreds = ▢
3. 5 tens and 10 = ▢
4. 5 hundreds and 10 tens = ▢
5. 7 tens and 11 = ▢
6. 7 hundreds and 11 tens = ▢

Regroup hundreds and tens. Then rewrite each number to show at least 10 tens and no more than 19 tens.

7. 900 = ▢ hundreds and ▢ tens
8. 310 = ▢ hundreds and ▢ tens
9. 220 = ▢ hundred and ▢ tens
10. 360 = ▢ hundreds and ▢ tens
11. 550 = ▢ hundreds and ▢ tens
12. 870 = ▢ hundreds and ▢ tens

Add or subtract.

13. $\begin{array}{r} 82 \\ +\ 46 \\ \hline \end{array}$

14. $\begin{array}{r} 58 \\ +\ 29 \\ \hline \end{array}$

15. $\begin{array}{r} 74 \\ -\ 33 \\ \hline \end{array}$

16. $\begin{array}{r} 58 \\ -\ 26 \\ \hline \end{array}$

17. $\begin{array}{r} 97 \\ -\ 29 \\ \hline \end{array}$

18. $\begin{array}{r} 65 \\ -\ 37 \\ \hline \end{array}$

19. $\begin{array}{r} 53 \\ 16 \\ +\ 31 \\ \hline \end{array}$

20. $\begin{array}{r} 214 \\ 121 \\ 343 \\ +\ \ 22 \\ \hline \end{array}$

Choose the correct answer.

21. How much money is this?

1 ten-dollar bill

3 five-dollar bills

2 one-dollar bills

2 dimes

3 nickels

6 pennies

Ⓐ $27.41 Ⓑ $18.16

Ⓒ $14.76 Ⓓ $11.96

22. How much money is this?

4 five-dollar bills

3 one-dollar bills

8 dimes

4 nickels

7 pennies

Ⓐ $24.07 Ⓑ $23.87

Ⓒ $15.17 Ⓓ $13.87

23. Josh has 4 one-dollar bills, 2 quarters, 4 dimes, 3 nickels, and 4 pennies. How much money does Josh have?

Ⓐ $3.89 Ⓑ $4.19

Ⓒ $4.99 Ⓓ $5.09

24. Joel has 1 twenty-dollar bill, 2 five-dollar bills, 2 quarters, 2 dimes, and 13 pennies. How much money does Joel have?

Ⓐ $30.83 Ⓑ $27.83

Ⓒ $22.13 Ⓓ $20.83

25. 5,564 + 4,237 =

Ⓐ 7,327 Ⓑ 8,901

Ⓒ 9,801 Ⓓ 9,810

26. 3,172 − 1,638 =

Ⓐ 4,872 Ⓑ 2,534

Ⓒ 1,534 Ⓓ 1,443

27. What is the Roman numeral for 34?

Ⓐ XXIV Ⓑ LIV

Ⓒ XXXIV Ⓓ XXXVI

28. What is the Roman numeral for 188?

Ⓐ CLXVI

Ⓑ CLXXXVIII

Ⓒ CLVIII

Ⓓ CLXXVIII

Practice Test

Use approximation to choose the correct answer.

29. 729 + 193 =

Ⓐ 822

Ⓑ 922

Ⓒ 1,022

30. 421 + 1317 =

Ⓐ 1,458

Ⓑ 1,568

Ⓒ 1,738

31. 73,289 + 12 ■ 70,289 + 30

Ⓐ $=$

Ⓑ $>$

Ⓒ $<$

32. 888,777 + 10 ■ 888,776 + 11

Ⓐ $=$

Ⓑ $>$

Ⓒ $<$

Choose the correct answer.

33. What does the number 4 represent in 42,831?

Ⓐ 4 hundreds

Ⓑ 4 thousands

Ⓒ 4 ten thousands

Ⓓ 4 ones

34. What is 315,080 in expanded form?

Ⓐ 300,000 + 10,000 + 4,000 + 0 + 80 + 0

Ⓑ 30,000 + 1,000 + 500 + 0 + 8

Ⓒ 300,000 + 10,000 + 5,000 + 0 + 80 + 0

Ⓓ 300,000 + 5,000 + 100 + 0 + 8

35. Tamlyn is 4 feet 7 inches tall. Max is 4 feet 9 inches tall. Keisha is 2 inches shorter than Tamlyn. How much taller is Max than Keisha?

Ⓐ 3 inches

Ⓑ 4 inches

Ⓒ 7 inches

Ⓓ 9 inches

Extended Response **Solve.**

36. The parents and teachers at Wilson School have four bake sales during the year to raise money for the library. They made $185 at the first sale. At the second sale, they made $87 more than they made at the first sale. At the fourth sale, they made $55 more than they made at the third sale and $19 less than they made at the second sale.

a. How much money did the parents and teachers make at the second sale?

b. How much more money did they make at the fourth sale than they made at the first sale?

c. How much money did they make altogether for the library?

d. The librarian wants to buy 2 more computers for the students to use. Each computer will cost $449. Did the parents and teachers earn enough money to pay for the computers? Tell how you know.

Thinking Story

How Close Is Close Enough?

Portia always likes to figure everything out exactly, but Ferdie doesn't mind using numbers that are "close enough."

"My way is better," said Portia, "because I always get the right answer."

"My way is better," said Ferdie, "because I get my answers quicker, and they are close enough. Besides, you sometimes make mistakes, and I never do."

Whose way do you think is better: Portia's way of always figuring things out exactly or Ferdie's way of using numbers that are close enough?

Ferdie and Portia decided to keep track for a whole day and see whose way worked better. It was Saturday, and they were in the store helping their mother with the shopping. She told them they could get supplies to decorate their tree house, but not to spend more than a dollar. Stickers cost 47¢ each. They had to figure out how many stickers they could get without spending more than a dollar.

"Let's see," said Portia, "47 and 47 is . . . I need a pencil for this one."

"I already have the answer," said Ferdie. "We can get 2 stickers and have a few cents left over."

Is Ferdie right?

How could he have figured it out so quickly?

"How do you know?" Portia asked.

"Because 47¢ is almost half a dollar," he said, "and 2 half-dollars make a dollar, so we can buy only

2 stickers for a dollar. There will be something left over, but not enough for another sticker."

"Your way worked better that time," said Portia, "but you were just lucky that 47¢ is so close to half a dollar; I didn't notice that."

Next their mother wanted them to get some small paintbrushes to use on the tree house. "We need 3 paintbrushes," their mother said, "but don't spend more than a dollar."

Ferdie and Portia found them. They cost 39¢ each.

"Oh, dear, I hope 3 of these don't cost more than a dollar," Portia said.

"Don't bother working it all out," said Ferdie. "We can't buy these paintbrushes. Three of them cost more than a dollar."

Can you think of a way that Ferdie could have figured out quickly that the paintbrushes cost more than a dollar?

"How can you be sure?" Portia asked.

"Easy," said Ferdie. "Thirty-nine is almost 40, which is 4 tens. Four tens and 4 tens and 4 tens makes 12 tens. That's 120¢, which is quite a bit more than a dollar."

The children looked around some more. At last they found some other paintbrushes that were almost as big, and they cost 29¢ apiece.

"Let's get these," said Ferdie.

"Not so fast," Portia said, getting out her pencil. "We need to figure out exactly how much 3 of them cost and make sure it isn't more than a dollar."

"Well, I'm ready to start painting the tree house. I'm going to pay for these so I can get started," said Ferdie.

While Portia was busy adding 29 and 29 and 29, Ferdie went up to the checkout counter and paid for the paintbrushes.

Will the 3 paintbrushes cost more or less than a dollar?

Try to figure it out Ferdie's way.

Ferdie came back just as Portia finished adding. "I knew I was right," he said. "I figured that 29 is almost 30. Thirty and 30 and 30 makes 90, so the 3 paintbrushes would cost less than 90¢. I paid the clerk, and I got 12¢ change from a dollar."

"Wait a minute," said Portia. "I've figured out that the 3 paintbrushes should cost 87¢. You didn't get the right amount of change."

If Portia is right, how much change should Ferdie have received?

"Eighty-seven from 100 is 13," Portia said. "You should have gotten 13¢ back, and you got only 12¢."

"I guess you're right," said Ferdie. He went back to the clerk, who said, "Oh, yes, I made a mistake," and gave him another penny in change.

"See," said Portia, "that proves it's important to figure out exactly how much things cost, even if it is more work and takes longer."

"You haven't proven it to me," said Ferdie. "All that work for just one penny! Twelve cents was close enough."

Who do you agree with—Ferdie or Portia? Why?

The End

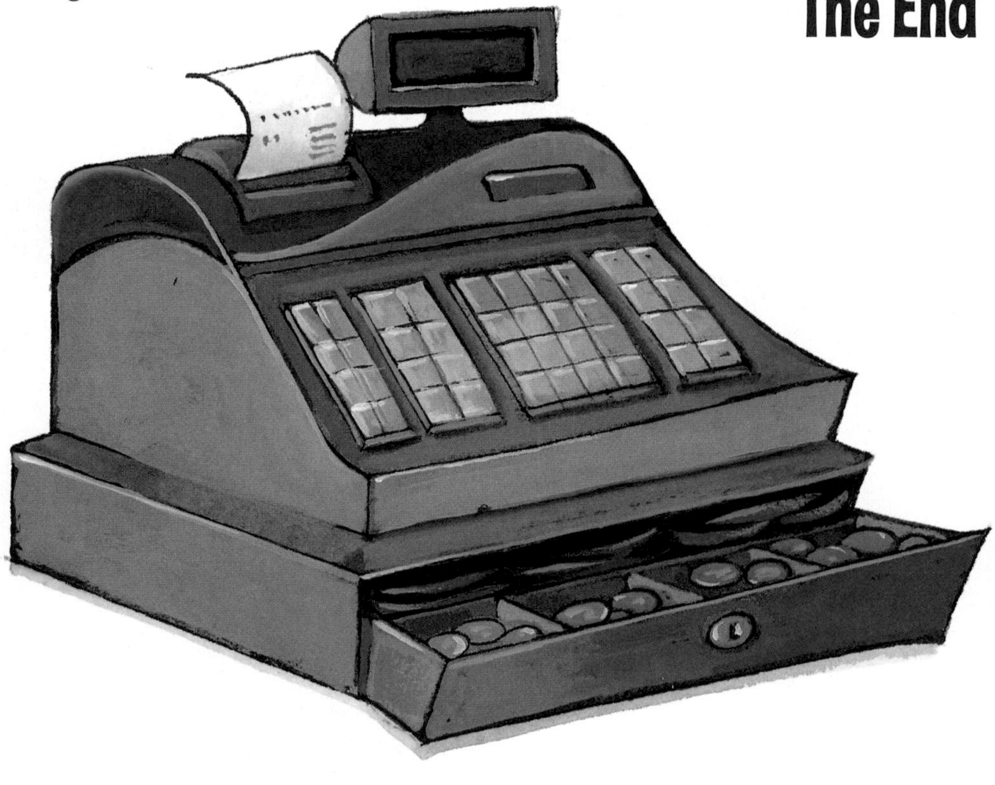

CHAPTER 3

Measuring and Graphing

In This Chapter You Will Learn

- how to tell time to the nearest minute.
- how to read a thermometer.
- how to measure length and compute perimeter and area.
- how to read and interpret graphs.

Problem Solving

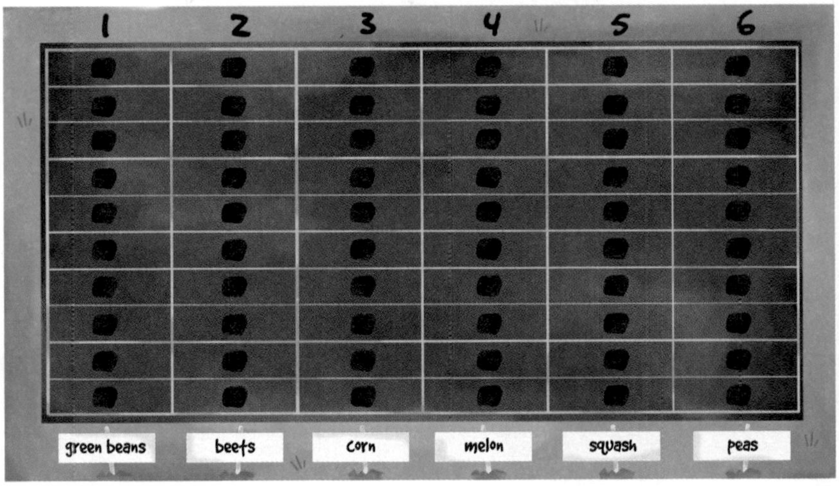

Speedy Gardener

Rules

Object: To see how many seedlings you can plant in half a minute

One partner rolls a ***Number Cube*** and calls out the number. The other partner puts a seedling in a hole in that row. Count and record how many seedlings are planted.

1. How many seedlings did you plant in half a minute?
2. How many seedlings do you think you could plant in a whole minute?
3. Play for a whole minute to check your prediction.

LESSON 3.1

Telling Time

Key Ideas

Remember: The long hand shows the minute or minutes. The short hand shows the hour.

What time is it? How many minutes after each hour? The first problem has been done for you.

1.  8:05

5 minutes after 8

2. 

minutes after

3. 

minutes after

4. 

minutes after

5. 

minutes after

6. 

minutes after

eTextbook This lesson is available in the *eTextbook.*

We can say the time in different ways.

45 minutes after 7

15 minutes to 8

7:45

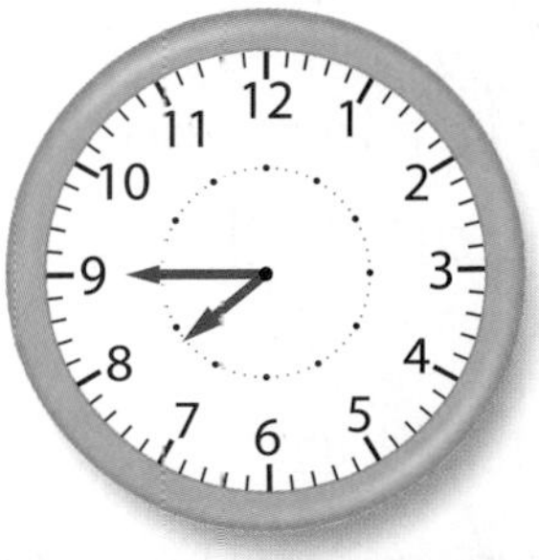

What time is it? How many minutes before the next hour? The first problem has been done for you.

7.  2:55

5 minutes to 3

8.  ___

___ minutes to ___

9. 

___

___ minutes to ___

10.  ___

___ minutes to ___

11. 

___

___ minutes to ___

12.  ___

___ minutes to ___

13. Penelope finished her homework at 7:30 P.M. She started at 6:45 P.M. How long did she spend on homework?

14. Chloe's walk to the bus stop takes her 15 minutes. She wants to arrive at the bus stop at 7:55 A.M. to ride the 8:00 A.M. bus. What time should Chloe leave her house?

15. Malik started eating lunch at 11:30 A.M. and was finished eating 50 minutes later. What time was he finished eating?

Tell which clocks show the same time. Match the analog clocks with the correct digital clocks.

16 

a. 

17 

b. 

18 

c. 

19 

d. 

20 

e. 

eTextbook This lesson is available in the ***eTextbook.***

Tell the time in three ways. The first one has been done for you.

21 

2:45

45 minutes after 2
15 minutes to 3

22 

___

___ minutes after ___
___ minutes to ___

23 

___

___ minutes after ___
___ minutes to ___

24 

___

___ minutes after ___
___ minutes to ___

25 

___

___ minutes after ___
___ minutes to ___

26 

___

___ minutes after ___
___ minutes to ___

27 

___

___ minutes after ___
___ minutes to ___

28 

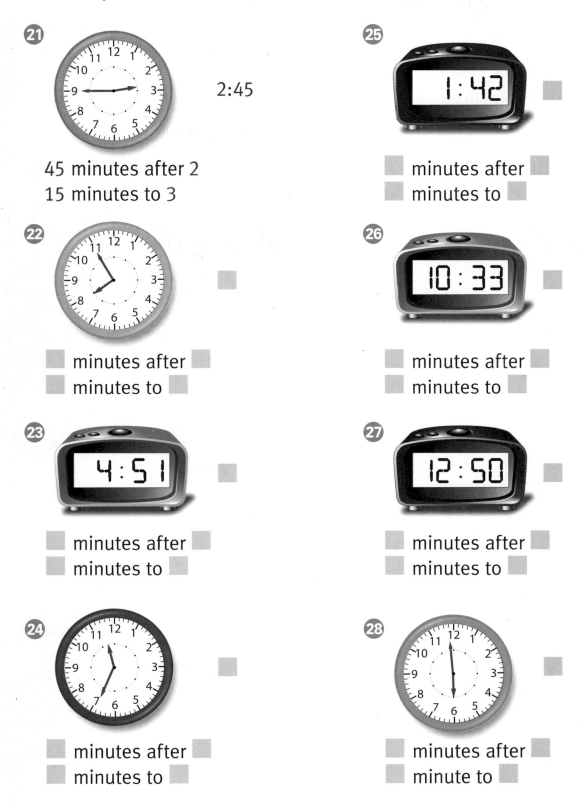

___

___ minutes after ___
___ minute to ___

LESSON 3.2

Reading a Thermometer

Key Ideas

Temperature is measured with a thermometer. In the United States, temperature is commonly measured in degrees Fahrenheit (°F). In most other countries, temperature is measured in degrees Celsius (°C). Celsius is sometimes called *Centigrade*.

Notice that on the thermometer below there are *two* degrees between the marks on the Fahrenheit side but only *one* degree between the marks on the Celsius side.

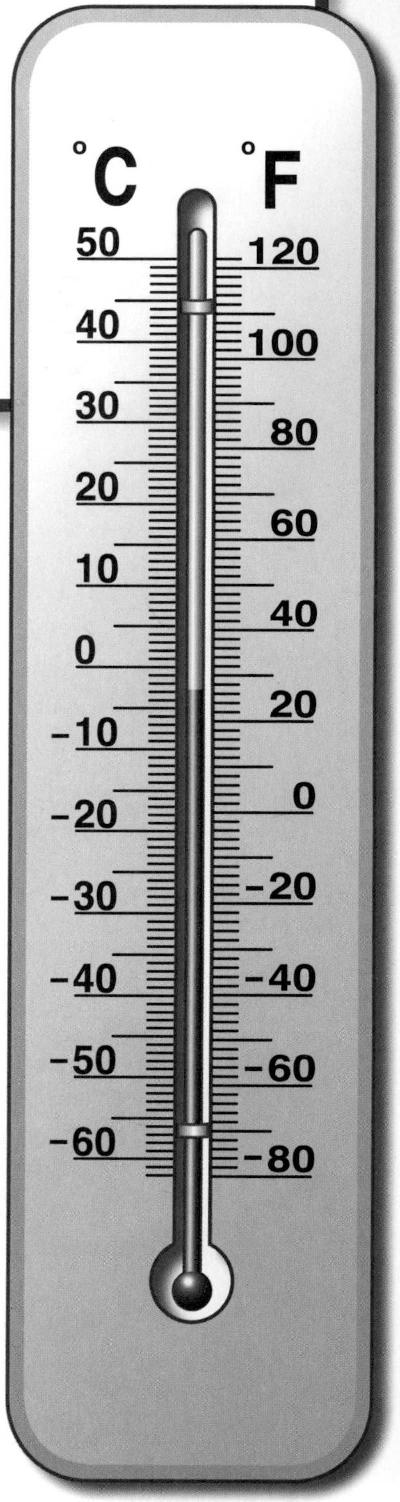

Use the Fahrenheit scale on the thermometer shown to answer the questions.

1. How many marks are there between 40 and 50 on this thermometer?
2. What does the first mark above the 40 stand for?
3. What does the third mark above the 20 stand for?
4. What does the fourth mark above the 20 stand for?
5. Does the temperature appear to be between 26 and 28 degrees?
6. What temperature does this thermometer show?
7. At that temperature, would you be comfortable in your swimsuit?
8. If the top of the red line were two marks below the 0, what would the temperature be? Would this be warm or cold?

Write the temperature shown on each Fahrenheit thermometer. Tell whether you think the temperature is *hot, comfortable,* or *cold.*

9 

10 

11 

12 

13 

14 

15 

16 

17 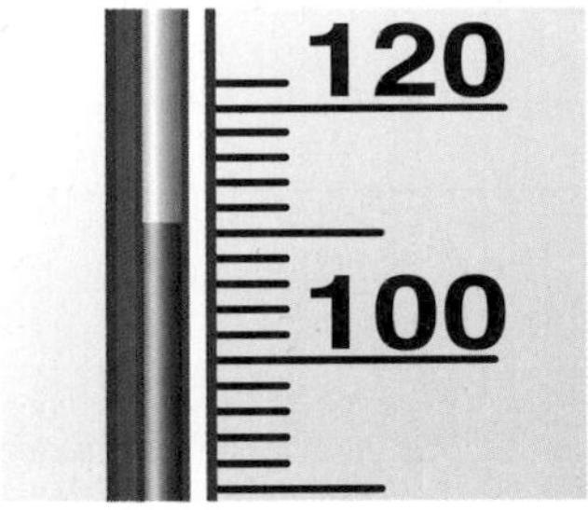

18 

LESSON 3.3 Measuring and Graphing

Key Ideas

Graphs are sometimes useful for displaying information.

A bar graph uses bars (rectangles) to represent data. You read a bar graph like the one below by first looking at the bottom for a category. Then you go to the top of that bar and trace over to the left axis for the number.

Each student in Libby's class measured the length of the room in shoe units. Libby made a bar graph of the results. Create a bar graph such as this for your class.

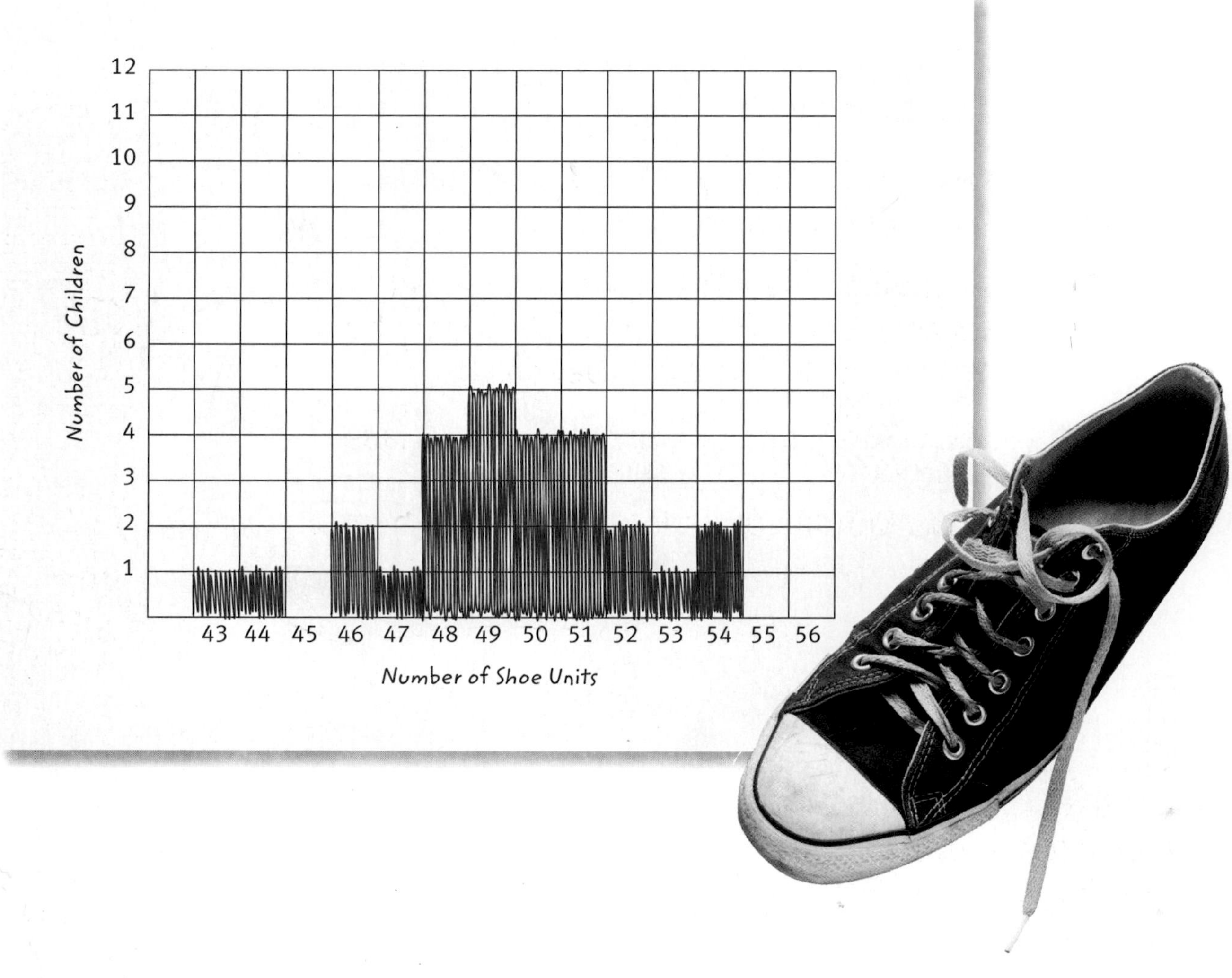

Use the graph on page 104 to answer Questions 1–10.

1. How many students measured 44 shoe units as the length of the room? How many students counted 54 shoe units? Which students do you think had longer shoes?
2. How many students measured the length of the room as 56 shoe units?
3. How many students measured the length of the room as 52 shoe units?
4. How many students measured the length of the room as 48 shoe units?
5. How many students measured the length of the room as 47 shoe units?
6. How many students measured the length of the room as 50 shoe units?
7. How many students measured the length of the room as more than 50 shoe units?
8. How many students measured the length of the room as less than 50 shoe units?
9. **Extended Response** Suppose a fifth-grade class had done the same activity. How would their graph be different? How would their graph be the same?
10. **Extended Response** Suppose that students in the class had measured the length of their classroom in inch units or in centimeter units. How would their measurements be the same? How would they be different?

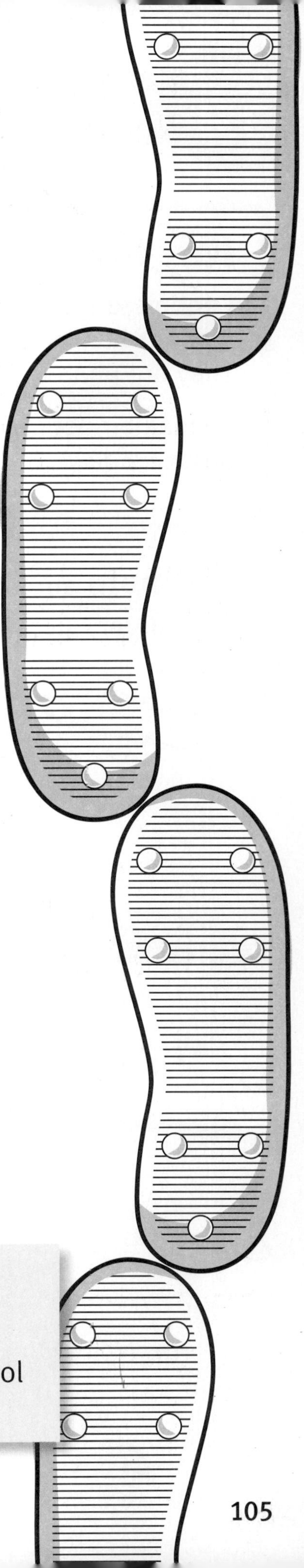

Writing + Math **Journal**

Predict how many of your shoe units it will take to measure the length of the room at the end of the school year. Explain how you made your prediction.

LESSON 3.4

Measuring Length—Centimeters and Meters

Key Ideas

Centimeters and meters are standard units used to measure length. They are units in the metric system.

A small binder clip is 2 centimeters long on one side.

Estimate and then measure each length with your centimeter ruler.

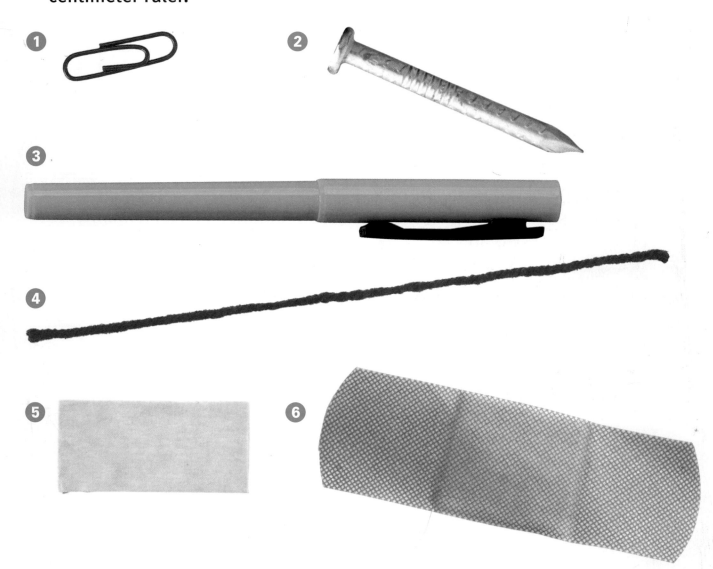

1. 

2. 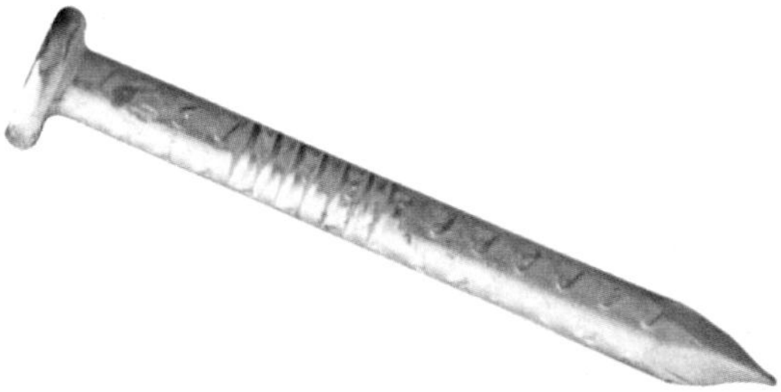

3. 

4. 

5. 

6. 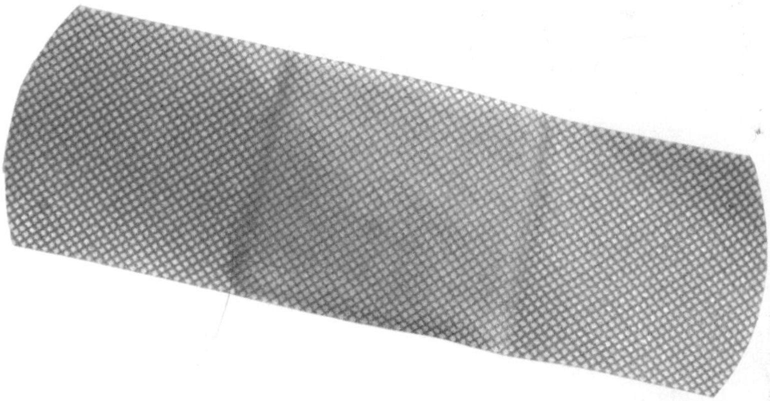

Andy is about 1 meter tall.

Study the picture on this page. Then discuss the answers to these questions.

7. About how many centimeters tall is Andy?
8. About how high is the floor of the tree house?
9. About how high is each rung on the tree house ladder?
10. **Extended Response** About how much rope was needed to hang the swing? Explain how you got your answer.

LESSON 3.5 Measuring Length—Inches, Feet, and Yards

Key Ideas

Inches, feet, and yards are standard units used to measure length.
They are units in the customary system.

This notebook is between 9 and 10 inches long (closer to 10 inches).

Estimate and then measure each length with your inch ruler.

1. 

2. 

3. 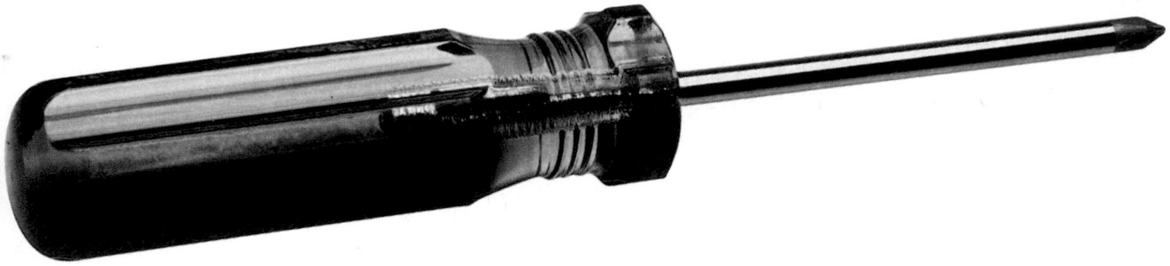

4. 

5. 

eTextbook This lesson is available in the ***eTextbook.***

Solve these problems.

Sasha can reach up to a height of 6 feet.

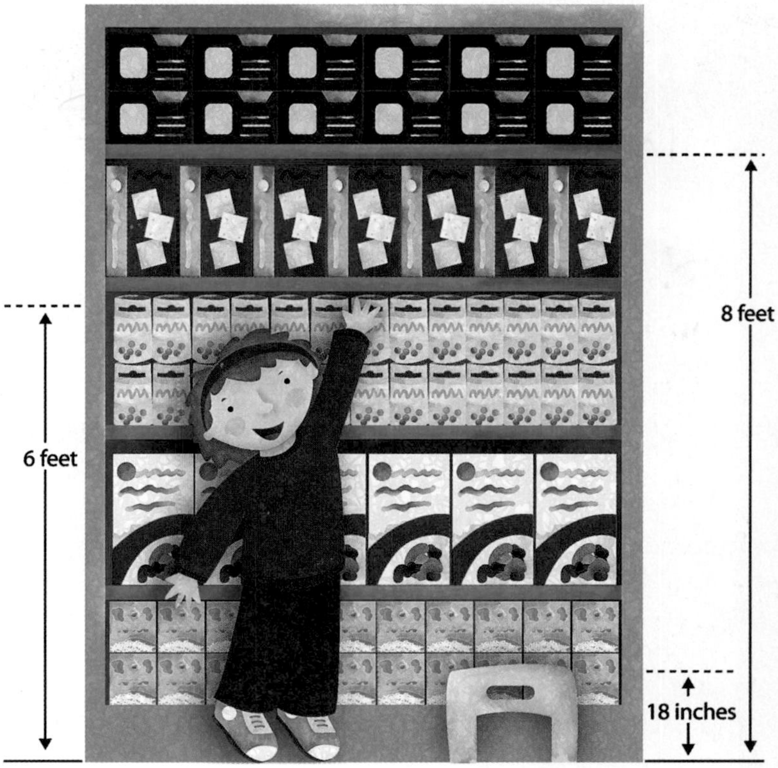

6 **Extended Response** If she stands on the stool, can she reach the top shelf? Explain your answer.

Mr. Cruz has a wooden board that is 2 feet long. He needs pieces that are 5 inches long.

7 How many 5-inch pieces can he get from the board?

8 How long will the leftover piece be?

9 **Extended Response** Meredith jumped 2 yards. Cora jumped 5 feet. Who jumped farther? How do you know?

10 **Extended Response** The Mount Baker Ski Area in Washington State reported 1,140 inches of snow during the winter of 1998–1999. That was the most snow ever recorded for one season in the United States. About how many feet is that? Explain your answer.

Writing + Math **Journal**

Is it easier to convert meters to centimeters or to convert feet to inches? Why?

Exploring Problem Solving

The students in Ms. Brown's class are planning a garden. They have 24 sections of fence to put around it. Each section is 1 yard long. What size and shape should they make the garden so that it has as much room for planting as possible?

Rachel used a pattern to make diagrams to solve the problem.

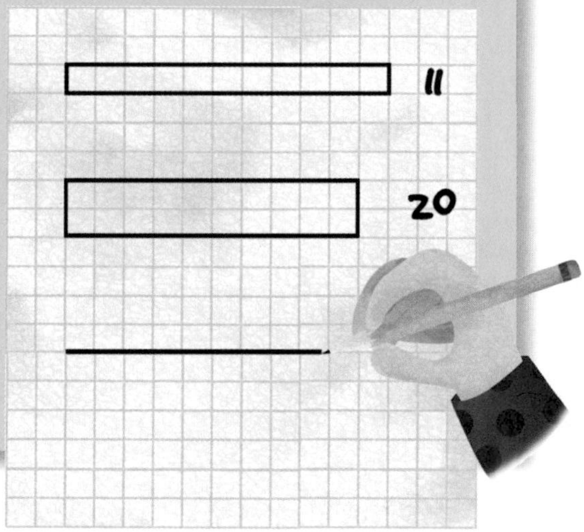

Think about Rachel's strategy.
Answer the following questions.

1. What does Rachel's first rectangle stand for?
2. Why has Rachel written 20 next to the second rectangle?
3. Which rectangle uses more fence sections, the first or the second? Which has more room?
4. Why doesn't Rachel make the second rectangle longer to give it more room?

eTextbook This lesson is available in the *eTextbook.*

5. What do you think Rachel will draw next?
6. How do you think Rachel is organizing her work on this problem?
7. Do you think Rachel's strategy will work? Why or why not?

Hector is making a physical model to solve the problem.

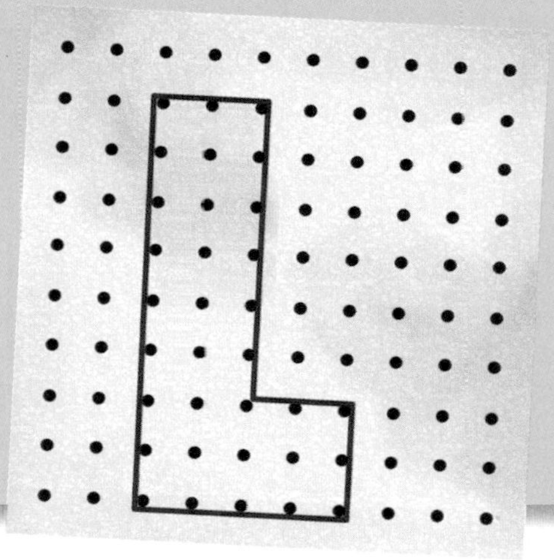

Think **about Hector's strategy. Answer the following questions.**

8. In Hector's model, what does the rubber band stand for?
9. How many sections of fence does Hector's *L*-shaped garden use? How can you tell?
10. Do you think it makes sense to try gardens that are not rectangles? Explain.
11. How can Hector keep track of what he is doing?
12. If you had the materials, would you use Hector's strategy? Why or why not?
13. Finish solving the problem. Use Rachel's strategy, Hector's strategy, or one of your own.

Cumulative Review

Patterns and Functions **Grade 2 Lesson 12.1**

Find the patterns. Fill in the blanks.

1. 112, 125, 138, 151, ___, ___, ___, ___, ___, ___, 242
2. 59, 51, 43, 46, 38, 30, ___, ___, ___, ___, 12
3. 37, 46, 55, 64, ___, ___, ___, ___, ___, 118
4. ___, 57, 43, 29, 69, 55, ___, ___, ___, 53, 39, 25
5. 69, 65, 61, ___, 59, 55, 57, ___, 49, 51, ___, ___, 45

Measurement—Yards, Feet, and Inches **Grade 2 Lesson 4.5**

How many?

6. 1 yard = ___ feet = ___ inches
7. 3 yards = ___ feet = ___ inches
8. 4 feet = ___ inches
9. 5 feet = ___ inches
10. 6 feet = ___ inches

Adding Two-Digit Numbers **Lesson 2.2**

Write the number sentence, and solve the problem.

11. 3 tens and 6 + 5 tens and 9

    ___ + ___ = ___

12. 8 tens and 2 + 2 tens and 5

    ___ + ___ = ___

13. 6 tens and 7 + 2 tens and 6

    ___ + ___ = ___

Place Value **Lesson 1.6**

Write the number on your paper in standard form. The table shows the number of hundred thousands, ten thousands, one thousands, hundreds, tens, and ones in each number.

	Hundred Thousands	Ten Thousands	One Thousands	Hundreds	Tens	Ones
14	0	6	6	8	4	5
15	1	2	3	1	2	7
16	7	5	7	3	8	9
17	3	8	2	4	7	6
18	2	0	7	7	6	9

Telling Time to the Minute **Grade 2 Lesson 10.9**

What time is it?

19

___ : ___

20

___ : ___

21

___ : ___

22

___ : ___

23

___ : ___

24

___ : ___

LESSON 3.6 Perimeter

Key Ideas

Perimeter is the length of the path around a figure.

The perimeter of the figure below is 20 centimeters because 4 + 6 + 4 + 6 = 20.

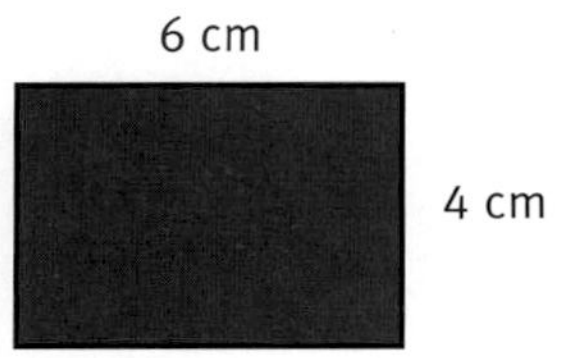

Find the perimeter of each figure.

1. 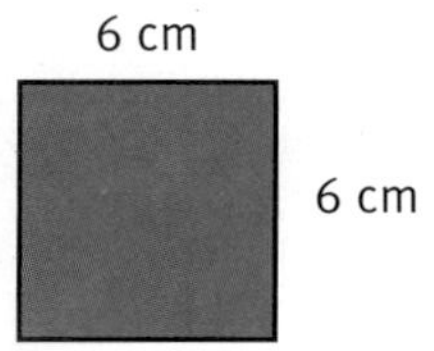

___ + 6 + 6 + ___ = ___

Perimeter: ___ centimeters

2. 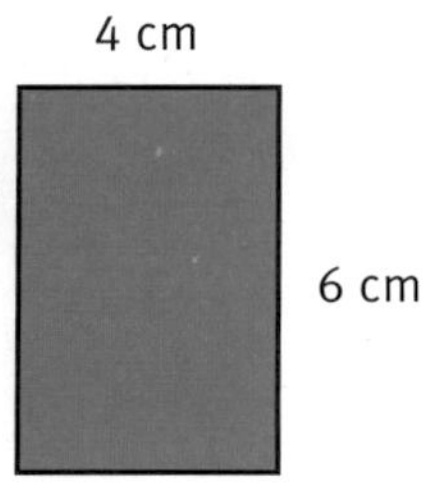

4 + ___ + ___ + 6 = ___

Perimeter: ___ centimeters

3. 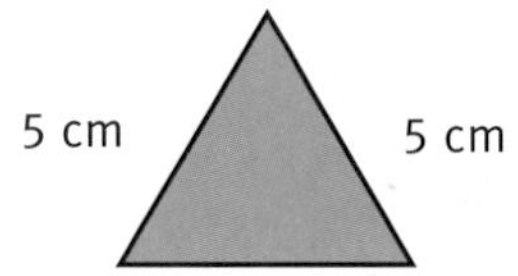

5 + ___ + ___ = ___

Perimeter: ___ centimeters

4. 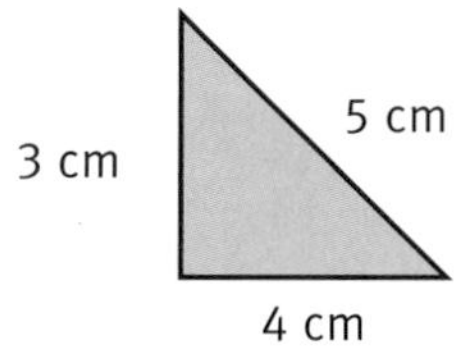

3 + ___ + ___ = ___

Perimeter: ___ centimeters

eTextbook This lesson is available in the ***eTextbook.***

Find the perimeter of each figure.

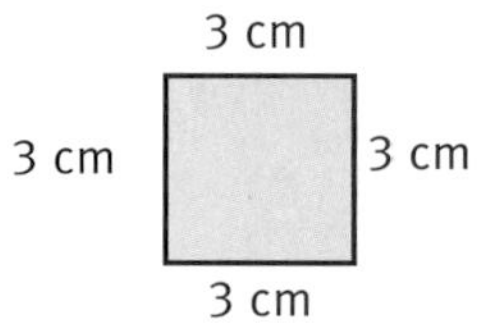

5 Square

Perimeter: ▢ centimeters

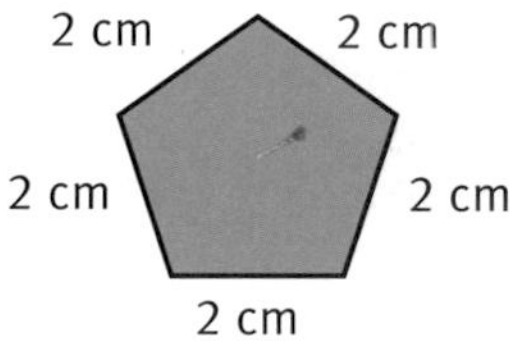

6 Regular pentagon

Perimeter: ▢ centimeters

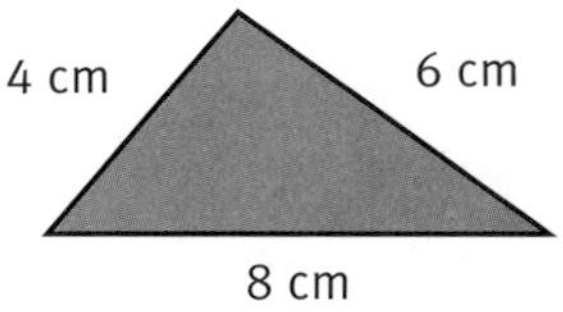

7 Triangle

Perimeter: ▢ centimeters

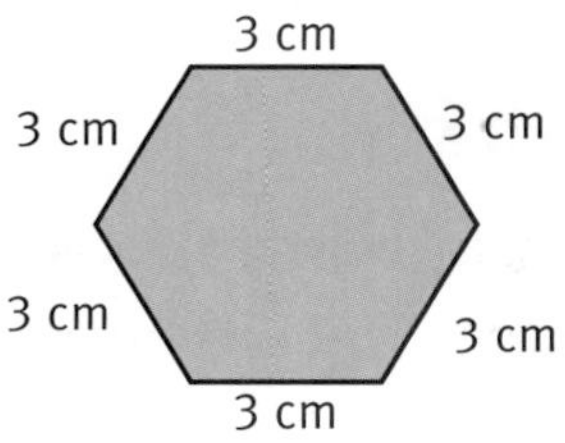

8 Regular hexagon

Perimeter: ▢ centimeters

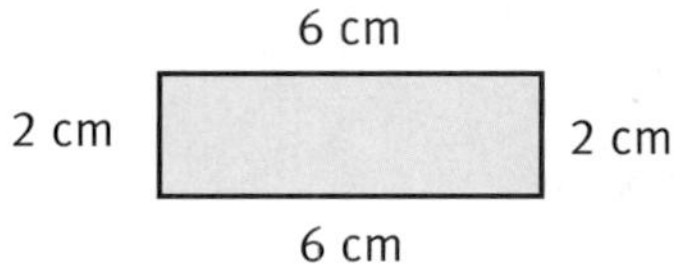

9 Rectangle

Perimeter: ▢ centimeters

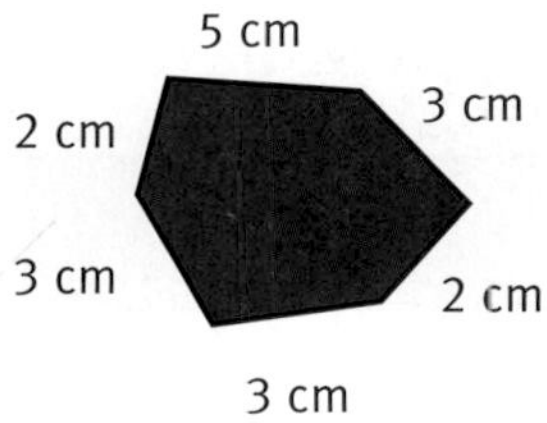

10 Hexagon

Perimeter: ▢ centimeters

LESSON 3.7

Perimeter and Area

Key Ideas

Area is the number of square units (such as square centimeters) that a figure covers. Area is *not* a length.

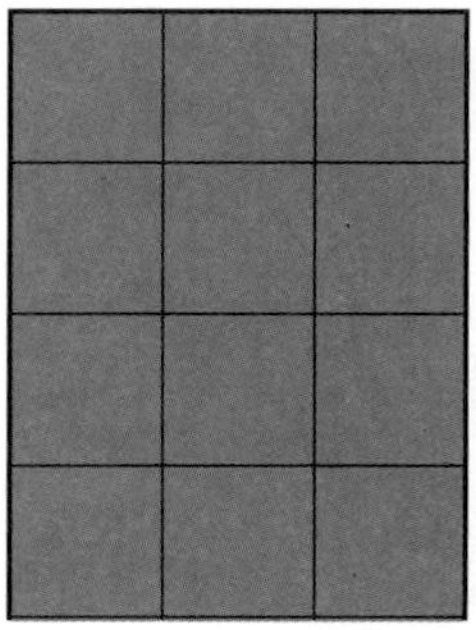

Count the squares inside the rectangle to find the area. Each square is 1 centimeter on each side.

The area of the rectangle is 12 square centimeters. The perimeter of the rectangle, which is the length of the path around the rectangle, is 14 centimeters.

Find the perimeter and the area for each figure. The first one has been done for you.

1. 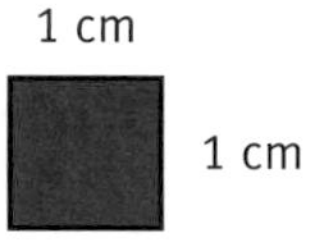

   Perimeter: 4 centimeters
   Area: 1 square centimeter

2. 

   Perimeter: ____ centimeters
   Area: ____ square centimeters

3. 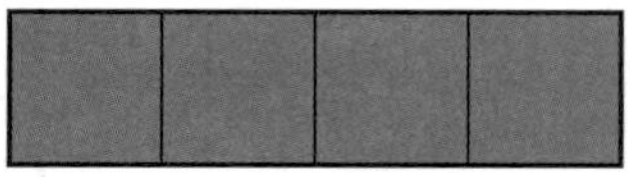

   Perimeter: ____ centimeters
   Area: ____ square centimeters

4. 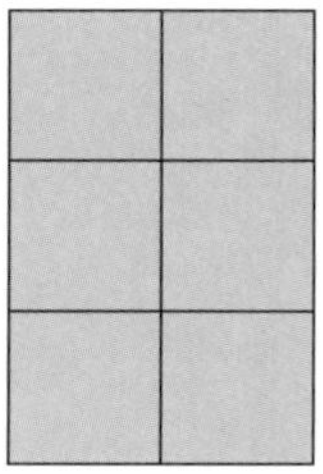

   Perimeter: ____ centimeters
   Area: ____ square centimeters

5. 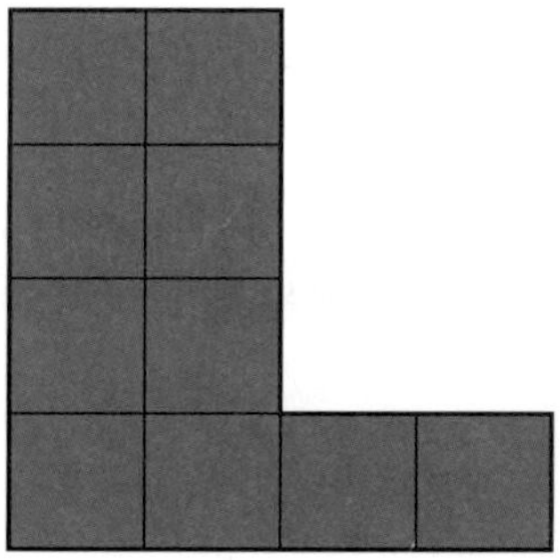

   Perimeter: ____ centimeters
   Area: ____ square centimeters

eTextbook This lesson is available in the *eTextbook.*

Solve.

6. What is the shape of Abby's garden?

7. How long a fence does Abby need to go around her garden?

8. Mr. Wing gave Abby 25 meters of fence. How many more meters of fence does she need?

9. Abby built a fence that divides her garden in half from left to right. What is the perimeter of one half of her garden?

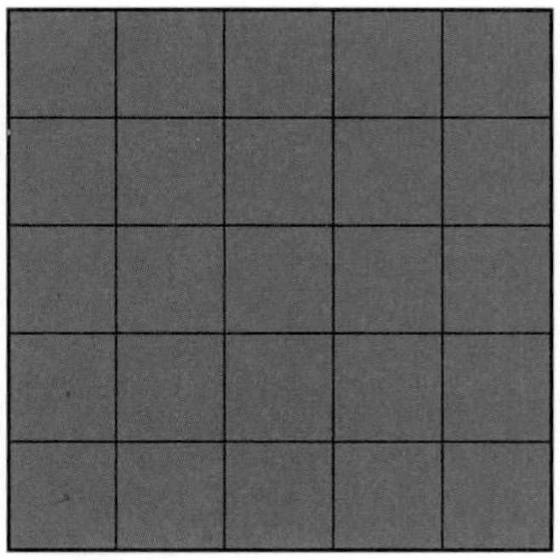

Marissa's older brother built her a square-shaped tree house in the backyard. He told Marissa he would take her to buy carpet if she knew the area. One side of her square tree house is 5 yards long.

10. What is the area of Marissa's tree house?

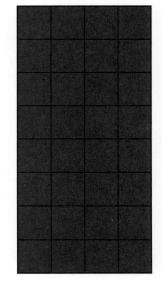

Rafael and his cousin are allowed to paint the top of the worktable in the garage. Rafael measures the top of the table and finds it to be 8 feet long and 4 feet wide.

11. How many square feet of the table will the paint cover?

12. **Extended Response** Rafael wants to set up a train track for his model train around the outer edge of the worktable. He will leave a 2-inch border around the track. About how many feet of track will he need?

LESSON 3.8 Estimating Area

Key Ideas

We can find or estimate the area of some figures by combining partial squares to make whole squares. We can also use this method to estimate area when we cannot find the exact area.

The four squares on the bottom are completely shaded. The four squares on the top are only partially shaded. However, we can combine the four partially shaded squares to make two whole squares. The area of this figure is 6 square centimeters.

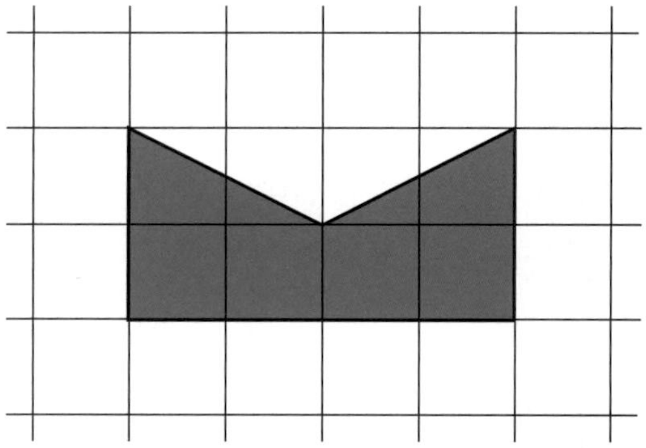

What is the area?

1. Exactly ▢ square centimeters

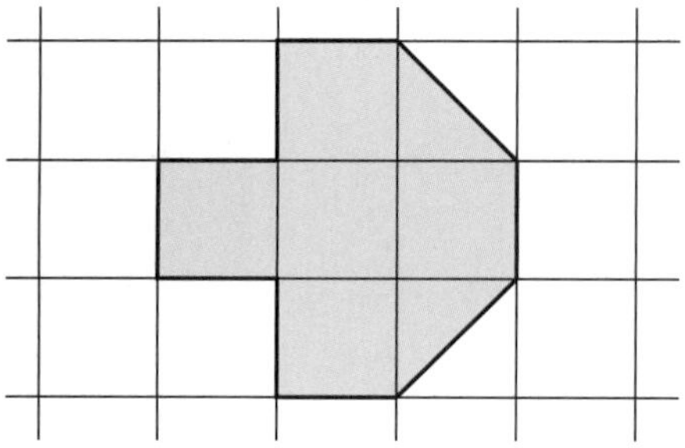

2. Exactly ▢ square centimeters

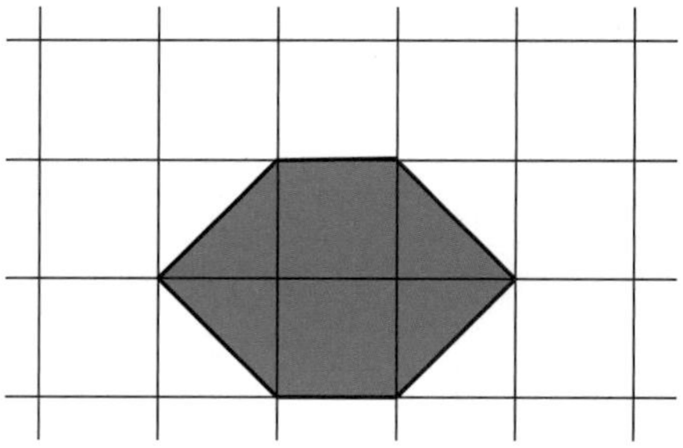

3. Exactly ▢ square centimeters

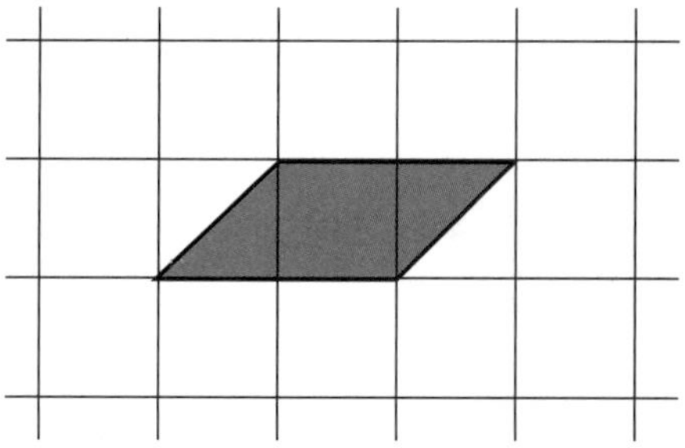

eTextbook This lesson is available in the ***eTextbook.***

4 Exactly ▢ square centimeters

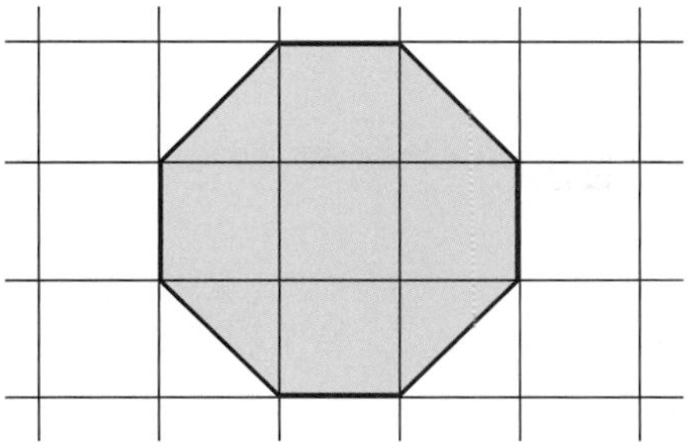

6 About ▢ square centimeters

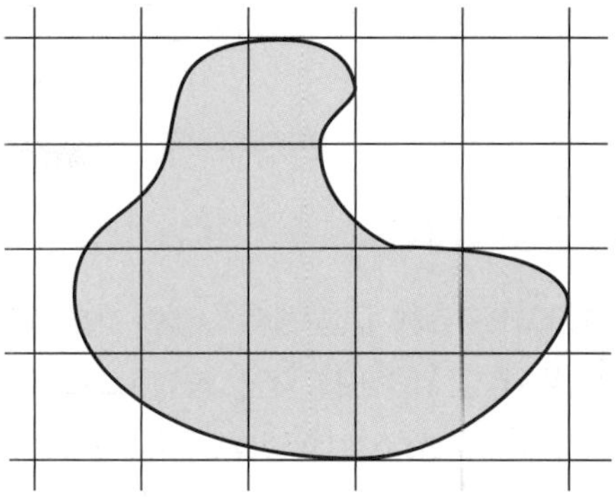

5 About ▢ square centimeters

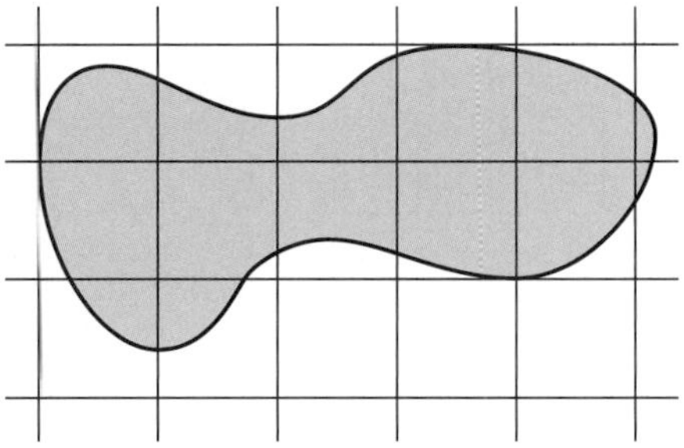

7 About ▢ square centimeters

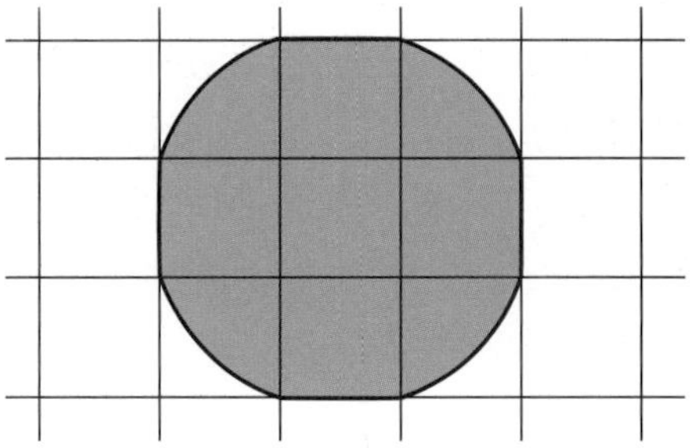

8 Find the area. About ▢ square centimeters

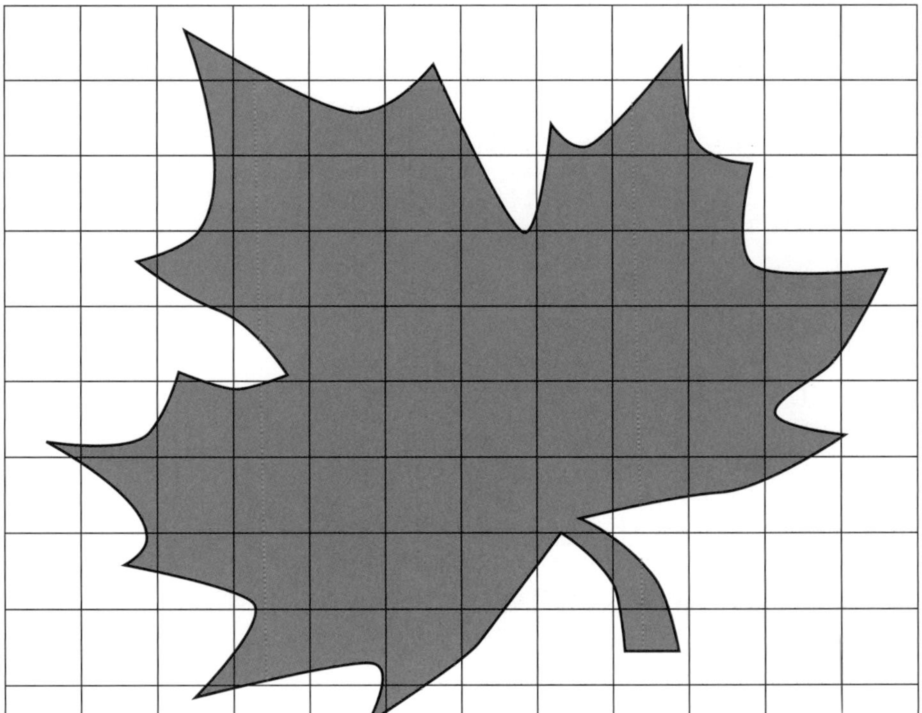

LESSON 3.9 Reading Graphs

Key Ideas

The graphs on these two pages show the cost of mailing a first-class letter for the years shown. Both graphs show the same information, but in different ways.

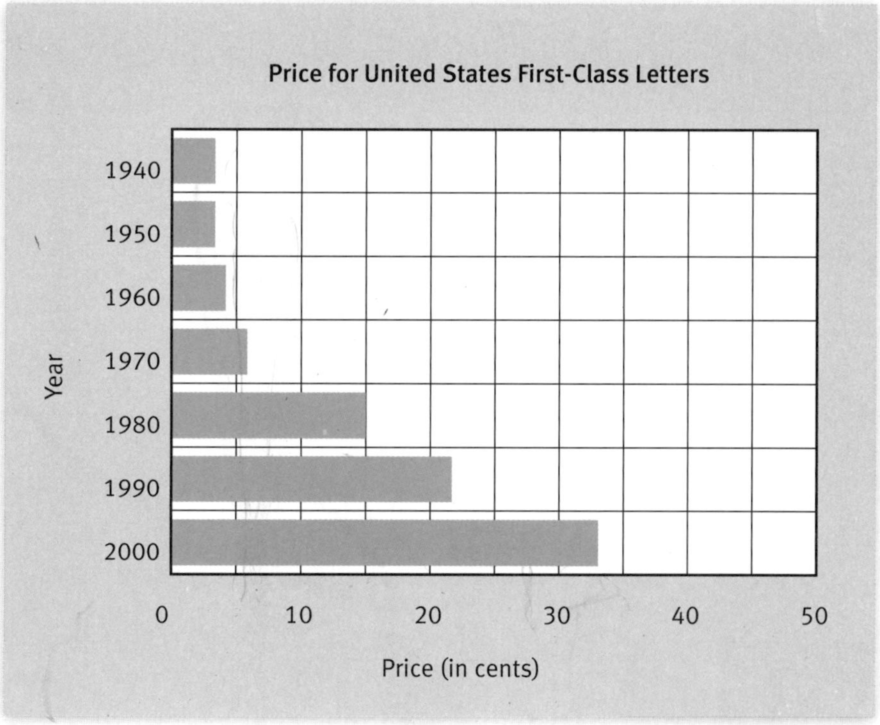

Use **the bar graph to answer the following questions.**

1. What was the cost of mailing a letter in 1970?
2. What was the cost of mailing a letter in 1990?
3. In which 20-year period did the cost double?
4. About what do you think the cost of postage was in 1975?
5. **Extended Response** What do you estimate the cost of mailing a letter will be in the year 2020? Explain your estimate.

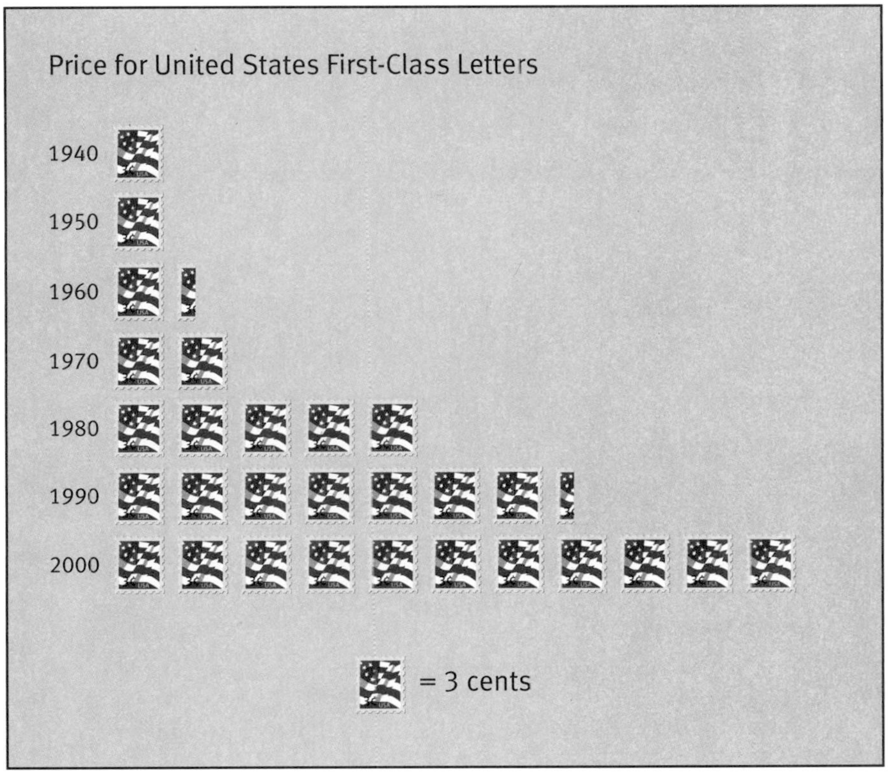

Use **the pictograph to answer the following questions.**

6. How many 3-cent stamps did it take to mail a letter in 1950?

7. How many 3-cent stamps did it take to mail a letter in 1980?

8. What was the cost for mailing a letter in 1950?

9. What was the cost for mailing a letter in 1980?

10. **Extended Response** How would you report the increase in the cost of postage from 1950 to 1980? Can you think of more than one way?

LESSON 3.10

Interpreting Bar Graphs

Key Ideas

It is often useful to organize and present information as a bar graph.

The principal of Northview Elementary School collected information about how students came to school. She reported what she found as a bar graph. Study the graph, and answer the questions.

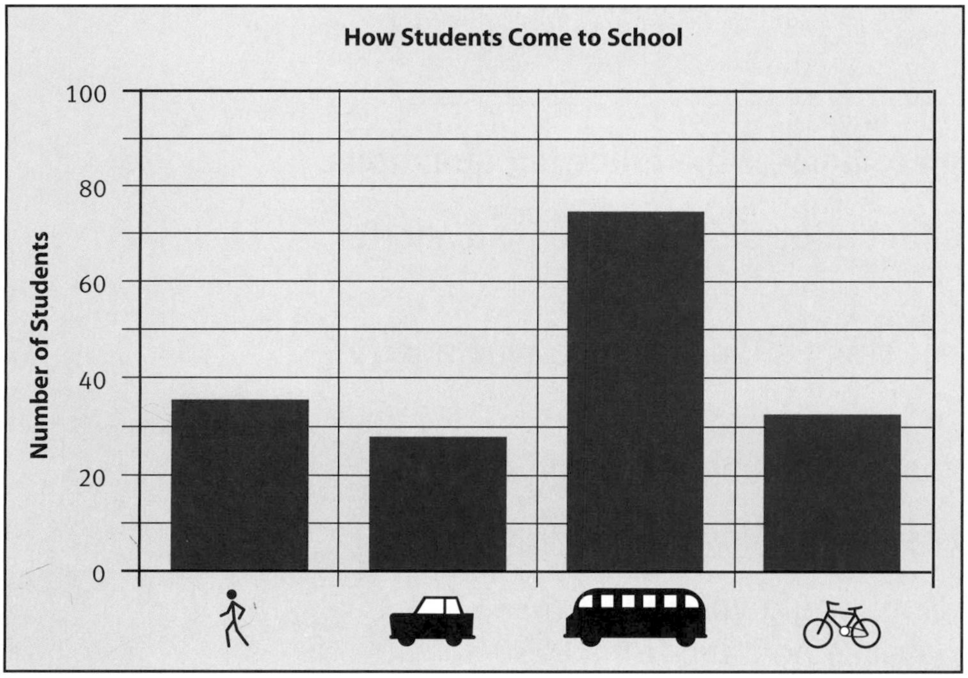

eTextbook This lesson is available in the ***eTextbook.***

Answer the following questions by studying the graph.

1. About how many students walk to school?
2. About how many students travel to school by car?
3. About how many students ride the school bus?
4. About how many students ride to school by bicycle?
5. **Extended Response** About how many students live within walking distance from school? Explain how you know.
6. **Extended Response** About how many students attend Northview Elementary School? Explain how you know.
7. **Extended Response** Northview Elementary School has grades 1–6. About how many students are in each grade? Write how you know.
8. **Extended Response** New houses are being built a few blocks from Northview Elementary School. How might this change the shape of the graph if the same information is collected three years from now?

The students from Ms. Nelson's class are planning next year's garden. They have permission to set up a garden along the back wall of the community center. They will use the wall as one side of the garden, so they need to buy fencing for only the other three sides. They have $36 to buy fencing, and they want a garden with as much area as possible.

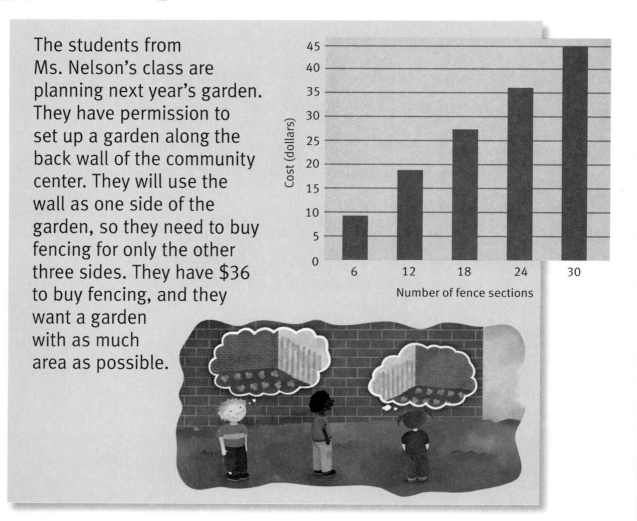

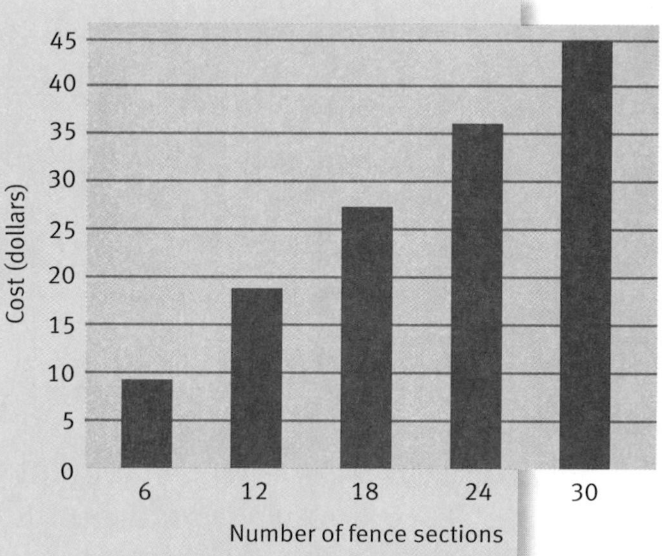

Work with your group to answer the following questions.

1. How many sections of fence will they be able to buy?
2. How many sides of the garden will the fence have to form?
3. How is this problem like the garden problem on page 110? How is it different?
4. How will you find the largest area that can be enclosed by 24 lengths of fence and one wall?

eTextbook This lesson is available in the *eTextbook.*

Cumulative Review

Counting and Estimating **Lesson 1.1**

Estimate how many roses are in this garden of roses. Then count the roses in the garden.

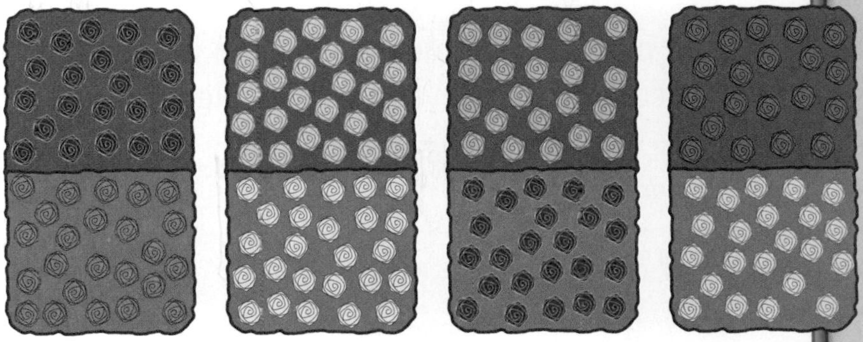

1. My estimate is that there are about ___ roses in the garden.
2. The actual number of roses in the garden is ___.

Applications with Money **Lesson 2.6**

Write how much.

3. 3 five-dollar bills
   4 one-dollar bills
   2 dimes
   7 nickels
   7 pennies ___

4. 1 one-dollar bill
   2 quarters
   5 dimes
   8 nickels
   1 penny ___

Measuring Perimeter **Grade 2 Lesson 10.3**

Find the perimeter.

5. 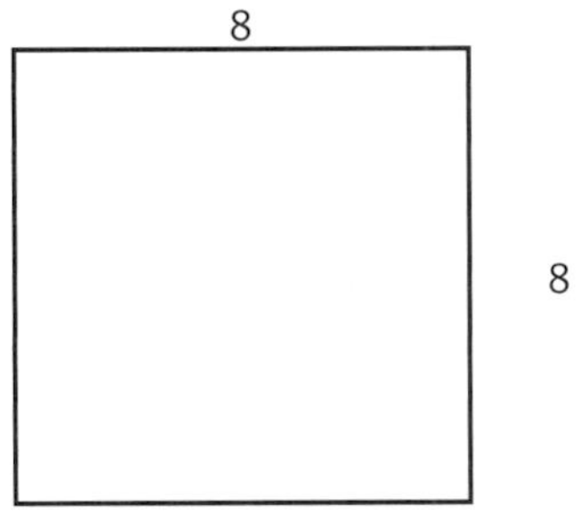

   perimeter = ___

6. 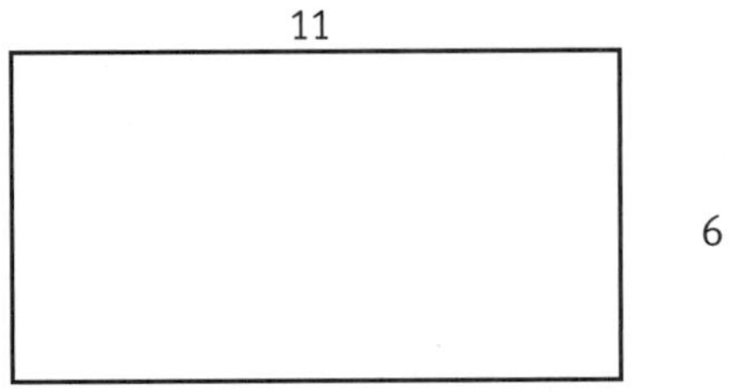

   perimeter = ___

Division and Multiplication **Grade 2 Lesson 11.8**

Complete the table.

7. Tyron sells flowers for $7 a bouquet.

   He made this table to help him know how much to collect. Help Tyron by completing the table.

Number of bouquets	1	2	3	4	5	6	7	8	9	10
Price (dollars)	7	14		28						70

Horizontal Bar Graphs **Grade 2 Lesson 4.11**

Transfer the data in the table to a horizontal bar graph. Then use the bar graph to answer the questions below. The data is a good-behavior table for Alia.

8. On which day did Alia get the most points?
9. How many points did Alia get all week?
10. **Extended Response** Why do you think the number of points on Tuesday was lower than any other day?

Pleasant and Polite Point Program

Day of the Week	Number of Points	Word of the Day
Saturday	卌 卌 卌 卌 卌 ||||	Helpful
Sunday	卌 卌 卌 卌 卌 卌	Courteous
Monday	卌 卌 卌 |||	Caring
Tuesday	卌 ||||	Hardworking
Wednesday	卌 卌 |	Understanding
Thursday	卌 卌 ||	Respectful
Friday	卌 卌 卌 卌 |||	Generous

CHAPTER 3 Key Ideas Review

In this chapter you explored measuring and graphing.

You reviewed telling time and reading a thermometer.

You estimated and measured length in nonstandard units and standard units.

You learned how to read and interpret bar graphs and pictographs.

Use **the bar graph to answer the questions.**

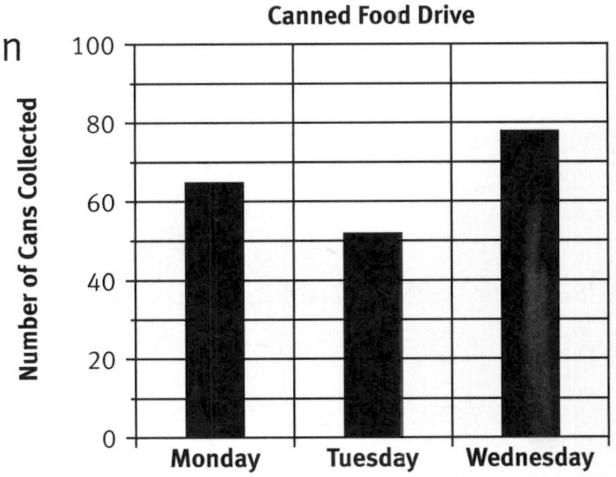

1. About how many cans were collected on Monday?
2. About how many more cans were collected on Monday than on Tuesday?
3. About how many cans were collected altogether on those three days?

Provide **a detailed answer for the following exercises.** Extended Response

4. Alex's bedroom is about 10 feet wide and 12 feet long. What is the area, in square feet, of his room? Draw a diagram, and then explain how you found the answer.
5. Danika's bulletin board is 1 foot 7 inches wide. How many pictures can she display in one row across the board if each picture is 5 inches wide? Explain your answer.
6. If the temperature outside were 55°F, would you wear a jacket? Tell why or why not.

CHAPTER 3 Chapter Review

Lesson 3.1 **Tell** how many minutes it is after the hour.

1. ___ minutes after ___
2. ___ minutes after ___
3. ___ minutes after ___

Lesson 3.2 **Write** the temperature shown on each Fahrenheit thermometer.

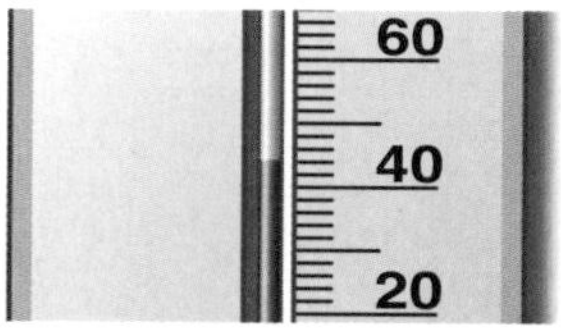

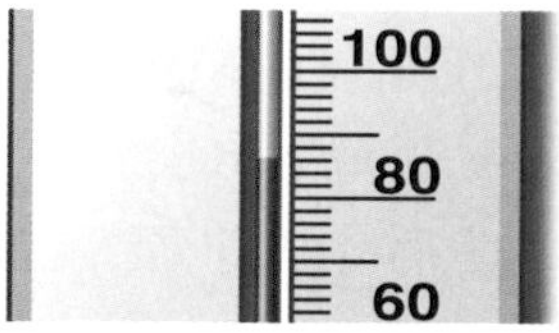

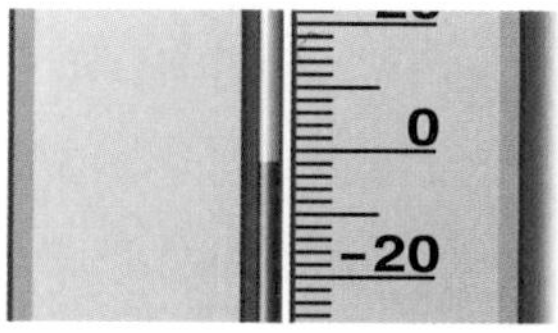

4.
5.
6.

Lesson 3.4 **Solve** each problem. Explain your answers.

7. **Extended Response** Ray estimated that the length from the floor to the surface of his desk is about 70 centimeters. Does his estimate make sense?

8. **Extended Response** Suki is measuring the perimeter of her grandmother's flower garden. Should she report her measure in centimeters or meters?

Lesson 3.5 **Solve** each problem.

9. J. D. has a piece of ribbon that is $3\frac{1}{2}$ feet long. He needs pieces that are 7 inches long. How many 7-inch pieces can he get from the long piece of ribbon? Will he have any ribbon left over?

10. The playground at Centerville School is 25 yards long. How many feet is that?

eTextbook This lesson is available in the ***eTextbook***.

Lesson 3.6

Find the perimeter of each figure.

11 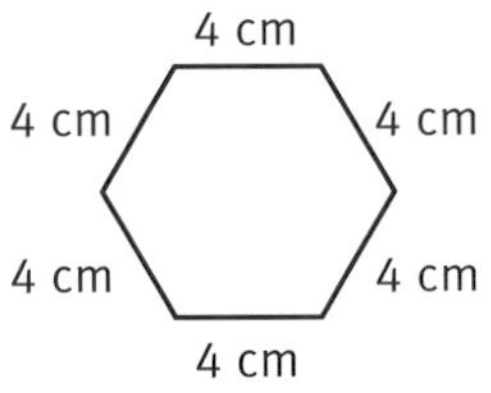

centimeters

12 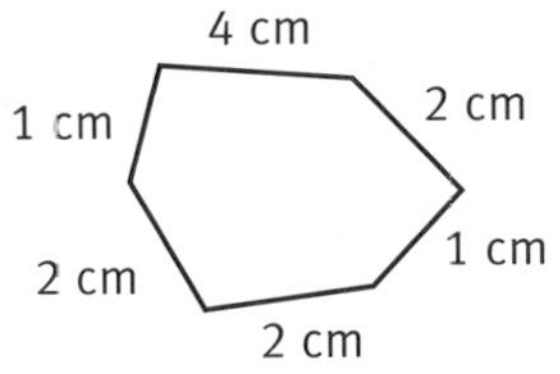

centimeters

Lesson 3.7

Answer the question.

13 What is the area of a rectangle that is 6 centimeters long and 2 centimeters wide? If you need to, draw the figure on graph paper to find the answer. Give your answer in square centimeters.

Lessons 3.3, 3.9, and 3.10

14 Petra and George are on one team. Lori and Kanye are on the other team. Which team has run more miles?

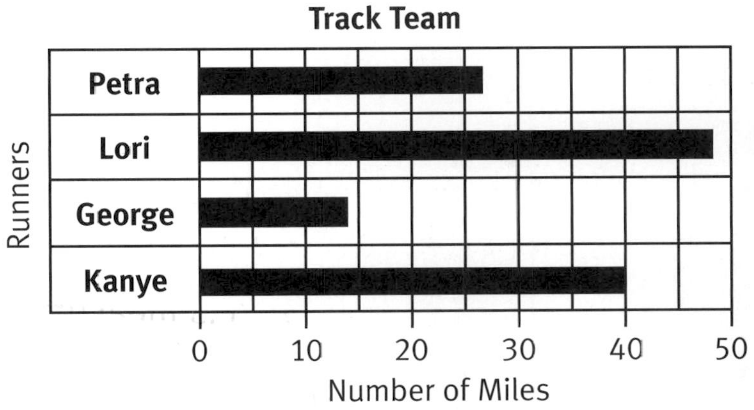

15 **Extended Response** Has Petra run more or less than half the number of miles Lori has run? Explain your answer.

CHAPTER 3 Practice Test

What time is it?

1. 

2. 

3. 

Write the temperature shown on each Fahrenheit thermometer. Tell whether the temperature is hot, comfortable, or cold.

4. 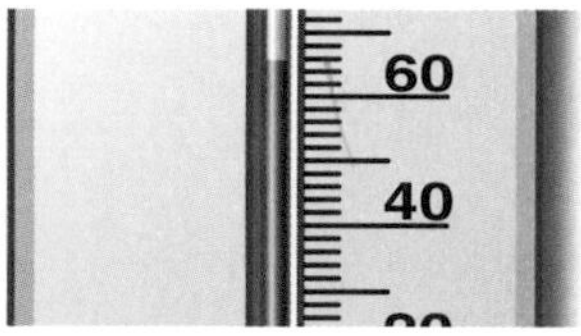

5. 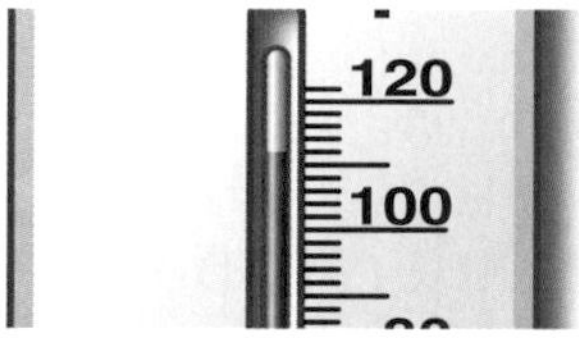

6. 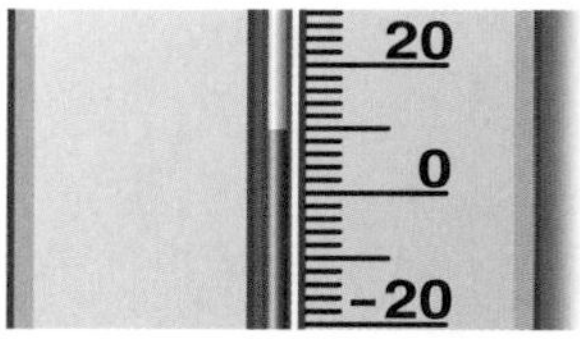

Find the perimeter of each figure.

7. ▢ centimeters

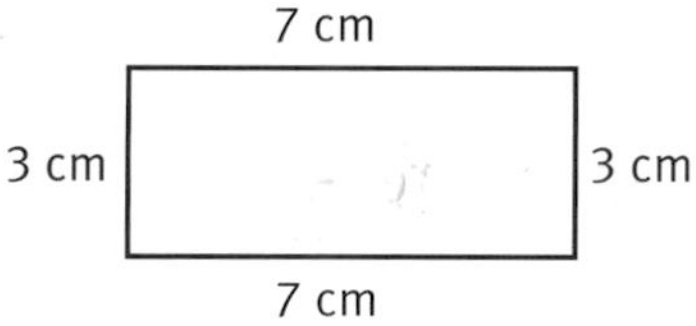

8. ▢ centimeters

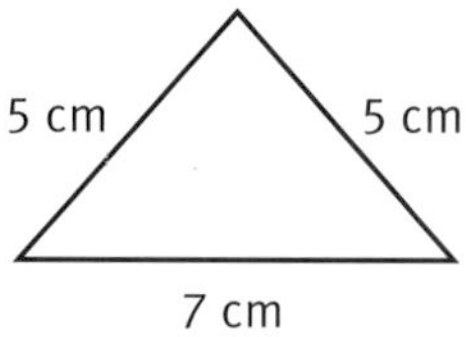

9. ▢ centimeters

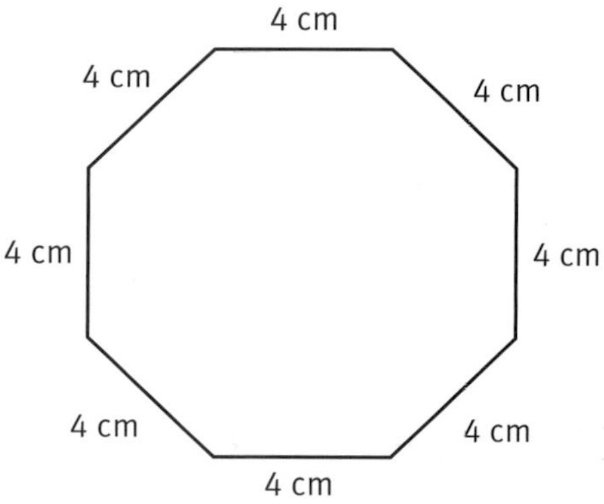

Find the perimeter and area of each figure.

10. Perimeter: ▢ centimeters
Area: ▢ square centimeters

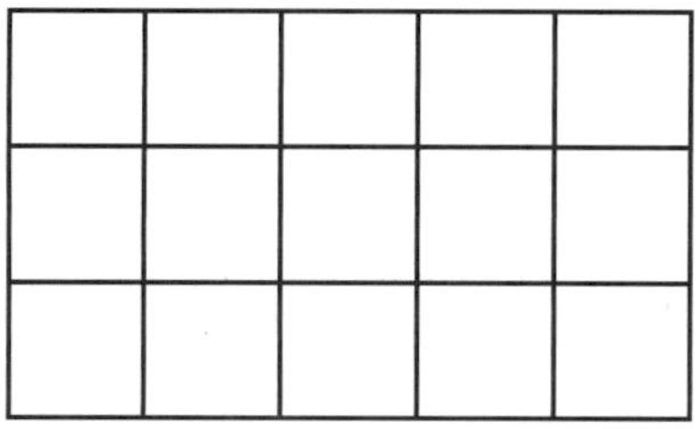

11. Perimeter: ▢ centimeters
Area: ▢ square centimeters

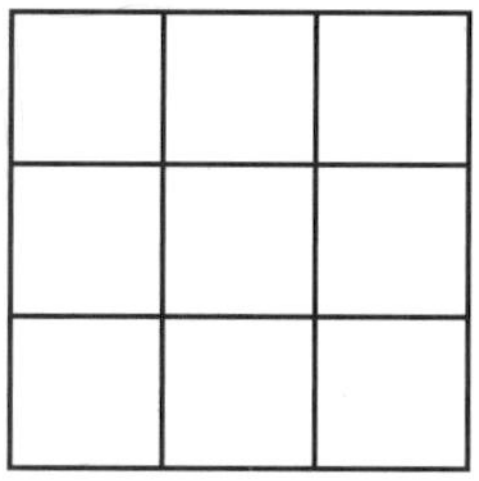

Choose the correct answer. Tell whether the temperature is hot, comfortable, or cold.

12. 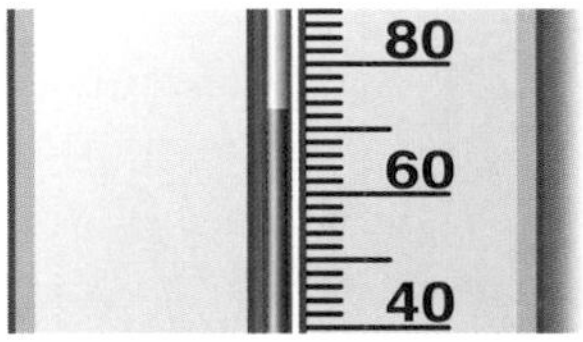

Ⓐ hot

Ⓑ cold

Ⓒ comfortable

13. 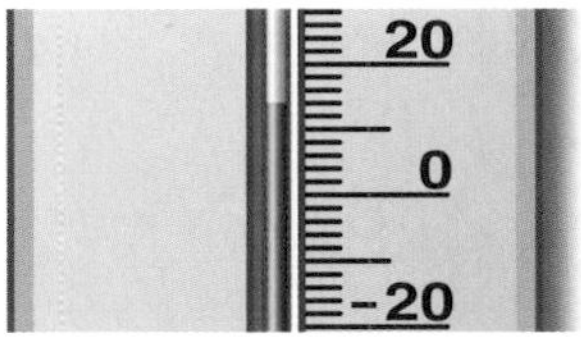

Ⓐ hot

Ⓑ cold

Ⓒ comfortable

Choose the correct answer.

14. Which is the largest unit?

Ⓐ feet Ⓑ inches

Ⓒ yards Ⓓ centimeters

15. Which is the smallest unit?

Ⓐ inches Ⓑ meters

Ⓒ feet Ⓓ yards

Estimate the length. (Hint: A paper clip is 3 centimeters long.)

16. 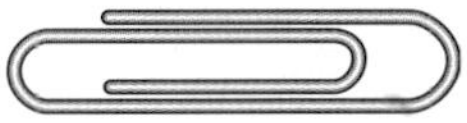

Ⓐ 1 centimeter

Ⓑ 2 centimeters

Ⓒ 4 centimeters

Ⓓ 10 centimeters

17. 

Ⓐ 20 centimeters

Ⓑ 15 centimeters

Ⓒ 9 centimeters

Ⓓ 5 centimeters

Practice Test

18. What is the perimeter?

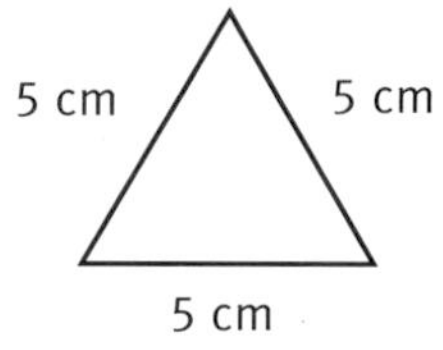

Ⓐ 5 centimeters

Ⓑ 10 centimeters

Ⓒ 15 centimeters

Ⓓ 20 centimeters

19. What is the best estimate of the area of the shape?

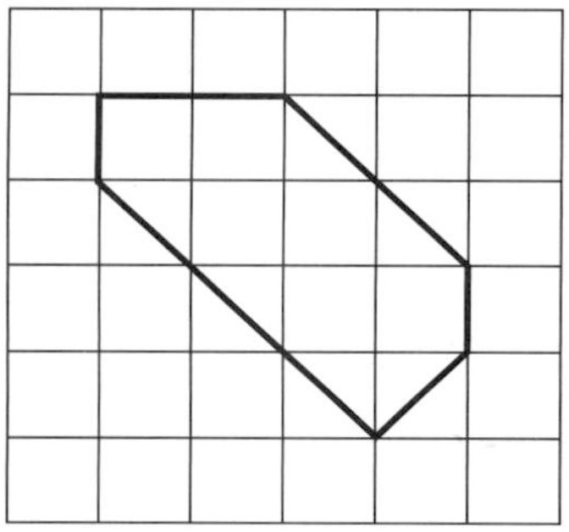

Ⓐ 5 square centimeters

Ⓑ 8 square centimeters

Ⓒ 9 square centimeters

Ⓓ 11 square centimeters

Choose the correct answer.

20. 71,495 + 99 ▢ 72,594 + 199

Ⓐ =

Ⓑ >

Ⓒ <

21. What does the number 5 represent in 1,582?

Ⓐ 5 hundreds

Ⓑ 5 thousands

Ⓒ 5 tens

Ⓓ 5 ones

22. Alfred bought 2 paintbrushes for 39¢ each and 3 jars of paint for 45¢ each. About how much did Alfred spend?

Ⓐ about $3.00

Ⓑ about $2.50

Ⓒ a little more than $2.00

Ⓓ a little less than $2.00

Add or subtract.

23. 56 + 22 + 35 = ?

Ⓐ 113 Ⓑ 115

Ⓒ 210 Ⓓ 211

24. 967 − 845 = ?

Ⓐ 113 Ⓑ 122

Ⓒ 223 Ⓓ 213

Use the graph to answer the questions.

25. The students in Mrs. Condall's class wanted to find out which kind of apple students in all of the third-grade classes preferred. They surveyed students and then drew a pictograph to display their results.

Third Graders' Favorite Kinds of Apples

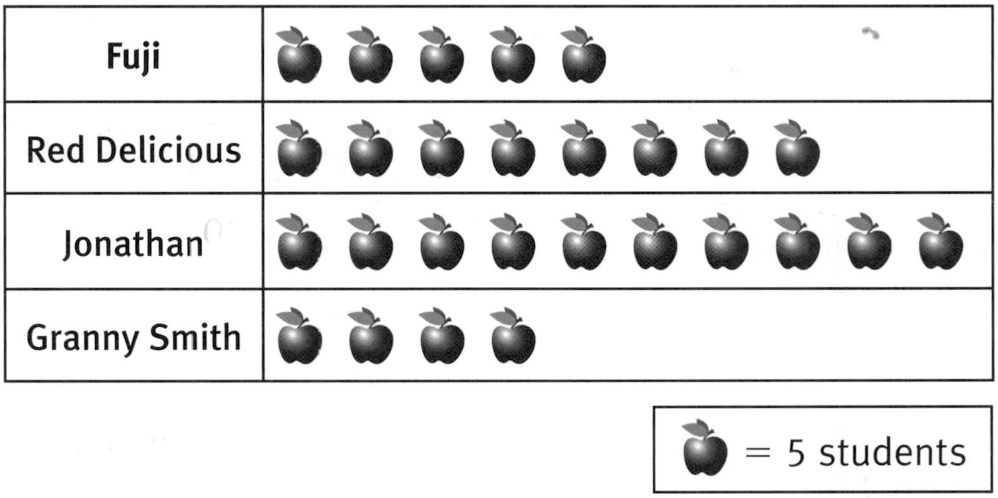

a. How many students prefer Red Delicious apples?

b. How many students prefer Granny Smith apples?

c. How many students took the survey?

d. **Extended Response** Would the pictograph look about the same if students in Mrs. Condall's class surveyed third graders at a different school? Explain your answer.

Thinking Story

The Case of the Fading Violets

"Something mysterious is going on," said Ms. Eng.

"I bought some violets and planted them in my backyard. The next morning there were only 6 plants left. Yesterday I bought some more violets and planted them. And this morning I counted, and there were only 8 violets left altogether."

"I'll help you look for them," said Mr. Muddle. "They couldn't have gone very far."

"Plants don't just get up and walk away," Ms. Eng said. "I think this is a case for Agatha Misty."

Ms. Eng telephoned the famous detective, and it was not long before Agatha Misty arrived in her limousine.

Ms. Eng, Mr. Muddle, and Agatha Misty went out to the backyard, where Ferdie, Portia, and Marcus were playing kickball. "Who are these suspicious-looking children?" Agatha Misty asked.

"They're friends of mine," said Ms. Eng. "I told them they could play in my backyard any time they wished."

"Now, children," said Agatha Misty, "I want you to tell the truth, because lying will only get you into more serious trouble than you're in now. Do any of you know what violets are?"

"I do," said Portia. "I have a violet plant in a flowerpot at home."

"Now we're getting somewhere," said Agatha Misty. "How high is your violet plant?"

"About 5 meters," said Portia.

"I thought I told you to tell the truth," the detective said sternly. "Five meters is as high as a tree! You're either quite mistaken or you're a very poor liar, young lady."

Could Portia be telling the truth?

How?

"You asked how high it is," Portia said. "The flowerpot is on a windowsill in our apartment, which is on the second floor, and that's about 5 meters from the ground."

What do you think Agatha Misty really wanted to know?

"I meant, what size is the plant?" Agatha Misty asked.

"Oh, it's about the same size as these violets here," said Portia.

"I'm glad you decided to tell the truth," said Agatha Misty. "The judge may treat you more kindly because of it. Now tell me, when and how did you get this violet plant?"

"I bought it a month ago with my allowance," said Portia.

"How much did you pay for it?"

"A dollar."

"And how much allowance do you get?"

"Fifty cents," said Portia.

"I've caught you lying again," said Agatha Misty.

Why might Agatha Misty think Portia wasn't telling the truth?

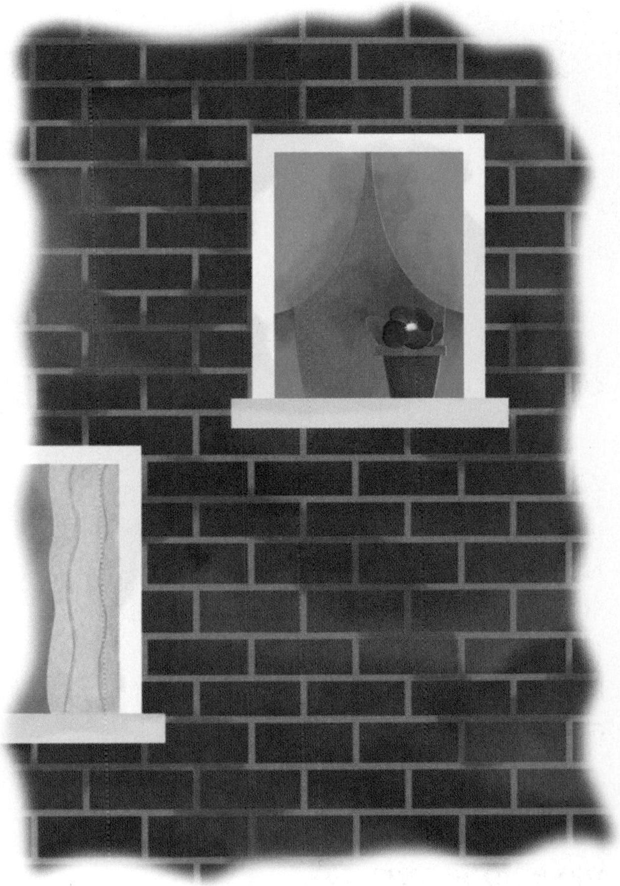

"If your allowance is only 50¢, you couldn't possibly buy something with it that costs a dollar, now could you?" said the detective.

How could Portia have bought something for a dollar if her allowance was only 50¢?

"I saved my allowance for one week," Portia explained, "and then when I got my next allowance, I had enough."

"A clever story," said Agatha Misty. "I can see this is going to be a difficult case." She looked over the flower bed. The violets were planted next to a wooden fence that was 2 meters high. On the other side of the fence was a sidewalk.

"When was the last time you walked along that sidewalk out there?" she asked Mr. Muddle.

"I go back and forth past there almost every day," he said.

"And how tall are you?"

"I'm about 2 meters tall when I stand straight," Mr. Muddle answered.

"Aha!" said the detective. "I begin to see the picture. This tall man is walking along the sidewalk. He glances over the fence and sees just what he has always wanted: some violet plants. In a flash he reaches over the fence, pulls up some of the plants, and hurries off with them.

"Mr. Muddle, I predict that we will find the stolen violets in your own backyard."

What is wrong with Agatha Misty's picture of what happened?

"You may be right," said Mr. Muddle, "but I don't understand. The fence is 2 meters tall. It comes right to the top of my head. I couldn't look over it, and I'm sure I couldn't reach over it and pull plants from the ground."

"Hmm," said the detective, "then we need to find someone a little taller."

About how tall would someone have to be to reach over a 2-meter fence and touch the ground?

Ferdie said, "Someone would have to be about twice as tall as Mr. Muddle to reach the plants by leaning over the fence!"

How tall is that?

"Nobody is that tall," said Ferdie. "A person that tall couldn't even stand up in a room."

Marcus had been silent up until then, but finally he had to ask some questions. "How many plants are missing?" he asked.

"I don't know," said Ms. Eng. "All I know is that there were only 6 plants left the first time, and there are only 8 plants left now."

What else would you need to know to figure out how many are missing?

"How many plants did you buy?" Marcus asked.

"I don't know," said Ms. Eng, "but it will be easy to find out. The bills are on the desk in the kitchen." She ran inside and returned in a moment with two bills. The first one said, "Half-dozen violet plants." The second one said, "Two violet plants."

Now can you figure out how many plants are missing?

"It's perfectly clear," said Agatha Misty. "Six and 2 are 8, so there are 8 violet plants missing."

What's wrong with that?

"Pardon me," said Marcus, "but 8 is how many plants Ms. Eng bought, and there are 8 plants in the ground, which means that none of the plants are missing!"

"This young man seems to know a great deal about the crime," Agatha Misty said. "Something is very suspicious about that. I believe that if I question him carefully I will begin to solve this mystery."

Is there really a mystery?

Why not?

The End

CHAPTER 4

Multiplication Concepts

In This Chapter You Will Learn

- how to apply skip counting and arrays to multiplication.
- how to use number grids and the Multiplication Table.
- the Commutative Law of Multiplication.

Problem Solving

Pretend you are starting your own dog-walking business. You plan to charge $3 for each hour you walk a dog. The bar graph shows how much you will charge for different numbers of hours.

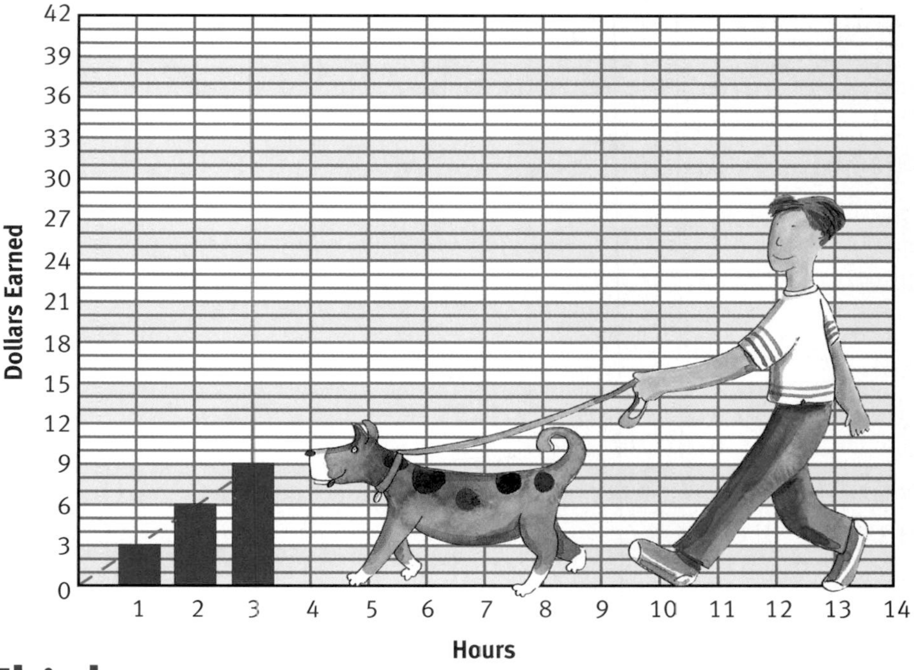

Think about and discuss these questions.

1. What pattern do you see in the graph?
2. Why do you think that pattern will or will not continue?

Work in groups. Use the graph or any other strategy you like to help you.

3. If you walk a dog from 3 P.M. to 4 P.M. every day for 2 weeks, how much will you earn?
4. How did you solve this problem?

LESSON 4.1

Understanding Multiplication

Key Ideas

Multiplication is a fast way of adding. It can be used when we have groups with equal numbers of objects in each group.

Each container of tennis balls has 3 balls. We can add the balls to see how many there are altogether.

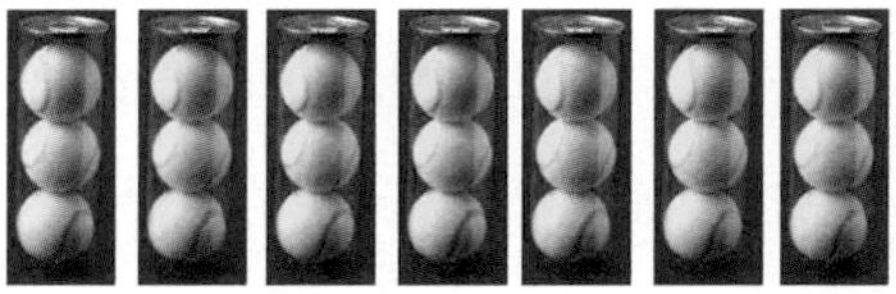

$3 + 3 + 3 + 3 + 3 + 3 + 3 = 21$

There are 21 tennis balls altogether.

We can write a multiplication sentence to describe this.

$7 \times 3 = 21$

Solve.

1. There are 2 marbles in each bag. How many marbles are there altogether?

$2 + 2 + 2 + 2 + 2$

$5 \times 2 = \square$

2. There are 6 crayons in each group. How many crayons are there altogether?

$6 + 6 + 6$

$3 \times 6 = \square$

3. Each package has 4 tomatoes. How many tomatoes are there altogether?

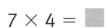

$4 + 4 + 4 + 4 + 4 + 4 + 4$

$7 \times 4 = \square$

eTextbook This lesson is available in the *eTextbook*.

Solve.

4. Each package has 6 bottles of fruit juice. How many bottles are there altogether?

   $4 \times 6 = \square$

6 + 6 + 6 + 6

5. There are 3 people seated in each row. There are 4 rows. How many people are seated altogether?

   $4 \times 3 = \square$

3 + 3 + 3 + 3

6. Each pile has 3 dollars. How many dollars are there altogether ?

   $3 \times 3 = \square$

3 + 3 + 3

7. How many lemons are there altogether?

8. Israel has 3 brothers, 2 sisters, a mom, and a dad. How many children are in his family, including himself?

Writing + Math **Journal**

In your own words, explain how you solved Problem 8.

LESSON 4.2
Skip Counting

Key Ideas

Skip counting can help us find multiplication patterns.

When you skip count, you are skipping over the numbers you are not counting.

When we skip count by 2s from 2 to 20, we say the following numbers:

2 4 6 8 10 12 14 16 18 20

When we skip count by 3s from 3 to 21, we say the following numbers:

3 6 9 12 15 18 21

Use skip counting to find the missing numbers and then to multiply. You may use the pictures to help.

1. 4, 8, ___, 16, ___, 24
2. $2 \times 4 =$ ___
3. $6 \times 4 =$ ___

4. 2, 4, 6, ___, ___, ___, 14
5. $7 \times 2 =$ ___
6. $5 \times 2 =$ ___

7. 6, 12, ___, ___, 30
8. $2 \times 6 =$ ___
9. $5 \times 6 =$ ___

eTextbook This lesson is available in the ***eTextbook.***

Find the missing numbers in each skip-counting exercise. Use the completed exercises to help you multiply.

10. 5, 10, 15, □, 25, □, □, 40
11. $3 \times 5 = $ □
12. $8 \times 5 = $ □

13. 10, 20, 30, □, □, 60, □, 80
14. $2 \times 10 = $ □
15. $8 \times 10 = $ □

16. 4, 8, 12, □, □, 24
17. $6 \times 4 = $ □
18. $3 \times 4 = $ □

19. 7, 14, □, 28, □, 42, □, 56
20. $3 \times 7 = $ □
21. $6 \times 7 = $ □

22. 3, 6, 9, □, □, 18
23. $6 \times 3 = $ □
24. $3 \times 3 = $ □

Use skip counting to find the number of jelly beans altogether. Then multiply.

25. 8, 16, 24, □, □, □, 56, □, □, 80
26. $9 \times 8 = $ □

Writing + Math **Journal**

In your own words, explain how addition and multiplication are related to each other.

LESSON 4.3

Multiplication and Number Patterns

Key Ideas

Looking for and finding patterns can help us learn about our number system.

Follow the directions for each exercise. Be sure to use three different 100 Tables.

1. On the first 100 Table, color the boxes you reach when counting by 2s. Circle the numbers in the boxes you reach when counting by 5s. Place an **X** in the boxes you reach when counting by 10s.

2. On the second 100 Table, circle the numbers in the boxes you reach when counting by 9s. Place an **X** in the boxes you reach when counting by 11s.

3. On the third 100 Table, circle the numbers in the boxes you reach when counting by 8s. Color the boxes you reach when counting by 12s.

0	1	2	3	4	5	6	7	8	9
10	11	12	13	14	15	16	17	18	19
20	21	22	23	24	25	26	27	28	29
30	31	32	33	34	35	36	37	38	39
40	41	42	43	44	45	46	47	48	49
50	51	52	53	54	55	56	57	58	59
60	61	62	63	64	65	66	67	68	69
70	71	72	73	74	75	76	77	78	79
80	81	82	83	84	85	86	87	88	89
90	91	92	93	94	95	96	97	98	99

eTextbook This lesson is available in the ***eTextbook.***

A Venn diagram is used to show patterns in a different way. Venn diagrams may have two or more circles to group information with a common area in the middle. This common area is for information that belongs in *both* groups.

Look at the Venn diagram below, and think about any patterns you may see.

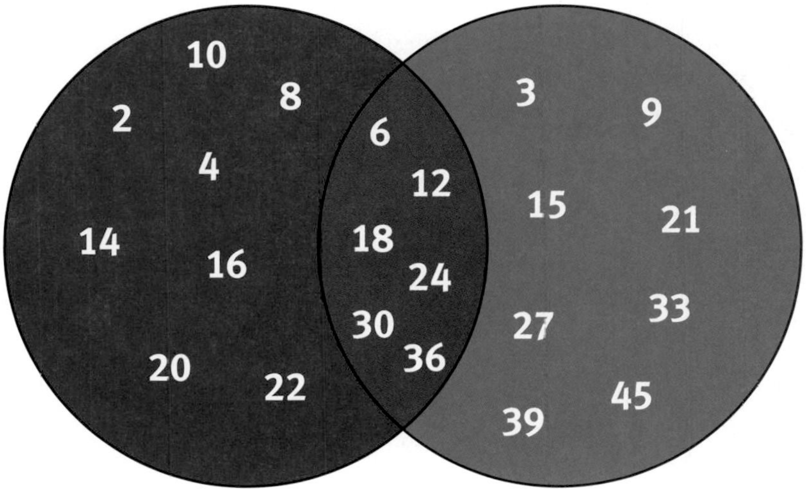

4. What is true of all the numbers in the left circle? What is true of all the numbers in the right circle?

5. What is true of all the numbers in the common (purple) area?

6. **Extended Response** Describe in your own words, the three parts of the above Venn diagram.

Writing + Math **Journal**

Write about a pattern you see in one of the 100 Tables.

LESSON 4.4

Multiplication Table

Key Ideas

Tables and charts help organize information. This is a Multiplication Table. It has the multiplication facts from 0 × 0 through 10 × 10.

×	0	1	2	3	4	5	6	7	8	9	10
0	0	0	0	0	0	0	0	0	0	0	0
1	0	1	2	3	4	5	6	7	8	9	10
2	0	2	4	6	8	10	12	14	16	18	20
3	0	3	6	9	12	15	18	21	24	27	30
4	0	4	8	12	16	20	24	28	32	36	40
5	0	5	10	15	20	25	30	35	40	45	50
6	0	6	12	18	24	30	36	42	48	54	60
7	0	7	14	21	28	35	42	49	56	63	70
8	0	8	16	24	32	40	48	56	64	72	80
9	0	9	18	27	36	45	54	63	72	81	90
10	0	10	20	30	40	50	60	70	80	90	100

Use the Multiplication Table above to find the answers.

1. 7 × 8 = ☐
2. 6 × 8 = ☐
3. 8 × 7 = ☐
4. 9 × 4 = ☐
5. 8 × 4 = ☐
6. 4 × 9 = ☐
7. 8 × 6 = ☐
8. 5 × 10 = ☐
9. 4 × 8 = ☐
10. 3 × 9 = ☐
11. 7 × 7 = ☐
12. 6 × 9 = ☐
13. 10 × 10 = ☐
14. 8 × 8 = ☐

eTextbook This lesson is available in the ***eTextbook.***

Solve.

15. Each bag has 3 lemons. How many lemons are in 5 bags?
16. Each eraser costs 4¢. How much will 7 erasers cost?
17. Each box has 5 pencils. How many pencils will be in 4 boxes?

Think about each problem and then solve. Use the Multiplication Table to help with your computation, if needed.

18. One pen costs 9¢. How much will 8 pens cost?
19. Marcia is 9 years old. How old will she be in 4 years?
20. One pack of gum has 7 pieces. How many pieces are there in 4 packs?

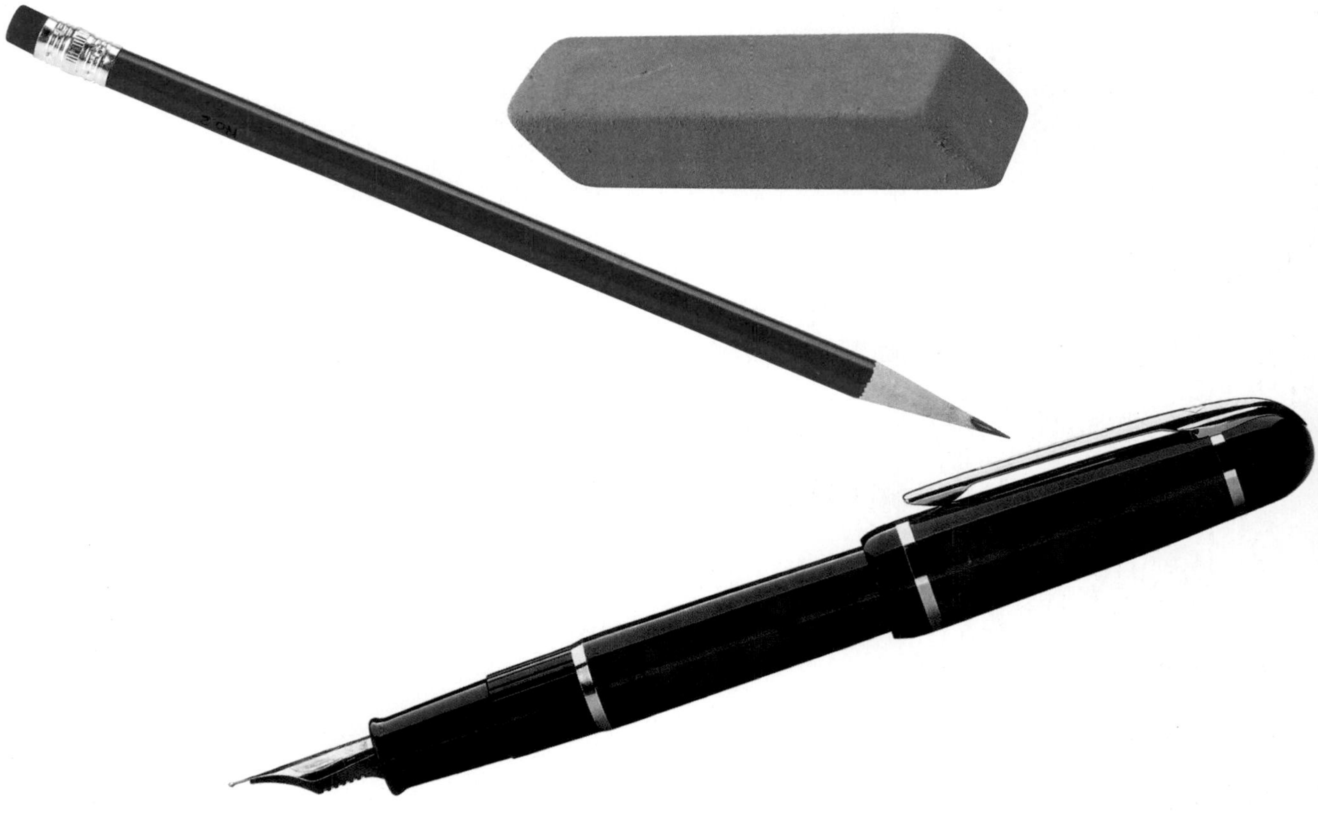

Read the problem. Think about how you might solve it.

You own a pet shop on a busy street where many people pass by. To catch their attention, you plan to make a changing display of dog-food can towers. You will always display towers with equal numbers of cans, but each day the towers will be a different size. You can tape the cans together so you can make very tall towers, but you have only 24 cans. How many days in a row can you keep the display changing in this way?

Sandra made a physical model to solve the problem.

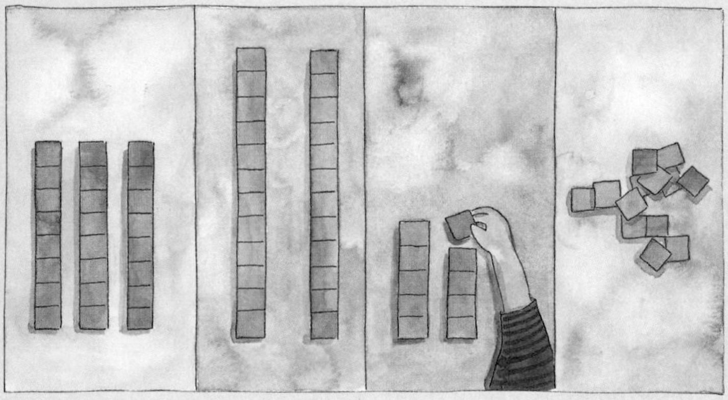

Think about Sandra's strategy. Answer the following questions.

1. What display did Sandra make first?
2. What display did Sandra make second?
3. How could Sandra keep track of the displays she makes?
4. Look at the third picture. Do you think towers of 5 will work? Why or why not?
5. Will Sandra's strategy work? Why or why not?

eTextbook This lesson is available in the *eTextbook.*

Barry used a physical model, and he used a pattern.

Think about Barry's strategy. Answer the following questions.

6. How is Barry's strategy like Sandra's strategy?
7. How is Barry's strategy different?
8. At what number do you think Barry should stop?
9. Finish solving the problem. Use Sandra's strategy, Barry's strategy, or a strategy of your own.
10. What strategy did you use? Why?

Cumulative Review

Introduction to Multiplication **Grade 2 Lesson 11.2**

Solve.

1. $3 + 3 + 3 + 3 + 3 + 3 =$ ____

   How many times does 3 appear in this addition? ____ times
   So, $6 \times 3 =$ ____

2. $5 + 5 + 5 + 5 + 5 + 5 =$ ____

   How many times does 5 appear in this addition? ____ times
   So, $6 \times 5 =$ ____

3. $2 + 2 + 2 + 2 + 2 + 2 + 2 + 2 =$ ____

   How many times does 2 appear in this addition? ____ times
   So, $8 \times 2 =$ ____

4. $7 + 7 + 7 + 7 + 7 =$ ____

   How many times does 7 appear in this addition? ____ times
   So, $5 \times 7 =$ ____

5. $8 + 8 + 8 + 8 + 8 + 8 =$ ____

   How many times does 8 appear in this addition? ____ times
   So, $6 \times 8 =$ ____

Understanding Multiplication **Lesson 4.1**

Solve.

6. There are 5 bags on each shelf. How many bags are there altogether?

   $4 \times 5 =$ ____

7. There are 9 packages of chew bones. Each package has 3 chew bones. How many chew bones are there altogether?

   $9 \times 3 =$ ____

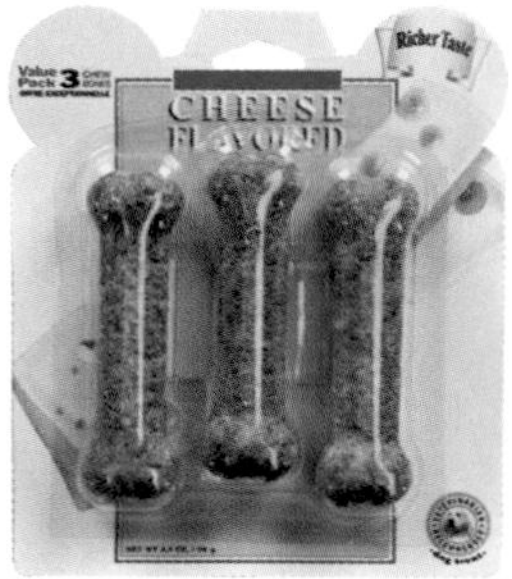

Telling Time **Lesson 3.1**

What time is it? How many minutes after each hour?

8

___

___ minutes after ___

9

___

___ minutes after ___

10

___

___ minutes after ___

Multiplication Table **Lesson 4.4**

Think about each problem, and then solve the problem. Use the Multiplication Table to help with your computation, if needed.

11. If 1 dog treat costs 6¢, how much will 15 treats cost?
12. We gave baths to 11 dogs, and then 4 more dogs needed baths. How many dogs will have baths?
13. Celia feeds her dog 8 ounces of dog food twice a day. How many ounces of dog food will she use in one day?
14. How many ounces of dog food will Celia need for 7 days?

LESSON 4.5 Arrays

Key Ideas

When you line up items in equal rows, you are creating an array.

Each row on this baker's counter has the same number of loaves of bread in it. The loaves of bread form an array.

$1 \times 5 = 5$

$2 \times 5 = 10$

$3 \times 5 = 15$

$4 \times 5 = 20$

$5 \times 5 = 25$

$6 \times 5 = 30$

There are 30 loaves of bread in this array.

eTextbook This lesson is available in the ***eTextbook.***

Brooklyn was trying to see if enough programs had been printed for her class play. She was counting the seats when a group of parents and teachers blocked her view of some of the seats. Quickly Brooklyn drew an array of the seats to find the total number of programs she might need.

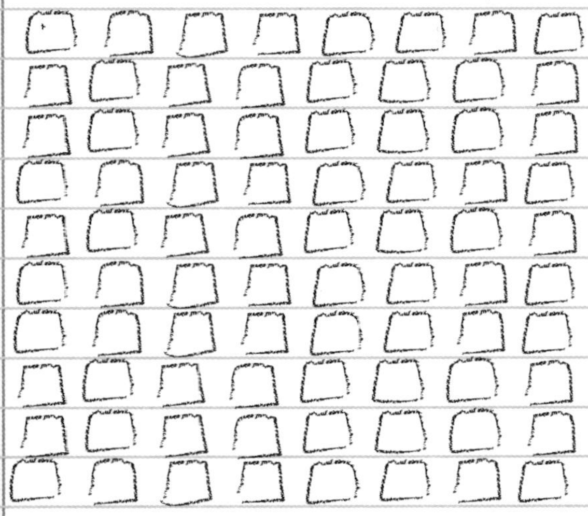

$1 \times 8 =$ ■

$2 \times 8 =$ ■

$3 \times 8 =$ ■

$4 \times 8 =$ ■

$5 \times 8 =$ ■

$6 \times 8 =$ ■

$7 \times 8 =$ ■

$8 \times 8 =$ ■

$9 \times 8 =$ ■

$10 \times 8 =$ ■

1. How many programs would Brooklyn need if all of the seats are filled?
2. There are 20 students in her class. If each person in her class invites 3 people, will there be enough seating for just the guests? $20 + 20 + 20 =$ ■
3. Ranier was excited about her grandfather's pumpkin patch this year. Her grandfather told her there were 8 rows of 8 pumpkins. Draw an array showing what the pumpkin patch looks like.
4. How many pumpkins are there?
5. Last year her grandfather had 55 pumpkins. Does he have more or fewer this year? How many more or fewer?
6. If Ranier's grandfather plants one more row of 8 pumpkins next year, how many pumpkins will he have?

LESSON 4.6

Arrays and Multiplication

Key Ideas

We can think of this array as a diagram of a tomato garden that contains 2 rows each with 3 tomato plants.

There are 6 tomato plants in the array.

$2 \times 3 = 6$

We can also think of the array as the contents of a rectangle, with each plant occupying one square unit.

The area of the garden is 6 square units.

$2 \times 3 = 6$

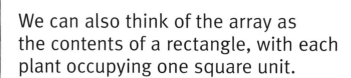

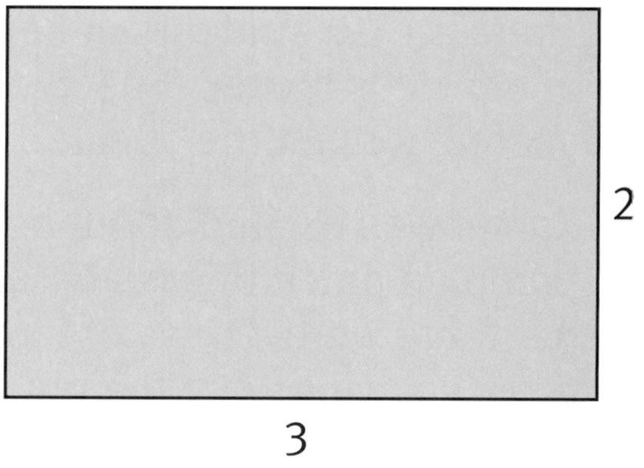

We can also think of the shape of the garden as a rectangle without thinking about the plants it contains.

The garden is shaped like a rectangle that is 3 units long and 2 units wide.

The area of the rectangle is 6 square units.

eTextbook This lesson is available in the ***eTextbook.***

Extended Response **Find** the area of these shapes.

1 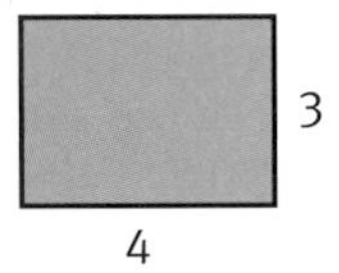

The area is ___ square units.
Write how you know.

2 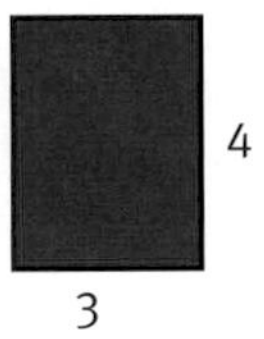

The area is ___ square units.
Write how you know.

3 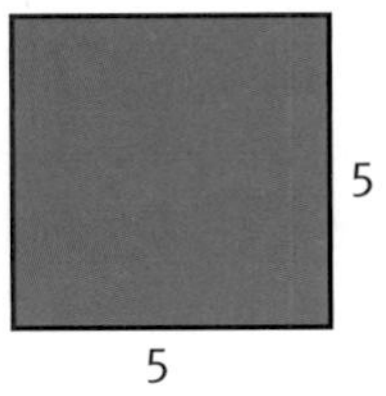

The area is ___ square units.
Write how you know.

4 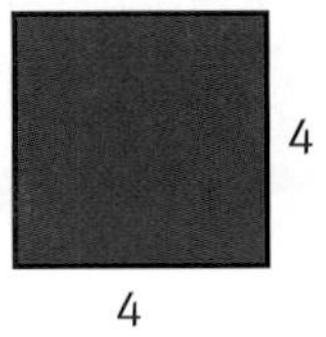

The area is ___ square units.
Write how you know.

5 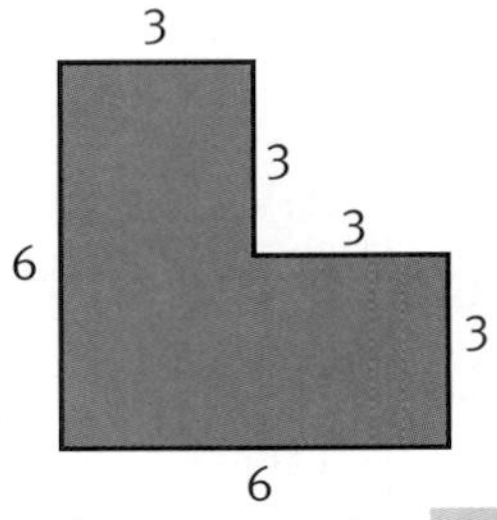

The area is ___ square units. Write how you know.

6 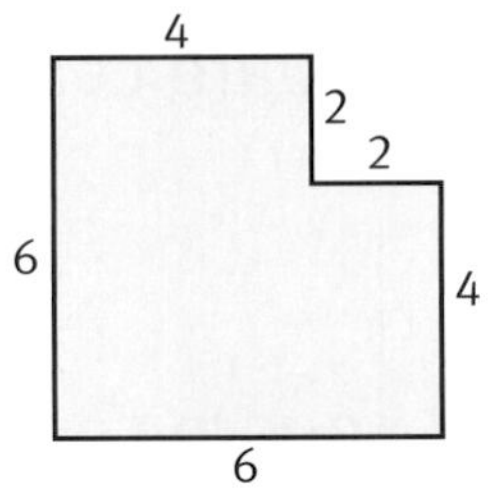

The area is ___ square units.
Write how you know.

Writing + Math **Journal**

Create a garden with 12 plants in it. Divide your garden to show a rectangular array. What multiplication sentence would best identify your garden?

LESSON 4.7 Area and Approximate Measure

Key Ideas

Area is the number of square units that fit inside a figure.

If you count the small squares in this rectangle, you will find its area is 32 square units.

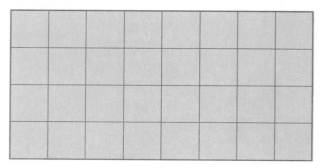

Because there are 4 rows, each 8 units long, we can think of the area as being equal to

$8 + 8 + 8 + 8 = 32$ or $4 \times 8 = 32$.

The area is 32 square units.

Find **the area of the orange shaded part of each rectangle.**

1. The area is ▭ square centimeters.

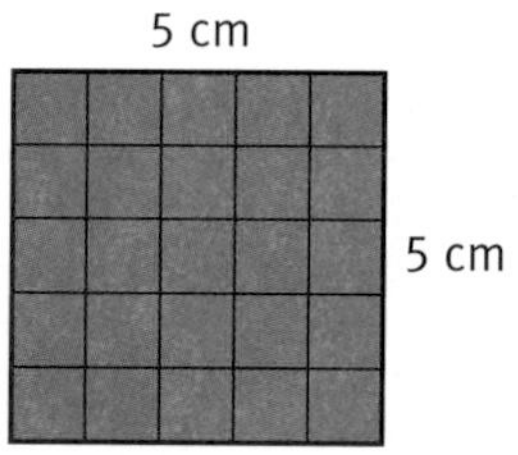

2. The area is ▭ square centimeters.

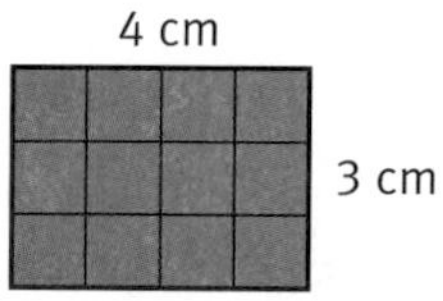

3. The area is ▭ square centimeters.

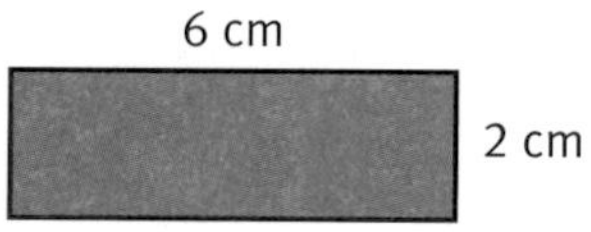

4. The area is ▭ square centimeters.

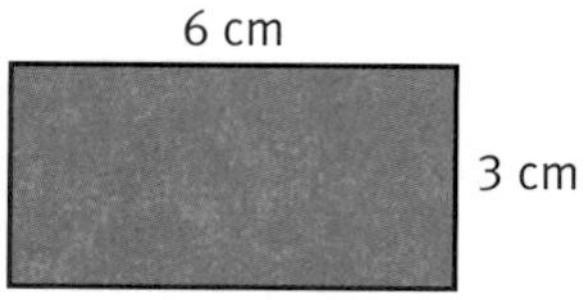

eTextbook This lesson is available in the *eTextbook*.

Find the area of the orange shaded part of the rectangle. Remember to label your answer correctly.

5 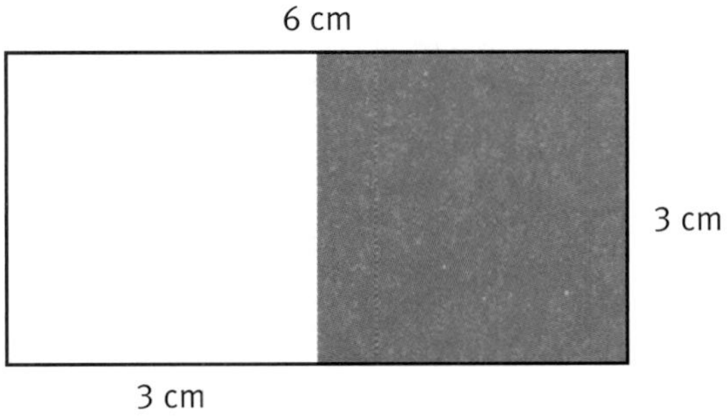

6 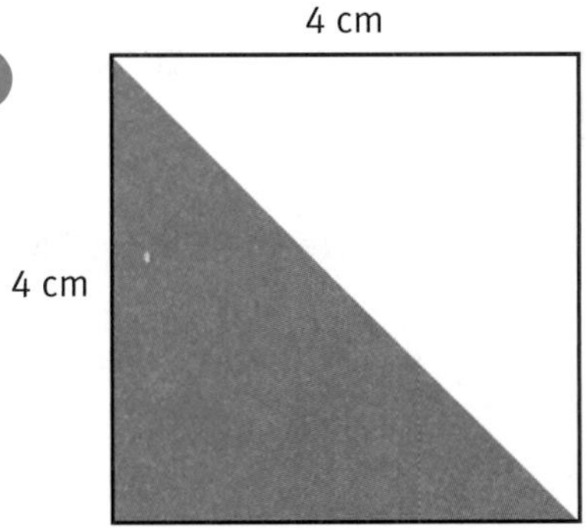

Extended Response Estimate the area of the orange part of each figure. Explain how you got your answers.

7 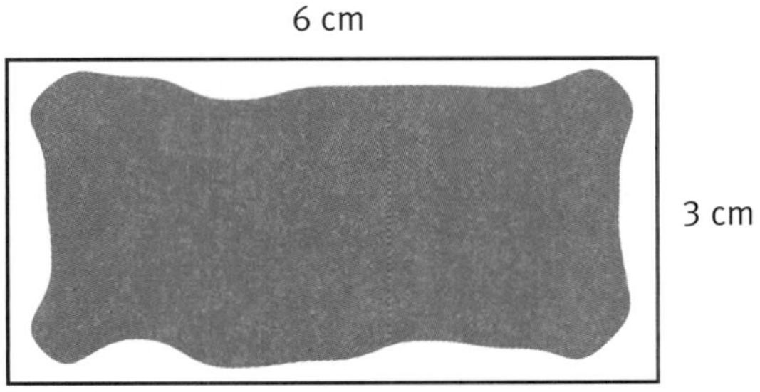

8 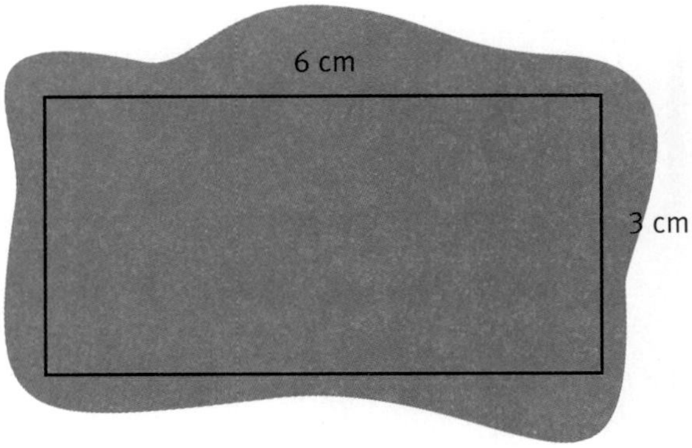

Writing + Math Journal

Estimate the area of the orange part of this figure. Explain how you got your answer.

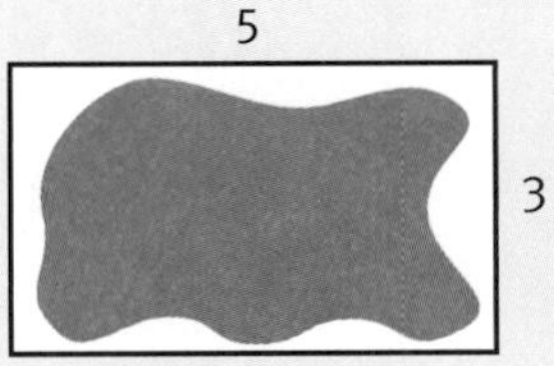

LESSON 4.8
Commutative Law of Multiplication

Key Ideas

Multiplication gives the same product no matter the order of the numbers being multiplied. We refer to this as the Commutative Law of Multiplication.

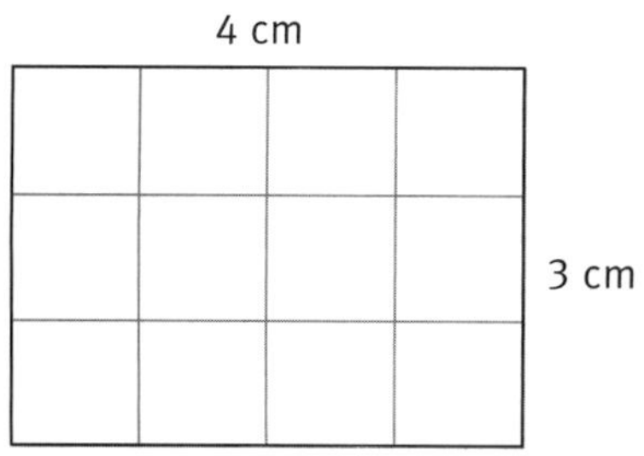

$3 \times 4 = 12$

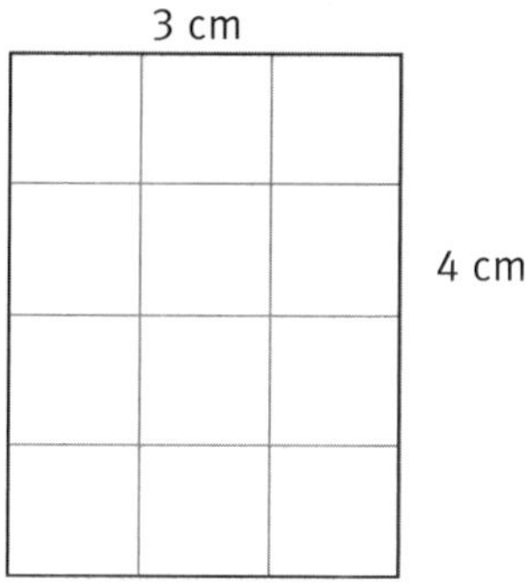

$4 \times 3 = 12$

Find the area of each of the following rectangles.

1. 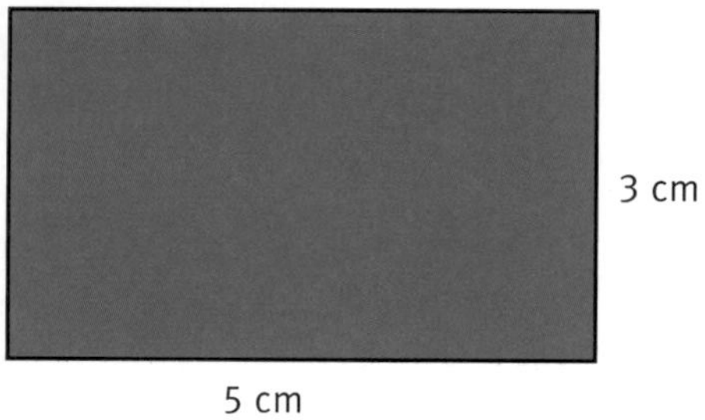

2. 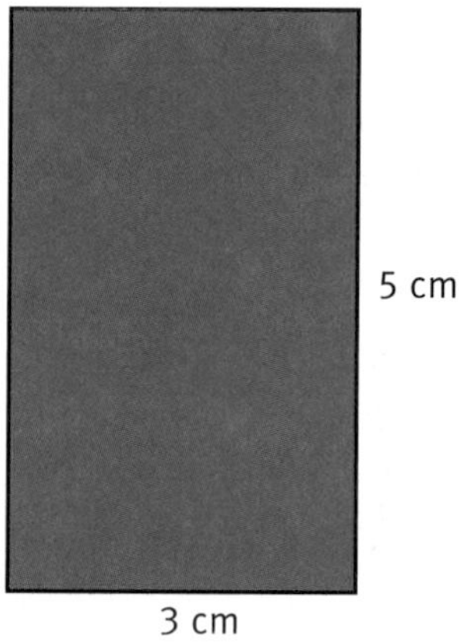

3. 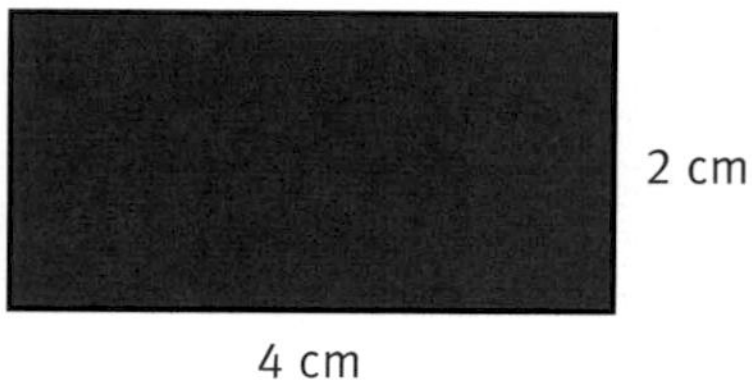

4. 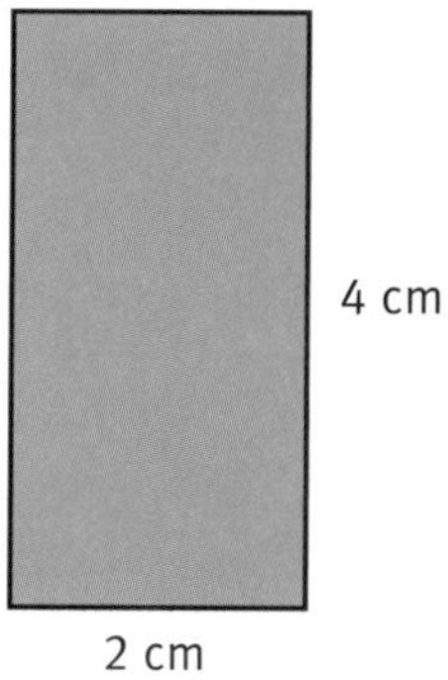

Find the products. Use repeated addition, skip counting, or the Multiplication Table on page 146 to check your answers.

5. $5 \times 4 = \square$
6. $4 \times 5 = \square$
7. $2 \times 9 = \square$
8. $9 \times 2 = \square$
9. $10 \times 3 = \square$
10. $3 \times 10 = \square$
11. $4 \times 0 = \square$
12. $0 \times 4 = \square$

Write a number sentence for each problem. Solve.

13. Nadia has 10 nickels. How much money does she have in cents?
14. Rachel has five \$10 bills. How much money does she have in dollars?
15. Brent has given 2 bouncy balls to each of his 9 friends. How many bouncy balls did he give?
16. There are 9 pairs of shoes in the hallway. How many shoes are there altogether?
17. Bart has six \$5 bills. How much money does he have in dollars?
18. There are 5 pencils in each package. Hailey bought 6 packages for school. How many pencils did Hailey buy altogether?
19. Dyane has 6 baseball cards and 7 football cards. How many cards is that all together?
20. Cameron had gift bags for his 8 friends. There were 5 noisemakers in each bag. How many noisemakers were there altogether?

Exploring Problem Solving

Read the problem. Think about how you might solve it.

You are a park planner who is designing a special park for dogs inside a city park. The dog park is supposed to have an area of 100 square yards. Also, it cannot get in the way of old trees, so the dog park must be shaped like a *U*, but with corners instead of curves:

1. Draw a plan for the dog park. Show exactly how many yards each side should be.
2. How do you know the area of your dog park is exactly 100 square yards?
3. What method did you use to make a plan that met all the conditions?
4. Compare and contrast your plan with others. Did everyone in your class draw the same plan?

Cumulative Review

Adding Two-Digit Numbers Lesson 2.2

Add. You can use craft sticks or other materials to help.

1. 65 + 43 = ▢
2. 79 + 15 = ▢
3. 28 + 47 = ▢
4. 62 + 31 = ▢
5. 35 + 35 = ▢
6. 37 + 19 = ▢
7. 33 + 22 = ▢
8. 44 + 56 = ▢
9. 14 + 67 = ▢
10. 13 + 68 = ▢

Regrouping for Subtraction Lesson 2.3

Solve.

Latisha has two $10 bills and four $1 bills. She is paying for a dog license that costs $9.

11. How much money does Latisha have?
12. How can Latisha pay $9?
13. How can Latisha get a $5 bill in her change?
14. How much will Latisha have left after paying for the license?

Counting and Estimating Lesson 1.1

Find the numbers that are written twice, and write them on your paper. Notice that the numbers are not written in order.

15. Start counting from 15.

    15 18 19 16 17 25 20 23 19 21 24 22 18

16. Start counting from 37.

    41 39 42 37 40 38 45 43 39 46 47 42 44

Cumulative Review

Multiplication and Number Patterns **Lesson 4.3**

Look at the Venn diagram below, and think about any patterns you may see.

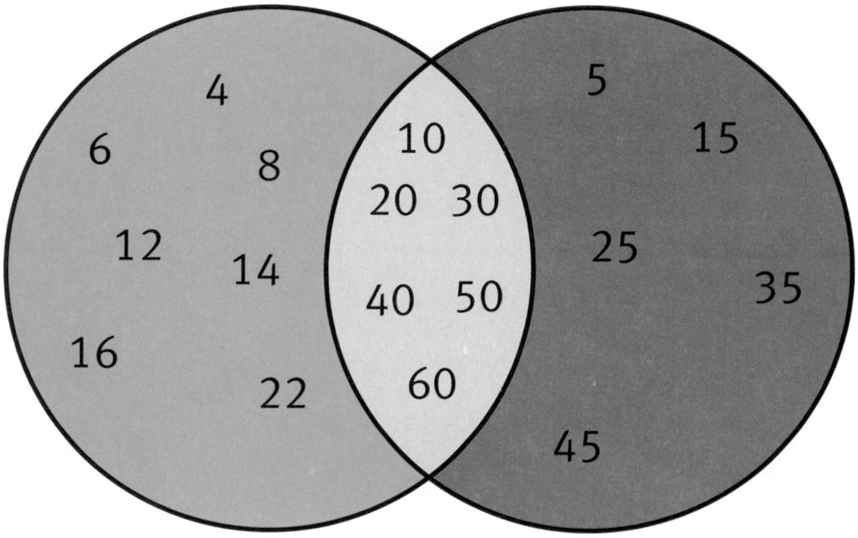

17. What patterns do you see among numbers in the left circle?
18. What patterns do you see among the numbers in the right circle?
19. What patterns do you see among the numbers in the common (yellow) area?
20. Write a number that would fit into the left circle.
21. Write a number that would fit into the right circle.
22. Write a number that would fit into the center space.

CHAPTER 4 Key Ideas Review

In this chapter you developed concepts of multiplication.

You learned basic multiplication facts.

You explored the relationship between multiplication, arrays, and area.

You explored the Commutative Law of Multiplication.

Solve or find the missing term.

1. $0 \times 9 = \square$
2. $\square \times 7 = 56$
3. $9 \times \square = 9$

Draw the following arrays.

4. Draw an array for 1×4.
5. Draw an array for 3×5.

Shade the area.

6. Charles wants to fit a small rectangle, with an area of 4 square units, into this larger rectangle. Shade the area of the smaller rectangle.

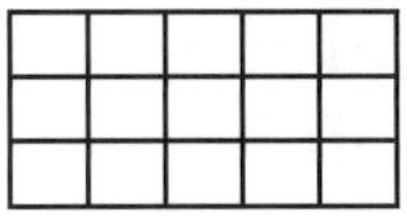

Extended Response **Provide** a detailed answer for the following exercises.

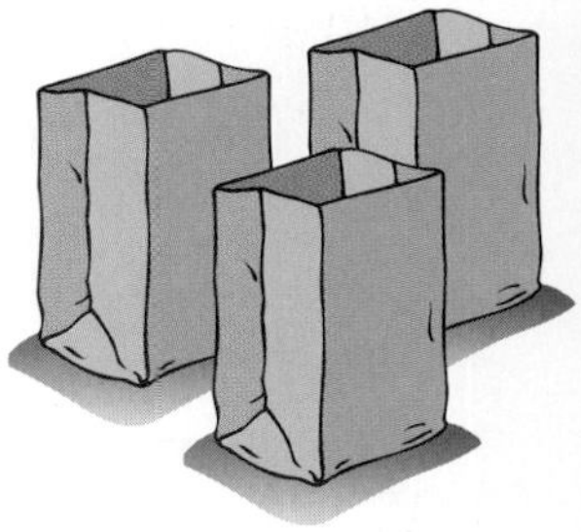

7. Sheri and Rachael want to buy 3 bags of peppers that each contain 6 peppers. To find the number of peppers to buy, Sheri multiplies 3 by 6. Rachael multiplies 6 by 3. Will Sheri and Rachael get the same answer? How do you know?

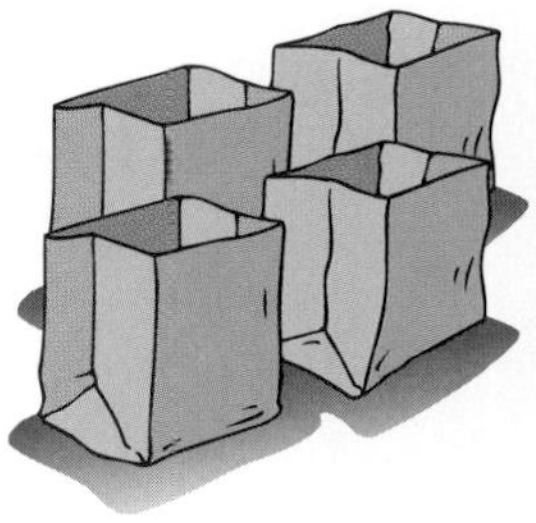

8. Sheri and Rachael decide to buy 4 bags of potatoes instead. Each bag of potatoes contains 10 potatoes. To find the number of potatoes altogether, Sheri multiplies 4 by 10. Rachael adds $10 + 10 + 10 + 10$. Will Sheri and Rachael get the same answer? How do you know?

CHAPTER 4

Chapter Review

Lesson 4.1 **Answer** true or false.

1. $7 \times 7 = 49$ is the same as $7 + 7 + 7 + 7 + 7 + 7 + 7 = 49$.
2. $2 \times 3 = 6$ is the same as $2 + 2 + 2 = 16$.
3. $3 + 3 = 6$ is the same as $3 \times 3 = 6$.
4. $4 \times 2 = 8$ is the same as $4 + 4 = 8$.
5. $2 \times 8 = 16$ is the same as $2 + 8 = 16$.
6. $3 \times 5 = 15$ is the same as $5 + 5 + 5 = 15$.
7. $3 + 0 = 3$ is the same as $3 \times 1 = 3$.

Lesson 4.2 **Fill** in the blank.

8. 3, 6, 9, ▢, 15
9. 10, 20, 30, ▢, 50
10. 2, 4, 6, ▢, 10
11. 6, 12, 18, ▢, 30
12. 12, 10, 8, ▢, 4
13. 5, 10, 15, ▢, 25
14. 1, 3, 5, ▢, 9
15. 12, 9, 6, ▢, 0

Lesson 4.4 **Use** the Multiplication Table to find the products.

16. $7 \times 8 =$ ▢
17. $8 \times 3 =$ ▢
18. $9 \times 2 =$ ▢
19. $0 \times 1 =$ ▢

×	0	1	2	3	4	5	6	7	8	9	10
0	0	0	0	0	0	0	0	0	0	0	0
1	0	1	2	3	4	5	6	7	8	9	10
2	0	2	4	6	8	10	12	14	16	18	20
3	0	3	6	9	12	15	18	21	24	27	30
4	0	4	8	12	16	20	24	28	32	36	40
5	0	5	10	15	20	25	30	35	40	45	50
6	0	6	12	18	24	30	36	42	48	54	60
7	0	7	14	21	28	35	42	49	56	63	70
8	0	8	16	24	32	40	48	56	64	72	80
9	0	9	18	27	36	45	54	63	72	81	90
10	0	10	20	30	40	50	60	70	80	90	100

Lesson 4.5 **Draw** two different arrays for the following numbers.

20. 9
21. 6

Draw three different arrays for the following numbers.

22 12

23 16

Lesson 4.7 **Find** the area of each rectangle.

24

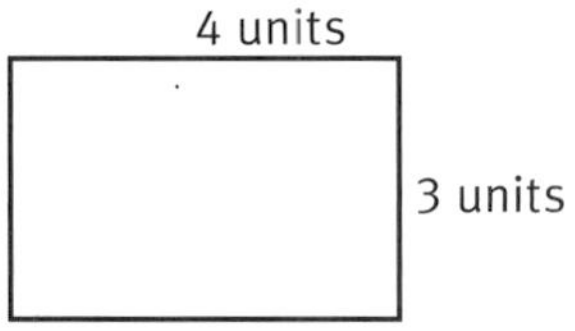

4 units

3 units

Area: _____

25
9 units

2 units

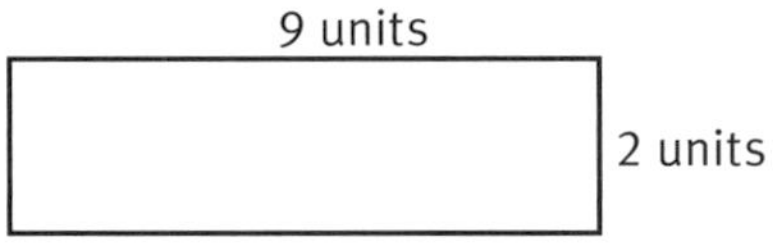

Area: _____

Lesson 4.8

Estimate the area of the shaded part and its upper bound.

26
4 units

2 units

Area of shaded part: _____

Upper bound: _____

27

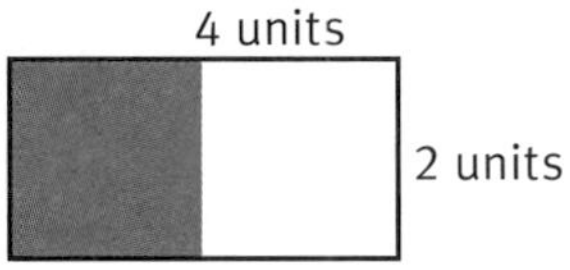

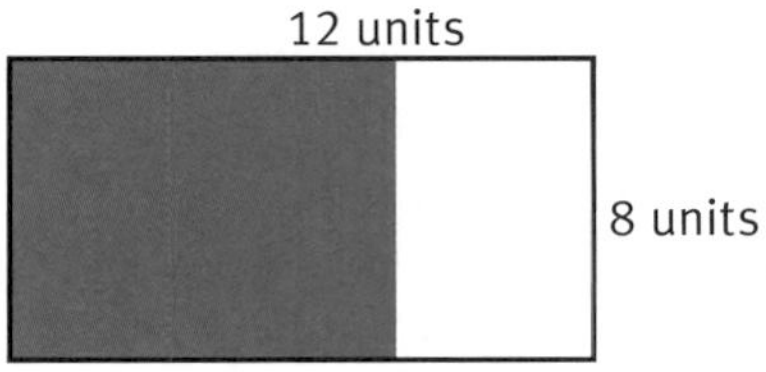

12 units

8 units

Area of shaded part: _____

Upper bound: _____

Lesson 4.9

Solve.

28 Rob and Bryan are trying to decide who has the most marbles. To count their marbles, they created the following arrays.

Rob's array:

● ● ● ● ● ● ● ● ●
● ● ● ● ● ● ● ● ●

Bryan's array:

● ● ● ● ● ●
● ● ● ● ● ●
● ● ● ● ● ●

Do Rob and Bryan have the same number of marbles? How do you know?

Practice Test

Answer the questions.

1. There are 4 children. Each child has 10 toes. How many toes are there altogether?

2. There are 4 children. Each child has 2 ears. How many ears are there altogether?

3. There are 4 children. Each child has 2 legs and 2 arms. How many arms and legs are there altogether?

4. There are 3 flowers. Each flower has 6 petals. How many petals are there altogether?

6. There are 4 cats each with 4 legs. How many legs are there altogether?

7. Sam sees 6 tricycles. How many wheels are there altogether?

8. Each window has 4 windowpanes. How many windowpanes are there in 5 windows?

9. Find the area.

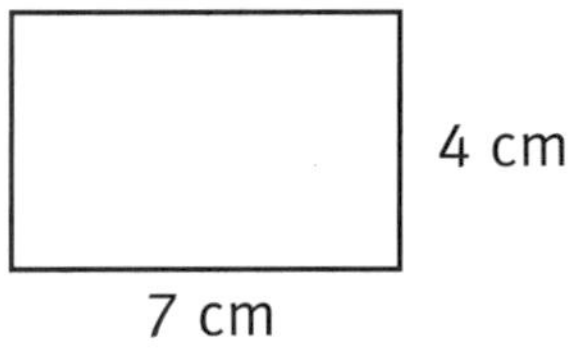

Tell whether the temperature is high, low, or comfortable.

5.
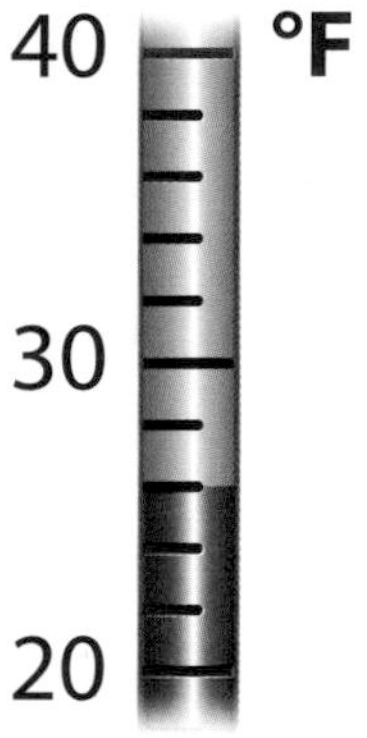

Write the Roman numeral for the standard number.

10. 759

Solve by using skip counting or repeated addition.

11. $4 \times 5 =$ ▢

Ⓐ 20 Ⓑ 10

Ⓒ 7 Ⓓ 6

12. $2 \times 4 =$ ▢

Ⓐ 24 Ⓑ 15

Ⓒ 12 Ⓓ 8

13. $4 \times 7 =$ ▢

Ⓐ 35 Ⓑ 28

Ⓒ 15 Ⓓ 10

14. $6 \times 7 =$ ▢

Ⓐ 42 Ⓑ 39

Ⓒ 35 Ⓓ 28

15. $3 \times 9 =$ ▢

Ⓐ 12 Ⓑ 15

Ⓒ 27 Ⓓ 30

16. $5 \times 5 =$ ▢

Ⓐ 10 Ⓑ 25

Ⓒ 35 Ⓓ 55

17. $8 \times 5 =$ ▢

Ⓐ 40 Ⓑ 45

Ⓒ 50 Ⓓ 60

Solve.

The parking lot has 5 rows of 8 cars.

18. $8 \times 1 =$ ▢

Ⓐ 8 Ⓑ 9

Ⓒ 11 Ⓓ 12

19. $8 \times 2 =$ ▢

Ⓐ 8 Ⓑ 10

Ⓒ 14 Ⓓ 16

20. $8 \times 3 =$ ▢

Ⓐ 12 Ⓑ 16

Ⓒ 24 Ⓓ 28

21. $8 \times 4 =$ ▢

Ⓐ 32 Ⓑ 28

Ⓒ 24 Ⓓ 16

22. $8 \times 5 =$ ▢

Ⓐ 45 Ⓑ 40

Ⓒ 30 Ⓓ 28

CHAPTER 4 Practice Test

Find the missing number.

23. 6, 12, ▢, 24, 30

Ⓐ 14 Ⓑ 18

Ⓒ 20 Ⓓ 22

24. 8, 16, 24, ▢, 40

Ⓐ 32 Ⓑ 30

Ⓒ 28 Ⓓ 25

25. 2, 4, 6, 8, ▢, 12

Ⓐ 9 Ⓑ 10

Ⓒ 11 Ⓓ 13

26. Which shows the same product as 9×2?

Ⓐ 2×8 Ⓑ 2×9

Ⓒ 3×9 Ⓓ 4×5

27. Which shows the same product as 3×8?

Ⓐ 3×7 Ⓑ 6×2

Ⓒ 3×9 Ⓓ 8×3

28. What is 550,081 in expanded form?

Ⓐ 500,000 + 5,000 + 0 + 80 + 1

Ⓑ 500,000 + 50,000 + 800 + 0 + 1

Ⓒ 500,000 + 50,000 + 0 + 0 + 80 + 1

Ⓓ 50,000 + 5,000 + 0 + 80 + 1

29. 8 + 6 + 9 = ▢

Ⓐ 14 Ⓑ 19

Ⓒ 23 Ⓓ 27

Estimate the length of the yellow crayon. (Hint: A paper clip is about 1 centimeter wide.)

30.

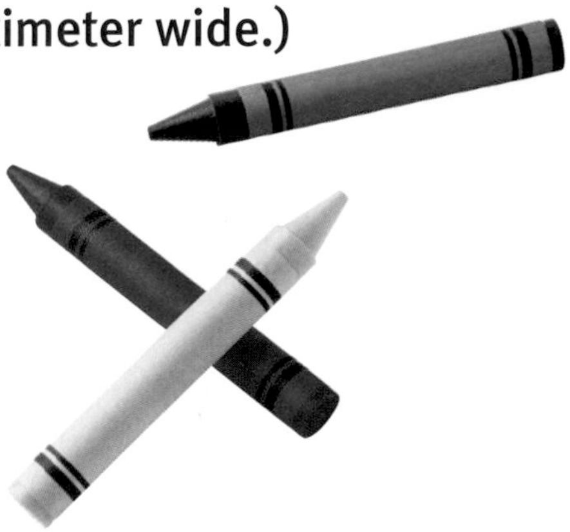

Ⓐ about 10 centimeters

Ⓑ about 25 centimeters

Ⓒ about 40 centimeters

Ⓓ about 2 centimeters

eTextbook This lesson is available in the *eTextbook*.

31. **Extended Response** **Use** the Venn diagram to answer the questions.

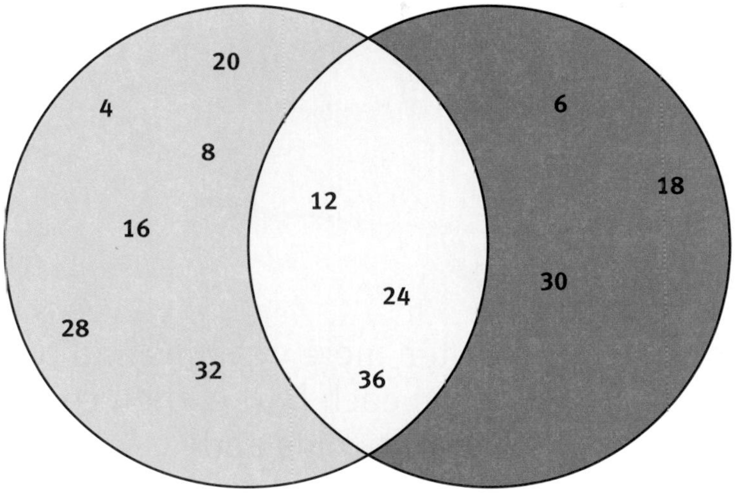

a. Describe the numbers in the common area.

b. Describe the numbers in the right circle.

32. **Extended Response** **Solve.**

Karen wants to plant a garden. Her father will let her use one of two spots in their yard. One area is 5 feet by 7 feet. The other is a 6-foot square.

a. What is the area of the rectangular spot?

b. What is the area of the square spot?

c. Which spot would give Karen a bigger garden? By how much? Explain how you got your answer.

Thinking Story

The Easy Way and the Breezy Way

Manolita wanted to earn some extra money to buy a new seat for her bicycle. “I know,” she thought, “there’s one person who always has jobs he wants done—that’s Mr. Breezy. And I know how to make Mr. Breezy’s hard jobs easy.”

Manolita found Mr. Breezy bustling around in the storeroom of his dog-training school. “I can’t talk to you now, Manolita,” he said. “I have such a hard job to do that I won’t be finished for hours.”

“But,” said Manolita, “I came to help you.”

“That’s just what I like to hear,” said Mr. Breezy. “I sure do need help. See this big bottle of dog vitamins? I need to dump them all out on the table and count to see how many there are altogether. Then I need to count out ten vitamins, then take ten little bottles all the same size, then take the ten vitamins and put one in each bottle, then count out ten more vitamins and put one in each bottle, then count ten more vitamins and . . .”

“Wait,” said Manolita, “I know what to do now.”

“How do you know what to do next when I haven’t finished telling you?” asked Mr. Breezy.

What do you think Mr. Breezy wants Manolita to do?

How can you tell?

"It was easy to figure out what to do," said Manolita. "I just have to keep doing the same thing over and over again until all the vitamins are divided into the ten little bottles. Right?"

"That's right," said Mr. Breezy.

"What if there aren't enough vitamins to put exactly the same number in each bottle?" asked Manolita.

"Don't worry about it," said Mr. Breezy, "as long as each bottle has about the same number. When you're done with all that counting, in about a half hour, then I'll tell you what else needs to be done."

"Half an hour!" thought Manolita. "It will take me that long just to find out how many vitamins there are altogether. I wonder if I can do this job without counting all the vitamins first."

How can Manolita divide the vitamins into ten bottles without knowing how many vitamins there are all together?

"I know," thought Manolita, "I'll just keep putting vitamins into the ten bottles one at a time. When I'm finished each bottle will have the same number—or some might have a few more."

How many more might some bottles have than others if Manolita does it just the way she plans?

After she had worked for a few minutes putting vitamins in bottles one at a time, Manolita noticed that the big bottle was still almost full. "There must be thousands of vitamins in that bottle," she thought. "This will take forever."

Is there a faster way for Manolita to end up with about the same number of vitamins in each bottle?

Then Manolita had an idea. She took the big bottle and just poured vitamins from it into each of the little bottles. Then she poured a few vitamins from one bottle to another until all the bottles looked as if they were filled to the same height. The whole job took only about five minutes.

Mr. Breezy was amazed at Manolita's fast work. "How many vitamins were there altogether?" he asked.

Do you know how many vitamins there were altogether?

Why or why not?

"Well, um, well . . .," stammered Manolita. "I changed the job a little and didn't count the vitamins."

Mr. Breezy said, "But now I have to know how many vitamins there are because I have to pay for them. I forget whether I ordered 1,000 or 2,000."

"I guess I'll have to count them," said Manolita. "That will take me a while."

Manolita started counting the vitamins in one bottle. She counted 100 and noticed that she had counted about half the vitamins in the bottle. "I have another idea," thought Manolita. "I can figure out about how many vitamins there are in this little bottle without counting any more."

How can Manolita figure out how many vitamins there are in the bottle?

About how many are there?

"If there are about 100 vitamins in half a bottle, she thought, "then there must be about 200 in the whole bottle. And now I know about how many vitamins there are altogether."

How could Manolita figure out how many vitamins there were altogether without counting them?

How many vitamins were there altogether?

"I already have the answer!" Manolita shouted to Mr. Breezy. "You ordered 2,000 vitamins."

"How could you have counted them so fast?" asked Mr. Breezy.

“I didn’t count them all,” Manolita explained. “I counted about half of one of the small bottles, and that was 100 vitamins. That means about 200 are in each bottle, and there are ten bottles, which makes 2,000.”

“But I need to know exactly how many vitamins I ordered, so that I can pay for them,” said Mr. Breezy. “And you only figured out about how many.”

“No,” said Manolita, “I figured out that you ordered 2,000 vitamins.”

How could Manolita be sure?

“You told me that you ordered either 1,000 or 2,000 vitamins,” said Manolita. “I figured out that the number is close to 2,000, and it isn’t close to 1,000 at all, so 2,000 must be the right answer.”

“Amazing!” said Mr. Breezy. “That’s all the work I have for you today. I thought it was going to be hard work, but everything turned out to be quick and easy.”

“It was hard work,” Manolita told him. “The hard part is figuring out how to make jobs easy.”

The End

CHAPTER 5

Multiplication and Division Facts

In This Chapter You Will Learn

- multiplication facts.
- division facts.
- about missing factors.

Problem Solving

You are planning an arts and crafts party for 10 people. You want to buy enough modeling clay for each person to have 2 bars of clay.

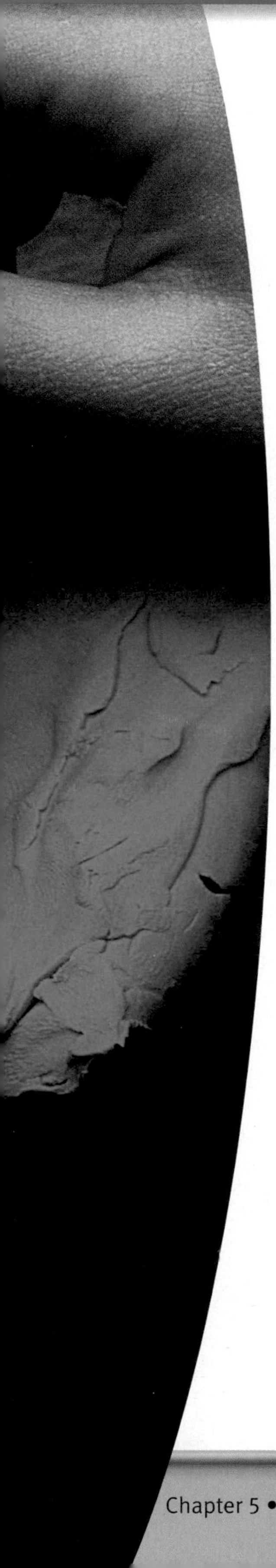

Work with your group to solve these problems.

1. Which boxes of clay will you buy?
2. How much will that cost? How do you know?
3. How else could you buy enough clay for 10 people?
4. Why did you choose the boxes you did?

LESSON 5.1 Multiplying by 2, 1, and 0

Key Ideas

A product is the result of multiplying numbers together.
The numbers being multiplied are called factors.

To find 2×7, you can skip count by 2s to 14.

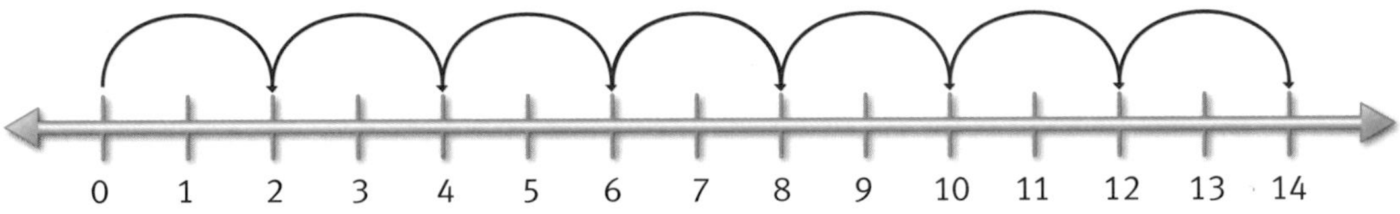

$7 \times 2 = 14$

You can also find the product of a number and 2 by doubling, or adding the number to itself.

7 plus 7 = 14
$2 \times 7 = 14$

Solve.

1. $\begin{array}{r} 2 \\ \times 8 \\ \hline \end{array}$ ___

2. $\begin{array}{r} 2 \\ \times 9 \\ \hline \end{array}$ ___

3. $\begin{array}{r} 2 \\ \times 3 \\ \hline \end{array}$ ___

4. $\begin{array}{r} 6 \\ \times 2 \\ \hline \end{array}$ ___

5. $\begin{array}{r} 5 \\ \times 2 \\ \hline \end{array}$ ___

Fill in the blanks.

6. 2, 4, 6, 8, ___, ___, ___, 16, ___, 20, ___, ___, 26

7. **Extended Response** Could you multiply a whole number by 2 and get a product of 29? Explain how you know.

When you multiply any factor and 1, the product is always that factor.

$1 \times 8 = 8$

When you multiply any factor by 0, the product is always 0.

$0 \times 8 = 0$

Multiply.

8. $8 \times 1 =$ ☐
9. $2 \times 6 =$ ☐
10. $0 \times 8 =$ ☐
11. $7 \times 8 =$ ☐
12. $9 \times 1 =$ ☐
13. $8 \times 7 =$ ☐

Solve each problem. REAL WORLD

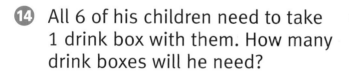

Mark is packing lunches for his 6 children. He is trying to figure out how much of each food he needs.

14. All 6 of his children need to take 1 drink box with them. How many drink boxes will he need?
15. Mark bought 24 drink boxes. How many will he have left after packing one day's lunches?
16. Mark's children get 2 large pretzels each. How many large pretzels will Mark need?
17. None of Mark's 6 children are taking carrot sticks. How many carrot sticks will he need?
18. **Extended Response** If 4 children each need 2 bananas and 2 children each need 1 banana, how many bananas will Mark need? Explain your answer.

Writing + Math Journal

How could you explain multiplying by 0 to a friend? Write your explanation using words, numbers, and pictures.

LESSON 5.2

Multiplying by 10 and 5

Key Ideas

For facts like 7 × 10, think of 7 sets of two hands.

For facts like 7 × 5, think of 7 hands.

Fill **in the tables. Look for patterns.**

1 Copy and fill in this table by skip counting by 10.

10	20	■	■	50	60	■	■	■	100

2 Copy and fill in this table by skip counting by 5.

5	10	15	■	■	■	35	■	■	50

Use **the patterns for the 5s and 10s facts and other patterns you have learned to find each multiplication fact.**

3 3 × 10 = ■

4 7 × 10 = ■

5 7 × 8 = ■

6 8 × 7 = ■

7 6 × 2 = ■

8 9 × 5 = ■

9 10 × 4 = ■

10 6 × 5 = ■

11 8 × 10 = ■

Solve **each problem. Then explain your answers.**

Extended Response Max has only nickels in his pocket.

12 Could he have 45¢? How do you know?

13 Could he have 52¢? How do you know?

eTextbook This lesson is available in the ***eTextbook.***

Copy and finish the tables to help Beth using the following information. Make enough rows for 10 packages.

REAL WORLD

Beth's computer store sells CDs in packages of 5 for $7 and packages of 10 for $13. To help her customers, she used a ×5 and a ×10 function machine to create a table showing how many CDs you would have if you bought different numbers of packages. Beth's printer ran out of ink.

14

5-pack	
1	5
2	10
3	

15

10-pack	
1	10
2	20
3	

Solve the following problems.

16. Which costs less, one 10-pack or two 5-packs?

17. How many 5-packs would you need to buy to have the same number of CDs as two 10-packs?

18. If you needed 20 CDs, how much money would you save by buying 10-packs instead of 5-packs?

19. **Extended Response** Suppose you wanted to buy exactly 25 CDs. What is the least you can pay? Explain how you found the lowest cost.

20. **Extended Response** Suppose you needed about 25 CDs. How many packs of each would you buy? Explain your answer.

Writing + Math **Journal**

Describe the patterns in the ×5 and ×10 facts. Write strategies to help you remember those facts.

Multiplying by 9

Key Ideas

Finding and using patterns can help you find the ×9 facts.

0	1	2	3	4	5	6	7	8	9
10	11	12	13	14	15	16	17	18	19
20	21	22	23	24	25	26	27	28	29
30	31	32	33	34	35	36	37	38	39
40	41	42	43	44	45	46	47	48	49
50	51	52	53	54	55	56	57	58	59
60	61	62	63	64	65	66	67	68	69
70	71	72	73	74	75	76	77	78	79
80	81	82	83	84	85	86	87	88	89
90	91	92	93	94	95	96	97	98	99

Every ninth number should be shaded.

1 What are the next four numbers in the pattern shown in the box above?

You already learned 9×1, 9×2, 9×5, and 9×10 because they are the same as 1×9, 2×9, 5×9, and 10×9.

2 Copy and complete the table to the right.

3 **Extended Response** Do you see any interesting patterns in the table? If so, describe them.

4 **Extended Response** Find 9×11 and 9×12. Explain whether they fit the patterns you found.

$$9 \times 1 = 9$$
$$9 \times 2 = 18$$
$$9 \times 3 = \square$$
$$9 \times 4 = \square$$
$$9 \times 5 = 45$$
$$9 \times 6 = \square$$
$$9 \times 7 = \square$$
$$9 \times 8 = \square$$
$$9 \times 9 = \square$$
$$9 \times 10 = 90$$

Solve.

5 $9 \times 3 = \square$ **6** $5 \times 9 = \square$ **7** $4 \times 9 = \square$ **8** $7 \times 9 = \square$

9 $9 \times 8 = \square$ **10** $2 \times 9 = \square$ **11** $9 \times 9 = \square$ **12** $9 \times 4 = \square$

e Textbook This lesson is available in the *eTextbook.*

An array is a set of objects arranged in rows and columns.

Describe each array in words (▢ groups of ▢) and in a multiplication sentence (▢ × ▢ = ▢).

13 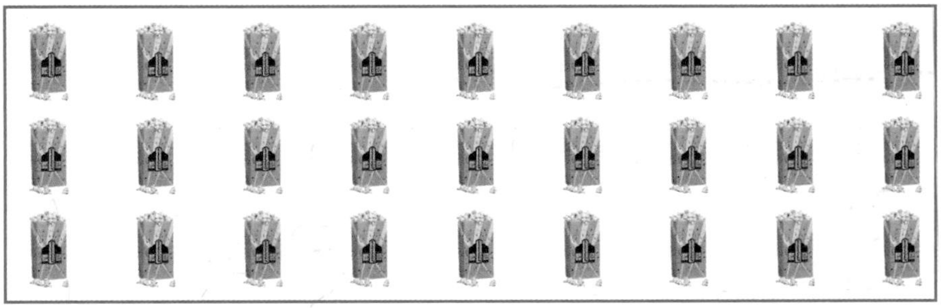

14 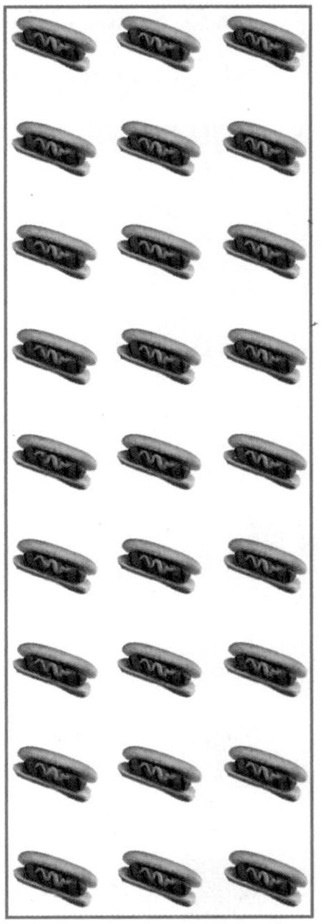

15 **Extended Response** How many pictures are there in each array? Did you have to count each picture? Explain.

16 Draw 7 × 9 and 9 × 7 as arrays.

Solve the following problems. REAL WORLD

The Cougars played 4 regular baseball games this week. Each game had 9 innings.

17 How many innings did the Cougars play this week?

18 The Cougars played 3 games at their home stadium. How many innings did they play there?

19 How many innings did the Cougars play at another team's stadium?

20 **Extended Response** In their last game, the Cougars scored a total of 9 runs in the third, sixth, and ninth innings. They scored twice as many runs in the sixth inning as in the third inning. In the last inning, they scored 3 runs. How many runs did they score in the third inning? Explain your answer.

Writing + Math **Journal**

Write about a strategy for multiplying by 9 and why it works.

LESSON 5.4 Square Facts

Key Ideas

When you multiply a whole number by itself, the product is called the square of a whole number. Any such number is a *square number*.

Study these diagrams. Then write about the patterns you see.

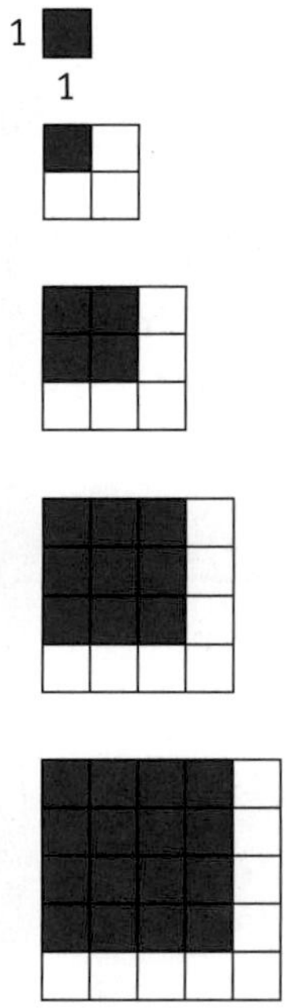

Area of Square	Pattern
$1 \times 1 = 1$	
$2 \times 2 = 4$	$1 + 3 = 4$
$3 \times 3 = 9$	$4 + 5 = 9$
$4 \times 4 = 16$	$9 + 7 = 16$
$5 \times 5 = 25$	$16 + 9 = 25$

Area of Square	Pattern
$1 \times 1 = 1$	
$2 \times 2 = 4$	$1 + 3 = 4$
$3 \times 3 = 9$	$4 + 5 = 9$
$4 \times 4 = 16$	$9 + 7 = 16$
$5 \times 5 = 25$	$16 + 9 = 25$

Complete the patterns for 6×6, 7×7, 8×8, and 9×9. Draw the squares if necessary.

Multiplication and Strategies Practice

Squares to 200

Players: Two

Materials:
Two 0–5 ***Number Cubes,*** two 5–10 ***Number Cubes***

Object: Accumulate a total equal to or greater than 200

Math Focus: Square multiplication facts and mathematical reasoning

HOW TO PLAY

1. Roll one ***Number Cube.*** The player with the greatest number goes first.
2. Players take turns rolling the 0–5 ***Number Cube.*** When the ***Number Cube*** is rolled, the player squares the number and adds the square to their running score.
3. On the second roll, after seeing the number rolled, the player may choose to roll the 5–10 ***Number Cube.*** The player may then decide to square the number rolled on the 0–5 ***Number Cube*** or square the number rolled on the 5–10 ***Number Cube.***
4. Play continues like this, with the players having the option of rolling the 5–10 ***Number Cube*** every other turn.
5. If both players pass 200 on the same turn, with each player having the same number of rolls, the player with the greater score wins.

Exploring Problem Solving

Mr. Smith makes pots for plants and grows plants in them. He waters the indoor plants once a week, and he waters the outdoor plants every three days. He did both chores on May 4. On which other days in May will he do both chores on the same day?

Lena made a diagram to solve the problem.

I made a calendar of the days in May. Then I used a different mark for each chore.

○ = *water outdoor plants (every 3 days)*

□ = *water indoor plants (every 7 days)*

1	2	(3)	4	5	(6)	[7]
8	(9)	10	11	(12)	13	[14]
15	16	17	18	19	20	[21]
22	23	24	25	26	27	[28]
29	30	31				

Think **about Lena's method. Answer these questions.**

1. If you used Lena's method, what date would you circle first?
2. What dates would you mark with a square?
3. Do you think Lena will get the correct answer? Why or why not?
4. Why is it important to look back after you have an answer to a problem?
5. What is useful about Lena's method even though she did not get the correct answer?

Spencer made lists and used patterns to solve the problem.

I made a list of the days in May that Mr. Smith does each chore.

I skip counted by 3 for the chore he does every 3 days.

I skip counted by 7 for the chore he does every 7 days.

I started both lists with 4 because he did both chores on May 4th.

outdoor plants → May 4, 7, 10, 13, 16, 19, 22, 25, 28, 31

indoor plants → May 4, 11

I stopped at 31.

Think about Spencer's method. Answer the following questions.

6. How is Spencer's method different from Lena's method?
7. What patterns did Spencer use?
8. Why did Spencer stop at 31?
9. What number will Spencer write next?
10. How can Spencer use his method to find the answer?
11. Solve the problem. Use Lena's method, Spencer's method, or your own method.

Cumulative Review

Skip Counting **Lesson 4.2**

Use skip counting to find the missing numbers and then to multiply.

1. 9, 18, ▢, 36, ▢, 54
2. $4 \times 9 =$ ▢
3. $6 \times 9 =$ ▢
4. 12, 24, 36, ▢, ▢, 72, 84
5. $3 \times 12 =$ ▢
6. $7 \times 12 =$ ▢
7. 7, 14, 21, ▢, 35, ▢, ▢ ,56
8. $3 \times 7 =$ ▢
9. $5 \times 7 =$ ▢

Approximation **Lesson 2.9**

Extended Response **Choose** the best approximate answer. In each problem, two of the answers are clearly wrong, and one is the best approximate answer.

10. $88 + 11 =$ ▢ **a.** 100 **b.** 90 **c.** 80
11. $717 + 180 =$ ▢ **a.** 827 **b.** 907 **c.** 1,017
12. $632 + 981 =$ ▢ **a.** 1,600 **b.** 180 **c.** 2,000
13. $774 + 809 =$ ▢ **a.** 3,713 **b.** 1,561 **c.** 5,608
14. $324 + 48 =$ ▢ **a.** 372 **b.** 423 **c.** 350
15. $567 + 262 =$ ▢ **a.** 569 **b.** 819 **c.** 809
16. $45 + 362 =$ ▢ **a.** 422 **b.** 589 **c.** 354
17. $488 + 288 =$ ▢ **a.** 797 **b.** 895 **c.** 8,904

Applying Multiplication **Grade 2 Lesson 11.6**

Solve these problems.

There are 4 ounces of glue in 1 bottle.

18 How many ounces are in 6 bottles?

19 How many ounces are in 8 bottles?

20 How many ounces are in 10 bottles?

One package of clay costs $6.

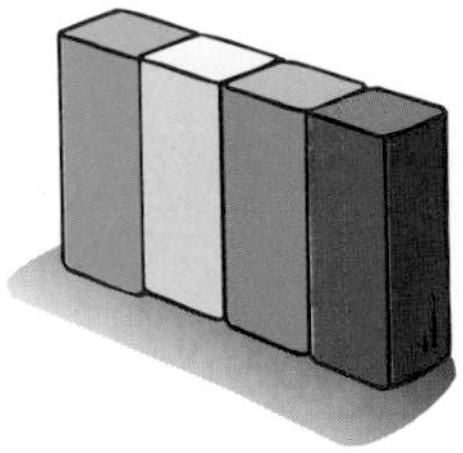

21 How much do 5 packages cost?

22 How much do 6 packages cost?

Perimeter and Area **Lesson 3.7**

Find the perimeter and the area for each figure.

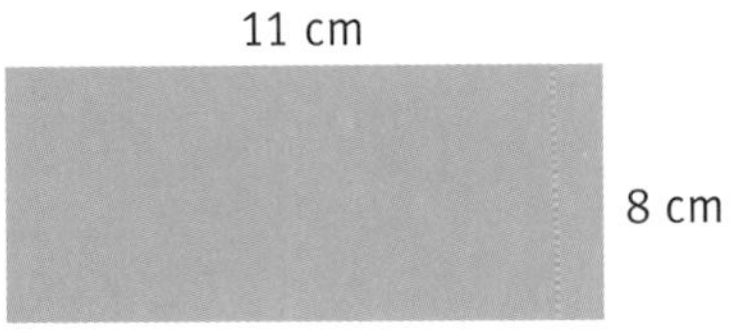

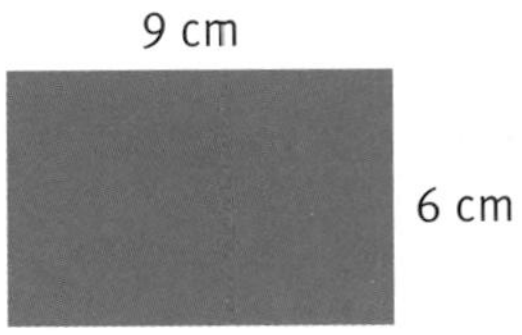

23 Perimeter: ☐ centimeters

Area: ☐ square centimeters

24 Perimeter: ☐ centimeters

Area: ☐ square centimeters

25 Tamira wants to border her page with lace ribbon. How long a piece of ribbon does she need to go around her page if each square sheet has one side measuring 12 inches?

26 Tamira has 27 inches of ribbon. How many more inches of ribbon does she need?

LESSON 5.5

Multiplying by 3 and 6

Key Ideas

Knowing the $\times 2$ facts may help you remember the $\times 3$ and the $\times 6$ facts.

For example, to help remember 3×7, think of 2×7 and then add one more 7.

How many watermelon seeds?

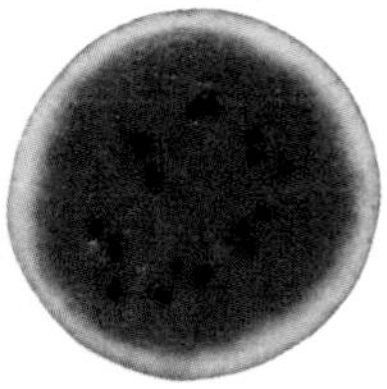

$2 \times 7 = 14$

$1 \times 7 = 7$

Altogether there are 2 rows of 7 and 1 more row of 7.

$(2 \times 7) + (1 \times 7) = 3 \times 7 = 21$

1. Draw an array to show 3×4.
2. Draw an array to show 3×8.

Multiply.

3. $3 \times 8 = \square$
4. $3 \times 2 = \square$
5. $9 \times 3 = \square$
6. $3 \times 0 = \square$
7. $3 \times 3 = \square$

Answer each question.

8. Last week melons were $4 each. Sara bought 3 melons. How much did Sara pay?
9. This week melons are $5 each. How much will Sara have to pay for 3 melons?
10. **Extended Response** Describe at least two ways to solve Problem 9.

One way to remember 6×7 is to think 3×7 and then double it.

How many ladybugs?

$3 \times 7 = 21$ plus $3 \times 7 = 21$

$6 \times 7 = 21 + 21 = 42$

Another way to remember 6×7 is recalling that $5 \times 7 = 35$. $(5 \times 7) + (1 \times 7) = 6 \times 7 = 42$

Copy **and complete each table.**

11 Tennis balls are sold 3 per can. Copy and complete the table to show how many tennis balls there are in different numbers of cans.

Cans	1	2	3	4	5	6	7	8	9	10
Tennis Balls	■	■	■	■	15	■	■	24	■	■

12 Each can of tennis balls costs $6. Copy and complete the table to show how much different numbers of cans will cost.

Cans	1	2	3	4	5	6	7	8	9	10
Cost (Dollars)	■	■	18	■	■	■	42	■	■	■

13 **Extended Response** Study the tables for Problems 11 and 12. How can knowing the $\times 3$ facts help with recalling the $\times 6$ facts? Write your answer. Draw diagrams if you wish.

14 Draw an array to show 6×4. Then draw a line to show that a 6×4 array is the same as two 3×4 arrays.

15 Draw an array to show 6×5. Then draw two lines showing the 6×5 array as three 2×5 arrays.

Multiply.

16. $6 \times 3 = \square$
17. $4 \times 6 = \square$
18. $7 \times 8 = \square$
19. $6 \times 8 = \square$
20. $3 \times 6 = \square$
21. $9 \times 3 = \square$
22. $6 \times 9 = \square$
23. $9 \times 6 = \square$
24. $6 \times 6 = \square$

In the American game of football, points can be scored in the following way:

6 points for each touchdown
1 extra point after a touchdown
3 points for each field goal
2 points for each safety

Extended Response **Give the number of points scored. Show how you found your answer.**

25. 3 touchdowns and 2 extra points
26. 3 field goals and 2 safeties
27. 3 touchdowns and 4 field goals

Extended Response **Solve each problem. Explain your answers.**

28. The Cougars scored 9 points. How many ways could they do that?
29. The Panthers beat the Bobcats by a score of 12 to 7. Which team scored more touchdowns?
30. The Leopards scored 26 points with no field goals or safeties. How many extra points did they score? Explain.

Game

Mul-Tack-Toe Game

Players: Two

Materials: Two **Mul-Tack-Toe** cards (like those below), two 0–5 ***Number Cubes*** (red), two 5–10 ***Number Cubes*** (blue), eight counters or coins for each player

Object: To cover three boxes in a line

Math Focus: Multiplication facts and mathematical reasoning

HOW TO PLAY

1. Each player chooses one of the two **Mul-Tack-Toe** cards.
2. Players take turns rolling any two ***Number Cubes***.
3. Both players calculate the product of the two numbers rolled. If the product is on a player's card, he or she puts a counter on that box.
4. The first player to cover three boxes in a line (horizontally, diagonally, or vertically) wins the round.

36	28	12
6	0	100
16	72	40

Card 1

18	56	30
1	0	8
20	63	24

Card 2

Writing + Math **Journal**

How did you decide which ***Number Cube*** to roll? Explain your strategy.

LESSON 5.6 Multiplying by 4 and 8

Key Ideas

You can use what you know about multiplying by 2 to multiply by 4 and 8.

To multiply by 4, you can first multiply by 2 and then double the product. To double a number, add the number to itself.

For example, to find the product of 4×7, first find 2 times 7.

$2 \times 7 = 14$

$2 \times 7 = 14$

$4 \times 7 = 28$

Write the product.

1. 4×8
2. 4×6
3. 4×9

Multiply.

4. $4 \times 5 = \square$
5. $3 \times 4 = \square$
6. $6 \times 4 = \square$
7. $3 \times 8 = \square$
8. $7 \times 8 = \square$
9. $9 \times 4 = \square$

Solve.

10. How many days in 2 weeks?
11. How many days in 4 weeks?
12. How many days in 8 weeks?
13. How many days in 10 weeks?
14. Alex bought 8 packs of pencils. There are 4 pencils in each pack. How many pencils did he buy?
15. Joan buys 4 CDs. Each CD costs \$9. How much does she spend on CDs?

eTextbook This lesson is available in the ***eTextbook.***

To multiply by 8, you can multiply by 4 and then double the product.

$4 \times 3 = 12$

$4 \times 3 = 12$

$8 \times 3 = 24$

Solve for ***n*** in each exercise. **Algebra**

16. $8 \times 8 = n$
17. $7 \times 2 = n$
18. $4 \times 8 = n$
19. $8 \times 7 = n$
20. $n \times 4 = 16$
21. $7 \times n = 14$

Mrs. Hancock ordered rainbowfish on the Internet for \$8 each. The company has a \$4 shipping and handling charge. That charge is the same no matter how many fish are ordered. Complete the table to show how much she will pay for different numbers of rainbowfish.

22.

Number	1	2	3	4	5	10
Cost (\$)	12					

23. Mrs. Hancock ordered 2 rainbowfish on Monday. The following week she ordered 3 more rainbowfish. How much did she pay in all?

24. **Extended Response** Explain how Mrs. Hancock could have spent less money for 5 rainbowfish.

Writing + Math Journal

Describe any patterns you see in the ×8 facts. Do you think that you could multiply any number by 8 and get a product of 153? Explain.

LESSON 5.7

Missing Factors and Division I

Key Ideas

Separating a set into equal parts is called division.
We can use division to describe sharing.

Kristin, Karen, and Jeff wish to share 24 pennies equally. How can they do it?

One way is to lay out 24 pennies equally and take turns removing and keeping one penny.

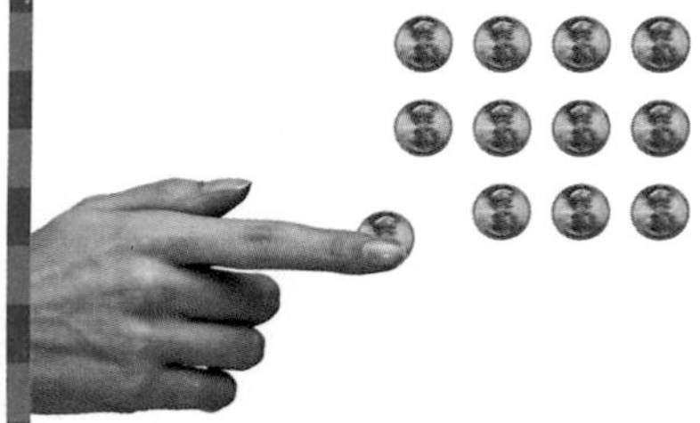

Another way is to think,

3 children

24 cents to share

$3 \times 8 = 24.$

How much will each child get?

Another way is to divide.

This is the number of cents to share.

$24 \div 3 = 8$

This is the number of children to share them.

This is the number of cents each child gets.

Solve each problem.

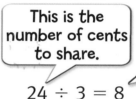

Rebecca and David are doing the Numbers on the Back Activity. Rebecca sees a 7 on David's back.

1. Suppose the product of the number on Rebecca's back and the number on David's back is 56. What number is on Rebecca's back?

2. Suppose the product of the number on Rebecca's back and the number on David's back is 42. What number is on Rebecca's back?

Solve each problem. You can use objects to act them out.

3. There are 24 shells and 3 children. How many shells are there for each child?

   $3 \times \square = 24$ $\quad$ $24 \div 3 = \square$

4. There are 12 coins in 3 rows. How many coins are in each row?

   $3 \times \square = 12$ $\quad$ $12 \div 3 = \square$

5. There are 35 cabbage plants. There are 5 rows. How many plants are there in each row?

   $5 \times \square = 35$ $\quad$ $35 \div 5 = \square$

6. There are 20 postcards on the table. Four children take turns picking cards until the cards are gone. Do they each have the same number of cards? How many postcards does each child have?

7. Jamal needs to pay 30¢. He has only nickels. How many nickels should he pay?

8. Rina had 18 marbles. She lost 3 marbles. How many marbles does she have left?

9. Donna has 3 sheets of stickers. Each sheet has 8 stickers. She wants to give the stickers to 4 friends so each friend gets the same number of stickers. How many stickers should each friend get?

10. **Extended Response** James bought some packs of baseball cards for $3 each. Then he bought an album for $15. He spent $27 in all. How many packs of cards did he buy? Explain how you found the answer.

Writing + Math **Journal**

Write a story or draw a picture to represent the problem $15 \div 3 = 5$.

LESSON 5.8 Missing Factors and Division II

Key Ideas

Multiplication and division are inverse (opposite) operations.

$2 \times 3 = 6$

$6 \div 3 = 2$ $\qquad \begin{array}{r} 2 \\ 3\overline{)6} \end{array}$

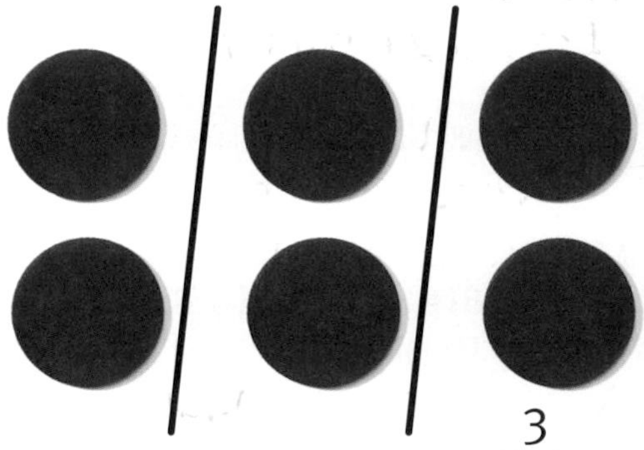

$6 \div 2 = 3$ $\qquad \begin{array}{r} 3 \\ 2\overline{)6} \end{array}$

Find the answers.

1. $4 \times 5 =$ ☐
2. $20 \div 4 =$ ☐
3. $\begin{array}{r} ☐ \\ 4\overline{)20} \end{array}$
4. $7 \times 6 =$ ☐
5. $42 \div 7 =$ ☐
6. $\begin{array}{r} ☐ \\ 7\overline{)42} \end{array}$
7. $35 \div 5 =$ ☐
8. $5 \times 7 =$ ☐
9. $\begin{array}{r} ☐ \\ 5\overline{)35} \end{array}$

Solve.

10. There are 16 computers. If 4 computers will fit on a table, how many tables are needed?
11. The servers at Leon's Restaurant share their tips equally. Last night they made $80 altogether. How much did each server earn?
12. Ricardo wants to share $48 with 5 friends. How much does each person get including Ricardo?

Solve.

13. From 1912 to 1959, there were 48 states in the United States. The flag had 48 stars, one for each state. The stars were in the shape of a rectangle with 6 rows. How many stars were in each row?

14. Between January and August of 1959, there were 49 states in the United States. The flag had 49 stars. The stars were in the shape of a rectangle. How many rows do you think there were? How many stars were in each row? What kind of rectangle was that?

15. Now the United States has 50 states. If the stars on the flag were in the shape of a rectangle with 5 rows, how many stars would be in each row? Draw how the flag would look.

16. What other rectangular shapes are possible with 50 stars?

LESSON 5.9
Understanding Division

Key Ideas

Just as multiplication can be thought of as repeated addition, division can be thought of as repeated subtraction.

To find the answer to 4×3, you can add 3 four times:

$3 + 3 + 3 + 3 = 12$

$\mathbf{4 \times 3 = 12}$

To find the answer to $12 \div 3$, keep subtracting 3 until you get to 0. Then count the number of times you subtracted 3.

$12 - 3 - 3 - 3 - 3 = 0$ (subtracted 3 four times)

$\mathbf{12 \div 3 = 4}$

Divide. **Use repeated subtraction if you need to.**

1. $24 \div 3 =$ ■
2. $24 \div 4 =$ ■
3. $24 \div 6 =$ ■
4. $24 \div 8 =$ ■
5. $27 \div 3 =$ ■
6. $81 \div 9 =$ ■
7. $72 \div 8 =$ ■
8. $42 \div 7 =$ ■
9. $16 \div 8 =$ ■
10. $25 \div 5 =$ ■
11. $64 \div 8 =$ ■
12. $35 \div 7 =$ ■

Solve.

13. **Extended Response** Jean, Val, and Todd wanted some ice cubes. They used 2 trays that made 12 ice cubes each. If they shared the ice cubes equally, how many did each person get? Explain.

14. **Extended Response** Mr. Marshall wants to take his 4 nieces to the movies. If he brings \$50, how much money can he spend equally on each niece and himself? Explain.

eTextbook This lesson is available in the *eTextbook*.

Each student in Ms. Warner's after-school class must choose exactly two clubs to join. Here's how many students are in each club.

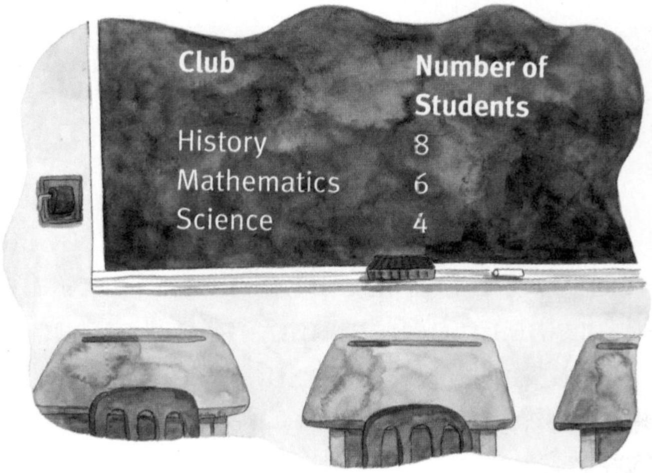

15. **Extended Response** How many students are in Ms. Warner's class? Explain.

16. The history club needed $24 for a field trip to the museum. How much was each student's share?

17. The math club worked on problems in groups of 3. How many groups were there?

18. **Extended Response** The science club had 8 model airplanes. How many could each student use? Explain.

19. Ms. Warner went to a teacher's convention and was given 19 pins that read "I Love Math!" She wanted to share the pins equally among all of her after-school students. How many should each student get?

20. **Extended Response** If the mathematics club and the science club decide to take a field trip together, how many students will go? Explain.

21. Suppose Ms. Warner required each student to belong to 3 clubs. How many students would belong to the history club?

22. The history club collected 40 old history books. They decided to donate 8 of the books to the school and share the remaining books equally among themselves.

    a. **Extended Response** How many books will each student get? Explain.

    b. The oldest book was published in 1929. How old was that book?

Exploring Problem Solving

Ms. Evans is buying a paintbrush for each student in her class for a special art project. There are 28 students in her class. She remembers that the price of a package of 8 brushes is $2 and some cents.

Work with your group to solve these problems. Explain how you got each answer.

1. How many extra paintbrushes do you think Ms. Evans will have?
2. Is $5 enough for Ms. Evans to buy 1 paintbrush for each student? Explain.
3. What is the least amount that Ms. Evans will need to spend on these brushes?
4. What is the most that Ms. Evans will need to spend on these brushes?

eTextbook This lesson is available in the *eTextbook*.

Cumulative Review

Basic Facts and Missing Terms **Lesson 1.3**

Solve.

1. Ethan was making a piñata. He needed to let the papier-mâché dry for 12 hours. He looked at the clock at noon and counted. It had been drying for 4 hours. How much more time does Ethan need to let it dry?

2. Emily's collage shows 31 different animals. The assignment is to show 63 different animals. How many more animals does Emily need in her collage?

Roman Numerals **Lesson 2.14**

Write the Arabic numeral for each Roman numeral. Show how to add numbers as you read the Roman numeral.

3. VI = ■ + ■ = ■
4. XIII = ■ + ■ + ■ + ■ = ■
5. CLV = ■ + ■ + ■ = ■
6. XXVII = ■ + ■ + ■ + ■ + ■ = ■

Division and Multiplication Functions **Grade 2 Lesson 11.9**

Find the function rules.

7. The function rule is ■.

in	*out*
5	10
12	■
16	■
18	36

8. The function rule is ■.

16	■
■	6
44	11
88	22

Cumulative Review

More Functions with Mixed Operations **Grade 2 Lesson 12.3**

Write the simplified rule for each problem.

9. The function rule is $\times 5 \div 5$.
The simplified rule is ___.

12	12
15	15
20	20
25	25

10. The function rule is $\times 10 \div 2$.
The simplified rule is ___.

7	35
9	45
12	60
16	80

Arrays and Multiplication **Lesson 4.6**

Find the area of these figures.

11. The area is ___ square units.
Write how you know.

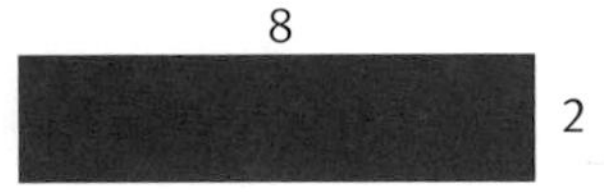

12. The total area is ___ square units.
Write how you know.

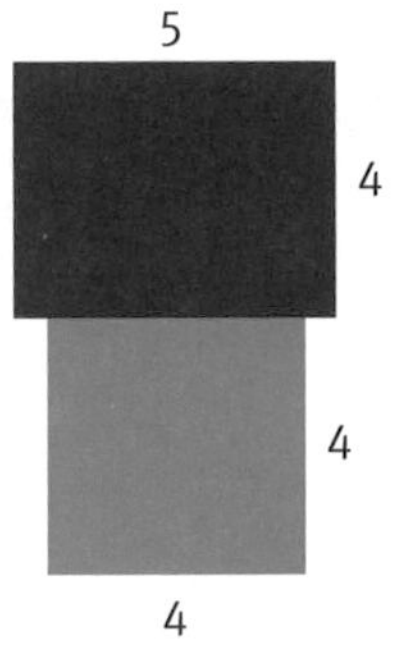

CHAPTER 5

Key Ideas Review

In this chapter you explored multiplication strategies.

You learned patterns to help you find multiplication facts.

You learned how to find missing factors.

Solve **the following. Identify the missing number as a *product*, *quotient*, or *factor*.**

1. $5 \times \square = 15$
2. $7 \times 3 = \square$
3. $12 \div 2 = \square$

4. Which of the following is an example of an array?

   a. $3 \times 4 = 12$

   b.
   * * *
   * * *
   * * *

   c. $4 + 4 + 4 = 12$

Extended Response **Solve each problem.**

5. Explain the difference between multiplication and division.
6. Does $3 \times 4 = 4 \times 3$? Explain.
7. Explain what skip counting is.
8. What is a factor?
9. Explain how to double a number.
10. Describe a pattern you could use to remember one of the multiplication facts.

CHAPTER 5

Chapter Review

Lessons 5.1 and 5.2

Solve or find the missing factor.

1. $2 \times 8 = \square$

   $\square \times 1 = 0$

2. $3 \times 1 = \square$

   $\square \times 10 = 10$

3. $3 \times 10 = \square$

   $2 \times \square = 10$

4. $8 \times 5 = \square$

   $\square \times 10 = 40$

Lessons 5.3 and 5.4

Solve or find the missing factors.

5. $9 \times 4 = \square$

   $\square \times 9 = 81$

6. $9 \times 8 = \square$

   $7 \times \square = 63$

7. $6 \times 6 = \square$

   $5 \times \square = 25$

8. $\square \times 7 = 49$

   $0 \times 0 = \square$

Lessons 5.5 and 5.6

Solve or find the missing factors.

9. $3 \times 6 = \square$

   $\square \times 9 = 54$

10. $9 \times 3 = \square$

    $3 \times \square = 24$

11. $8 \times 8 = \square$

    $4 \times \square = 28$

12. $7 \times \square = 56$

    $8 \times 5 = \square$

Lesson 5.7 **Solve** or find the missing term.

13. $64 \div 8 = n$

    $60 \div n = 10$

    $56 \div n = 8$

14. $27 \div 3 = n$

    $48 \div n = 8$

    $81 \div n = 9$

Lesson 5.8

15. Austin has 35 paper clips to give to 7 people.

    a. How many paper clips will each person receive?

    b. Tomorrow each person who received paper clips will get 8 times as many paper clips as he or she received today. How many paper clips will each person get?

    c. **Extended Response** Each paper clip is one inch long, and each person must arrange all of his or her paper clips in the shape of a square. Draw a picture of the square, and mark the number of inches for each side. How long is one side of the square? Explain why you cannot make a small square using all the paper clips.

CHAPTER 5 Practice Test

Solve.

1. There are 7 tricycles. Each tricycle has 3 wheels. How many wheels are there altogether?
2. There are 2 spiders. Each spider has 8 legs. How many legs are there altogether?
3. There are 5 ants. Each ant has 6 legs. How many legs are there altogether?
4. $3 \times 3 = \square$
5. Draw a square to model your answer to Problem 4.

Solve.

6. Melanie bought a book and a bookmark for each of her 5 nieces and nephews. How many gifts did she buy?
7. How many books did she buy?
8. Melanie also bought everyone a package of stickers. How many gifts will there be altogether?
9. What whole number times 2 equals 17?
10. When you multiply any number by 10, what digit is always in the ones place in the answer?
11. Doris put 6 nickels into the parking meter for her mother. How much money did she put into the parking meter?

Write the correct answer.

12. $4 \times 9 =$ ▢

Ⓐ 13 Ⓑ 27

Ⓒ 28 Ⓓ 36

13. $7 \times 8 =$ ▢

Ⓐ 63 Ⓑ 56

Ⓒ 50 Ⓓ 45

14. $3 \times 5 =$ ▢

Ⓐ 20 Ⓑ 18

Ⓒ 15 Ⓓ 8

15. $5 \times 6 =$ ▢

Ⓐ 11 Ⓑ 15

Ⓒ 27 Ⓓ 30

16. $3 \times 9 =$ ▢

Ⓐ 27 Ⓑ 28

Ⓒ 30 Ⓓ 33

17. $8 \times 9 =$ ▢

Ⓐ 88 Ⓑ 80

Ⓒ 72 Ⓓ 17

18. $4 \times 3 =$ ▢

Ⓐ 7 Ⓑ 8

Ⓒ 12 Ⓓ 19

19. $8 \times 3 =$ ▢

Ⓐ 11 Ⓑ 12

Ⓒ 20 Ⓓ 24

20. $31 + 9 =$ ▢

Ⓐ 40 Ⓑ 39

Ⓒ 38 Ⓓ 36

21. Mr. Hayes bought 36 cookies for the students in his room. There were 6 cookies in each package. How many packages did he buy?

Ⓐ 3 Ⓑ 4

Ⓒ 6 Ⓓ 7

22. There were 64 apples in the produce section of the store. They were arranged in 8 rows. How many apples were in each row?

Ⓐ 10 Ⓑ 8

Ⓒ 6 Ⓓ 4

CHAPTER 5

Practice Test

23. There are 6 dogs on Sarah and Mandy's street. The girls picked up 18 tennis balls in the neighborhood. If they divide the balls equally among the dogs, how many balls will each dog get?

Ⓐ 24 Ⓑ 12

Ⓒ 6 Ⓓ 3

24. The shoe store had 4 shelves filled with 20 shoes. How many shoes were on each shelf?

Ⓐ 80 Ⓑ 24

Ⓒ 5 Ⓓ 8

25. Ron has 5 dimes in his pocket. How much money does he have?

Ⓐ 25¢ Ⓑ 30¢

Ⓒ 5¢ Ⓓ 50¢

26. What is 2 thousands + 8 hundreds + 7 tens + 4 ones in standard form?

Ⓐ 2,784 Ⓑ 2,874

Ⓒ 20,874 Ⓓ 20,784

27. What does the number 5 represent in 5,306,241?

Ⓐ 5 millions

Ⓑ 5 ten thousands

Ⓒ 5 hundreds

Ⓓ 5 tens

28. Keiko has 5 red pencils, 3 green pencils, and 4 blue pencils. Jung Hyun has 6 red pencils and 2 brown pencils. How many more pencils does Keiko have than Jung Hyun?

Ⓐ 20 Ⓑ 12

Ⓒ 4 Ⓓ 2

29. Which shows the same product as 4×7?

Ⓐ 6×5 Ⓑ 7×4

Ⓒ 8×3 Ⓓ 3×8

30. Which shows the same product as 5×8?

Ⓐ 9×4 Ⓑ 7×6

Ⓒ 8×5 Ⓓ 6×7

31. $211 + 425 + 181 = \blacksquare$

Ⓐ 708 Ⓑ 817

Ⓒ 827 Ⓓ 917

32. $548 - 309 = \blacksquare$

Ⓐ 857 Ⓑ 587

Ⓒ 249 Ⓓ 239

33. **Extended Response** Solve, and then write a word problem to match each number sentence.

a. $48 \div 8 = \square$

b. $5 \times 7 = \square$

34. Mr. Jones is bringing food for a class party in his daughter's after-school group. There are 7 children in the group. Mr. Jones will bring 2 bottles of juice, 3 granola bars, and 7 pretzel rods per child. How many of each snack does he need?

a. bottles of juice

b. granola bars

c. pretzel rods

Ashley, his daughter, wants him to bring 1 big cookie for each child. One cookie costs $1.

d. How much will Mr. Jones spend on cookies?

Thinking Story

A Sticky Problem

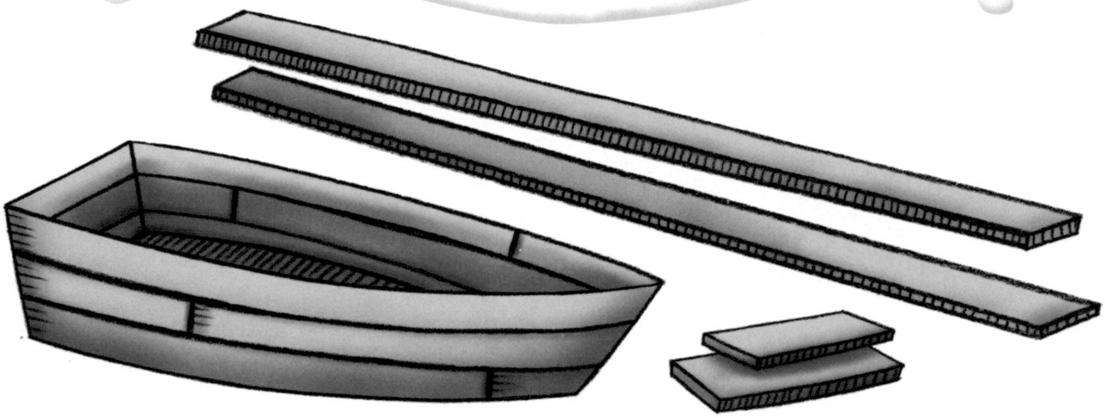

"Have you finished your model ship yet?" Portia asked.

"No," said Manolita. "I've run into a problem. I have to cut this stick of wood into 5 equal pieces, and I don't know how to figure out how long each piece should be. We haven't learned that kind of thing yet at school."

"How long is the stick?" Marcus asked.

"I've never measured it," said Manolita. "I didn't see how that would help."

How would measuring the stick help solve the problem?

Willy had a tape measure in his pocket, and with it he and Manolita measured the stick of wood. It was 65 centimeters long. "That's no help," said Manolita, "because I don't know how to divide 65 into 5 equal parts either."

While the children were walking along the sidewalk, thinking hard, they met Miss Asker. "Are you having a problem?" she asked.

"A very hard problem," Ferdie said. "Manolita has a stick 65 centimeters long, and we need to figure out how to divide it into 5 equal parts."

"My goodness, that is a hard problem," said Miss Asker. "It's too bad the stick isn't 50 centimeters long, isn't it?"

"Yes, it is," said Manolita. "Then I would know exactly how long each of the 5 pieces should be."

How long would each of the pieces be if the stick were 50 centimeters long?

"I know too," said Willy. "Each piece would be 10 centimeters long."

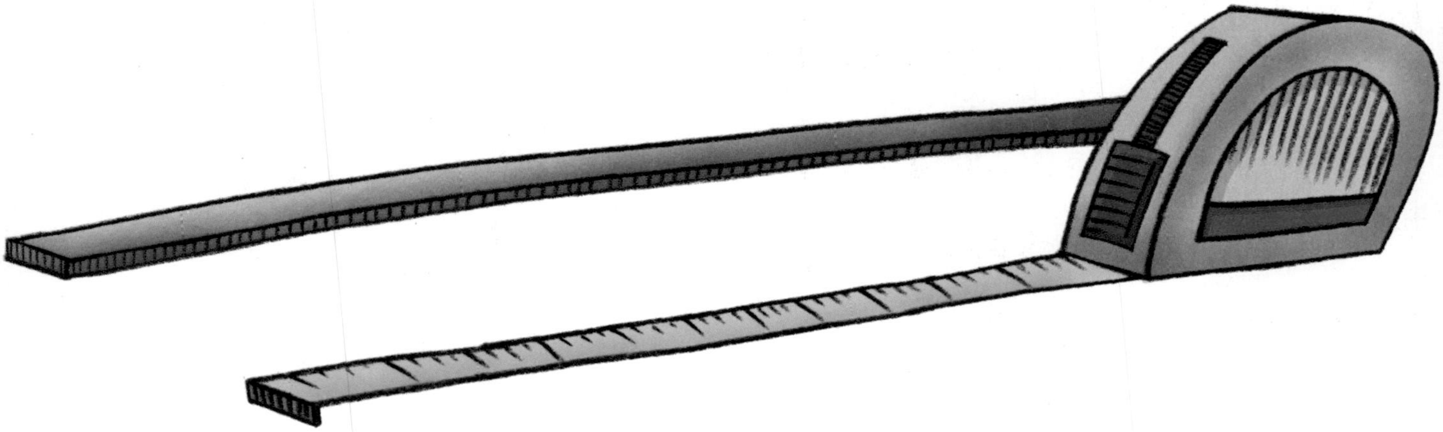

"But my stick isn't 50 centimeters long," said Manolita. "It's 65 centimeters, and I have to use all of it. If I made 5 pieces that were each 10 centimeters long, there would still be some left over."

"How much would be left over?" asked Miss Asker.

Can you figure out the answer?

"There'd be 15 centimeters left over," said Ferdie. "Sixty-five minus 50 is 15."

"Ah, yes," said Miss Asker, "that's quite a bit left over. I wonder what would happen if you tried to divide the leftover part into 5 equal pieces?"

How could you divide 15 centimeters into 5 equal parts?

"I know," Portia said. "You'd get pieces that were 3 centimeters long. Five 3s is 15: 3, 6, 9, 12, 15."

"That's very clever," said Miss Asker. "Now we have 5 pieces that are each 10 centimeters long and 5 pieces that are each 3 centimeters long. Is there any way to put those pieces together to get what we want?"

How could you put the pieces together to get the length Manolita needs?

"You could use glue," said Marcus. "You could take each of the 10-centimeter pieces and glue a 3-centimeter piece to one end of it. Then you'd have 5 pieces."

"Would each piece be the same length?" Miss Asker asked.

Would each piece be the same length?

How do you know?

How long would each piece be?

"They'd all be the same length, which is what I want," said Manolita. "Each piece would be 13 centimeters long, and the whole stick would be used up. But it wouldn't work. With so many parts glued together, the piece might be too weak."

"That's too bad," said Miss Asker. "I thought we had the problem solved. Is there any way we could do it without having to glue pieces of wood together?"

Can you think of a way?

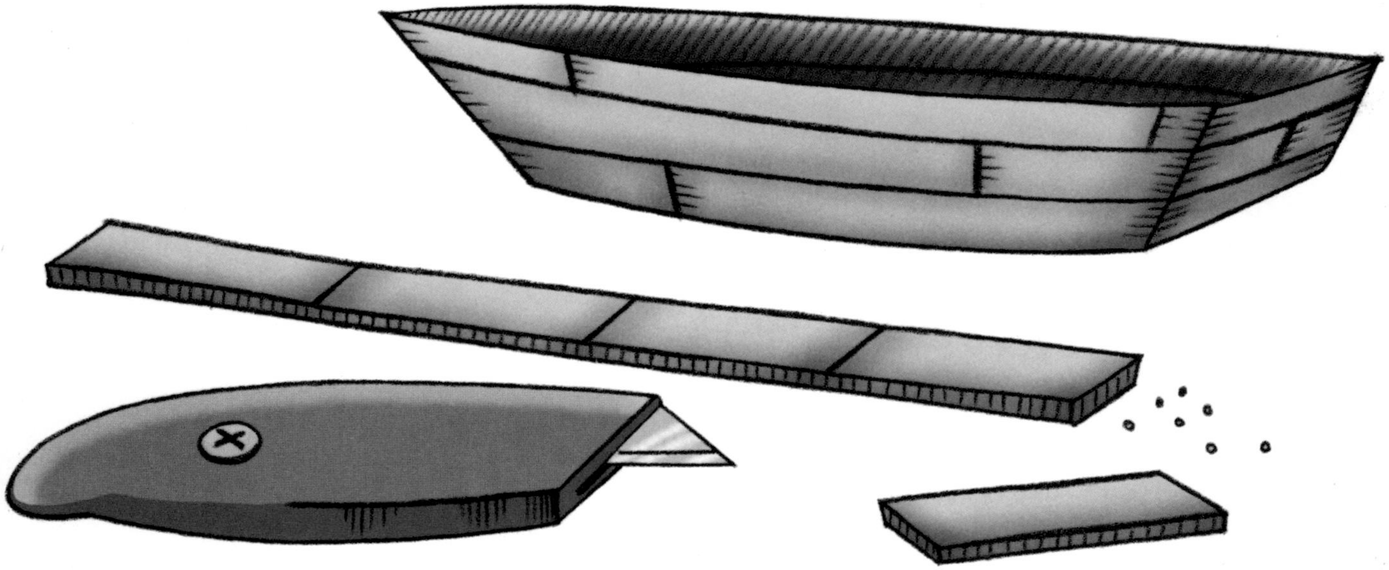

"I have an idea," said Portia. "We know that if we cut up the stick and then glue the parts back together, we can get 5 sticks that are each 13 centimeters long, so why don't we just cut 5 pieces that are 13 centimeters long in the first place? Then we won't have to glue."

"That sounds like a fine idea," said Miss Asker. "I wish I'd thought of it, but you children are very good at solving problems by yourselves."

The children thanked her anyway and hurried over to Manolita's house to try out Portia's idea. On the stick they marked off pieces that were exactly 13 centimeters long. Then Manolita asked her father to cut the stick where they had marked. When he finished, he gave her the 5 pieces that were each the same length, and nothing was left over.

"I wish Miss Asker was still here," said Manolita, "because I have another problem."

"She isn't much help anyway," said Ferdie. "She never knows the answers. She just asks questions."

Is it true that Miss Asker wasn't much help?

Why do you think so?

"My new problem," said Manolita, "is that I have this other stick that is 60 centimeters long. I need to cut it up into 5 equal parts too."

"That's easy," said Ferdie. "I can solve that one with my eyes closed." He thought and thought, and finally he said, "I think I'll open my eyes." None of the others knew how to solve the problem either.

What is it they need to figure out?

"It's too bad the stick isn't 50 centimeters long," said Marcus. "Then I'd know how long each of the 5 pieces should be."

How long would each piece be if the stick were 50 centimeters long?

"Everybody knows that," said Ferdie. "The pieces would be 10 centimeters long, because 5 times 10 is 50. But that's no help, because the stick is 60 centimeters long."

How much would be left if Manolita cut off 5 pieces that were each 10 centimeters long?

"We have 10 centimeters left to worry about," said Willy. Then he thought of something. "Hey," he said, "this problem is almost the same as the first problem we solved! I think I can work it out now!"

Can you? Work on it today by yourself or with your classmates. Find out tomorrow if you got it right. Remember, the problem is how to divide a stick 60 centimeters long into five equal pieces.

If the piece were 50 centimeters, how long would each of the five small pieces be?

How much would be left of the long piece?

If you divided that into five equal pieces, how long would each piece be?

Now, how could you put the small pieces together to make just five the same length?

So, in the end, how long should each piece be?

The End

CHAPTER 6

Functions

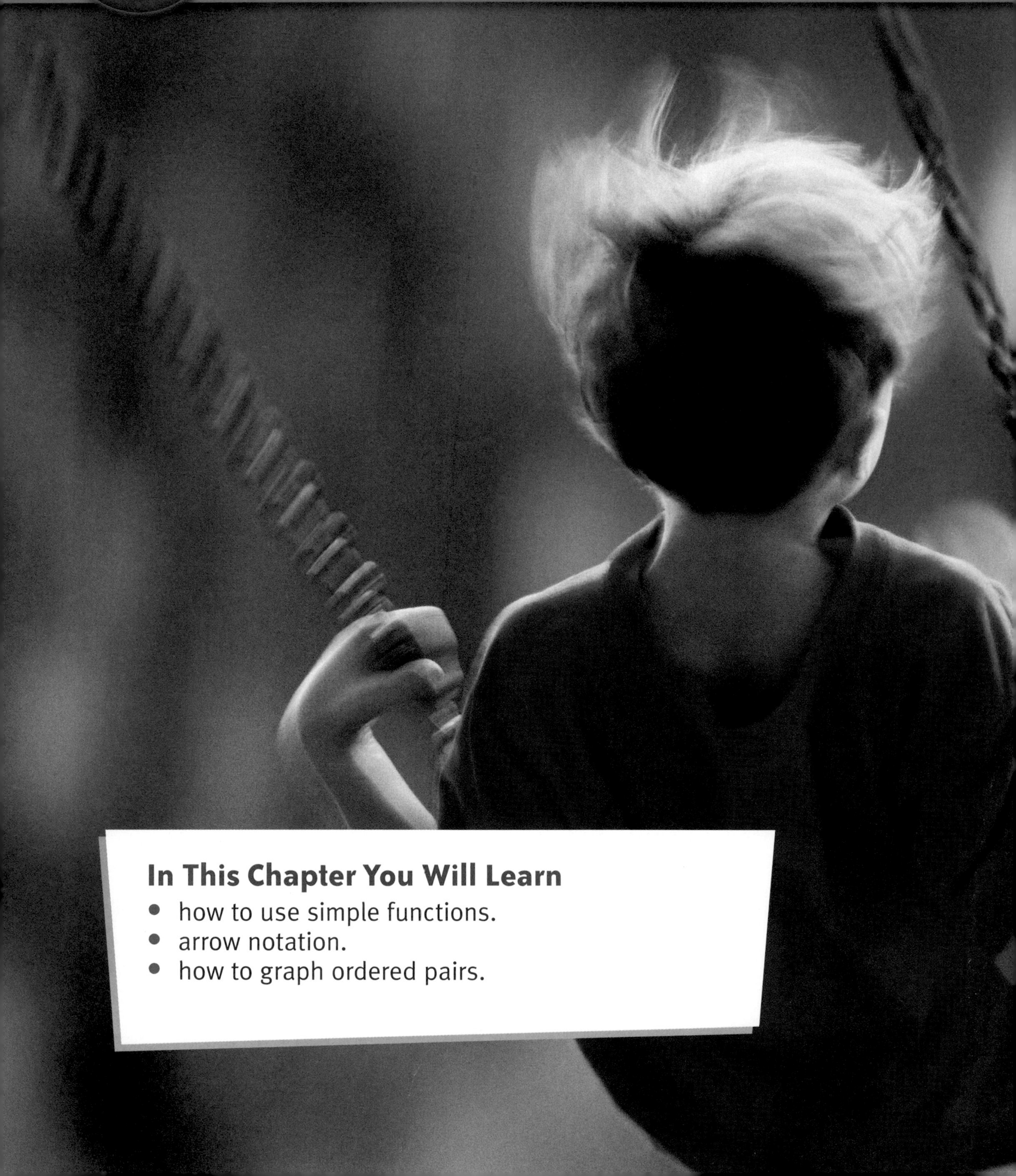

In This Chapter You Will Learn

- how to use simple functions.
- arrow notation.
- how to graph ordered pairs.

Problem Solving

It takes 5 seconds to make 1 swing back and forth on this swing set.

Solve and discuss.

1. How long will it take to make 2 swings?
2. Write how you would find how long it takes to make 6 swings.
3. Copy and complete these sentences to show how the number of swings you make and the number of seconds it takes are related.

   If you ______ the number of swings by ___, you get the number of seconds.
4. Trevor drew a diagram as a shorter way to show how the number of swings and the number of seconds are related. Copy and complete Trevor's diagram.

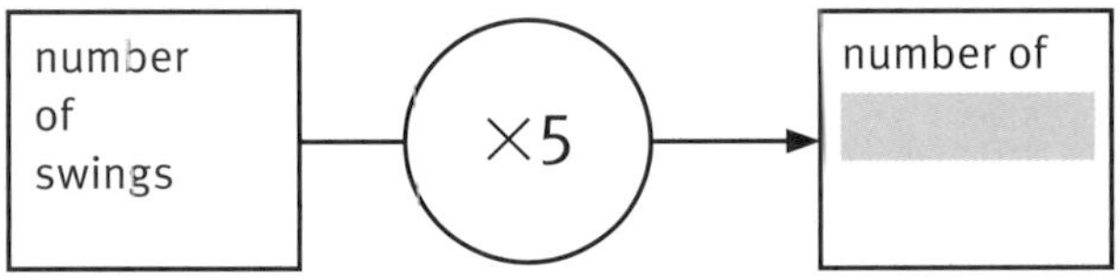

5. This taller swing set takes 8 seconds to make 1 swing. Show how the number of swings and the number of seconds are related for this swing set. Make a diagram like Trevor's, write a word equation, or use some other way.

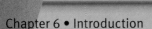

LESSON **6.1**

Simple Functions

Key Ideas

A function machine changes any number that is put into it. It changes the number based on a rule.

Roger put a 5 into the same machine, and a 20 came out. Then he put in a 7, and a 28 came out. He determined that the rule for the machine must be $\times 4$.

The table below shows the numbers that went into a function machine. It also shows some of the numbers that came out.

Write **what you think the function rule is. Then complete the table.**

Function Rule: ▢

In	Out
3	15
6	30
9	45
1 7	▢
2 8	▢
3 1	▢
4 4	▢
5 5	▢

e Textbook This lesson is available in the ***eTextbook.***

Manolita dreamed about a machine that makes pencils. The machine could make 4 pencils every minute.

Fill in the table. Show how many pencils the machine could make in 2 minutes, in 3 minutes, and so on.

Number of Minutes	Number of Pencils
1	4
6 2	■
7 3	■
8 4	■
9 5	■
10 6	■
11 7	■
12 8	■
13 9	■
14 10	■

Solve.

15. Sylvia wants to hang 5 posters. Each poster needs 4 tacks. How many tacks does she need?
16. Each crate holds 8 containers of milk. There are 6 empty crates. How many containers can they hold?
17. Bananas come in bunches of 7. There are 6 bunches left on the shelf. How many bananas are there?
18. There are 4 quarters in 1 dollar. Jill has 9 dollars' worth of quarters. How many quarters does she have?

LESSON 6.2

Introducing Arrow Notation

Key Ideas

You can use an arrow to represent a function machine.
The function rule is inside the circle.

9 —(×7)→ 63

Answer each question.

1. If 3 is put in, what number will come out?

   3 —(×3)→

2. If 7 is put in, what number will come out?

   7 —(×3)→

3. If 16 is put in, what number will come out?

   16 —(−7)→

4. If 7 is put in, what number will come out?

   7 —(−7)→

Dari made a table. She wrote each number that she put into this function machine. She also wrote each number that came out. Then she found the function rule.

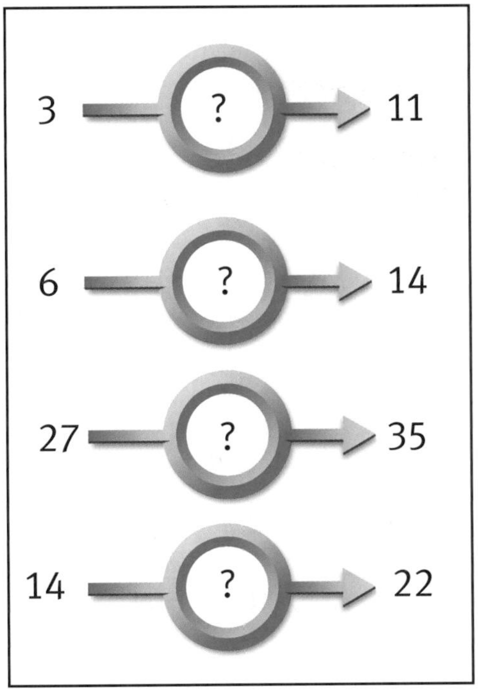

The function rule is +8.

Find **the function rule for each set of numbers.**

5

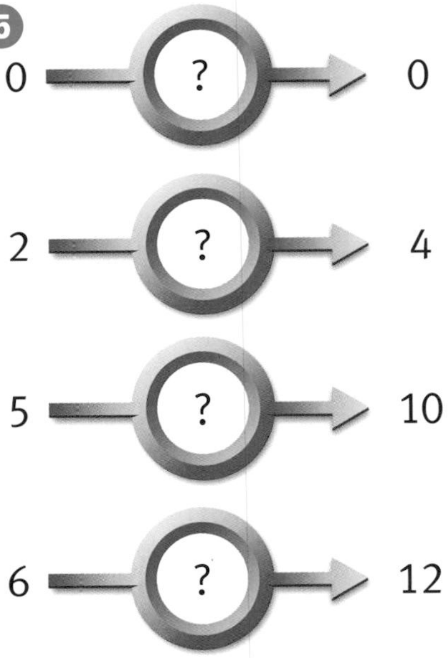

The function rule is ▢.

6

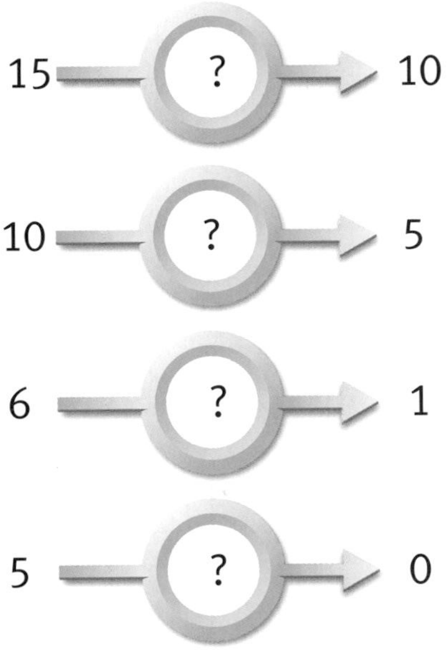

The function rule is ▢.

LESSON 6.3

Using Arrow Notation to Solve Equations

Key Ideas

A letter can stand for an output or an input.

$4 \xrightarrow{\times 9} n$

The letter *n* stands for the output. The value of *n* is 36.

In the function below, *x* stands for the input. What is the value of *x*?

$x \xrightarrow{\times 6} 42$

The value of *x* is 7.

Find the value of *n*. **Algebra**

1. $4 \xrightarrow{+6} n$

   $n =$ ▢

2. $6 \xrightarrow{-5} n$

   $n =$ ▢

3. $n \xleftarrow{\times 2} 5$

   $n =$ ▢

4. $n \xleftarrow{\div 3} 21$

   $n =$ ▢

5. $n \xrightarrow{+6} 10$

   $n =$ ▢

6. $n \xrightarrow{-5} 2$

   $n =$ ▢

eTextbook This lesson is available in the *eTextbook*.

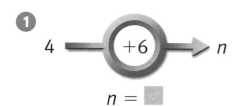

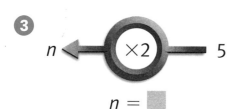

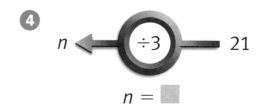

Algebra

Find the values of *n*, *x*, and *y*.

7. 10 ← (×2) — *n*

   n = ▢

8. *x* — (÷3) → 7

   x = ▢

9. 8 ← (+8) — *x*

   x = ▢

10. *y* — (×8) → 56

    y = ▢

11. 21 — (÷3) → *n*

    n = ▢

12. *y* ← (×3) — 7

    y = ▢

13. 4 — (+2) → *n* — (×3) → *m*

    n = ▢
    m = ▢

14. 5 — (+2) → *n* — (×3) → *m*

    n = ▢
    m = ▢

15. 2 — (+83) → *n* — (×0) → *m*

    n = ▢
    m = ▢

16. *m* ← (×2) — *n* ← (÷3) — 12

    n = ▢
    m = ▢

Exploring Problem Solving

Some students were playing at the playground. Then 7 more students came, and 2 left. All the students at the playground decided to play a team game. There were enough students to have 4 teams with 6 on each team. How many students were there to begin with?

Clara decided to use guess, check, and revise to solve the problem.

1: I'll try 7 as the answer. $7 + 7 = 14$	2: $7 + 7 = 14$ $14 - 2 = 12$	3: $7 + 7 = 14$ $14 - 2 = 12$ $12 \div 4 =$

Think about Clara's strategy. Answer the following questions.

1. Why did Clara write $7 + 7$ as her first step?
2. Why did Clara compute $14 - 2$ next?
3. Why did Clara compute $12 \div 4$ next?
4. Did Clara's guess of starting with 7 students work? Explain.
5. How should Clara make her next guess? Why?

Warren wrote an equation, drew a diagram, and worked backward to solve the problem.

number to start —> 7 more came —> 2 left —> made 4 teams —> 6 on each team

n —> +7 —> -2 —> ÷4 —> 6	n —> +7 —> -2 —> ÷4 —> 6 [x4] 6	n —> +7 —> -2 —> ÷4 —> 6 [+2] [x4] 6

Think about Warren's strategy. Answer the following questions.

6. How does Warren's word equation model the problem?
7. What does n stand for in Warren's diagrams?
8. How does Warren's first diagram model the problem?
9. In his second diagram, why has Warren drawn a backward arrow and written $\times 4$?
10. Why is Warren drawing another backward arrow and writing $+2$?
11. What do you think Warren will do next? Why?
12. When Warren gets an answer, what can he do to make sure it is correct?
13. Finish solving the problem. Use Clara's strategy, Warren's strategy, or a strategy of your own.
14. What strategy did you use? Why?

Cumulative Review

Simple Function Machines **Lesson 1.5**

Find the in values, the out values, or the rule.

1. Rule: −7

in	out
15	
16	
17	
13	

2. Rule: +9

in	out
19	
22	
35	
58	

3. Rule: +6

in	out
20	
19	
18	
17	
16	

4. Rule: ___

in	out
11	25
9	
21	
	34

5. Rule: ___

in	out
31	18
53	
65	
	66

6. Rule: ___

in	out
	30
	29
	28
7	27
6	26

7. Rule: ___

in	out
30	12
28	10
	7
	5

8. Rule: −6

in	out
	0
12	
8	
	8

9. Rule: ___

in	out
	14
	12
12	
9	

Multiplication and Number Patterns Lesson 4.3

Follow the directions for each exercise. Be sure to use three different 100s Tables.

10. On the first 100s Table, color the boxes you reach when counting by 3s. Ring the number in the boxes you reach when counting by 6s. Place an **X** in the boxes you reach when counting by 12s.

11. On the second 100s Table, ring the number in the boxes you reach when counting by 4s. Place an **X** in the boxes you reach when counting by 8s.

12. On the third 100s Table, ring the number in the boxes you reach when counting by 2s. Color the boxes you reach when counting by 10s.

Missing Factors and Division II Lesson 5.8

Find the answers.

13. $8 \times 3 = \square$
14. $24 \div 8 = \square$
15. $8\overline{)24} = \square$
16. $3 \times 9 = \square$
17. $27 \div 3 = \square$
18. $3\overline{)27} = \square$
19. $48 \div 8 = \square$
20. $6 \times 8 = \square$
21. $8\overline{)48} = \square$

Solve.

22. Eight volunteers plan to paint shapes and maps on the playground. There are 48 paintbrushes divided equally among the 8 volunteers. How many paintbrushes will each volunteer receive?

LESSON 6.4

Inverse Functions (Reversing the Arrow)

Key Ideas

***Inverse* means about the same thing as *opposite*.** The inverse of +6 is −6 because they undo each other.

—(+6)→

←(−6)—

Write the inverse arrow operation. The first one has been done for you.

1. —(+8)→
   ←(−8)—

2. ←(−12)—
   —(■)→

3. ←(+9)—
   —(■)→

4. ←(−16)—
   —(■)→

5. —(■)→
   ←(×3)—

6. —(÷7)→
   ←(■)—

7. —(÷4)→
   ←(■)—

8. —(+10)→
   ←(■)—

9. —(×0)→
   ←(■)—

Use inverse arrow operations to find the value of n. **Algebra**

10 $n \xrightarrow{\times 3} 12$

$\xleftarrow{\div 3}$

$n =$ ■

11 $n \xrightarrow{\times 5} m \xrightarrow{+8} 38$

$\xleftarrow{\div 5}$ $\xleftarrow{-8}$

$n =$ ■

12 $n \xrightarrow{\times 2} 14$ $n =$ ■

13 $13 \xleftarrow{-7} n$ $n =$ ■

14 $n \xrightarrow{-7} m \xrightarrow{-6} 1$ $n =$ ■

15 $10 \xleftarrow{+4} m \xleftarrow{\times 3} n$ $n =$ ■

16 $n \xrightarrow{\div 4} m \xrightarrow{\div 2} 1$ $n =$ ■

LESSON 6.5

Variables and Arrow Notation

Key Ideas

In the function below, *x* and *y* are variables. If you are given the value of *y*, you can use the inverse arrow operation to solve for *x*.

$$x \xrightarrow{\times 5} y$$

If you know that the value of *y* is 35, you can determine that the value of *x* is 7 by dividing 35 by 5.

Solve **these problems. Work down the page.** **Algebra**

$$x \xrightarrow{+3} y$$

1. If $x = 3$, what is *y*?
2. If $y = 3$, what is *x*?
3. If $x = 6$, what is *y*?
4. If $y = 6$, what is *x*?

$$y \xleftarrow{-7} x$$

5. If $x = 56$, what is *y*?
6. If $x = 42$, what is *y*?
7. If $y = 63$, what is *x*?
8. If $y = 35$, what is *x*?

$$y \xleftarrow{\times 3} x$$

9. If $x = 6$, what is *y*?
10. If $y = 6$, what is *x*?
11. If $x = 9$, what is *y*?
12. If $y = 9$, what is *x*?

$$x \xrightarrow{\times 8} y$$

13. If *x* is 6, what is *y*?
14. If *x* is 9, what is *y*?
15. If *y* is 32, what is *x*?
16. If *y* is 64, what is *x*?

eTextbook This lesson is available in the ***eTextbook.***

Copy and complete the function tables. **Algebra**

17 $x \rightarrow \times 4 \rightarrow y$

x	y
5	■
■	16
9	■
4	■
■	32

18 $x \rightarrow \div 2 \rightarrow y$

x	y
4	2
10	5
16	8
6	■
■	6
■	0

19 $x \rightarrow -7 \rightarrow y$

x	y
8	1
12	■
■	0
■	4
13	■

20 $x \rightarrow \times 0 \rightarrow y$

x	y
1	0
7	0
4	■
■	0
173	0

Writing + Math **Journal**

Choose a number for y that is a multiple of 2, and solve for x. Explain why x and y are variables.

$x \rightarrow \times 2 \rightarrow y$

LESSON 6.6

Graphing Ordered Pairs

Key Ideas

An ordered pair is a set of numbers that describes the location of a point on a graph.

Manolita lives in Graph Town. Her house is located at Point D on the map. Point D is located where 4th Street meets 5th Avenue. A shorter way to describe this location on the map is by using the ordered pair (4, 5).

Look at the map of Graph Town, and answer the questions.

Graph Town

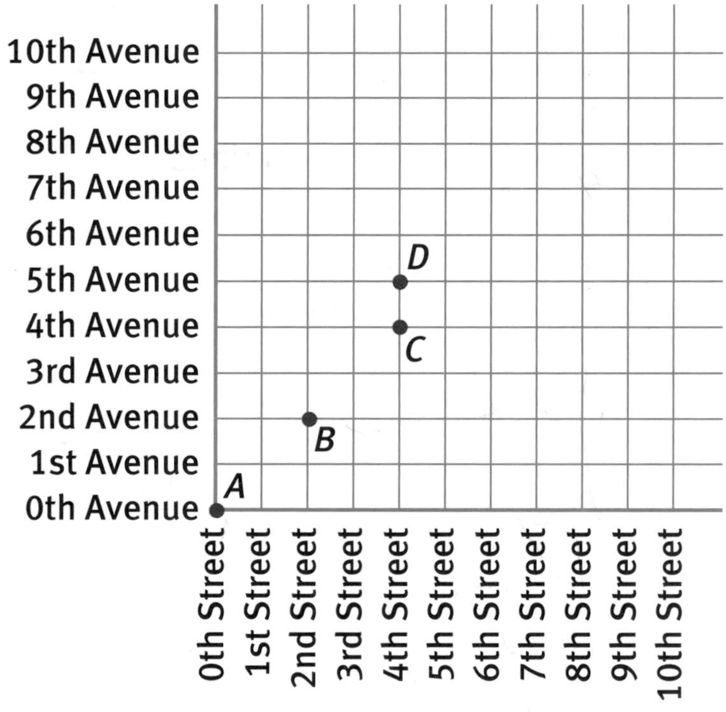

1. Which point is located at (0, 0)?

2. A new school is being built where 8th Street meets 7th Avenue. What is the ordered pair that describes this location?

3. **Extended Response** Manolita needs directions from her house to the new school. What is the shortest route she can take?

4. **Extended Response** Manolita used to go to a school located at Point B. What ordered pair describes Point B? How many more blocks must she travel to get to her new school, if she always takes one of the shortest routes? Explain your answer.

5. How many blocks would Manolita travel if she started at (0, 0) and took the shortest route to (10, 10)?

6. Manolita is going to visit her friend Lara. Lara gave her these directions to her house: Start at your house. Go five blocks east to 9th Street. Then go two blocks south to 3rd Avenue and you will be at Lara's house. What is the ordered pair that describes the location of Lara's house?

7. Manolita's class is taking a field trip to an art museum. They leave the new school at 10:00 and go two blocks west and two blocks north to get to the museum. What is the ordered pair that describes the location of the museum?

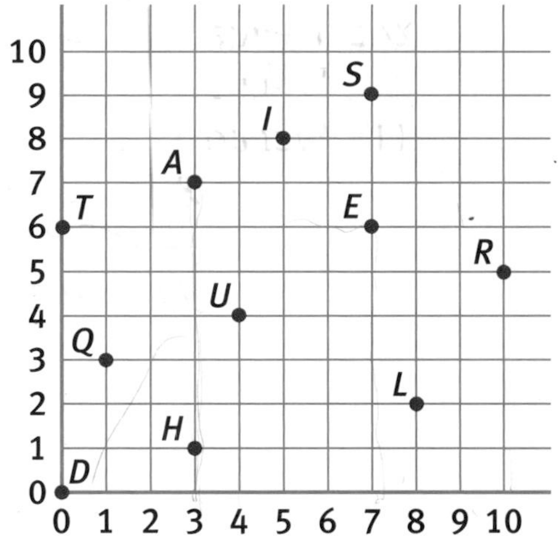

Fill in the blanks by finding the letters in the graph that match the ordered pairs.

A silly definition of this word is "money for your brain to spend."

8. __ __ __ __ __ __ __ __ __ __ __ __

(3, 1) (7, 6) (3, 7) (0, 0) (1, 3) (4, 4) (3, 7) (10, 5) (0, 6) (7, 6) (10, 5) (7, 9)

Functions and Graphing

Key Ideas

A graph can show how the input and output values of a function are related.

Jamaal and Ana earn money by collecting seashells, and selling them at a local flea market for $3 each.

To estimate how much money they might earn, they decided to use the following function:

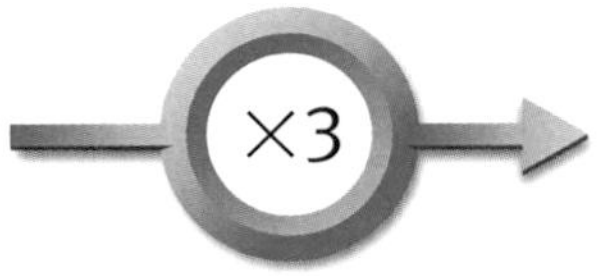

1. What does x represent?
2. What does y represent?

Then they made the following function table to help them see how much money they might earn.

Copy and complete the table.

	Number of Seashells Sold (x)	Dollars Earned (y)
	2	6
	4	12
3	6	
4	8	
5	10	
6	12	
7	14	
8	16	
9	18	

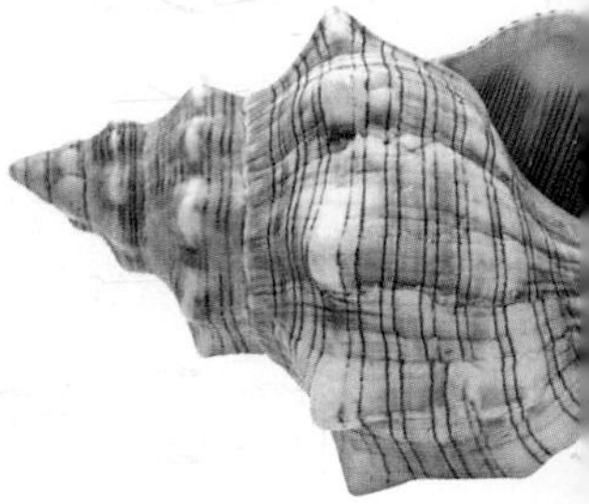

Finally, Jamaal and Ana decided to make a line graph to show how many dollars they might earn for selling different numbers of seashells. They drew the following graph and noticed that each row on the table shows an ordered pair for the function rule $\times 3$. For example, these are some of the ordered pairs:

(2, 6) (4, 12) (6, 18)

These ordered pairs are plotted on the following graph. Copy and complete the graph by plotting the rest of the ordered pairs from the function table.

Jamaal and Ana's Profit for Selling Different Numbers of Seashells

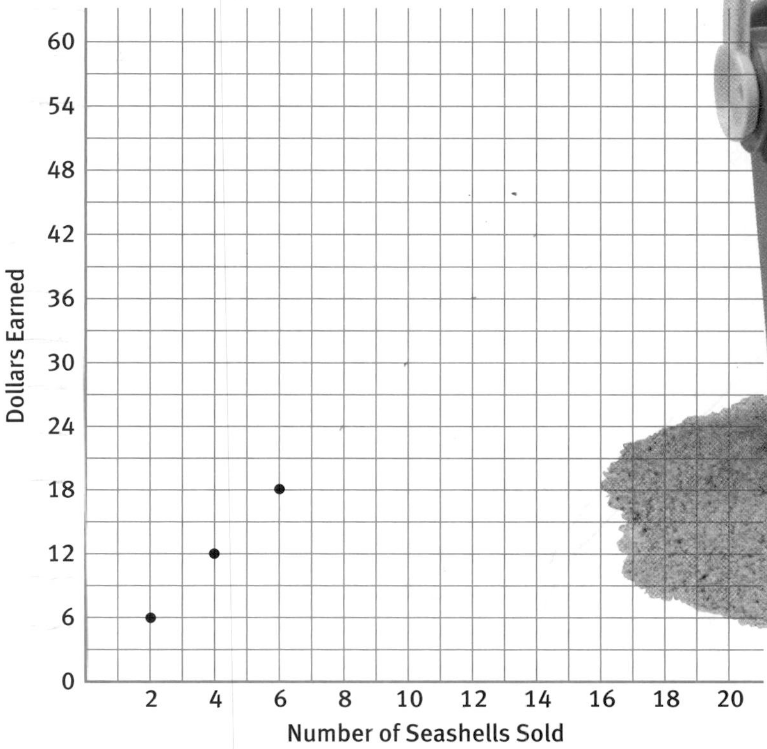

10. Using only the completed graph, find out how much money Jamaal and Ana would earn if they sold 14 shells. If they sold 8 shells?

11. Using only the completed graph, find out how many shells they sold if they earned $36.

12. **Extended Response** Suppose that Jamaal and Ana earned $50. Is that possible? Why or why not?

Exploring Problem Solving

You are designing a new kind of slide for a playground. The slide will have a special water sprayer to keep children cool and wet as they go down the slide. You want to know how high it will be at the point where you slide above the sprayer. Here is what you know so far about the slide.

HEIGHT:
The ladder is 14 feet above the ground, just enought to reach the high end of the slide.

STEEPNESS:
The slide will be straight. For every 3 feet the slide goes across, it will go down 2 feet.

SPRAYER:
The sprayer will be on the ground 12 feet from the ladder.

Solve these problems.

1. Design the slide, and draw a plan for it. Show how high above the sprayer the slide will be.
2. How do you know the height shown on your plan is correct?
3. Compare your answer with others. Did everyone in your class get the same height?
4. What strategies did you use to solve the problem?

Cumulative Review

Commutative Law of Multiplication Lesson 4.8

Find the product. Use repeated addition, skip counting, or the Multiplication Table on page 146 to check your answers.

1. $6 \times 3 = \square$
2. $3 \times 6 = \square$
3. $4 \times 9 = \square$
4. $9 \times 4 = \square$
5. $7 \times 10 = \square$
6. $10 \times 7 = \square$
7. $8 \times 1 = \square$
8. $1 \times 8 = \square$

Basic Facts and Missing Terms Lesson 1.3

Solve. For Problems 25–28, write the correct math sentence, and then solve the problem.

9. $17 - 3 = \square$
10. $21 + 6 = \square$
11. $9 + 7 = \square$
12. $9 + \square = 13$
13. $6 + \square = 14$
14. $5 - 5 = \square$
15. $8 + 9 = \square$
16. $4 + \square = 16$
17. $12 - \square = 9$
18. $7 + 3 = \square$
19. $18 + 7 = \square$
20. $12 - \square = 8$
21. $18 - 5 = \square$
22. $10 + 8 = \square$
23. $5 + 17 = \square$
24. $14 - 9 = \square$

25. Fifteen ladders on the playground needed to be repainted. Three workers painted 7 ladders altogether. How many more ladders need to be painted?

26. There are 27 slides on the playground, and 12 of the slides are metal. The rest of the slides are plastic. How many plastic slides are on the playground?

27. The cat jungle gym has 16 ledges. Cats are sleeping on 7 of the ledges. How many ledges are empty?

28. During recess, 26 students were playing around the jungle gym. Then 8 of the students decided to play with jump ropes. How many students did not play with the jump ropes?

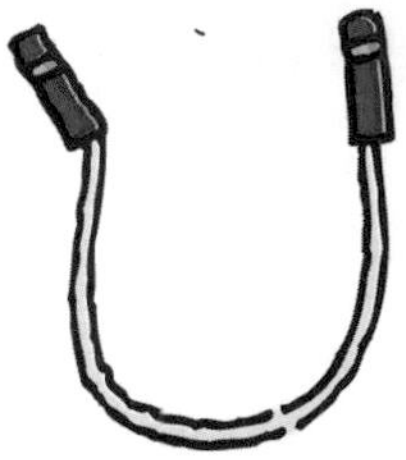

Cumulative Review

Multiplication Table Lesson 4.4

Find the product. Use repeated addition, skip counting, or the Multiplication Table on page 146 to check your answers.

29. $8 \times 7 =$ ▢
30. $9 \times 9 =$ ▢
31. $3 \times 7 =$ ▢
32. $5 \times 8 =$ ▢
33. $8 \times 8 =$ ▢
34. $5 \times 10 =$ ▢
35. $6 \times 4 =$ ▢
36. $7 \times 6 =$ ▢
37. $8 \times 9 =$ ▢
38. $9 \times 6 =$ ▢
39. $6 \times 7 =$ ▢
40. $7 \times 7 =$ ▢

Measuring and Graphing Lesson 3.3

Follow the directions, and answer the question.

Mrs. Burger had her students measure the length of the board with 7 different pencils.

Pencil Number	Pencil Unit Tally	Number of Pencil Units
1	𝍸 𝍸 𝍸 𝍸 𝍸	
2	𝍸 𝍸 𝍸 ||	
3	𝍸 𝍸 |	
4	𝍸 𝍸 𝍸 |	
5	𝍸 𝍸 |||	
6	𝍸 𝍸 ||	
7	𝍸 𝍸 𝍸 ||||	

41. Complete the table, and create a bar graph of the results.
42. Which pencil was used to measure 25 pencil units as the length of the board? Which pencil was used to measure 17 pencil units? Which pencil is the shorter pencil?

CHAPTER 6 Key Ideas Review

In this chapter you explored functions and graphing.

You learned how to use an arrow to represent a function machine.

You learned how a variable can represent an input or an output value of a function.

You learned how to graph ordered pairs to show how the input and output values of a function are related.

Find the function rule for each set of numbers.

Solve these problems.

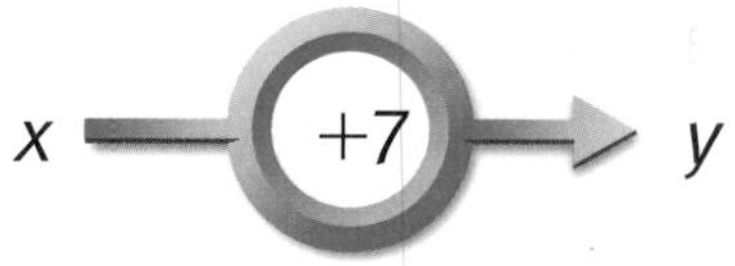

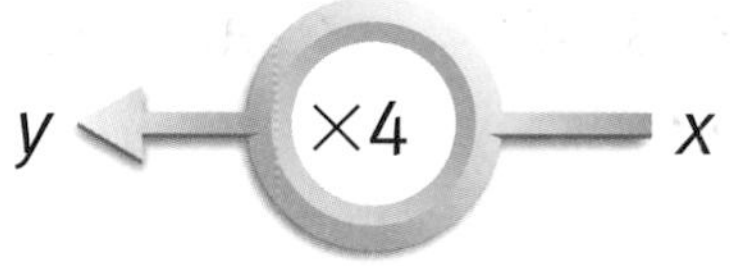

1. If $x = 21$, what is y?
2. If $y = 21$, what is x?
3. If $x = 9$, what is y?
4. If $y = 36$, what is x?

Use the graph to solve the exercises below.

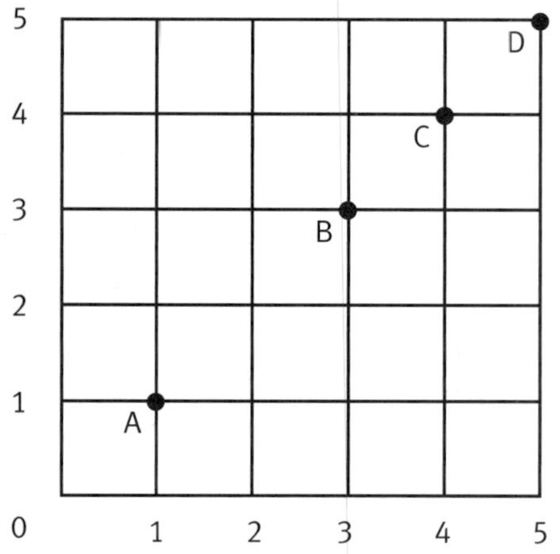

5. Which point is located at (1, 1)?
6. Which point is located at (5, 5)?
7. Which point is located at (3, 3)?
8. **Extended Response** If the ordered pairs on the graph represent the input and output values of a function, could +1 be the function rule? Tell how you know.

CHAPTER 6

Chapter Review

Lessons 6.1–6.3 **Find** the value of n. Then find the value of m.

1. 2 —(+6)→ n —(×2)→ m $n =$ ■ $m =$ ■

2. 35 —(÷5)→ n —(×4)→ m $n =$ ■ $m =$ ■

Lesson 6.4 **Use** inverse arrow operations to find the value of n.

3. n ←(×9)— m ←(−9)— 18 $n =$ ■

Lesson 6.5 **Copy** and complete the function tables.

4. x —(+5)→ y

x	y
1	■
■	9
9	■
10	■
■	17

5. x —(×7)→ y

x	y
2	■
■	70
9	■
7	■
■	28

6. x —(÷4)→ y

x	y
40	■
■	9
16	■
24	■
■	1

eTextbook This lesson is available in the *eTextbook*.

Lessons 6.6 and 6.7

Arthelle and Vijay made pillows to sell at their school's craft fair. They decided to sell them for $4 each.

7. Write the function Arthelle and Vijay can use to estimate how much money they might earn. Use an arrow to represent the function machine.

Arthelle and Vijay made a line graph to show how many dollars they might earn for selling different numbers of pillows.

8. Using only the completed graph, can you find out how much money Arthelle and Vijay would earn if they sold 12 pillows?

9. Using only the completed graph, can you find out how much money Arthelle and Vijay would earn if they sold 16 pillows?

10. **Extended Response** Suppose Arthelle and Vijay earned $80. Is that possible? Why or why not?

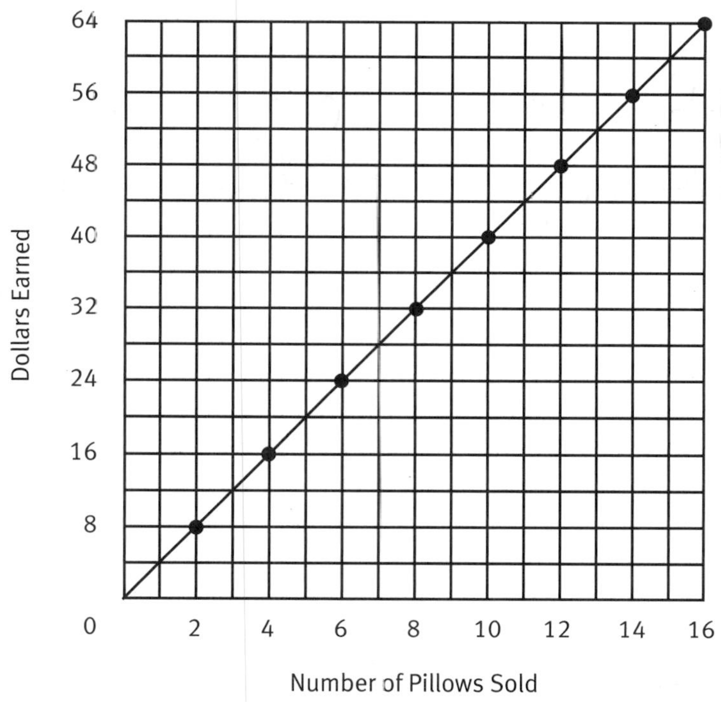

Practice Test

Find the function rule for each this set of numbers.

1. What is the function rule?

3 → ? → 18

4 → ? → 24

2 → ? → 12

0 → ? → 0

2. What is the function rule?

25 → ? → 5

15 → ? → 3

10 → ? → 2

5 → ? → 1

Jan enjoys running. She runs 1 mile every 8 minutes. Fill in the table to show how long it will take her to run 2, 3, 5, and 7 miles.

Number of Miles	Number of Minutes
1	8
2	**3.** ☐
3	**4.** ☐
5	**5.** ☐
7	**6.** ☐

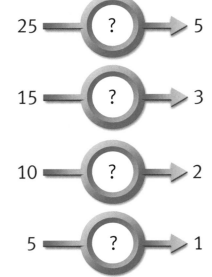

Choose the correct answer. Find the value of *x*.

7.

35 ——(−8)——➤ x

Ⓐ 27 Ⓑ 17

Ⓒ 7 Ⓓ 3

8.

8 ——(×2)——➤ x

Ⓐ 4 Ⓑ 8

Ⓒ 10 Ⓓ 16

9.

55 ——(÷5)——➤ x

Ⓐ 1 Ⓑ 5

Ⓒ 11 Ⓓ 15

10.

18 ——(+9)——➤ x

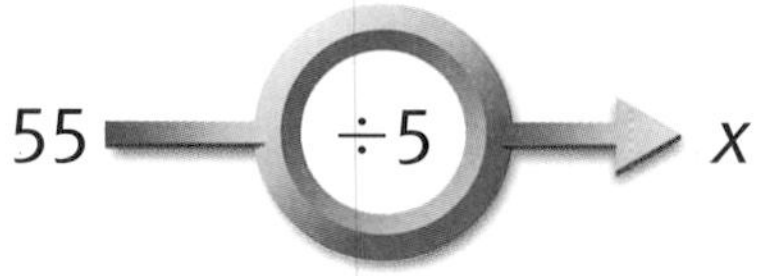

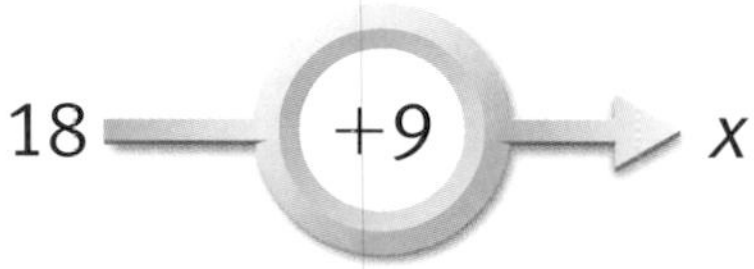

Ⓐ 36 Ⓑ 27

Ⓒ 19 Ⓓ 9

11. If 49 is put in, what number will come out?

49 ——(÷7)——➤ ▪

Ⓐ 49 Ⓑ 24

Ⓒ 7 Ⓓ 1

12. If 7 is put in, what number will come out?

7 ——(−7)——➤ ▪

Ⓐ 1 Ⓑ 0

Ⓒ 7 Ⓓ 49

13. If 17 is put in, what number will come out?

17 ——(+12)——➤ ▪

Ⓐ 29 Ⓑ 21

Ⓒ 15 Ⓓ 5

14. If 0 is put in, what number will come out?

0 ——(×0)——➤ ▪

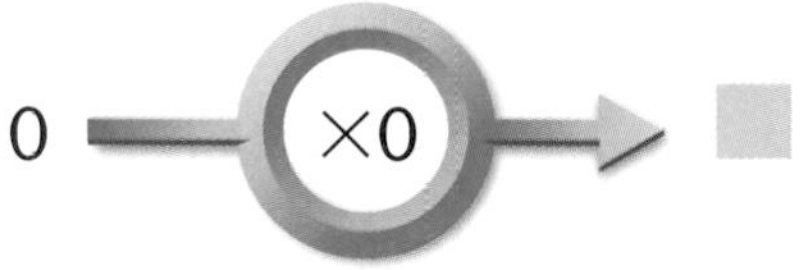

Ⓐ 0 Ⓑ 12

Ⓒ 1 Ⓓ 24

CHAPTER 6 Practice Test

Find the value of *x* or *y*.

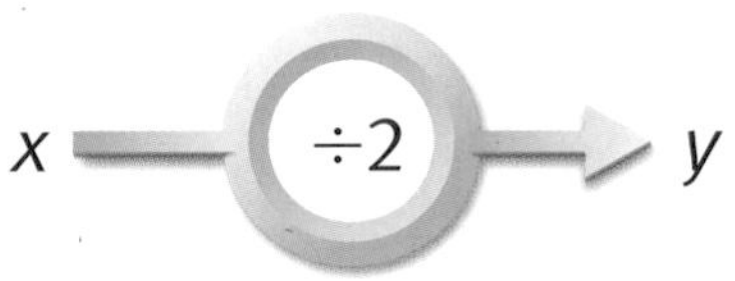

15. If $x = 2$, what is y?

Ⓐ 0 Ⓑ 1
Ⓒ 2 Ⓓ 8

16. If $x = 24$, what is y?

Ⓐ 48 Ⓑ 24
Ⓒ 12 Ⓓ 6

17. If $y = 16$, what is x?

Ⓐ 32 Ⓑ 16
Ⓒ 8 Ⓓ 2

Find the inverse operation.

18. ×11

Ⓐ ×11 Ⓑ +11
Ⓒ −11 Ⓓ ÷11

19. −6

Ⓐ −6 Ⓑ +6
Ⓒ ×6 Ⓓ ÷6

20. ÷5

Ⓐ ×5 Ⓑ +5
Ⓒ −5 Ⓓ ÷5

Choose the correct answer.

21. 274 + 589 =

Ⓐ 368 Ⓑ 683
Ⓒ 863 Ⓓ 963

22. 107 + 621 + 239 =

Ⓐ 679 Ⓑ 967
Ⓒ 769 Ⓓ 976

23. 38 − 17 =

Ⓐ 55 Ⓑ 17
Ⓒ 21 Ⓓ 11

24. 6,187 − 2,050 =

Ⓐ 4,137 Ⓑ 3,187
Ⓒ 2,037 Ⓓ 1,187

25. Which is the smallest unit?

Ⓐ meters
Ⓑ kilometers
Ⓒ millimeter
Ⓓ centimeters

26. Naomi can move 3 boxes at one time. How many trips will she need to make to move 27 boxes?

Ⓐ 3 Ⓑ 6
Ⓒ 9 Ⓓ 12

Use **the map to answer the following questions.**

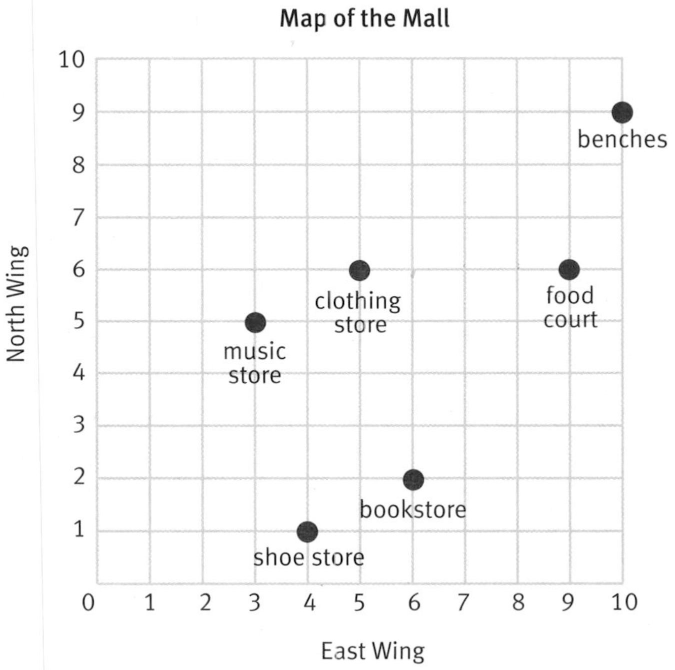

27. a. What are the points that show the location of the bookstore?

b. What is located at (4, 1)?

28. a. Use the map to write directions to get from the food court to the benches.

b. If you are at the food court and walk left 4 spaces, where are you?

c. What are the three shortest ways to get from the music store (3, 5) to the clothing store (5, 6)?

Thinking Story

Swing Low, Sweet Willy

"Dad," said Willy, "will you help me build a swing in the backyard?"

"I'll help you put it up," his father said, "but you'll need to figure it all out and get the materials yourself. You'll need to think about where you want the swing to be, what you want it to look like, and exactly what you need to make it. When you have everything ready, I'll help you."

Willy spent several days planning the swing. He thought about many things. He thought, "I want the swing to hang from a tree, and I want it to look nice, and I want it to work right, and I hope it doesn't fall out of the tree, and I want everyone to tell me what a great swing it is."

Is that the kind of planning Willy's father told him to do?

What kinds of things did Willy's father want Willy to think about?

The next day Willy went with his father to the hardware store and asked for some rope.

"How long does the piece need to be?" the salesperson asked him.

"I don't know," said Willy. "I guess I'll have to go back and plan some more."

He went home and looked at the big tree in the backyard.

His little sister, Wendy, asked him, "Why do you keep staring at that tree? I thought you were going to make a swing today."

"I'm wishing I knew how tall that big old tree is," said Willy.

"Are you planning to hang the swing from the very top of the tree?" asked Wendy.

Would it work to hang a swing from the top of a tree?

Why or why not?

"Well, no," said Willy. "Now that I think about it, I guess the branches at the top aren't strong enough, and besides, the rope would get tangled in the lower branches. I guess I'll hang the swing from that big branch up there. But how do I find out how high the branch is?"

Can you think of some ways to find out how high the branch is?

First Willy found a long stick. Willy measured the stick. It was 2 yards long. "Now," he said, "all I have to do is figure out how high I can reach by myself."

How can Willy do that?

Willy took a piece of chalk. Holding it in his hand, he reached as high up on the side of the garage as he could and made a mark with the chalk. He measured from the ground up to the mark and found the distance was about 2 yards.

How high can Willy reach?

How high can he reach holding the stick in his hand?

"I can reach 2 yards by myself," said Willy. "If I hold the stick in my hand, I can reach 2 yards more. That's 4 yards altogether."

Willy took the stick and tried to reach the branch of the tree with it, but the stick wasn't long enough. "I wish I'd tried first to see if it reached," Willy said. "Now I've wasted all that time measuring, and I still have no way to find out how high the branch is."

"I'll bet you could touch the branch with your stick if you reached out my bedroom window," said Wendy. "The branch comes right up close to my window."

"It wouldn't help to touch the branch from your window," Willy said. "That wouldn't tell me how high the branch is. But you have given me an idea."

He got a ball of string and went upstairs to his sister's bedroom. He found that the tree branch was just about even with the middle of the window.

How can Willy use the string to find out how high the branch is?

Willy unwound the string until it reached from the window all the way down to the ground. He had Wendy hold the string on the ground while he pulled it tight and held it as high as the middle of the window. Then he cut the string just where he was holding it and measured the piece he had cut off. It was 5 yards long.

The next day he was heading to the hardware store to buy 5 yards of rope when he stopped himself. "I forgot about something," he said. "I almost bought a rope that was too short."

What had Willy forgotten?

"I forgot that the rope has to be tied around the branch and that it also has to be tied to the bottom of the board. I'd better allow another yard for that. I'm glad I thought to add another yard; otherwise, the rope wouldn't have reached the ground."

How much rope will Willy buy now?

Do you think that is enough?

Willy bought 6 yards of rope. He also asked for a thick board to use for the seat of the swing.

"How long do you want the board to be?" the salesperson asked him.

"I haven't thought about that," said Willy. "Now I have to go home and do some more planning."

How would you decide how long the board should be?

"Do you want a seat for a swing?" asked the salesperson. "I don't think you need to go home to figure that out." The salesperson placed a yardstick on the floor. "Here, sit on this . . . Fine, I think 2 feet will be a good length."

How could the salesperson tell?

When Willy got home, he marked two places near each end of the board, just big enough to put a rope through. He would ask his father to drill holes in the four spots.

Why would he need to have two holes in the board near each end?

"At last I have everything ready," Willy said. He laid the piece of rope and the board out under the tree. As soon as his father came home from work, Willy asked him to drill the holes in the board and to help put up the swing.

"You did a good job marking the seat," said his father, "but it looks as if you have only about half enough rope."

"I forgot that I needed two ropes," said Willy. "Well, I want to get this swing finished tonight, so let's just cut this rope in half and use one-half on each side."

What would be wrong with the swing if he did that?

"You'd have a swing so high up in the air that you could never get on it," his father said. "You'd better buy another piece of rope tomorrow, and then we'll put up the swing."

The next day Willy bought 6 more yards of rope. He tied one end of each rope to the board so that everything was ready when his father got home. Willy held up the swing while his father climbed a high ladder and tied both ropes to the tree branch. Then Willy set the swing down on the ground.

"Success!" Willy shouted. "I measured everything just right. The swing reaches exactly to the ground."

What did Willy forget about when he was measuring?

"Your swing is fine if you want to sit on the ground," his father said. "But if you want to swing on it, we'll have to raise it a half yard or so. I'll just wrap each rope around the tree branch once more. That should raise the swing enough."

Soon Willy was swinging happily on his swing. "I planned everything," he said, "except that I didn't plan on having to think so much."

The End

CHAPTER 7

Multidigit Multiplication and Division

In This Chapter You Will Learn

- how to multiply multidigit numbers.
- how to divide multidigit numbers.

Problem Solving

Roger is going to take his pennies to the bank. He piled them into equal stacks. He has 6 stacks that are all the same height. He wants to know if he has enough pennies to make $1.

Think **about, answer, and discuss the following questions.**

1. In each stack, how many pennies are below the dotted line?
2. How many pennies are above the dotted line in each stack?
3. Do you think there are enough pennies to make $1? How could you find out without counting them all?
4. Use your method to find out if there are more than 100 pennies.
5. How would you find the total if there were 23 pennies in each stack?

LESSON 7.1

Multiplying by 10, 100, and 1,000

Key Ideas

When multiplying by 10, 100, or 1,000, it is important to remember that multiplication is related to skip counting and repeated addition.

$5 \times 10 = ?$

5 tens = 50

$5 \times 10 = 50$

1. 8 tens = ▢
   $8 \times 10 =$ ▢
2. 7 tens = ▢
   $7 \times 10 =$ ▢
3. 4 hundreds = ▢
   $4 \times 100 =$ ▢
4. 9 thousands = ▢
   $9 \times 1{,}000 =$ ▢
5. 10 thousands = ▢
   $10 \times 1{,}000 =$ ▢

eTextbook This lesson is available in the *eTextbook*.

Use your knowledge of base ten to do these exercises mentally.

6. $20 \times 10 = \square$
7. $16 \times 1{,}000 = \square$
8. $100 \times 21 = \square$
9. $1{,}000 \times 19 = \square$
10. $100 \times 93 = \square$
11. $1{,}000 \times 63 = \square$
12. $92 \times 100 = \square$
13. $65 \times 1{,}000 = \square$

14. Mr. Baccari, the park ranger, has 3,500 yards of fencing. The park has 4 sides. Each side is 1,000 yards long. Does Mr. Baccari have enough fencing to surround the park?

15. **Extended Response** Sharla has thirteen $10 bills. Does she have enough money to buy the skates? Explain.

16. Estefan and Miguel collected soda pop tabs. On Monday and Tuesday they collected 123 soda pop tabs. On Wednesday and Thursday they collected 184 soda pop tabs. How many soda pop tabs did they collect in those 4 days?

17. **Extended Response** There are 7 boxes of balloons. Each box has 100 balloons. There are 629 children. Can each child have a balloon? Explain.

18. Northview School is 30 years old. Do they have enough classrooms for 400 students?

Writing + Math **Journal**

Explain how you would find the product of 40×6.

LESSON 7.2 Multiplying Two-Digit Numbers by One-Digit Numbers

Key Ideas

To help understand how to multiply two-digit numbers, we can use an area model and break the whole area into partial areas. For example:

Ms. Chaccupa wants to carpet her hallway. Her hallway is a rectangle that is 27 feet long and 6 feet wide. How much carpeting will Ms. Chaccupa need for her hallway?

She knows that the answer is the product of 6×27, but she doesn't know how to do the multiplication.

Here is what she does:

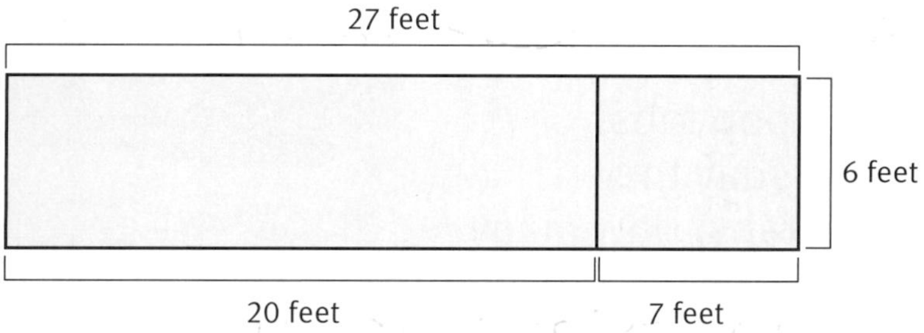

Ms. Chaccupa realizes that when she divides the hallway into sections, she has numbers she can multiply in her head.

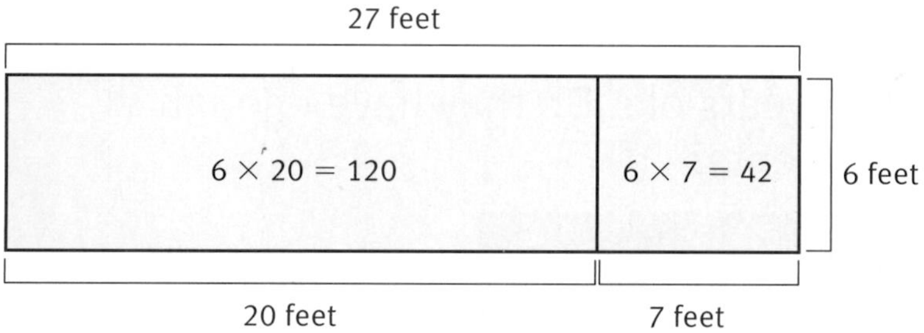

Ms. Chaccupa adds the partial area together to get the whole area.

$$120 + 42 = 162$$

Ms. Chaccupa needs 162 square feet of carpet.

If you want to know the area of a rectangle that is 27 units long and 6 units wide, you would multiply 6×27.

$6 \times 27 = ?$

Ann's Work

Step 1 $6 \times 20 = 120$

$$\begin{array}{r} 27 \\ \times\ 6 \\ \hline 120 \end{array}$$

120 is a partial product.

Step 2 $6 \times 7 = 42$

$$\begin{array}{r} 27 \\ \times\ 6 \\ \hline 120 \\ 42 \end{array}$$

42 is a partial product.

Step 3 $120 + 42 = 162$

$$\begin{array}{r} 27 \\ \times\ 6 \\ \hline 120 \\ +\ 42 \\ \hline 162 \end{array}$$

Martin's Work

Step 1 $6 \times 7 = 42$

$$\begin{array}{r} 27 \\ \times\ 6 \\ \hline 42 \end{array}$$

42 is a partial product.

Step 2 $6 \times 20 = 120$

$$\begin{array}{r} 27 \\ \times\ 6 \\ \hline 42 \\ 120 \end{array}$$

120 is a partial product.

Step 3 $120 + 42 = 162$

$$\begin{array}{r} 27 \\ \times\ 6 \\ \hline 42 \\ +\ 120 \\ \hline 162 \end{array}$$

Adding the partial products gives us the whole product.

Multiply. You may draw pictures to help.

1. $\begin{array}{r} 83 \\ \times\ 5 \\ \hline \end{array}$
2. $\begin{array}{r} 11 \\ \times\ 4 \\ \hline \end{array}$
3. $\begin{array}{r} 30 \\ \times\ 8 \\ \hline \end{array}$
4. $\begin{array}{r} 47 \\ \times\ 5 \\ \hline \end{array}$
5. $\begin{array}{r} 38 \\ \times\ 5 \\ \hline \end{array}$
6. $\begin{array}{r} 30 \\ \times\ 9 \\ \hline \end{array}$
7. $\begin{array}{r} 26 \\ \times\ 1 \\ \hline \end{array}$
8. $\begin{array}{r} 29 \\ \times\ 7 \\ \hline \end{array}$
9. $\begin{array}{r} 58 \\ \times\ 9 \\ \hline \end{array}$

Solve.

10. If Donna gets $6 a week, how much money will she receive in a year (52 weeks)?
11. How much will Donna receive in 2 years?

Students from Los Amigos School are going on a field trip. Altogether, 350 people are going. Each bus can seat 45 people.

12. How many people can 7 buses seat?
13. **Extended Response** How many buses should the school use? Why?
14. If the school rents 8 buses, how many extra seats will there be?
15. It costs $52 to rent 1 bus for a day. How much will it cost to rent 8 buses for a day?
16. **Extended Response** Suppose that each person going on the trip pays $2. Will that be enough to pay for 8 buses for one day each? How much is left after paying for the buses? Explain.

Game

Roll a Problem Game (Multiplication)

Players: Two or more

Materials: One 0–5 ***Number Cube***

Object: To get the greatest product

Math Focus: Multiplying two-digit numbers by one-digit numbers, place value, and mathematical reasoning

HOW TO PLAY

1. Use blanks to outline a multiplication problem on your paper like this:

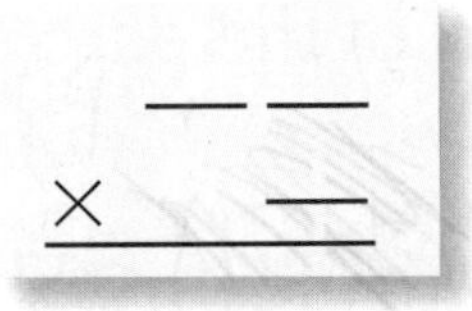

2. The first player rolls the cube three times.
3. Each time the cube is rolled, all players write that number in one of the blanks in their outline. Once a number has been written in a blank, it cannot be moved.
4. The player with the greatest product wins the round.

Variations:

- Use a 5–10 ***Number Cube.*** If you roll a 10, roll again.
- **Object:** To get the smallest product

Multiplying Three-Digit Numbers by One-Digit Numbers

Key Ideas

Multiplying a three-digit number by a one-digit number is done almost exactly like multiplying by a two-digit number.

Ms. Chaccupa wants to carpet her hallway. Her hallway is a rectangle 27 feet long and 6 feet wide. In Lesson 7.2 when Ms. Chaccupa added all of the parts together, she found out the area of her hallway was 162 square feet.

She called the carpet store and found a sale on the carpet she wants. If she buys more than 100 square feet of carpet, she can purchase the carpet at $5 per square foot. She needs 162 square feet, so she is eligible for the discount. How much money will she spend on carpet for her hallway?

Step 1:

$$\begin{array}{r} 162 \\ \times \quad 5 \\ \hline \mathbf{500} \end{array}$$

$100 \times 5 = 500$
500 is a partial product.

Step 2:

$$\begin{array}{r} 162 \\ \times \quad 5 \\ \hline 500 \\ \mathbf{300} \end{array}$$

$60 \times 5 = 300$
300 is a partial product.

Step 3:

$$\begin{array}{r} 162 \\ \times \quad 5 \\ \hline 500 \\ 300 \\ \mathbf{10} \end{array}$$

$2 \times 5 = 10$
10 is a partial product.

Step 4:

$$\begin{array}{r} 162 \\ \times \quad 5 \\ \hline \mathbf{500} \\ \mathbf{300} \\ + \ \mathbf{10} \\ \hline \mathbf{810} \end{array}$$

$500 + 300 + 10 = 810$
Add the partial products to get the product.

Ms. Chaccupa's carpet will cost $810.

e Textbook This lesson is available in the ***eTextbook.***

Multiply. You may draw pictures to help.

1. $\begin{array}{r} 247 \\ \times \quad 3 \\ \hline \end{array}$
2. $\begin{array}{r} 248 \\ \times \quad 3 \\ \hline \end{array}$
3. $\begin{array}{r} 732 \\ \times \quad 0 \\ \hline \end{array}$
4. $108 \times 7 = \square$
5. $111 \times 7 = \square$
6. $909 \times 9 = \square$

Solve. Be sure to label your answers correctly.

7. There are 365 days in a year. How many days are in 2 years if neither year is a leap year?
8. Mr. Ruiz manages a clothing store. Yesterday he ordered 4 cartons of shirts. Each carton has 250 shirts. How many shirts did he order?
9. The distance around the city race track is 250 meters. Mark ran 4 laps around the track. How far did he run?
10. The distance around the country race track is 500 meters. Sarah ran 4 laps around the track. How far did she run?
11. Yesterday Amanda collected 876 pennies. How much money did she collect?
12. When José was 6, he collected 282 soda pop tabs for a local charity. Now that he is 5 years older, he plans on collecting over 1,000. What is José's age now?
13. There were 611 students at Ridgeview South Elementary. In one week 5 students enrolled. How many students now attend Ridgeview South Elementary?

LESSON 7.4

Applications of Multiplication

Key Ideas

If there are several equal sets of objects, we can find how many there are altogether by multiplying.

A bag of lemons has 12 lemons in it. If Janelle bought 6 bags, how many lemons does she have?

$12 \times 6 = ?$

$$\begin{array}{r} 12 \\ \times\ 6 \\ \hline 60 \\ +\ 12 \\ \hline 72 \end{array}$$

$12 \times 6 = 72$

Janelle has 72 lemons.

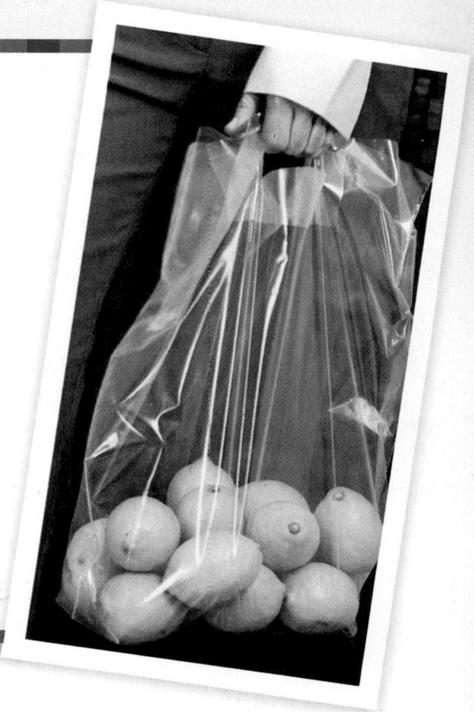

Solve.

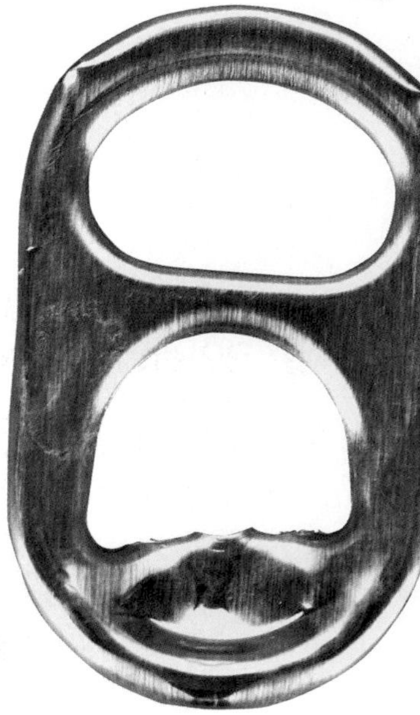

1. Latisha needs 125 large binder clips. She bought 8 packs with 15 binder clips in each box. Will she have enough binder clips? Why or why not?
2. Ms. Chen earns $325 each week. How much money does she earn in 4 weeks?
3. Phyllis and Michele were collecting clothing for a clothing drive. Phyllis collected 19 sweatshirts, and Michele collected 8 pairs of jeans. How many articles of clothing did the girls collect altogether?
4. The Nuts and Bolts Factory can make 534 bolts in 1 hour. How many bolts are made in 8 hours?
5. The Brown Cow Dairy Company produces about 450 gallons of milk each day. About how much milk does it produce in 7 days?
6. There are 356 children at Hidden Hollow Camp. The kitchen staff prepares breakfast, lunch, and dinner for each child. How many meals are prepared for the children every day?

Adam wanted to know about how many hours he spent doing certain things each year. He made some estimates and wrote them in a table.

7 Write the missing amounts.

Adam's Activity	Hours Each Day	Number of Days Each Year	Hours Each Year
Sleeping	8	365	
Eating	2	365	
Reading at home	2	250	
Being in school	5	180	
Watching television	1	175	

8 Does Adam spend more time eating or reading each year?

9 Does Adam spend more time sleeping than he spends doing the other activities shown in the table?

10 **Extended Response** About how many hours do you spend reading each year? Explain how you got your answer.

Most years have 365 days. Leap years have 366 days. Leap years come every 4 years. In a leap year, February has 29 days instead of 28 days.

11 Alonzo is exactly 3 years old. One of those years was a leap year. How many days old is Alonzo?

12 Ruth is exactly 6 years old. She has lived through 1 leap year. How many days old is Ruth?

Writing + Math **Journal**

Calculate about how many days old you are. The years 2000, 2004, 2008, and 2012 are leap years. Explain how you got your answer.

Exploring Problem Solving

Vera and her brothers want to buy a special present for their parents' anniversary. They have $43 so far. If they save $24 each week, how long will it be before they can buy the grill?

Miriam is making a table to solve the problem.

Now	1 Week	2 weeks	3 weeks	4 weeks
$43	$67	$91	■	■

1. Why did Miriam write $43 in the first column of her table?
2. Why did she write $67 in the second column?
3. What do you think Miriam will do next?
4. Do you think Miriam's strategy will work? Explain.
5. What happens if Miriam keeps adding $24 but doesn't get $247 exactly?

…n equation to solve the problem.

Neil is …

…What will Neil find out by using his equation?

7. How will he use his equation to find that out?

8. After he finds out how much the children need to save, what do you think Neil will try to figure out next?

9. What equation could Neil write to help him figure that out?

10. Do you think Neil's strategy will work? Explain.

11. Work with your group to solve the problem. Use any strategy you like.

Cumulative Review

Multiplying by 10 and 5 **Lesson 5.2**

Fill in the tables. Look for patterns.

1. Copy and fill in this table by skip counting.

35	40	45	■	■	■	65	■	■

2. Copy and fill in this table by skip counting.

110	120	■	■	150	160	■	■	■	200

Measuring and Graphing **Lesson 3.3**

Use the graph to answer the questions. Each cashier at the store had a different amount in his or her cash register at the end of the day. The bar graph shows the amounts in each cashier's drawer.

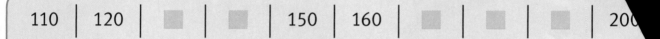

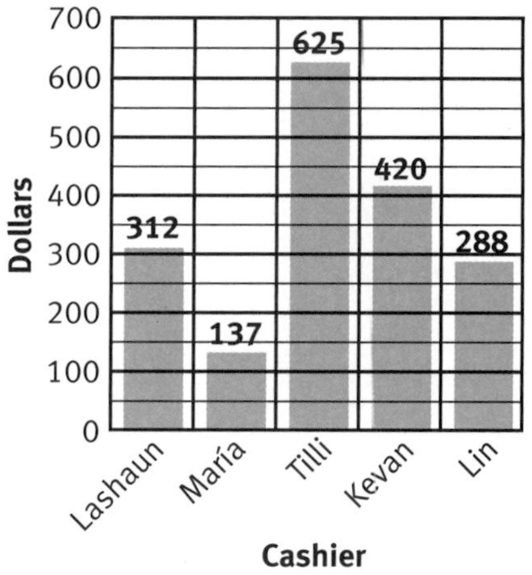

3. How many cashiers had more than $300 in their register at the end of the day? How many had more than 400?

4. How much money was in Lin's drawer?

5. Who had the least amount of money in his or her drawer at the end of the day?

6. How much money was there altogether?

Area and Approximate Measure **Lesson 4.7**

Find the area of each figure. Remember to label your answer correctly.

7. The area is ____ square feet.

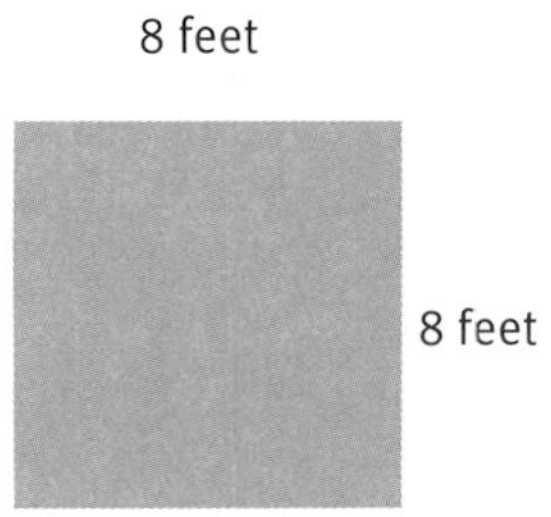

8. The area is ____ square feet.

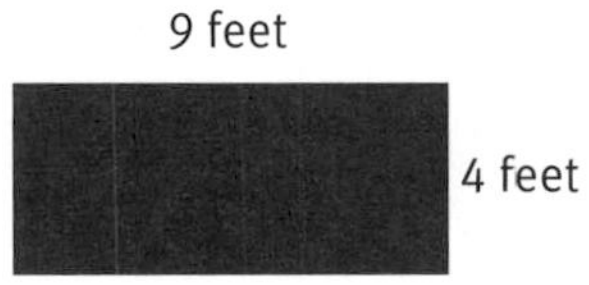

9. The area is ____ square feet.

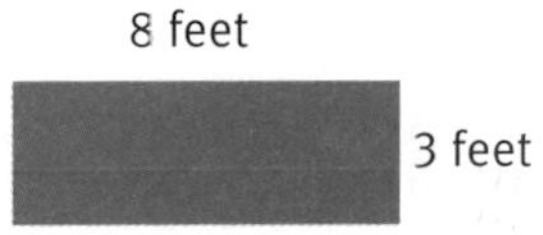

10. The area is ____ square feet.

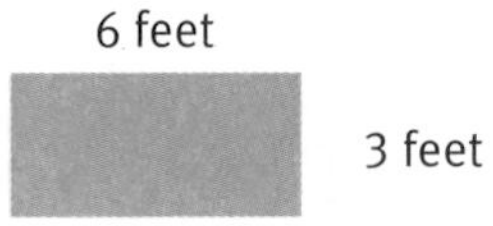

Variables and Arrow Notation **Lesson 6.5**

Solve these problems.

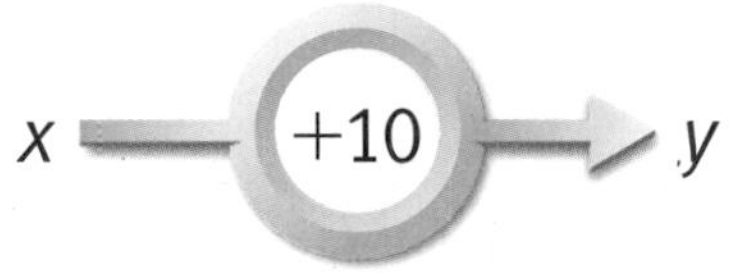

11. If $x = 8$, what is y?
12. If $y = 25$, what is x?
13. If $x = 36$, what is y?

14. If $x = 88$, what is y?
15. If $x = 101$, what is y?
16. If $x = 72$, what is y?

LESSON 7.5

Division with Remainders

Key Ideas

When a number does not divide exactly, we say the leftover amount is the remainder.

Rafael has a dozen muffins to share among 3 friends and himself. How many muffins will each person get?

$12 \div 4 = n$

Rafael passed the muffins out one at a time. When he was finished passing them out, he saw that each person got 3 muffins. $12 \div 4 = 3$

$13 \div 4 = n$

Next Saturday Rafael opened his box of muffins to find there were 13 muffins. When he finished passing them out to his 3 friends and himself, Rafael discovered each person again had 3 muffins but there was one muffin left over. $13 \div 4$ is 3 R1

This answer can be read *3 with a remainder of 1.*

Divide. **Use craft sticks or other manipulatives to divide. The first one has been done for you.**

1. $7 \div 4$ is 1 R3

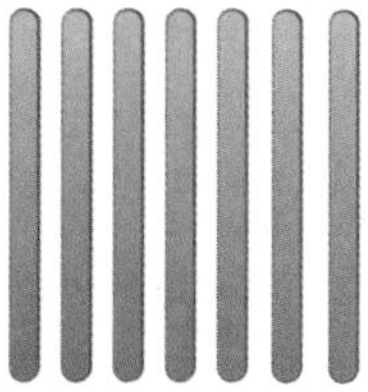

2. $8 \div 3$ is ▢
3. $20 \div 5$ is ▢
4. $20 \div 6$ is ▢
5. $24 \div 5$ is ▢
6. $30 \div 8$ is ▢
7. $54 \div 9$ is ▢
8. $56 \div 9$ is ▢
9. $50 \div 7$ is ▢
10. $10 \div 4$ is ▢

Answer the questions.

11. Joanne and her 2 friends want to share 20 baseball cards equally.

    How many baseball cards should each of the 3 children get? How many baseball cards will be left over?

12. Mrs. Sarton has 11 balloons to divide equally among 4 children.

    How many balloons should each child get? How many balloons will be left over?

13. Arnaldo has 40 shells to divide equally among 5 friends.

    How many shells should each child get? How many shells will be left over?

14. **Extended Response** Mr. Bailey, a zookeeper, has 40 bananas for Koko the ape. Koko eats 5 bananas each day.

    How many days will the bananas last? How much does Koko weigh?

15. At the flower shop, Mr. Kane is putting 17 roses into bouquets of 6 flowers each.

    How many bouquets can he make? How many roses will be left over?

LESSON 7.6

Reasonable Answers to Division Problems

Key Ideas

It is often useful in real life to approximate the answer to a math problem. It is helpful, when answering multiple choice questions, to eliminate answers that are obviously incorrect. You should assume, unless told otherwise, that exactly one answer is correct.

Look at this exercise:

Choose the correct answer.

$345 \div 3 = n$

a. $n = 15$

b. $n = 115$

c. $n = 1{,}150$

Even though you may not know how to divide this large number, you do know $3 \times 15 = 45$, so choice *a* is too small. You also know that $3 \times 1{,}150$ is greater than 3,000, so choice *c* is too great. This leaves choice *b* as the correct answer.

Is each of the following possible? If yes, give the answer. If no, explain why not.

1. The lunch cost \$15. Abigail and Dan each paid half.
2. There are 15 softball players. They are on 2 teams. Each team has the same number of players.
3. Joe and Heika have 15 cookies. They share them equally.

e Textbook This lesson is available in the ***eTextbook.***

Extended Response **Solve each problem. Then explain your answer.**

4. Each motorcycle can hold 2 people, and 15 people want to ride. How many motorcycles are needed?

5. Paulette had 15 marbles. She gave Peter and Nicholas each an equal number of marbles. What is the most marbles Paulette could have given Peter?

6. Anna and Laura wanted to share equally 15 ounces of orange juice. How many ounces should each get?

7. Ben and Helena are both 15 years old. They each have $2. If they share their money, how much will each have?

8. David and Gay want to share $15 equally. What is each person's share?

9. Steve and Joe paid $15 for a book. They want to share it equally. How can they do that?

10. Each car can carry 7 people, and 55 people must be taken to the airport in a car. How many cars are needed?

LESSON 7.7

Dividing Two-Digit Numbers by One-Digit Numbers

Key Ideas

Using play money, we can find a way to divide one number by another.

Felipe's family wanted to divide $96 equally among the 4 members. How much money should each person get?

First, Felipe decided that $96 was close to $100, so each person would get *about* $25. He knew that $25 \times 4 = 100$.

Then he began dividing the money.

Step 1: Felipe starts by giving each person a $10 bill. He is able to do this 2 times altogether.

Felipe	Sister	Mom	Dad
$10	$10	$10	$10
$10	$10	$10	$10

Step 2: He has one $10 bill and six $1 bills left. He asks his dad to exchange the $10 bill for ten $1 bills. Counting the $1 bills, Felipe discovers he now has sixteen $1 bills.

Step 3: He gives each person a $1 bill. He is able to do this 4 times until he runs out of money.

Felipe	Sister	Mom	Dad
$1	$1	$1	$1
$1	$1	$1	$1
$1	$1	$1	$1
$1	$1	$1	$1

Step 4: They count their money and find they have $24 each.

eTextbook This lesson is available in the ***eTextbook.***

Here is the record Felipe kept when passing out the money.

Step 1: When he divided the $10 bills, each person got two $10 bills. Altogether it was eight $10 bills, which left Felipe with one $10 bill.

$$\begin{array}{r l}
 & \text{2 } \quad \text{?} \\
4 \overline{)} & \text{9 tens 6 ones} \\
 & \underline{\text{8 tens}} \\
 & \text{1 ten}
\end{array}$$

Step 2: Before exchanging money, he had one $10 bill and six $1 bills. He exchanged the $10 bill for 10 $1 bills. Altogether it was $16.

$$\begin{array}{r l}
 & \text{2 } \quad \text{?} \\
4 \overline{)} & \text{9 tens 6 ones} \\
 & \underline{\text{8 tens}} \\
 & \text{1 ten 6 ones} = \text{16 ones}
\end{array}$$

Step 3: Felipe gave four $1 bills to each member of his family. This used all 16 ones and left him with no money.

$$\begin{array}{r l}
 & \text{2 } \quad \text{4} \\
4 \overline{)} & \text{9 tens 6 ones} \\
 & \underline{\text{8 tens}} \\
 & \text{16 ones} \\
 & \underline{\text{16 ones}} \\
 & \text{0}
\end{array}$$

Step 4: They counted their money. They each had $24.

An abbreviated record of Felipe's division looks like this:

$$\begin{array}{r r}
 & 24 \\
4 \overline{)} & 96 \\
 & \underline{8} \\
 & 16 \\
 & \underline{16} \\
 & 0
\end{array}$$

Divide. Keep records like Felipe's records to show your answer.

1. $57 \div 3 = \square$
2. $36 \div 2 = \square$
3. $85 \div 5 = \square$
4. $84 \div 4 = \square$
5. $64 \div 4 = \square$
6. $81 \div 3 = \square$
7. $96 \div 6 = \square$
8. $95 \div 5 = \square$

Solve. Be sure to label your answer correctly.

9. If 4 students divided $76 equally, how much money did each student get?

10. In Ms. Hopkins's class, there are 17 girls and 16 boys. How many students are in Ms. Hopkins's class?

11. There are 6 boys who want to divide 78 trading cards equally among them. How many cards should each boy get?

12. The 5 girls want to divide 65 stickers equally among themselves. How many stickers should each girl get?

Writing + Math **Journal**

The 5 girls want to divide 66 stickers equally among themselves. Is it possible? Why or why not?

Dividing Three-Digit Numbers by One-Digit Numbers

Key Ideas

Dividing a three-digit number by a one-digit number is like dividing a two-digit number by a one-digit number.

Alfred and his 5 friends broke Mr. McGinty's window with a baseball while playing next door. The cost to replace the window is $474. How much will each person contribute if Alfred and his friends are going to split the cost of the replacement window equally?

Alfred knew that $474 was a bit less than $600, so first he estimated that each person was going to contribute a bit less than $100, because $6 \times 100 = 600$.

Then he began to find the actual cost with play money.

6)4 hundreds 7 tens 4 ones

Alfred noticed there are not enough $100 bills to divide equally. He decides to exchange all four $100 bills for forty $10 bills. He now has forty-seven $10 bills.

6)47 tens 4 ones

When he divides the $10 bills one at a time into piles, each group gets seven $10 bills. He records this amount.

```
     7 tens
  6)47 tens  4 ones
  − 42 tens
     5 tens  4 ones   → 54 ones
```

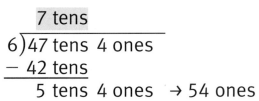

Alfred is left with 5 tens and 4 ones. He exchanges the tens for fifty $1 bills. He now has fifty-four $1 bills.

Alfred distributes the $1 bills and each pile gets 9 altogether.

```
     7 tens 9 ones
  6)47 tens  4 ones
    42 tens
   ----------
            54 ones
            54 ones
            -------
             0
```

He has divided all the money. Each person will contribute $79.

Divide. **Keep records like Alfred's to show your answer.**

1. 125 ÷ 5 = ■
2. 324 ÷ 6 = ■
3. 314 ÷ 2 = ■

Solve. **Use play money or other manipulatives if you wish. Be sure to label your answer correctly.**

4. Gretchen, Hank, Isaac, Judith, Kevin, Liam, Maggie, and Nell have 584 smelly stickers that they wish to divide equally among themselves. How many stickers will each person get?
5. There are 3 feet in a yard. How many yards are there in 852 feet?
6. How many feet are in 300 yards?
7. How many feet are in 280 yards?
8. How many yards are in 282 feet?

LESSON 7.9

Problem-Solving Applications

Key Ideas

When solving a problem, be sure you understand the situation, and be sure your answer makes sense when you finish. After deciding which operation to use, estimate your answer. Once you have solved the problem or exercise, be sure to compare your answer to your estimation. Some problems may not be possible to solve, but be sure to try all of your options before deciding an answer cannot be found.

Solve.

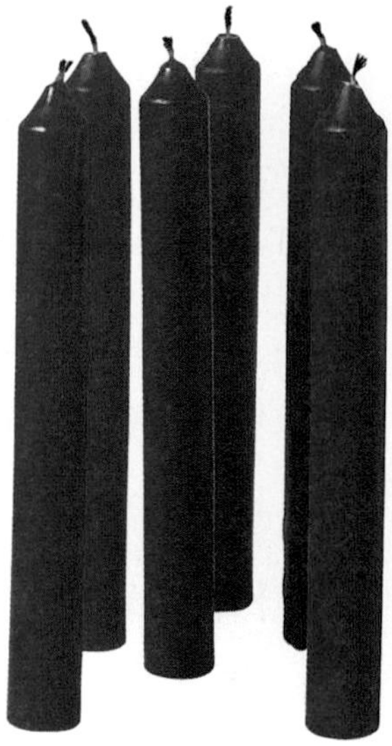

1. Three months ago Chris weighed 89 pounds. Now he weighs 92 pounds. How many pounds did he gain in the last 3 months?
2. Chelsea had 24 balloons. Some of them burst. Now she has 4 balloons. How many burst?
3. Mrs. James bought 13 packages of candles. Each package holds 6 candles. How many candles did she buy?
4. It usually takes Benjamin 2 hours to do his homework. It usually takes his twin sister 1 hour to do hers. If they work together, how long will it take to do their homework?
5. Stickers cost 11¢ each. Lana has 45¢. How many stickers can she buy? Will she have any change and if so, how much?
6. **Extended Response** Abigail used a calculator to calculate 345×3. Her answer was 105. What mistake did Abigail most likely make?

Solve.

7 Jorge, Phillip, and Cody had a race. Each child finished the race in about 20 seconds. About how long did the race take?

8 Maria bought 9 packages of paper cups. Each package has 25 cups. How many paper cups did Maria buy?

9 The area of a rectangle is 72 square meters. One side is 9 meters long. How long is the adjacent side?

10 What is the perimeter of the rectangle in Problem 9?

Solve.

Most years have 365 days. Leap years have 366 days. Leap years come every four years. In a leap year, February has 29 days instead of 28 days. The years 1988, 1992, 1996, 2000, 2004, and 2008 are leap years.

February

SUN	MON	TUE	WED	THU	FRI	SAT
		1	2	3	4	5
6	7	8	9	10	11	12
13	14	15	16	17	18	19
20	21	22	23	24	25	26
27	28	29				

11 **Extended Response** Mohammed just had his second birthday. Could he have been alive during a leap year? Explain your answer.

12 Bridget was born exactly 4 years before her cousin Angie. One of those years was a leap year. Bridget is how many days older than her cousin?

Elliot's grandfather gave him a coin collection. Each coin is in a clear plastic holder. Elliot will store the holders in a box until he gets a display cabinet. How many holders can he pack in the box?

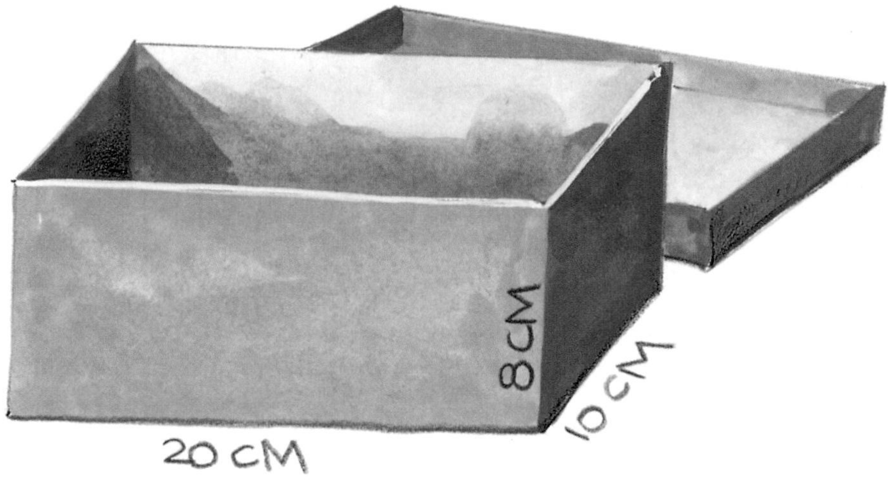

Work **with your group to solve the following problems.**

1. Is there more than one way to arrange the holders in the box?
2. How will you arrange the coin holders in the box?
3. If you arrange the holders that way, how many can fit in the box?
4. What is the greatest number of holders that will fit in the box? How do you know?

Cumulative Review

Rounding **Lesson 1.8**

Round to the nearest ten in Problems 1–5. Round to the nearest thousand in Problems 6–10.

1. 54
2. 29
3. 369
4. 888
5. 537
6. 5,137
7. 4,713
8. 7,248
9. 3,634
10. 2,492

Missing Factors and Division I **Lesson 5.7**

Solve each problem.

11. There are 36 employees and 4 banks. How many employees are there for each bank?

    $4 \times \square = 36$ $36 \div 4 = \square$

12. There are 30 ATMs in the entire county. There are 6 ATMs in each city in the county. How many cities are in the county?

    $6 \times \square = 30$ $30 \div 6 = \square$

Division and Multiplication Functions Grade 2 **Lesson 11.9**

Find the function rules.

13.

in	*out*
18	6
33	11
42	14
9	3

14.

40	10
36	9
32	8
28	7

Cumulative Review

Commutative Law of Multiplication **Lesson 4.8**

Write the multiplication sentence for each problem. Then solve the problem.

15. Rosa has eight $5 bills. How much money does she have in dollars?

16. Moisha drove to 4 different banks each day for 6 days. How many banks did she visit?

More Functions with Mixed Operations **Grade 2 Lesson 12.3**

Find the simplified function rules.

17. The rule is $\times 8 \div 2$.
The simplified rule is ■.

2	8
4	16
6	24
8	32

18. The rule is $\times 9 \div 3$.
The simplified rule is ■.

in	*out*
3	9
6	18
7	21
8	24

CHAPTER 7

Key Ideas Review

In this chapter you learned multidigit multiplication and division.

You learned two- and three-digit multiplication before exploring applications of multiplication.

You learned about remainders in division before being introduced to two-digit and three-digit division, as well as applications of division.

Solve the following multiplication problems.

1. $100 \times 3 = \blacksquare$
2. $123 \times 5 = \blacksquare$
3. $14 \times 2 = \blacksquare$
4. $901 \times 3 = \blacksquare$

Solve the following division problems. Write the remainders if necessary.

5. $9 \div 2$
6. $78 \div 3$
7. $64 \div 7$
8. $103 \div 3$

Provide a detailed answer for the following exercises. Extended Response

9. Josh and Mary want to divide a pile of 28 baseball cards into 3 equal piles. Are there any extra baseball cards after they divide them into piles? How do you know?
10. Jurgen has 28 marbles, and Juan gave him 3 times as many marbles. How many marbles does Jurgen have now? If Jurgen wants to divide all of his marbles into equal piles, what is one way he could divide them?

CHAPTER 7 Chapter Review

Lesson 7.1 **Find** the missing terms.

1. 1,000; 2,000; 3,000; ▢; 5,000

   8,000; 9,000; 10,000; ▢; 12,000

   120; 110; 100; ▢; 80

2. 90; 100; 110; ▢; 130

   500; 600; 700; ▢; 900

   160; 170; 180; ▢; 200

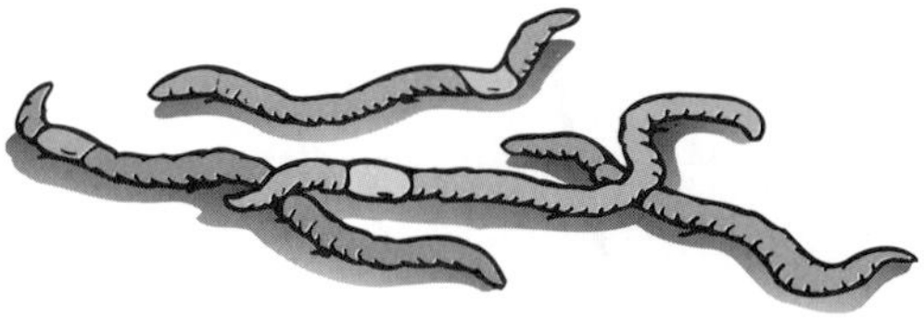

Lesson 7.2 3. At a bait shop, Bonnie bought 4 bags of earthworms. Each bag had 46 earthworms.

   a. How many earthworms did Bonnie buy?

   b. If Sue and Nancy each bought 2 bags of earthworms with 46 earthworms in each bag, how many earthworms do Bonnie, Sue, and Nancy have altogether?

   c. If Jon buys 3 bags of earthworms with 10 earthworms in each bag, how many earthworms do Jon and Sue have altogether?

Lesson 7.3 **Multiply.**

4. $123 \times 2 =$ ▢

   $123 \times 3 =$ ▢

   $123 \times 4 =$ ▢

5. $500 \times 3 =$ ▢

   $250 \times 3 =$ ▢

   $125 \times 3 =$ ▢

Lesson 7.5 **Determine** the remainder.

6. $34 \div 5$ 7. $38 \div 3$ 8. $48 \div 6$ 9. $13 \div 7$

Lesson 7.6

Choose the correct answer.

10. Lance has 32 buttons, and he wants to make suits with 4 buttons each. How many suits can he make?

    a. 2

    b. 4

    c. 6

    d. 8

11. Andy wants to split a pizza among 3 friends and himself. The pizza has a total of 10 slices. If each receives an equal number of whole slices, how many whole slices will each person have?

    a. 1

    b. 2

    c. 3

    d. 4

Lessons 7.7 and 7.8

Divide.

12. $32 \div 2$ 13. $32 \div 8$ 14. $126 \div 6$ 15. $120 \div 5$

Lesson 7.9

Answer the questions.

16. Marilyn bought a pack of 36 crayons. Danielle took 2 crayons, Bob took 6 crayons, and Matt took 7 crayons. How many crayons does Marilyn have left?

17. Bob bought 3 times more crayons than he took from Marilyn. Matt bought 4 times more crayons than he took from Marilyn. How many crayons did Bob and Matt buy?

18. Matt wants to divide his 28 crayons among Marilyn, Danielle, Bob, and himself. How many crayons does each person get?

Practice Test

Solve.

1. $9 \times 1{,}000 = \blacksquare$
2. $142 \times 100 = \blacksquare$
3. Grandpa gave each of his 5 grandchildren a $10 bill. How much money did he give away?
4. One of the children will exchange his $10 for dimes. How many dimes will he get?
5. Georgia's brother spends $8 a day on lunch. If he spends the same amount every day, how much does he spend on lunch in 1 year?
6. Lisa made 6 batches of cookies. Each batch makes 96 cookies. How many cookies did Lisa make altogether?
7. Marc's brother is 4 years old. How many months old is he?
8. Marc's brother is 4 years old. How many days old is he? (Hint: Count one leap year.)
9. $63 \div 9 = \blacksquare$
10. $155 \div 4 = \blacksquare$
11. Sara's aunt gave her $40 to share evenly with her sister. How much will Sara and her sister each get?
12. How many feet are there in 187 yards?

Find the correct answer.

13. $74 \times 7 = \blacksquare$

Ⓐ 141 Ⓑ 518

Ⓒ 718 Ⓓ 441

14. $100 \times 18 = \blacksquare$

Ⓐ 18 Ⓑ 180

Ⓒ 1,800 Ⓓ 18,000

15. $46 \times 1{,}000 = \blacksquare$

Ⓐ 460 Ⓑ 4,600

Ⓒ 46,000 Ⓓ 60,000

16. $153 \times 5 = \blacksquare$

Ⓐ 312 Ⓑ 515

Ⓒ 155 Ⓓ 765

17. $218 \times 7 = \blacksquare$

Ⓐ 225 Ⓑ 1,308

Ⓒ 1,519 Ⓓ 1,526

18. $231 \times 4 = \blacksquare$

Ⓐ 824 Ⓑ 924

Ⓒ 1,024 Ⓓ 876

19. $144 \times 8 = \blacksquare$

Ⓐ 1,152 Ⓑ 1,072

Ⓒ 832 Ⓓ 152

20. $87 \div 3 = \blacksquare$

Ⓐ 18 Ⓑ 29

Ⓒ 30 Ⓓ 20

CHAPTER 7

Practice Test

In the equations below, *a* stands for the unknown number. Find the value of *a*.

21. $78 \div a = 13$

Ⓐ 10 Ⓑ 8

Ⓒ 6 Ⓓ 3

22. $175 \div 5 = a$

Ⓐ 35 Ⓑ 25

Ⓒ 15 Ⓓ 5

23. There were 102 pairs of shoes in the storeroom. They were arranged equally on 6 shelves. How many pairs of shoes were on each shelf?

Ⓐ 17 Ⓑ 17 R3

Ⓒ 18 R3 Ⓓ 19

24. What is the perimeter?

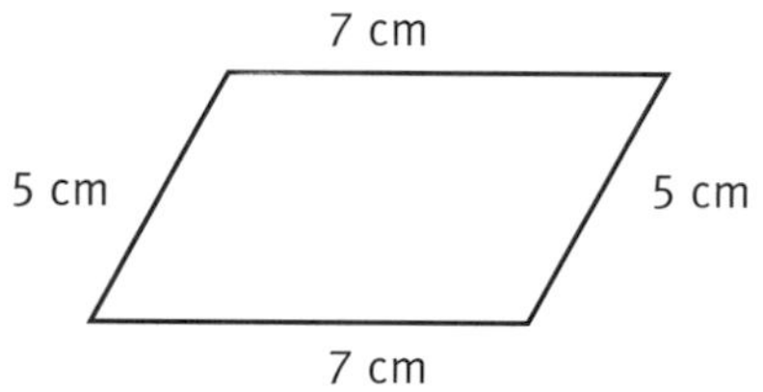

Ⓐ 12 centimeters

Ⓑ 14 centimeters

Ⓒ 24 centimeters

Ⓓ 35 centimeters

25. Would this temperature be high, low, or comfortable?

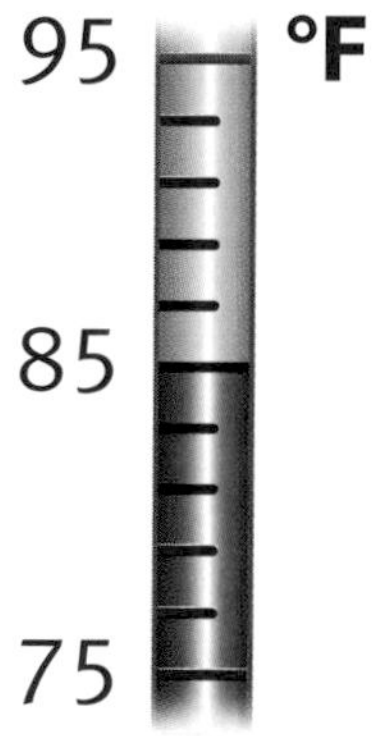

Ⓐ high

Ⓑ low

Ⓒ comfortable

Complete the following comparison using <, >, or =.

26. 47,142 ☐ 48,142

Ⓐ <

Ⓑ >

Ⓒ =

27. Which shows the same product as 3×8?

Ⓐ 9×2 Ⓑ 8×3

Ⓒ 8×4 Ⓓ 7×4

28. What is 58,004 in expanded form?

Ⓐ 50,000 + 8,000 + 0 + 0 + 4

Ⓑ 50,000 + 800 + 0 + 4

Ⓒ 500,000 + 80,000 + 0 + 0 + 4

Ⓓ 500,000 + 0 + 800 + 0 + 0 + 4

29. How would you write 1,410 as a Roman numeral?

Ⓐ CCXXX Ⓑ DDDDX

Ⓒ DCDX Ⓓ MCDX

30. Find the sum.

819 + 236 = ▢

Ⓐ 1,275 Ⓑ 1,255

Ⓒ 1,155 Ⓓ 1,055

Extended Response **Solve.**

31. Ralph is making small bouquets for Mother's Day. He groups 3 roses with 2 carnations. Each bouquet has 20 flowers.

a. How many roses and how many carnations does he use for each bouquet? Explain your answer.

b. Ralph made 8 bouquets. How many flowers did he use in all? How many were roses? How many were carnations? Explain your answer.

32. Ralph later got 30 orchids. He put 3 orchids in each bouquet.

a. How many orchids did he use in the bouquets? Explain your answer.

b. Did he have any orchids left over? If so, how many?

Thinking Story

Clever Consuela

Manolita's mother worked with computers. She did part of her computer work at home, but she let Manolita use the computer when she wasn't working. She even taught Manolita how to write programs that would make the computer do what Manolita wanted it to do. Manolita loved number tricks, so she wrote a program that made the computer do tricky things with numbers. When the computer was running her programs, Manolita thought of it as her computer. She even gave it a name. She called it Clever Consuela. When she wrote a new program, she thought of that as teaching Clever Consuela a new trick.

"Come see the new trick I have taught Clever Consuela," she said to Marcus one day.

"I didn't know you have a dog," Marcus said.

What would make Marcus think Clever Consuela was a dog?

"Clever Consuela is my computer," Manolita said. "When I write programs for it, it does neat things that I want it to do. That's like teaching it to do new tricks. Type any number, and see what Clever Consuela does."

Marcus typed the number 1, and it started dancing across the screen. "That's nice," Marcus said, "but I wouldn't call it clever. It just shows the number that you press and makes it dance."

"Type another number," Manolita said.

Marcus typed a 2, and immediately a number 3 started dancing across the screen. "It made a mistake," Marcus said. "I typed a 2, and a 3 came up instead."

"That's no mistake," Manolita said. "That's what it's supposed to do."

What could the computer be doing that made a 3 come up?

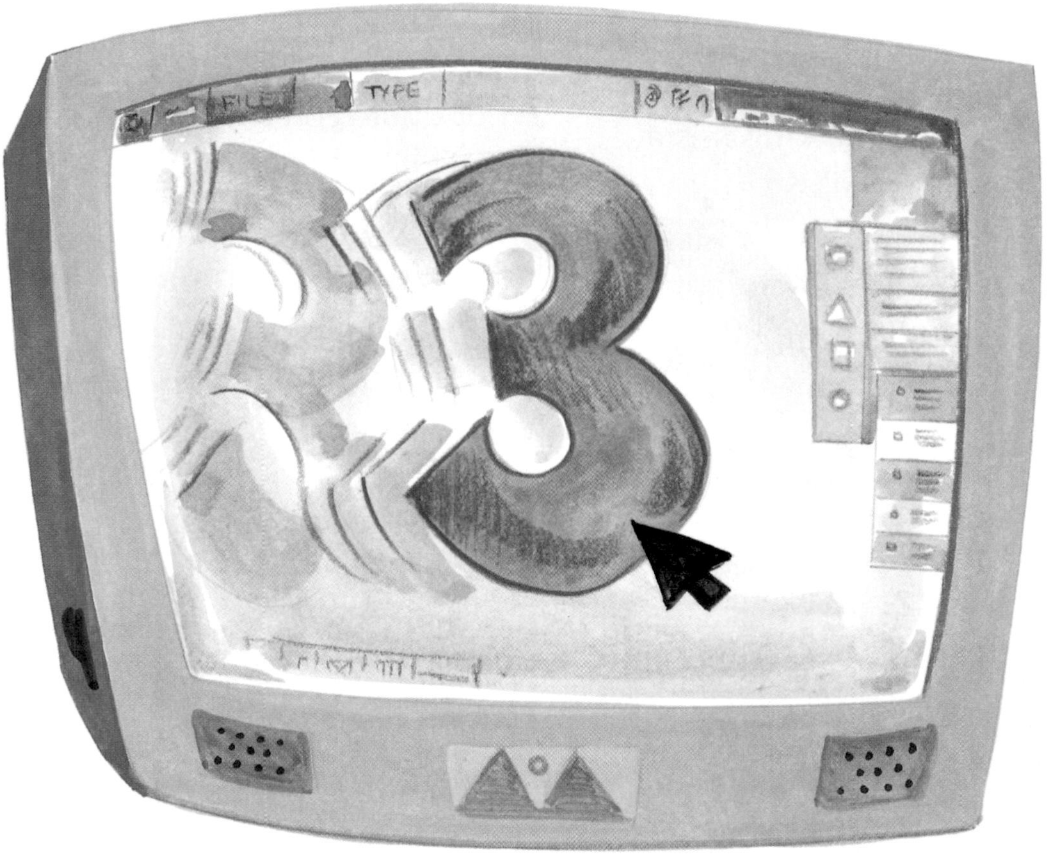

"I get it," Marcus said. "It's adding the numbers. What's so great about that? My little calculator can do that."

"Type another number," Manolita said.

"I'm typing a 4," he said, "so a 7 should come up." But a 6 came up instead. "See, it is making mistakes; 1 plus 2 plus 4 is 7, not 6."

"Clever Consuela never makes mistakes," Manolita said.

What could the computer be doing that made a 6 come up?

"I don't get it," Marcus said.

"Type another number," Manolita said.

This time Marcus typed a 10, and the number that danced across the screen was 14. "I'm starting to get an idea," Marcus said. He typed a 4 and a 14 danced across the screen, just as it had before.

"That's just what I expected," Marcus said.

What could the computer be doing that made 14 come up after Marcus typed 10, and that also made 14 come up after he typed 4?

Marcus typed again. "This time an 8 should come up," he said, and he was right. "Consuela is clever, but not too clever for me," he said. "Now I know what the computer will do every time. If I type a 3, 7 will come up. See, it did. Now if I type 2, 5 will come up. Now if I type 1 . . . "

What number will dance across the screen if Marcus types 1 after he typed 2 the time before?

"Three comes up, just the way it should," Marcus said. "Consuela just adds the number I type to the number I typed before. That's all there is to it. But how did you get the computer to do that?"

"There are things called variables," Manolita said. "I programmed Clever Consuela to recognize three variables. One is called *Old Number,* one is called *New Number,* and one is called *Dancing Number.* New Number is the number you type in. The computer figures out what Dancing Number is."

How could the computer figure out what Dancing Number should be?

"That part is easy," said Marcus. "Dancing Number equals Old Number plus New Number. But how does the computer know what Old Number is? It keeps changing."

"That's the tricky part," said Manolita. "When you start the program, Old Number is always 0. That's why, when you typed 1 the first time, a 1 danced across the screen. Zero plus 1 is 1. When you type a number, two things happen. First, Consuela adds the New Number to the Old Number, like you said. Then Consuela changes the New Number into the Old Number."

"I get it," said Marcus. "When I typed 2 after typing 1 the time before, 1 became Old Number, New Number was 2, and Dancing Number was 1 plus 2, which is 3."

"That's right," said Manolita. "And then Old Number became 2, and when you type in another number, Dancing Number is 2 plus that new number."

"Now that I understand it," said Marcus, "I don't think Consuela is very clever at all. The clever one is Manolita."

Do you agree that Manolita is the clever one, not the computer? Why or why not?

The End

CHAPTER 8

Fractions

In This Chapter You Will Learn

- about fractions of geometric figures, linear measure, sets, and time.
- how to compare fractions.
- how to add and subtract fractions.
- about tenths, hundredths, and percents.

Problem Solving

A designer at an advertising company wants to paint three circular signs that look alike but use different amounts of red, blue, and green. She set aside enough paint for each sign, but she lost her notes. Can you help her?

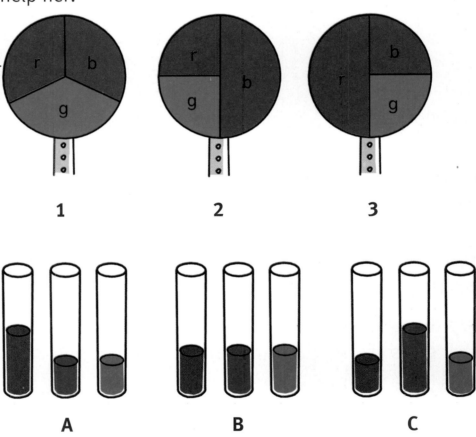

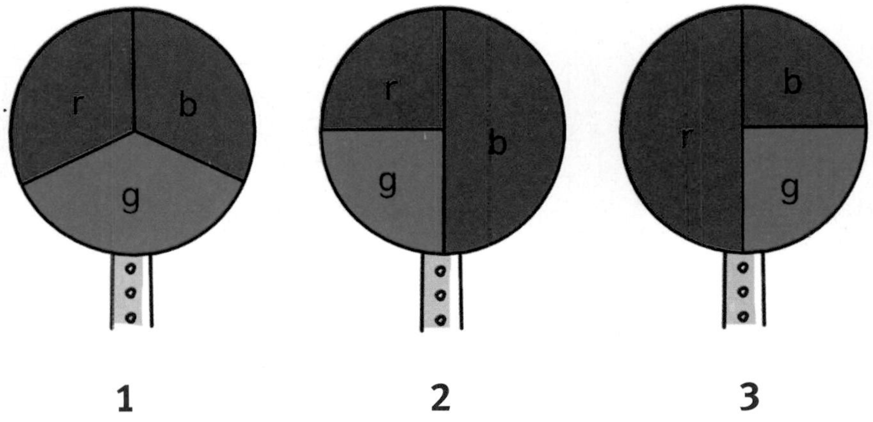

1. Which set of paints should be used for which sign?
2. How did you decide which paints go with which sign?
3. How could you use the words *half, third,* and *fourth* to prove that your answer is correct?

LESSON 8.1

Fractions of Geometric Figures

Key Ideas

A fraction represents a specific part of a whole. The numerator, or top number of a fraction, tells the number of equal parts being referenced. The denominator, or bottom number of a fraction, tells the total number of equal parts.

Look at the following picture and its related fraction.

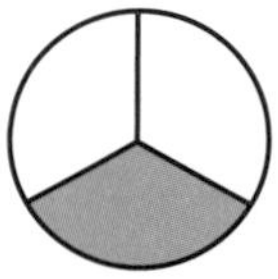

The fraction $\frac{1}{3}$, read as *one-third,* represents the shaded part of this circle.

The 1 is the numerator, showing we are referring to 1 part of the entire circle.

The 3 is the denominator, showing there are 3 equal parts total in the circle.

Copy the following shapes. Then listen as your teacher gives you specific directions for the following figures.

1. 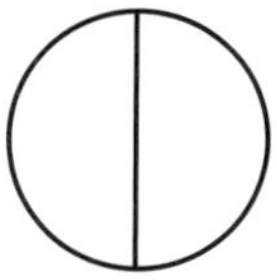
2. 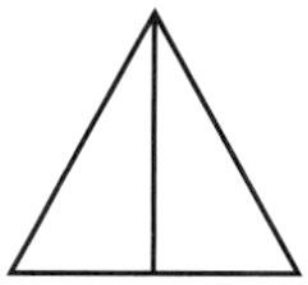
3. 
4. 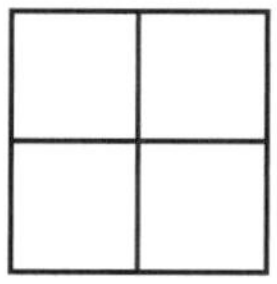
5. 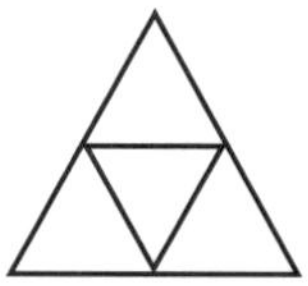
6. 

What fraction of each figure is shaded?

7 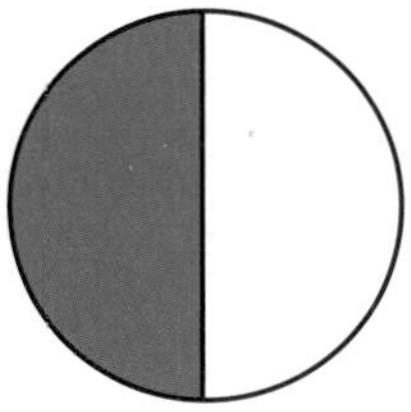

8 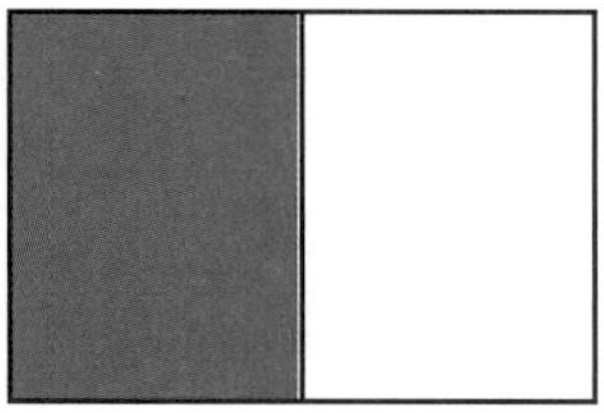

9 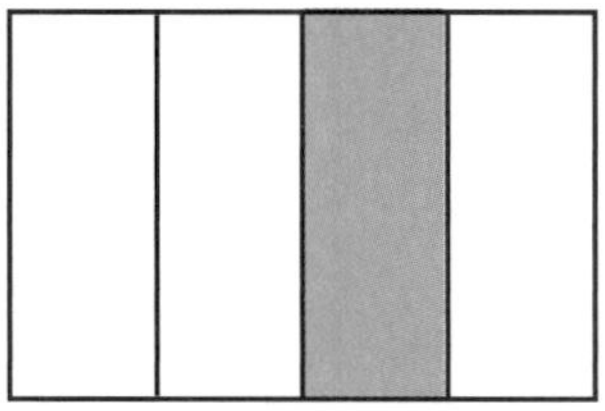

10 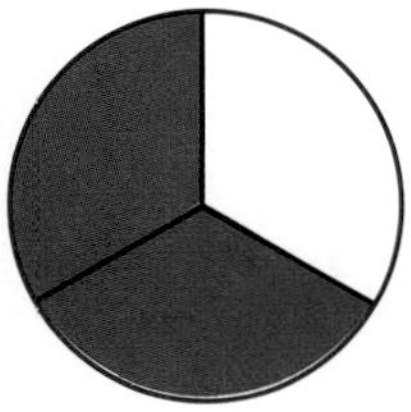

11 

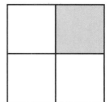

12 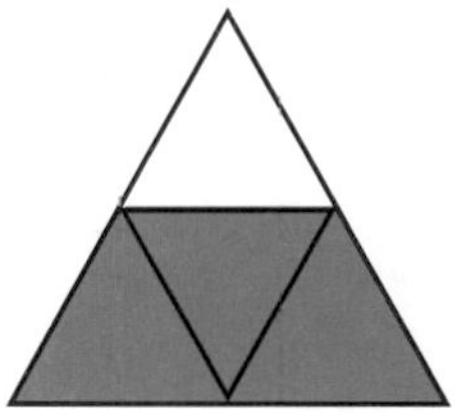

13 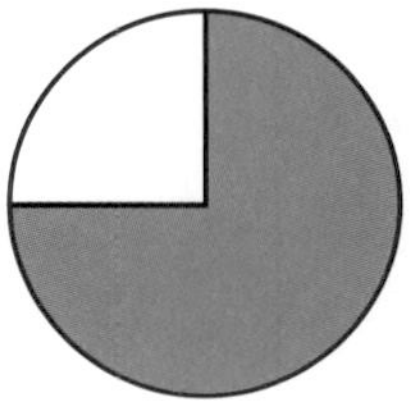

14 

What fraction is colored?

15 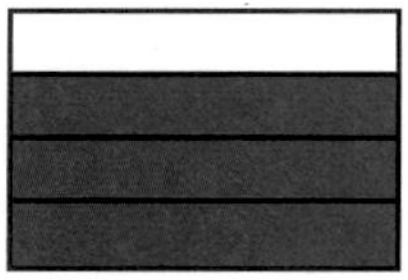

16 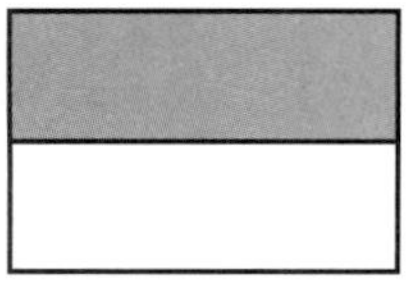

17 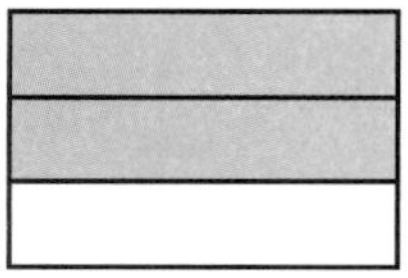

18 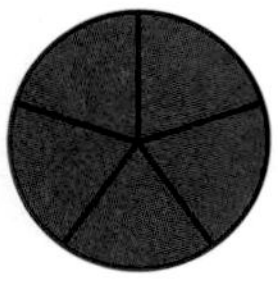

19 

20 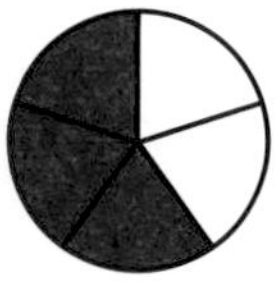

21 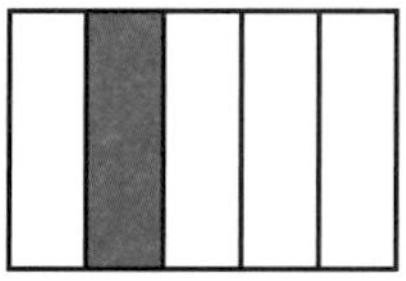

22 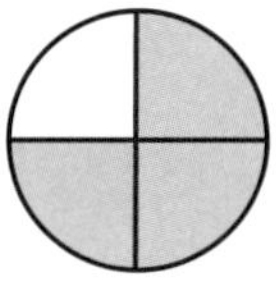

23 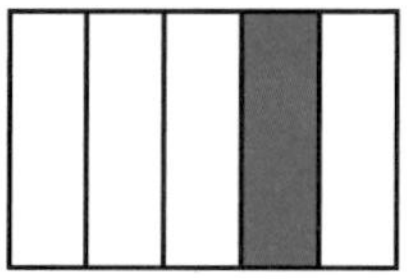

24 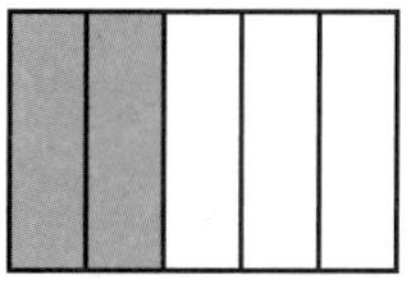

25 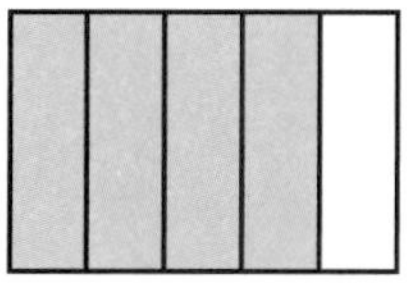

26 

27 Copy or trace this figure four times. Color $\frac{1}{4}$ in four different ways.

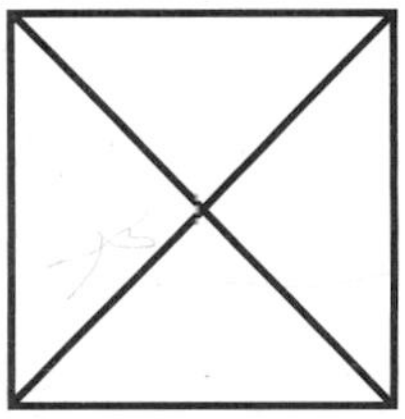

28 Copy or trace this figure six different times. Color $\frac{2}{4}$ in six different ways.

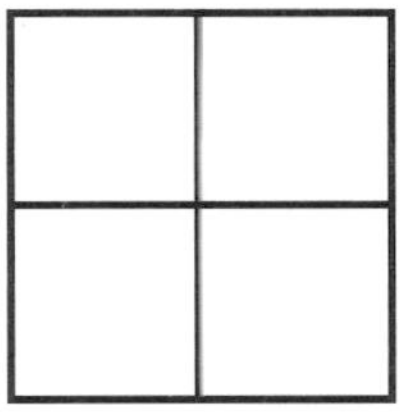

29 Copy or trace this figure four times. Color $\frac{3}{4}$ in four different ways.

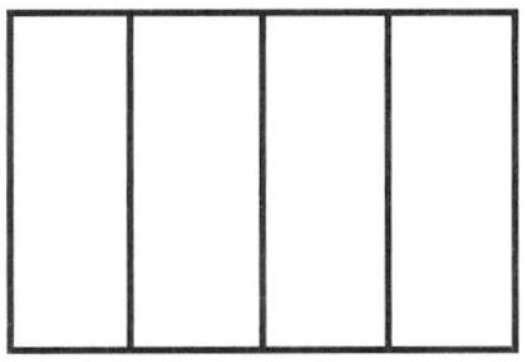

30 Copy or trace this figure. Color in $\frac{4}{4}$.

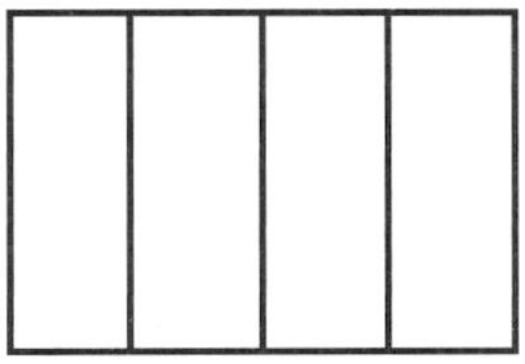

Writing + Math **Journal**

Copy or trace the figure in Problem 28 six different times. Color in $\frac{1}{2}$ of the square in six different ways. Describe any similarities and/or differences you notice between the response to Problem 28 and the response to your Journal.

Fractions of Linear Measure

Key Ideas

Any distance or length can be divided into equal parts. A fraction can be used to tell how many equal parts there are and how many of those parts are being considered.

| $\frac{1}{6}$ | $\frac{1}{6}$ | $\frac{1}{6}$ | $\frac{1}{6}$ | $\frac{1}{6}$ | $\frac{1}{6}$ |

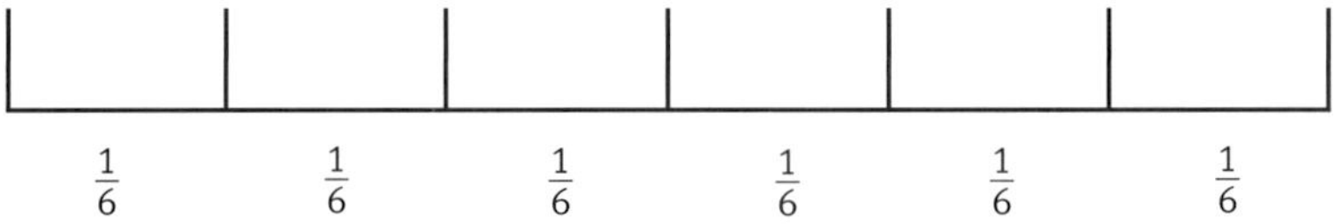

This section of a line is divided into 6 parts. Each part is $\frac{1}{6}$ of the specific section of the line.

What fraction of the line is shaded?

1

| $\frac{1}{6}$ | $\frac{1}{6}$ | $\frac{1}{6}$ | $\frac{1}{6}$ | $\frac{1}{6}$ | $\frac{1}{6}$ |

2
| $\frac{1}{6}$ | $\frac{1}{6}$ | $\frac{1}{6}$ | $\frac{1}{6}$ | $\frac{1}{6}$ | $\frac{1}{6}$ |

3

| $\frac{1}{8}$ | $\frac{1}{8}$ | $\frac{1}{8}$ | $\frac{1}{8}$ | $\frac{1}{8}$ | $\frac{1}{8}$ | $\frac{1}{8}$ | $\frac{1}{8}$ |

4

| $\frac{1}{8}$ | $\frac{1}{8}$ | $\frac{1}{8}$ | $\frac{1}{8}$ | $\frac{1}{8}$ | $\frac{1}{8}$ | $\frac{1}{8}$ | $\frac{1}{8}$ |

e Textbook This lesson is available in the *eTextbook*.

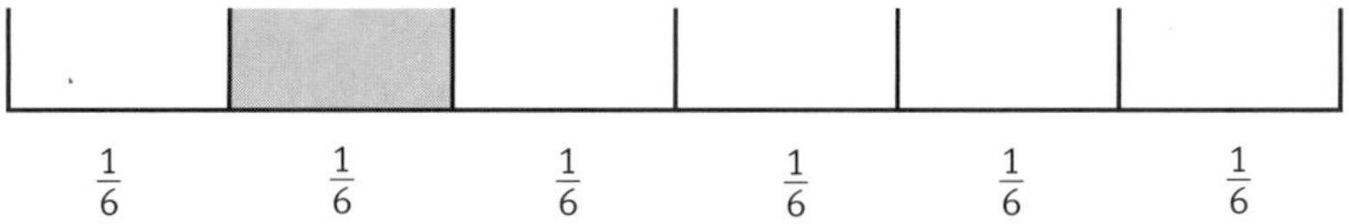

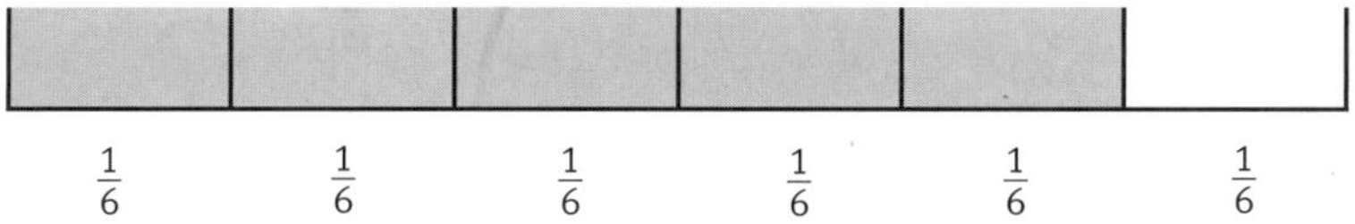

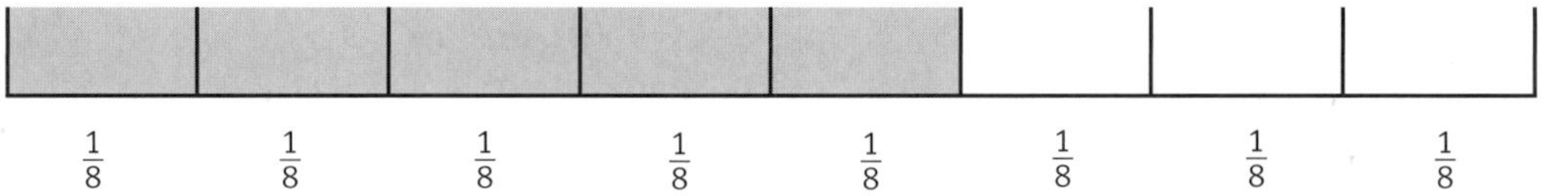

A ruler is often divided into sections. To read the fractional parts on a ruler, first count the total parts, which will be your denominator. Then count the parts you are working with, which will be your numerator.

Each of the following rulers has been divided into twelfths, so each section is $\frac{1}{12}$. How much of a whole is each ribbon?

5 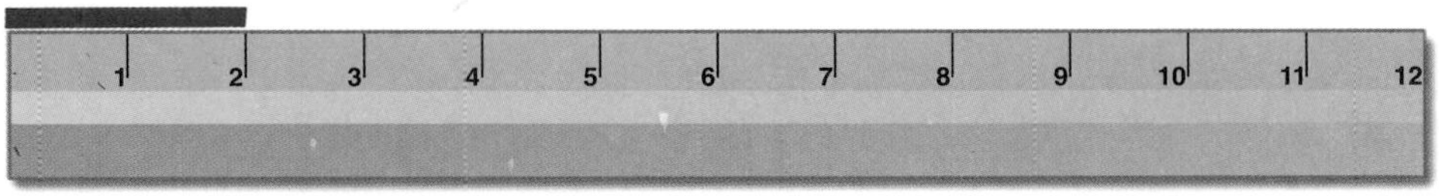

6 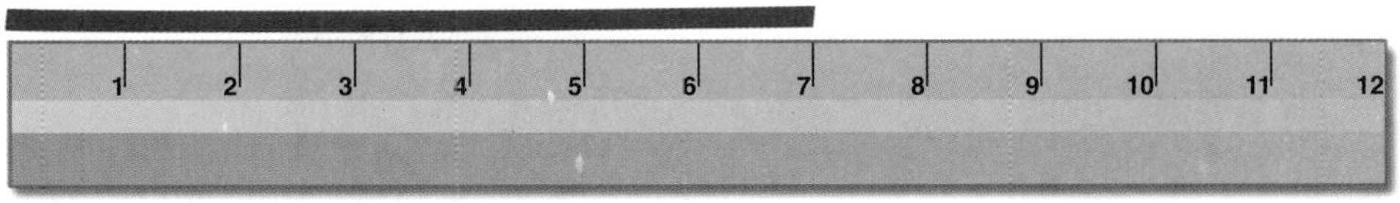

7 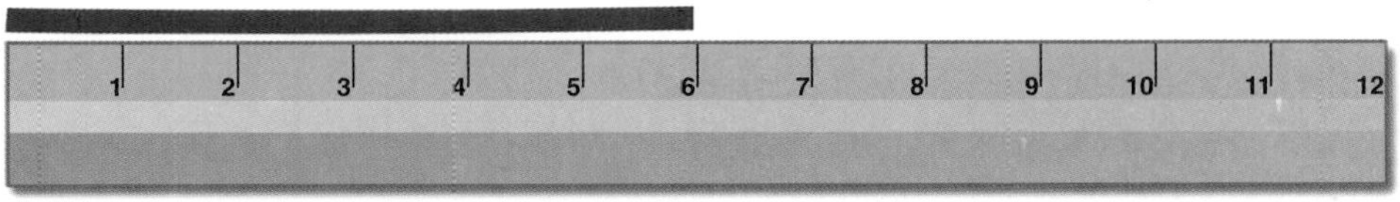

8 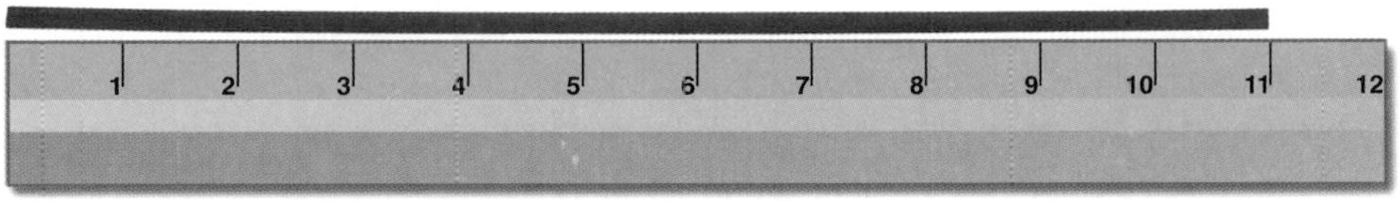

Each of the following rulers has been divided into tenths, so each section is $\frac{1}{10}$. How much of a whole is each ribbon?

9 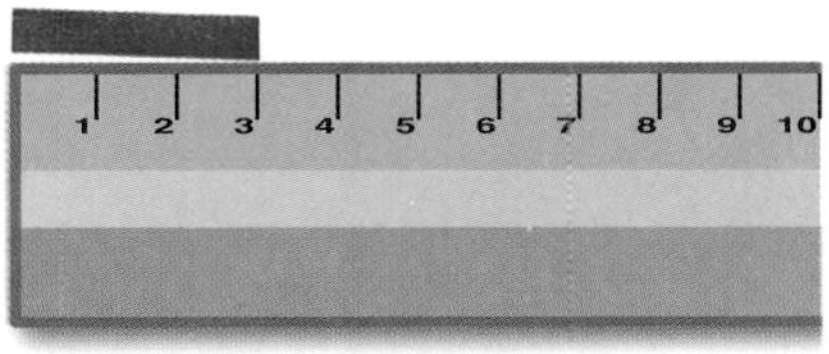

10 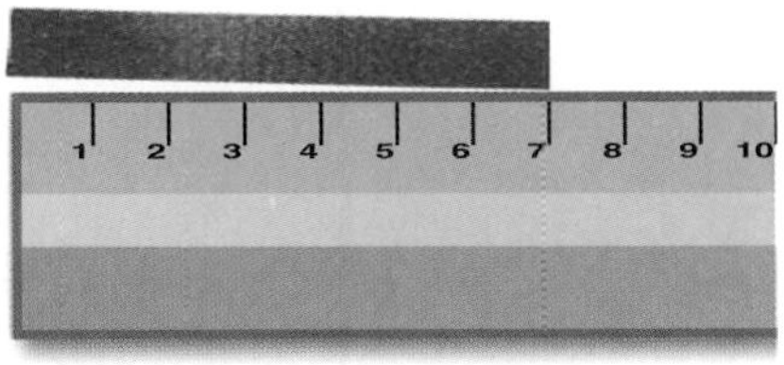

11 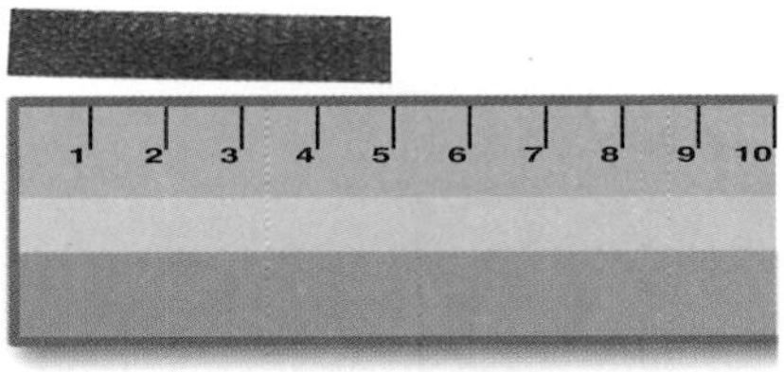

12 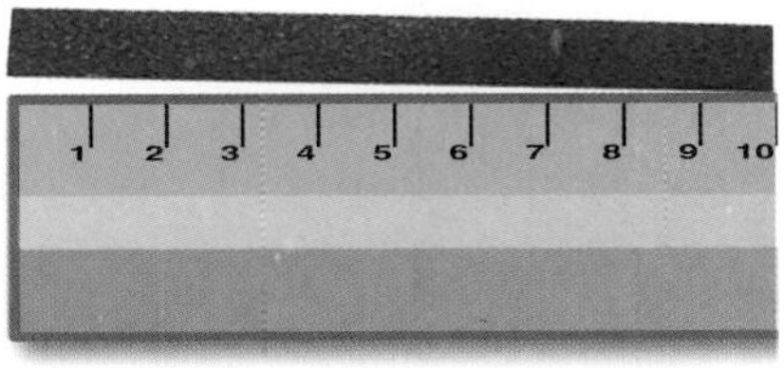

LESSON
8.3 Fractions of Sets

Key Ideas

Recall that a fraction represents a specific part of a whole. This can be a whole shape, or it can be a whole collection, or set, of items.

Rosalie divided 15 coins into 3 equal piles.

Because there are 3 equal piles total, we would say 1 pile is $\frac{1}{3}$ of the whole collection, or set, of pennies.

Count the number of pennies in 1 pile. There are 5 pennies in 1 pile.

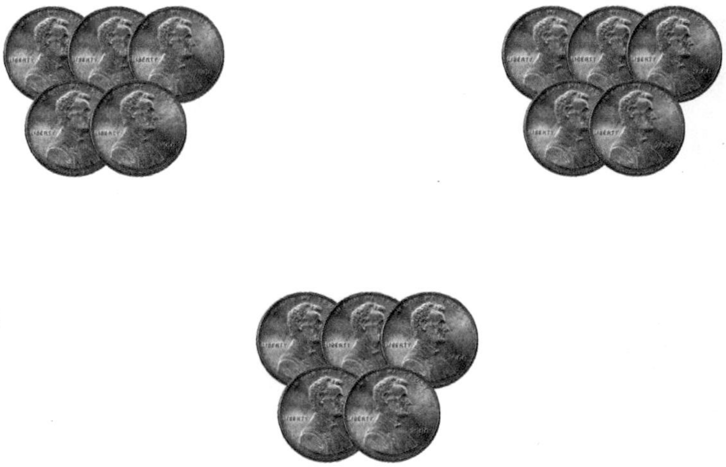

$\frac{1}{3}$ of 15 = 5

Solve. **You may use manipulatives to act out these problems.**

Lola divided 10 coins into 5 equal piles.

1. Draw the 5 piles.
2. How many coins are there in each pile?
3. $\frac{1}{5}$ of 10 is ▢.
4. $\frac{1}{4}$ of 16 is ▢.

5. $\frac{1}{2}$ of 12 = ■.

6. $\frac{1}{5}$ of 15 = ■.

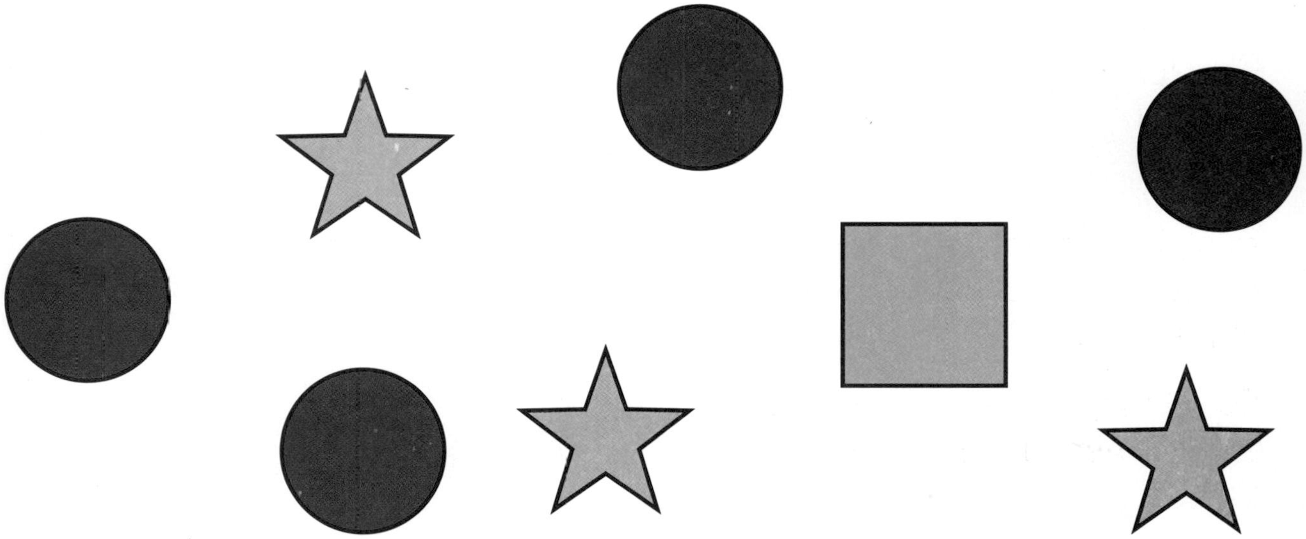

Use the picture to answer the questions.

7. What fraction of the set is stars?
8. What fraction of the set is circles?
9. What fraction of the set is squares?
10. What fraction of the set includes all the stars and all the circles?
11. What fraction of the set includes all the stars, circles, and squares?
12. What fraction of the set includes no stars, circles, or squares?
13. What fraction of the set is not squares?
14. What fraction of the set is not circles?

You may use manipulatives to help you solve these problems. Work down the page.

15. $\frac{1}{6}$ of 12 is ____.
16. $\frac{2}{6}$ of 12 is ____.
17. $\frac{3}{6}$ of 12 is ____.
18. $\frac{4}{6}$ of 12 is ____.
19. $\frac{1}{8}$ of 24 is ____.
20. $\frac{2}{8}$ of 24 is ____.
21. $\frac{3}{8}$ of 24 is ____.
22. $\frac{4}{8}$ of 24 is ____.
23. $\frac{1}{5}$ of 25 is ____.
24. $\frac{2}{5}$ of 25 is ____.
25. $\frac{3}{5}$ of 25 is ____.
26. $\frac{4}{5}$ of 25 is ____.
27. $\frac{1}{5}$ of 30 is ____.
28. $\frac{3}{5}$ of 30 is ____.
29. $\frac{1}{3}$ of 30 is ____.
30. $\frac{2}{3}$ of 30 is ____.

Solve.

31. In Michael's class, $\frac{1}{3}$ of the students are boys. What fraction of the students are girls?

There are 20 students in Bev's class; $\frac{1}{2}$ of them are girls.

32. How many girls are in Bev's class?

33. How many boys are in Bev's class?

34. Julius lives 30 miles from where he works. He has driven $\frac{1}{3}$ of the way there. How many miles has he driven?

35. Keiko and her 4 friends want to share a pizza equally. What fraction of the pizza should each person get?

36. **Extended Response** There are 400 pages in the book Shamika is reading for her summer reading program. She has 8 weeks to read the book. How many pages should she read weekly if she wants to read an equal amount each week? Explain how you got your answer.

Writing + Math **Journal**

Determine what fraction each shape is of the whole area. Explain how you got your answer.

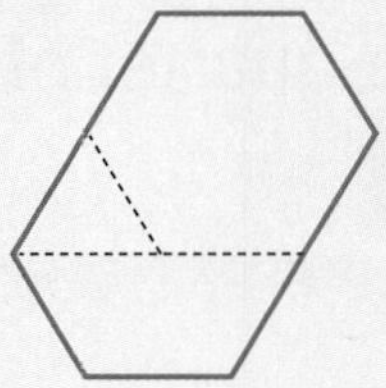

a. Hexagon

b. Triangle

c. Trapezoid

LESSON 8.4 Fractions of Time

Key Ideas

Time can be represented as fractions of an hour. We often use the phrases *half hour* and *quarter hour*. What do these phrases actually mean when referring to fractions of time?

If we look at the face of a clock, we can see how it could be divided into halves and quarters.

This clock face is divided into 2 equal sections, so each section would be $\frac{1}{2}$ of the whole.

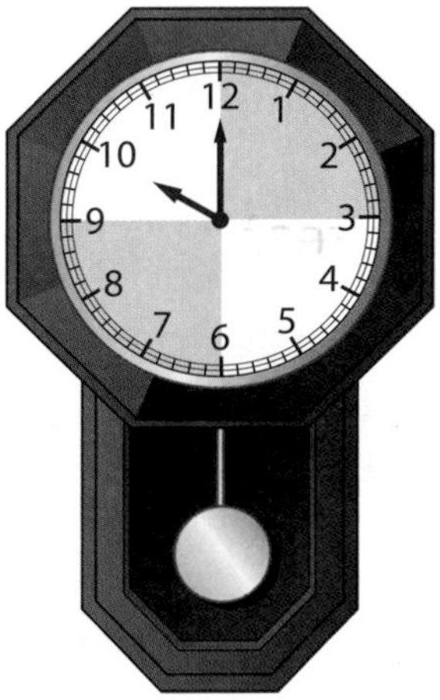

This clock face is divided into 4 equal sections, so each section would be $\frac{1}{4}$ of the whole. Another way of saying $\frac{1}{4}$ is to refer to it as one-quarter of the whole.

Think about how much time passes in an hour. There are 60 minutes in one hour.

$\frac{1}{2}$ of $60 = 30$

Therefore, $\frac{1}{2}$ of an hour is 30 minutes.

What fraction is represented by the shaded part of each clock?

1. 

2. 

3. 

How many minutes? The first one is done for you.

4. 1 hour $=$ 60 minutes
5. $\frac{2}{2}$ of an hour
6. $\frac{2}{4}$ of an hour
7. $\frac{3}{4}$ of an hour
8. $\frac{4}{4}$ of an hour
9. $\frac{1}{3}$ of an hour
10. $\frac{2}{3}$ of an hour

Which is longer?

11. $\frac{1}{2}$ of an hour or $\frac{2}{4}$ of an hour?
12. $\frac{1}{2}$ of an hour or $\frac{1}{4}$ of an hour?
13. $\frac{1}{2}$ of an hour or $\frac{3}{4}$ of an hour?
14. $\frac{2}{2}$ of an hour or $\frac{1}{1}$ of an hour?
15. $\frac{2}{2}$ of an hour or $\frac{4}{4}$ of an hour?
16. $\frac{2}{4}$ of an hour or $\frac{2}{3}$ of an hour?

Writing + Math **Journal**

Describe how you would find $\frac{1}{5}$ of an hour.

LESSON 8.5 Equivalent Fractions

Key Ideas

When two or more fractions represent the same part of a whole, we call them equivalent fractions.

Each of the following circles has the same amount shaded. However, each shaded part is represented by a different fraction.

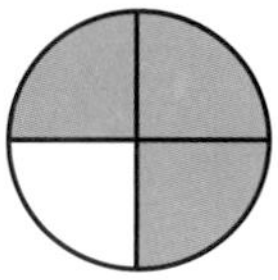

$\frac{3}{4}$

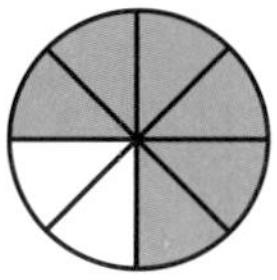

$\frac{6}{8}$

Because $\frac{3}{4}$ and $\frac{6}{8}$ represent the same amount, we would say they are equivalent fractions.

What fraction of each circle is colored?

1. 

2. 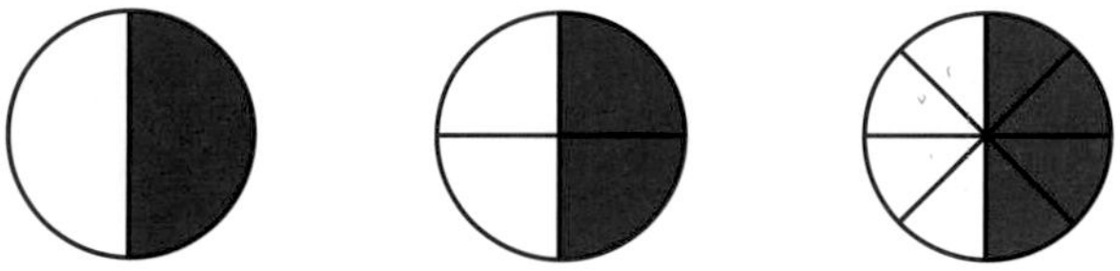

3. 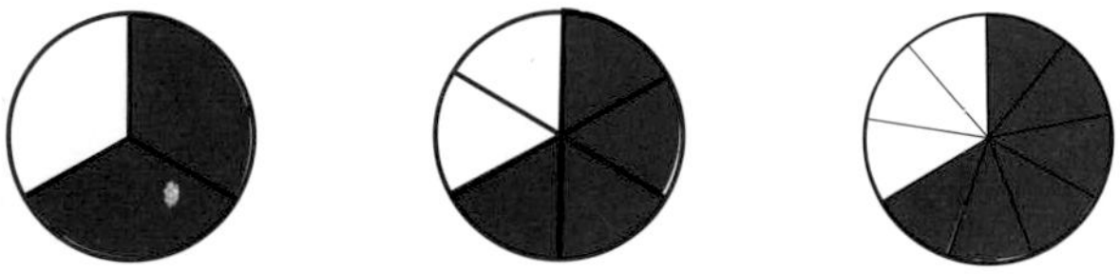

What fraction of each rectangle is colored?

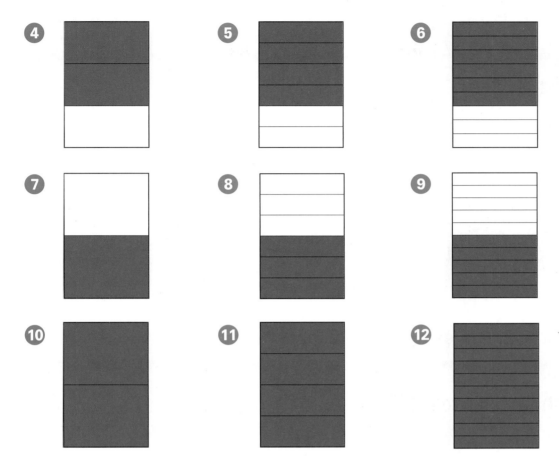

4

5
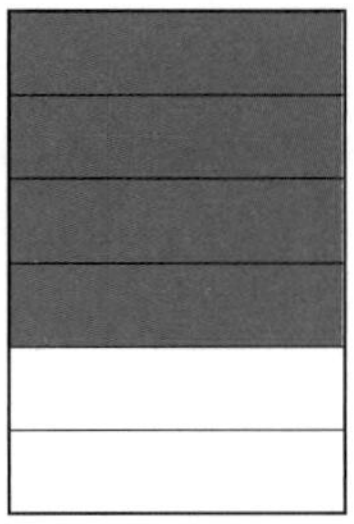

6
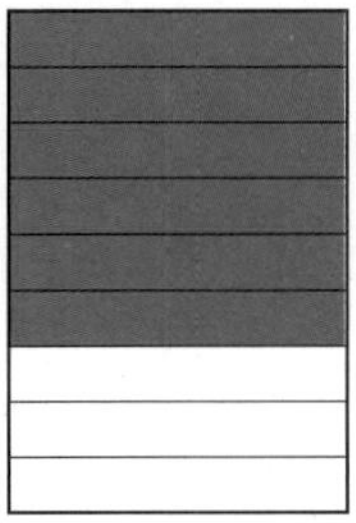

7
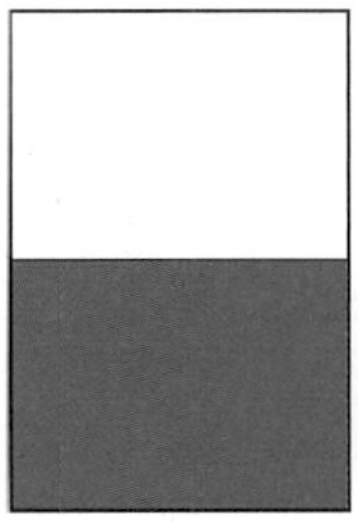

8
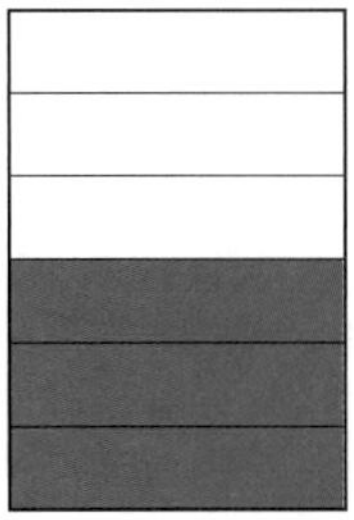

9
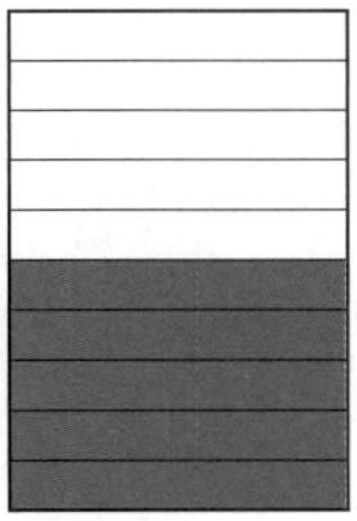

10

11

12

Writing + Math **Journal**

List or draw five fractions that are equivalent to $\frac{1}{2}$.

LESSON 8.6 Comparing Fractions

Key Ideas

When we compare fractions, we decide which fraction of something is bigger and which is smaller, or if both fractions of a thing are the same.

Which is bigger, $\frac{1}{2}$ of the cake or $\frac{1}{3}$ of the cake?

We could draw a picture using circles for the two cakes.

By looking at the pictures, we can see that $\frac{1}{2}$ is bigger.

Answer these questions.

1. Which is bigger, $\frac{1}{2}$ of the pie or $\frac{1}{5}$ of the pie?
2. Which is bigger, $\frac{1}{3}$ of the loaf of bread or $\frac{1}{5}$ of the loaf?
3. Which is bigger, $\frac{1}{3}$ of the pizza or $\frac{1}{4}$ of the pizza?
4. Which is bigger, $\frac{1}{2}$ of the muffin or $\frac{1}{4}$ of the muffin?
5. Which is bigger, $\frac{1}{4}$ of the apple or $\frac{1}{2}$ of the apple?
6. Which is bigger, $\frac{1}{5}$ of the banana or $\frac{1}{2}$ of the banana?
7. Which is bigger, $\frac{1}{3}$ of the sandwich or $\frac{1}{4}$ of the sandwich?
8. **Extended Response** Explain how you got your answer to Problem 7.

Symbols are also used sometimes to compare fractions. These symbols are $<$, $>$, or $=$.

Copy each statement, and replace the ■ with $<$, $>$, or $=$ to make a true statement. The pictures may help you.

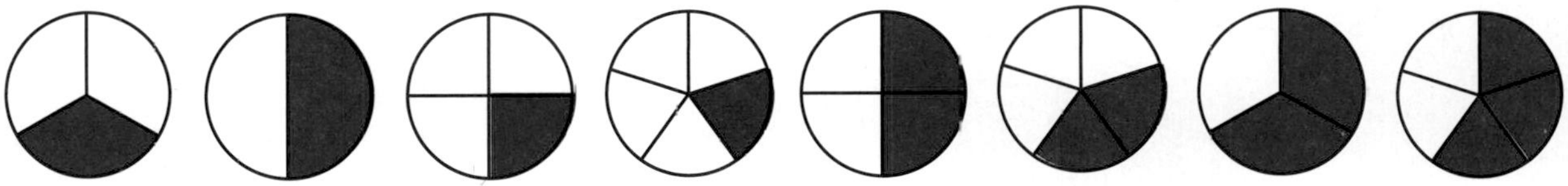

9. $\frac{1}{3}$ ■ $\frac{1}{2}$
10. $\frac{1}{2}$ ■ $\frac{2}{5}$
11. $\frac{2}{3}$ ■ $\frac{2}{2}$
12. $\frac{1}{3}$ ■ $\frac{1}{4}$
13. $\frac{1}{2}$ ■ $\frac{3}{5}$
14. $\frac{2}{4}$ ■ $\frac{1}{3}$
15. $\frac{1}{3}$ ■ $\frac{1}{3}$
16. $\frac{2}{4}$ ■ $\frac{3}{5}$
17. $\frac{3}{4}$ ■ $\frac{1}{5}$
18. $\frac{1}{2}$ ■ $\frac{1}{4}$
19. $\frac{2}{4}$ ■ $\frac{2}{5}$
20. $\frac{1}{2}$ ■ $\frac{2}{4}$

Writing + Math **Journal**

Which of the following would have the most juice if all the glasses are the same size: a glass $\frac{1}{2}$ full, a glass $\frac{1}{5}$ full, a glass $\frac{1}{4}$ full, or a glass $\frac{1}{6}$ full? Explain.

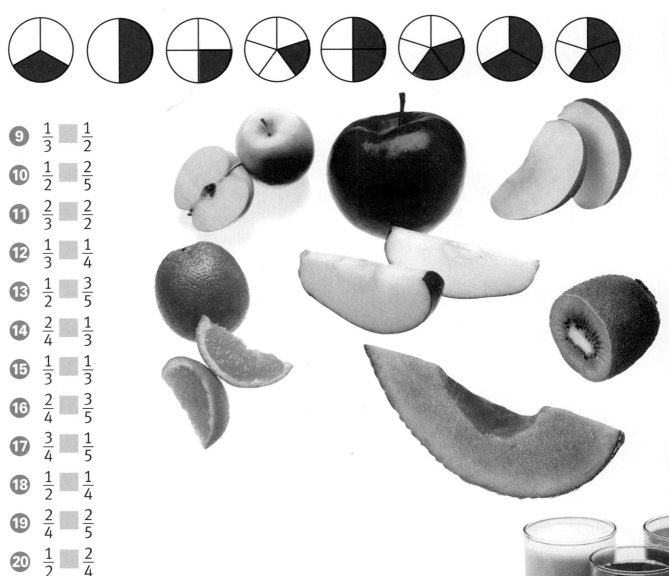

Read the problem. Think about how you might solve it.

You are going to advertise a sale where a customer can buy one robot at the regular price and then buy an identical one for half off. What fraction of the cost of two robots will people save if they take advantage of this sale?

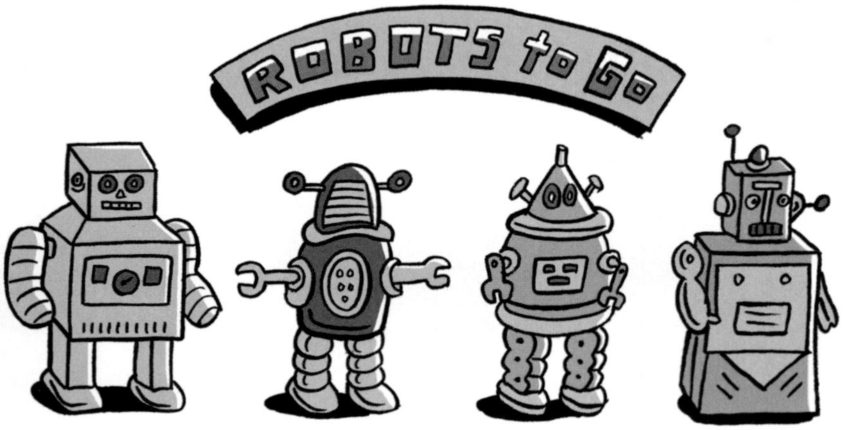

Claudia used simple numbers to solve the problem.

My Plan

A. I will choose a simple number for the price: $1.

B. I will figure out how much I would pay for 2 robots with the sale.

C. I will figure out how much I save from the regular price for 2 robots.

D. I will compare the amount I save to the regular price.

Think about Claudia's strategy. Answer the following questions.

1. What do you think of Claudia's choice for a simple number?
2. How can Claudia figure out the amount in step C?
3. How do you think Claudia will figure out the fraction off the whole price in step D?

e Textbook This lesson is available in the *eTextbook*.

Trenton made a diagram to solve the problem.

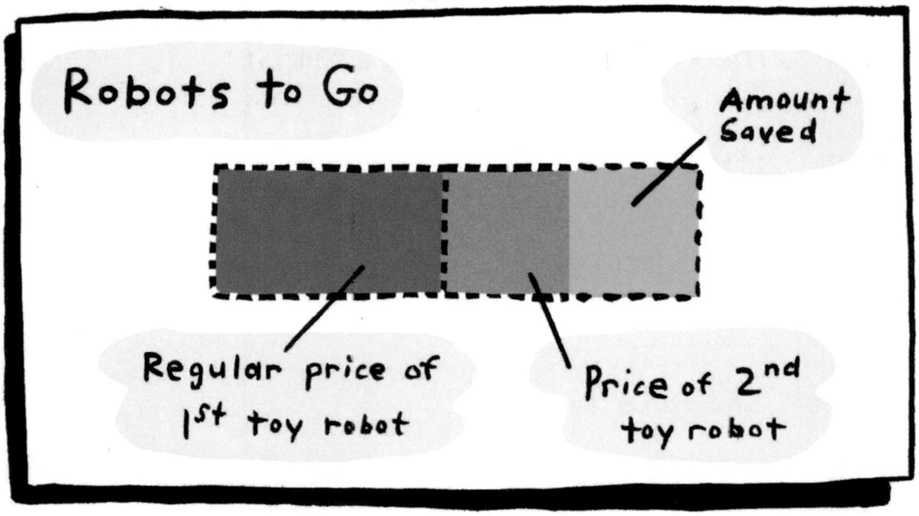

Think about Trenton's strategy. Answer these questions.

4. What did Trenton use to stand for the regular price of a robot?
5. What did Trenton use to stand for the price of the second robot at Robots to Go?
6. Should you compare the amount saved to the regular price of 1 robot or 2 robots? Why?
7. How will Trenton figure out what fraction of the regular price is saved in the sale?

Work with a partner to solve these problems.

8. Finish solving the problem. Use Claudia's strategy, Trenton's strategy, or a strategy of your own.
9. Would you write in your advertisement that this is a $\frac{1}{2}$-off sale? Why or why not?
10. What strategy did you use to solve the problem? Why?

Cumulative Review

Skip Counting Lesson 4.2

Find the missing numbers. Then use the completed exercise to help multiply.

1. 6, 12, 18, ▢, 30, ▢, ▢, 48
2. $12 \times 3 =$ ▢
3. $6 \times 6 =$ ▢

Measuring Length—Inches, Feet, and Yards Lesson 3.5

Solve.

4. **Extended Response** This ad shows a stuffed animal. Use the scale in the ad to determine the height of the stuffed animal. How tall is it in feet? How tall is it in yards? Explain your answer.

Adding with Three or More Addends Lesson 2.10

Add. Use shortcuts if you can.

5. $444 + 263 + 188 =$ ▢
6. $130 + 230 + 430 + 630 =$ ▢

Telling Time Lesson 3.1

Write the time in two ways.

7. 

▢

▢ minutes after ▢

8. 

▢

▢ minutes after ▢

Multiplying by 2, 1, and 0 Lesson 5.1

Find the product.

9. $8 \times 0 = \blacksquare$
10. $12 \times 2 = \blacksquare$
11. $8 \times 7 = \blacksquare$
12. $100 \times 0 = \blacksquare$

Estimating/Reasonable Answers to Division Problems Lesson 7.6

Extended Response **Answer** the problems. If it is not possible to solve the problem, explain why.

13. There were 20 advertisements. The teacher wanted to divide them equally among 3 students. How many did each student get?

14. There are 28 pairs of white shorts. Each volleyball player will get 2 pairs of shorts. How many players are there?

15. Ms. Reeve said each student could check out 5 books. There are 35 books in the checkout pile. How many students are checking out books?

16. Our neighborhood is having a community yard sale. There are 7 people hanging the 28 signs for the sale. How many signs will each person hang?

17. The students wanted to make a picture for the craft show. They wanted an equal number of girls and boys in the picture. They wanted a total of 37 students in the photo. How many girls and how many boys are in the picture?

LESSON 8.7 Adding and Subtracting Fractions

Key Ideas

When we add fractions, we are combining the number of parts of the whole.

For example, if you ate $\frac{1}{3}$ of a pizza and your brother ate $\frac{1}{3}$ of the same pizza, together the two of you have eaten $\frac{2}{3}$ of the pizza.

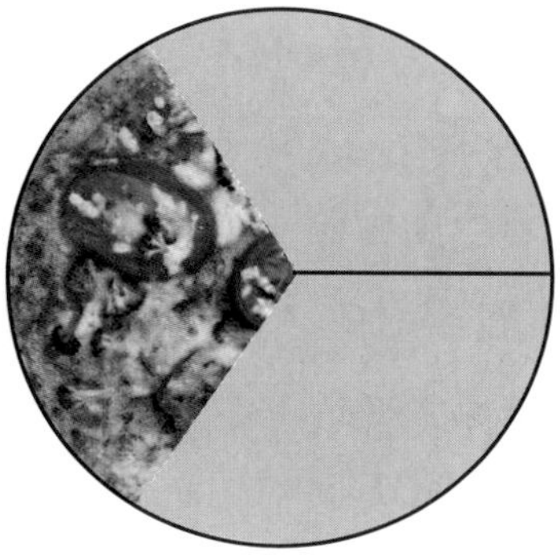

$\frac{1}{3} + \frac{1}{3} = \frac{2}{3}$

Use the following illustrations to complete the addition sentences.

1. 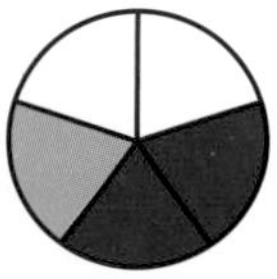

$\frac{2}{5} + \frac{1}{5} =$ ▢

2. 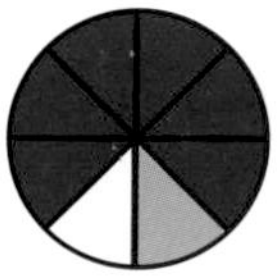

$\frac{1}{8} + \frac{6}{8} =$ ▢

eTextbook This lesson is available in the ***eTextbook.***

Solve. You may draw pictures to help.

3. Randoph's mom divided her vegetable garden into sixths. She planted $\frac{2}{6}$ with green beans and $\frac{3}{6}$ with tomatoes. What fraction of her total garden is planted with beans or tomatoes?

4. Alfonso walked $\frac{5}{8}$ of the way to school. He stopped for a rest, and then walked another $\frac{3}{8}$. What fraction of the way to school did Alfonso walk?

5. Mary Ann lined up her stuffed animals on her shelf. She noticed $\frac{1}{3}$ of them are teddy bears and $\frac{1}{3}$ of them are polar bears. The remaining stuffed animals are dolphins. What fraction of her total stuffed-animal collection is bears?

6. If Mary Ann has 30 stuffed animals total, how many are teddy bears? How many are polar bears? How many are dolphins?

Replace each ■ with <, =, or > to make a true statement. The pictures may help you.

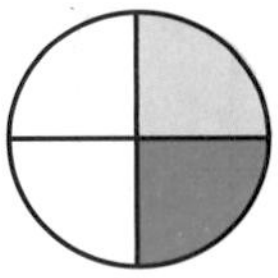

7. $\frac{1}{4} + \frac{1}{4}$ ■ $\frac{1}{2}$

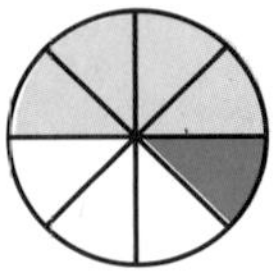

8. $\frac{4}{8} + \frac{1}{8}$ ■ $\frac{1}{2}$

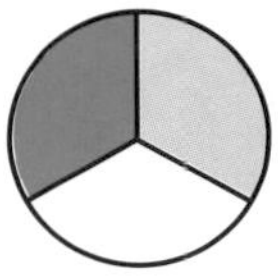

9. $\frac{1}{3} + \frac{1}{3}$ ■ $\frac{1}{2}$

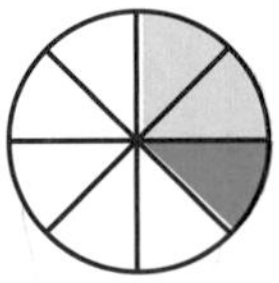

10. $\frac{2}{8} + \frac{1}{8}$ ■ $\frac{1}{2}$

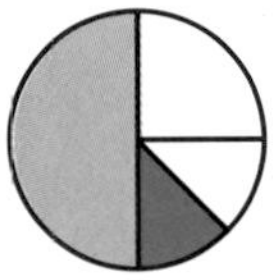

11. $\frac{1}{2} + \frac{1}{8}$ ■ $\frac{3}{4}$

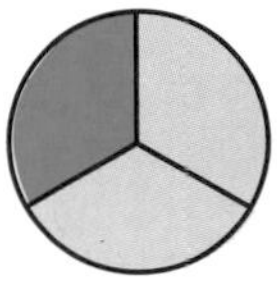

12. $\frac{2}{3} + \frac{1}{3}$ ■ $\frac{3}{4}$

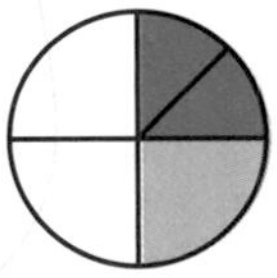

13. $\frac{2}{8} + \frac{1}{4}$ ■ $\frac{1}{2}$

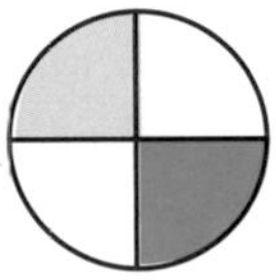

14. $\frac{1}{4} + \frac{1}{4}$ ■ $\frac{3}{4}$

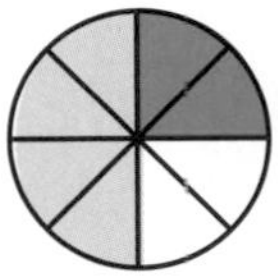

15. $\frac{1}{2} + \frac{2}{8}$ ■ $\frac{3}{4}$

Replace each ■ with <, >, or = to make a true statement. The pictures may help you.

16 $\frac{1}{4} + \frac{1}{4}$ ■ $\frac{1}{2}$

17 $\frac{1}{4} + \frac{1}{2}$ ■ $\frac{1}{8}$

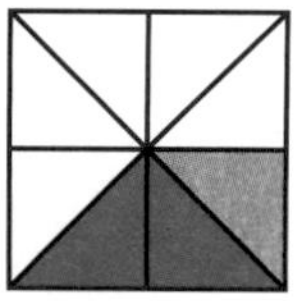

18 $\frac{1}{8} + \frac{1}{8} + \frac{1}{8}$ ■ $\frac{1}{2}$

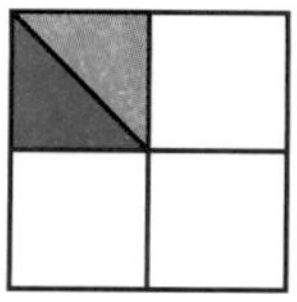

19 $\frac{1}{8} + \frac{1}{8}$ ■ $\frac{1}{4}$

20 $\frac{3}{8} + \frac{1}{8}$ ■ $\frac{1}{2}$

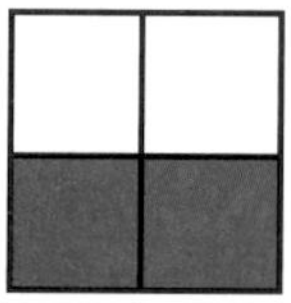

21 $\frac{1}{4} + \frac{1}{4}$ ■ $\frac{3}{4}$

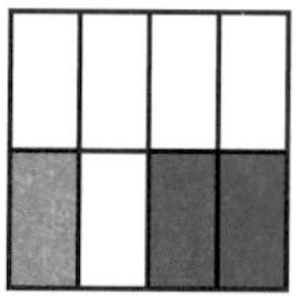

22 $\frac{1}{4} + \frac{1}{8}$ ■ $\frac{1}{2}$

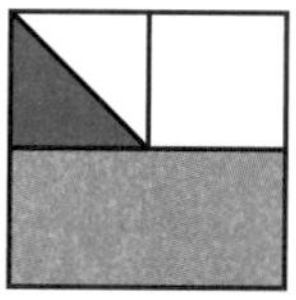

23 $\frac{1}{2} + \frac{1}{8}$ ■ $\frac{3}{4}$

24 $\frac{1}{2} + \frac{1}{4} + \frac{1}{8}$ ■ $\frac{3}{4}$

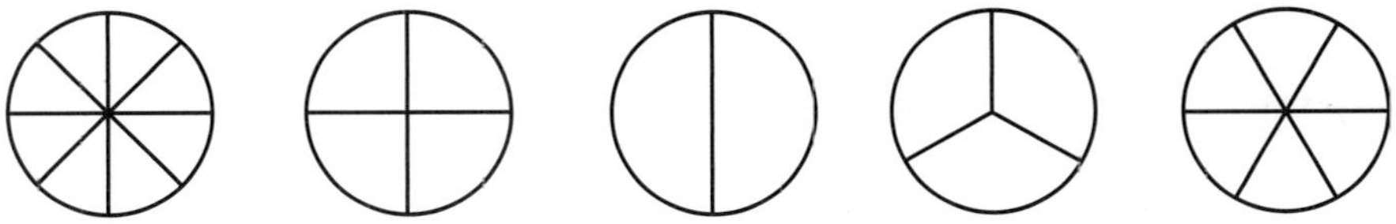

Add. The pictures may help you.

25. $\frac{1}{2} + \frac{1}{2} =$ ■
26. $\frac{1}{2} + \frac{1}{4} =$ ■
27. $\frac{1}{4} + \frac{1}{4} + \frac{1}{4} =$ ■
28. $\frac{1}{4} + \frac{1}{8} =$ ■
29. $\frac{1}{4} + \frac{1}{8} + \frac{1}{8} =$ ■
30. $\frac{1}{3} + \frac{1}{3} =$ ■
31. $\frac{2}{6} + \frac{1}{3} =$ ■
32. $\frac{1}{6} + \frac{1}{6} + \frac{1}{6} =$ ■
33. $\frac{1}{3} + \frac{1}{6} + \frac{1}{6} =$ ■
34. $\frac{3}{6} + \frac{2}{6} =$ ■
35. $\frac{1}{2} + \frac{1}{3} =$ ■

Subtract. The pictures may help you.

36. $\frac{3}{4} - \frac{1}{2} =$ ■
37. $\frac{3}{8} - \frac{1}{4} =$ ■
38. $\frac{1}{3} - \frac{1}{6} =$ ■
39. $\frac{1}{2} - \frac{1}{6} =$ ■
40. $1 - \frac{1}{3} =$ ■

Writing + Math **Journal**

Which picture is $\frac{3}{5}$ shaded? Explain why the other pictures don't show $\frac{3}{5}$.

a.

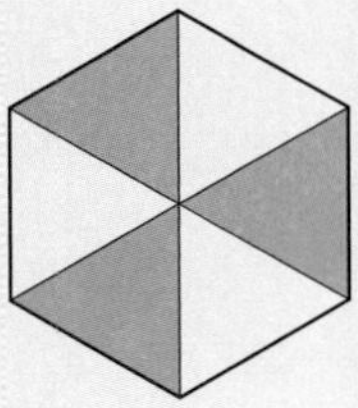

b.

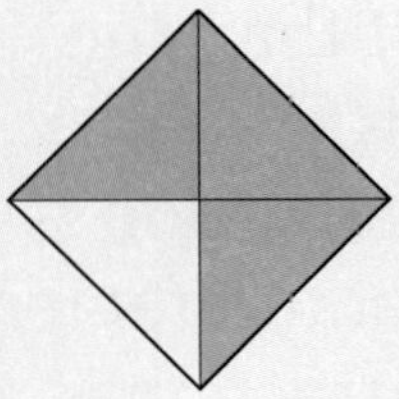

c.

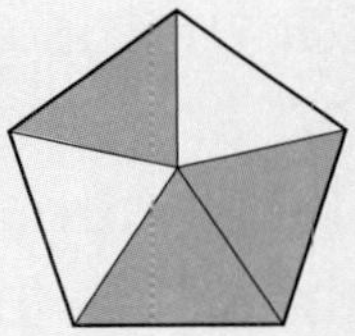

LESSON 8.8 Fractions Greater Than a Whole

Key Ideas

Fractions can be used to represent amounts greater than a whole. A fraction that represents an amount greater than a whole can be just a whole number, or the fraction can be a whole number *and* a fraction.

The amount represented by the above fraction circles can be written two ways. If we count the shaded parts, there are 12 shaded parts total. Each circle is divided into 6 sections. We can write this fraction as $\frac{12}{6}$.

We also can tell there are 2 whole fraction circles that are shaded. We can write this fraction as 2.

If we count the shaded parts of these fractions, we find there are 7 shaded parts total. Each circle is divided into 5 equal sections. We can write this fraction as $\frac{7}{5}$.

We can also tell there is 1 whole fraction circle shaded, and $\frac{2}{5}$ of another fraction circle is shaded. We can write this fraction as $1\frac{2}{5}$.

A fraction with a numerator that is greater than the denominator is often called an improper fraction. A fraction that has a whole number and a fraction is often called a mixed number. It is important to remember that the amount is the same whether the fraction is written as an improper fraction or a mixed number.

Name the fraction represented by the shaded sections in two ways.

1. 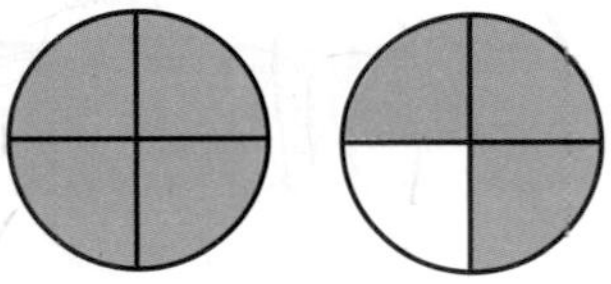

2. 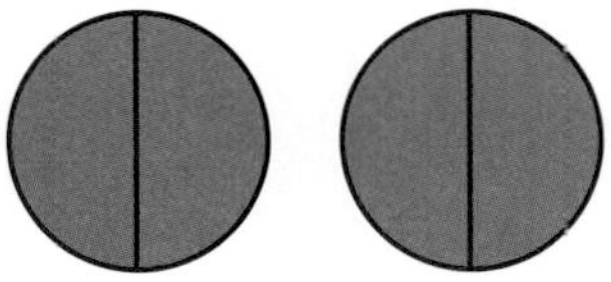

3. 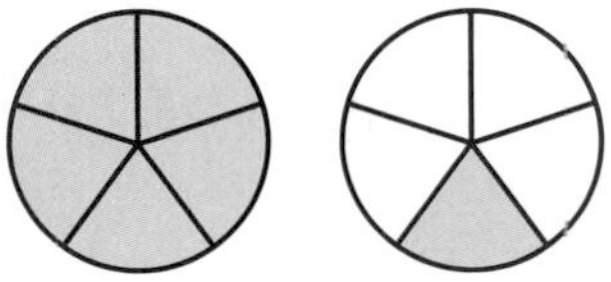

4. 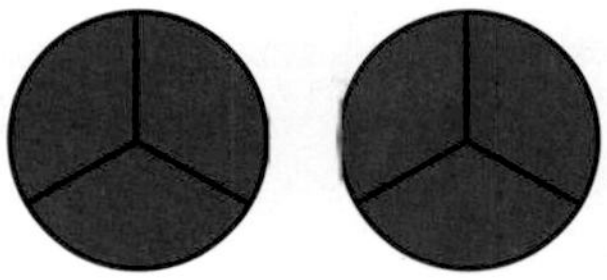

5. 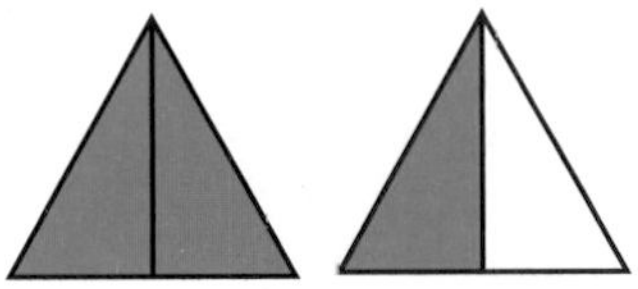

6. 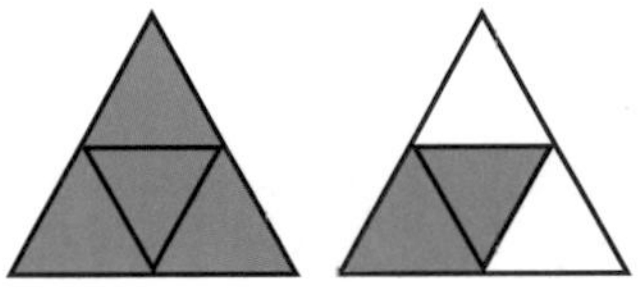

Writing + Math Journal

Which is greater, $2\frac{1}{2}$ or $3\frac{1}{3}$? Explain.

LESSON 8.9

Comparing Fractions Greater Than a Whole

Key Ideas

Even though fractions greater than a whole may contain a whole number or a whole number and a fraction, compare them as you would any other type of number.

Look at the following fractions. Determine which fraction is larger.

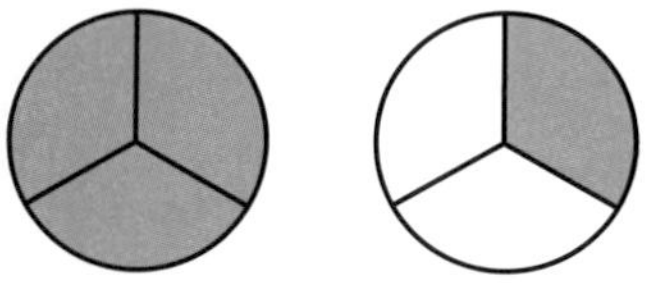

The fraction represented here is $1\frac{1}{3}$, read *one and one-third.*

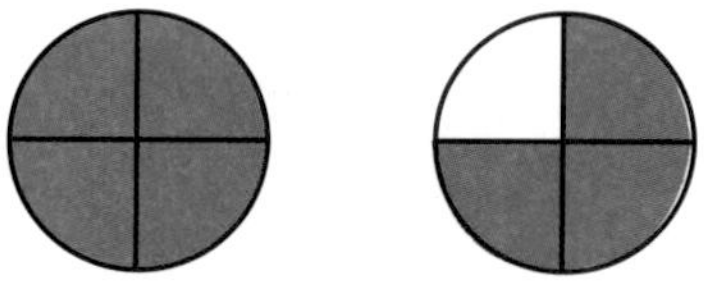

The fraction represented here is $1\frac{3}{4}$, read *one and three-fourths.*

We can determine by looking at the fraction circles that $1\frac{3}{4}$ is the larger fraction. This mathematical statement can be written as $1\frac{3}{4} > 1\frac{1}{3}$, read *one and three-fourths is greater than one and one-third*, or $1\frac{1}{3} < 1\frac{3}{4}$, read *one and one-third is less than one and three-fourths.*

Copy and replace the ■ with $<$, $>$, or $=$ to make a true statement. The first one has been done for you.

1. $5 < 5\frac{2}{3}$. This is read *5 is less than five and two-thirds.*
2. $\frac{4}{5}$ ■ $\frac{3}{4}$
3. $2\frac{4}{5}$ ■ $2\frac{3}{4}$
4. $6\frac{2}{5}$ ■ $6\frac{3}{4}$

eTextbook This lesson is available in the ***eTextbook.***

Copy and replace the ■ with $<$, $>$, or $=$ to make a true statement. Use fraction circles, fraction tiles, or drawings if needed.

5. $4\frac{1}{2}$ ■ $3\frac{1}{3}$
6. $7\frac{2}{3}$ ■ $7\frac{4}{6}$
7. $5\frac{4}{5}$ ■ $5\frac{3}{4}$
8. $\frac{2}{3}$ ■ $\frac{3}{4}$
9. $1\frac{1}{2}$ ■ $1\frac{2}{4}$
10. $7\frac{2}{3}$ ■ $7\frac{3}{4}$
11. $5\frac{4}{5}$ ■ $6\frac{3}{4}$
12. $5\frac{2}{3}$ ■ $5\frac{3}{4}$
13. $\frac{3}{5}$ ■ $1\frac{1}{5}$
14. $7\frac{2}{3}$ ■ $6\frac{3}{4}$
15. $5\frac{4}{5}$ ■ $4\frac{3}{4}$
16. $3\frac{1}{5}$ ■ $2\frac{3}{5}$

Solve.

17. Margaret has 3 boxes of green pens and $\frac{3}{4}$ of a box of red pens. How many boxes of pens does she have?
18. Natasha has 3 boxes of green pens and $\frac{1}{2}$ box of red pens. How many boxes of pens does she have?
19. Which girl has more pens?
20. Write one mathematical statement comparing the fractions $3\frac{1}{4}$ and $2\frac{1}{2}$.

Writing + Math Journal

Explain how you determine which fraction is greater when comparing two or more fractions.

LESSON 8.10

Tenths and Hundredths

Key Ideas

This circle is divided into 100 equal parts.

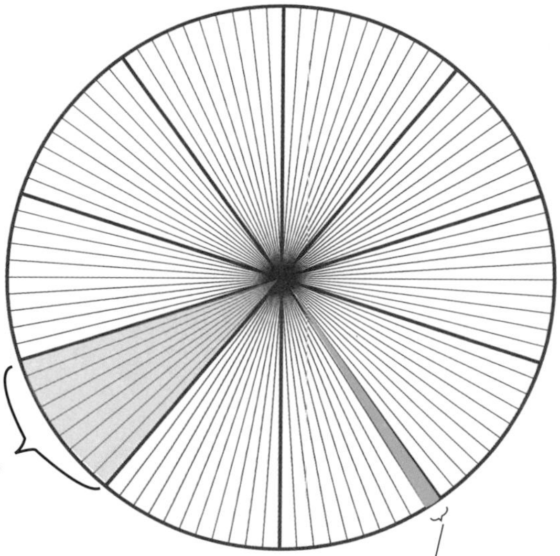

This part is one-tenth $\left(\frac{1}{10}\right)$ of the circle.

This part is one-hundredth $\left(\frac{1}{100}\right)$ of the circle.

Use the circle graph to help answer the following questions.

1. How many $\frac{1}{100}$ sections are there in this graph?
2. How many $\frac{1}{10}$ sections are there in this graph?
3. In $\frac{1}{10}$ of the circle, how many $\frac{1}{100}$ sections are there?
4. In $\frac{3}{10}$ of the circle, how many $\frac{1}{100}$ sections are there?
5. In $\frac{5}{10}$ of the circle, how many $\frac{1}{100}$ sections are there?
6. What is another fraction to represent $\frac{5}{10}$ of the circle?

eTextbook This lesson is available in the ***eTextbook.***

Fill in the table.

Tenths		Hundredths	Tenths		Hundredths
$\frac{1}{10}$	=	$\frac{10}{100}$	$\frac{6}{10}$	=	■
$\frac{2}{10}$	=	$\frac{20}{100}$	■	=	$\frac{70}{100}$
$\frac{3}{10}$	=	■	■	=	$\frac{80}{100}$
$\frac{4}{10}$	=	■	$\frac{9}{10}$	=	■
■	=	$\frac{50}{100}$	■	=	$\frac{100}{100}$ or ■ whole

Solve.

7. What is $\frac{1}{10}$ of 100?
8. What is $\frac{1}{10}$ of 200?
9. What is $\frac{1}{10}$ of 300?
10. What is $\frac{2}{10}$ of 100?
11. What is $\frac{2}{10}$ of 200?
12. What is $\frac{2}{10}$ of 300?
13. What is $\frac{3}{10}$ of 100?
14. What is $\frac{5}{10}$ of 200?
15. What is $\frac{10}{10}$ of 300?

Writing + Math Journal

Describe how to find $\frac{1}{10}$ of 500.

LESSON 8.11

Percents and Hundredths

Key Ideas

A percent is a fraction with 100 as the denominator.

The term 1% is read *one percent.*

The term 1% can be written as the fraction $\frac{1}{100}$. The fraction $\frac{1}{100}$ is read *one one-hundredth.*

Write the fraction for the following percents.
Remember, a percent is a fraction with a denominator of 100.

1. 46%
2. 6%
3. 21%
4. 100%
5. 89%
6. 0%

Write the percent for the following fractions.

7. $\frac{87}{100}$
8. $\frac{19}{100}$
9. $\frac{33}{100}$
10. $\frac{2}{100}$
11. $\frac{100}{100}$
12. $\frac{99}{100}$

Determine which of the following benchmark percents, 0%, 25%, 50%, 75%, or 100%, would be closest to the given fraction.

13. $\frac{5}{100}$
14. $\frac{98}{100}$
15. $\frac{76}{100}$
16. $\frac{60}{100}$
17. $\frac{21}{100}$
18. $\frac{75}{100}$

eTextbook This lesson is available in the ***eTextbook.***

Use the graph to answer the following questions. Remember, a percent is a fraction with a denominator of 100.

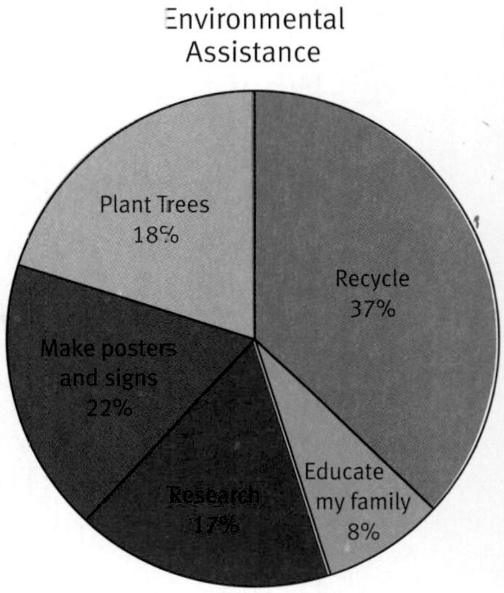

19 What fraction is each section of this circle graph?

a. Recycle

b. Make my family more aware

c. Research

d. Make posters and signs

e. Plant trees

20 What was the most popular way to help the environment? What was the least popular way?

21 **Extended Response** If there were 5,829 students in grades K–5 surveyed in all, would the number who chose recycling be more or less than 5,000? Explain.

22 **Extended Response** Of the following percents, 0%, 25%, 50%, or 100%, which would you choose to describe about how many students voted for *make posters, research,* or *make* family more aware? Explain.

Use the graph to answer the following questions.

23 What fraction is each section of this circle graph?

a. Preprimary School

b. Elementary or High School

c. College or Graduate School

d. Not in School

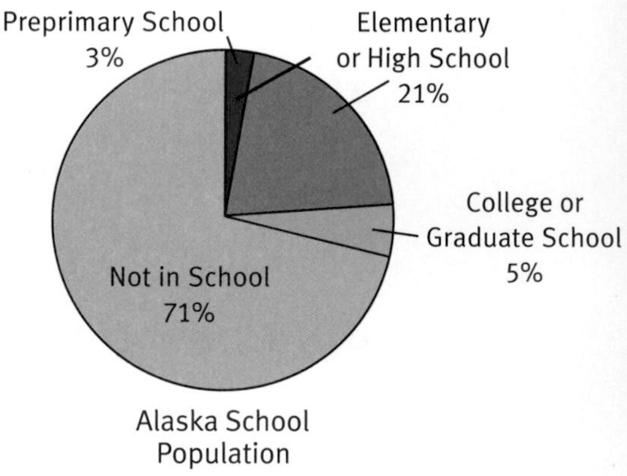

24 **Extended Response** This is a graph of the population of Alaska during the 2000 Census. There were 626,932 residents in Alaska. Why do you think 71% of the residents are not enrolled in school?

25 Of the three sections representing Alaskan residents *in school* for the 2000 Census (ages 3 and up), which group had the greatest number of students?

26 **Extended Response** If there were 185,760 students enrolled in school in Alaska during the 2000 Census, would the number who were in the *College or Graduate School* section be more or less than 100,000? Explain.

27 **Extended Response** In 2000, the percent of Alaskans in elementary or high school was closest to which of these: 0%, 25%, 50%, 75%, or 100%?

28 **Extended Response** In 2000, the percent of Alaskans not in school was closest to which of these: 0%, 25%, 50%, 75%, 100%?

Use the graph to answer the following questions.

29 What fraction is each section of this circle graph?

a. Mom

b. Dad

c. Sibling

d. Grandparent

e. Other

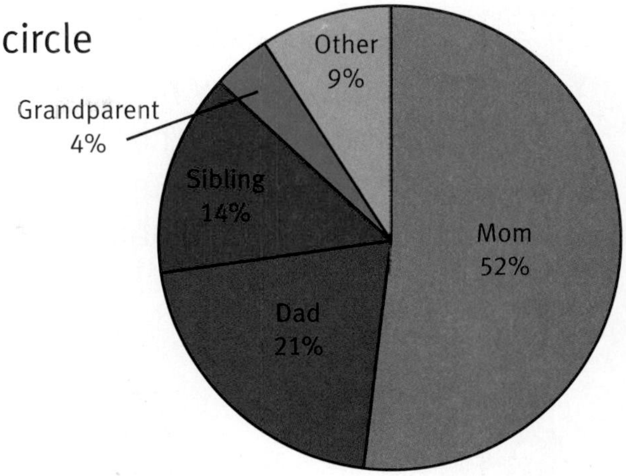

Time Spent with Family Member

30 In this survey, who is the family member the students spend the most amount of time with?

31 In this survey, who is the family member the students spend the least amount of time with?

32 **Extended Response** If there were 428 students surveyed, would the number who chose *Other* be more or less than 500? Explain how you know.

33 **Extended Response** Of the following percents, 0%, 25%, 50%, 75%, or 100%, which would you choose to describe about how many students chose *Sibling* as the family member they spend the most time with? Explain.

34 **Extended Response** Of the following percents, 0%, 25%, 50%, 75%, or 100%, which would you choose to describe about how many students chose *Mom* or *Dad* as the family member they spend the most time with? Explain.

Writing + Math Journal

Write one true statement and one false statement about the graph above.

Exploring Problem Solving

Your advertising agency has created four new T-shirt colors for a company that sells clothing on the Internet. The formulas for the four colors got mixed up. Your job is to figure out which formula goes with which shirt color. You also get to give each color a special name.

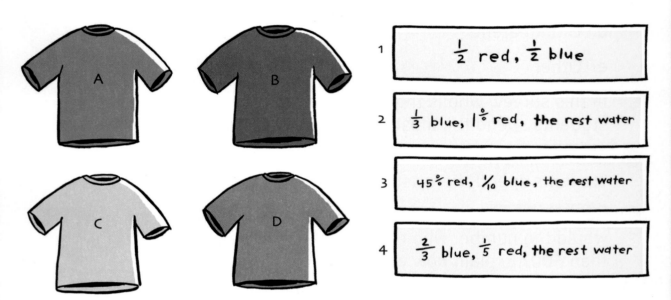

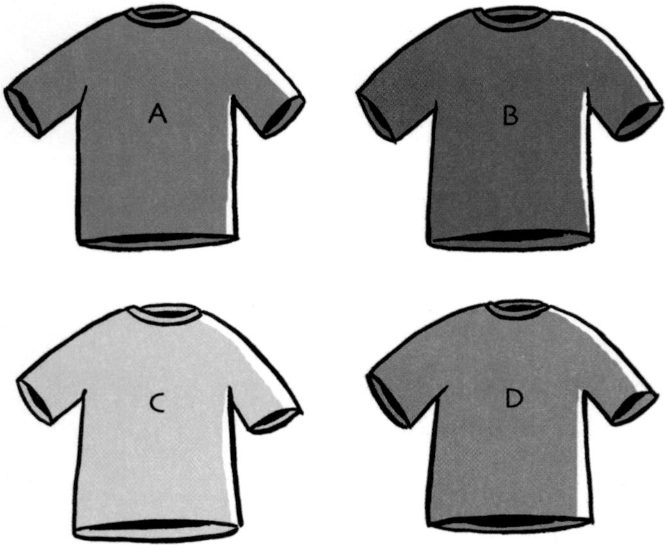

1 $\frac{1}{2}$ red, $\frac{1}{2}$ blue

2 $\frac{1}{3}$ blue, 1% red, the rest water

3 45% red, $\frac{1}{10}$ blue, the rest water

4 $\frac{2}{3}$ blue, $\frac{1}{5}$ red, the rest water

Answer these questions to help match up the formulas and the shirts.

1. Which formula has the most red? How do you know?
2. Which formula has the most blue? How do you know?
3. Which formula has the most water? How do you know?
4. Which formula goes with each shirt?
5. How can you prove that you matched each formula with the correct color?
6. Make up a name for each color.

Cumulative Review

Reading a Thermometer Lesson 3.2

Use the Fahrenheit scale on the thermometers shown to answer the questions.

1. What temperature is it? Is it comfortable, cold, or hot?

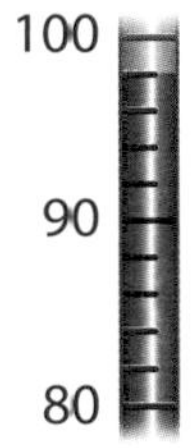

2. What temperature is it? Is it comfortable, cold, or hot?

Multiplying by 2, 1, and 0 Lesson 5.1

Solve each problem.

3. Each student is making 2 signs for the craft fair. If there are 24 students, how many signs will there be altogether?

4. Adina and her sister are making 6 loaves of banana bread. Each loaf requires 2 bananas. How many bananas do they need?

Multiplying by 10, 100, and 1,000 Lesson 7.1

Multiply.

5. $1{,}000 \times 10 = \square$
6. $60 \times 10 = \square$
7. $10 \times 110 = \square$
8. $100 \times 83 = \square$
9. $240 \times 1{,}000 = \square$
10. $1{,}000 \times 16 = \square$
11. $1{,}000 \times 43 = \square$
12. $100 \times 2 = \square$

Cumulative Review

Adding with Three or More Addends Lesson 2.10

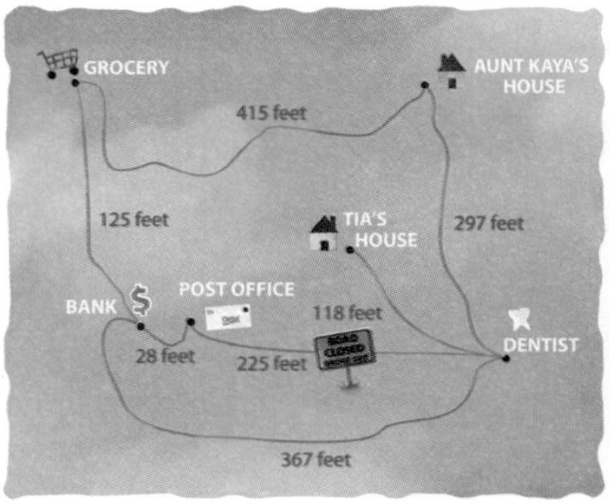

Add. Use shortcuts if you can.

13. Tia had two errands on Monday. She had to go to the grocery store and to her Aunt Kaya's house. How far did she travel to get to the store?

14. When she stops by her aunt's house, her aunt asks her to drop off a check at the bank. How many feet must she go to get to the bank from her Aunt Kaya's house?

15. On Tuesday, Tia made two stops. First, she stopped at the dentist. The dentist asked Tia to get a special toothpaste at the grocery store. Tia went to the grocery store and then went home. If she took the shortest route, how many feet did Tia travel altogether on Tuesday?

16. On Wednesday, Tia went to the post office. When the bridge was not under construction, the distance to the post office was only 343 feet. How many feet is it now?

17. **Extended Response** Which one-way route is a total distance of 610 feet? Explain how you found your answer.

Inverse Functions (Reversing the Arrow) Lesson 6.4

Write the inverse operation.

18. $+20$
19. $+3$
20. $\times 6$
21. $\div 9$
22. $\div 30$
23. $+100$
24. $+4$
25. $\div 14$

CHAPTER 8 Key Ideas Review

In this chapter you learned about fractions.

You learned about properties of fractions.

You learned how to compute with fractions.

Copy the following. Shade the fractional amounts.

1. $\frac{2}{5}$

2. $\frac{1}{2}$

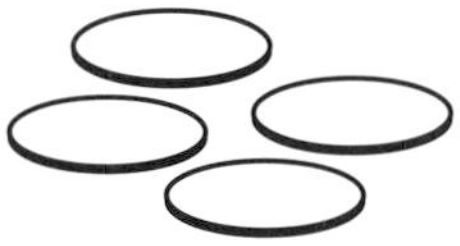

3. $\frac{6}{10}$

4. $\frac{2}{5}$

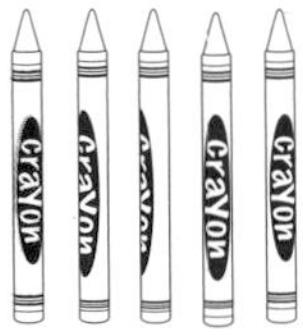

Add or subtract.

5. $\frac{4}{8} + \frac{1}{8} = \square$

6. $\frac{4}{6} - \frac{3}{6} = \square$

Answer true or false.

7. $\frac{1}{2}$ is greater than $\frac{3}{4}$.

8. $\frac{5}{6}$ is less than $\frac{6}{6}$.

Extended Response **Provide** a detailed answer for the following exercises.

9. Mary bought a pack of 16 pens and gave $\frac{1}{4}$ of them away.

   a. How many pens does she have now?

   b. Then she gave $\frac{1}{2}$ of her leftover pens away. How many pens does she have left?

10. Charles added the following:

    $\frac{4}{8} + \frac{2}{8} = \frac{3}{4}$

    Explain how you know Charles is correct.

Chapter Review

Lesson 8.1 **Divide** the figures.

1

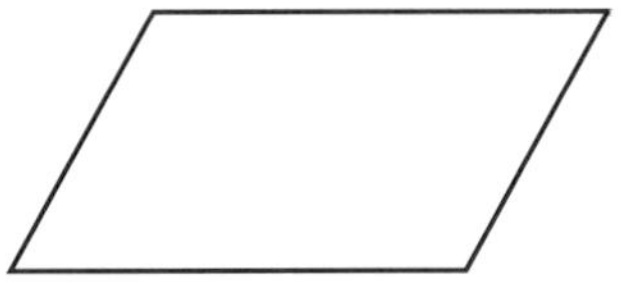

Copy the figure, and shade in about two-thirds of the figure.

2

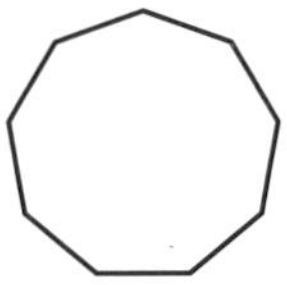

Copy the figure, and shade in half of the figure.

Lesson 8.4 **Determine** the fractions of time.

3

a. How many minutes is it until 4:00?
b. What fraction of an hour is left until 4:00?

4

a. What time is it?
b. What fraction of an hour has passed since 5:00?

Lesson 8.5 **State** true or false.

5 $\frac{1}{2} = \frac{5}{8}$ $\square$

6 $\frac{2}{10} = \frac{1}{5}$ $\square$

Lesson 8.6 **Fill** in the blank using $<$, $=$, or $>$.

7 $\frac{3}{3}$ $\square$ $\frac{1}{2}$

8 $\frac{6}{18}$ $\square$ $\frac{1}{2}$

Lesson 8.7

9 **Extended Response** Tricia, Patty, Mike, and Josh want to split a pizza equally among themselves.

Draw a diagram showing how they would split the pizza.

Lesson 8.10

Fill in the blank with *tenths* or *hundreddths*.

10 80¢ = 8 ▢ of a dollar

11 1¢ = one ▢ of a dollar

12 40¢ = 4 ▢ of a dollar

13 95¢ = 9 ▢ and 5 ▢ of a dollar

Lesson 8.11

Answer the questions.

14 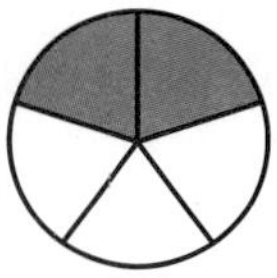

a. If 40% of this circle is shaded, what percent is *not* shaded?

b. What fraction of the circle is shaded?

CHAPTER 8

Practice Test

What fraction of each picture is shaded?

1. 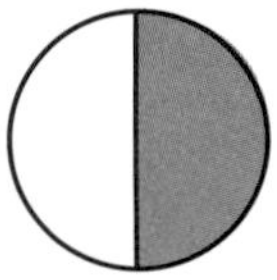

2. 

3. 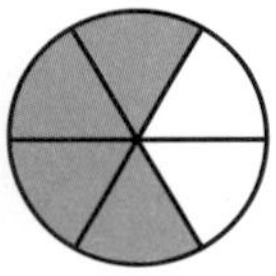

4. Color in the empty grid to show $\frac{4}{6}$.

Answer.

5. What fraction do the pictures represent?

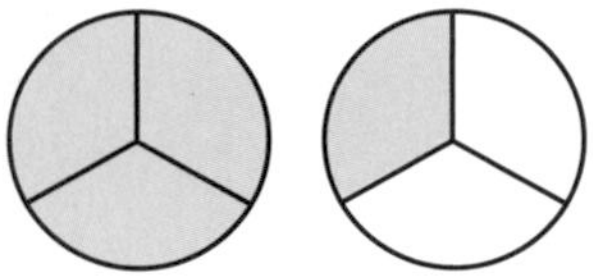

6. What fraction does the picture represent?

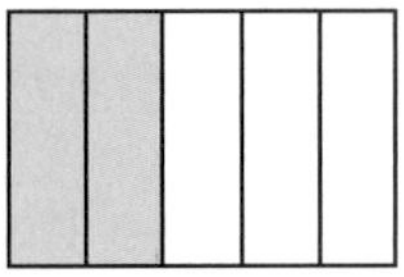

7. The following ruler has been divided into twelfths. What fraction of the ruler is the pencil?

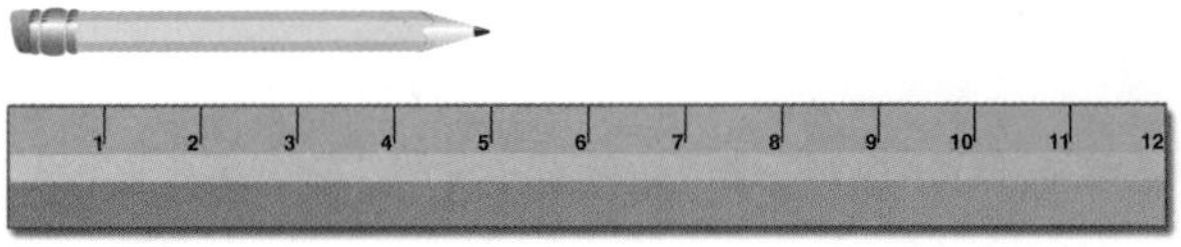

8. The following ruler has been divided into tenths. What fraction of the ruler is the pencil?

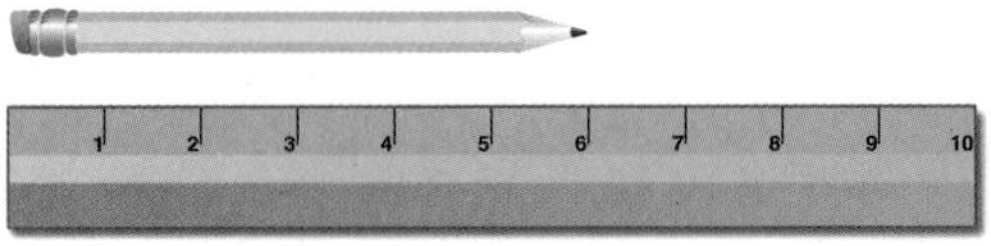

Choose the correct answer.

9. What is $\frac{1}{3}$ of 30?

Ⓐ 10 Ⓑ 9

Ⓒ 8 Ⓓ 5

10. What is $\frac{2}{4}$ of 16?

Ⓐ 2 Ⓑ 4

Ⓒ 8 Ⓓ 12

11. How many minutes is $\frac{2}{4}$ of an hour?

Ⓐ 15 Ⓑ 12

Ⓒ 30 Ⓓ 35

12. How many minutes is $\frac{1}{5}$ of an hour?

Ⓐ 10 Ⓑ 12

Ⓒ 20 Ⓓ 30

13. Which is bigger: $\frac{1}{4}$ of the pizza or $\frac{3}{8}$ of the pizza?

Ⓐ They are the same.

Ⓑ $\frac{3}{8}$

Ⓒ $\frac{1}{4}$

Ⓓ $\frac{1}{8}$

14. Which is bigger: $\frac{1}{2}$ of the pizza or $\frac{4}{8}$ of the pizza?

Ⓐ They are the same.

Ⓑ $\frac{4}{8}$

Ⓒ $\frac{1}{2}$

Ⓓ $\frac{1}{8}$

Which sign makes each statement true?

15. $2\frac{2}{4}$ ▇ $2\frac{1}{2}$

Ⓐ $=$

Ⓑ $>$

Ⓒ $<$

16. $4\frac{2}{3}$ ▇ $4\frac{1}{5}$

Ⓐ $=$

Ⓑ $<$

Ⓒ $>$

CHAPTER 8 Practice Test

Solve.

17. $\frac{3}{4} - \frac{2}{4} = $ ■

Ⓐ $\frac{6}{8}$ Ⓑ $\frac{5}{8}$

Ⓒ $\frac{1}{4}$ Ⓓ $\frac{1}{8}$

18. $\frac{5}{8} + \frac{2}{8} = $ ■

Ⓐ $\frac{7}{8}$ Ⓑ $\frac{6}{8}$

Ⓒ $\frac{3}{8}$ Ⓓ $\frac{2}{8}$

19. $\frac{2}{3} + \frac{1}{3} = $ ■

Ⓐ $\frac{1}{3}$ Ⓑ $\frac{2}{3}$

Ⓒ $\frac{3}{3}$ Ⓓ $\frac{4}{3}$

20. Which mixed number is equal to $\frac{13}{5}$?

Ⓐ $1\frac{1}{5}$ Ⓑ $1\frac{3}{5}$

Ⓒ $2\frac{2}{5}$ Ⓓ $2\frac{3}{5}$

21. What is the value of the 4 in 83,142?

Ⓐ 4 ten thousands

Ⓑ 4 thousands

Ⓒ 4 hundreds

Ⓓ 4 tens

22. Find the sum. 299 + 173 = ■

Ⓐ 492 Ⓑ 472

Ⓒ 461 Ⓓ 453

23. Find the difference.
912 − 347 = ■

Ⓐ 565 Ⓑ 574

Ⓒ 635 Ⓓ 646

24. Find the product of 7 × 8.

Ⓐ 15 Ⓑ 32

Ⓒ 49 Ⓓ 56

25. Harrison has 7 dimes in his pocket. How much money does he have?

Ⓐ 70¢ Ⓑ 75¢

Ⓒ 80¢ Ⓓ 90¢

26. Find the quotient of 81 ÷ 9.

Ⓐ 12 Ⓑ 11

Ⓒ 9 Ⓓ 8

27. Find the inverse function of −3.

Ⓐ +3 Ⓑ −3

Ⓒ ÷3 Ⓓ ×3

28. 2 + 8 + 5 + 7 = ■

Ⓐ 22 Ⓑ 30

Ⓒ 28 Ⓓ 19

Use the graph to answer the following questions.

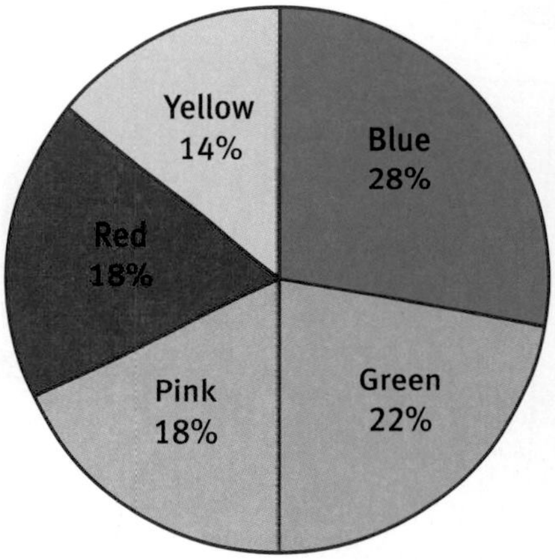

Favorite Colors

29. Ari surveyed his classmates about their favorite colors. He made a circle graph to show the results of his survey.

a. What color did the most of Ari's classmates choose as their favorite? What percent of his classmates chose it?

b. What color did the fewest of Ari's classmates choose as their favorite? What percent of his classmates chose it?

c. Which two colors were equally popular among Ari's classmates? What percent of his classmates chose them?

d. Of the following benchmark percents, 0%, 5%, 25%, 50%, 75%, or 100%, which percent benchmark is closest to how many of Ari's classmates chose green as their favorite color?

30. Ryan and his friends are making wall hangings out of cloth and felt. A small wall hanging uses $\frac{3}{4}$ yard of black felt and $\frac{1}{4}$ yard each of red, blue, and green felt. A large wall hanging uses $1\frac{1}{4}$ yards of black felt and $\frac{1}{2}$ yard each of red, blue, and green felt.

a. How much felt does a small wall hanging use altogether? Explain.

b. How much felt does a large wall hanging use altogether? Explain.

c. Ryan wants to make a small wall hanging and a large wall hanging. How much felt will he need altogether?

Thinking Story

Bargains Galore

Portia and Ferdie's cousin Trixie had a summer job in a store. One day Willy and his mother went to the store.

"Hi, Willy!" said Cousin Trixie when they walked in the door. "You've come to the perfect store. I have bargains galore."

"I don't know what that means," said Willy.

"It's what our advertising manager told me to say. I don't know what it means either," said Cousin Trixie. "But I know you'll save money by shopping in my store."

"I'm getting more confused," said Willy. "How can I save money by spending it?"

What does it mean when people say that you'll save money by shopping somewhere?

"What I mean," said Trixie, "is that you'll get more for your money if you buy things from me than if you buy them someplace else. For instance, I have a special on big packs of chewing gum. They usually cost 30¢ apiece, but today you can buy 3 packs for a dollar."

Will Willy save money if he buys 3 packs of gum?

Why or why not?

"I think I'll buy 3 packs at the regular price," said Willy. "Then I'll save 10¢."

Will Willy really save 10¢?

Willy's mother was standing nearby. She whispered to Willy, "You can buy 3 packs of chewing gum in any store for 90¢, so you're not saving any money."

"Thanks," said Willy. "Then I guess I won't buy the gum. I want to save money."

"I'll tell you what I'll do," said Trixie. "If you buy 3 packs of gum for a dollar, I'll throw in a 10¢ package of mints free. You can't turn down a bargain like that!"

Is that a real bargain?

Why or why not?

As Willy left the store with his 3 packs of gum and the mints, he began thinking out loud. "I didn't really save money. I got 3 packs of gum worth 30¢ each and a 10¢ package of mints for a dollar. That's just what they usually cost. Besides, I don't like mints very much, and I don't need all this gum."

Trixie's next customer was Manolita. "I need a pound of salted peanuts," she said. "We're having a party."

"You're in luck," said Cousin Trixie. "I have a special bargain today. Usually I sell a pound bag of peanuts for $2, but today peanuts are half off."

"Half off!" said Manolita. "That's great. My dad will be happy when he finds out I've saved him money."

Cousin Trixie opened a pound bag of peanuts and poured half of them out. "That will be $2," she said, handing the half-empty bag to Manolita.

What did Trixie do wrong?

"Didn't you take half off the wrong thing?" asked Manolita. "You should charge me half as much money, not give me half as many peanuts."

"Just to make you happy, I'll take half off the price too," Trixie said. "That will be $1 for half a pound of peanuts. You can't say that doesn't save you money. You've saved a whole dollar."

Does that really save Manolita money?

Why or why not?

"It sounds as if I'm saving money," said Manolita, "but I'm not sure. Now I have to take the dollar I saved and buy another half pound of peanuts with it. So I'm still spending $2 and getting only a pound of peanuts. I don't think my dad will be very impressed."

Later that afternoon, Mr. Eng went to Trixie's store to buy a purple lamp for his favorite purple room. "You came to the right store," said Cousin Trixie. "I have bargains galore on lamps. All the lamps are a dollar less than the regular price."

"Very good," said Mr. Eng, "but I can't find any purple lamps."

"In that case, you're luckier yet," said Trixie. "I also have a bargain on purple paint. A $3 spray can of paint will cost you only $2. You're really saving money today, Mr. Eng. You're saving money on the lamp and on the paint too."

How much is Mr. Eng saving on the lamp?

How much money does he have to spend for the paint?

Is he really saving money?

Why or why not?

When Mr. Eng got back home, he told his wife about his lucky bargain. "But," said Ms. Eng, "you saved a dollar on the lamp and had to spend $2 for paint. So the lamp is costing a dollar more than the regular price. What kind of bargain is that?"

"It's a Trixie-type bargain," said Mr. Eng. "That means you spend more than you should to get more than you need."

The End

AISLE D
LAMPS
$54
$34
$67
$85
MILK
PURPLE
NET WT 12oz.

CHAPTER 9

Measurement

In This Chapter You Will Learn

- how to use standard units of metric length, weight, and capacity.
- how to estimate and measure lengths to the nearest inch, foot, or yard.
- how to calculate elapsed time.

Problem Solving

You are helping a youth organization build a new campground. You are in charge of planning a brick border along the path from the swimming pool to the ropes. How will you decide the number of bricks you need?

Pretend your classroom is as long as the path and a crayon is as long as a brick.

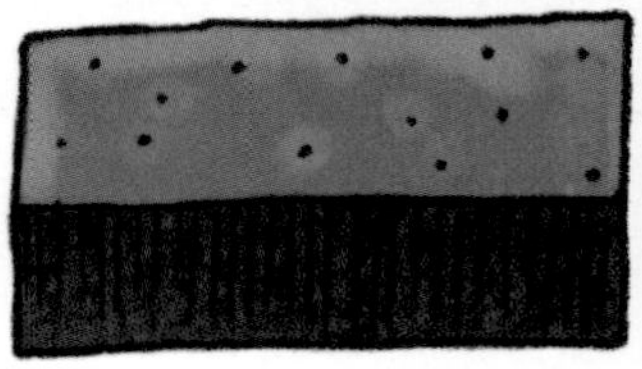

Work with your group to solve these problems. You may make things to help you measure.

1. How many bricks do you need? How did you find out?
2. How many bricks would you need to go all the way around your classroom?

LESSON 9.1

Metric Length

Key Ideas

The meter is the basic unit of length in the metric system. The height from the floor to the doorknob of your classroom door is probably about 1 meter.

We often measure shorter lengths using centimeters. There are 100 centimeters in 1 meter. Each edge of your ***Number Cube*** is about 2 centimeters long.

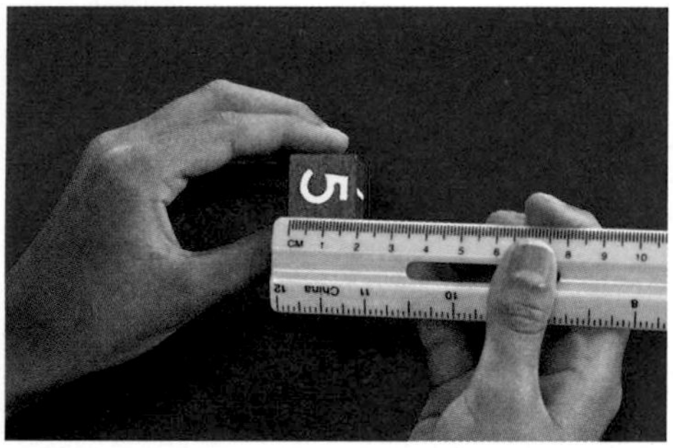

Very short lengths are often measured in millimeters. There are 1,000 millimeters in 1 meter. A nickel is about 2 millimeters thick.

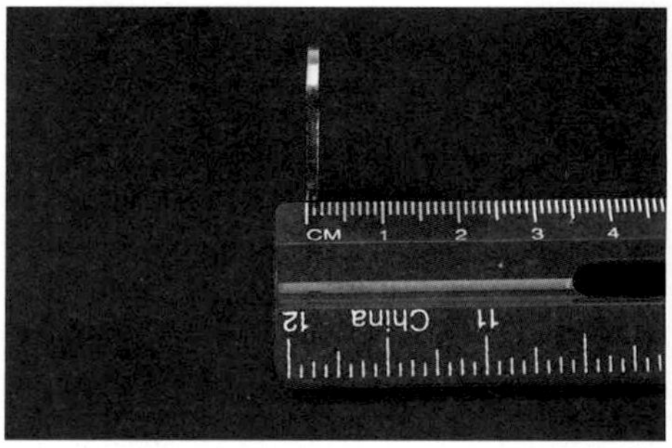

Longer distances are often measured in kilometers. There are 1,000 meters in 1 kilometer.

Which unit (millimeters, centimeters, meters, or kilometers) would you use to measure these lengths or distances?

1. the length of a large pool
2. the distance from where you live to the next town or city
3. the length of your index finger
4. the length of a sharp pencil point
5. the wingspan of a monarch butterfly

Grady is 125 centimeters tall. The apple he is about to pick is 160 centimeters high.

Discuss and solve these problems.

6 **Extended Response** Can Grady pick the apple without standing on something to make him taller? Explain.

7 **Extended Response** What if the apple were 200 centimeters high? Would Grady be able to reach it without standing on something? Explain.

8 **Extended Response** If he jumped, could Grady reach the apple that is 200 centimeters high? Explain.

Do this activity. Work in groups of two or three.

- Measure and record your height in centimeters.
- Estimate how high you can reach. Record your estimate.
- Reach as high as you can, and measure the height. Record that measurement.
- Estimate how high you can reach if you jump. Record your estimate.
- Measure how high you can reach if you jump. Record that measurement.

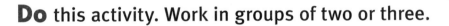

Discuss the following questions with your group.

- Were your estimates accurate? Why or why not?
- How much higher will you be able to reach next year? In five years? In twenty years? Explain.

LESSON 9.2 Customary Length

Key Ideas

The inch, foot, and yard are customary units of length.

There are 12 inches in 1 foot.

12 in. = 1 ft

There are 3 feet in 1 yard.

There are 36 inches in 1 yard.

There are 1,760 yards in 1 mile.

Answer the following questions.

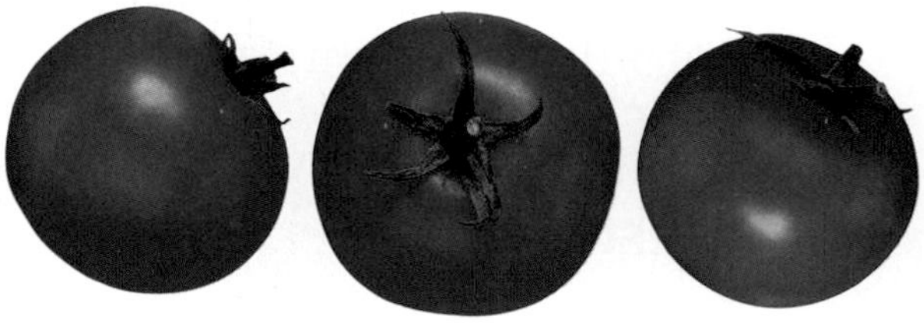

1. Edward was able to jump about 36 inches. How many feet is that?
2. David's desk is 6 feet long. How many yards is that?
3. Shawn's garden is about 3 yards long. How many feet is that?
4. Darlene wants to buy fencing for her tomato garden. The garden is shaped like a rectangle and is 3 yards wide and 6 yards long. How many yards of fencing does she need?
5. **Extended Response** The type of fence Darlene wants to buy is packaged in 6-foot rolls. How many rolls must she buy? Explain.

eTextbook This lesson is available in the ***eTextbook.***

REAL WORLD

Shea Stadium is located in Flushing, New York. It is the home ballpark of the New York Mets.

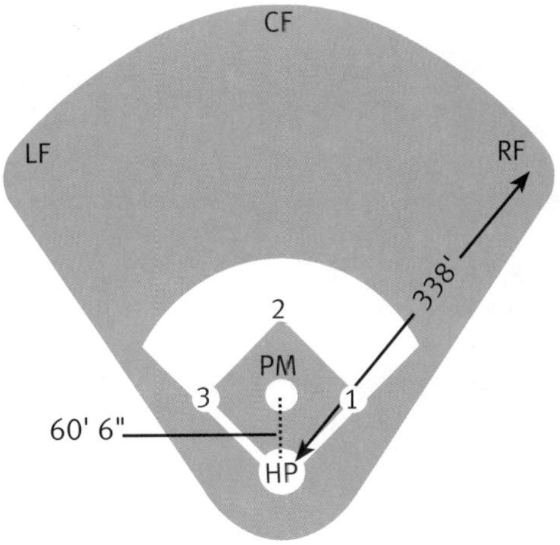

Study **the map of Shea Stadium. Then make your best estimates of the distances shown on the table. Check your estimates by researching the distances in an almanac or on the Internet.**

Distance	Estimate	Actual
Pitcher's mound to home plate		60 feet, 6 inches
Home plate to right field post		338 feet
First base to second base		6
Second base to third base		7
First base to third base		8
Home plate to farthest point in center field		9

10 About how many yards is it from first base to second base?

11 **Extended Response** How many yards is it from home plate to the farthest point in center field? Tell how you know.

12 How many inches is it from first base to second base? How do you know?

13 If you could draw lines from home plate to first base to second base to third base and back to home plate, what shape would you make?

14 About how far does a player run if he or she hits a home run?

LESSON 9.3

Metric Weight

Key Ideas

The gram and the kilogram are metric units of weight.

There are 1,000 grams in 1 kilogram.

1,000 g = 1 kg

Convert each measure from kilograms to grams or from grams to kilograms. Write the new measure.

1. ■ g = 5 kg
2. ■ g = 2 kg
3. 1 kg = ■ g
4. 4 kg = ■ g
5. 6 kg = ■ g
6. ■ g = 3 kg
7. ■ g = 10 kg
8. 11 kg = ■ g

Write whether you would use grams or kilograms to report the weight of each of the following.

9. a slice of bread
10. an adult cat
11. a dime
12. a bag of groceries

Copy and complete the table.

Number of Nickels	Weight (grams)	Number of Dollars
20	about 100	1
100	13	5
1,000	14	50
2,000	15	100
10,000	16	500
100,000	17	5,000

Write the weight in kilograms.

18. 1,000 nickels = about ___ kilograms
19. 2,000 nickels = about ___ kilograms
20. 3,000 nickels = about ___ kilograms
21. 10,000 nickels = about ___ kilograms
22. 100,000 nickels = about ___ kilograms
23. 1000,000 nickels = about ___ kilograms
24. **Extended Response** Because 1 nickel weighs about 5 grams, do you think 1 dime weighs about 10 grams? Why or why not?

Writing + Math **Journal**

One penny weighs about $2\frac{1}{2}$ grams. If most third-grade students can carry about 2,000 nickels (10 kilograms), about how many pennies do you think you can carry? Explain your answer. How much money is that?

LESSON 9.4 Customary Weight

Key Ideas

The ounce and the pound are customary units of weight.

There are 16 ounces in 1 pound.

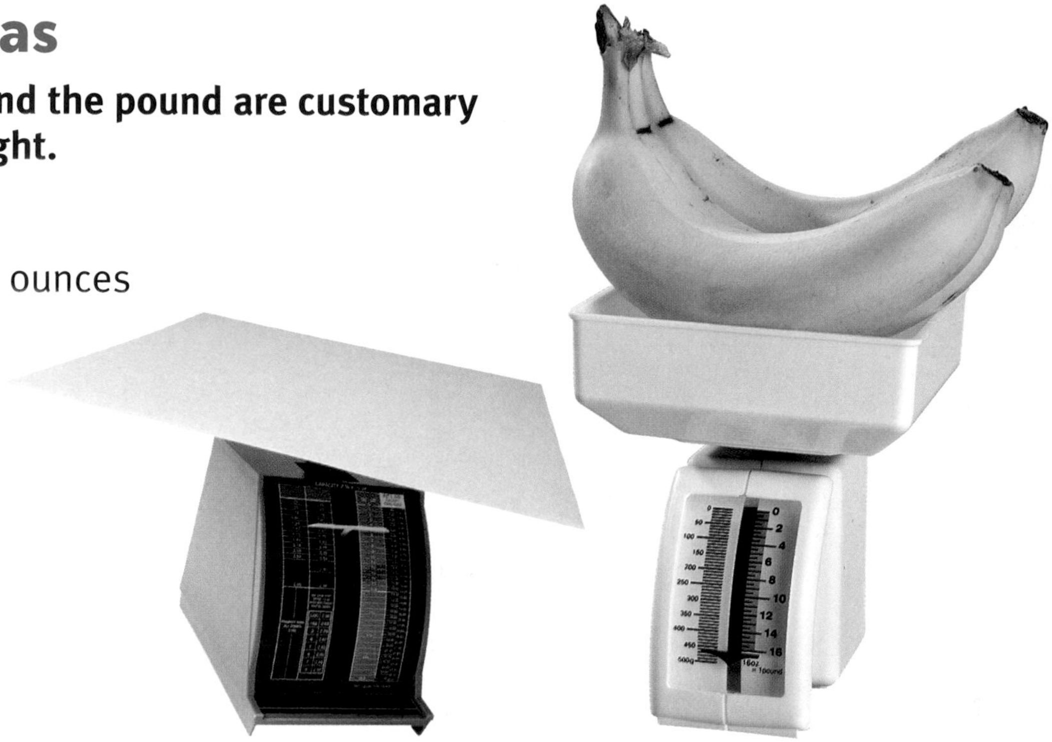

Convert each measure from pounds to ounces or from ounces to pounds. Write the new measure.

1. 2 lb = ☐ oz
2. 10 lb = ☐ oz
3. 8 oz = ☐ lb
4. 24 oz = ☐ lb
5. 4 lb = ☐ oz
6. 8 lb = ☐ oz
7. 100 lb = ☐ oz
8. 50 lb = ☐ oz

Write whether you would use ounces or pounds to report the weight of each of the following.

9. a bag of flour
10. a paper clip
11. an adult dog
12. a toothbrush

Choose the number that makes the most sense.

13  weighs about ___ pounds

a. 10 **b.** 100 **c.** 1,000

14  weighs about ___ pounds

a. 2 **b.** 25 **c.** 250

15 

weighs about ___ ounces

a. 32 **b.** 16 **c.** 1

16  weighs about ___ ounces

a. 25 **b.** 250 **c.** 2,500

17  weighs about ___ pounds

a. 400 **b.** 40 **c.** 4

18  weighs about ___ ounces

a. 10 **b.** 100 **c.** 1,000

The owners of Cherry Lake are going to build a campground. They plan to put campsites around three sides of the lake. Each campsite will be a square 10 meters wide. How many campsites will fit?

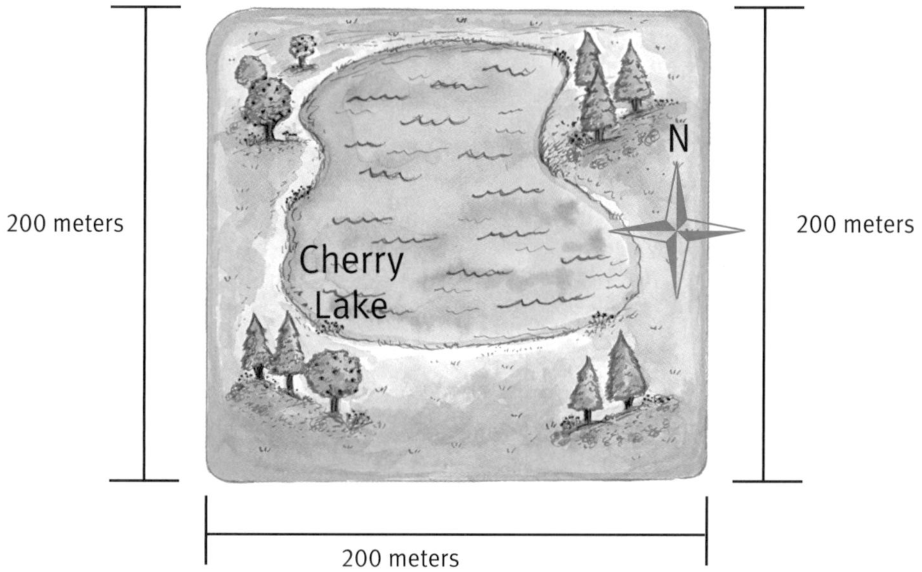

Gloria made a diagram to solve the problem

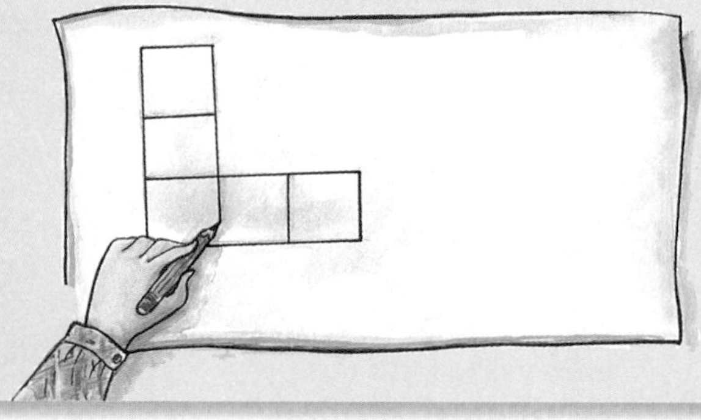

Think about Gloria's strategy. Answer the following questions.

1. What do the squares in Gloria's diagram represent?
2. How could Gloria use her diagram to help solve the problem?
3. How could Gloria solve the problem without drawing every campsite?

James wrote an equation to solve the problem.

Numbers of campsites on one side = Length of side ÷ Length of campsite

Total number of campsites = Number of campsites on west side + Number of campsites on south side + Number of campsites on east side − 2

Think about James's strategy. Answer the following questions.

4. Does James's first equation make sense? Why or why not?
5. What numbers should James use in his first equation to find the number of campsites along one side of the lake?
6. In James's second equation, why is he subtracting 2 from the sum?
7. How might James write his equation in a shorter way?
8. Finish solving the problem. Use Gloria's strategy, James's strategy, or a strategy of your own.
9. What strategy did you use? Why?
10. How many fewer campsites would fit if each campsite was 20 meters wide instead of 10 meters wide?

Cumulative Review

Measuring Length—Inches, Feet, and Yards Lesson 3.5

Solve these problems.

1. **Extended Response** Angel put his tent 5 yards from the creek. Sofía put her tent 15 feet from the creek. Whose tent is closer to the creek?

2. How do you know?

3. Taylor has a wooden board that is 1 yard long. He needs pieces that are 6 inches long. How many 6-inch pieces can he get from the board?

4. How long will the leftover piece be?

Fractions of Sets Lesson 8.3

What fraction is colored?

5.
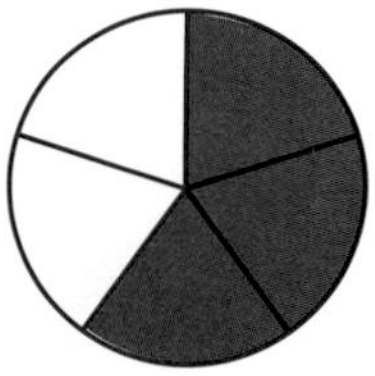

6.
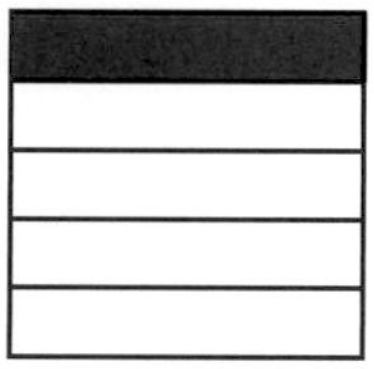

7.
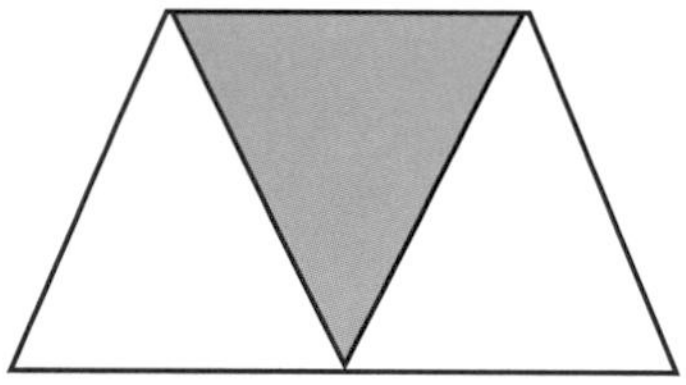

8.
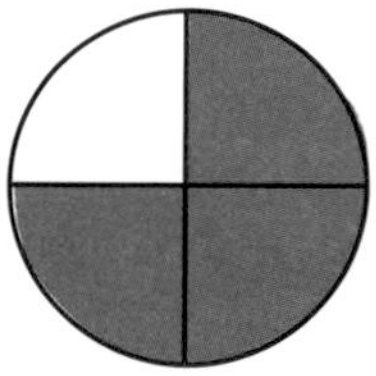

9.
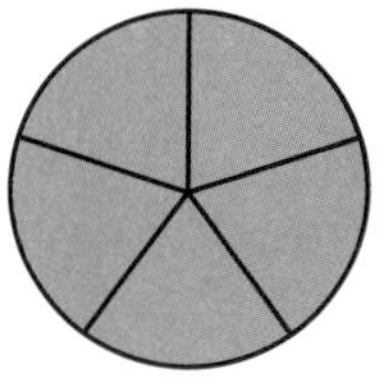

10.
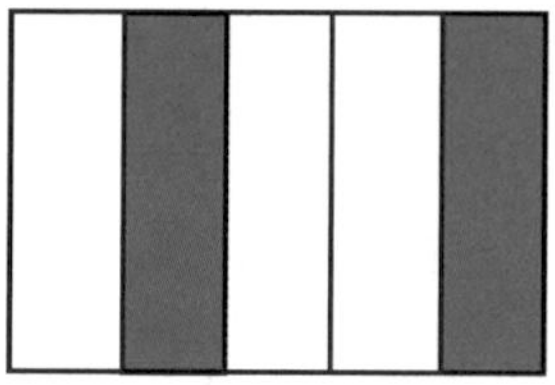

eTextbook This lesson is available in the ***eTextbook.***

Customary Length **Lesson 9.2**

3 feet = 1 yard

Answer the following questions.

11. Élan has a rope that is 72 inches long. How many feet is that?

12. Fátima must stay 6 feet from the campfire. How many yards is that?

13. My family's camper is about 6 yards long. How many feet is that?

14. **Extended Response** For her camping trip, Jo wants to make tablecloths for the picnic tables. There will be 3 picnic tables at her campsite. Each table is 6 *feet* long. How many *yards* of fabric does she need? Explain your answer.

Multiplying Two-Digit Numbers by One-Digit Numbers **Lesson 7.2**

Read the problem, and answer the question.

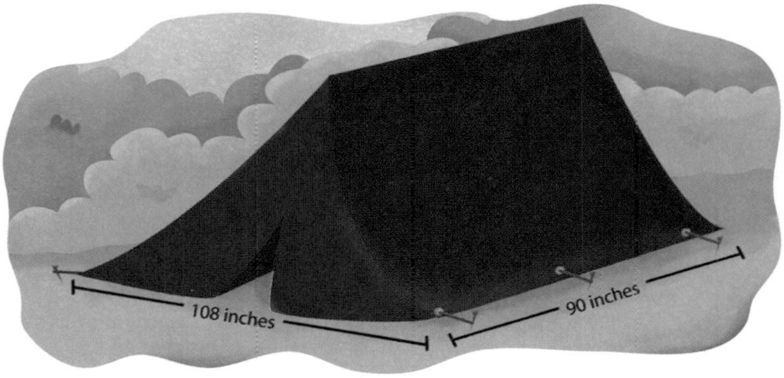

15. The Cho family wants to buy a tarp to put under their tent. One tarp is 2 yards long and 2 yards wide. Another tarp is 3 yards long and 3 yards wide. The tent is 90 inches by 108 inches. Which tarp will be closer in size to covering the bottom of the tent completely?

    a. 2 yards by 2 yards

    b. 3 yards by 3 yards

LESSON 9.5 Metric Capacity

Key Ideas

The liter and the milliliter are metric units of capacity.
Capacity is the amount (of anything) a container can hold.

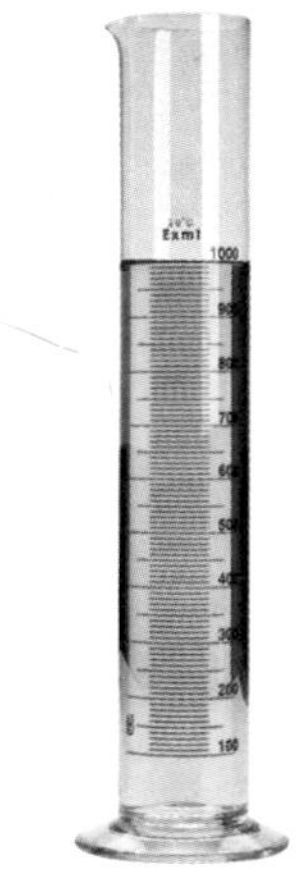

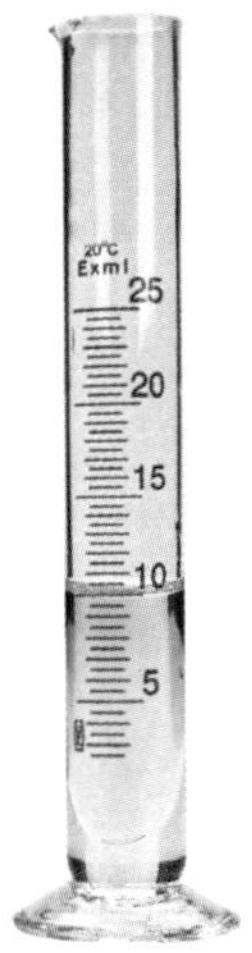

There are 1,000 milliliters in 1 liter.

1000 mL = 1 L

Convert **each measure from liters to milliliters or from milliliters to liters. Write the new measure.**

1. 1 L = ___ mL
2. ___ L = 1,000 mL
3. 2 L = ___ mL
4. ___ L = 3,000 mL
5. 7 L = ___ mL
6. ___ L = 5,000 mL
7. 4 L = ___ mL
8. ___ L = 8,000 mL
9. **Extended Response** Ming sells lemonade at her juice stand. Each glass contains 240 milliliters of lemonade. If she sold 20 glasses of lemonade, about how many liters is that?

Write the name of the unit that makes sense.
Use milliliters or liters.

⑩ About 250 ___ of juice

⑫ About 100 ___ of perfume

⑪ About 10 ___ of water

⑬ About 1 ___ of stew

⑭ About 800 ___ of water

LESSON 9.6 Customary Capacity

Key Ideas

The cup, pint, quart, and gallon are customary units of capacity. They are usually used for measuring liquids.

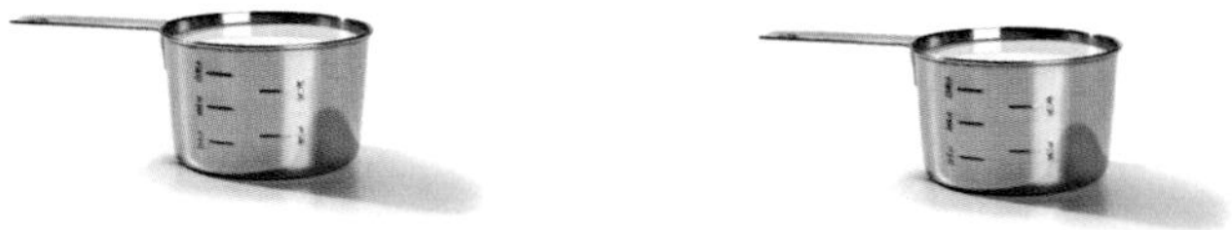

=

There are 2 cups in 1 pint.

There are 2 pints in 1 quart.

=

There are 4 quarts in 1 gallon.

Convert each measure. Write the new measure.

1. 1 quart = $\square$ cups
2. $\frac{1}{2}$ gallon = $\square$ pints
3. 2 quarts = $\square$ cups
4. $\frac{1}{2}$ gallon = $\square$ quarts
5. 1 gallon = $\square$ cups
6. $\frac{1}{4}$ gallon = $\square$ quart
7. 1 gallon = $\square$ pints
8. 8 pints = $\square$ quarts

Which unit makes more sense?

9. About 1 (gallon, cup)

10. About $\frac{1}{2}$ (gallon, pint)

11. About 1 (quart, cup)

12. About 3 (gallons, cups)

LESSON 9.7

Choosing the Correct Unit

Key Ideas

The measurement unit you choose depends on what you want to measure and how you want to use the results.

If you were measuring these people and things in real life, what metric units would you use? Write *kilometers, meters, centimeters, kilograms,* or *grams*. Work down the page.

1. About 2 ___ tall
2. Weighs about 80 ___

3. About 2 ___ across
4. Weighs about 3 ___

5. About 18 ___ long
6. Weighs about 6 ___

7. About 130 ___ tall
8. Weighs about 27 ___

9. About 30 ___ long
10. Weighs about 500 ___

11. About 2 ___ long
12. Weighs about 8 ___

eTextbook This lesson is available in the ***eTextbook.***

If you were measuring these people and things in real life, what customary units would you use? Write *inches, feet, yards, ounces,* or *pounds.*

13 About 18 ___ long

14 Weighs about 3,500 ___

19 About 1 ___ long

20 Weighs about 24 ___

15 About 6 ___ tall

16 Weighs about 160 ___

21 About 1 ___ long

22 About 2 ___ thick

17 About 100 ___ long

18 About 50 ___ wide

23 About 7 ___ long

24 Weighs about 2 ___

LESSON 9.8

Measuring Elapsed Time

Key Ideas

The time difference between the start of an event and the end of the event is called elapsed time. It is the amount of time that has passed.

Start Time	End Time	Elapsed Time
11:25	12:10	45 minutes

Think: The time from 11:25 to noon is 35 minutes. Noon to 12:10 is 10 minutes. So, the elapsed time is 45 minutes.

Copy and complete the table by filling in the elapsed times. The first one is done for you.

Daily Schedule for Art Camp

Activity	Time	Elapsed Time
Campers Arrive	8:45–9:00 A.M.	1 15 minutes
Morning Meeting	9:00–9:10 A.M.	2
Puppetry	9:15–9:55 A.M.	3
Dance Class	10:00–10:55 A.M.	4
Making Your Own Movie	11:05–11:55 A.M.	5
Lunch	12:00–12:30 P.M.	6
Special Guest	12:35–1:50 P.M.	7
World Music	1:55–2:35 P.M.	8
Soccer	2:40–3:40 P.M.	9
Farewell Meeting	3:45–3:55 P.M.	10
Campers Depart	4:00 P.M.	

e Textbook This lesson is available in the ***eTextbook.***

Daily Bus Schedule from San Antonio, TX, to Dallas, TX

Bus	Departs	Arrives
A	1:45 A.M.	7:00 A.M.
B	5:00 A.M.	10:45 A.M.
C	7:00 A.M.	12:55 P.M.
D	9:15 A.M.	3:00 P.M.
E	12:45 P.M.	6:00 P.M.
F	3:15 P.M.	8:50 P.M.
G	4:30 P.M.	10:15 P.M.
H	6:00 P.M.	11:25 P.M.
I	8:00 P.M.	1:20 A.M.
J	10:05 P.M.	3:00 A.M.
K	10:45 P.M.	4:30 A.M.

Use the bus schedule to answer the questions.

11. Bus D arrived 15 minutes early. What time was that?

12. Bus F arrived 10 minutes late. What time was that?

13. Which buses could you take if you need to depart from San Antonio before noon?

14. What is the elapsed time between the time Bus E departs and the time the next bus departs?

15. If you take Bus K to Dallas, how many hours travel time will you have?

16. If you take Bus J to Dallas, how many hours travel time will you have?

Writing + Math **Journal**

Why do you think the number of hours of travel time is different depending on which bus you take?

LESSON
9.9 Understanding the Metric System

Key Ideas

Relating the metric system of measures to United States currency can help you remember how to convert metric units.

Use the table on the next page to answer these questions.

1. How many cents are in $1?
2. How many centimeters are in 1 meter?
3. How many dollars are in $1,000?
4. How many grams are in 1 kilogram?
5. How many liters are in 1 kiloliter?
6. How many centiliters are in 1 liter?
7. How many dimes are in $1?
8. How many cents are in 1 dime?
9. How many decimeters are in 1 meter?
10. How many centigrams are in 1 decigram?

The highway department in President County has decided to replace old signs. Look at the old signs to the right. Then help the highway department create the new sign by converting the units to kilometers. Use the table on the next page to help.

This table shows how metric units can be related to United States currency.

Length Units	Weight Units	Capacity Units	U.S. Currency
millimeter (mm)	milligram (mg)	milliliter (mL)	mill
centimeter (cm)	centigram (cg)	centiliter (cL)	cent
decimeter (dm)	decigram (dg)	deciliter (dL)	dime
meter (m)	**gram (g)**	**liter (L)**	**dollar bill ($1)**
dekameter (dam)	dekagram (dag)	dekaliter (daL)	10-dollar bill
hectometer (hm)	hectogram (hg)	hectoliter (hL)	100-dollar bill
kilometer (km)	kilogram (kg)	kiloliter (kL)	1,000-dollar bill

15 **Extended Response** What's wrong with the sign that is advertising Super Soda?

16 **Extended Response** There is a sale on cheese at the Metric Market. Should you buy 500 grams of cheese for $3.75 or 1 kilogram of cheese for $8.00? Explain.

Exploring Problem Solving

On a camping trip with their group, three children are filling a water barrel. They walk to the stream to fill their containers. Then they carry them back and pour the water into the barrel. The pictures show their first trip.

Work in groups to solve this problem. Show how you solved it.

1. If the children keep working at this rate, when will the barrel be full?
2. What will happen on the last trip?

eTextbook This lesson is available in the *eTextbook*.

Cumulative Review

Multiplying Three-Digit Numbers by One-Digit Numbers **Lesson 7.3**

Multiply. You may draw pictures to help.

1. 523×4
2. 122×5
3. 801×7
4. 869×0
5. 374×6
6. 752×9

Perimeter **Lesson 3.6**

Find the perimeter for each figure.

7. 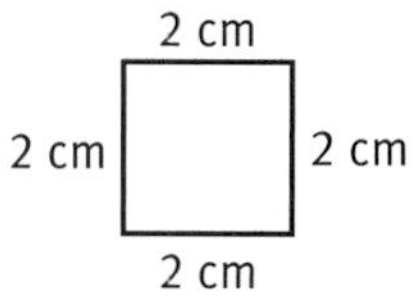

Perimeter: □ centimeters

8. 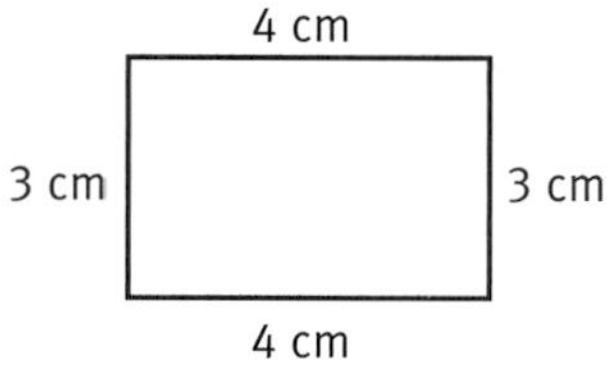

Perimeter: □ centimeters

9. 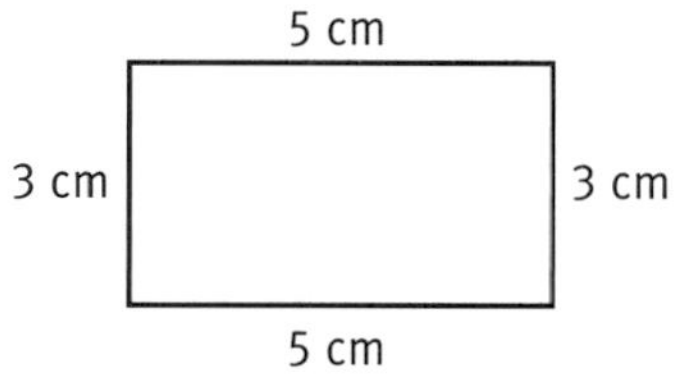

Perimeter: □ centimeters

10. 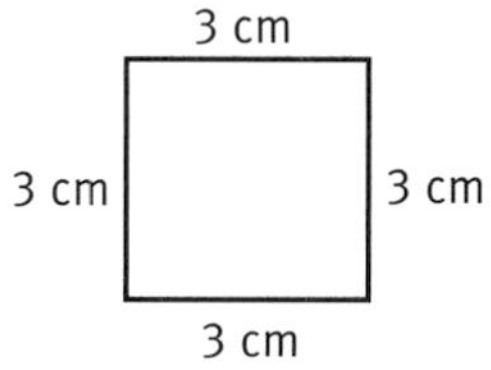

Perimeter: □ centimeters

Metric Length **Lesson 9.1**

Write the metric unit (millimeters, centimeters, meters, or kilometers) you would use to measure these lengths or distances.

11. the length of the Pacific Coast Highway
12. the length of an airplane
13. the distance from one state capital to the next state capital
14. the length of a shoelace
15. the thickness of a quarter

Cumulative Review

Fractions of Time Lesson 8.4

How many minutes?

16. $\frac{3}{4}$ of an hour = ☐ minutes
17. $\frac{1}{2}$ of an hour = ☐ minutes
18. 1 hour = ☐ minutes
19. $\frac{1}{3}$ of an hour = ☐ minutes

Customary Weight Lesson 9.4

Convert each measure from pounds to ounces or from ounces to pounds. Write the new measure. Then answer the questions.

Lillia is going camping in the mountains. She must take a plane to get to the mountains. The plane has a weight limit for each passenger. With all of her luggage, she cannot weigh more than 265 pounds.

20. food 240 ounces = ☐ pounds
21. first aid kit 32 ounces = ☐ pounds
22. sleeping bag 48 ounces = ☐ pounds
23. tent 128 ounces = ☐ pounds
24. ropes 32 ounces = ☐ pounds
25. backpack 80 ounces = ☐ pounds
26. Lillia 1,920 ounces = ☐ pounds
27. shelter gear 80 ounces = ☐ pounds
28. clothes 160 ounces = ☐ pounds
29. cooking gear 80 ounces = ☐ pounds
30. How many pounds does she have altogether? How many more pounds of equipment could she bring with her?

CHAPTER 9 Key Ideas Review

In this chapter you learned about the customary and metric systems of measure.

You learned to estimate and measure length, weight, and capacity in these systems.

You learned how to convert from one measure to another within each system.

Solve each problem.

1. Sanjay is laying square tiles on his bathroom floor. Each tile is 10 centimeters wide, and the floor is 2 meters wide. If Sanjay lays the tiles across the width of the floor, about how many tiles can he lay end to end in each row?

2. The length of one of the walls in John's bedroom is 8 feet. The length of his bed is 65 inches. If he places the bed along the wall, how much space will be left along the wall for other things?

3. Ms. Maples is making cookies. The recipe calls for 1 cup of milk, and she has $\frac{1}{2}$ pint of milk left. Does she have enough milk to make the cookies?

Extended Response **Provide a detailed answer for the following exercises.**

4. Aileen measured the length of her classroom and reported that the length was a bit more than 13 yards but less than 14 yards. Could the length of the classroom be 40 feet? Why or why not? Explain your answer.

5. Taylor weighed a bag of apples. It weighed a bit more than 5 pounds. Could its weight be 82 ounces? Why or why not? Explain your answer.

CHAPTER 9

Chapter Review

Lessons 9.1–9.6

Convert.

1. ☐ centimeters = 5 meters
2. ☐ meters = 6 kilometers
3. 2 kilometers = ☐ meters
4. 300 centimeters = ☐ meters

5. ☐ inches = 5 feet
6. 10 yards = ☐ feet
7. 36 feet = ☐ yards
8. ☐ feet = 2 miles

9. 5,000 grams = ☐ kilograms
10. ☐ grams = 10 kilograms

11. ☐ ounces = 2 pounds
12. 6 pounds = ☐ ounces

13. ☐ milliliters = 3 liters
14. 16 liters = ☐ milliliters

15. ☐ cups = 3 pints
16. 4 pints = ☐ quarts
17. ☐ cups = 2 quarts
18. ☐ quarts = 10 gallons

Lesson 9.7

Solve each problem.

19 **Extended Response** Tricia wants to buy a fish tank that could fit on her desk. What customary measuring unit should she use to measure the fish tank and her desk? Explain your answer.

If Tricia could measure the weight of her new goldfish, which customary measuring unit would she use? Why?

20 **Extended Response** A zookeeper needs to weigh a new baby elephant. What metric measuring unit should he use to weigh the baby elephant? Explain your answer.

Would the zookeeper use the same measuring unit to measure the amount of water the baby elephant drinks every day? Why?

Lesson 9.8

Measure the elapsed time.

21 Bob read a book from 7:50 to 9:15. How long did he spend reading?

22 Karl wanted to get a good night's sleep. He went to bed at 9:45 P.M. and woke up at 6:15 A.M. How long did he sleep?

CHAPTER 9

Practice Test

Answer each question.

1. Francis ran 1 kilometer. How many meters did he run?
2. How many centimeters are in 1 meter?
3. Bob counted 250 pennies. How can he write this amount of money in dollars and cents?
4. Marcus has a 2-liter bottle of sports drink. How many milliliters of sports drink does he have?
5. Casey's mother is making fruit punch. She needs 3 quarts of lemonade. How many cups is this?
6. What is the inverse function of $+7$?
7. What is an expression that has the same product as 9×7?
8. Paul is 4 feet tall. How many inches tall is he?
9. Karla's new football weighs 15 ounces. About how many pounds does it weigh?
10. Rafael's piano lesson lasts 60 minutes. How many hours is that?
11. Should you use a gram or a kilogram to measure the weight of a stamp?
12. Should you use inches or yards to measure the perimeter of your classroom?
13. Should you use cups or quarts to measure the amount of coffee in a coffee mug?
14. Should you use kilometers or meters to measure the length of the Potomac River.

eTextbook This lesson is available in the *eTextbook.*

Choose the unit that makes sense.

15. A deck of cards is about 1.6 ___ thick.

Ⓐ kilometers

Ⓑ meters

Ⓒ centimeters

Ⓓ yards

16. A deck of cards weighs about 50 ___.

Ⓐ grams

Ⓑ kilograms

Ⓒ kilometers

Ⓓ inches

17. A standard ruler is usually 12 ___ long.

Ⓐ kilometers

Ⓑ meters

Ⓒ inches

Ⓓ yards

18. The distance from first base to second base in baseball is 90 ___.

Ⓐ inches

Ⓑ feet

Ⓒ yards

Ⓓ kiloliters

19. A baseball weighs about 5 ___.

Ⓐ pounds

Ⓑ ounces

Ⓑ inches

Ⓓ kilograms

20. A whale is about 8 ___ long.

Ⓐ kilometers

Ⓑ meters

Ⓒ centimeters

Ⓓ inches

21. A whale can weigh up to 5,000 ___.

Ⓐ kilograms

Ⓑ grams

Ⓒ ounces

Ⓓ milliliters

CHAPTER 9 Practice Test

Convert. Then choose the correct answer.

22. 1 gallon = ☐ pints

Ⓐ 2

Ⓑ 4

Ⓒ 8

Ⓓ 10

23. ☐ dimes = 3 dollars

Ⓐ 10

Ⓑ 30

Ⓒ 50

Ⓓ 60

24. 2 meters = ☐ centimeters

Ⓐ 2

Ⓑ 20

Ⓒ 200

Ⓓ 2,000

25. ☐ inches = 2 yards

Ⓐ 72

Ⓑ 60

Ⓒ 48

Ⓓ 36

26. ☐ kilograms = 7,000 grams

Ⓐ 7,000

Ⓑ 700

Ⓒ 70

Ⓓ 7

27. If 3 is the input, what is the output?

Ⓐ 3

Ⓑ 6

Ⓒ 9

Ⓓ 12

28. If 6 is the output, what is the input?

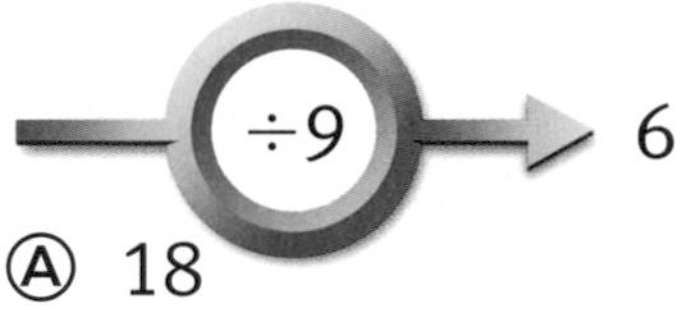

Ⓐ 18

Ⓑ 32

Ⓒ 54

Ⓓ 56

29. Which mixed number is equal to $\frac{17}{6}$?

Ⓐ $3\frac{1}{6}$

Ⓑ $2\frac{5}{6}$

Ⓒ $2\frac{2}{6}$

Ⓓ $2\frac{1}{6}$

eTextbook This lesson is available in the ***eTextbook.***

Answer this question.

30. **Extended Response** Mr. Davis is deciding on a schedule for the new school year. The school day begins at 8:10 A.M. and ends at 2:35 P.M. Here is his proposed schedule:

Subject	Time
Reading and Language Arts	8:15–10:15
Math	10:15–11:30
Lunch and Recess	11:30–12:00
Specials	12:00–12:45
Science	12:45–1:30
Social Studies	1:30–2:15
Cleanup	2:15–2:30

a. How long is math class?

b. Mr. Davis wants to set aside at least 45 minutes for science and 45 minutes for social studies every day. Does his schedule show that? Explain.

c. Which subject does he plan to spend the most time on each day?

d. Mr. Davis wants his students to study reading and language arts for at least 6 hours each school week. Does his schedule show that? Explain.

Thinking Story

Mosquito Lake

"Hooray!" shouted Ferdie. "We're going camping at Mosquito Lake."

"I wish we were going camping someplace else," said Portia. "It always rains at Mosquito Lake."

"How do you know that?" asked Ferdie.

"Because it has rained every time I've been there," she said.

"Oh," said Ferdie, "then I guess you're right."

Does Portia have a good reason for saying it rains all the time at Mosquito Lake?

What do you need to know before you can decide if Portia has a good reason?

"How many times have you been to Mosquito Lake?" their mother asked.

"Lots of times," said Portia. "Well, let me see ... just twice, I guess."

Is that enough times to know how often it rains at Mosquito Lake?

If Portia had been there 20 times and it had rained every time, would you be more willing to believe her?

"I've been going to Mosquito Lake for years and years," their mother said, "and it hardly ever rains. It just happened to rain the two times you were along. According to the weather report, it isn't likely to rain this weekend."

"Good," said Ferdie. "Then we won't have to take along anything to protect us from the rain."

Can they be sure it isn't going to rain?

Why or why not?

"I think we'll take raincoats and a waterproof tent, just in case," their mother said. "It probably won't rain, but you can never be sure, and it's best to be prepared."

Saturday morning the three of them piled into a car and headed for Mosquito Lake. As soon as they arrived, Ferdie ran down to the water and put his foot in it. "This lake is cold," he complained.

"You can't be sure," said Portia. "You just tested one little part of it. Maybe the rest of the lake is warm."

Could Portia be right?

Why or why not?

"That's silly," Ferdie said. "If one part of the lake is cold, it's all cold." But the children ran down the beach anyway and tested the water in different places. Strangely enough, the rest of the lake water was warmer. Ferdie and Portia investigated and found a spring of cold water bubbling up out of the ground where Ferdie had tested the first time. That was why the lake water was colder there.

As soon as the sun went down, the mosquitoes came out. Portia sprayed her arm to keep the mosquitoes off. "This stuff doesn't work," she said. "I sprayed my arm all over, and right away two mosquitoes came and landed on it."

Does Portia have a good reason for saying the spray doesn't work?

"You can't tell from that," Ferdie said. "You sprayed only one part of you. If you tried your other arm and your legs, you might find it worked there."

Do you agree with Ferdie's argument?

Why or why not?

Portia tried spraying herself all over, but still the mosquitoes kept landing and biting her. Her mother looked at the can and said, "Someone brought the wrong thing. This isn't mosquito spray; it's hairspray. No wonder it doesn't keep the mosquitoes off!"

Ferdie and Portia went off to gather wood for the outdoor fireplace. They found many long pieces of wood and brought back as many as they could carry. Their mother took the shortest one and tried to lay it in the fireplace. It wouldn't fit. "I'm afraid all the pieces of wood you brought are too long," she said.

Does their mother have a good reason for saying all the pieces of wood are too long?

Why or why not?

"You just tried one of them," Ferdie said. "Maybe the rest of them will fit."

Which piece of wood did their mother try?

Could the other pieces fit if the shortest one didn't?

"I tried the shortest one," their mother said. "If it's too long, then all the others must be even longer. Since we don't have an ax, I guess you'll have to go find shorter pieces of wood."

It was a hot night, but Ferdie and Portia slept with the tent closed to keep the mosquitoes away. In the morning Portia took the big jug of milk they had kept in the tent with them and poured herself a cupful to drink. "This milk is all sour!" she said.

"You can't tell for sure," Ferdie said. "You tried only one cupful. I'm going to pour myself some, and I'll bet it will be all right."

Do you think the milk Ferdie pours will be sour?

Why or why not?

The milk Ferdie poured was sour. He tried some more, and it was sour too. "We have no milk to drink," Ferdie complained. "It's all sour."

"Don't give up yet," said their mother. "There's another carton of milk in the cooler. Maybe it is still good."

"No, it isn't," Ferdie said. "I just found out that if some of the milk is sour, it's all sour."

Why could Ferdie be wrong about the carton of milk?

They opened the new carton of milk and found that it was still good. "Milk keeps better when it stays cold," their mother said. "That's probably why this milk is still good."

"I'm confused," Ferdie said. "Sometimes everything is like the part you try, and sometimes it isn't. How can you tell?"

"You can't always tell," their mother said. "You have to think about whether the other parts could be different or whether they are probably the same. I think you have the right idea that it's usually good to test things more than once."

The End

CHAPTER 10

Decimals

In This Chapter You Will Learn

- how to use decimals with money and with measurements.
- about the relationship between decimals and fractions.
- how to add, subtract, multiply, and divide decimals and to solve problems that involve decimals.

Problem Solving

A totem pole begins with a straight tree with few branches. Before figures can be carved, the tree must be cut, the branches removed, and the bark stripped.

The picture below shows six tree trunks that will become totem poles. For some of the trunks, the task of stripping the bark is further along than for others.

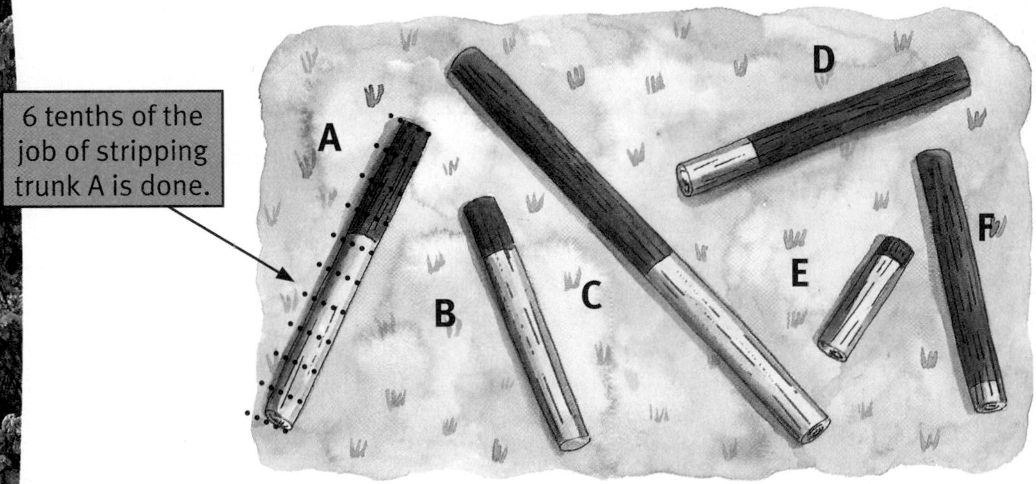
6 tenths of the job of stripping trunk A is done.
A
B
C
D
E
F

Think about, answer, and discuss the following questions.

1. For each trunk, estimate how many tenths of the job is done.
2. How could you check your estimates?
3. Check your estimates. How close were your estimates?
4. For which trunk, C or E, is a greater fraction of the job done?
5. Which trunk has taken longer so far to strip, C or E?
6. Why does it make sense that the answers to Questions 4 and 5 are different?

LESSON 10.1 Where Do We See Decimals?

Key Ideas

We see decimal numbers often.

What do decimal numbers mean? Let's consider the price tag on the bicycle.

The 7 represents 7 tens, or 70 dollars. It is in the tens place.

The 6 represents 6 ones, or 6 dollars. It is in the ones place.

The **decimal point** separates ones and tenths.

The 9 represents $\frac{9}{10}$ of 1 dollar, or 90 cents. It is in the **tenths** place.

The 8 represents $\frac{8}{100}$ of 1 dollar, or 8 cents. It is in the **hundredths** place.

$$\mathbf{76.98 = 70 + 6 + 0.9 + 0.08}$$

Let's look at another example, the number of kilograms of ketchup.

The 1 represents 1 kilogram. It is in the ones place.

The 8 represents $\frac{8}{10}$ of 1 kilogram, or 8 hectograms. It is in the tenths place.

The 1 represents $\frac{1}{100}$ of 1 kilogram, or 1 dekagram. It is in the hundredths place.

The 4 represents $\frac{4}{1,000}$ of 1 kilogram, or 4 grams. It is in the thousandths place.

$$\mathbf{1.814 = 1 + 0.8 + 0.01 + 0.004}$$

eTextbook This lesson is available in the ***eTextbook.***

Answer these questions.

1. One box of crayons costs 253¢. How much do 2 boxes cost? Write the answer using dollars and cents.

2. Bowser the dog eats about 750 grams of dog food each day. About how much does he eat in one week? Write your answer in kilograms.
3. Memorial Park is shaped like a triangle. Each side is 432 meters long. What is the perimeter of the park? Write your answer in kilometers.
4. One box of crackers weighs 375 grams. How much do 5 boxes weigh? Write your answer in grams and in kilograms.
5. The distance around a racetrack is 320 meters. How many kilometers is a race of 4 laps?
6. If Nick saves 10¢ every day, how long will it take him to save $1.00? How long will it take him to save $2.00?
7. Sugar the cat is 9 years old and weighs about 3 kilograms. She eats about 100 grams of cat food each day. How old will Sugar be next year?
8. **Extended Response** Shelley is making punch for a party. She needs 5 liters of juice like the one shown in the picture. How many bottles must she buy? Explain your answer.

9. Raulito is about 173 centimeters tall. About how many meters is that?
10. Juanita is 15 years old. She runs 2 laps around the track every morning. How many miles is that?

LESSON 10.2

Decimals and Money

Key Ideas

We use a decimal point when writing amounts of money.

$4.58

A dime is one-tenth of a dollar. A cent is one-hundredth of a dollar.

Solve these problems. REAL WORLD

1. 3 dimes = ___¢
2. 17 dimes = $___
3. 200 dimes = $___
4. $___ = 80 dimes
5. $___ = $8 and 7 dimes
6. $4.20 = ___ dimes
7. If you have $8, how many dimes could you get for it at the bank?
8. If you have $7.60, how many dimes could you get?
9. If you take 253 dimes to the bank to exchange for $1 bills, how many $1 bills will you get? Will you have any dimes left over?
10. How many dimes could you get for 73¢? Would you have any cents left over?

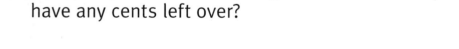

Solve these problems. Make the least number of dimes and cents possible in each case.

11. $8.47 = $___ and ___ dimes and ___¢
12. $___ = $7 and 15 dimes and 8¢
13. $17.93 = $___ and ___ dimes and ___¢
14. $___ = $43 and 9 dimes and 10¢

15. Jean is thinking about her savings plan for the next year (which is not a leap year).

    a. If she saves 1¢ each day, how much money is that?

    b. If she saves 10¢ each day, how much money is that?

    c. If she saves $1 each day, how much money is that?

    d. If she saves $2 each day, how much money is that?

David buys umbrellas and sells them when it is raining. He sells the umbrellas at a profit. He pays $4.00 for each small umbrella and $6.00 for each large umbrella. He makes a profit of $1.50 on each small umbrella and a $2.00 profit for each large umbrella.

16. **Extended Response** Is it fair to make a greater profit on the large umbrellas? Why or why not?

17. If David sells 10 large umbrellas and 5 small umbrellas, how many dollars is that in sales? What is his profit?

18. On one rainy day David's sales totaled $64.50. He knew he sold 3 small umbrellas but forgot how many large umbrellas he sold. How many large umbrellas did he sell? What was his profit that day?

LESSON 10.3

Decimals and Metric Measures

Key Ideas

We can use the decimal point with measurements as well as with money.

With money, we could write $3.4 for 3 dollars and 4 dimes because a dime is one-tenth of a dollar.

With measurement, we write 3.4 meters for 3 meters and 4 decimeters because a **decimeter** is one-tenth of a meter. You can read 3.4 as *three and four-tenths* or *three point four.*

We write 3.46 for 3 meters, 4 decimeters, and 6 centimeters because a **centimeter** is one-hundredth of a meter. You can read 3.46 as *three and forty-six hundredths* or *three point four six.*

Answer these questions.

1. How many decimeters are in 1 meter?
2. How many decimeters are in 2.5 meters?
3. How many meters are 15 decimeters?
4. How many decimeters are in 7.3 meters?
5. How many decimeters are in 73 meters?
6. How many meters are 125 decimeters?

eTextbook This lesson is available in the ***eTextbook.***

There are 10 decimeters in 1 meter.

10 dm = 1 m

There are 10 centimeters in 1 decimeter.

10 cm = 1 dm

Write the equivalent measures.

7. 2 m = ___ dm
8. 200 dm = ___ m
9. 37 dm = ___ m and ___ dm
10. ___ m and ___ dm = 9.2 m
11. 4.5 m = ___ dm
12. ___ dm = 6.5 m
13. 2 m and 3 dm = ___ m
14. ___ m = 6 m and 1 dm

Mr. Thompson wants to buy fencing for his garden. The garden is shaped like a rectangle with one side 12 meters and another side 4 meters in length. Fencing is sold in lengths of 80 centimeters.

15. What is the perimeter of Mr. Thompson's garden?
16. How many lengths of fencing must Mr. Thompson buy?
17. If each length of fencing costs $20, how much will the fencing cost?
18. **Extended Response** Mr. Thompson was thinking of enlarging his garden. He needed to keep the width the same but could extend the length to between 17 and 22 meters. He decided to make the garden 20 meters long. Why might Mr. Thompson have chosen 20 meters rather than one of the other possible lengths?

Comparing Decimals and Fractions

Key Ideas

Tenths and hundredths can be written as fractions or decimals.

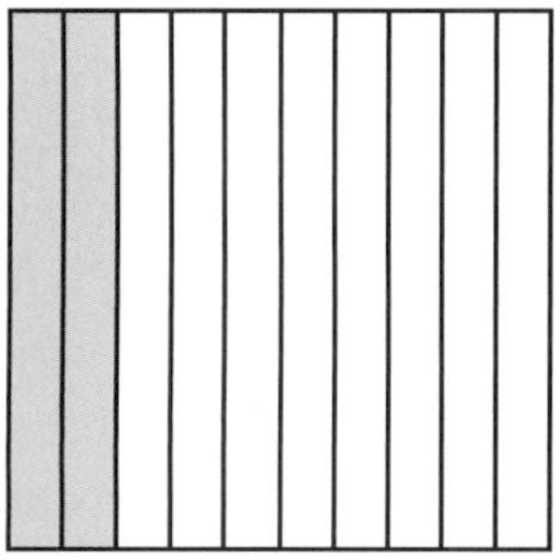

Fraction	Decimal	Percent
$\frac{2}{10}$	0.2	20%

Two-tenths of the square is shaded.

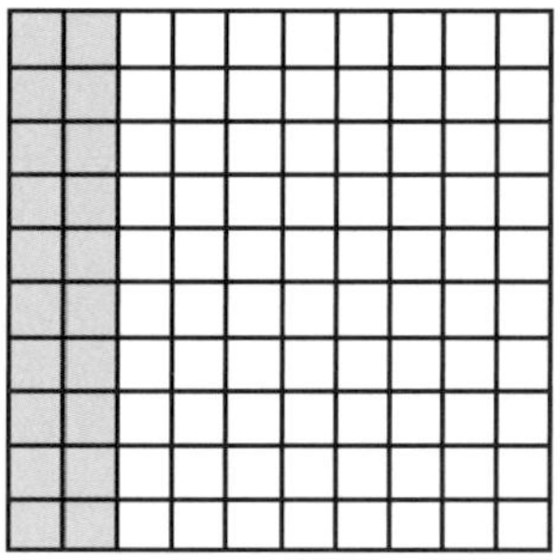

Fraction	Decimal	Percent
$\frac{20}{100}$	0.20	20%

Twenty-hundredths of the square is shaded.

Notice that $\frac{20}{100}$ of the square and $\frac{2}{10}$ of the square is the same amount.

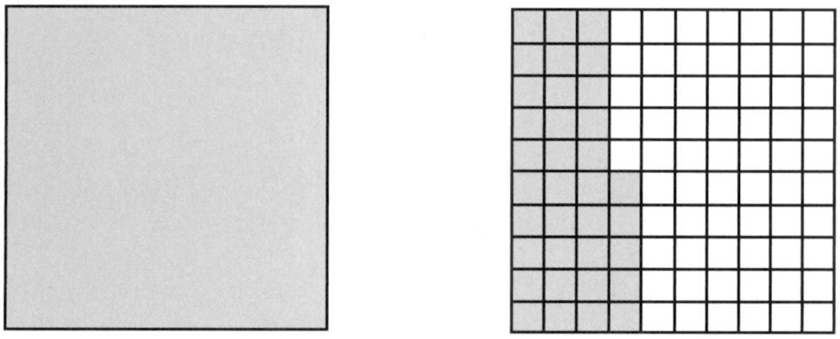

Fraction	Decimal	Percent
$1\frac{35}{100}$	1.35	135%

Write these fractions as decimals.

1. $\frac{3}{10}$
2. $\frac{5}{10}$
3. $1\frac{5}{10}$
4. $\frac{6}{100}$
5. $\frac{65}{100}$
6. $4\frac{32}{100}$
7. $\frac{20}{100}$
8. $\frac{2}{10}$

Write these decimals as fractions. Do not reduce the fraction.

9. 0.10
10. 0.25
11. 0.5
12. 0.05
13. 0.67
14. 0.60
15. 0.04
16. 1.25
17. 4.58
18. 5.01

Solve these problems.

19. Mark earned $4\frac{1}{2}$ dollars running errands. His sister earned \$4.50 delivering newspapers.

    a. Who earned more?

    b. How much money did they earn together?

20. Henry was paid \$2.00 each hour he worked in his mother's garden. He worked for $3\frac{3}{4}$ hours.

    a. Did he earn more than \$6.00?

    b. Did he earn less than \$8.00?

    c. Did he earn more than \$7.00?

    d. How much did he earn?

LESSON 10.5 Adding Decimals

Key Ideas

Before adding decimals, line up the decimal points.

If you had \$3.86 and you earned \$4.75 raking leaves, how much money would you have now? Add the two numbers to find out.

\$3.86 + \$4.75 = ?

$$\begin{array}{r} 3.86 \\ +\ 4.75 \\ \hline \end{array}$$ Line up the decimal points.

$$\begin{array}{r} \scriptstyle 1\ 1\ \ \\ 3.86 \\ +\ 4.75 \\ \hline 8.61 \end{array}$$ Add.

6.39 + 2.4 = ?

$$\begin{array}{r} 6.39 \\ +\ 2.4\ \ \\ \hline \end{array}$$ Line up the decimal points.

$$\begin{array}{r} 6.39 \\ +\ 2.40 \\ \hline \end{array}$$ If it helps, put in a 0 (because 2.4 and 2.40 have the same value), but be sure to add ones to ones, tenths to tenths, and so on.

$$\begin{array}{r} 6.39 \\ +\ 2.40 \\ \hline 8.79 \end{array}$$ Add.

Add.

1. $\begin{array}{r} 3.27 \\ +\ 2.48 \\ \hline \end{array}$

2. $\begin{array}{r} 7.63 \\ +\ 1.54 \\ \hline \end{array}$

3. $\begin{array}{r} 5.4 \\ +\ 2.55 \\ \hline \end{array}$

4. $\begin{array}{r} 8.31 \\ +\ 4.24 \\ \hline \end{array}$

5. $\begin{array}{r} 7.45 \\ +\ 6.7 \\ \hline \end{array}$

6. $\begin{array}{r} 1.30 \\ +\ 2.74 \\ \hline \end{array}$

7. $\begin{array}{r} 10.28 \\ +\ 17.94 \\ \hline \end{array}$

8. $\begin{array}{r} 12.34 \\ +\ 19.8 \\ \hline \end{array}$

9. $\begin{array}{r} 43.72 \\ +\ 56.28 \\ \hline \end{array}$

10. $\begin{array}{r} 2.4 \\ +\ 1.65 \\ \hline \end{array}$

11. $\begin{array}{r} 325.6 \\ +\ 35.3 \\ \hline \end{array}$

12. $\begin{array}{r} 98.6 \\ +\ 98.6 \\ \hline \end{array}$

Add. Work down the page.

13. 4.3 + 1.5 =
14. 2.5 + 4 =
15. 25.6 + 30.2 =
16. 86.8 + 2.7 =
17. 25.6 + 30.2 =
18. 25.7 + 30.2 =
19. 257 + 302 =
20. 2.57 + 3.02 =

Solve.

21. Olga ran 100 meters in 14.3 seconds. Jenny ran the same distance, but 3.7 seconds slower. What was Jenny's time?

22. Bill wants to run 20 kilometers this week. Monday he ran 8.4 kilometers. Tuesday he ran 4.8 kilometers. How far has Bill run so far this week?

Solve these problems.

23. Serena worked for $3\frac{1}{2}$ hours. She needs to earn \$14.25 to buy a present for her mother. Will she earn enough money?

24. Grant is 67 centimeters tall. How many meters is that?

25. Mr. Bourne drives to work and back each day. If he lives 76.54 kilometers from work, how far does he drive in a day?

26. Building laws in Shasta say that a house cannot be more than 6.5 meters from front to back. Ms. Soto measured her house. It was exactly 5.75 meters from front to back. But she forgot to measure the small front porch. The porch floor sticks out 7 decimeters from the house. The porch railing sticks out another 4 centimeters. Does the house follow the law? If so, how much extra room does Ms. Soto have? If not, how far over the limit is the house?

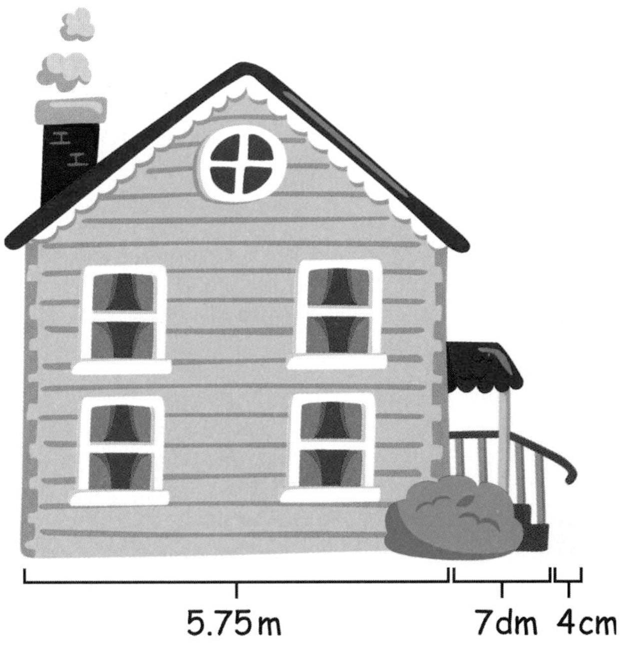

27. Sonia can usually jump about 2.6 meters. She marked a spot 2.6 meters from the starting line. On her first jump, she landed 53 centimeters past that mark. How far did she jump?

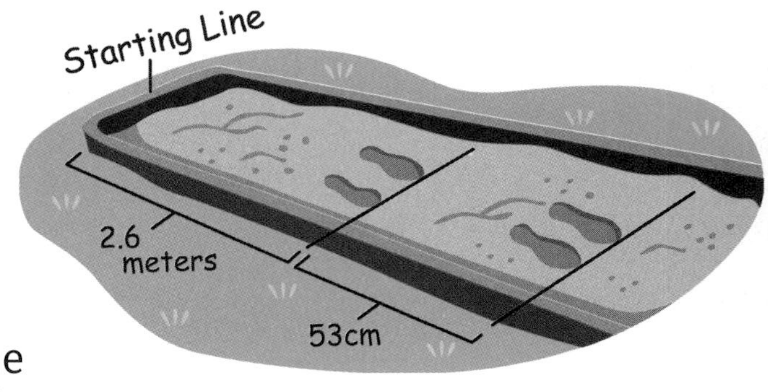

28. The next time Sonia jumped, she landed 53 centimeters short of the 2.6-meter mark. How far did she jump this time?

Game

Addition and Strategies Practice

Roll a Problem (Decimals) Game

Players: Two or more

Materials: ***Number Cube:*** one 5–10

Object: To get the sum that is closest to 100

HOW TO PLAY

1. Use blanks to outline an addition exercise on your paper, such as this:

   ___ ___ ___ + ___ ___ ___ = 100

2. One player rolls the ***Number Cube*** six times.
3. Each time the ***Number Cube*** is rolled, all players write that number in one of the blanks in their outlines. If a 10 is rolled, don't count it, and roll again. Once a number is placed, it cannot be moved.
4. When all of the blanks have been filled in, place a decimal point in each number so that the sum is as close as possible to 100. The sum can be less than or more than 100.
5. Determine the greatest sum. Do exact calculations only if you need to. The player with the sum closest to 100 is the winner.

SAMPLE GAME:

Numbers Rolled

8	6	7	8	8	7

Libby 87.6 + 8.78 = 96.38

Devin 88.7 + 8.67 = 97.37

Devin's sum is closer to 100. He is the winner.

Exploring Problem Solving

Omak is carving a totem pole that is 17.0 meters tall. He wants to carve ten figures to fill the pole, and he wants them all to be the same height. How high should he make each figure?

Tracy is using guess, check, and revise to solve the problem.

Guess	Check	Result
1 meter	10 meters	Too short
2 meters	■	■

Think **about Tracy's strategy. Then answer and discuss these questions.**

1. Why did Tracy write *10 meters* when she checked her first guess?
2. What do you think Tracy will write when she checks her second guess?
3. What do you think Tracy will guess next?
4. How can Tracy check her next guess?
5. Do you think Tracy's strategy will work?

Ross is using a physical model to solve the problem.

Think **about Ross's strategy. Then answer and discuss the following questions.**

6. In Ross's model, what does each strip stand for?
7. What does each small square on a strip stand for?
8. How could Ross use his model to solve the problem?
9. What do you think of Ross's strategy?
10. Work with your group to solve the problem. Use any strategy you like.

Cumulative Review

Customary Capacity Lesson 9.6

Convert each measure. Write the new measure.

1. 6 quarts = ▢ cups
2. 4 quarts = ▢ cups
3. 1 gallon = ▢ pints
4. 7 gallons = ▢ quarts
5. $\frac{1}{4}$ gallon = ▢ quart
6. 1 pint = ▢ quart

Applications with Money Lesson 2.6

Match the dollar amounts to the money listed.

a. $32.38 **b.** $32.35 **c.** $4.80

d. $70.60 **e.** $44.05 **f.** $53.02

7. 4 one-dollar bills
   2 quarters
   3 dimes
8. 5 five-dollar bills
   4 one-dollar bills
   9 quarters
   2 dimes
   3 nickels
   78 pennies
9. 6 five-dollar bills
   1 one-dollar bill
   5 quarters
   1 dime
10. 2 twenty-dollar bills
    1 ten-dollar bill
    3 five-dollar bills
    4 one-dollar bills
    6 quarters
    2 nickels
11. 4 ten-dollar bills
    2 five-dollar bills
    3 one-dollar bills
    2 pennies
12. 1 twenty-dollar bill
    22 one-dollar bills
    6 quarters
    5 dimes
    1 nickel

eTextbook This lesson is available in the *eTextbook*.

Understanding the Metric System Lesson 9.9

Use the table on page 365 to answer the following questions.

13 **Extended Response** There is a sale on juice at the Metric Market. Should you buy 2,000 milliliters of juice for $4.35 or 1 liter of juice for $2.00? Explain your answer.

14 **Extended Response** There are two options for buying salt at the Metric Market. You can buy a 1-kilogram container of salt for $3.50, or you can buy a 500-gram container of salt for $1.75. Which container should you buy? Explain your answer.

15 **Extended Response** The Metric Market also sells rope. The green rope is sold by the meter. The black rope is sold by the centimeter. This week the price for the green rope is $3.80 per meter. The price of the black rope is $0.03 per centimeter. Which rope is more expensive? Explain your answer.

Comparing Fractions Lesson 8.6

Write $<$, $>$, or $=$ to make each statement true.

16 $\frac{1}{3}$ ■ $\frac{1}{2}$

17 $\frac{2}{5}$ ■ $\frac{1}{2}$

18 $\frac{2}{6}$ ■ $\frac{1}{3}$

19 $\frac{3}{4}$ ■ $\frac{2}{3}$

Adding and Subtracting Fractions Lesson 8.7

Add or subtract.

20 $\frac{1}{2} + \frac{1}{2} =$ ■

21 $\frac{1}{4} + \frac{1}{8} =$ ■

22 $\frac{3}{4} - \frac{1}{4} =$ ■

23 $\frac{1}{5} - \frac{1}{10} =$ ■

LESSON 10.6

Subtracting Decimals

Key Ideas

When you subtract decimals, remember to line up the decimal points.

If you had \$23.79 and you bought a book for \$10.82, how much money would you have left? Subtract to find out.

\$23.79 − \$10.82 = ?

$$\begin{array}{r} 23.79 \\ -\ 10.82 \\ \hline \end{array}$$

Line up the decimal points.

$$\begin{array}{r} 2\overset{2}{\cancel{3}}.\overset{17}{\cancel{7}}9 \\ -\ 10.82 \\ \hline 12.97 \end{array}$$

Subtract.

4.6 − 3.25 = ?

$$\begin{array}{r} 4.6 \\ -\ 3.25 \\ \hline \end{array}$$

Line up the decimal points.

$$\begin{array}{r} 4.60 \\ -\ 3.25 \\ \hline \end{array}$$

If it helps, put in a 0 (because 4.6 and 4.60 have the same value).

$$\begin{array}{r} 4.\overset{5}{\cancel{6}}\overset{10}{\cancel{0}} \\ -\ 3.25 \\ \hline 1.35 \end{array}$$

Subtract.

eTextbook This lesson is available in the ***eTextbook***.

Subtract.

1. 12.73 − 9.06	2. 5.45 − 2.9	3. 10.00 − 2.50	4. 43.85 − 27.8
5. 63.5 − 18.55	6. 2.05 − 1.38	7. 5.09 − 4.92	8. 6.43 − 2.31
9. 4.7 − 4	10. 10.00 − 0.03	11. 17.4 − 15.26	12. 12.07 − 9.38

13. 7.0 − 3.5 = ■	17. 80.3 − 41.7 = ■	21. 12.2 − 6.6 = ■
14. 8.30 − 4.17 = ■	18. 80.4 − 41.7 = ■	22. 5.06 − 1.43 = ■
15. 11.7 − 2.9 = ■	19. 804 − 417 = ■	23. 0.42 − 0.39 = ■
16. 4.2 − 1.75 = ■	20. 8.04 − 4.17 = ■	24. 0.03 − 0.03 = ■

Solve.

25. On Monday Nikki bought a pair of sneakers for $42.99. On Tuesday the same sneakers went on sale for $40.50. How much would Nikki have saved if she had waited a day to buy the sneakers?

26. Agatha spent $3.43 for milk and bread. The bread cost $1.39. How much was the milk?

There is only one correct answer to each exercise. Can you use shortcuts to find it?

27. $4.35 - 2.1 = \square$
    a. 4.14
    b. 2.25
    c. 2.24

28. $106 - 5.43 = \square$
    a. 437
    b. 51.7
    c. 100.57

29. $3.7 + 4.65 = \square$
    a. 5.02
    b. 7.35
    c. 8.35

30. $3.74 + 8.79 = \square$
    a. 11.53
    b. 12.53
    c. 13.53

31. $10.3 + 4.76 = \square$
    a. 15.06
    b. 57.9
    c. 5.79

32. $8.79 - 3.74 = \square$
    a. 5.05
    b. 4.95
    c. 4.05

33. $10.3 - 4.76 = \square$
    a. 3.73
    b. 5.54
    c. 15.06

34. $73.2 - 6.47 = \square$
    a. 8.5
    b. 67.73
    c. 66.73

35. $106 + 5.43 = \square$
    a. 111.43
    b. 160.3
    c. 649

36. $73.2 + 6.47 = \square$
    a. 79.67
    b. 13.79
    c. 137.9

Solve these problems.

37 Helena is 9 years old. Last year she was 110 centimeters tall. How tall is she this year?

38 Sid is saving his money to buy a football. It costs $12. He has $5.65 in his bank. How much more money does he need?

39 Mr. Rice bought some gum for 55¢. He gave the cashier a $5 bill. How much change should the cashier give Mr. Rice?

40 Before today, Andrea had ridden her bicycle a total of 274.8 kilometers. Now she has ridden her bicycle a total of 275.4 kilometers. How far did Andrea ride today?

41 Jack earned $10.50 babysitting. Does he have enough money to buy the book he wants?

42 Megan had $7.43. She bought a book. She had $1.48 left. How much did the book cost?

LESSON 10.7

Multiplying Decimals by Whole Numbers

Key Ideas

When you multiply a decimal by a whole number, remember to estimate first and to place the decimal point in the answer.

Solve.

1. One book costs 347¢. How many cents do 8 books cost?
2. One book costs \$3.47. How much do 8 books cost?
3. Each table is 127 centimeters long. How many centimeters long are 6 tables placed end to end?
4. Each table is 1.27 meters long. How many meters long are 6 tables placed end to end?
5. One ticket to the movie costs \$7.25. How much do 4 tickets cost?
6. One lap around the racetrack is 1.25 miles. How many miles is 6 laps?

eTextbook This lesson is available in the ***eTextbook.***

Multiply.

7. $7.5 \times 2 =$ ▢
8. $7.5 \times 4 =$ ▢
9. $7.50 \times 4 =$ ▢
10. $75.0 \times 4 =$ ▢
11. $7.5 \times 8 =$ ▢
12. $2.43 \times 5 =$ ▢
13. $3.02 \times 7 =$ ▢
14. $4.25 \times 4 =$ ▢
15. $1.75 \times 5 =$ ▢
16. $4.42 \times 6 =$ ▢
17. $6.33 \times 3 =$ ▢
18. $4.5 \times 6 =$ ▢
19. $3.7 \times 9 =$ ▢
20. $7.5 \times 4 =$ ▢
21. $2.43 \times 7 =$ ▢
22. $3.00 \times 8 =$ ▢
23. $2.5 \times 4 =$ ▢
24. $1.25 \times 8 =$ ▢
25. $3.2 \times 7 =$ ▢
26. $8.1 \times 2 =$ ▢
27. $13.61 \times 5 =$ ▢
28. $8.12 \times 2 =$ ▢
29. $7.33 \times 9 =$ ▢
30. $5.8 \times 6 =$ ▢
31. $1.48 \times 3 =$ ▢
32. $3.1 \times 2 =$ ▢
33. $9.9 \times 6 =$ ▢
34. $1.3 \times 8 =$ ▢
35. $2.04 \times 5 =$ ▢
36. $1.01 \times 9 =$ ▢
37. $2.29 \times 4 =$ ▢
38. $3.47 \times 7 =$ ▢

Writing + Math **Journal**

Cakes at the bakery cost $10.00 each, but people can buy portions that are $\frac{1}{4}$ of a whole cake. A $\frac{1}{4}$ section of a cake sells for $3.50. If 8 people want a $\frac{1}{4}$ portion of a cake, should they purchase 2 whole cakes and cut the cakes themselves, or should they purchase eight $\frac{1}{4}$ portions? Explain.

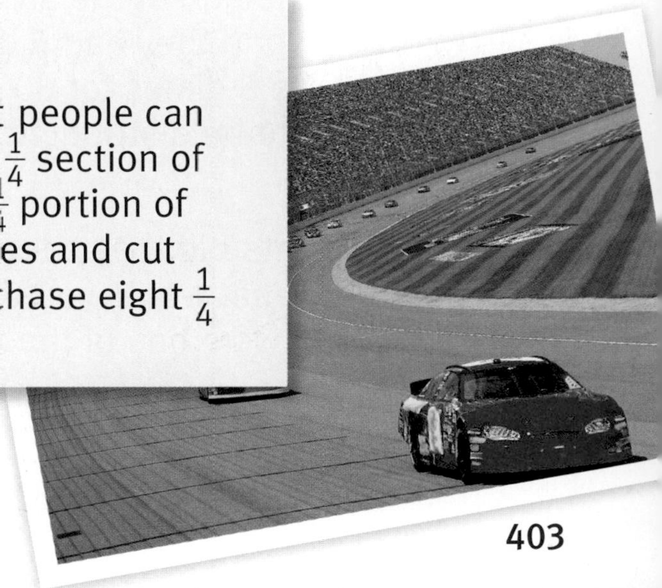

LESSON 10.8 Dividing Decimals

Key Ideas

Dividing decimal numbers is very similar to dividing whole numbers.

A group of 8 students earned $573.47 and decided to divide it equally among themselves. There were 5 hundred-dollar bills, 7 ten-dollar bills, 3 one-dollar bills, 4 dimes, and 7 pennies. How much should each get?

```
   7 1.___
8 )5 7 3.4 7
   5 6
     1 3
       8
       5
```

Because the students could not share the 5 hundred-dollar bills, they exchanged them for 50 ten-dollar bills. Now they had a total of 57 ten-dollar bills. Each student took 7 tens. That left 1 ten-dollar bill. Then they exchanged the remaining ten-dollar bill for 10 one-dollar bills.

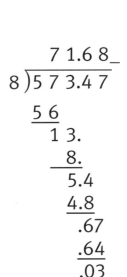

The students now had 13 one-dollar bills. Each one took 1 one-dollar bill, leaving 5 one-dollar bills. Does the record at the right show what has happened so far?

Because the students could not share the 5 one-dollar bills, they exchanged them for 50 dimes. Now they had a total of 54 dimes. Each student took 6 of the 54 dimes. That used up 48 dimes, and they had 6 dimes left. They exchanged the 6 dimes for 60 cents, so they had 67 cents to be distributed. Each student got 8 cents.

```
   7 1.6 8_
8 )5 7 3.4 7
   5 6
     1 3.
       8.
       5.4
       4.8
        .67
        .64
        .03
```

How many cents did they have left to be distributed? What would you do with the 3 cents if you were one of the 8 students?

Solve.

1. A recipe for 6 people calls for 1.2 kilograms of flour. Mitchell is making the recipe for one person. How many kilograms of flour should she use? How many grams is that?

2. There are 5 students who will share a 1-liter bottle of apple juice. How much is each person's share?

3. The 9 members of the history club were preparing for a trip to Washington, D.C. They estimated that the trip would cost $500. About what is each person's share?

4. **Extended Response** Raulito is a member of the history club that is going to visit Washington, D.C. He reported that his share of the $500 would be $55.56. Is Raulito correct? Why or why not?

5. There are 9 classrooms and about 200 students in Northview School. How many of the students walk to school?

6. A wooden board measures 5.75 meters in length. If the board is cut into 5 equal-sized pieces, how long will each piece be? How many centimeters is that?

7. Suzie read that if you jog around the perimeter of Seward Park, you will have jogged about 2.5 miles. The park is shaped like a square. What is the length of each side of the park?

8. Tammy, Brandt, and Sally want to share equally the cost of a new bicycle. If the full price of the bicycle is $375.96, what is each person's share?

LESSON 10.9 Decimal Applications

Key Ideas

You can use what you have learned about decimals to solve problems. Problems dealing with money and measurement often involve decimals.

Solve these problems.

1. Wei made curtains for one window. She used 2.68 yards of cloth. How many yards of cloth will she need to make curtains for 4 more windows the same size?
2. Wei is buying 10.8 yards of cloth. The piece at the store is 14.5 yards long. What length of cloth will be left?
3. The cloth costs $35.26. Wei gave the storekeeper two $20 bills. How much change should Wei get?
4. Wei decided to buy 2 yards of fancy cloth to make a pillowcase. The fancy cloth costs $8.99 per yard. How much did Wei spend?
5. How much would she spend if she bought 3 yards of the fancy cloth?

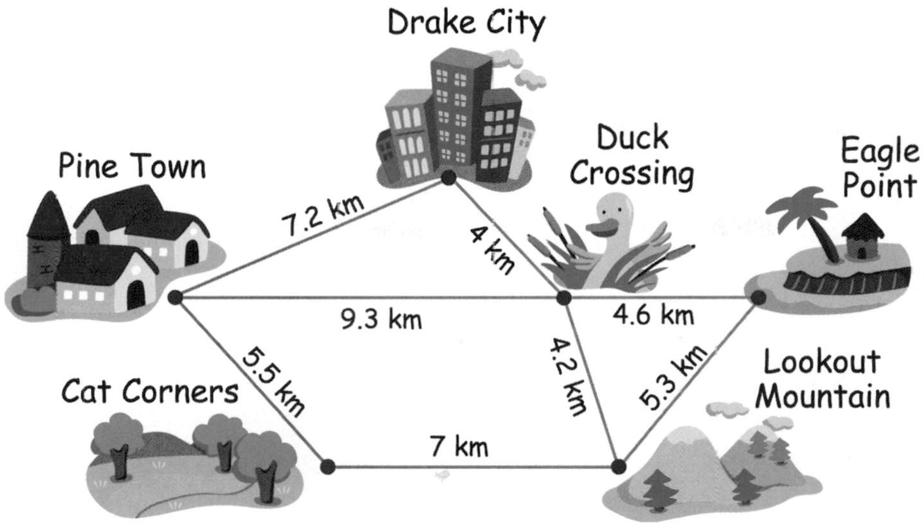

Solve.

6. How far is it from Pine Town to Duck Crossing?
7. How far is it from Pine Town to Eagle Point?
8. How far is it from Pine Town to Lookout Mountain if you go through Duck Crossing?
9. How far is it from Pine Town to Lookout Mountain if you go through Cat Corners?
10. Suppose you are going from Duck Crossing to Pine Town. How much farther would it be to go through Drake City?
11. What is the shortest route from Eagle Point to Cat Corners?
12. How many kilometers is that route?
13. **Extended Response** New City is located about 10 kilometers from Cat Corners and 10 kilometers from Pine Town.

    a. Is New City closer to Duck Crossing or Eagle Point?

    b. What other information do you need to know to locate New City?
14. **Extended Response** If a bird flew directly between Cat Corners and Duck Crossing, about how far would it fly? Explain.

Exploring Problem Solving

Suppose you are going to carve a talking stick that is 10.0 centimeters wide. You are designing one of the faces that you will carve on the stick. You want the eyes to be placed realistically when you look at the face straight on.

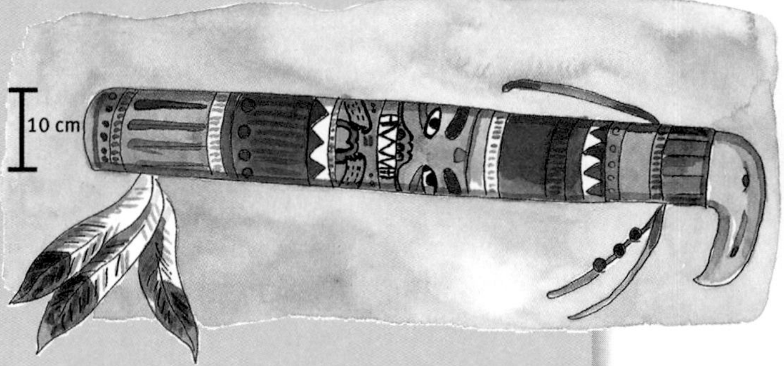

- Each eye will be 2.6 centimeters wide.
- The distance between the eyes will be twice the distance between an eye and the side of the face.

Solve these problems.

1. How many centimeters will there be between the eyes?
2. How many centimeters will there be on each side of the eyes?
3. How can you prove that your answers are correct?

Cumulative Review

Adding and Subtracting Very Large Numbers **Lesson 2.12**

Add or Subtract.

1. $627534373 + 322447972$
2. $726419397 + 453627428$
3. $770361529 - 524643011$

Fractions Greater Than a Whole **Lesson 8.8**

Name the fraction represented by the shaded sections. Give the name in at least two ways.

4. 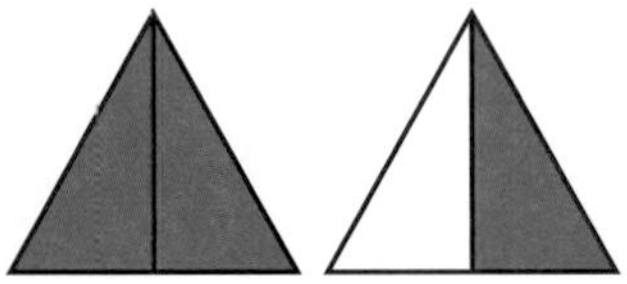

5. 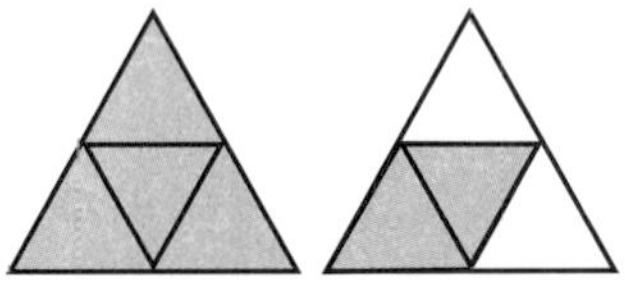

Division with Remainders **Lesson 7.5**

Solve. If it is not possible to solve the problem, tell why.

6. $5\overline{)37}$ 7. $8\overline{)61}$ 8. $3\overline{)88}$ 9. $9\overline{)59}$ 10. $6\overline{)77}$ 11. $4\overline{)47}$

Nia's class has been assigned group projects. Each group has 4 students and must tell about 37 different monuments.

12. If the group members are splitting the task equally, how many monuments should each of the 4 students research? How many monuments will still need to be researched?

13. **Extended Response** How should the students in the group deal with the remainder?

Cumulative Review

Measuring Elapsed Time **Lesson 9.8**

Copy and complete the table by filling in the elapsed time.

Schedule for Monument Day

Activity	Time	Elapsed Time
Students Arrive	8:45 A.M.–9:00 A.M.	14
Discuss Day's Events and Safety	9:00 A.M.–9:15 A.M.	15
Inside Tour of Monument	9:15 A.M.–10:30 A.M.	16
Guest Speaker	10:30 A.M.–11:45 A.M.	17
Lunch	11:45 A.M.–12:30 P.M.	18
Outside Tour of Monument	12:30 P.M.–1:40 P.M.	19
Making Monumental Crafts	1:40 P.M.–3:05 P.M.	20
Gift Shop Visit	3:05 P.M.–3:15 P.M.	21
Students Depart	3:15 P.M.	

22 What is the total amount of elapsed time from the time the students arrive to the time they finish their lunches? Write your answer in hours and minutes (not just minutes).

CHAPTER 10 Key Ideas Review

In this chapter you explored decimals and some of their uses.

You learned how to use decimals with money and with measurements.

You learned how tenths and hundredths can be written as fractions or decimals.

You learned how to add, subtract, multiply, and divide decimals.

Solve each problem.

1. Marsha wants to hang 2 pictures on a wall that is 1.2 meters wide. Each picture frame is 30 centimeters wide, and Marsha would like to have 10 centimeters of space between each picture. Will that be possible? Draw a diagram to show why or why not.

Extended Response **Provide a detailed answer for the following exercises.**

2. Suppose your friend added 7.8 and 3 and got an answer of 8.1. Explain the error your friend made, and tell how you might be able to help him get the right answer.
3. Each ticket to the zoo costs $8.75. Will 4 tickets cost more than $32?
4. Sam and two of his friends want to buy a collection of old postage stamps to share equally. The stamps cost $6.75. If Sam has $2, will the cost of the stamps be shared equally among he and his friends?

CHAPTER 10

Chapter Review

Lessons 10.2-10.3 **Answer** each question.

1. How many dimes are in \$7.00?
2. How many dimes are in \$3.80?
3. How many decimeters are in 3 meters?
4. How many decimeters are in 3.5 meters?

Lesson 10.4 **Write** true or false.

5. $0.5 = \frac{5}{100}$
6. $0.02 = \frac{2}{100}$
7. $0.78 = \frac{78}{100}$
8. $0.67 = \frac{67}{10}$

Write each fraction as a decimal or each decimal as a fraction.

9. $3\frac{25}{100}$
10. 0.08
11. $\frac{6}{10}$
12. 0.80
13. $\frac{40}{100}$
14. 0.9

Lesson 10.5 **Add.**

15. $3.67 + 7.5$
16. $4.43 + 7.58$
17. $60.3 + 2.24$
18. $198.5 + 98.5$

Lesson 10.6 **Subtract.**

19. $2.2 - 0.06$
20. $39.87 - 17.5$
21. $3.2 - 0.3$
22. $74.6 - 29.06$

eTextbook This lesson is available in the ***eTextbook.***

Lesson 10.7

Multiply.

23. $\begin{array}{r} 6.8 \\ \times\ 4 \\ \hline \end{array}$

24. $\begin{array}{r} 14.52 \\ \times\ 3 \\ \hline \end{array}$

25. $\begin{array}{r} 4.03 \\ \times\ 8 \\ \hline \end{array}$

26. $\begin{array}{r} 2.9 \\ \times\ 9 \\ \hline \end{array}$

Lesson 10.8

Solve.

27. A wooden board measures 3.65 meters in length. If the board is cut into 5 equal-sized pieces, how long will each piece be? How many centimeters is that?

28. A. J., Micah, and Brandi want to share equally the cost of a new stereo. If the full price of the stereo is $214.98, what is each person's share?

Lesson 10.9

Solve each problem.

29. Mr. Morales spent $45.18 at the grocery store. Then he spent $25.87 at the gasoline station. He had $100 before going to the grocery store and the gasoline station. How much of the $100 did he have left after going to both places?

30. The 11 members of the art club were preparing for a trip to New York City to see an art exhibit. They estimated that the trip would cost $800. Miles reported that his share of the $800 would be about $70. Is he correct? Why or why not?

Practice Test

Answer each question.

1. How many decimeters are in 1 meter?
2. How many decimeters are in 58 meters?
3. How many meters are in 42 decimeters?
4. Paula had $14.00 in dimes. How many dimes did she have?
5. Carol has 83 dimes. She wants to trade in her dimes for dollar bills. How many dollar bills can she get for her dimes? How many dimes will she still have?
6. There are 50 dimes in 1 roll of dimes. There are 40 nickels in 1 roll of nickels. REAL WORLD
   a. How much money is 1 roll of dimes worth?
   b. How much money is 1 roll of nickels worth?
   c. Mason wants to exchange 5 rolls of dimes and 3 rolls of nickels for dollar bills. How much money is that?

Convert.

7. ▢ meters = 80 decimeters
8. 2.7 meters = ▢ decimeters
9. $5.30 = ▢ dimes
10. 100 dimes = ▢¢
11. 65 dimes = $▢

Choose the correct answer.

12. Which fraction is equivalent to 3.38?

Ⓐ $38\frac{3}{100}$ Ⓑ $3\frac{38}{100}$

Ⓒ $\frac{38}{100}$ Ⓓ $\frac{338}{100}$

13. Which fraction is equivalent to 0.06?

Ⓐ $\frac{6}{1000}$ Ⓑ $\frac{6}{100}$

Ⓒ $\frac{1}{6}$ Ⓓ $\frac{6}{10}$

14. Which decimal is equivalent to $5\frac{2}{10}$?

Ⓐ 520 Ⓑ 52

Ⓒ 5.2 Ⓓ 0.52

15. Which decimal is equivalent to $\frac{64}{100}$?

Ⓐ 64.4 Ⓑ 6.4

Ⓒ 0.64 Ⓓ 0.064

16. Find the product. $8 \times 7 = ?$

Ⓐ 15 Ⓑ 16

Ⓒ 56 Ⓓ 65

17. Ali has a box of books that weighs 9.1 pounds. He adds to the box another book that weighs 1.4 pounds. How much does the box weigh now?

Ⓐ 7.7 pounds

Ⓑ 9.5 pounds

Ⓒ 10.5 pounds

Ⓓ 13.1 pounds

18. Caroline has 5.76 centimeters of ribbon. She uses 0.65 centimeter of ribbon for a project. How much ribbon does Caroline have left?

Ⓐ 6.41 centimeters

Ⓑ 5.41 centimeters

Ⓒ 5.31 centimeters

Ⓓ 5.11 centimeters

CHAPTER 10 Practice Test

Choose the correct answer.

19. Find the product. $8.2 \times 7 = ?$

Ⓐ 15.2 Ⓑ 56.4

Ⓒ 57.4 Ⓓ 87.2

20. Polly has 6 boxes of fruit juice. Each box holds 2.4 ounces. How many ounces of juice does Polly have in all?

Ⓐ 24.2 Ⓑ 14.4

Ⓒ 8.4 Ⓓ 3.6

21. Find the quotient. $10.25 \div 5 = ?$

Ⓐ 2.05 Ⓑ 2.5

Ⓒ 5.25 Ⓓ 15.30

22. Find the difference.
$3.53 - 1.80 = ?$

Ⓐ 1.33 Ⓑ 1.73

Ⓒ 2.73 Ⓓ 5.33

23. How many inches are in 5 feet?

Ⓐ 17 Ⓑ 36

Ⓒ 48 Ⓓ 60

24. How many kilograms equal 4,600 grams?

Ⓐ 4.6 Ⓑ 46

Ⓒ 460 Ⓓ 4,600

25. Which mixed number is equal to $\frac{19}{5}$?

Ⓐ $2\frac{1}{5}$ Ⓑ $2\frac{4}{5}$

Ⓒ $3\frac{1}{5}$ Ⓓ $3\frac{4}{5}$

26. Which symbol makes this sentence true?

$5\frac{2}{5}$ ■ $5\frac{1}{3}$

Ⓐ $=$

Ⓑ $<$

Ⓒ $>$

Solve.

27. Brendan lives 0.85 kilometer from his school. He lives 0.45 kilometer from the park.

a. Brendan walks to and from school every day. How far does he walk to school each week?

b. Two school days each week, Brendan has soccer practice at the park. He walks from his house to the park and back. How far does he walk each week for soccer practice?

c. On average, how far does Brendan walk each school day? Round to the nearest tenth.

28. Nancy works at the library for 4 hours on Saturdays. She earns $6.25 an hour. She wants to buy a new bike that costs $187.00.

a. How many Saturdays will she have to work before she has enough money to buy the bike?

b. How much money will Nancy have left after she buys the bike?

Muddle the Engineer

Mr. Muddle went to many different places looking for a job, but no one hired him. They would ask him a few questions, then say "Thank you" and send him away. But one day the president of a large engineering company called him in and offered him a job as chief engineer. The president of the company said, "We're very happy to hire a famous engineer like you, Mr. Nuddle, to help us build bridges and skyscrapers."

Mr. Muddle wondered why the president called him "Mr. Nuddle," but Mr. Muddle was too polite to correct the president. He also wondered why the president called him a famous engineer, because Mr. Muddle couldn't remember ever having built any bridges or large buildings.

What do you think has happened?

The president gave Mr. Muddle a large office and introduced him to the engineers who would be taking directions from him. The first engineer brought in a small model bridge made out of toothpicks. "This is the bridge we are going to build across Roaring River," said the young engineer.

"It's very nice," said Mr. Muddle, holding it in his hands, "but don't you think it's a little small to reach across such a big river?"

What is it that Mr. Muddle doesn't understand?

"This is just a model," said the engineer. "The real bridge will be 500 times as big."

"I see," said Mr. Muddle. "This is a kind of toy bridge, and we're going to make a real one just like it, only 500 times as big."

"If you approve," said the engineer.

"I certainly do," said Mr. Muddle. "I think it's a very clever idea. Now to get down to business. How many toothpicks did you use to make this little bridge?"

"About a thousand."

"Then if the real bridge is going to be 500 times as big, we'll need 500 times as many toothpicks. That will be about 500,000. Right?" said Mr. Muddle.

Is Mr. Muddle right?

"I thought we would make the bridge out of steel," said the engineer.

"Another clever idea," said Mr. Muddle. "Steel toothpicks—they should be much stronger than wooden ones."

How would you describe the pieces of steel that bridges are usually made of?

The engineer looked a little puzzled, but she explained that the bridge was going to be made of large pieces of steel, like most other bridges. Then she and Mr. Muddle went down to the river to look at the place where the bridge was supposed to be built.

"Do you see any problems with building the bridge here?" the young engineer asked.

"Just one," said Mr. Muddle. "The river is full of water. People will get all wet trying to build a bridge here. We'll have to get rid of the water. Send a thousand people down with buckets, and have them empty all the water out of the river."

Would that work?

Why or why not?

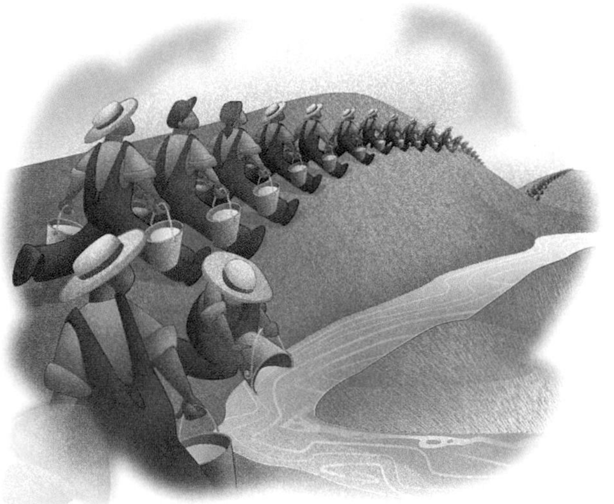

The engineer thought Mr. Muddle was joking and didn't bother to explain that the river would keep filling up with water if they tried to empty it. Instead they went back to the office. Another engineer came in and showed Mr. Muddle the plans for a hotel they were building.

"We want the hotel to have as many rooms as possible," he said, "but the building itself isn't very large."

"I see," said Mr. Muddle. "You want a building that is big on the inside but small on the outside."

The engineer gave Mr. Muddle a strange look.

What do you think is bothering the engineer?

"The building can be only about 100 meters high," said the engineer. "So how many stories do you think it can have?"

"That's simple," said Mr. Muddle. "It can be 100 stories high."

Is that right?

Why or why not?

How high would the rooms be?

"One meter ought to be high enough," said Mr. Muddle. "After all, people use hotels to sleep in, so everyone will be lying down."

Why do the rooms really have to be more than 1 meter high?

"According to the law," said the engineer, "the rooms have to be at least $2\frac{1}{2}$ meters high so that people can walk around." The engineer left the room and went to talk to the other engineer. Together they went to see the president of the company. "We don't think Mr. Nuddle knows anything about engineering," they told him.

What things has Mr. Muddle said that show he doesn't know how to do his job?

"Something will have to be done about this," said the president, after he heard of all the strange things Mr. Muddle had said. "I'll give him an impossible problem, and then when he can't solve it we'll have an excuse to ask him to leave."

The president brought Mr. Muddle a model of a skyscraper his company had built. "We built a skyscraper like this several years ago," the president said, "and now someone wants us to build another one. The new one is supposed to be exactly like the old one in every way, but every part of the new one must be different from the same part of the old one. Can you design such a skyscraper for us?"

"The whole skyscraper exactly the same but every part different?" asked Mr. Muddle. "That sounds pretty hard, but I'll try to have it worked out for you by tomorrow."

What is impossible about the problem?

Mr. Muddle worked hard all night. The next morning he showed the president the model he had made.

"This skyscraper is exactly like the other one!" the president said.

"That's what you wanted, isn't it?" said Mr. Muddle.

"Yes," he said, "but every part is supposed to be different, and I don't see anything different. Look, your roof is just the same as this other roof."

"Pardon me," said Mr. Muddle, "but that's not the roof of my skyscraper. That's the front door."

"Furthermore," the president went on, "the front of your skyscraper is exactly the same as the front of the other skyscraper."

"Pardon me," said Mr. Muddle, "but that's not the front of my skyscraper. That's the roof."

"And I suppose the back wall of your skyscraper is really the floor!"

"Now you're getting the idea," Mr. Muddle said.

What has Mr. Muddle done to make every part of his skyscraper different?

"This is ridiculous," said the president. "All you've done is call every part something else. But you can't do that. The roof can't be on the front of the skyscraper. It has to be on the top."

"That's simple," said Mr. Muddle, turning the model over on its side. "Now the roof is on the top, just the way you want it. And the door, which I admit looks very much like a roof, is on the front where it should be. You see, the two skyscrapers are exactly alike, but every part is different."

The End

CHAPTER 11

Geometry

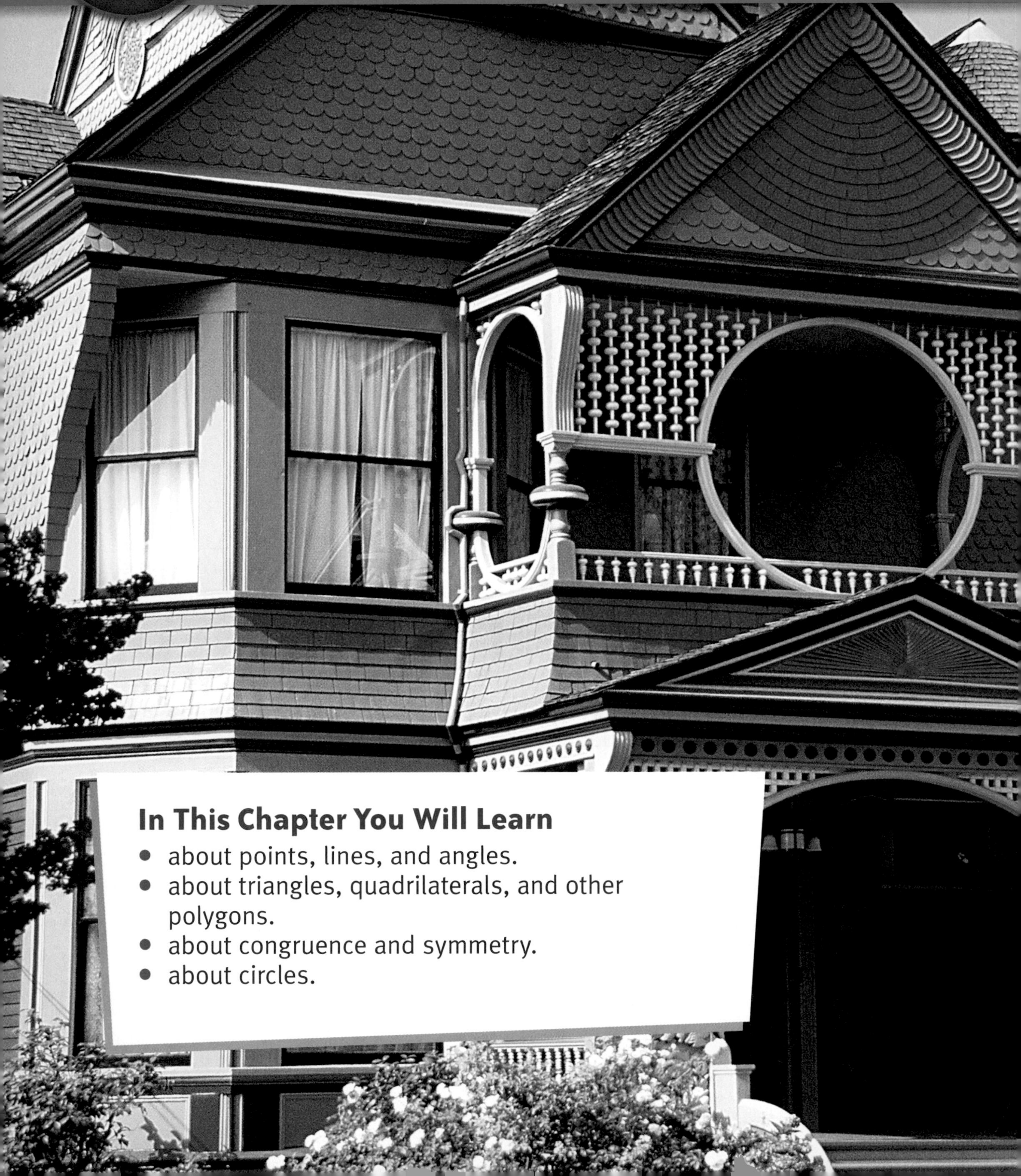

In This Chapter You Will Learn

- about points, lines, and angles.
- about triangles, quadrilaterals, and other polygons.
- about congruence and symmetry.
- about circles.

Problem Solving

Have you ever wished you could design your own room or even your entire house? How would you describe to the builder what you want? Try this activity to see how well you can use words to describe a design.

Work with a partner.

1. On graph paper, draw a design to show the shape and size of the room or house you would like to live in. Do not let your partner see your design.

2. On a separate sheet of paper, write step-by-step instructions for drawing your design.

3. Exchange instructions with your partner. Try drawing each other's design by following the instructions.

4. Compare each drawing to the original design.

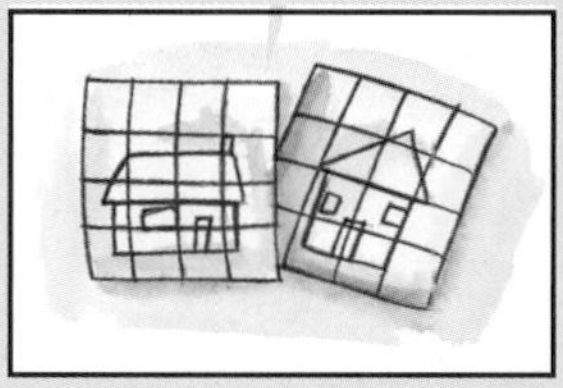

LESSON 11.1
Points and Lines

Key Ideas

A point marks an exact position. We represent a point with a dot, similar to a period: .

A straight path that goes on forever in opposite directions is called a line. We indicate infinite length by the arrows at the end of the line. This represents a line: 

Any section of the line is called a line segment.
A line segment always has two endpoints. This is a line segment: 

Label each of the following as *point, line,* or *line segment.*

1. 

2. 

3. 

4. 

5. 

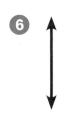

6. 

eTextbook This lesson is available in the *eTextbook.*

Lines that cross each other at one point are called intersecting lines. These are intersecting lines: 

Parallel lines are lines in the same plane that will never cross each other. These are two parallel lines: 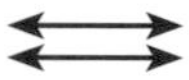

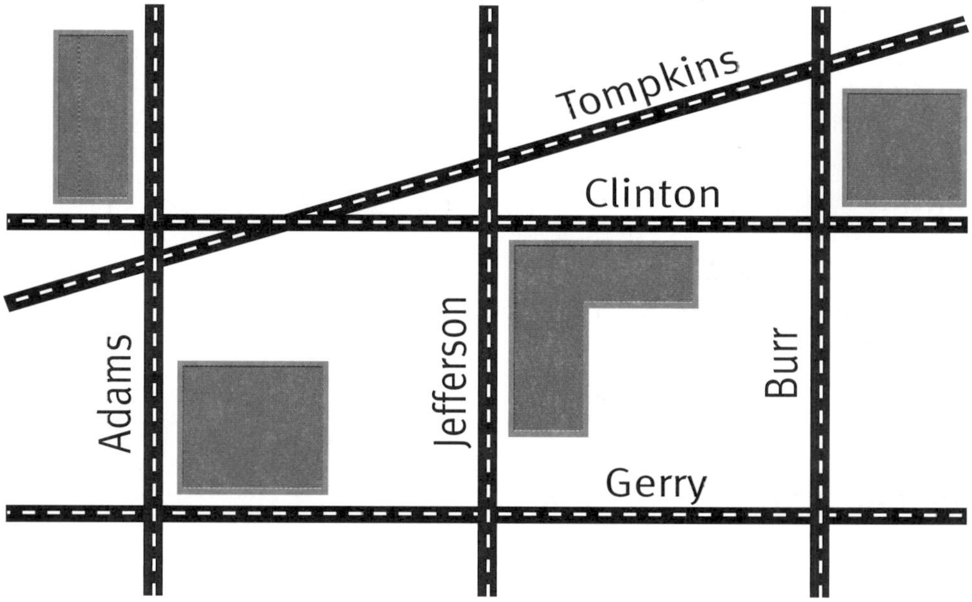

Answer these questions by studying the map.

7. Name one set of streets that are parallel to each other.

8. Name another set of streets that are parallel to each other.

9. Name the streets that intersect Burr Street.

10. Name the streets that are intersected by four streets.

Extended Response Point to where the two lines in each exercise will meet. Explain how you know. Label each of the following as *intersecting lines* or *parallel lines.*

11

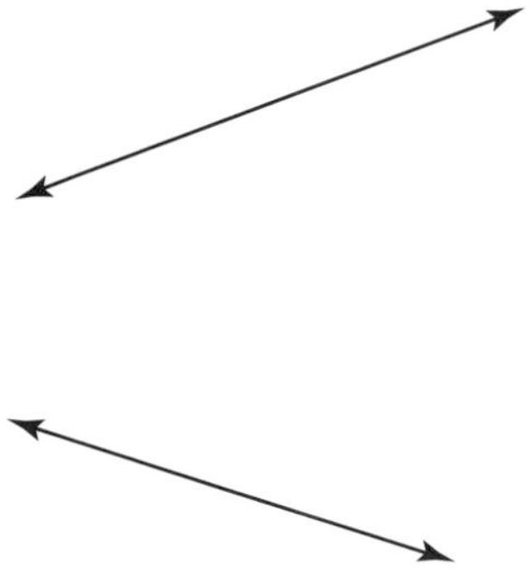

12

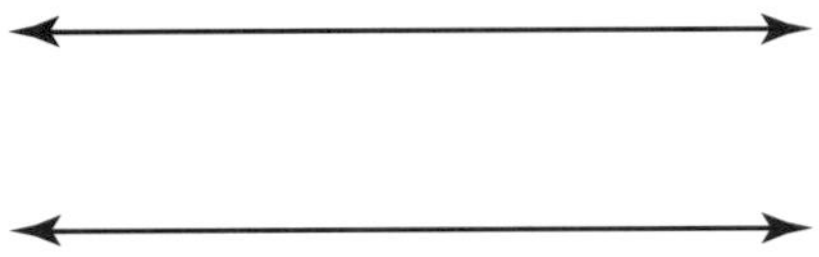

13

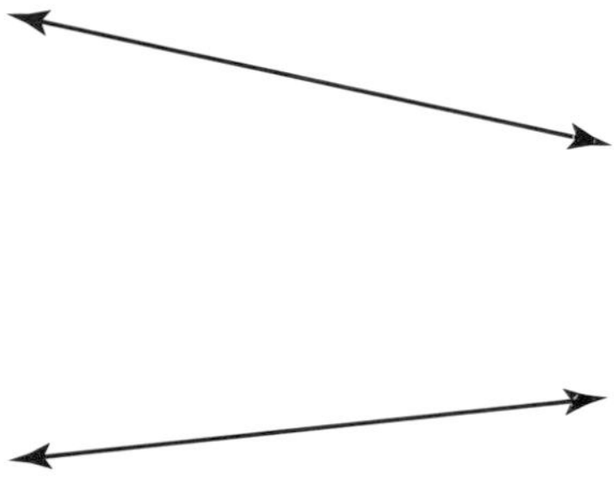

Extended Response Point to where the two lines in each exercise will meet. Explain how you know. Label each of the following as *intersecting lines* or *parallel lines*.

14

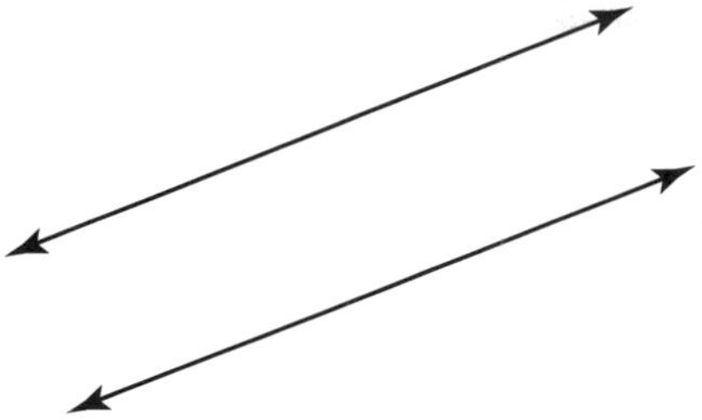

15

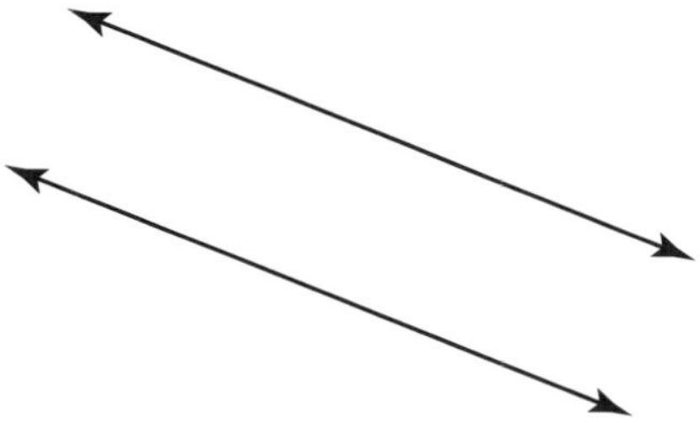

16

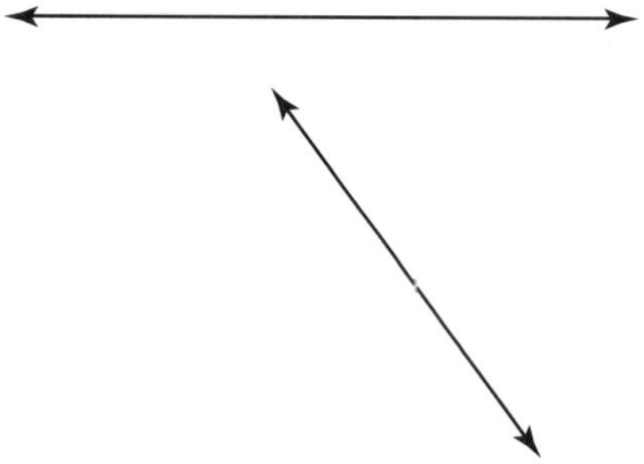

Writing + Math **Journal**

In your own words, define *point, line segment, line, parallel lines,* and *intersecting lines*. Include an illustration with each definition.

LESSON 11.2 Angles

Key Ideas

A ray is part of a line that goes on forever in one direction but ends at a point in the other direction.

This represents a ray: 

An angle is formed by two rays that have the same endpoint. The point where the two rays meet is called the vertex of the angle. This is an angle with its vertex labeled *Q*.

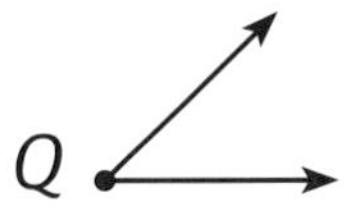

This is an angle with the vertex labeled *S*.

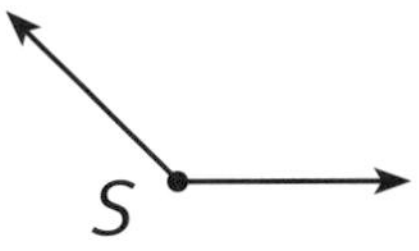

Label the following as *ray, line,* or *angle.*

1. 

2. 

3. 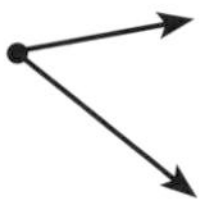

4. 

5. 

6. 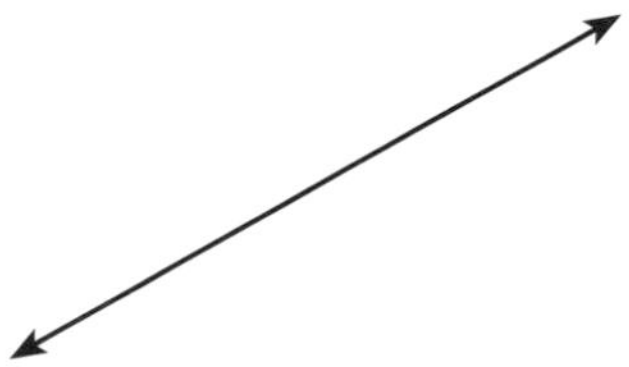

Two intersecting lines form four angles.

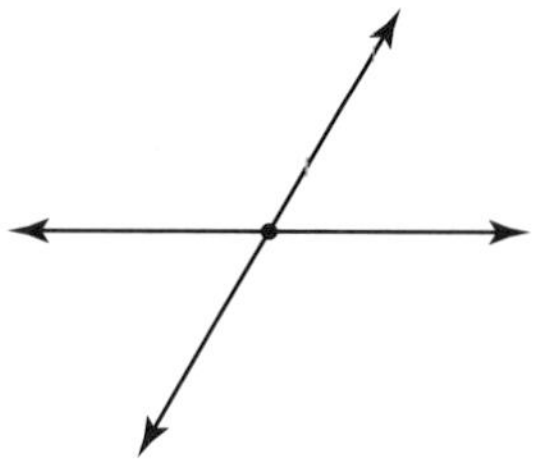

When two intersecting lines form four *identical* angles, the lines are perpendicular. The angles formed in this way are called right angles.

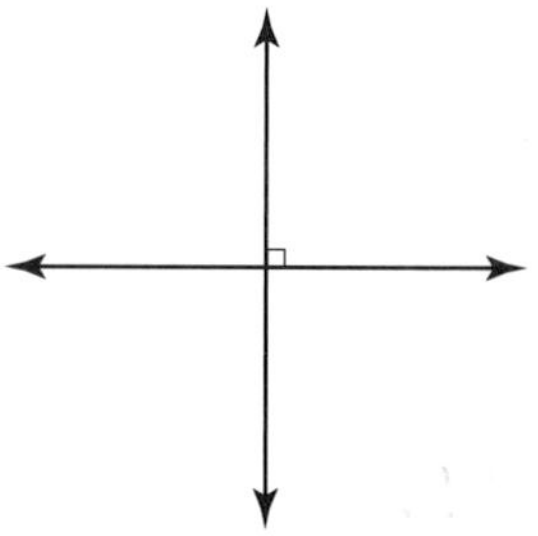

All of these are right angles.

None of these are right angles.

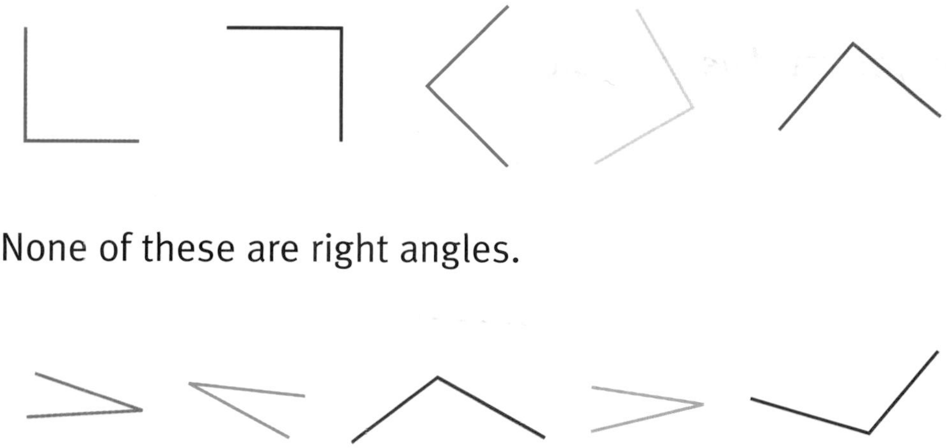

7 Which of the following are right angles?

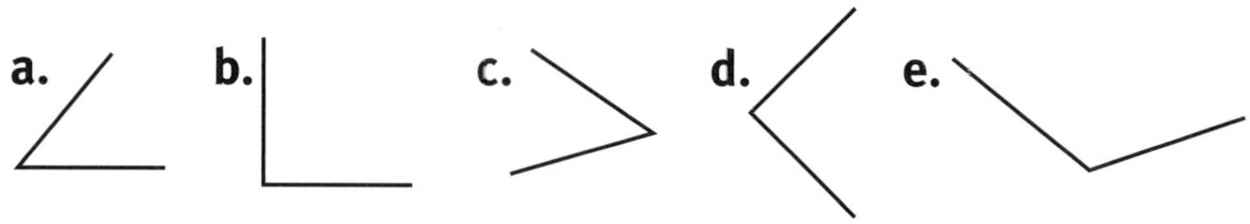

Create a two-column chart. In one column, list the angles that are greater than a right angle. In the second column, list the angles that are smaller than a right angle. The remaining angles will be right angles. Estimate first, but use the corner of a book or page to check.

8
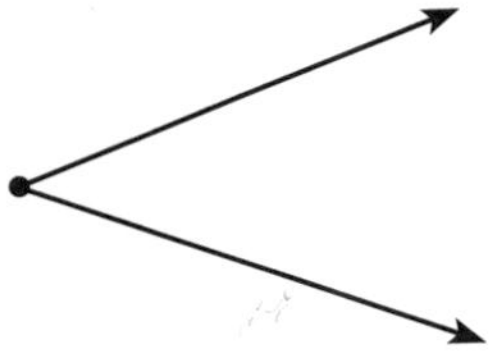

9
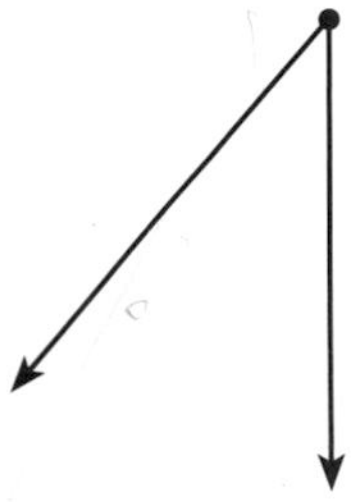

10

11
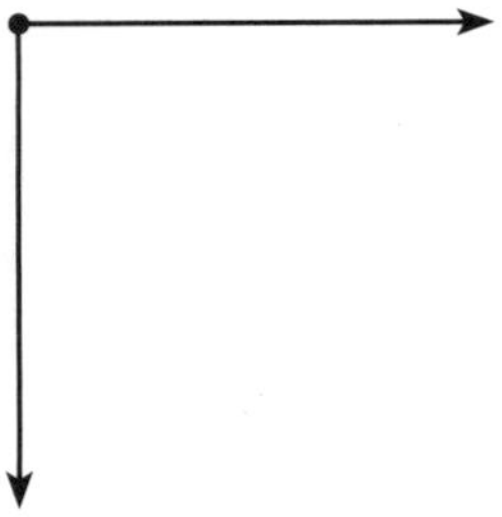

12
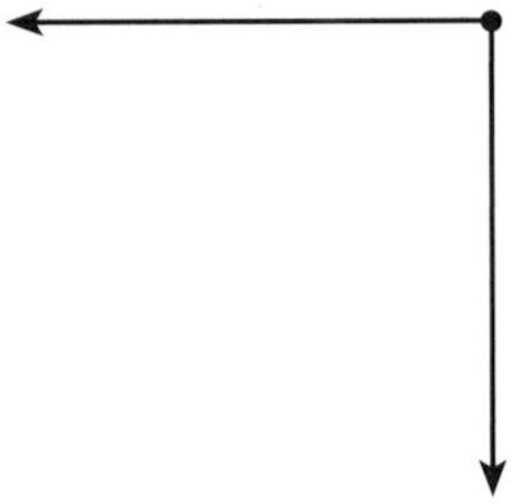

13

14
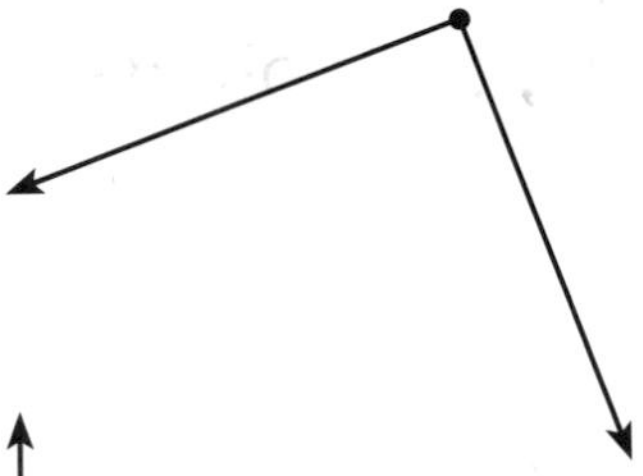

15
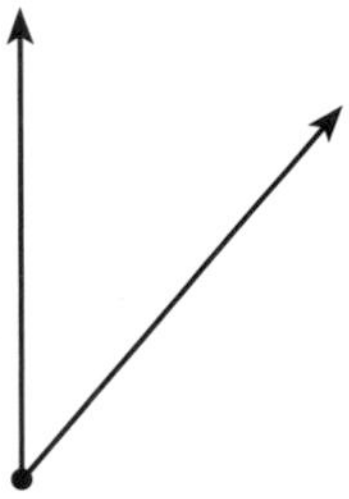

16
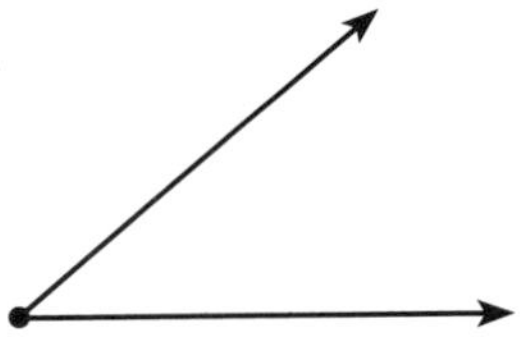

17
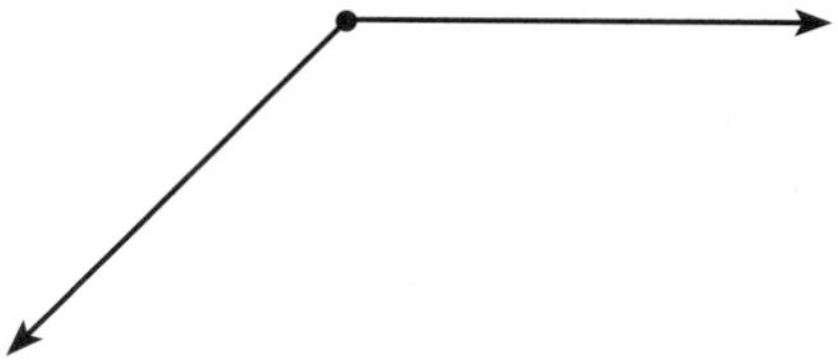

18
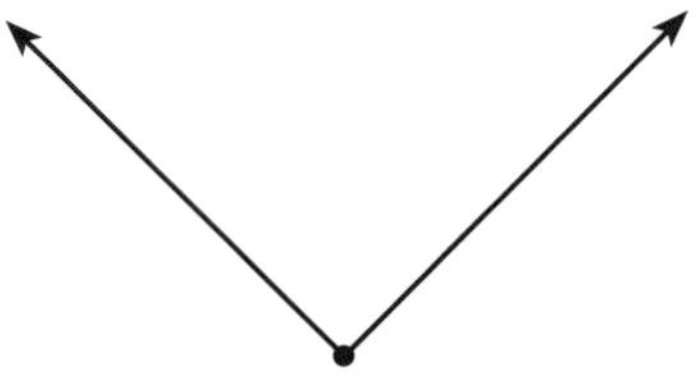

An angle that is smaller than a right angle is called an *acute angle*. An angle that is greater than a right angle is called an *obtuse angle*.

Write the correct time for each clock face. Then tell if the measure of the angle of the clock hands is a right angle, an acute angle, or an obtuse angle.

19 

20 

21 

22 

23 

24 

25 

26 

Writing + Math **Journal**

Describe the measure of the angle of the clock hands when it is 6:00.

LESSON 11.3 Triangles

Key Ideas

A figure that has three sides and three angles is a triangle. Triangles, like angles, can have special names. Three names of triangles, based on the lengths of their sides, or the size of their angles are *equilateral, isosceles,* and *right.*

All of these are equilateral triangles.

None of these are equilateral triangles.

1. Which of the following are equilateral triangles?

a. b. c. d. e.

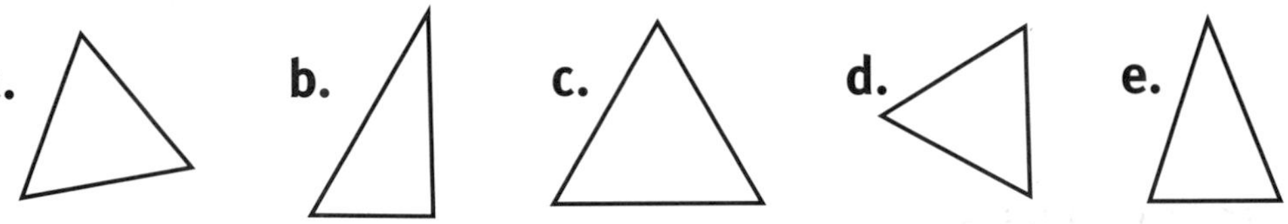

All of these are isosceles triangles.

None of these are isosceles triangles.

2. Which of the following are isosceles triangles?

a. b. c. d. e.

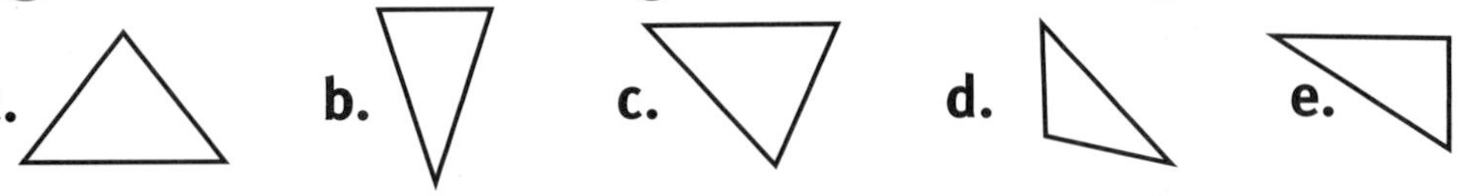

All of these are right triangles.

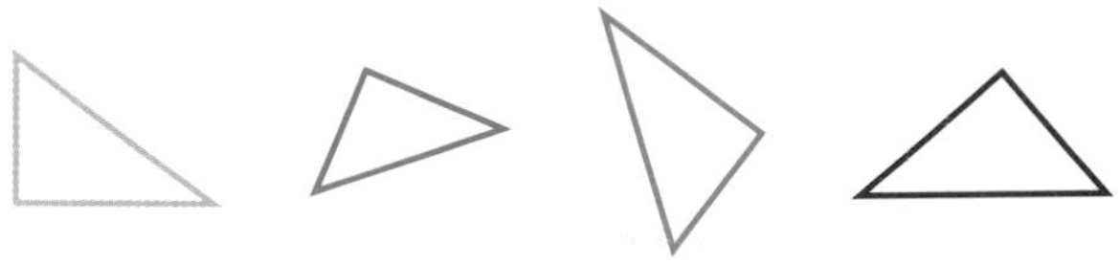

None of these are right triangles.

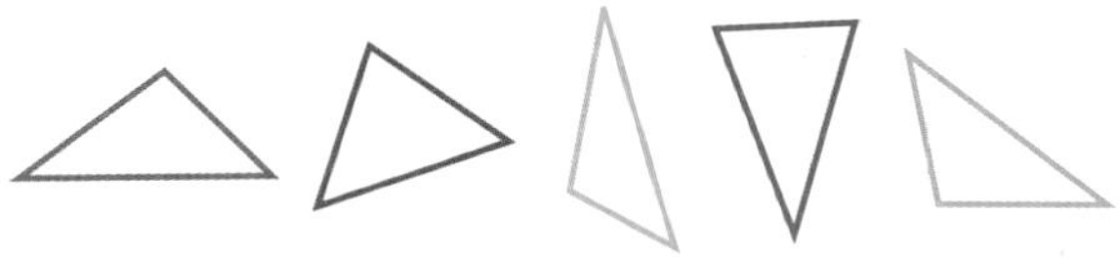

❸ Which of the following are right triangles?

a. 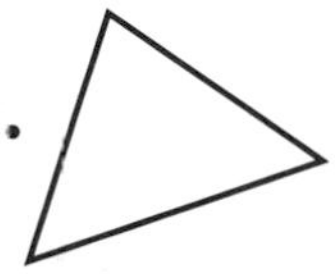 b. 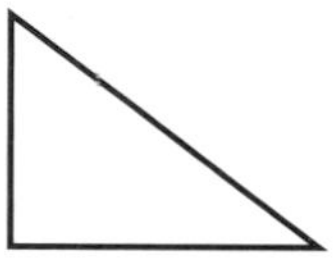 c. 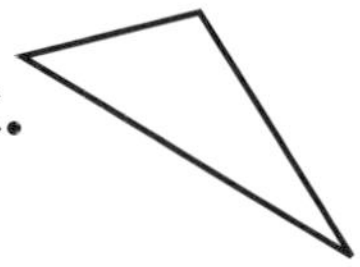 d. 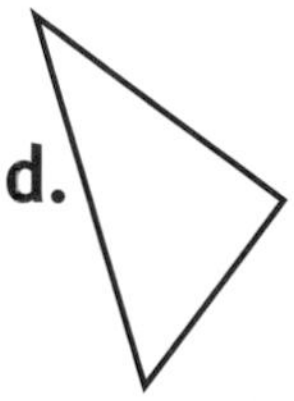 e. 

Find the perimeters of these triangles. Then identify the type of triangle.

❹

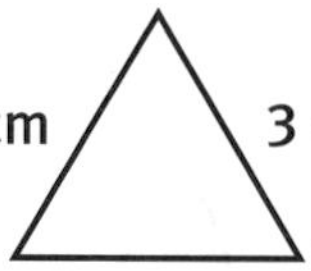

❺

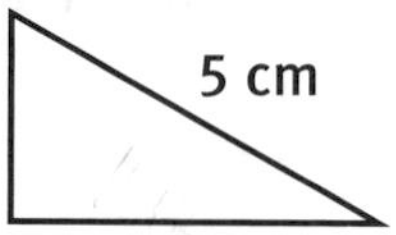

❻ Jobrack Park is shaped like an equilateral triangle. Julie jogs around the perimeter of the park every day. About how far does she jog in 3 days?

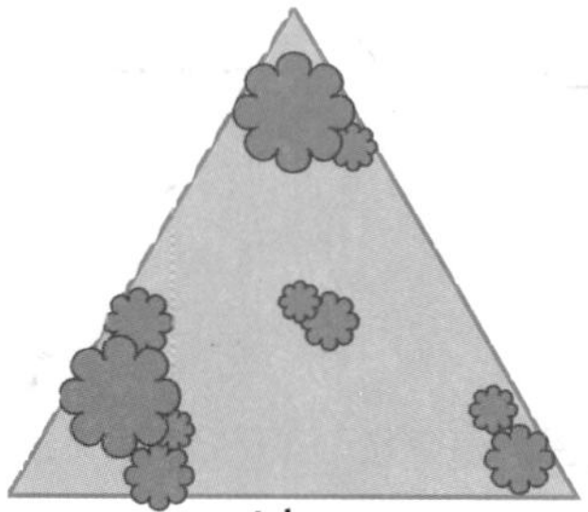

Writing + Math

Journal

In your own words, define *triangle, equilateral triangle, isosceles triangle,* and *right triangle.* Include an illustration with each definition.

LESSON 11.4
Quadrilaterals

Key Ideas

Parallelograms, trapezoids, squares, rectangles, and rhombuses are special kinds of quadrilaterals.

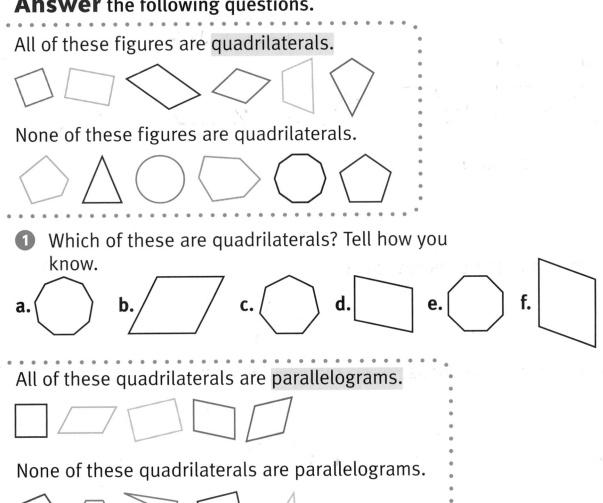

Answer the following questions.

All of these figures are quadrilaterals.

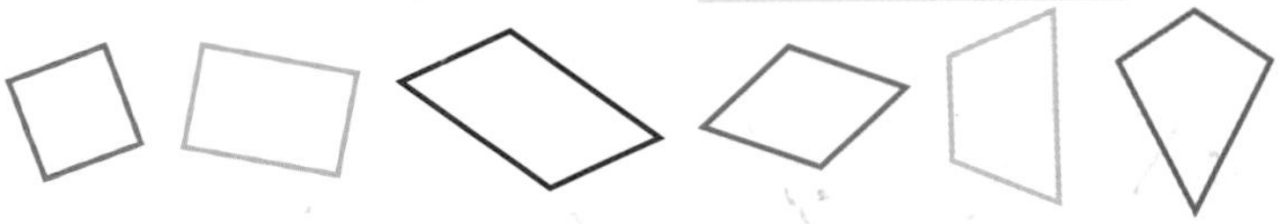

None of these figures are quadrilaterals.

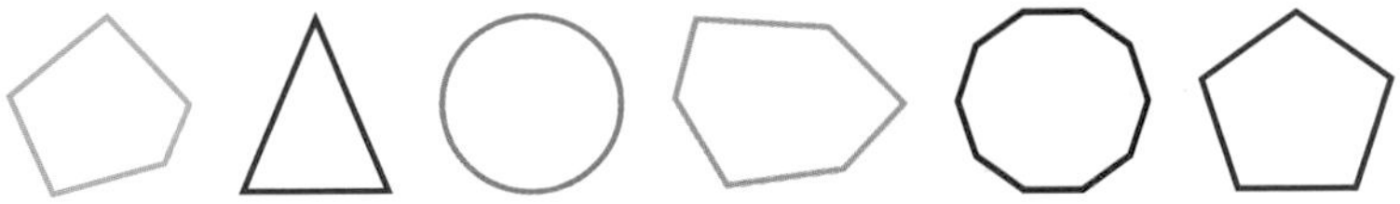

1. Which of these are quadrilaterals? Tell how you know.

a. 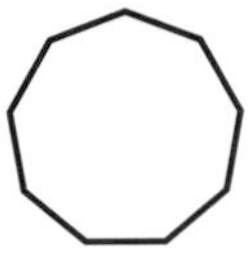 **b.** 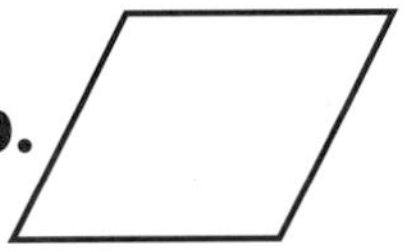 **c.**  **d.** 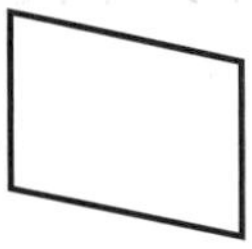 **e.** 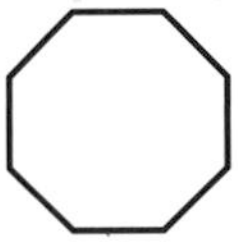 **f.** 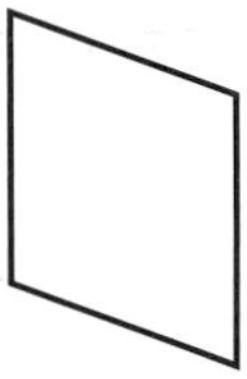

All of these quadrilaterals are parallelograms.

None of these quadrilaterals are parallelograms.

2. Which of these quadrilaterals are parallelograms? Write how you know.

a.  **b.**  **c.** 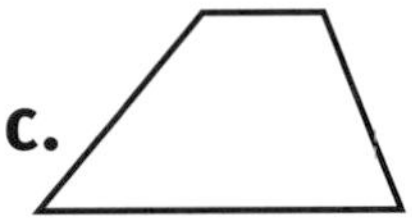 **d.**  **e.** 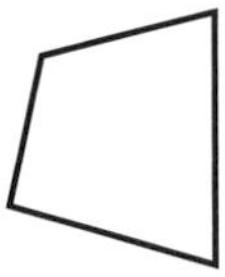 **f.** 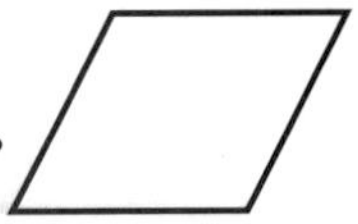

eTextbook This lesson is available in the ***eTextbook.***

Answer the following questions.

All of these parallelograms are rhombuses.

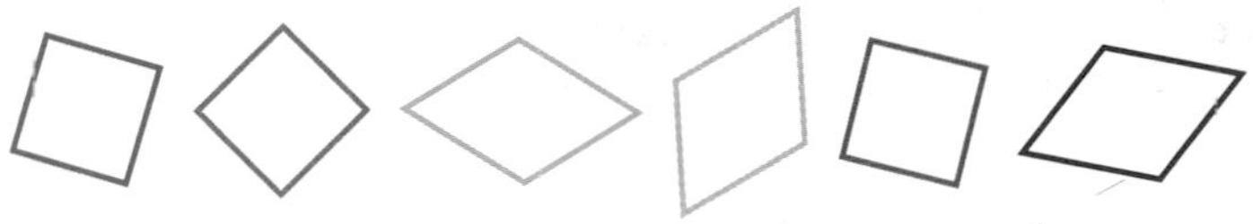

None of these parallelograms are rhombuses.

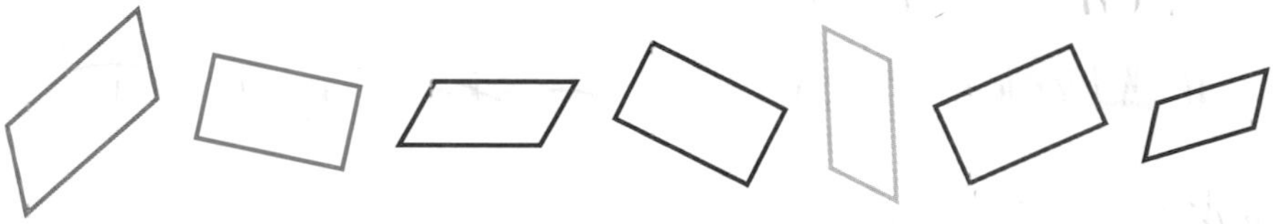

3. Which of these parallelograms are rhombuses? Write how you know.

All of these rhombuses are squares.

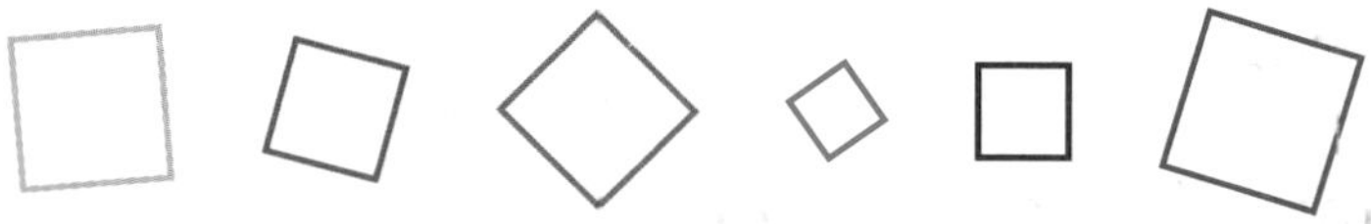

None of these rhombuses are squares.

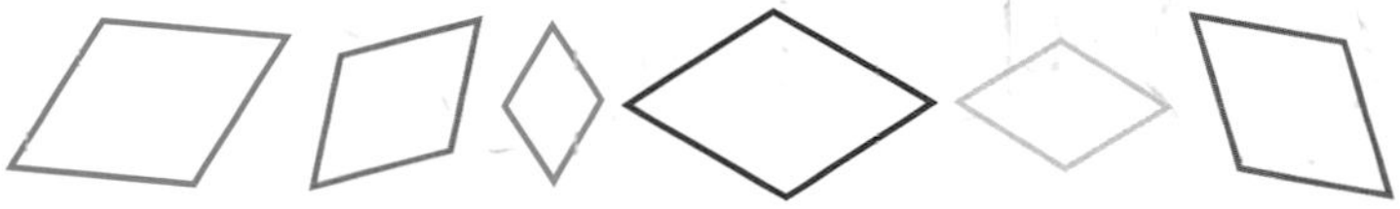

4. Which of these rhombuses are squares? Tell how you know.

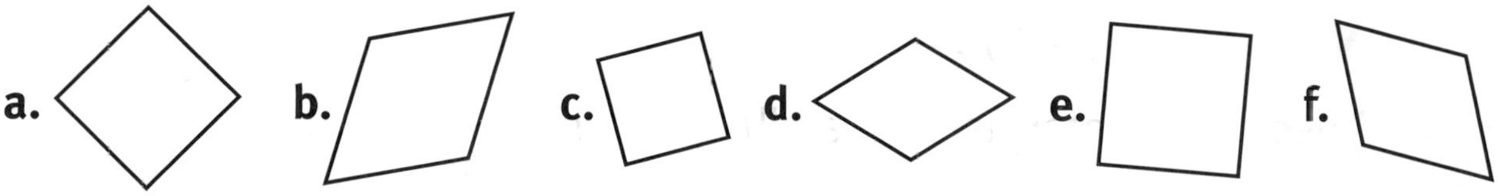

Answer the following question. Use a separate sheet of paper to record your answers.

All of these quadrilaterals are trapezoids.

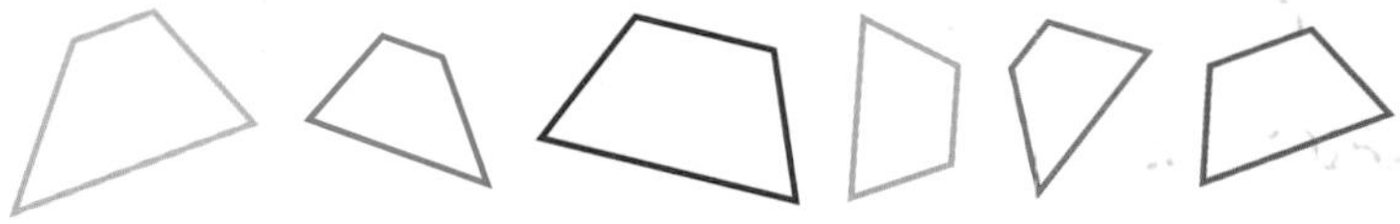

None of these quadrilaterals are trapezoids.

5 Which of these quadrilaterals are trapezoids? How do you know?

a.

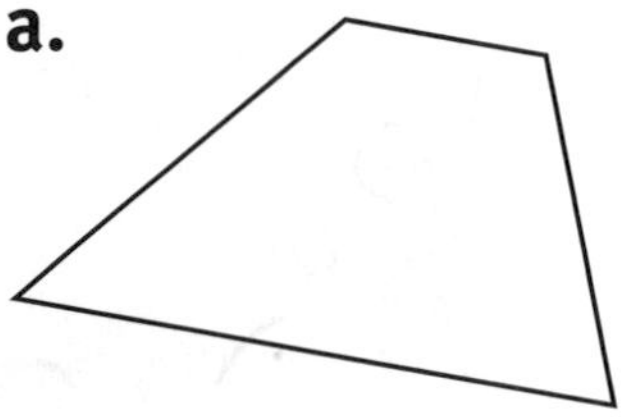

b.

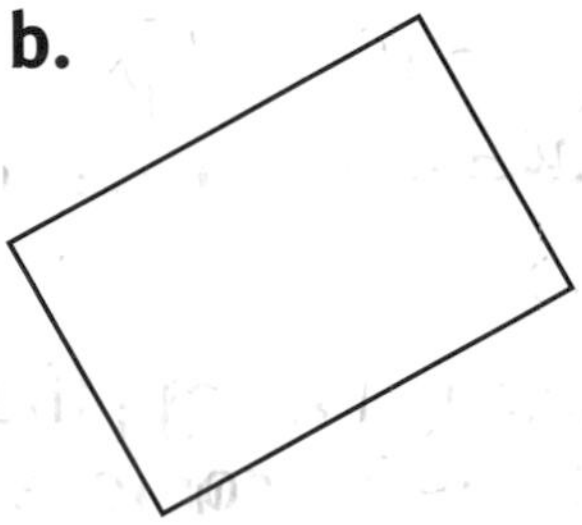

c.

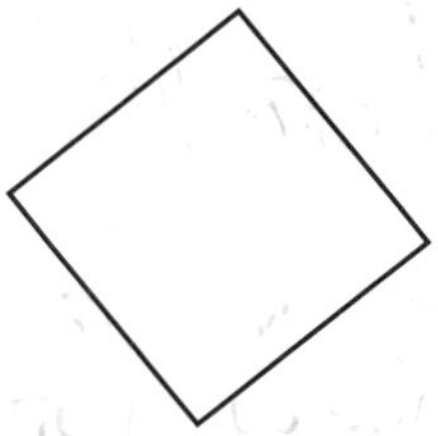

d.

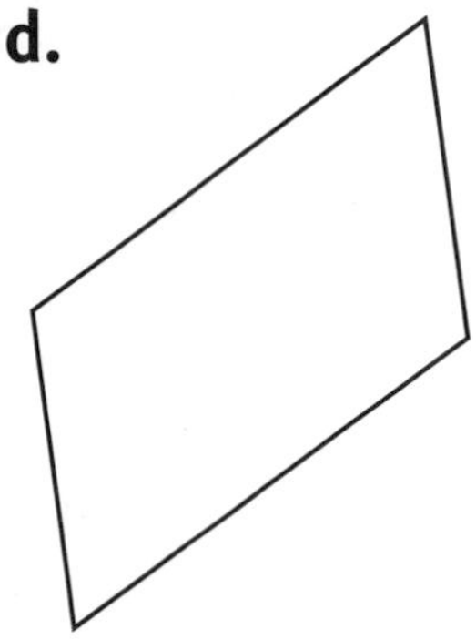

e.

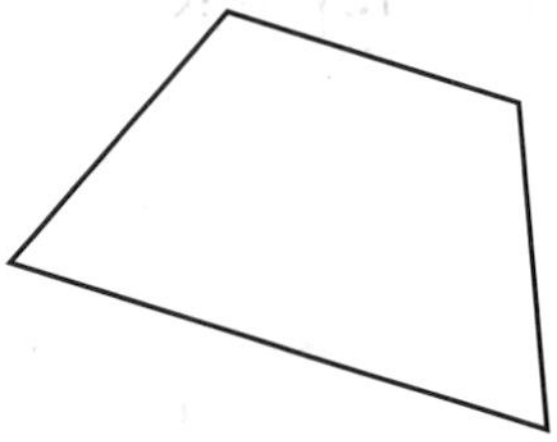

f.

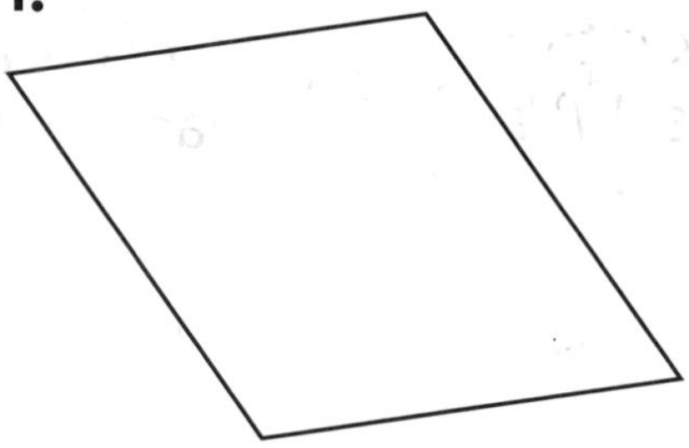

Extended Response **Label** each of the following as *true* or *false*. How do you know?

6 All rectangles are parallelograms.

7 All parallelograms are rectangles.

8 All trapezoids are quadrilaterals.

9 All squares are also rhombuses and parallelograms.

10 All quadrilaterals are parallelograms.

11 **Extended Response** Sayeski Park is shaped like a rectangle. Its perimeter is 12 kilometers. Melissa jogs along the longer side of the park each day and then takes the bus home. About how far does Melissa jog each day?

12 Moss Park is shaped like a square. Its perimeter is 28 kilometers. What is the measurement of the sides?

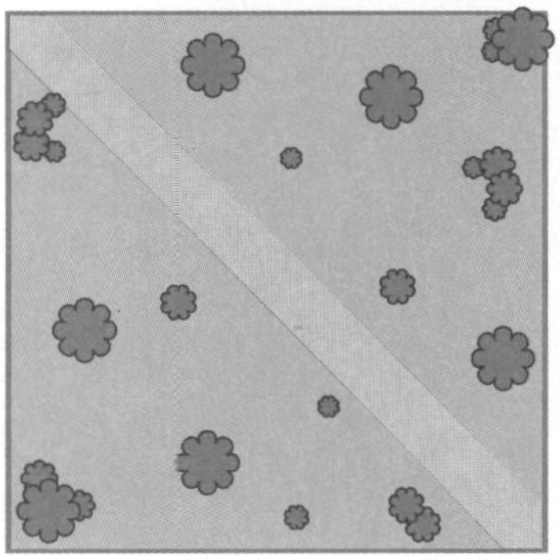

13 **Extended Response** Moss Park has a jogging path that runs from one corner of the park to the corner at the opposite end. Notice that the jogging path divides the park into two regions that are shaped like triangles. What kind of triangles are they? How do you know?

Writing + Math **Journal**

In your own words, define *quadrilateral, parallelogram, trapezoid, square, rectangle,* and *rhombus*. Include an illustration with each definition.

LESSON 11.5

Polygons

Key Ideas

A polygon is a closed plane figure having at least three sides.

Write the names of each of the following polygons.

1. 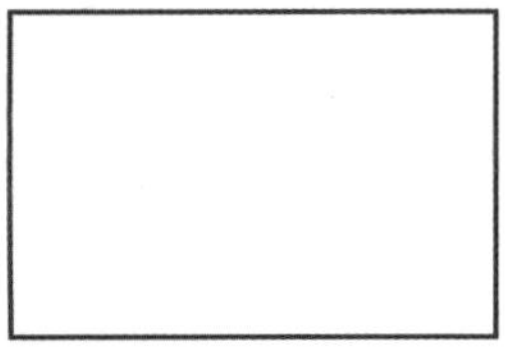

2. 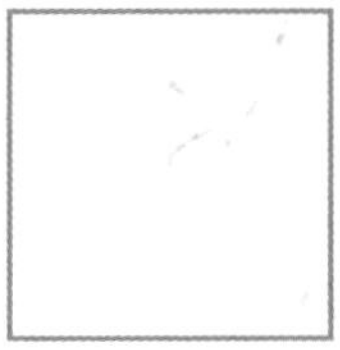

3. 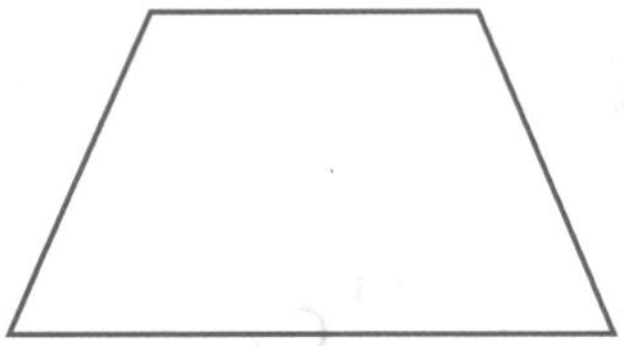

4. 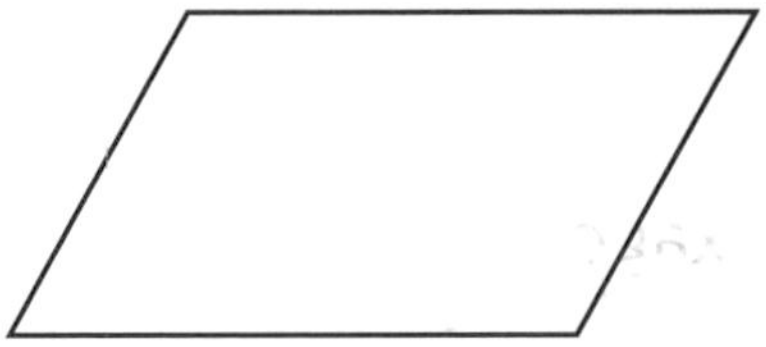

5.

6. 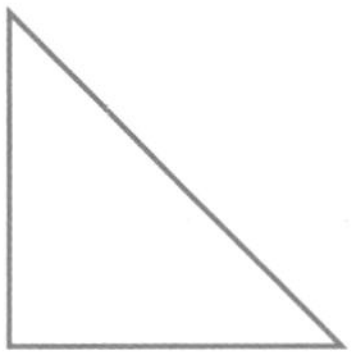

All of these are triangles.

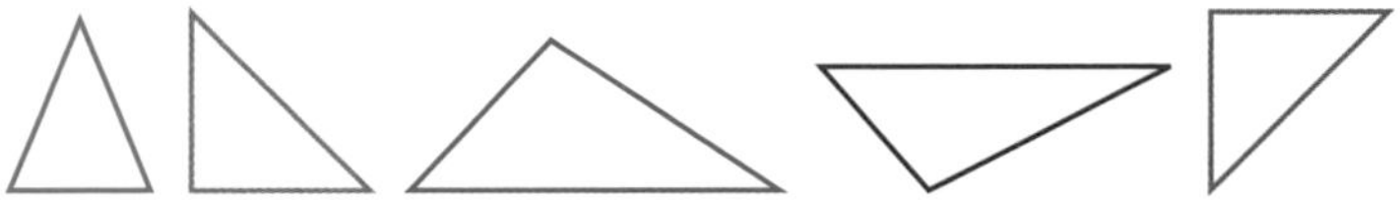

None of these are triangles.

7. Which of the following are triangles?

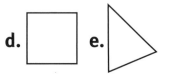

a. 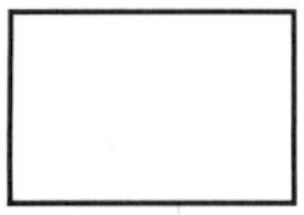 **b.** 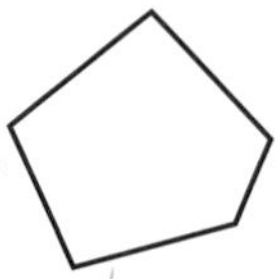 **c.** 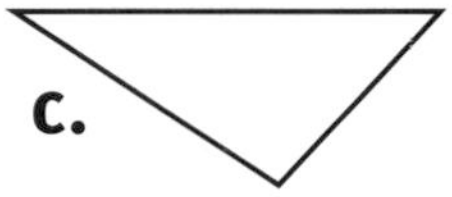 **d.**  **e.** 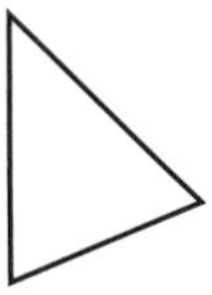

eTextbook This lesson is available in the ***eTextbook.***

All of these are pentagons.

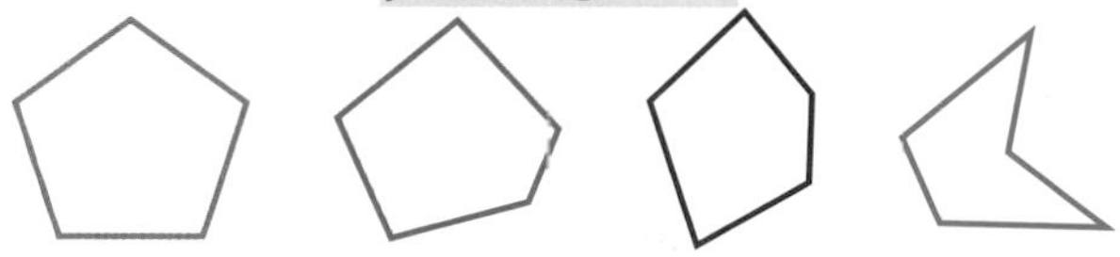

None of these are pentagons.

8 Which of the following are pentagons?

a. 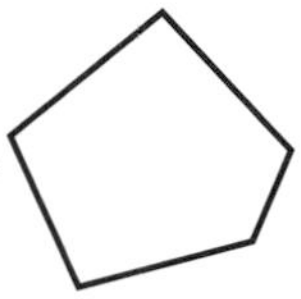 **b.** 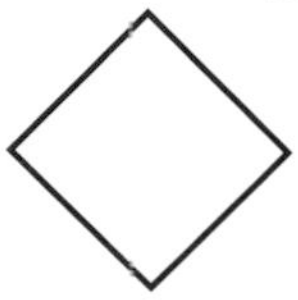 **c.**  **d.** 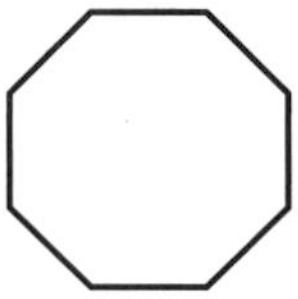 **e.** 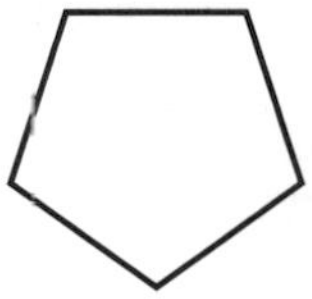

All of these are hexagons.

None of these are hexagons.

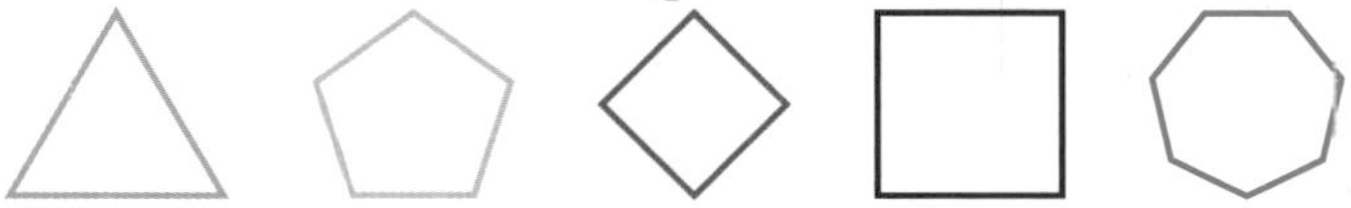

9 Which of the following are hexagons?

a. 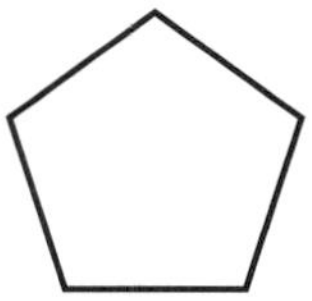 **b.** 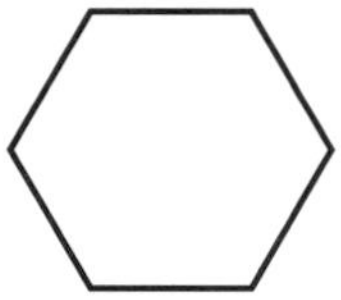 **c.** 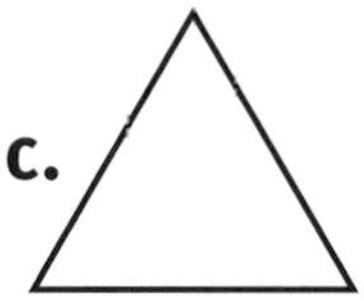 **d.** 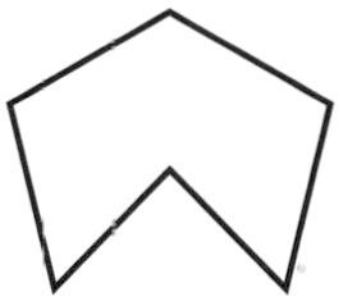 **e.** 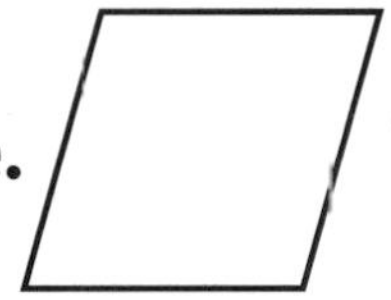

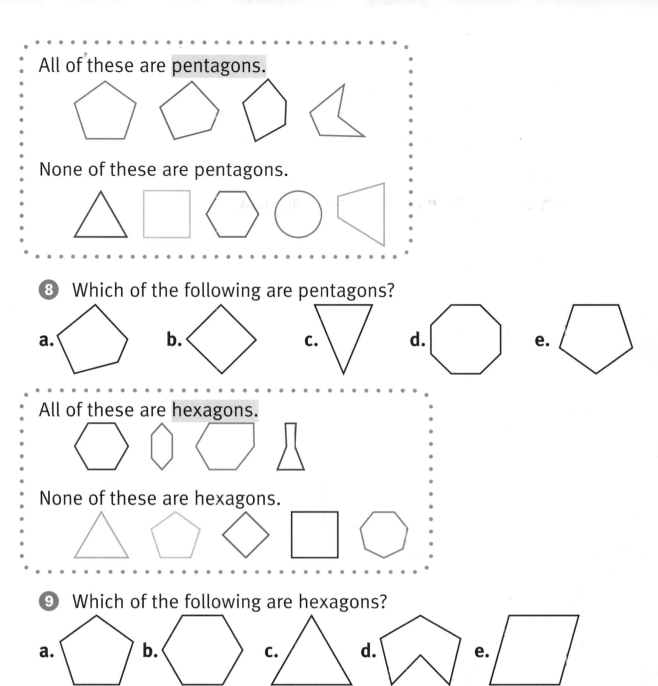

All of these are octagons.

None of these are octagons.

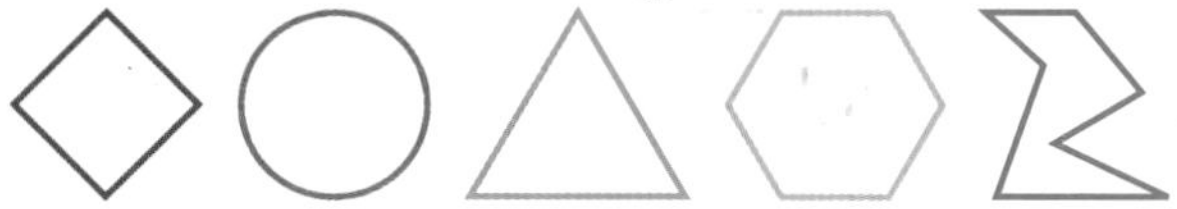

⑩ Which of the following are octagons?

a. 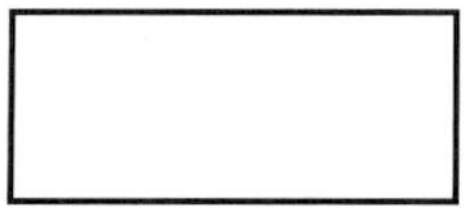 **b.** 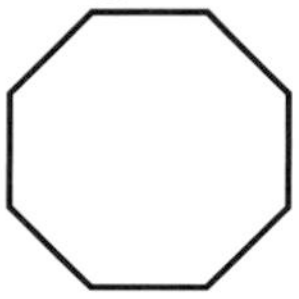 **c.** 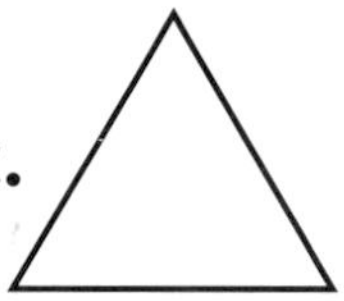 **d.** 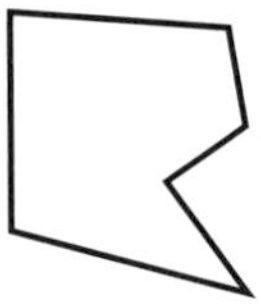

Predict which shape comes next. Include a drawing and the name of the polygon in your answer.

⑪ 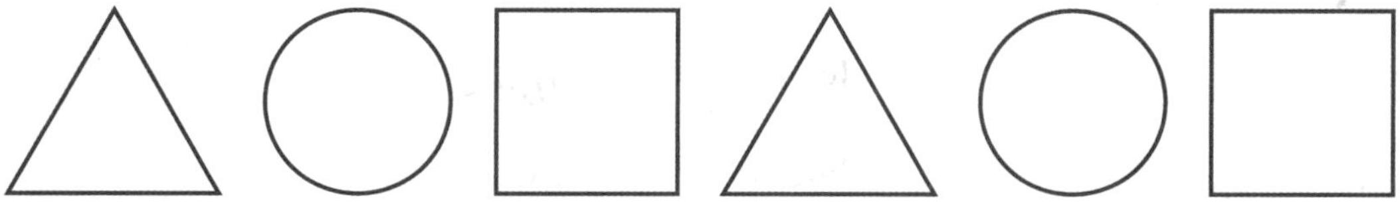 ▢

⑫ 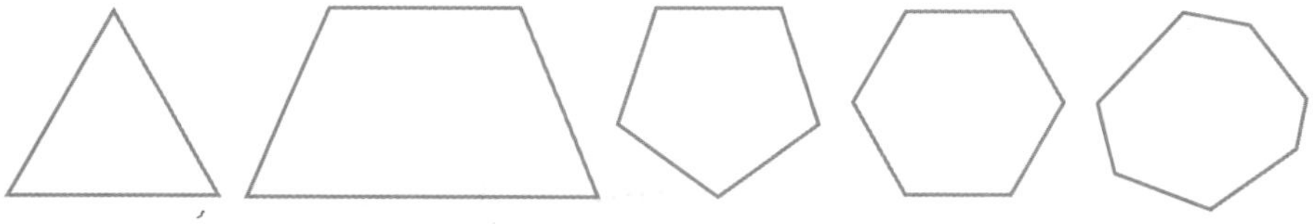 ▢

How many of the following polygons can you find in this picture?

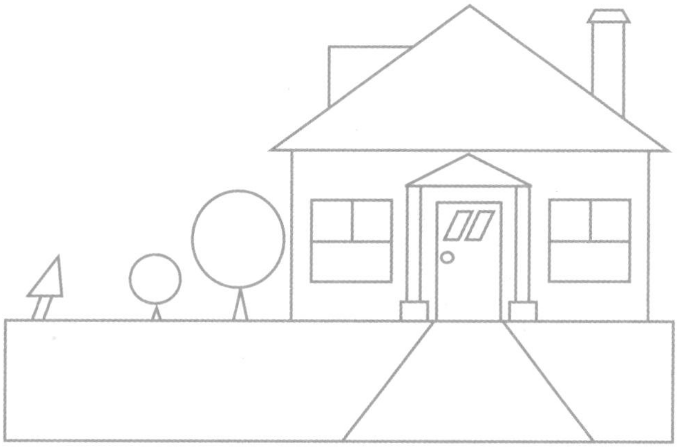

⑬ Squares ▢

⑭ Non-square Rectangles ▢

⑮ Non-rectangular Parallelograms ▢

⑯ Trapezoids ▢

⑰ Triangles ▢

eTextbook This lesson is available in the *eTextbook*.

Use the pictures to find the number.

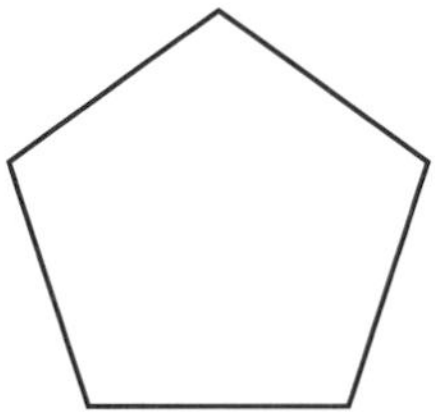

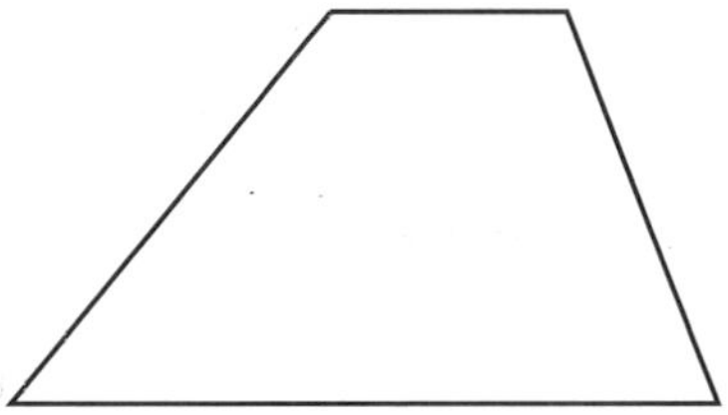

18 Number of sides

19 Number of angles

20 Name of shape

21 Number of sides

22 Number of angles

23 Name of shape

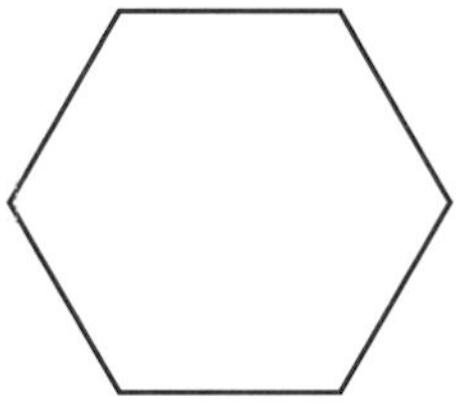

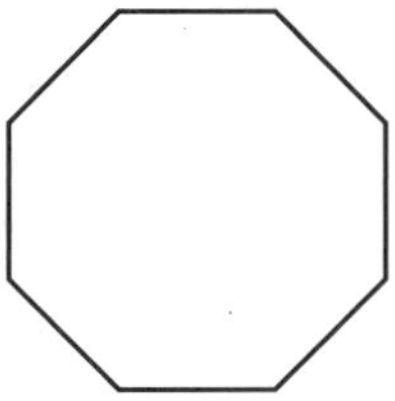

24 Number of sides

25 Number of angles

26 Name of shape

27 Number of sides

28 Number of angles

29 Name of shape

Writing + Math **Journal**

A polygon with ten sides is called a *decagon*. Draw three decagons in your journal that are not all alike.

Congruence

Key Ideas

Two figures are congruent if they are the same shape *and* the same size.

You can check to see if two figures are congruent by tracing one figure and seeing if the tracing fits on top of the other figure. Flip the tracing paper to see that these two right triangles are congruent.

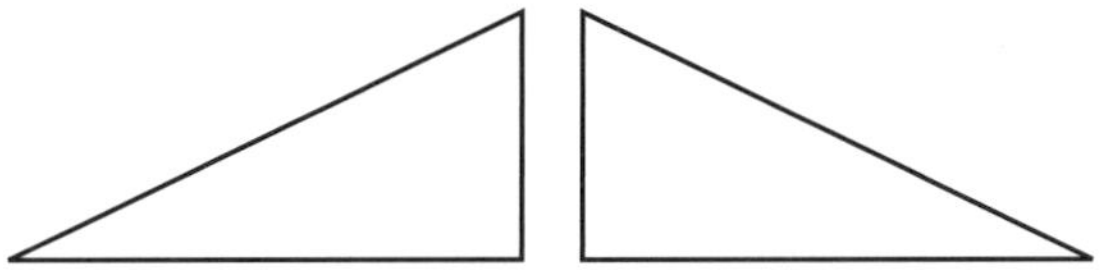

Look at the figures. Use tracing paper if needed to help you see which are congruent. List each pair of congruent figures.

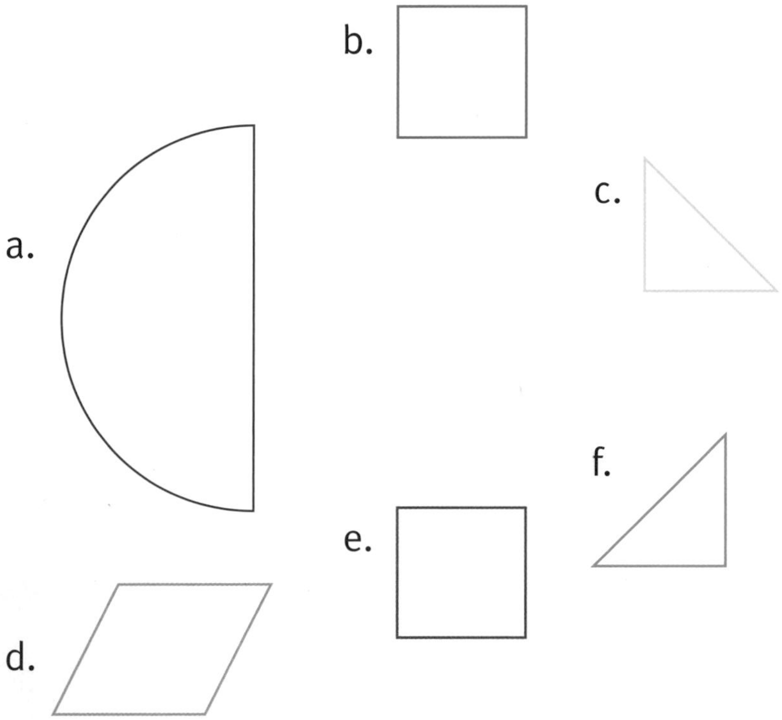

List each pair of congruent figures.

a.

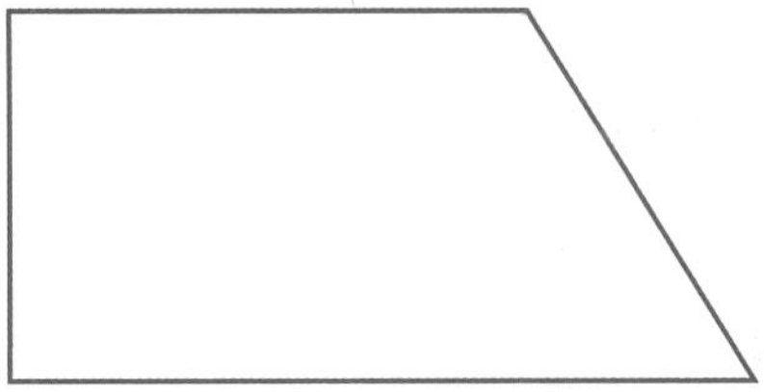

b.

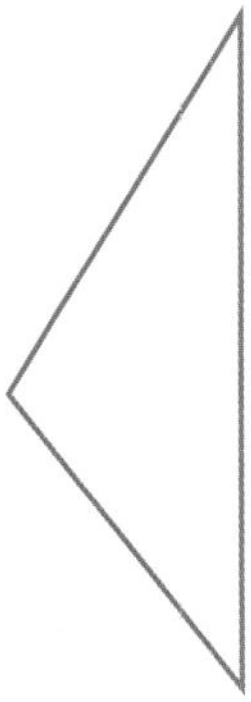

c.

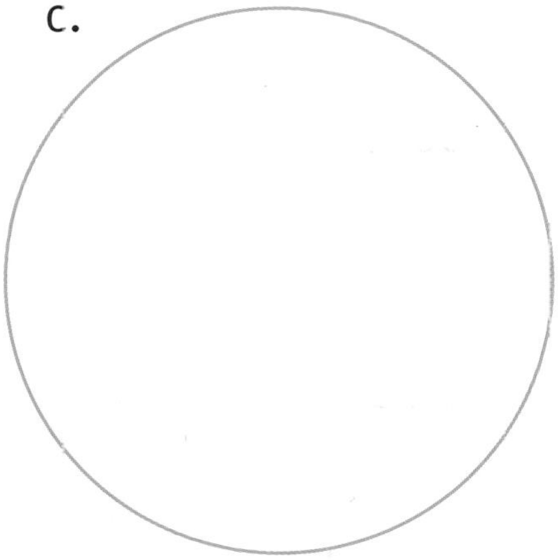

e.

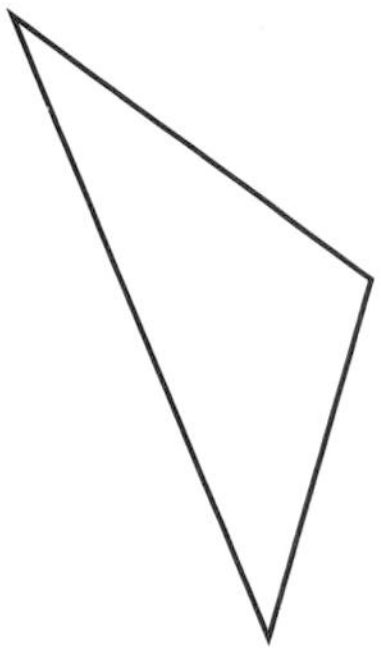

d.

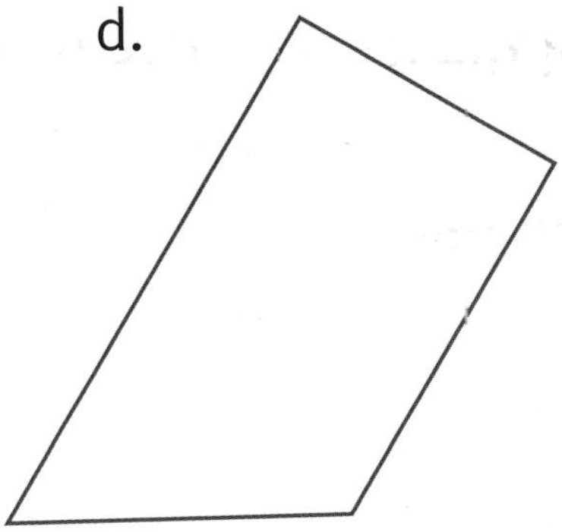

f.

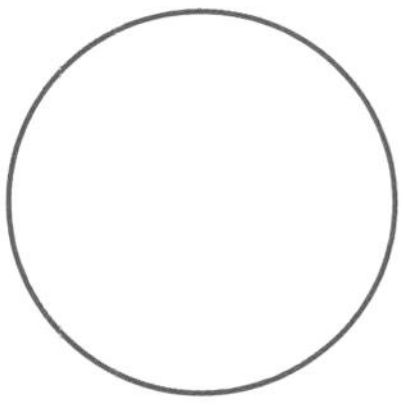

g.

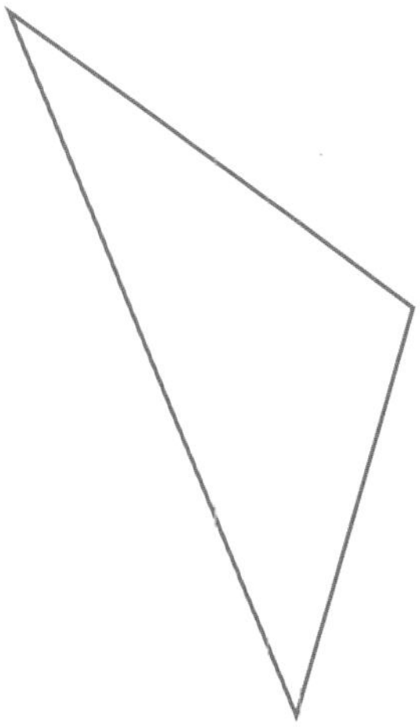

h.

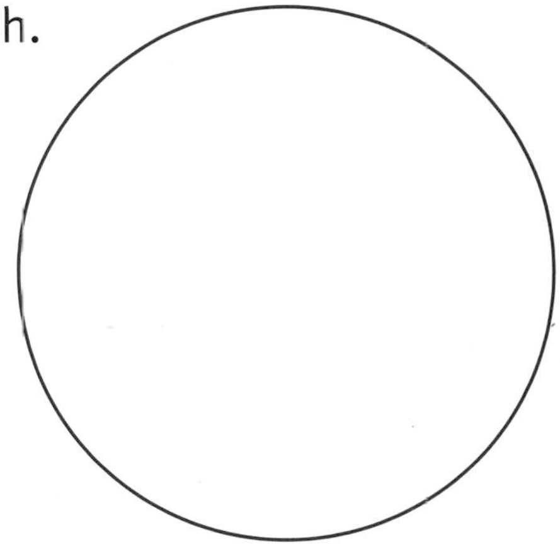

Do you remember designing your own room or house on page 423? Now you are going to decorate one of the walls. You will use triangle tiles in a pattern like the one shown at the right. You have 10 boxes of tiles with 25 tiles in each box. Each tile is 3 inches high. How high can you make your tile design?

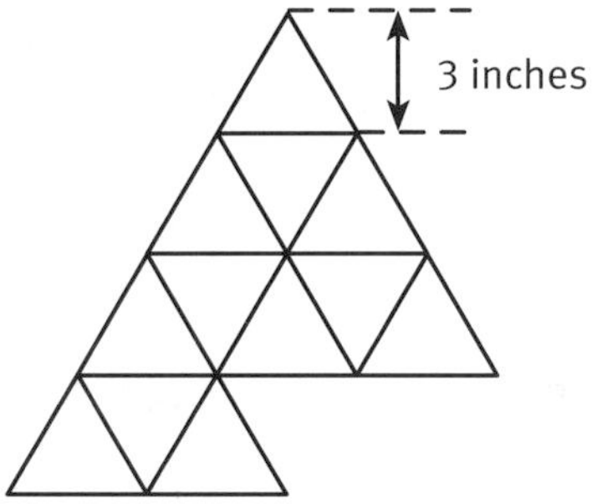

Jasmine started to solve the problem by making a physical model.

My Plan

1. *Cut out 250 triangle pieces.*
2. *Build a design like the one in the picture, only bigger.*

Think **about Jasmine's strategy. Answer the following questions.**

1. Why did Jasmine decide to make 250 triangles?
2. Do Jasmine's triangles have to be 3 inches high? Explain.
3. Would you use Jasmine's strategy to solve the problem? Explain.

Javier used simple numbers, made a table, and looked for a pattern to solve the problem.

My Plan

1. Draw the design with just a few tiles. Record the results in a table.
2. Look for a pattern.
3. Use the pattern to find how big the design can be with 250 tiles.

Design	Number of Rows in the Design	Number of Tiles Used
	1	1
	2	1+3=4
	3	

Think about Javier's strategy. Answer the following questions.

4. What equation do you think Javier is about to write?
5. How many tiles will be in the design if it has 4 rows?
6. How many complete rows can be made with 15 tiles?
7. What pattern do you see in the number of tiles in each row?

Cumulative Review

Customary Length **Lesson 9.2**

Answer the following questions.

1. Mrs. Jiménez has a window that is 64 inches wide. How many feet is that?
2. She wants to make 9-foot-long curtains for the window. How many yards is that?
3. Hannah is making beanbag chairs with 12 yards of fabric. How many feet is that?

Percents and Hundredths **Lesson 8.11**

Write the fraction for each percent.

4. 53%
5. 18%
6. 22%
7. 88%
8. 100%
9. 79%

Multiplying Three-Digit Numbers by One-Digit Numbers **Lesson 7.3**

Solve. Be sure to label your answers correctly.

10. In one week's time, Alejandra and her 4 sisters each planted 235 tulip bulbs. How many tulip bulbs did the girls plant altogether?
11. Mr. Norman is an ornithologist. He loves to study birds. He studied 187 bird species each week for 4 weeks. How many bird species did he study altogether?

Perimeter **Lesson 3.6**

Find the perimeter of each figure.

12 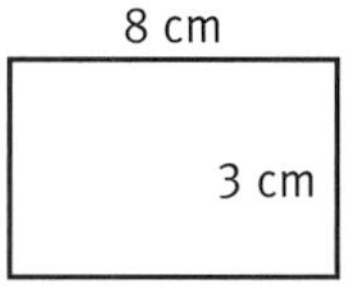

Perimeter: ___ centimeters

13 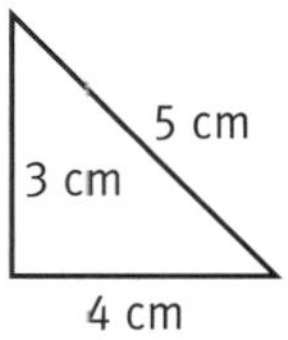

Perimeter: ___ centimeters

14 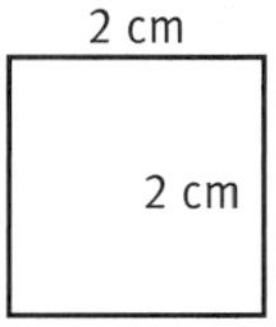

Perimeter: ___ centimeters

15 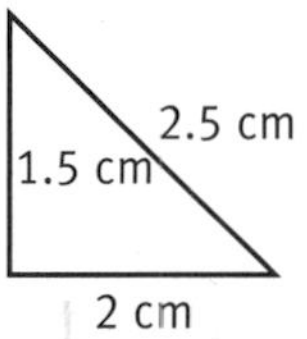

Perimeter: ___ centimeters

16 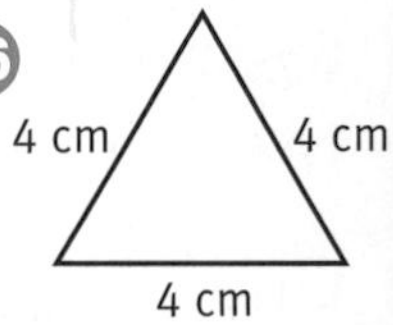

Perimeter: ___ centimeters

Decimals and Metric Measures **Lesson 10.3**

Answer these questions.

17. How many decimeters are in 4 meters?
18. How many decimeters are in 3.5 meters?
19. How many meters are in 65 decimeters?
20. How many decimeters are in 5.7 meters?
21. How many decimeters are in 21 meters?

Equivalent Fractions **Lesson 8.5**

What fraction of each figure is shaded?

22 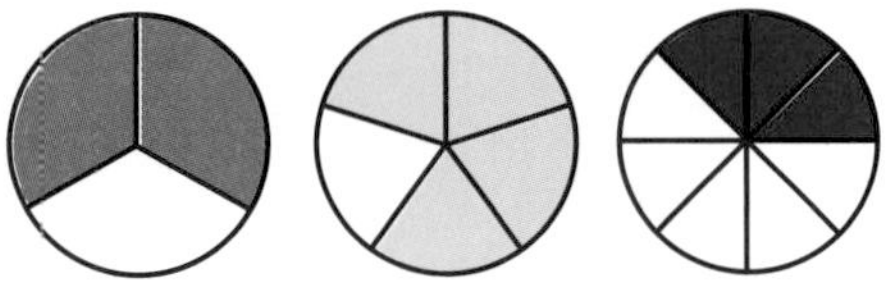

24 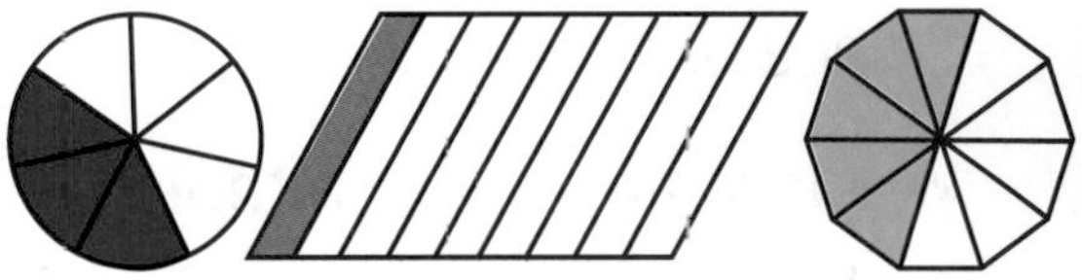

23 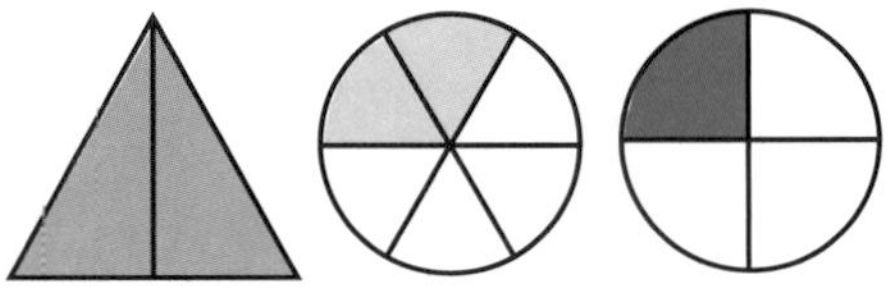

25 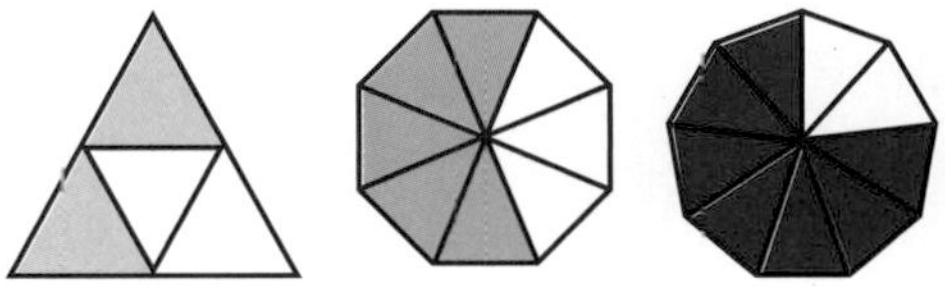

LESSON 11.7

Slides, Flips, and Turns

Key Ideas

There are three ways to move a figure from one place to another without changing the size or the shape of the figure.

One way is to *slide* the figure in any direction. Another name for a slide is translation.

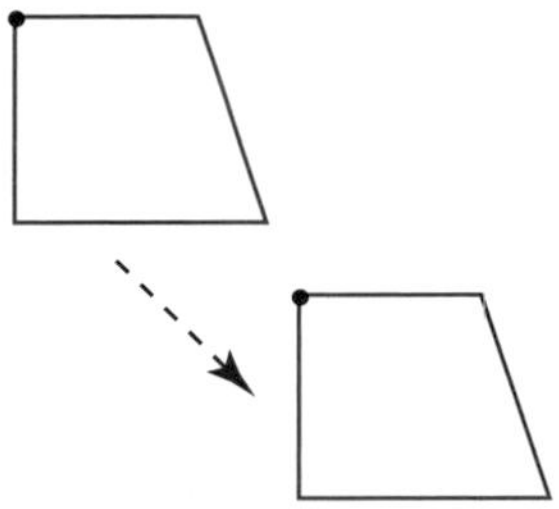

A second way is to *flip* the figure over a line. Another name for a flip is reflection.

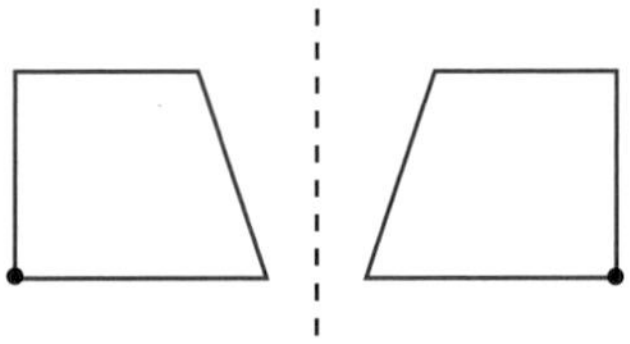

A third way is to *turn* the figure around a point, either to the right or to the left. Another name for a turn is rotation.

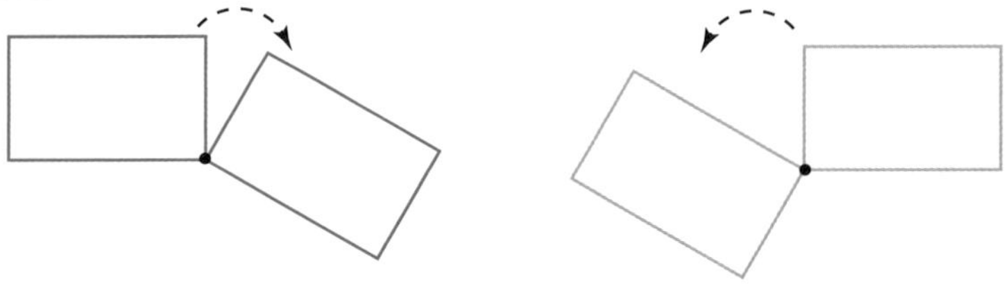

Translations, reflections, and rotations are also called transformations. These transformations can also be combined.

Look closely at each change. Determine if the change was due to a *translation*, a *reflection*, or a *rotation*.

1. 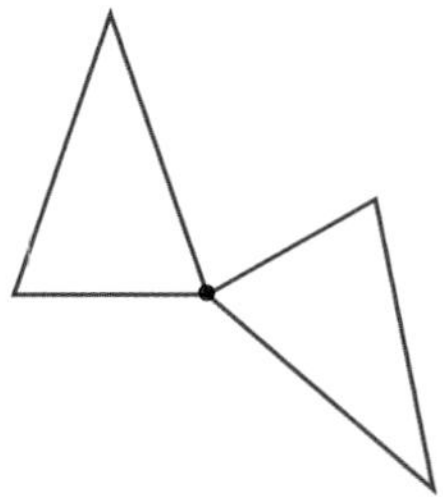

2. 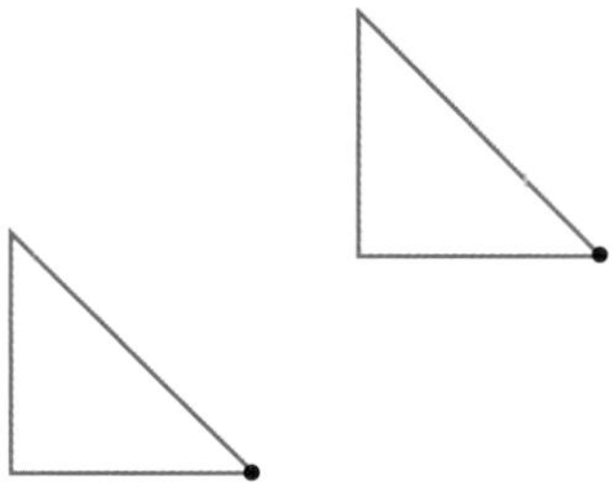

3. 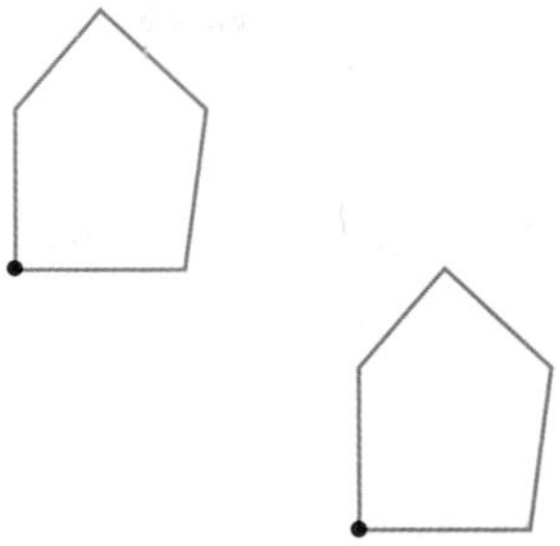

4. 

Describe the change from one position to the other for the figure.

5. 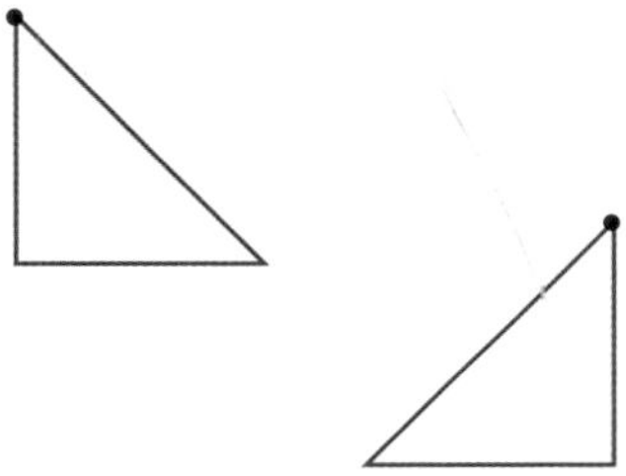

6. 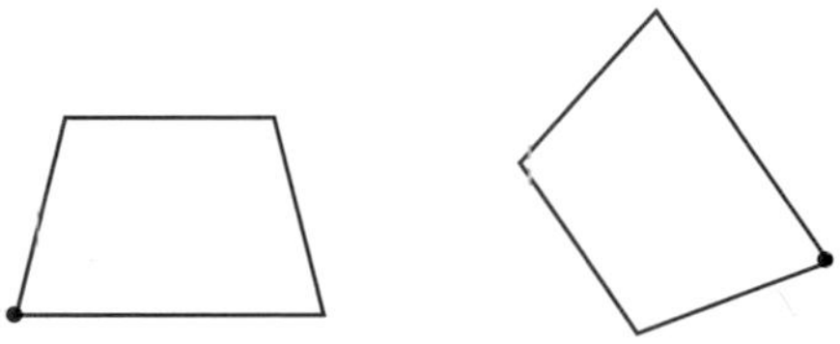

7. 

8. 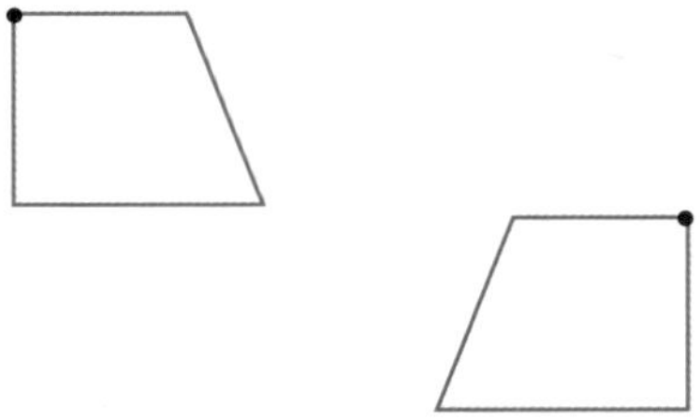

Writing + Math **Journal**

Trace this triangle. Then draw a picture of this triangle after it is reflected and then rotated any amount.

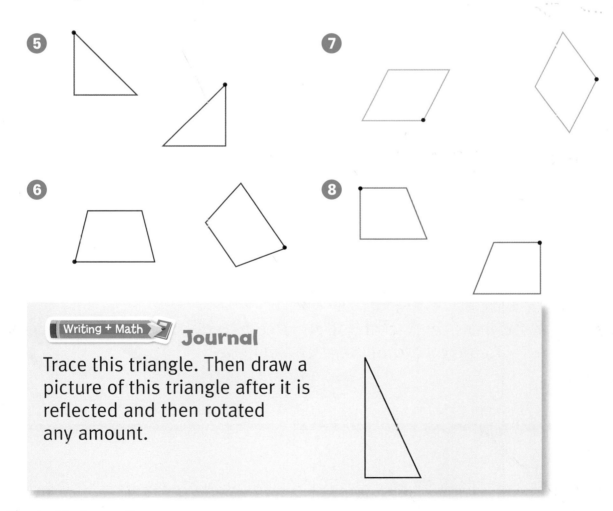

LESSON
11.8 Symmetry

Key Ideas

An object is symmetric if it looks the same on one side of a line as it does on the other.

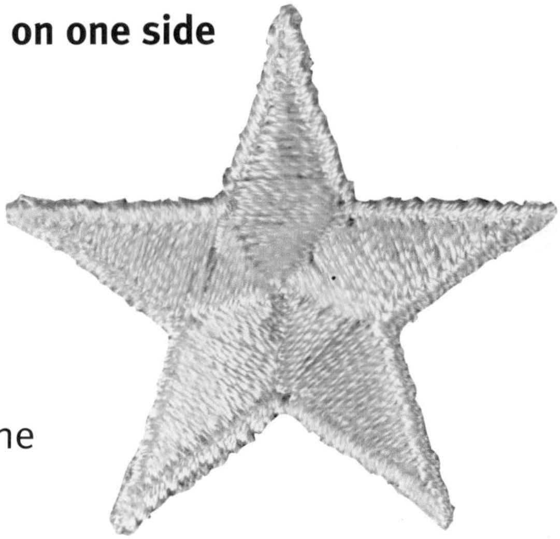

If you can trace the part of a figure on one side of a line and flip the tracing so it fits on the other half of the figure, the figure is symmetric about that line.

The flip line is the line of symmetry.

All lines of symmetry have been drawn in the following figures. Notice there is no line of symmetry for the third figure.

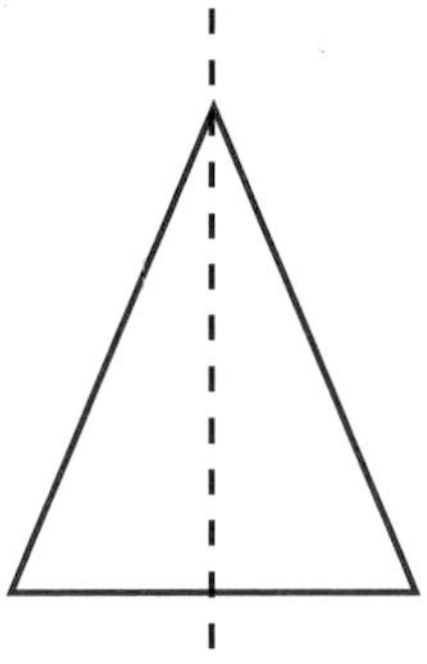

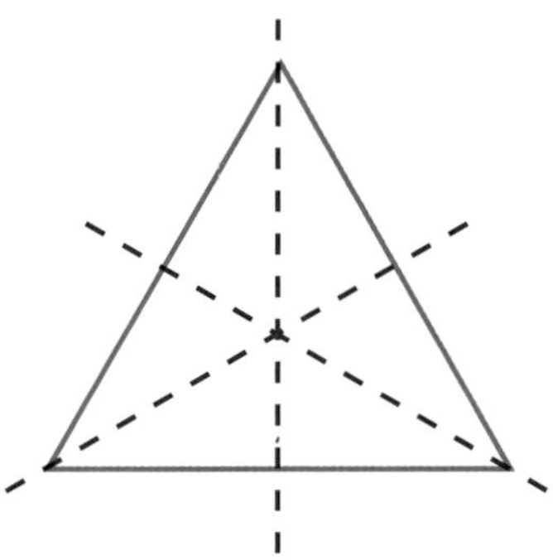

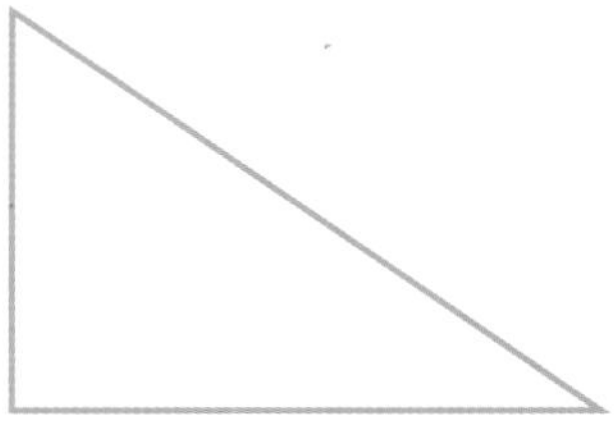

eTextbook This lesson is available in the ***eTextbook.***

Copy the figures on your paper. Use a second color to draw all the lines of symmetry.

1. 

2. 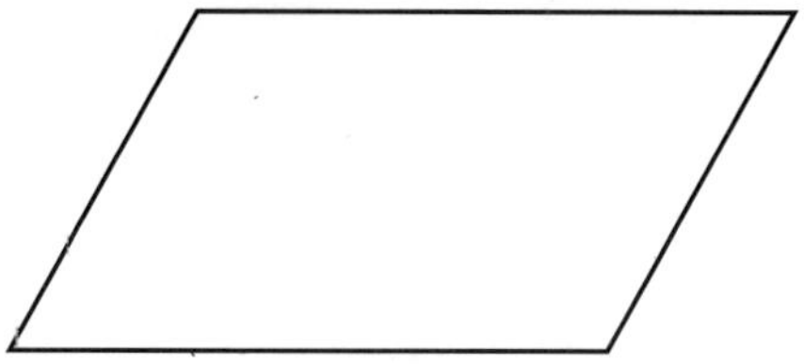

3. 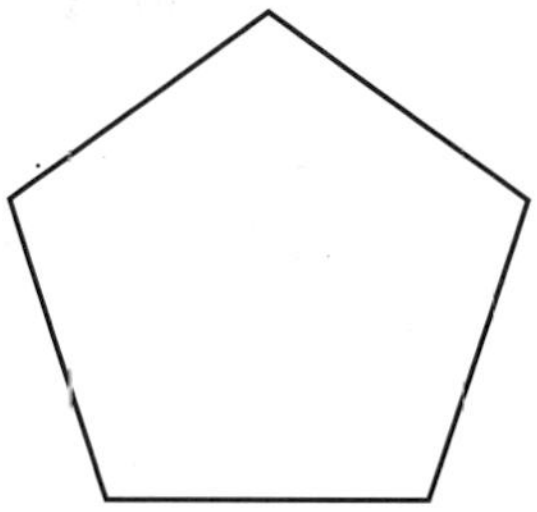

4. 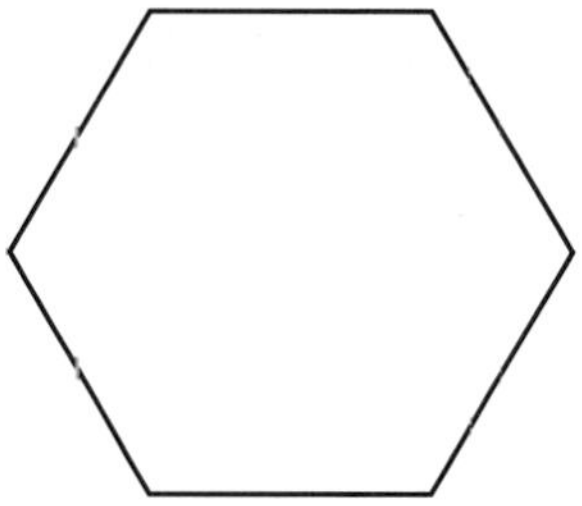

5. 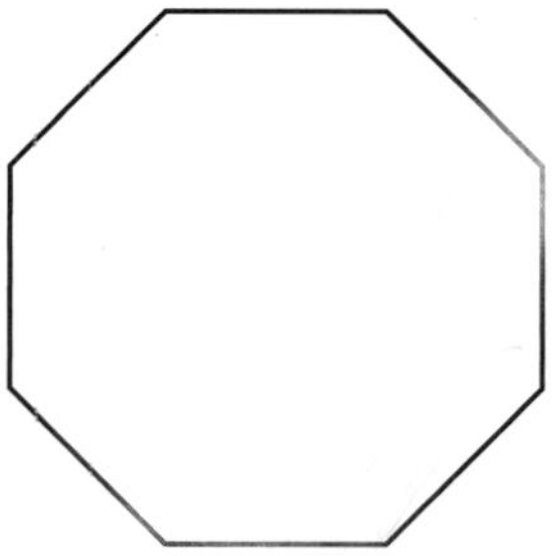

6. 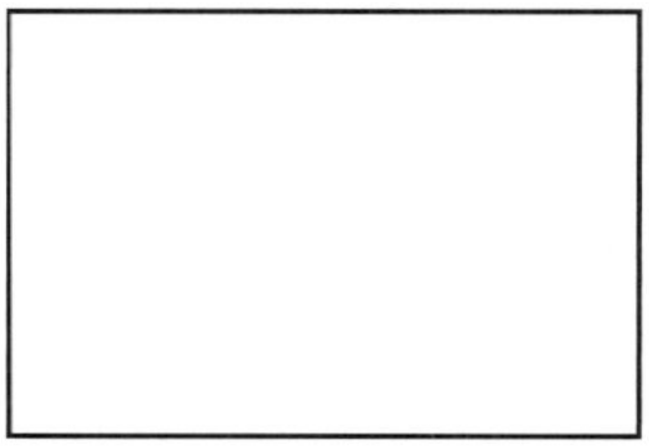

Use mirrors to find the lines of symmetry. Draw all figures and lines of symmetry in a different color on your paper.

7. A

8. E

9. 8

10. W

11. C

12. F

13. H

14. M

15. N

16. X

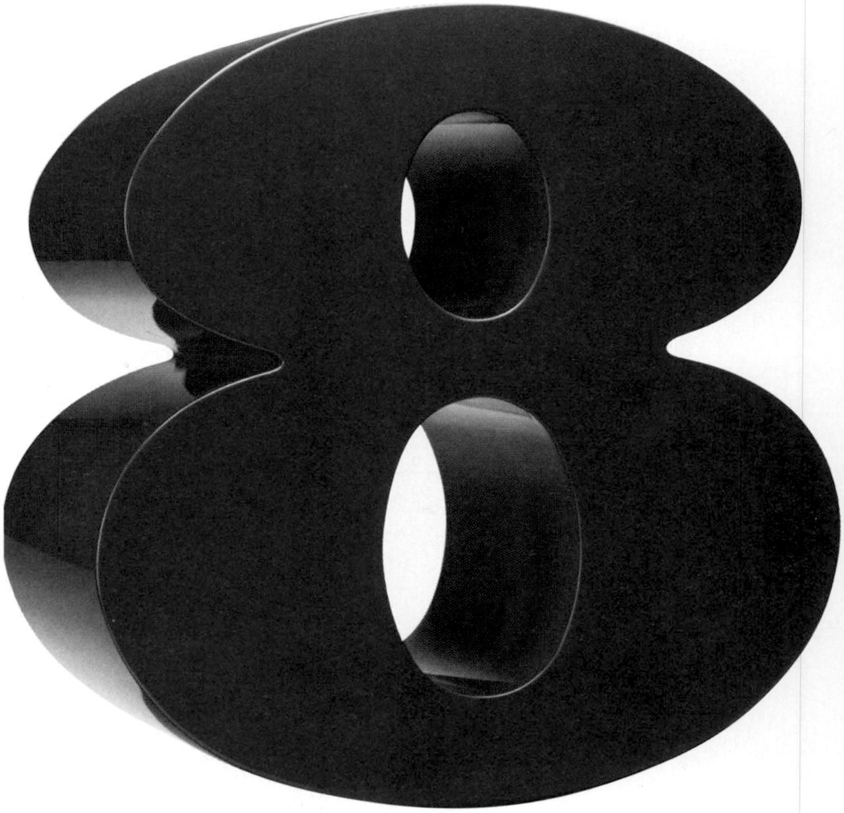

Textbook This lesson is available in the ***eTextbook.***

Is the dotted line a line of symmetry? First estimate, and then use your mirrors to check if you are not sure.

17 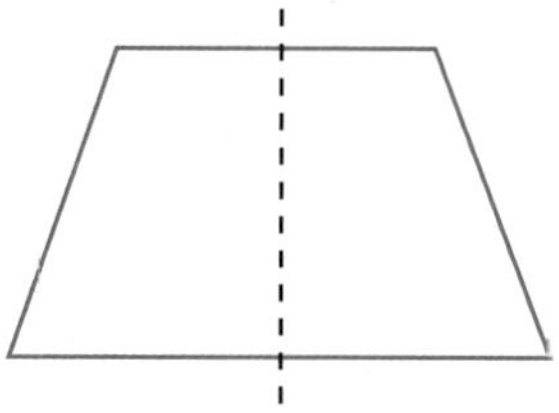

20 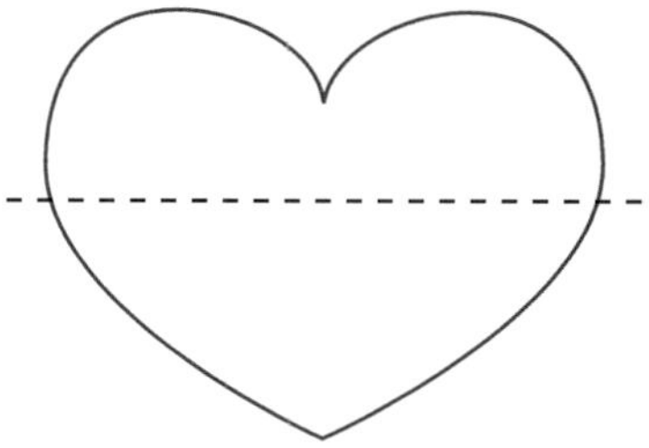

18 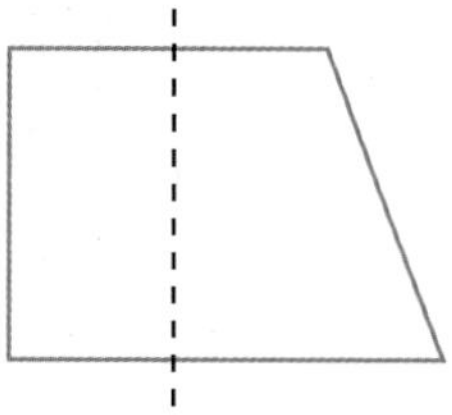

21 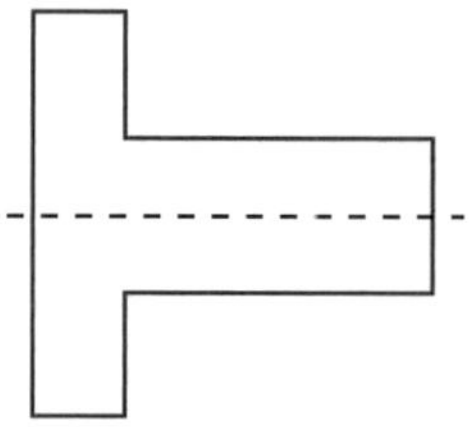

19 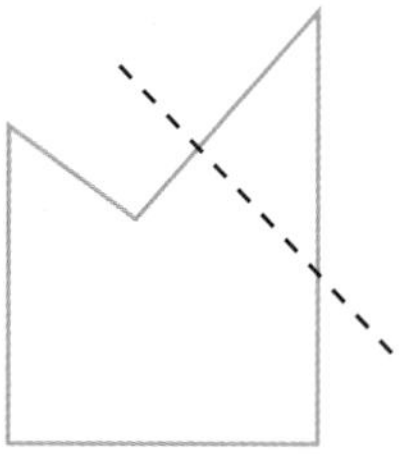

22 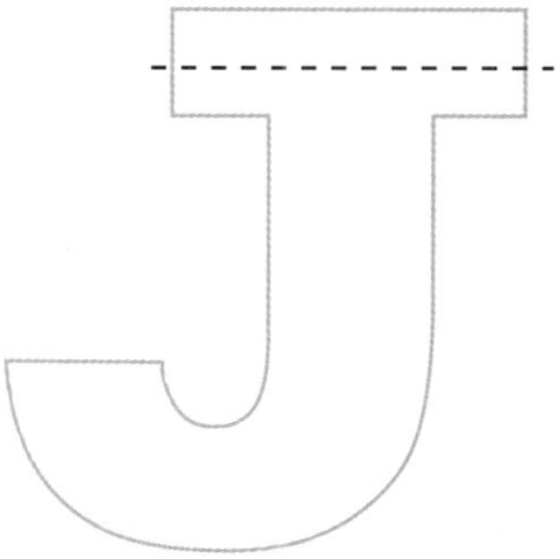

Writing + Math **Journal**

Trace the circle. How many lines of symmetry does a circle have? Use your mirrors if needed. Explain where they are.

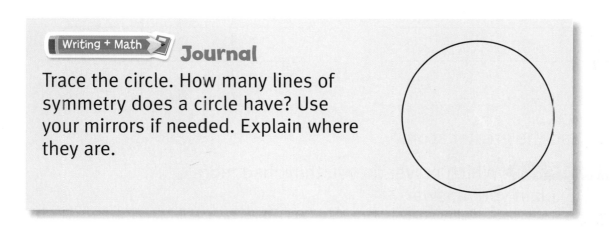

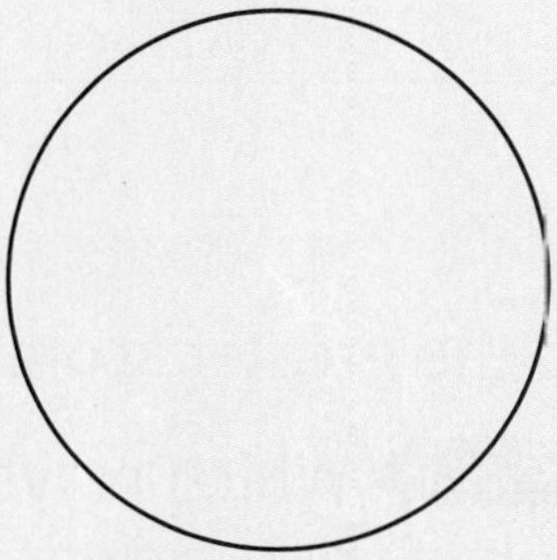

LESSON 11.9 Circles I

Key Ideas

Polygons are closed plane figures that have three or more sides. A common shape that is not a polygon is a circle. Circles have special properties of their own.

Carmen and Dee each made a dartboard. Study both boards and decide which board gives a fairer score.

Dee's board

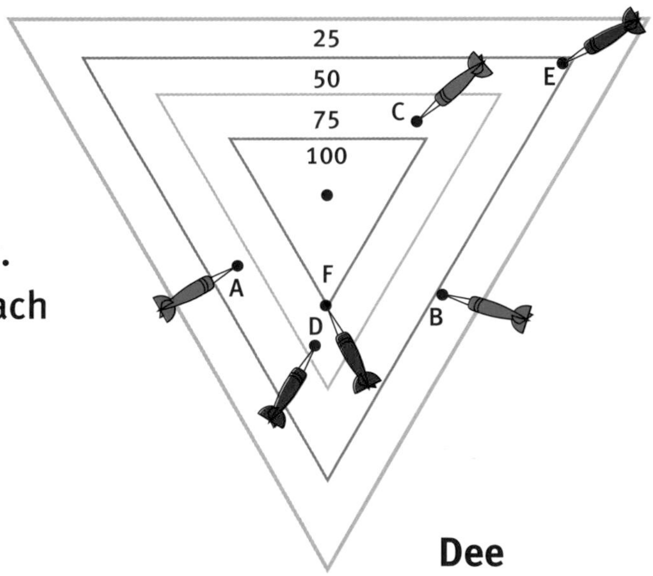

Find the score for each dart. **Measure the distance from each dart to the center.**

Carmen

Dart	Score	Distance from Center
A		cm
B		cm
C		cm
Total		cm

Dee

Dart	Score	Distance from Center
D		cm
E		cm
F		cm
Total		cm

1. Who had the greater score?
2. **Extended Response** Which player do you think had more skill? Explain your answer.
3. **Extended Response** What is a fairer way to design a dartboard?

Find the score for each dart. Measure the distance from each dart to the center.

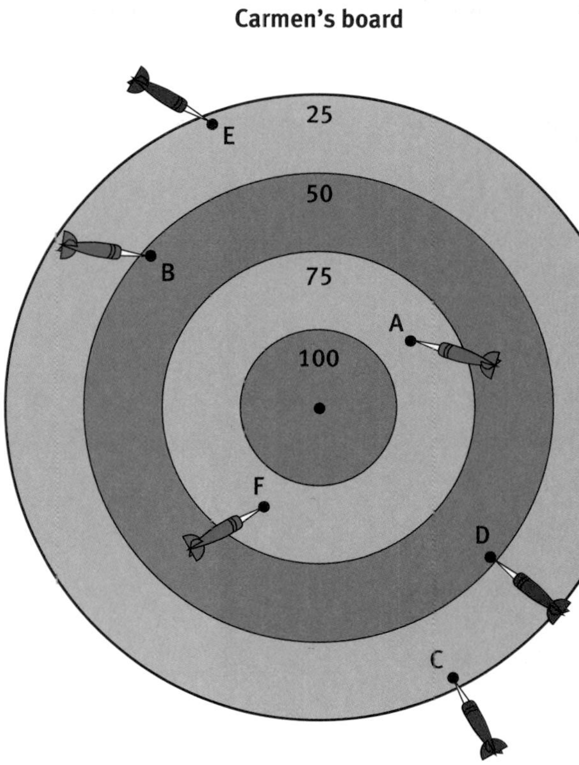

Carmen

Dart	Score	Distance from Center
A	■	■ cm
B	■	■ cm
C	■	■ cm
Total	■	■ cm

Dee

Dart	Score	Distance from Center
D	■	■ cm
E	■	■ cm
F	■	■ cm
Total	■	■ cm

4. Who had the greater score?

5. **Extended Response** Which player do you think had more skill? Explain your answer.

6. **Extended Response** To you, does the triangular dartboard or the circular dartboard seem more fair?

LESSON 11.10

Circles II

Key Ideas

A circle is a special figure that has every point an equal distance from the center. The center point of this circle is point *P*.

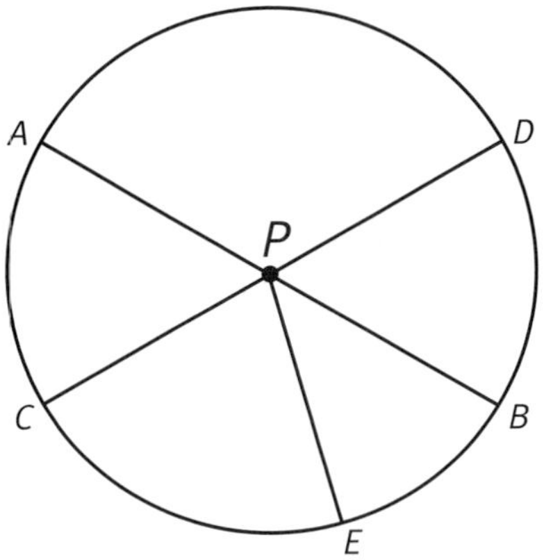

A diameter of a circle is a line segment that passes through the center of the circle and whose endpoints are on the circle. One diameter of the circle above is *CD*. Another is *AB*.

A radius of a circle is a line segment that has one endpoint on the center of the circle and the other on the circle. The plural of *radius* is *radii*.

Use **Circle *P* to measure.**

1. Diameter *AB* is ▢ centimeters long.
2. Diameter *CD* is ▢ centimeters long.
3. Radius *PE* is ▢ centimeters long.
4. Radius *PB* is ▢ centimeters long.

Use the picture to name the following.

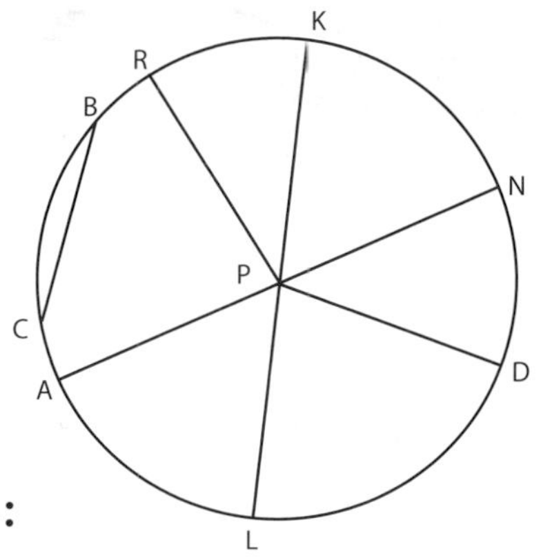

5. Name a diameter.

6. Name a radius.

7. Name a line segment that is not a diameter or radius.

8. Create one circle with the following attributes:
   - Center labeled point *R*
   - Diameters labeled *NS* and *QL*
   - Radii labeled *FR*, *RD*, and *SR*
   - A line segment (neither a diameter nor a radius) labeled YZ

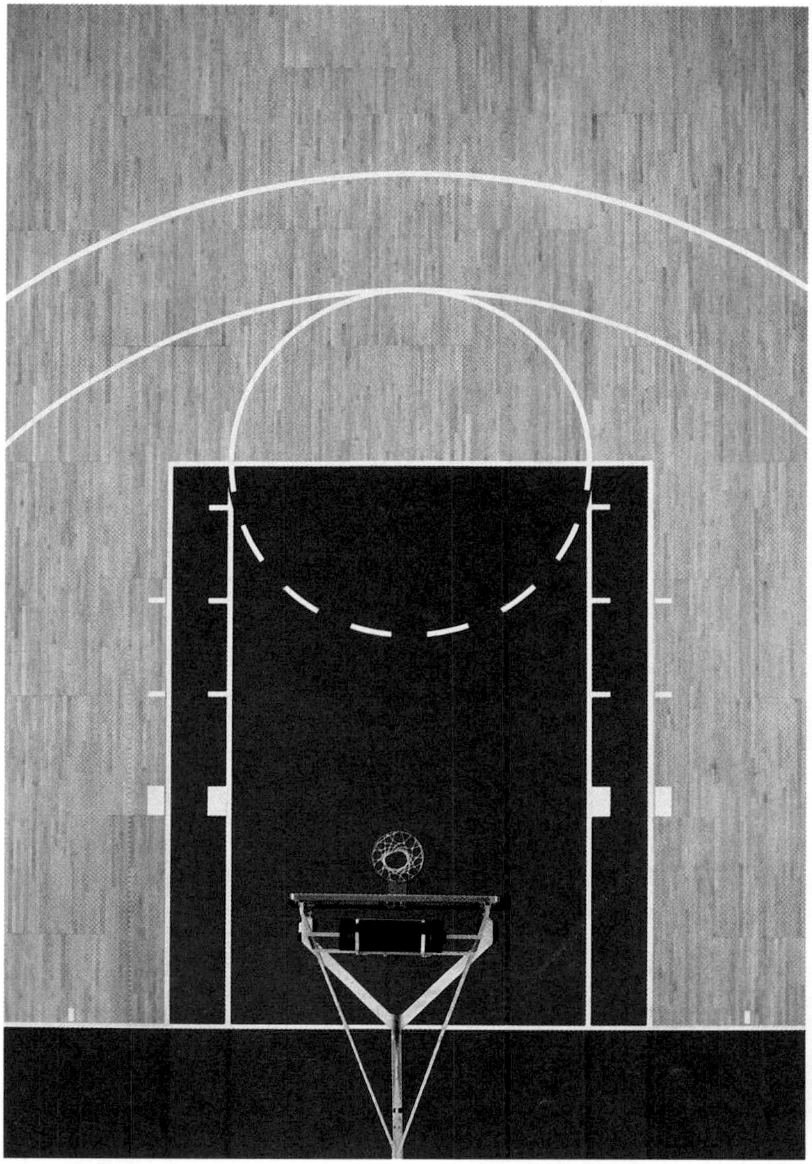

LESSON 11.11

Space Figures

Key Ideas

Space figures are figures that cannot fit in a plane.

Look at the following pictures of space figures. How many do you recognize? List some things that look like each object.

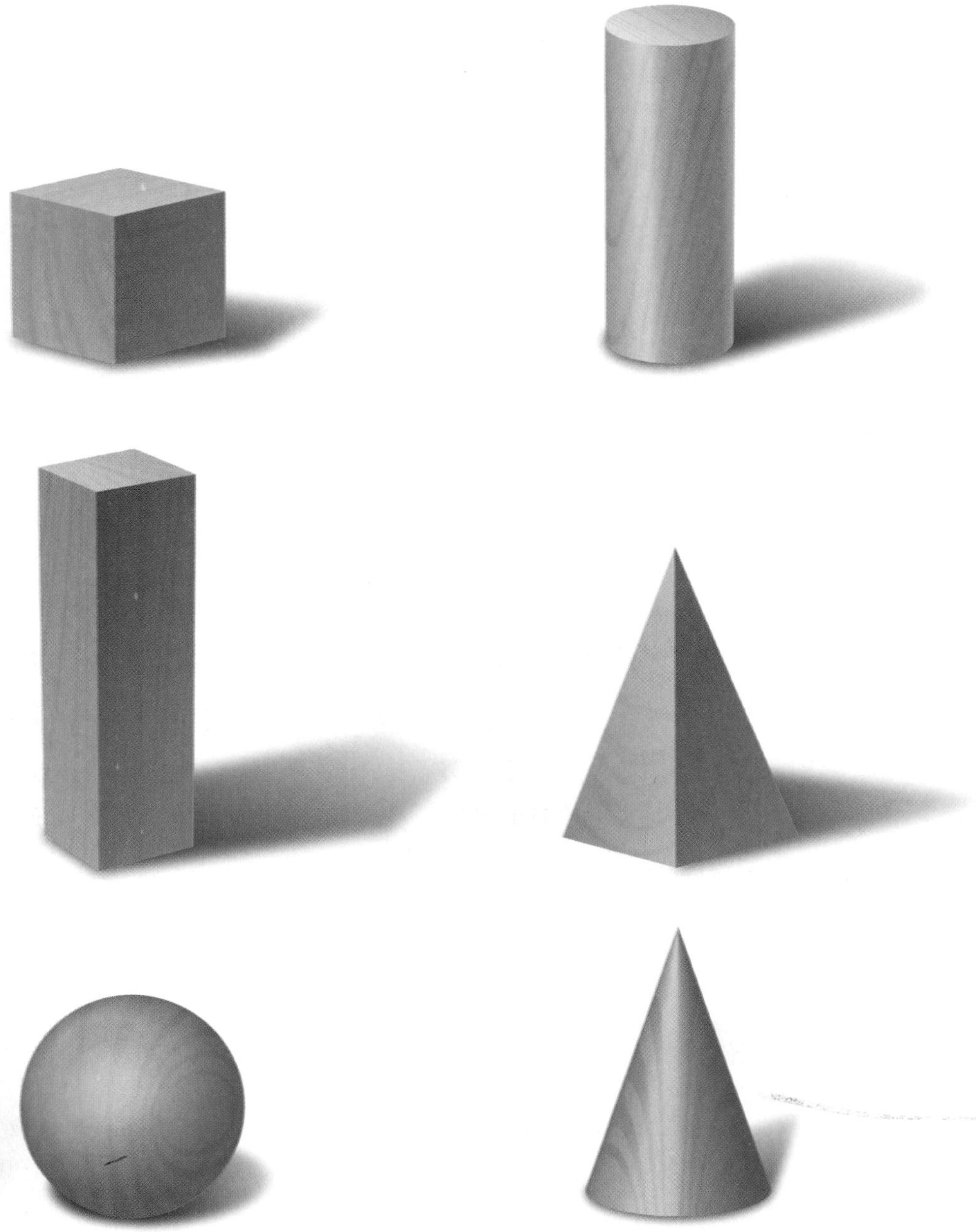

A flat surface of a space figure is called a face. Faces are usually polygons. A line segment where two faces meet is called an edge. The point where three or more edges meet is called a vertex.

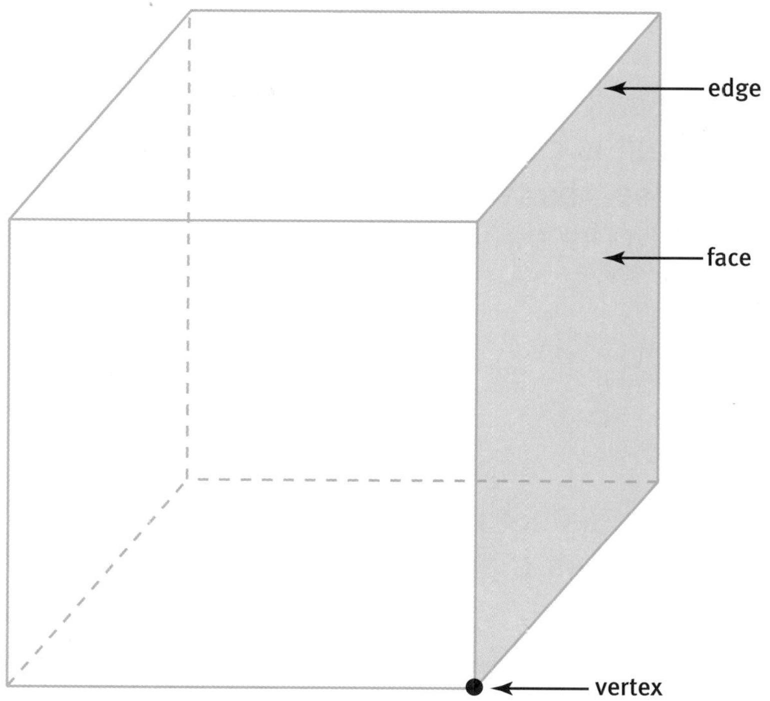

Answer the following questions. Use models of the figures if needed.

1. How many faces does a cube have?
2. How many edges does a cube have?
3. How many vertices does a cube have?
4. How many faces does a rectangular prism have?
5. How many edges does a rectangular prism have?
6. How many vertices does a rectangular prism have?
7. How many faces does a square pyramid have?
8. How many edges does a square pyramid have?
9. How many vertices does a square pyramid have?
10. How many faces does a triangular pyramid have?
11. How many edges does a triangular pyramid have?
12. How many vertices does a triangular pyramid have?

LESSON 11.12

Nets and Surface Area

Key Ideas

Any space figure can be taken apart to show all of its surfaces. The pattern that is created is called the net of the space figure. Likewise, the two-dimensional drawing, or net, can be folded into the three-dimensional space figure.

Look at the following net:

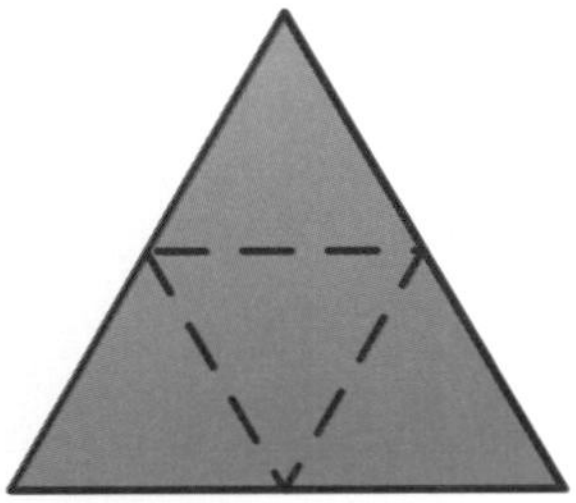

When this net is folded, it creates a triangular pyramid.

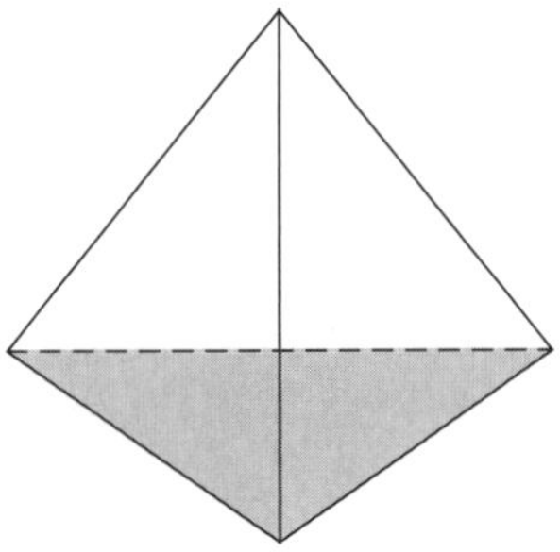

Trace the following net on a piece of unlined paper. Cut along the solid lines, and fold along the dotted lines.

1. What space figure does it make?

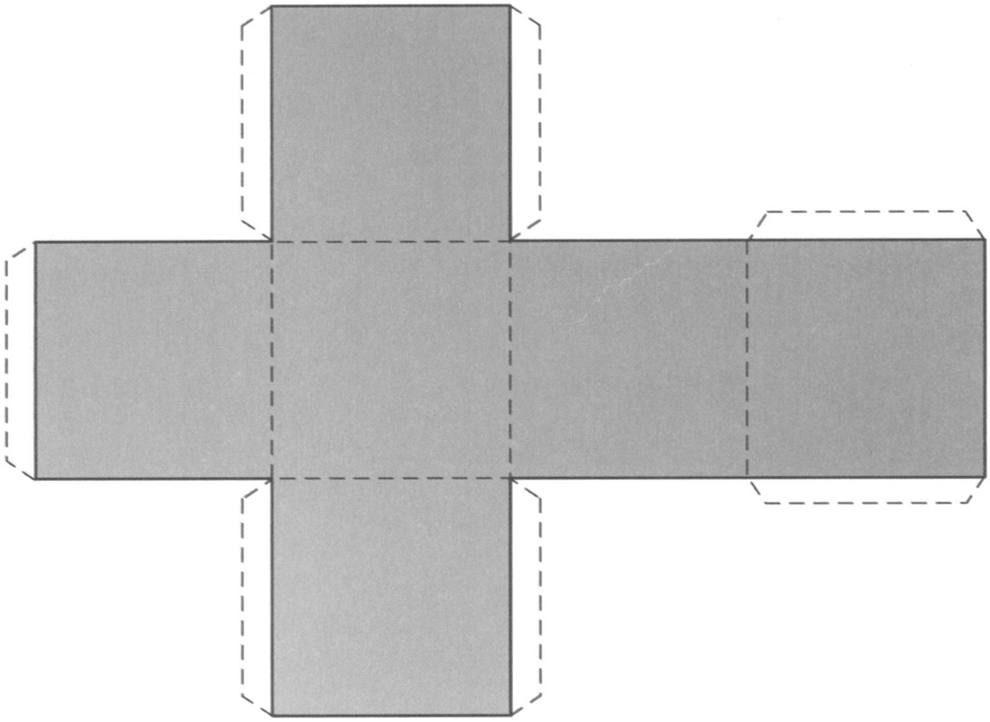

eTextbook This lesson is available in the *eTextbook.*

In previous lessons, we learned that the area of a rectangle is the length times the width. For example, the area of this rectangle would be 24 square units because $6 \times 4 = 24$.

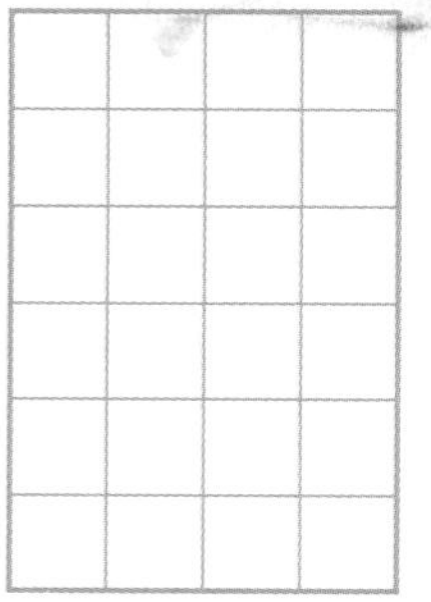

The same idea applies to a square. For example, the area of this square would be 16 square units because $4 \times 4 = 16$.

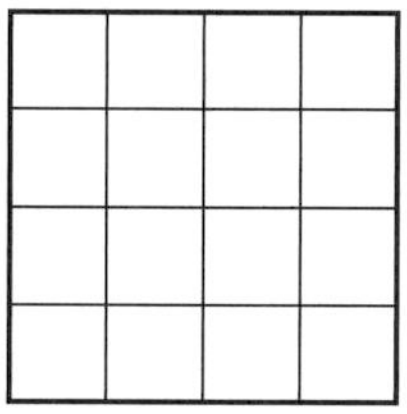

Look at the net of a cube. Use the net to answer the following questions:

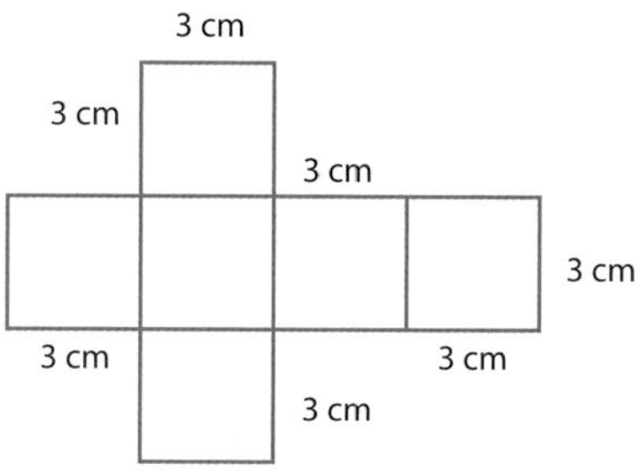

2. What shape are all of the polygons in this net?

3. What is the area of one polygon in the net? ___ square centimeters

4. **Extended Response** Another name for the total area of a cube is surface area. Describe how you would find the total area, or surface area, of the cube. What is the surface area for the cube?

LESSON 11.13

Volume

Key Ideas

The volume of a rectangular prism can be measured by counting the number of cubes that will fit inside the solid. We often measure volume in cubic units.

The volume of this cube is 8 cubic units. Count each of the cubes to verify the volume.

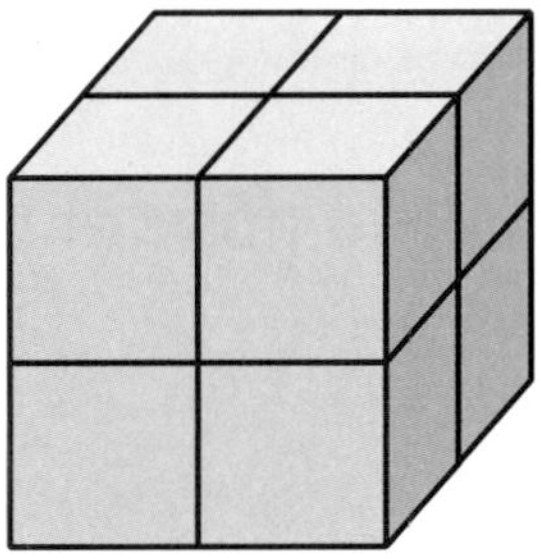

What is the volume? Count the cubes in an orderly manner to determine the volume. You might want to use cubes to build the solid figures if you need help.

1. 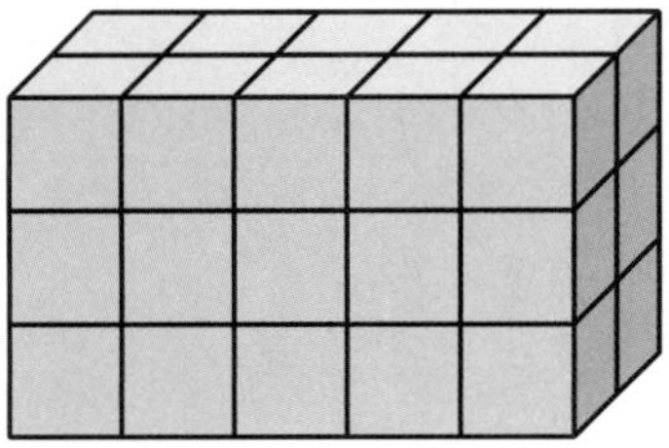

2. 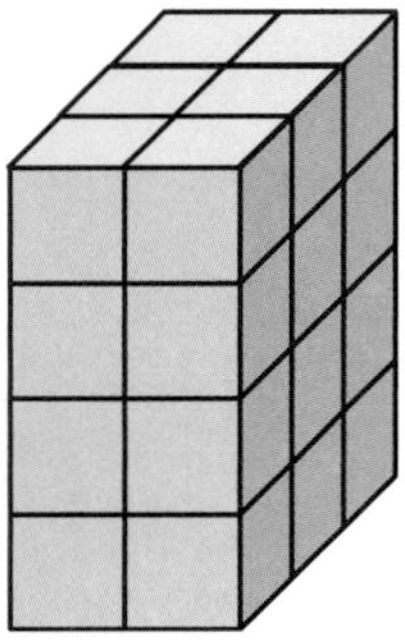

3. 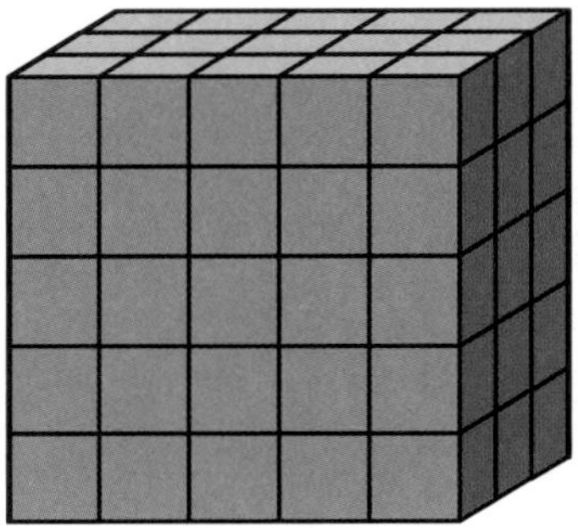

4. 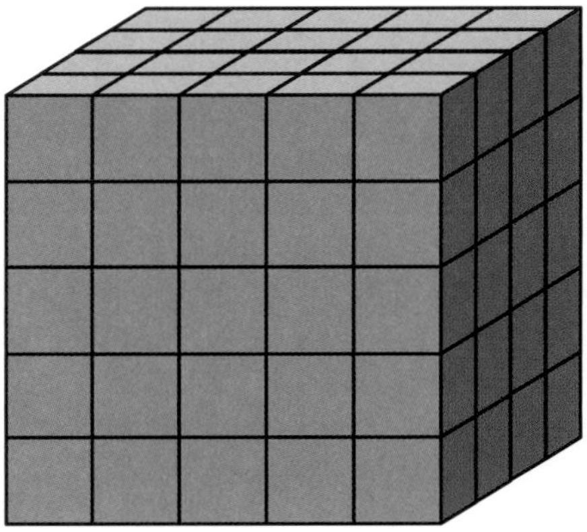

eTextbook This lesson is available in the ***eTextbook.***

What is the volume? Count the cubes.

5 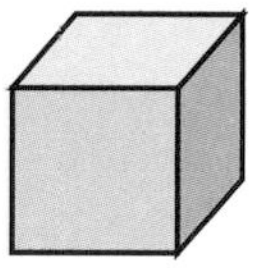

6 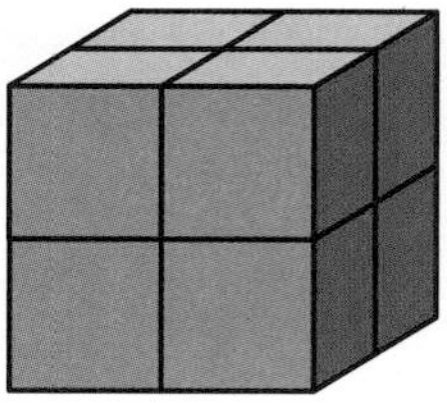

7 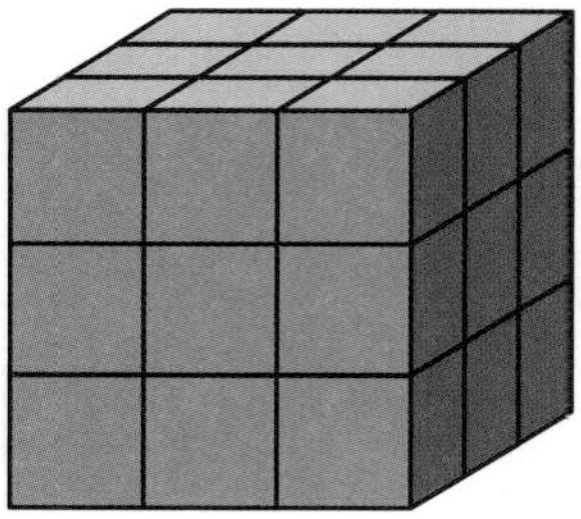

8 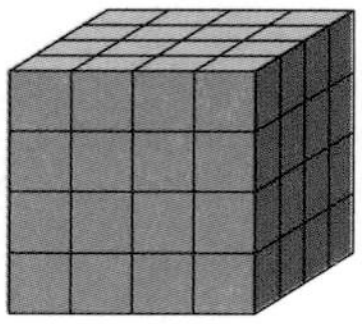

9 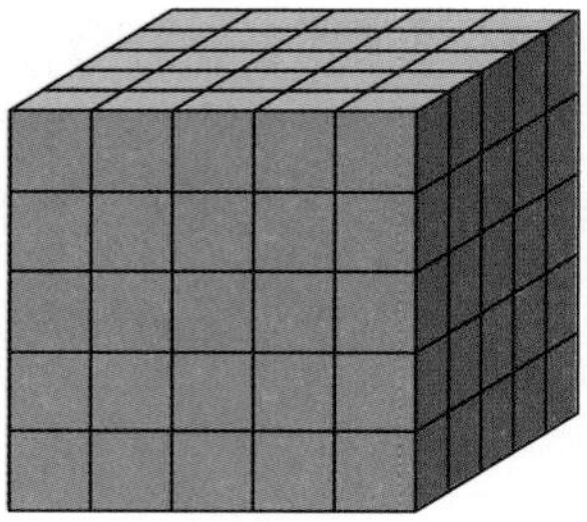

10 In Problems 5–9, the space figures are cubes. Describe any patterns you might have noticed.

The cubic centimeter is a unit of volume. This cube has a volume of 1 cubic centimeter.

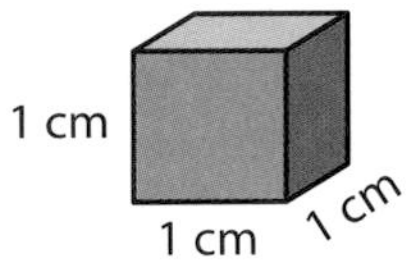

1 cubic centimeter

Find out how many cubic centimeters are in each box. Then give the volume of the box.

11 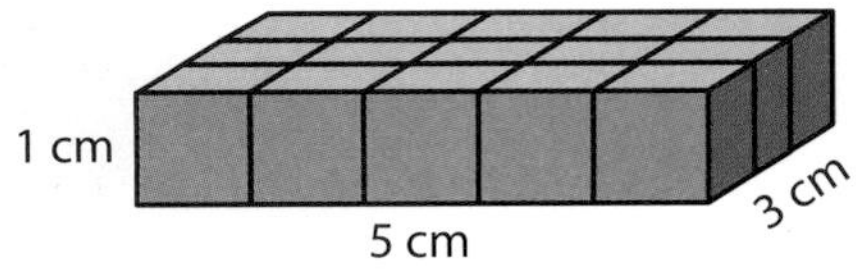

12 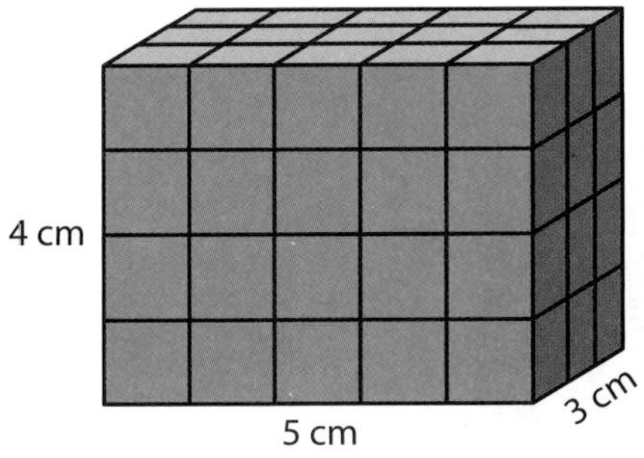

13 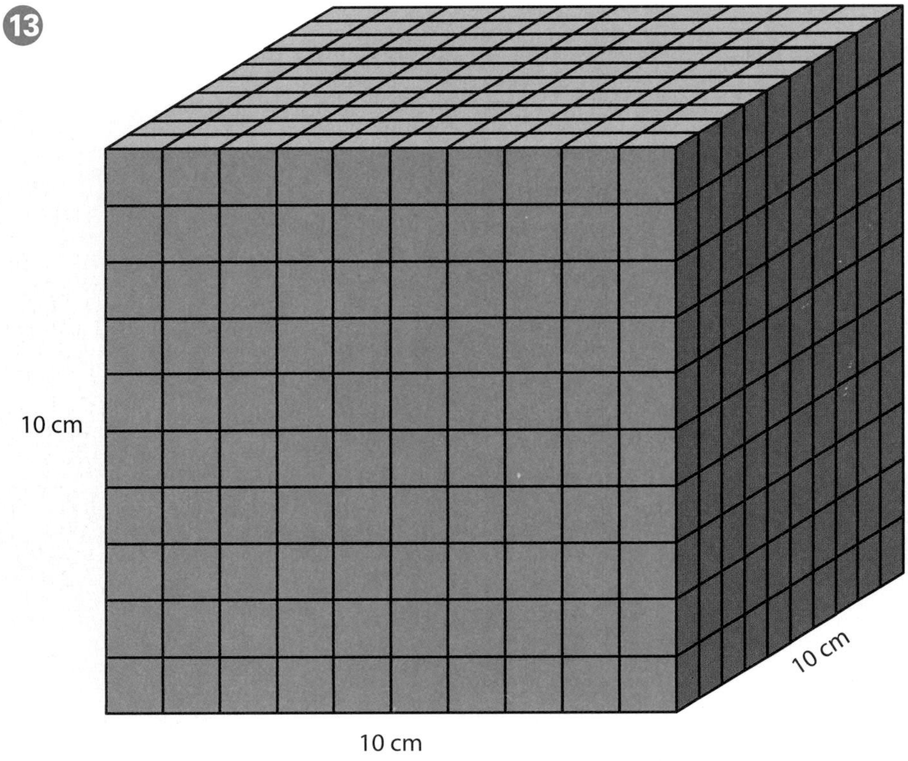

eTextbook This lesson is available in the *eTextbook.*

The liter and milliliter are units of volume.

There are 1,000 milliliters in 1 liter.

1,000 milliliters (mL) = 1 liter (L)

One milliliter is about the same volume as 1 cubic centimeter.

Write the equivalent amounts.

14. 1 L = ☐ mL
15. ☐ L = 1,000 mL
16. 2 L = ☐ mL
17. ☐ L = 3,000 mL
18. 7 L = ☐ mL
19. ☐ L = 5,000 mL
20. 4 L = ☐ mL
21. ☐ L = 8,000 mL
22. 1 L = ☐ cubic centimeters
23. ☐ L = 5,000 cubic centimeters
24. 2 L = ☐ cubic centimeters
25. ☐ L = 8,000 cubic centimeters

Exploring Problem Solving

You are designing a playhouse for your backyard. The playhouse will be in the shape of a rectangular box. To explore possible shapes, you are using cubes to build different models.

Each model will

- be a rectangular box.
- use exactly 64 cubes.

Work with your group to answer the following questions.

1. How many different playhouse shapes can you make?
2. Which playhouse shape will cost the least to paint? How do you know?
3. Suppose the side of each cube in your model stands for 1 yard. What will be the volume of your playhouse?
4. Does the answer to Problem 3 depend on which of the shapes you choose? Explain.

Cumulative Review

Inverse Functions (Reversing the Arrow) **Lesson 6.4**

Use inverse-arrow operations to find the value of *n*.

1. $n \longrightarrow (\times 11) \longrightarrow 110$ $n = \square$

2. $n \longrightarrow (\div 5) \longrightarrow m \longrightarrow (\times 3) \longrightarrow 9$ $n = \square$

Dividing Decimals **Lesson 10.8**

Solve. If you cannot solve, explain why.

3. The girls from the Pink team bought a present for one of the team members. Including tax, the gift cost $22.05. If 5 girls are sharing the cost equally, what is each person's share?

4. The children in the neighborhood organized a 5-kilometer relay race. Each relay team has 4 children. How far will each child run? Write your answer in kilometers and meters.

Multiplying by 9 **Lesson 5.3**

Solve the following problems.

Mr. and Mrs. Hoffman challenged their 5 children to read 9 stories per week.

5. In 2 weeks how many stories will 1 child read?

6. How many stories will 2 of the children read in 2 weeks?

7. How many stories will all the children read in 1 week?

Cumulative Review

Fractions of Time **Lesson 8.4**

Which is a longer period of time?

8. $\frac{1}{5}$ of an hour or $\frac{1}{4}$ of an hour?
9. $\frac{3}{4}$ of an hour or $\frac{3}{3}$ of an hour?
10. $\frac{2}{2}$ of an hour or 1 hour?

Where Do We See Decimals? **Lesson 10.1**

Solve these problems.

11. At the aviary, the average African gray parrot weighs about 520 grams. About how much do 3 parrots weigh? Write your answer in kilograms.
12. If 1 bag of apples costs 321 cents, how much do 2 bags cost? Write the answer using dollars and cents.
13. The nature preserve is shaped like a square. Each side is 942 meters long. What is the perimeter of the nature preserve? Write your answer in kilometers.

Dividing Three-Digit Numbers by One-Digit Numbers **Lesson 7.8**

Divide.

14. $654 \div 6$
15. $2\overline{)578}$
16. $798 \div 7$
17. $8\overline{)344}$
18. $216 \div 9$

Metric Capacity **Lesson 9.5**

Convert each measure.

19. 6 L = ▢ mL
20. ▢ L = 2,500 mL

CHAPTER 11

Key Ideas Review

In this chapter you learned about different geometrical terms and figures, such as angles, triangles, quadrilaterals, polygons, and circles.

You learned about the properties of different polygons and how their appearances change when translated, rotated, or reflected.

You learned about symmetry, congruency, and some characteristics of space figures.

Identify the geometrical figures.

1 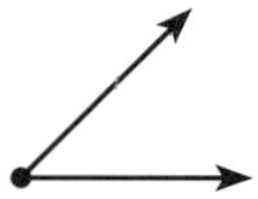

2 

3 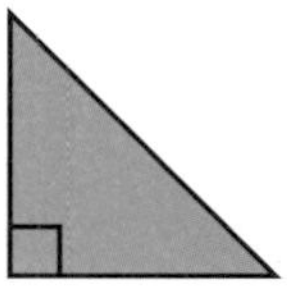

4 

5 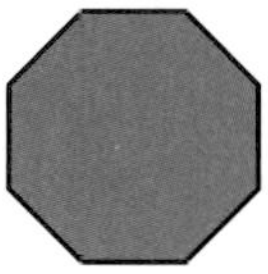

Determine whether these are examples of translation, rotation, or reflection.

6 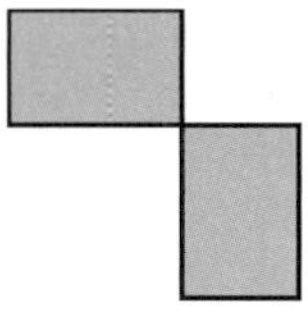

7 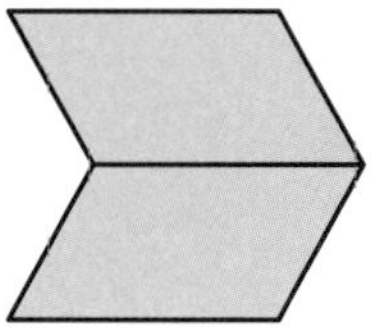

List the number of lines of symmetry for each figure.

8 

9 

Provide a detailed answer for the following exercise.

10 Draw the net of this space figure:

CHAPTER 11

Chapter Review

Lesson 11.1

1. Draw a line, and label two points on the line.

Lesson 11.2

2. Perpendicular lines intersect to form what kind of angles?
3. Draw two rays intersecting to form an angle.
4. Label the vertex in your angle from Problem 3 as point Q.

Lesson 11.3

5. Isosceles triangles have ☐ equal sides.
6. ☐ triangles have 3 equal sides.
7. Right triangles have how many right angles?
8. **Extended Response** Draw an example of an isosceles triangle. Draw an example of an equilateral triangle.

Lesson 11.4

Answer yes or no.

9. Is a rhombus a parallelogram?
10. Is a trapezoid a quadrilateral?
11. Is a rhombus a quadrilateral?
12. Is a trapezoid a parallelogram?

Lesson 11.5

Fill in the blank.

13. A triangle has ☐ sides.
14. A rectangle has ☐ sides.
15. A parallelogram has ☐ sides.
16. A hexagon has ☐ sides.
17. A rhombus has ☐ sides.
18. An octagon has ☐ sides.
19. An isosceles triangle has ☐ sides.
20. A pentagon has ☐ sides.

Lesson 11.7

Determine whether the following diagrams show a reflection, a rotation, or a translation.

21. 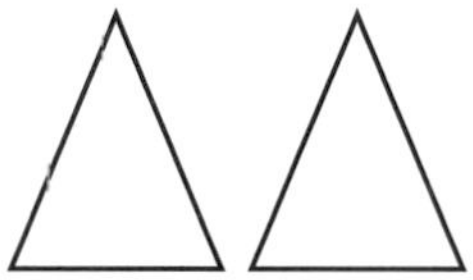

22. 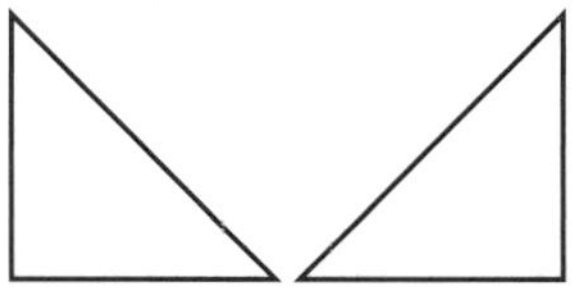

23. 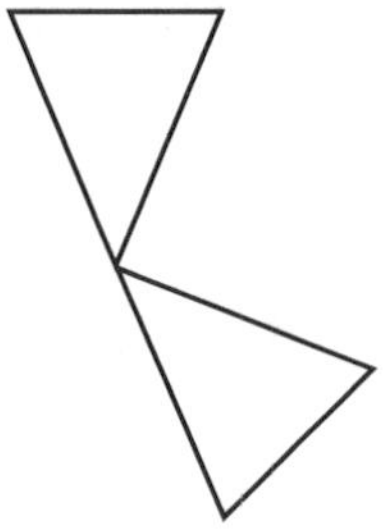

Lesson 11.10

24. **Extended Response** Draw a circle, and label the center point *P*. Draw a diameter, and label it *AD*. Draw a radius, and label it *PL*.

Lesson 11.11

25. What is the name of this space figure?

26. What is the name of this space figure?

27. What is the name of this space figure?

Lesson 11.13

28. What is the volume of this figure?

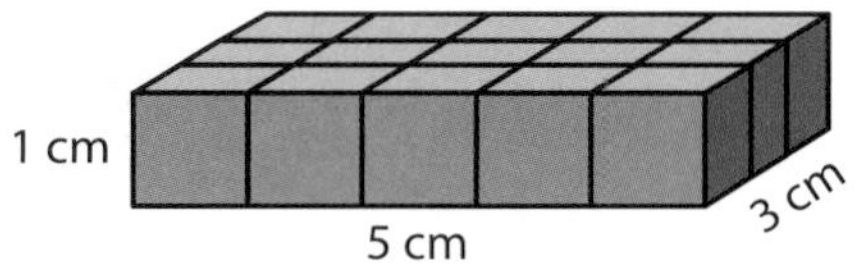

CHAPTER 11

Practice Test

Write the word or words that make the sentences true.

1. This is an example of ___ lines.

2. Lines that are the same distance apart and will never cross one another are ___ lines.

3. This cube has ___ faces and ___ vertices.

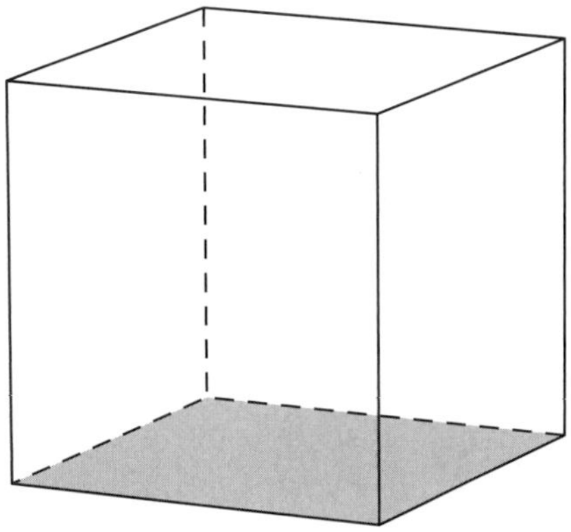

4. A square pyramid has ___ faces and ___ edges.

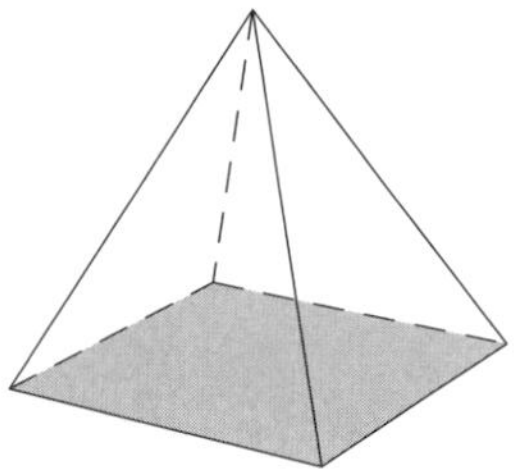

5. What would the area of a square be if one side measured 5 inches?

Answer these questions.

6. How many milliliters are in 5 liters?

7. How many liters equal 12,000 milliliters?

Write the letter of the correct answer.

8. What kind of angle is formed by the hands on this clock?

Ⓐ acute Ⓑ obtuse
Ⓒ right Ⓓ straight

9. Gisele says the hands on the clock form a right angle. Of the following choices, what time could it be?

Ⓐ 11:35 Ⓑ 12:30
Ⓒ 3:00 Ⓓ 10:00

10. What kind of angle is formed by the hands on this clock?

Ⓐ acute Ⓑ obtuse
Ⓒ right Ⓓ straight

11. Donna drew this triangle. What kind of triangle did she draw?

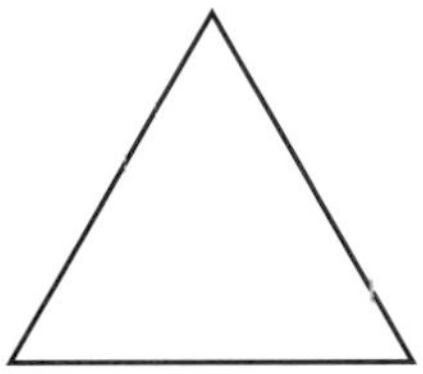

Ⓐ equilateral
Ⓑ isosceles
Ⓒ right
Ⓓ obtuse

12. What is the name of this shape?

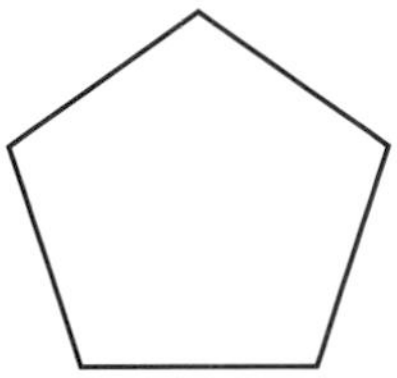

Ⓐ hexagon Ⓑ square
Ⓒ triangle Ⓓ pentagon

13. What is the name of this shape?

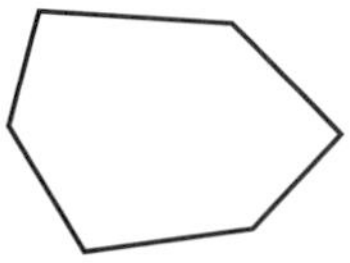

Ⓐ hexagon Ⓑ square
Ⓒ triangle Ⓓ pentagon

Practice Test

14. Maya turned a shape around a point. How did she transform the shape?

Ⓐ translation

Ⓑ reflection

Ⓒ rotation

Ⓓ tessellation

15. Peter flipped his shape over an imaginary line. How did he transform his shape?

Ⓐ translation

Ⓑ reflection

Ⓒ rotation

Ⓓ tessellation

16. What transformation was carried out on the trapezoid?

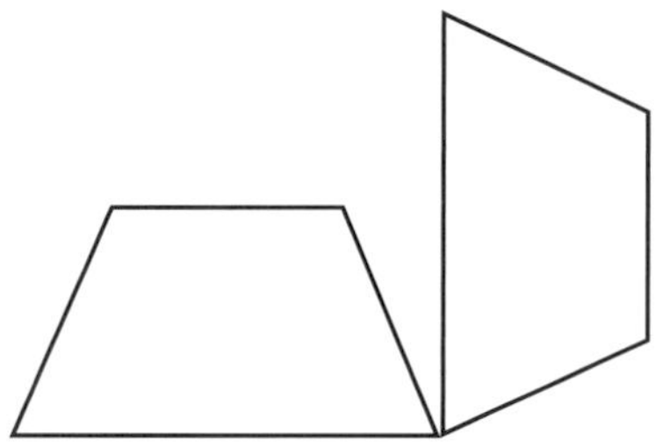

Ⓐ rotation

Ⓑ translation

Ⓒ tessellation

Ⓓ reflection

Use this circle to answer Questions 17–19.

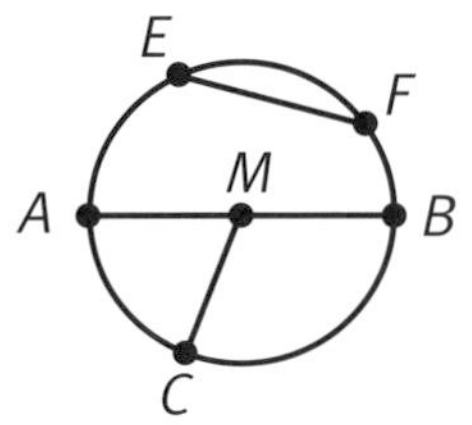

17. How can this circle be named?

Ⓐ Circle *M* Ⓑ Circle *AB*

Ⓒ Circle *CM* Ⓓ Circle *EF*

18. Which is the diameter?

Ⓐ *M* Ⓑ *AB*

Ⓒ *CM* Ⓓ *EF*

19. Which is neither the radius nor the diameter?

Ⓐ *AM* Ⓑ *AB*

Ⓒ *CM* Ⓓ *EF*

20. Find the quotient. $72 \div 8 = \square$

Ⓐ 12 Ⓑ 11

Ⓒ 9 Ⓓ 8

21. How many pints are in 3 gallons?

Ⓐ 12 pints Ⓑ 24 pints

Ⓒ 38 pints Ⓓ 40 pints

Extended Response **Solve.**

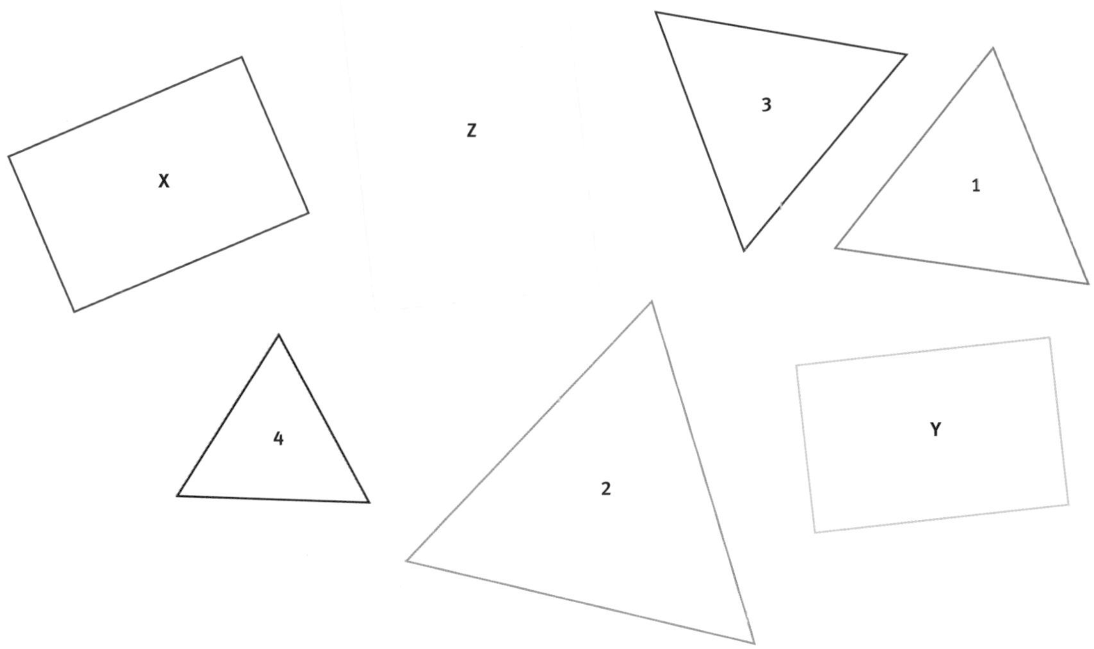

Look at the pictures, and list pairs of congruent figures.

22. Which rectangles are congruent? How do you know?

23. Draw a rectangle that is congruent to rectangle Z.

24. Which triangles are congruent? How do you know?

25. Draw a triangle that is congruent to triangle 4.

Thinking Story

A Paneful Story

A fly kept buzzing around Mr. Breezy's window at his house in the country. Every time Mr. Breezy tried to hit it with the fly swatter, he missed. He would take careful aim, but by the time he swatted, the fly would always be somewhere else on the window.

"I know what the trouble is," said Mr. Breezy. "Every time the fly is on one pane of the window and I swat at it there, it zips over to another pane of the window. I need something so that I can swat at all the panes of the window at the same time. Then I'll get the fly."

What could Mr. Breezy use to do this?

Mr. Breezy found a board that was as big as the whole window, and he waited for the fly to land.

What do you think happened when he swatted at the fly?

"Oh, oh," said Mr. Breezy. "That fly was a little problem, but now I have a big problem. I've broken every pane of glass in the window. But at least I taught that fly a lesson it won't forget."

Mr. Breezy went to a hardware store. "I broke a window, and I need some panes of glass to fix it," he said. "The window is square, and all the panes are square too."

The woman in the hardware store said she could cut squares of glass that were just the right size for Mr. Breezy's window. "How many do you need?" she asked.

"Let me think," said Mr. Breezy. "All the panes in the window are broken, so I need 2 pieces of glass for the top of the window, 2 pieces for the left-hand side of the window, 2 pieces for the bottom, and 2 pieces for the right-hand side."

How many pieces of glass do you think Mr. Breezy needs altogether?

Be careful. Draw the window before you answer.

"You say you need 2 pieces for the top, 2 for the left-hand side, 2 for the bottom, and 2 for the right-hand side," said the woman. "That makes 8 pieces of glass. Something must be wrong. I thought you said the window was square and all the panes in it were square."

"That's right," said Mr. Breezy.

What's wrong?

Try to draw a square window with 8 panes that are all square.

"You can't make a square window out of 8 squares," said the woman. "Are you sure there aren't 9 squares?"

"No," said Mr. Breezy. "As a matter of fact, there are only 4 squares."

"But you said there were 2 on the top, 2 on the bottom, and 2 on each side."

How is that possible? Draw a picture of the window to show how.

"It's very simple," said Mr. Breezy. He drew a picture of a square window divided into 4 squares. "You see, there are 4 squares—2 on the top, 2 on the bottom, and 2 on each side."

"I think you could have told me that a little more clearly at the beginning," said the woman.

How could Mr. Breezy have told what he wanted in a way that would have been easier to understand?

After Mr. Breezy fixed his window, he went for a walk to where a new house was being built. He asked one of the workers what he was doing. "I'm trying to figure out how many different-colored pieces of glass I need to put in this stained-glass window," said the worker.

"You're very lucky," said Mr. Breezy. "I happen to be an expert on windows and can help you with any window problem."

"I could use some help," said the worker. "These plans don't tell me how many pieces of glass I need. I know the window is square and all the panes of glass are square, and they're all the same size. I know there are more than 7 panes and fewer than 15, but I don't know exactly how many."

Draw a picture to show how many panes the window might have. Remember, the window is square, and all the panes are square too, and the same size. There must be more than 7 panes and fewer than 15. How many panes could there be?

Mr. Breezy looked at the plans. "These plans show three sizes of square windows," he said. "One has 4 panes of glass, just like my window back home. Another has 9 panes. And the other has

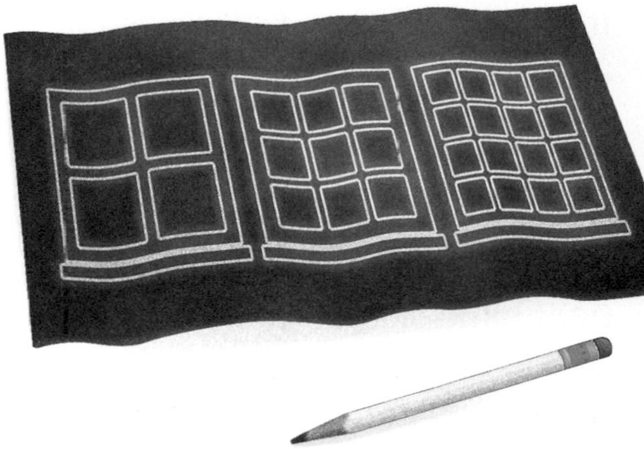

16 panes. The window you're making must have 9 panes."

How could Mr. Breezy decide that?

"You might be right," said the worker, "because 9 is the only one of the sizes that's more than 7 and fewer than 15. Thanks a lot. You really seem to know everything about windows."

"Only square windows," said Mr. Breezy. "I'm a smashing success with them."

The next day, Mr. Breezy went back to the house where the worker was making a window. "How is your stained-glass window coming along?" Mr. Breezy asked.

"I think I need your help again," the worker said. "I'm making a square window, and I know I need 9 panes of glass in it—you helped me figure that out yesterday, remember? And I know that some panes are supposed to be blue and some green and some red, but when I read the plans, I can't figure out how many I need of each kind."

"I'll try to help," said Mr. Breezy, reading over the plans. "Ah, I see. It's easy. You need 3 pieces of blue glass for the top of the window. You need 3 pieces of green glass for the bottom of the window. You need 2 pieces of blue glass on the left-hand side of the window and 2 pieces of green glass on the right-hand side of the window. And you need 1 piece of red glass."

Draw a picture of the window the way you think it is supposed to look. Color in the panes.

Where does the piece of red glass go?

"This doesn't work," said the worker. "You said I need 3 blue pieces for the top and 2 blue pieces for one side. That's 5 blue panes. Then you said I need 3 green pieces for the bottom and 2 green pieces for the other side. That's 5 more panes, which makes 10, plus a pane of red glass, which makes 11. I thought we'd already decided there were only 9 panes in the whole window!"

Can you explain why the numbers don't work out right?

How many blue panes should there be altogether?

How many green panes should there be altogether?

"It's very simple. I'll draw you a picture," said Mr. Breezy, taking some colored pencils from his pocket. He drew a square divided into 9 little squares. He colored all the top squares blue and all the bottom squares green. Then he colored the left-hand square in the middle row blue and the right-hand square in the middle row green. He colored the square in the middle red.

Is your picture just like the one Mr. Breezy drew? If not, draw another picture.

"I see," said the worker. "There are just 4 panes of blue glass altogether."

"Yes," said Mr. Breezy. "That's what I've been telling you: 3 blue panes on top and 2 blue panes on the left side."

"But," protested the worker, "you counted one of the panes twice."

Which pane was counted twice?

"Now you're getting the idea," Mr. Breezy told him. "This pane up in the corner is on the top and on the left-hand side at the same time."

"And the same thing happened with the green panes," said the worker. "There are only 4, and this one was counted twice."

Which green pane was counted twice?

"Very good," said Mr. Breezy. "This green pane down in the corner is on the bottom and on the right-hand side at the same time."

"It's all clear to me now," said the worker, "and I think I'll figure out the rest of the windows myself."

"Good luck," said Mr. Breezy. "If you need any more expert help, just get a telephone book, open it to where the Bs are, find the name Breezy, look at the third Breezy on the list, then count down two more Breezys, then ..."

"Never mind," said the worker, "I don't think I'll need more help. I think I'll get out of the window-making business and do something simpler—like build spaceships."

The End

CHAPTER 12

Data Analysis and Probability

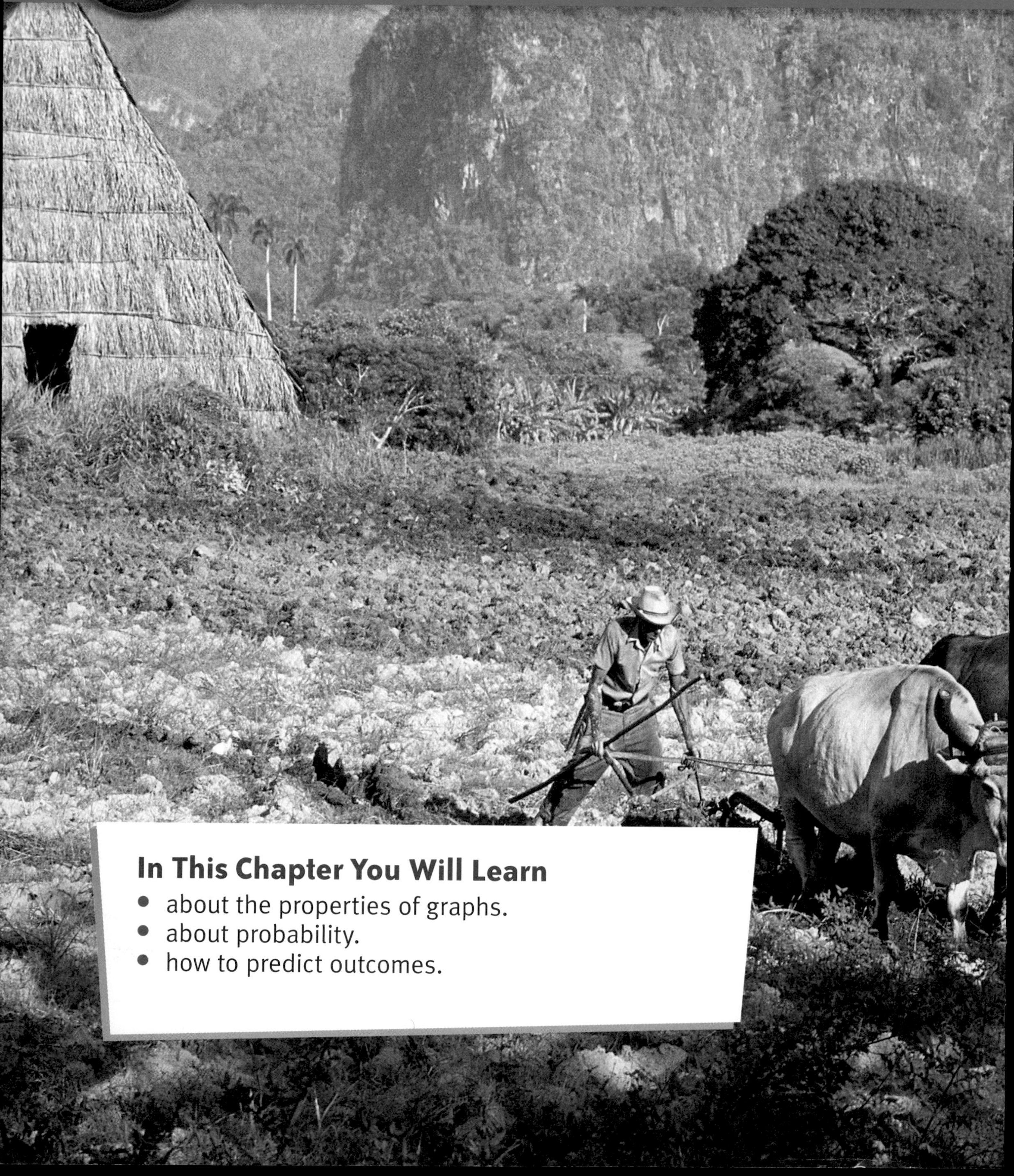

In This Chapter You Will Learn

- about the properties of graphs.
- about probability.
- how to predict outcomes.

Problem Solving

Have you ever tasted a papaya? It is a sweet and nutritious fruit picked from fast-growing plants that can grow 6 to 10 feet tall in less than a year.

Areas of the world where papayas are grown.

González Farm **Castillo Farm**

This illustration shows papayas from two different farms in Puerto Rico.

1. How many papayas are there from each farm?
2. Which group of papayas do you think weighs more?
3. If you picked 7 papayas from each farm, which group of papayas do you think would weigh more? Explain.
4. Which farm do you think is growing larger papayas?

LESSON 12.1

Collecting Data—Samples

Key Ideas

When you collect information about a topic, you are collecting data. Data can be collected in many different ways and for many different reasons.

If you are collecting a large group of data, such as from the students in your school or about the animals in your neighborhood, you often take a sample. A sample is a smaller portion of a larger set of data; it allows you to make an estimate of what the data would show if you collected and analyzed all of it. Since it is impossible to ask questions of every single person, it is important that your sample reflects properties of the larger group of data as much as possible.

Extended Response **Answer the following questions.**

Imagine that your teacher has a can that is filled with 24 marbles.

1. Your teacher pulls out 2 marbles and they are both blue. Based on this, what portion of the marbles in the can do you think are blue? Are there other colors of marbles in the can?

2. Your teacher replaces the two marbles, shakes the can, and then pulls out 6 marbles — 3 blue and 3 red. Based on this, what portion of the marbles in the can do you think are blue?

3. Your teacher replaces the 6 marbles, shakes the can, and then pulls out 18 marbles — 6 blue and 12 red. Which color of marble do you think there is more of in the can, red or blue?

4. How could you know the exact amount of each color of marble in the can? Would you want to do that for a can with 1,000 marbles in it?

eTextbook This lesson is available in the ***eTextbook.***

Sometimes the surveys and samples have already been gathered for you; it is up to you to organize the data. Putting the information in a chart or a table will help you organize the information and find important items from the data.

Create a table for the information below.

5. Mr. Anakin's science class saw the following birds on their field trip two weeks ago. The class also recorded how many times they saw each type of bird.
Cardinal—6 times
Blue Jay—8 times
Robin—10 times
Woodpecker—2 times
Canary—7 times
Red-Tailed Hawk—1 time
Turkey Vulture—3 times
Barn Owl—1 time
Hummingbird—4 times
Finch—4 times
Bald Eagle—1 time
Peregrine Falcon—1 time

6. Write one true and one false statement about the information above.

LESSON 12.2

Collecting Data—Tally Marks

Key Ideas

One of the easiest ways to collect data is to create a table using tally marks. The total number of tally marks in each category represents the frequency, or how often a particular response occurred.

Marc surveyed his third-grade class to see what transportation they used most often to arrive at school. The results are as follows:

Method	Tally	Frequency
Bus	卌 卌 卌	15
Car	||||	4
Walk	卌 |	6
Other	|||	3
	Total	28

Use the table to answer the following questions.

1. **Extended Response** How many students did Marc survey? Explain how you know.
2. What is the most common method of getting to school?
3. How many students in Marc's class do *not* get to school by bus?
4. **Extended Response** What methods of transportation to school might the *Other* category include?

Use the following information to create a table using tally marks.

5 **Extended Response** Star surveyed her gym class to see what their favorite colors are. She chose the top four colors and then decided on an *Other* category for the remaining colors. The top four colors are *blue*, *green*, *yellow*, and *red*. When Star counted each category, she found that 11 students liked blue, 9 students liked red, 7 students liked green, and 8 students liked yellow. There are 38 students in her gym class.

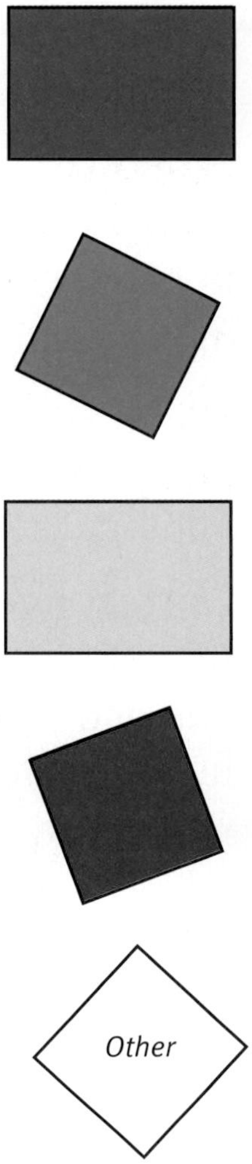

Answer the following questions about your completed table from Star's survey.

6 **Extended Response** What would be a good title for this survey?

7 What is the most common favorite color in the survey?

8 **Extended Response** Do you think this is the favorite color of the entire school? Why or why not?

9 Are there more students who like blue and green or students who like yellow, red, and *Other*?

10 **Extended Response** Write a true statement about the table you made from Star's survey.

Writing + Math **Journal**

In your own words, describe what a table with tally marks is and when you might use one.

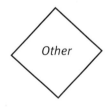

LESSON 12.3

Summarizing Data

Key Ideas

The numbers in a set can be written in order from least to greatest. How much the data are spread out is called the variability. The *variability* of the data also can be measured by the range and the outliers.

The range of a set of numbers is the difference between the greatest number in the data and the smallest number in the data. A small number for the range means the data are close together.

An outlier is a number that seems to be too far out at one end of the range. Sometimes an outlier can affect how we interpret the data.

The following is a table showing the number of student sick days at Valley Alternative Elementary School for the 2008–2009 school year.

Month	Student Sick Days
August	17
September	21
October	28
November	25
December	22
January	30
February	45
March	35
April	34
May	26
June	4

Use the table to answer the following questions.

1. What is the least number of student sick days? What is the greatest number of student sick days?
2. What is the range for the student sick days for the 2008–2009 school year?
3. Extended Response What number or numbers might be considered an outlier? What might be a reason for the outlier? Explain.
4. True or False. You could say the number of student sick days varied greatly from month to month.

The 1919 World Series between the Chicago White Sox and the Cincinnati Reds was an infamous World Series due to eight White Sox players being accused of cheating (trying to lose the World Series on purpose). It is also a unique series because, due to the country being happy about the end of World War I, the baseball commissioner declared this particular series would be the best of nine games, instead of the normal best of seven games. This meant the World Series champion would be the first team to win five games—which the Reds did in the eighth game. Listed below are the attendance numbers for the eight games of the 1919 World Series.

Game	Attendance
Game 1	30,511
Game 2	29,690
Game 3	29,126
Game 4	34,363
Game 5	34,379
Game 6	32,006
Game 7	13,923
Game 8	32,930

5. What was the least attendance? What was the greatest attendance?

6. What is the range for the attendance numbers in the 1919 World Series?

7. True or False. You could say the number of people in attendance for the 1919 World Series varied greatly from game to game.

8. Which attendance number might be considered an outlier?

LESSON 12.4

Mean, Median, Mode

Key Ideas

Median, mode, and mean are often used to represent data.

Thom measured the 7 plants in the classroom greenhouse. Their heights, measured in centimeters, were 11, 7, 3, 18, 7, 8, and 9. When Thom put them in order from shortest to tallest, he was able to find the middle value, or the median.

3 7 7 **8** 9 11 18

The median for this group of measurements is 8 centimeters.

The mode, or most frequently occurring height, is 7 centimeters.

Thom was also able to find the average, or mean, of the measurements by adding their heights and dividing by the total number of plants. The sum of their heights is 63 centimeters, and there are 7 plants total.

$63 \div 7 = 9$

The average, or *mean,* of the plant heights is 9 centimeters.

Mrs. Hartman's third-grade class recorded their ages in months. Here are the ages of all the students.

134	137	127	134	128	129	136	132	130	130
129	134	128	131	132	125	128	126	135	132
126	142	130	130	139	137	136	126	130	129

Use the table of ages of Mrs. Hartman's students (on page 488) to answer the following questions.

1. List the numbers in order from least to greatest.
2. What is the least number in your list? What is the greatest number?
3. Which number appears most often (the mode)?
4. What is the mean, or average age, for the students (in months)?
5. What is the range?

Here are the students' scores on Mrs. Hartman's math test.

83 85 91 62 85 74 95 68 92 94

85 97 73 78 80 86 88 91 93 87

81 79 76 83 82 96 84 82 85 86

6. What is the mode for this group of scores?
7. What is the average score (the mean)?
8. What are the least and greatest scores?
9. What score is the median, or middle, score?
10. What is the range?

Writing + Math **Journal**

Describe in your own words the terms *mean, median,* and *mode.*

LESSON 12.5 Displaying Data

Key Ideas

Data can be displayed in various kinds of graphs or tables.

> **The Local County Fair was held this past weekend. Here are the results from Sunday's competitions.**
>
> The Happy Valley Farms took home 8 first-place ribbons, 2 second-place ribbons, and 9 third-place ribbons. Merry Acres Meadows acquired 7 first-place ribbons, 4 second-place ribbons, and 1 third-place ribbon. First-time contestant Weary Wanderer's Rest received 3 first-place ribbons, 1 second-place ribbon, and 3 third-place ribbons.

Copy the following table. Use the information from the newspaper clipping to complete the table.

Contestant	1st Place	2nd Place	3rd Place
1. Happy Valley Farms	■	■	■
2.	7	■	■
3. Weary Wanderer's Rest	■	■	■

4. How many second- and third-place ribbons did Merry Acres Meadows win?
5. How many ribbons did Weary Wanderer's Rest win total?
6. Who won the most ribbons?

This grid shows a small section of Anytimetown. Each location can be named with an ordered pair—a number from the bottom number line, (axis) of the graph and a number from the left-hand number line (axis) of the graph.

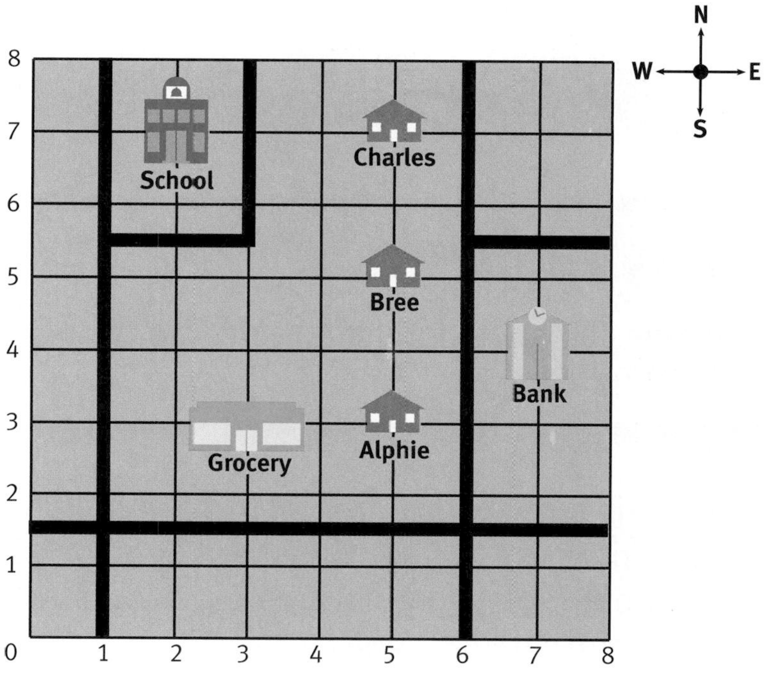

Answer **the following questions by using the section map of Anytimetown. The first one has been done for you.**

7. Where is the school located? (2, 7) Once you locate the school, go down to the bottom axis to find the first number, 2. From the school, go to the left axis to find the second number, 7.
8. Where is Bree's house located?
9. Who lives farther north, Alphie or Charles?
10. Where is the grocery store located?
11. If you were traveling from the grocery store to the bank, would you travel east or west?
12. **Extended Response** What would be a good title for this graph?

Writing + Math **Journal**

Describe a situation in which you might use a table to organize your information.

LESSON 12.6

Graphs That Compare

Key Ideas

Three common kinds of graphs are pictographs, bar graphs, and circle graphs.

Qmariz surveyed 50 fellow students on their favorite type of sport to play. Basketball got 14 votes, baseball/softball got 12 votes, soccer got 16 votes, and football got 8 votes.

1. Create a table of tallies using Qmariz's information on a separate piece of paper.
2. Use the information from the table you created in Problem 1 to copy and complete the pictograph. Remember to refer to the key to determine the number of figures to use.

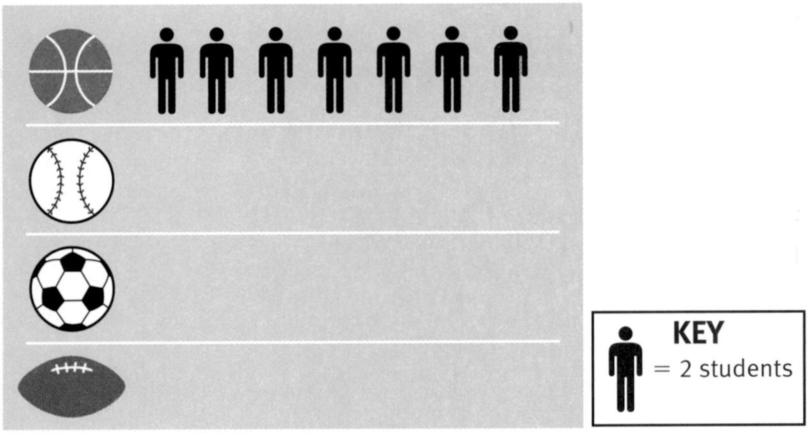

Copy the following bar graph on your paper. Use the information from page 492 to complete the bar graph.

3 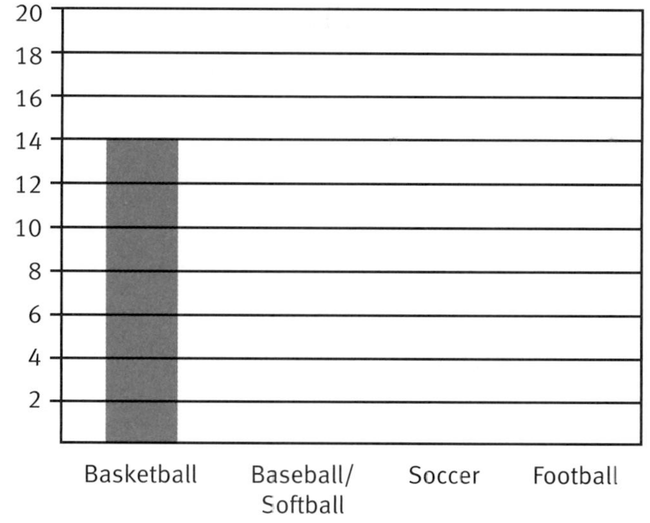

Qmariz also created a circle graph to show the percentages of the total votes for each favorite sport to play.

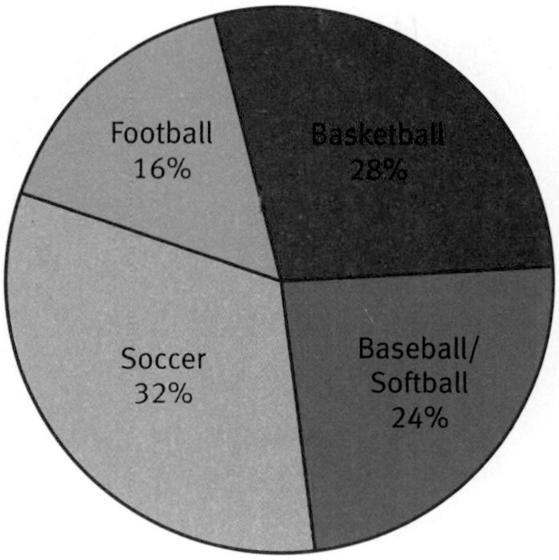

Answer the following questions.

4 Write each of the percents as fractions.

5 How many students were surveyed altogether?

6 **Extended Response** Write one true statement and one false statement about the information from the circle graph.

Writing + Math **Journal**

How are pictographs, bar graphs, and circle graphs alike? How are they different?

LESSON 12.7

Graphs Showing Change

Key Ideas

A line graph shows change over a period of time.

Along the bottom line, or *axis*, of a line graph is the measure of time (minutes, hours, years, centuries, and so on). On the left line, or *axis*, is usually another type of measurement (pounds, amount of something, number of something, and so on). It is important that in any graph, the spaces always represent equal amounts; if not, your graph may be misleading.

This line graph shows the change in Todd's height from his birth, which could be considered 0 years, through age 15. Notice the bottom axis is labeled *Age in Years*, and the left-hand axis is labeled *Height in Centimeters*.

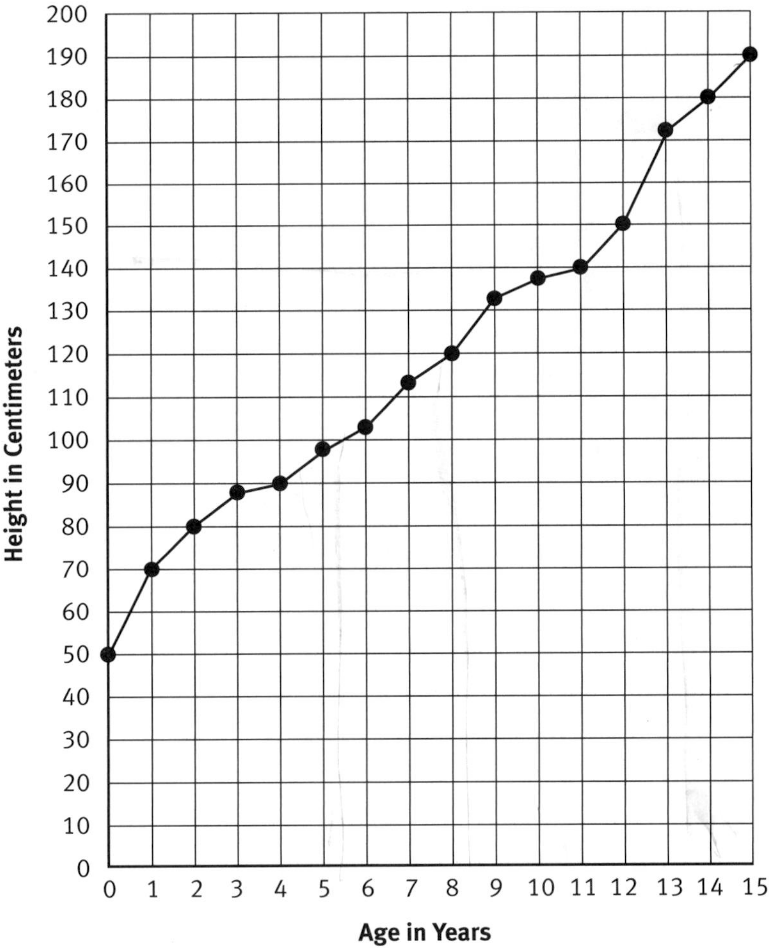

1. **Extended Response** What would be a good title for this graph?
2. Does this line graph show an *increase* in Todd's height or a *decrease* in Todd's height over the years?

eTextbook This lesson is available in the ***eTextbook.***

Use the graph to answer these questions.

About how tall was Todd on his

3. first birthday?
4. fifth birthday?
5. eighth birthday?
6. fourteenth birthday?

How old was Todd when he was

7. 90 centimeters tall?
8. 115 centimeters tall?
9. 140 centimeters tall?
10. 180 centimeters tall?

About how many centimeters did Todd grow between his

11. first and fifth birthdays?
12. fifth and eighth birthdays?
13. eighth and fourteenth birthdays?
14. first and fourteenth birthdays?
15. If Todd continues to grow at the same rate as he grew between his thirteenth and fifteenth birthdays, how tall do you think he will be on his sixteenth birthday?

This line graph shows the change in Wendy's weight from her birth.

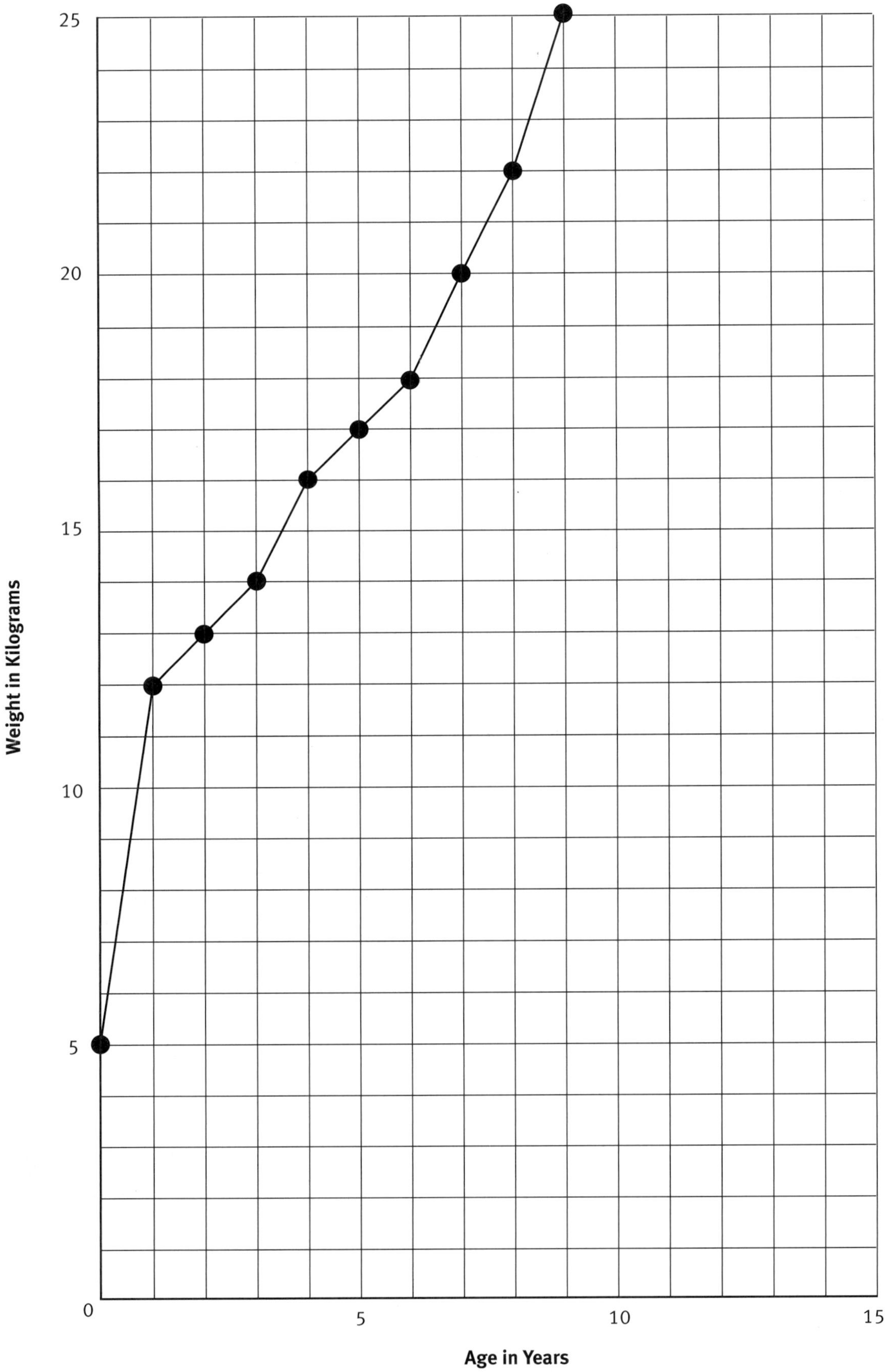

eTextbook This lesson is available in the ***eTextbook.***

16 **Extended Response** What would be a good title for this graph?

17 Does this line graph show an *increase* in her weight or a *decrease* in her weight over the years?

Use the line graph to answer these questions.

About how much did Wendy weigh on her

18 first birthday?

19 third birthday?

20 seventh birthday?

21 ninth birthday?

22 About how much do you think Wendy weighed when she was $7\frac{1}{2}$ years old?

23 About how old do you think Wendy was when she weighed 24 kilograms?

24 **Extended Response** Write one true statement about this graph.

25 When will Wendy reach 100 kg?

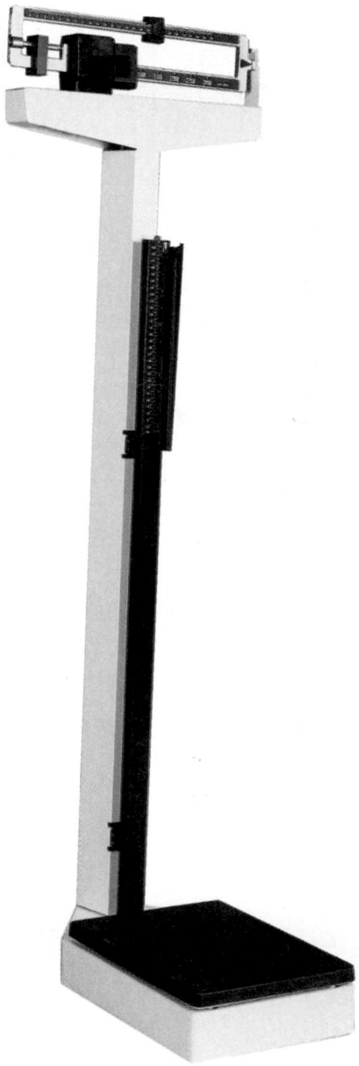

Exploring Problem Solving

Ms. Riley sells baskets of star fruit that she grows on her farm in Thailand. People tell her how many kilograms they want, and she makes up a basket with that amount. She keeps records such as the ones below so she knows the different amounts people order.

Ms. Riley has decided to make her business simpler. She will sell baskets of star fruit in only three sizes—small, medium, and large. How many kilograms should she put in each size?

Tuesday

Number of Baskets	Amount in Each Basket
1	2 kg
1	4 kg
2	10 kg
1	15 kg

Wednesday

Number of Baskets	Amount in Each Basket
2	3 kg
1	5 kg
1	8 kg
1	12 kg

Thursday

Number of Baskets	Amount in Each Basket
2	4 kg
1	7 kg
2	8 kg
1	15 kg

Friday

Number of Baskets	Amount in Each Basket
2	3 kg
1	9 kg
3	10 kg
2	15 kg

Saturday

Number of Baskets	Amount in Each Basket
2	2 kg
1	6 kg
2	8 kg
3	15 kg
1	18 kg

Eric organized the data in a table to help solve the problem.

Amount	Number of Baskets
2 kg	3
3 kg	4
4 kg	

Think about Eric and LeAnne's strategies. Answer the following questions.

1. Why did Eric write the number 3 next to 2 kg?
2. What number do you think Eric is about to write? Why?
3. Do you think Eric's way of organizing the data helps?
4. How would you solve the problem?

LeAnne organized the data in a different way.

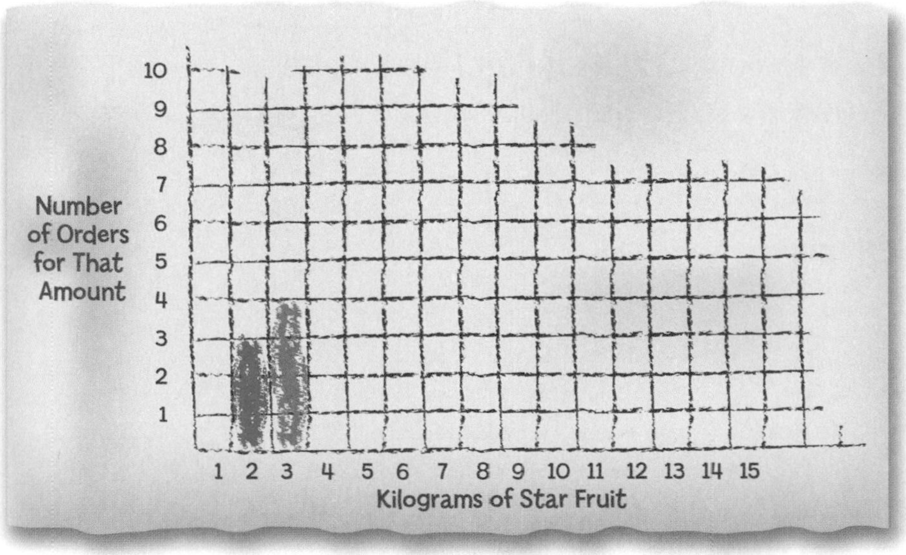

5. What do the two bars that LeAnne made so far show?
6. How is LeAnne's strategy different from Eric's?
7. How are the two strategies alike?
8. How could LeAnne use her graph to solve the problem?
9. Use one of the strategies shown or a strategy of your own to decide how heavy each size should be. Explain your reasoning.

Cumulative Review

Metric Weight Lesson 9.3

Convert each measure from kilograms to grams or from grams to kilograms. Write the new measure.

1. ☐ g = 10 kg
2. 4 kg = ☐ g
3. 17 kg = ☐ g
4. ☐ g = 8 kg
5. ☐ g = 3 kg

Arrays Lesson 4.5

Draw the array, and then answer the question.

6. In the winter, Amanda uses straw to help keep her llamas warm. She has 6 rows with 12 bales of straw each. Draw the array.
7. Amanda uses 3 bales to cover each shelter floor. If she used all the straw, how many shelter floors could she cover?

Subtracting Three-Digit Numbers Lesson 2.8

Subtract.

8. $261 - 199 = \square$
9. $354 - 275 = \square$
10. $613 - 535 = \square$
11. $707 - 488 = \square$

Dividing Two-Digit Numbers by One-Digit Numbers Lesson 7.7

Divide.

12. $96 \div 2$
13. $69 \div 3$
14. $49 \div 7$
15. $68 \div 4$
16. $96 \div 4$
17. $52 \div 4$

Graphing Ordered Pairs Lesson 6.6

Fill in the blanks by finding the letters in the graph that match the ordered pairs.

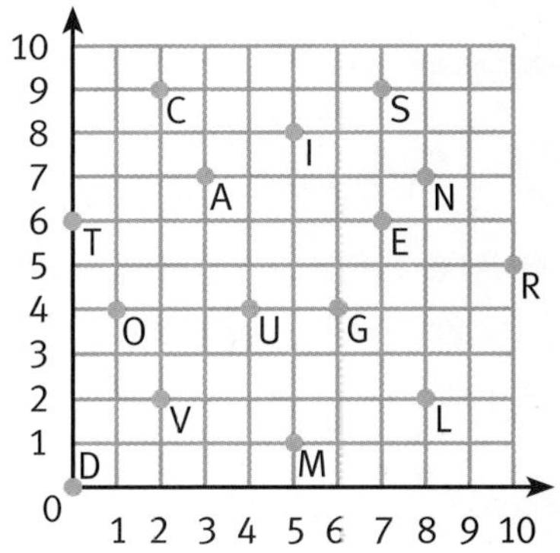

18 To move animals, a farmer might use this.

____ ____ ____ ____ ____ ____ ____

(0, 6) (10, 5) (3, 7) (5, 8) (8, 2) (7, 6) (10, 5)

19 Many horse ____ ____ ____ ____ ____ ____ ____ are made of leather.

(7, 9) (3, 7) (0, 0) (0, 0) (8, 2) (7, 6) (7, 9)

20 You might find this shelled animal at a reptile farm.

____ ____ ____ ____ ____ ____

(0, 6) (4, 4) (10, 5) (0, 6) (8, 2) (7, 6)

Equalities and Inequalities Lesson 1.4

Use $<$, $>$, or $=$ to make a true comparison.

21 875 ____ 877

22 9 + 185 ____ 12 + 186

23 4,325 ____ 4,442

24 86 − 8 ____ 68 − 6

25 1,235 ____ 1,235

26 617 − 9 ____ 619 − 7

Angles Lesson 11.2

Label each angle as either *right, obtuse,* or *acute*.

27 

28 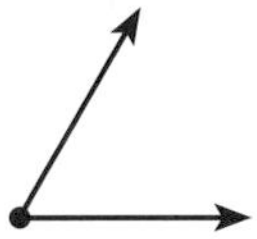

29 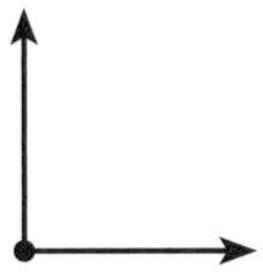

30 

LESSON 12.8

Graphs Showing How Data is Grouped

Key Ideas

There are times when you want to show the spread of data quickly to help identify the range, mode, or any outliers. One easy way to do this is by creating a line plot.

To create a line plot, begin by drawing a number line. Make sure your number line has a scale that includes the greatest value and the least value you need to graph. For each piece of information to graph, draw an *x* above the corresponding value. Look at the following line plot Zampa made of the pairs of shoes the students counted in their houses.

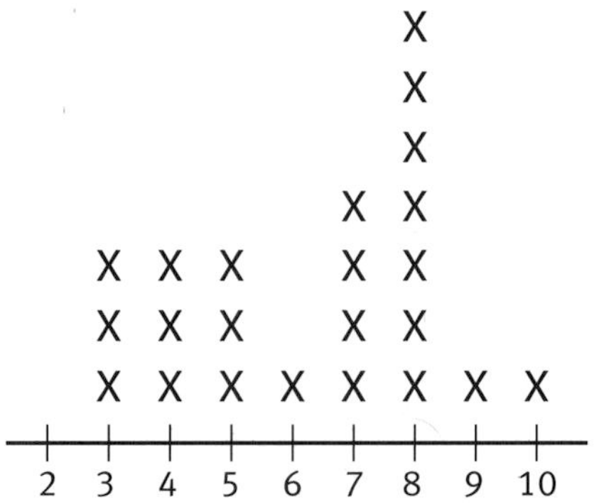

Use the information from Zampa's line plot to answer the following questions.

1. Create a bar graph showing how frequently you would expect to find a certain number of pairs of shoes in a student's house.
2. What is the mode? What is the range?
3. What number of pairs of shoes might be considered an outlier?
4. **Extended Response** Write one true and one false statement about the line plot.

Another type of plot that allows you to organize and group data is a stem-and-leaf plot.

The following are the ages of ten faculty at the News Review Journalism Camp.

35, 28, 19, 45, 51, 48, 31, 34, 18, 50

When we put the ages in numerical order, they are 18, 19, 28, 31, 34, 35, 45, 48, 50, and 51. The least value is 18, and the greatest value is 51. This will help us determine our first and last stem.

In this stem-and-leaf plot, the stems will be the digits in the tens place and the leaves will be the digits in the ones place.

Copy and list the stems to the left of the dividing line. Then list the leaves to the right of the dividing line so that they match up with the appropriate stem.

Stem	Leaves
1	8 9
2	8
3	1 4 5
4	5 8
5	0 1

The row 1 | 8 9 represents 18 and 19, 2 | 8 represents 28, and so on. By looking at this stem-and-leaf plot, we can tell that the most frequently occurring ages are between 30 and 39 and the median is 34.

The following are extra-credit points awarded in Ms. Pi's third-grade class for the entire year: 10, 21, 26, 8, 33, 41, 43, 28, 19, 17, 7, 22, 25, 31, 30, 20, 17, 50, and 44.

5. Use the extra-credit points listed above to create a stem-and-leaf plot.

6. Is it now easier to find the least, greatest, and most common number of extra-credit points?

7. How many students had extra credit this year in Ms. Pi's third-grade class?

8. **Extended Response** Write one true statement about the stem-and-leaf plot.

LESSON 12.9 Interpreting and Analyzing Data

Key Ideas

One way to see how closely two sets of data are related is to use a scatter plot. If the information is closely related, then the graph will resemble a line.

Julia recorded the age and height of twenty-five girls. Rather than make two separate graphs for age and height, she created a scatter plot comparing a girl's age to that girl's height.

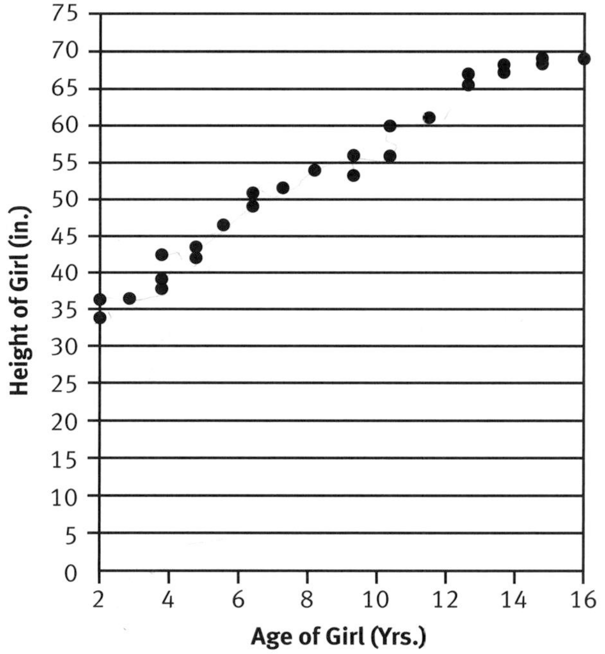

1. As a girl's age increases, does her height generally increase or decrease?
2. True or False. The points are fairly close to being on a line.
3. Based on your answer to Problem 2, would you consider the age and height of a girl to be closely related?
4. What would be a good title for this scatter plot?

Julia also recorded how many members were in each girl's family. She decided to plot that information compared to each girl's age on a different scatter plot.

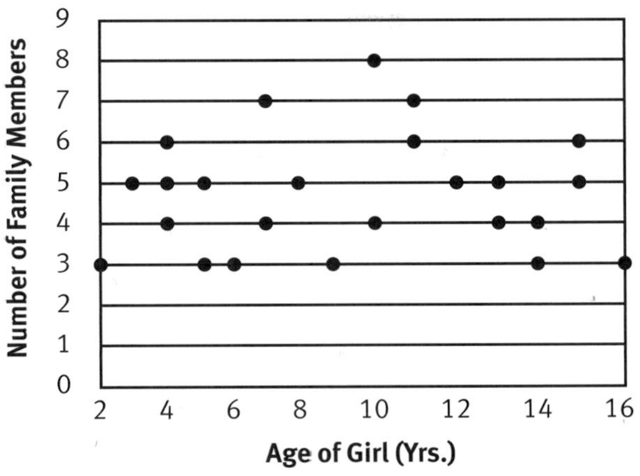

5. As a girl's age increases, does the number of members in her family generally increase or decrease?

6. True or False. The points are fairly close to being on a line.

7. Based on your answer to Problem 6, would you consider the age of a girl and the number of members in her family to be closely related?

8. What would be a good title for this scatter plot?

LESSON 12.10

Probability—Impossible to Certain

Key Ideas

People often make predictions about the future that are based on the probability that an event will happen.

If an event is certain to happen, such as the sun rising the next morning, we say it has a probability of 1.

If an event is impossible, such as rolling a 6 on a ***Number Cube*** which only has the numbers 0–5, we say that it has a probability of 0.

Most events are neither certain nor impossible, and they have a probability between 0 and 1.

Use the term *certain, impossible,* or *neither certain nor impossible* to label each of the following scenarios.

1. If today is May 3, then tomorrow is May 4.
2. If today is the 30th day of the month, then tomorrow is the 31st day of the month.
3. The day school starts has a name (in English) that doesn't end with the letter *"y."*
4. If I walk into a family restaurant, the first person I see will be a male.
5. When I roll a 5–10 ***Number Cube***, I will roll an even number or an odd number.

eTextbook This lesson is available in the ***eTextbook.***

Probabilities are expressed with fractions.

What is the probability that you will roll a 4 with a fair 0–5 ***Number Cube?*** There are 6 possible outcomes—0, 1, 2, 3, 4, and 5—but only 1 of the outcomes is a 4. We say that the probability of rolling a 4 is $\frac{1}{6}$.

What is the probability that you will roll a 7? The probability of rolling a 7 is $\frac{0}{6}$ or 0. It is impossible to roll a 7 with a 0–5 **Number Cube.**

What is the probability of rolling either a 0, 1, 2, 3, 4, or 5? The probability of rolling one of those numbers is $\frac{6}{6}$, or 1. It is certain that one of those numbers will be rolled.

Answer the following based on a 0–5 *Number Cube.*

6. What is the probability of rolling a 2?
7. What is the probability of rolling a 5?
8. What is the probability of rolling a 6?

Answer the following based on a regular penny with heads and tails.

9. How many possible outcomes are there when you flip the penny?
10. What is the probability of the penny landing on heads?
11. What is the probability of the penny landing on tails?
12. What is the probability of the penny landing on either heads or tails?

Writing + Math **Journal**

Describe how you would determine the probability of rolling a 7 on a 5–10 ***Number Cube.***

LESSON 12.11

Probability—Predictions and Experiments

Key Ideas

The probability of an event occurring can be written as a fraction from 0 through 1. The probability of a fair penny landing on heads when flipped is $\frac{1}{2}$, which can be read *one out of two.*

What would happen if you flipped a penny 10 times? The number of times you expect the penny to land heads would be $\frac{1}{2}$ of 10, or 5 times. If you flipped the penny 20 times, the number of times you expect the penny to land on heads would be $\frac{1}{2}$ of 20, or 10 times. In general, it will not land heads *exactly* $\frac{1}{2}$ the time, but in the long run we expect it to land heads *about* $\frac{1}{2}$ the time.

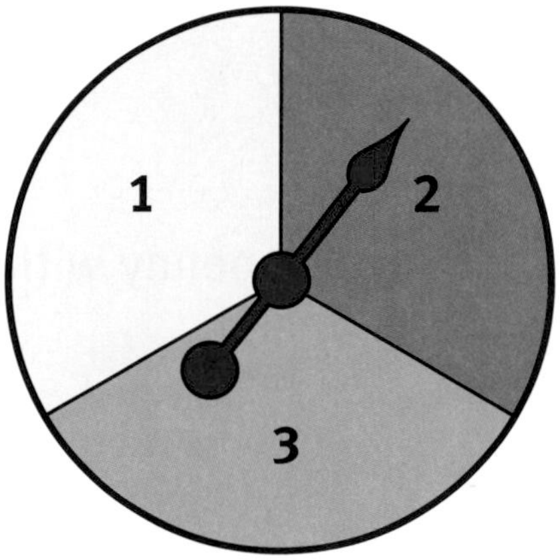

Use the spinner to answer the following questions.

1. What is the probability that you will spin a 1? A 2? A 3?
2. If you were to spin the spinner 6 times, what is the number of times that you would expect to spin a 1? A 2? A 3?
3. If you were to spin the spinner 12 times, what is the number of times that you would expect to spin a 3?
4. If you were to spin the spinner 8 times, what is the number of times that you would expect to spin a 5?

Suppose you roll a 0–5 ***Number Cube*** and a 5–10 ***Number Cube.***

5. Copy the following table and use your knowledge of sums to complete the table.

+	5	6	7	8	9	10
0	5	6	7			
1	6					
2	7	8				
3						
4	9	10				
5						

6. What is the probability that you would roll a sum of 5?
7. What is the probability that you would roll a sum of 15?
8. What is the probability that you would roll a sum of 0?
9. What is the probability that you would roll a sum of 10?
10. What is the probability that you would roll a sum of 13?

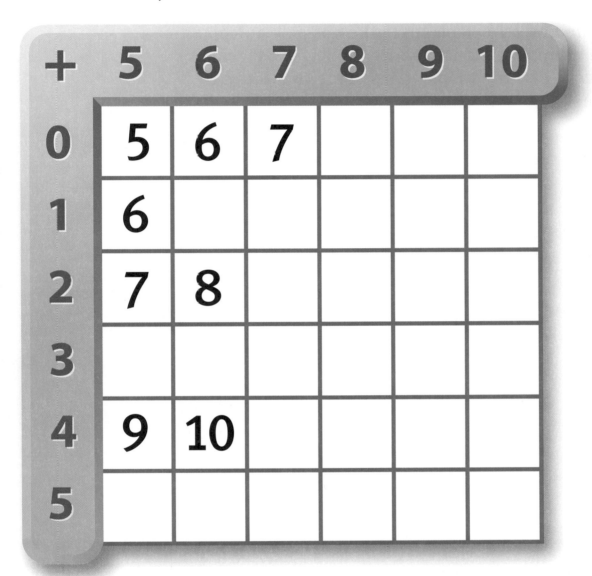

LESSON 12.12

Displaying and Analyzing Outcomes

Key Ideas

There are times when counting the possible outcomes can be confusing. Making a diagram might help you organize the information and make the counting a little easier.

Janice had the following choices for painting her room: blue, red, and green.

Her choices for decorations were flowers, animals, and shapes.

She made a diagram to show all the combinations (possible outcomes) she had for her new room.

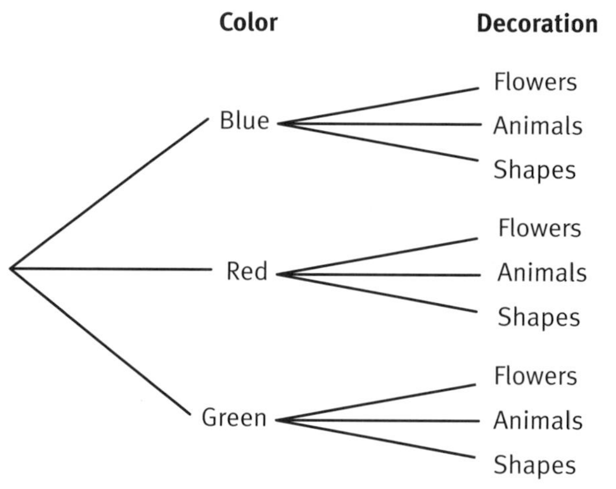

Use **the diagram above to answer the following questions.**

1. How many possible color and decoration combinations (for example, blue and animals) are there for Janice's room?

2. **Extended Response** Describe what mathematical sentence would give the same answer and why it would describe this diagram.

The name for this type of diagram is a tree diagram. A tree diagram helps to give the total number of possible outcomes.

Mrs. Godbey offered her class the following options for their free-writing assignment. They could choose the setting as the beach, the mountains, or the ocean; their characters could be robots or children; and their story genre could be science fiction or mystery.

3. Create a tree diagram with the information offered by Mrs. Godbey.

Use your completed tree diagram to answer the following questions.

4. How many possible outcomes are there?
5. If a student wants to write only a science fiction story, how many possible outcomes are there?
6. If a student wants to write only about a story on the beach, how many possible outcomes are there?
7. Is it possible for a student to write a mountain story about robots?
8. If a student wants to write only about robots in the mountains, how many possible outcomes are there?

Exploring Problem Solving

All over the world, people grow food on farms. Some farming methods are different from country to country. But some things are the same, such as the need to do chores.

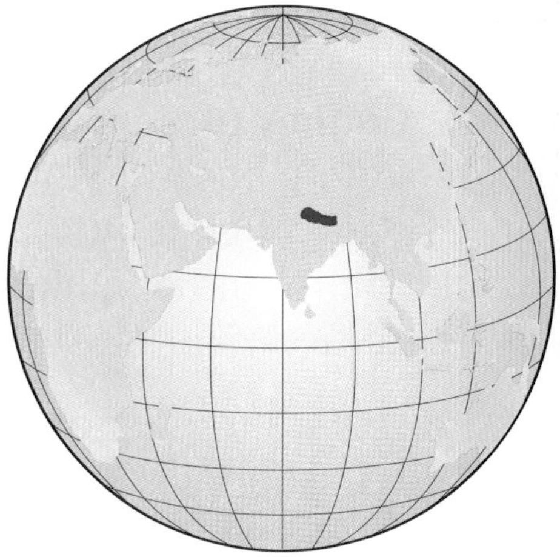

Suppose you are visiting a small farm thousands of miles away in Nepal. You are going to get a chance to help with farm chores. The names of five chores are placed in a paper bag, and you will reach in and pick two of them.

Work with your group to solve this problem.

1. What is the probability that you will pick milking buffalos and feeding goats?
2. How did you solve the problem?
3. Make up and exchange your own problem about chores on a farm in Nepal.

Cumulative Review

Subtracting Decimals Lesson 10.6

Subtract.

1. 18.53 − 11.26
2. 8.79 − 6.32
3. 20.00 − 10.5
4. 1.33 − 0.88
5. 9.17 − 3.4
6. 81.38 − 26.5

Fractions of Linear Measure Lesson 8.2

What fraction of the line is shaded?

7. 
8. 
9. 
10. 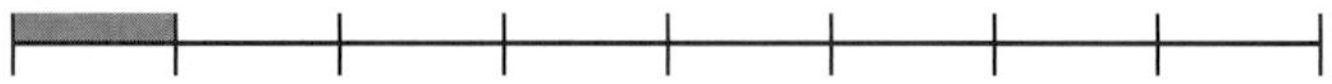

Problem-Solving Applications Lesson 7.9

Tell whether you would add, subtract, multiply, or divide to solve each problem. Then solve each problem. If it is not possible to solve the problem, tell why.

11. **Extended Response** Every five years the Tucker family moves half of their livestock to another farm. They moved 68 head of cattle this time. How many cattle did they have this year before they moved the livestock?
12. **Extended Response** Emma milked 3 cows every morning. She collected about 12 liters of milk each day. About how many liters of milk did she collect from each cow?
13. **Extended Response** Now Emma has 4 cows to milk. About how many liters of milk will she collect each day?

Cumulative Review

Slides, Flips, and Turns Lesson 11.7

Describe the change from position A to position B for each figure. Determine if the change was from a translation, reflection, rotation, or a combination of two different changes.

14

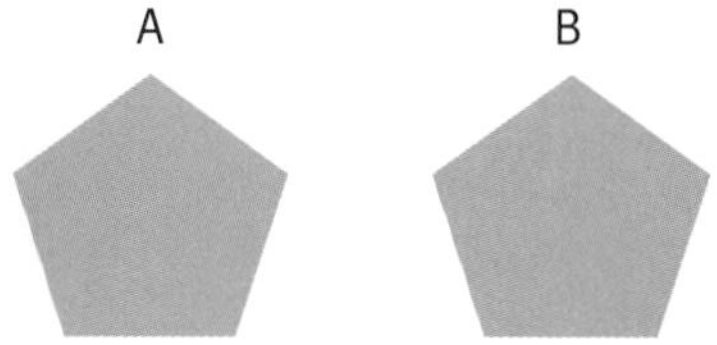

15

16
•••

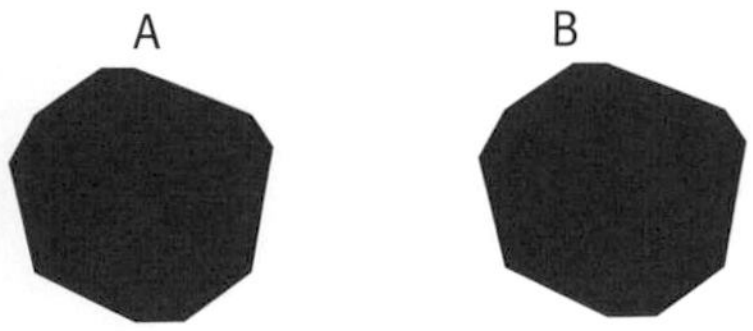

Using Arrow Notation to Solve Equations Lesson 6.3

Find the value of *n*. In Problem 20, find the value of *n* and the value of *m*.

17

$48 \longrightarrow \boxed{\div 4} \longrightarrow n$

$n = \blacksquare$

19

$9 \longrightarrow \boxed{\times 11} \longrightarrow n$

$n = \blacksquare$

18

$n \longleftarrow \boxed{\times 8} \longleftarrow 20$

$n = \blacksquare$

20

$7 \longrightarrow \boxed{+8} \longrightarrow n \longrightarrow \boxed{\times 4} \longrightarrow m$

$n = \blacksquare$
$m = \blacksquare$

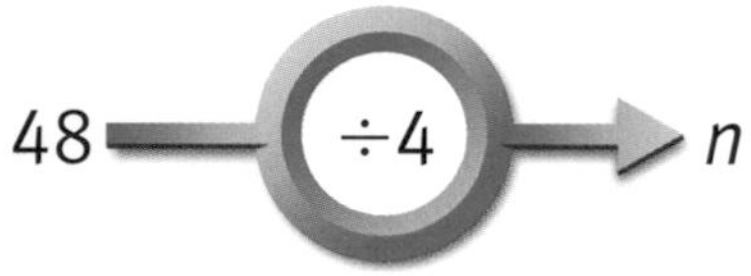

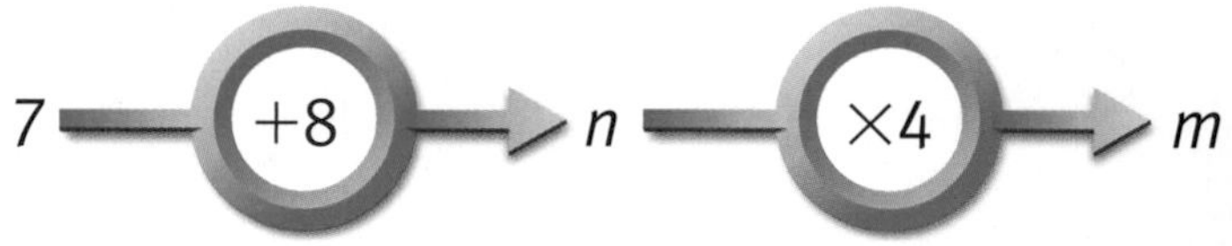

CHAPTER 12 Key Ideas Review

In this chapter, you explored various graphs and their properties and probability.

You learned about collecting and summarizing data. You learned about many types of graphs. You learned about predictions, probability, and outcomes.

Use the following information about Susanne's class's favorite seasons.

In Susanne's class 3 people chose winter, 7 people chose spring, 12 people chose summer, and 6 people chose fall.

1. Create a tally table and a single bar graph from the information gathered in Susanne's class.
2. **Extended Response** Write one true statement and one false statement from the data in Susanne's class.

Use the list of heights (in inches) of Shane's classmates to answer the following questions.

Height in inches of Shane's class:
36, 36, 48, 48, 41, 50, 57, 38, 32, 42, 43, 55, 42, 41, 36

3. What is the range? The mode? The median? The mean?
4. What is the probability (as a fraction) of the spinner landing on red with only one spin? What is the probability (as a fraction) of the spinner *not* landing on red with only one spin?

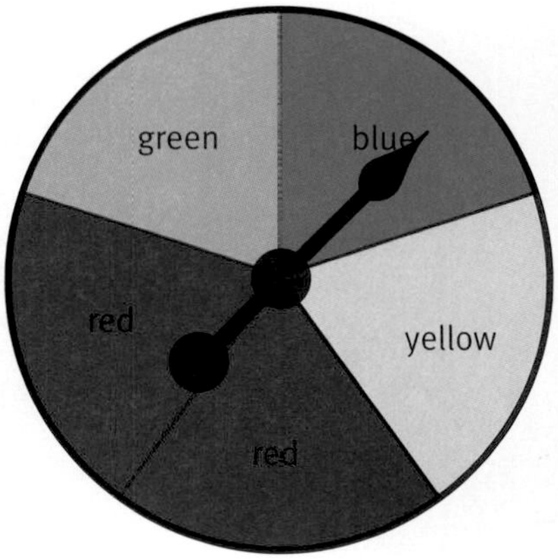

5. **Extended Response** If you spin the spinner ten times, what is the number of times that you would expect to land on yellow? Explain your answer.
6. **Extended Response** If you spin the spinner twenty times, what is the number of times that you would expect to land on red? Explain your answer.

CHAPTER 12 Chapter Review

Lesson 12.1 **Decide if each of the following shows a good sample by answering *yes* or *no*. If it is not a good sample, explain why.**

1. Students in Mr. Young's health class asked every fourth student entering the school cafeteria questions about the school lunch menu.

2. **Extended Response** Three students from Ms. Theus's homeroom stood in the hallway asking girls wearing glasses to list their favorite class in school.

Lesson 12.2 **Use the following information to create a tally table.**

3. Sara surveyed her art class to see what their favorite pastime activity is. The top five pastime activities are *Television, Games, Reading, Drawing,* and *Biking*. When Sara counted her results, she found that 9 students like television, 11 students like games, 2 students like reading, 3 students like drawing, 4 students like biking, and 3 students like activities other than the ones mentioned.

Lesson 12.3 **Answer the questions using the following data from Hydepark Elementary School.**

For the current school year, there are 117 kindergartners, 121 first graders, 105 second graders, 110 third graders, 108 fourth graders, 43 fifth graders, and 120 sixth graders at Hydepark Elementary School.

4. How many students are there total? What is the range of students?

5. Is there an outlier amount? If so, what is it?

Lesson 12.4 **Solve.**

Judith listed the number of days in each month on a piece of paper: 31, 28, 31, 30, 31, 30, 31, 31, 30, 31, 30, 31.

6. What is the mode? What is the median?

7. **Extended Response** Describe how you would find the mean.

Lesson 12.8 **Create a line plot and a stem-and-leaf plot using the following information.**

Misty counted the genres of books she had in her family library. She discovered there were 23 poetry books, 17 mysteries, 10 science fiction books, 21 romance novels, 12 biographies, 14 other types of nonfiction, and 17 other types of fiction.

Lesson 12.10 **Using the terms *certain, neither certain nor impossible,* and *impossible,* label each of the following scenarios.**

8. If today is March 3, then yesterday was March 2.

9. If I have a box with a pair of shoes, what is the probability I will pick out the left shoe?

Lesson 12.11 **Answer questions 10 and 11 based on a 5–10 *Number Cube.***

10. What is the probability (as a fraction) that you will roll a 10?

11. What is the probability (as a fraction) that you will roll a 0?

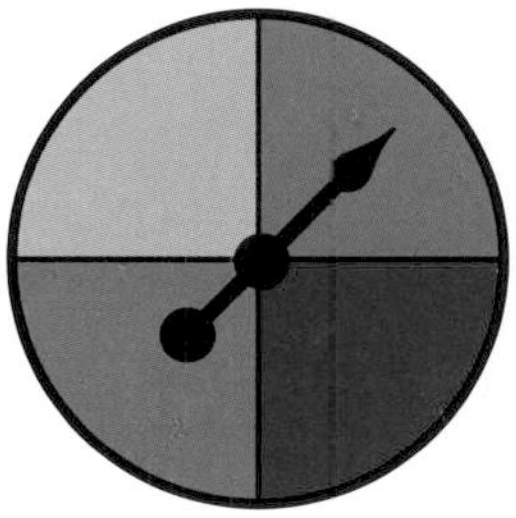

12. What is the probability (as a fraction) that your one spin will land on a green section? On a red section? On a blue section?

13. If you were to spin the spinner 8 times, what is the number of times that you would expect it to land on a green section? On a red section? On a blue section?

CHAPTER 12 Practice Test

Answer the questions.

1. Look at this set of data. What is the range?

   3, 7, 5, 8, 2, 9, 10, 12

2. Look at this set of data. Which number is an outlier?

   42, 44, 73, 36, 40, 38, 40

Use this set of data for Problems 3–6.

10, 8, 14, 14, 15, 9, 17

3. What is the mode?
4. What is the median?
5. What is the range?
6. Ally collected data about her friends' favorite sports and put them in this tally chart. She wants to display the data in a graph. What kind of graph should she use?

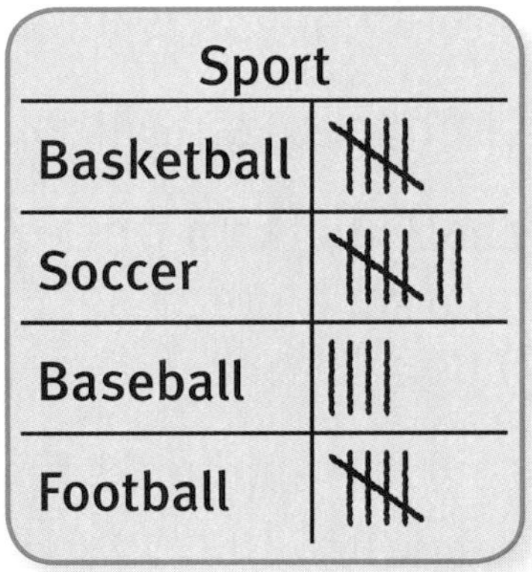

7. Carla has a 0–5 ***Number Cube.*** Using the terms *certain, impossible,* or *neither,* what is the probability that she will roll a number greater than 5?
8. Maya will flip a coin. What is the probability, as a fraction, that the coin will land heads up?

Use this table to answer the following questions.

Mr. Krishnan's Room (Eye Colors)

Eye Color	Number of Students
Blue	12
Brown	10
Hazel	2
Green	1

9. What is the most common eye color in Mr. Krishnan's class?

   Ⓐ blue　Ⓑ brown

   Ⓒ hazel　Ⓓ green

10. How many students are in Mr. Krishnan's class?

    Ⓐ 22　Ⓑ 25

    Ⓒ 23　Ⓓ 20

Choose the situation that shows an example of good sampling.

11. An ice-cream shop wants to test a new flavor.

Ⓐ The owner gives a sample to one person every 30 minutes for 2 hours.

Ⓑ The owner gives a sample to every third person who comes to the store.

Ⓒ The owner gives a sample to each boy who comes to the store.

Ⓓ The owner gives a sample to his next-door neighbor.

12. A student wants to find out what color car is most popular. What is the best way to get a good sample?

Ⓐ She tallies the colors of the cars that pass by her school for one hour each day for a week.

Ⓑ She tallies the colors of the cars owned by her family.

Ⓒ She asks all the girls in her class what their favorite color is.

Ⓓ She tallies the color of every car that passes by her school in a thirty-minute period.

Use this bar graph to answer the following questions.

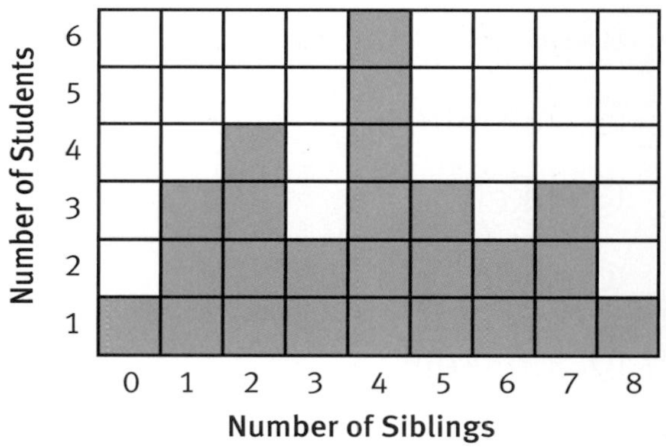

13. What is the mode?

Ⓐ 4 Ⓑ 6 Ⓒ 1 Ⓓ 8

14. What is the range?

Ⓐ 6 Ⓑ 10 Ⓒ 8 Ⓓ 7

Use this bar graph to answer the following questions.

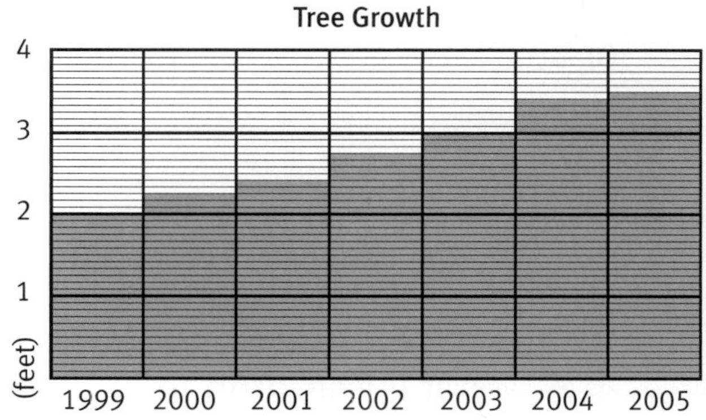

15. In what year did the tree grow the most?

Ⓐ 2001 Ⓑ 2003

Ⓒ 2004 Ⓓ 2005

CHAPTER 12

Practice Test

Find the probability of each event.

16. If today is Monday, then tomorrow will be Tuesday.

Ⓐ certain

Ⓑ likely

Ⓒ impossible

Ⓓ unlikely

17. After you turn ten, you will be nine on your next birthday.

Ⓐ certain

Ⓑ likely

Ⓒ impossible

Ⓓ unlikely

18. You roll a 0–5 ***Number Cube.*** What is the probability, as a fraction, of rolling either a 3 or a 4?

Ⓐ $\frac{1}{6}$ Ⓑ $\frac{2}{6}$

Ⓒ $\frac{4}{6}$ Ⓓ $\frac{5}{6}$

19. You roll a ***Number Cube*** with sides numbered 2, 2, 2, 3, 4, 6. What is the probability, as a fraction, of rolling an even number?

Ⓐ $\frac{1}{6}$ Ⓑ $\frac{2}{6}$

Ⓒ $\frac{3}{6}$ Ⓓ $\frac{5}{6}$

20. How many minutes is $\frac{3}{5}$ of an hour?

Ⓐ 24 minutes

Ⓑ 30 minutes

Ⓒ 36 minutes

Ⓓ 42 minutes

21. Find the quotient of 72 ÷ 9.

Ⓐ 5 Ⓑ 8

Ⓒ 9 Ⓓ 7

22. Find the sum of 7 + 6 + 4 + 3.

Ⓐ 18 Ⓑ 16

Ⓒ 20 Ⓓ 24

23. How many decimeters are in 72 meters?

Ⓐ 70 Ⓑ 7.2

Ⓒ 7,200 Ⓓ 720

24. There are 6 shelves filled with 120 books. If each shelf holds the same number of books, how many books are on each shelf?

Ⓐ 20 Ⓑ 26

Ⓒ 12 Ⓓ 6

Extended Response **Create the graph described.**

25. Make a bar graph using the information in this tally chart.

Favorite Animal	
Lion	~~||||~~ ~~||||~~ ||
Tiger	~~||||~~ ~~||||~~
Giraffe	~~||||~~ ||||
Seal	~~||||~~ ||

26. **Extended Response** The frozen yogurt shop has 3 flavors—strawberry, chocolate, and vanilla. The shop offers waffle cones, sugar cones, and bowls. Darcy wants to get one scoop of frozen yogurt.

   a. Draw a tree diagram to show all the combinations she can choose from.

   b. How many possible combinations can Darcy choose from?

   c. Darcy has decided she will get a cone with vanilla ice cream. How many combinations does she have to choose from now?

   d. Is it possible to get a 1-scoop bowl with chocolate and vanilla ice cream? Explain.

   e. The ice-cream shop can also top the ice cream with sprinkles. How does this affect the number of possible combinations?

Thinking Story

A Chancy Birthday Party

"I've been wishing for a surprise birthday party," said Willy, "but I'm afraid my wish won't come true. My birthday is only a week away, and no one has said anything about a party for me yet."

Is that a good reason for Willy to think he won't have a surprise birthday party?

How long will he have to wait to see if his wish comes true?

What makes you think so?

Seven days later there was a knock on Willy's door. When Willy opened the door, he heard a loud "Surprise!"

"What a big surprise," said Willy, as the crowd of people came in. "I'm glad no one told me about my party."

"Since you like to wish so much," Portia told him, "Ferdie and I brought you a special present. Here are 4 packages."

"That's more than I could have wished for," Willy said.

"But there's a catch," said Ferdie. "Only 3 of the packages have presents in them. One of the packages is empty."

"That's all right," said Willy. "Three presents are enough."

"But you may not get all 3," Portia explained. "It depends on how lucky you are. You have to point to and then open the packages one at a time, and when you open the empty package you have to stop. You get only the presents that you open."

"This is going to take some hard wishing," said Willy. "If my wishing works, I'll get lots of presents."

If Willy is really lucky, how many presents will he get from Portia and Ferdie?

"I wish I knew which package is empty," said Willy. "I wouldn't open it until the end. That way I'd get 3 presents."

If Willy is really unlucky, how many presents will he get from Portia and Ferdie?

Willy picked one of the packages and started to open it. "I hope my wishing works," he said. "If this package is empty, I won't get any presents."

Is the package more likely to be empty or more likely to have a present in it?

Why?

"The wishing worked!" screamed Willy. "I got a present!"

"I'm glad you did," said Marcus, "but that was pretty easy. There were 4 packages, and only 1 is empty. So you had 3 chances of picking a present and only 1 chance of picking the empty box."

"I hope I'm lucky again," said Willy. "Here goes."

How many packages are left?

How many packages have presents in them?

Is Willy more likely to pick a present or an empty box?

"I got another present!" shouted Willy. "Now do you believe wishing works, Marcus?"

"I doubt it very much," said Marcus. "There were 3 packages, and 2 of them had presents in them. You had 2 chances of picking a present and only 1 chance of picking an empty box."

How many packages are left now?

Is Willy more likely to pick the one with a present in it or the one that is empty?

This time when Willy opened the package, he found it was empty. "I wish I had one more chance," he said. "I'm sure my luck would work next time, and I'd pick the package with a present in it."

How can Willy be so sure?

How many packages did Willy open?

How many presents did he get?

Would you say he was very lucky, somewhat lucky, or not lucky at all? Why?

The End

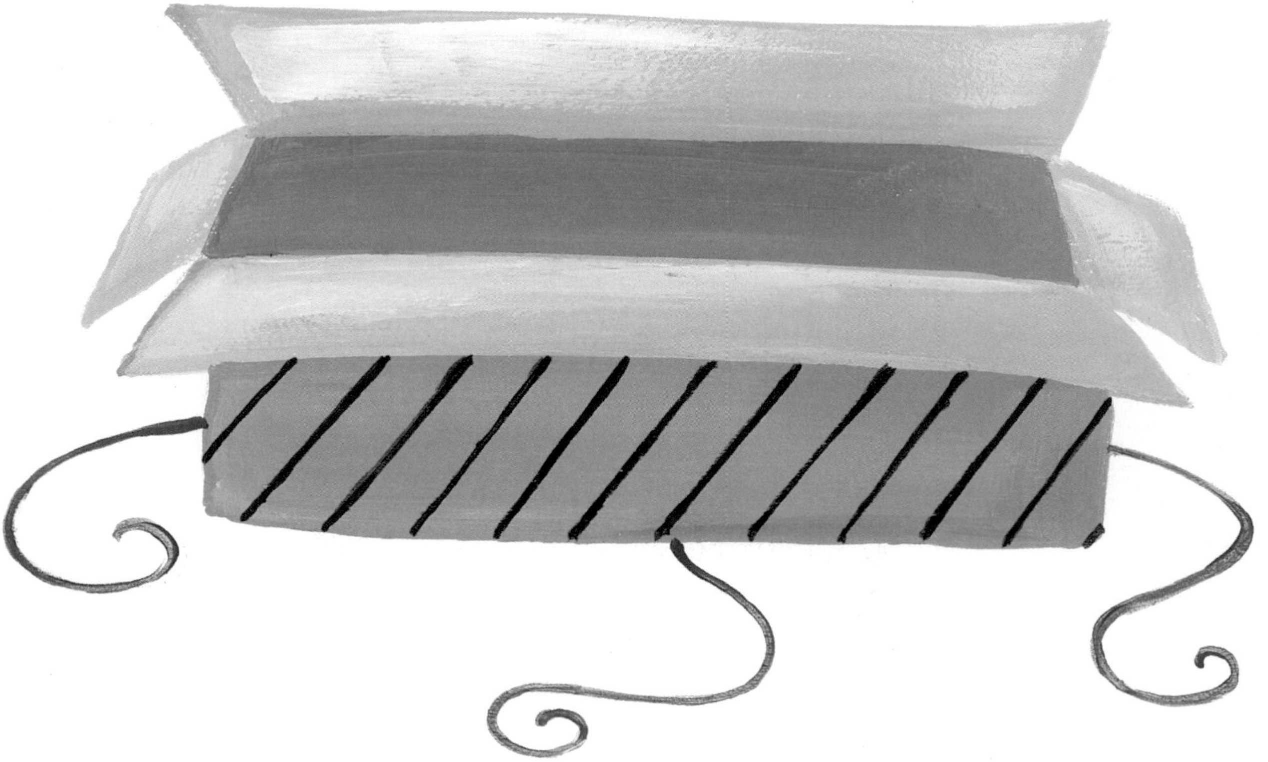

SRA Real Math

Student Handbook

Problem-Solving Tips

If you need help solving a math problem, try this:

- Write the problem in your own words.
- Write what you are trying to find out.
- List the information you already know.
- List the information you need to find out.
- Discuss the problem with other people.
- Write possible ways you can find out what you need to know.
- Have you solved problems like this before? If so, how did you do it?
- Try to solve the problem.

After you think you have solved the problem, ask yourself:

- Does the answer make sense?
- Is there more than one answer?
- Is there a different way to solve the problem?
- Would a different way have been easier or better for some reason?
- What have you learned that will help you solve other problems?

Handwriting Models

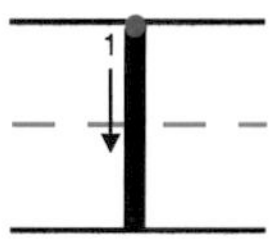

Starting point, straight down

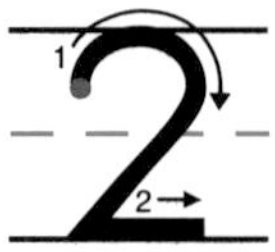

Starting point, around right, slanting left and straight across right

Starting point, around right, in at the middle, around right

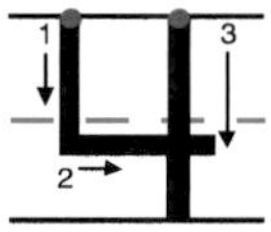

Starting point, straight down, straight across right. Starting point, straight down, crossing line

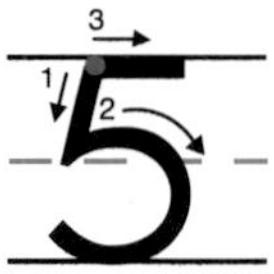

Straight down, curve around right and up. Starting point, straight across right

Starting point, slanting left, around the bottom curving up around left and into the curve

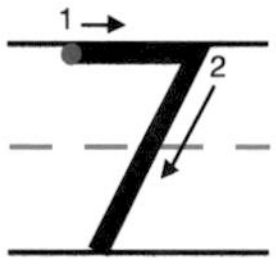

Starting point, straight across right, slanting down left

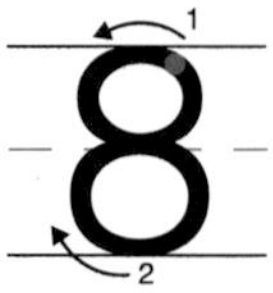

Starting point, curving left, curving down and around right, slanting up right to starting point

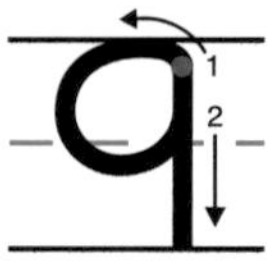

Starting point, curving around left all the way, straight down

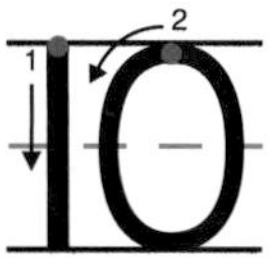

Starting point, straight down. Starting point, curving left all the way around to starting point

Number Line

Number lines show numbers in order.

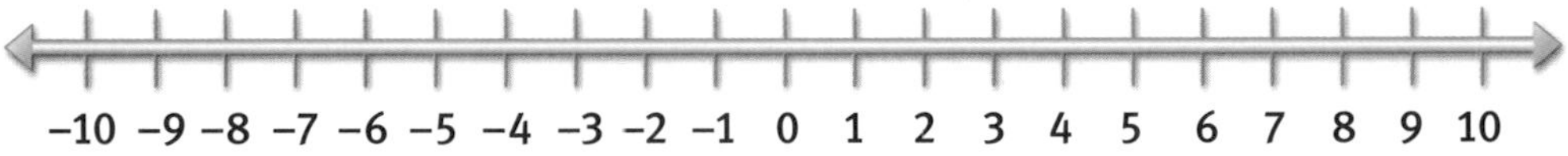

You can use a number line to

- count on.
- count back.
- skip count by 2s or 3s or any number.
- add.
- subtract.

Number Names

0	Zero			
1	One		1st	First
2	Two		2nd	Second
3	Three		3rd	Third
4	Four		4th	Fourth
5	Five		5th	Fifth
6	Six		6th	Sixth
7	Seven		7th	Seventh
8	Eight		8th	Eighth
9	Nine		9th	Ninth
10	Ten		10th	Tenth
11	Eleven	Ten and one	11th	Eleventh
12	Twelve	Ten and two	12th	Twelfth
13	Thirteen	Ten and three	13th	Thirteenth
14	Fourteen	Ten and four	14th	Fourteenth

15	Fifteen	Ten and five	15th	Fifteenth
16	Sixteen	Ten and six	16th	Sixteenth
17	Seventeen	Ten and seven	17th	Seventeenth
18	Eighteen	Ten and eight	18th	Eighteenth
19	Nineteen	Ten and nine	19th	Nineteenth
20	Twenty	Two tens	20th	Twentieth
30	Thirty	Three tens	30th	Thirtieth
40	Forty	Four tens	40th	Fortieth
50	Fifty	Five tens	50th	Fiftieth
60	Sixty	Six tens	60th	Sixtieth
70	Seventy	Seven tens	70th	Seventieth
80	Eighty	Eight tens	80th	Eightieth
90	Ninety	Nine tens	90th	Ninetieth
100	One hundred	Ten tens	100th	One hundredth

Place Value

A place-value table tells you how many hundreds, tens, and ones. Place value is important. Look what happens when the 5 is in the hundreds place or the ones place.

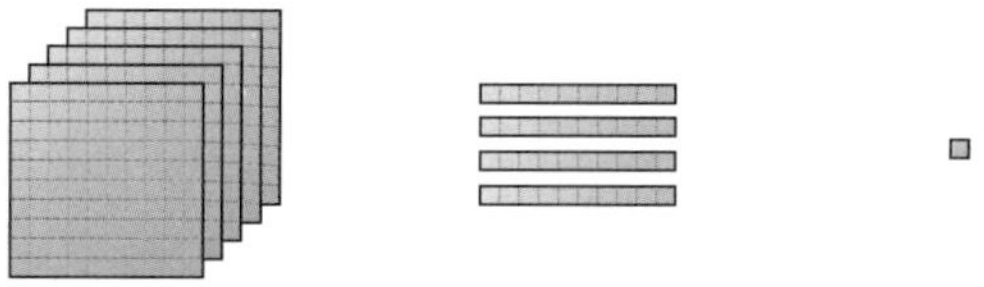

Hundreds	Tens	Ones
5	4	1

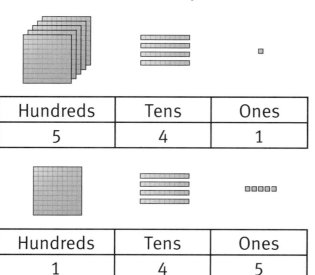

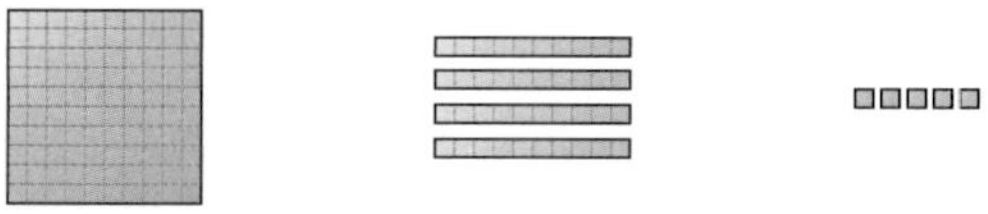

Hundreds	Tens	Ones
1	4	5

Big Numbers

Numbers go on forever. After trillions come quadrillions and then quintillions. A googol is written as 1 followed by 100 zeros. A googolplex is written as 1 followed by one googol zeros.

1	One
10	Ten
100	One hundred
1,000	One thousand
10,000	Ten thousand
100,000	One hundred thousand
1,000,000	One million
10,000,000	Ten million
100,000,000	One hundred million
1,000,000,000	One billion
10,000,000,000	Ten billion
100,000,000,000	One hundred billion
1,000,000,000,000	One trillion

Addition Table

You can use the Addition Table to find basic addition and subtraction facts.

+	0	1	2	3	4	5	6	7	8	9	10
0	0	1	2	3	4	5	6	7	8	9	10
1	1	2	3	4	5	6	7	8	9	10	11
2	2	3	4	5	6	7	8	9	10	11	12
3	3	4	5	6	7	8	9	10	11	12	13
4	4	5	6	7	8	9	10	11	12	13	14
5	5	6	7	8	9	10	11	12	13	14	15
6	6	7	8	9	10	11	12	13	14	15	16
7	7	8	9	10	11	12	13	14	15	16	17
8	8	9	10	11	12	13	14	15	16	17	18
9	9	10	11	12	13	14	15	16	17	18	19
10	10	11	12	13	14	15	16	17	18	19	20

Addition and Subtraction Facts

Addition Fact Helpers

These strategies can help with many of the addition facts.

To add:	Think of:
0	No change
1	Counting on 1
2	Counting on 2
4	One less than adding 5
5	Finger sets—one more hand
6	One more than adding 5
9	One less than adding 10
10	Write 1 in the tens place

Subtraction Fact Helpers

These strategies can help with some of the subtraction facts. For other subtraction facts, think of the corresponding addition fact.

To subtract:	Think of:
0	No change
1	Counting back 1
5	Finger sets—taking away one hand
9	One more than subtracting 10
10	Subtracting 1 from the tens digit

Addition

One Way to Add

$$\begin{array}{r} 685 \\ +\ 267 \\ \hline \end{array}$$

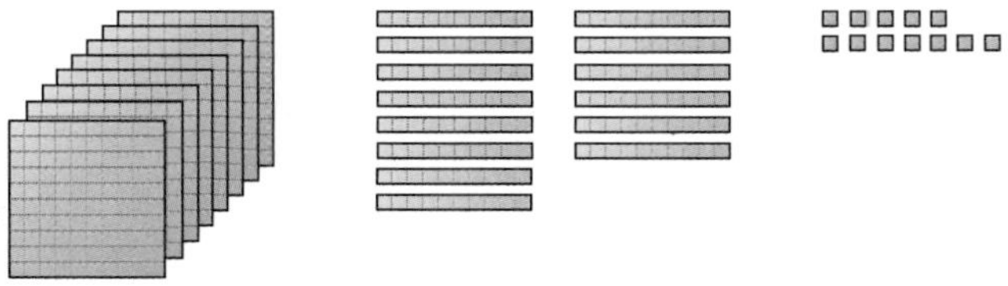

We start at the right because it is easier that way. Add ones.
5 + 7 = 12. 12 ones = 1 ten and 2 ones.

$$\begin{array}{r} 1 \\ 685 \\ +\ 267 \\ \hline 2 \end{array}$$

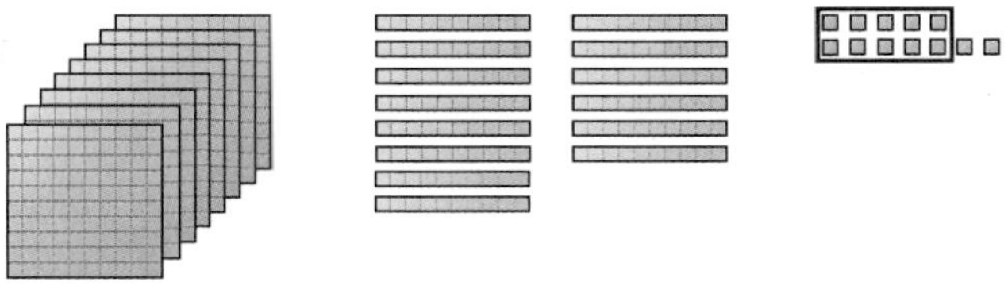

Add tens. 1 + 8 + 6 = 15. 15 tens = 1 hundred and 5 tens.

$$\begin{array}{r} 11 \\ 685 \\ +\ 267 \\ \hline 52 \end{array}$$

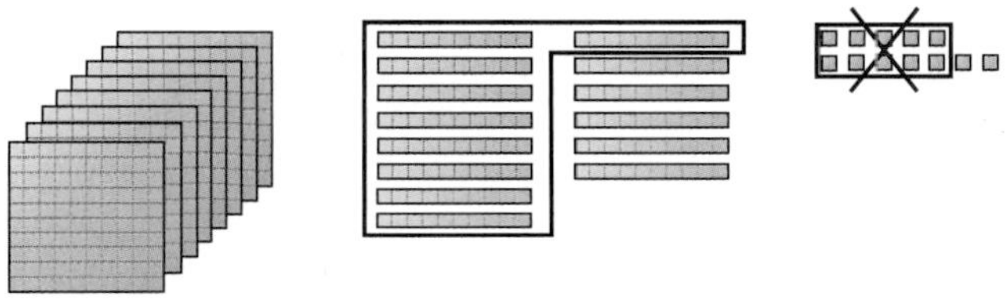

Add hundreds. 1 + 6 + 2 = 9.

$$\begin{array}{r} 11 \\ 685 \\ +\ 267 \\ \hline 952 \end{array}$$

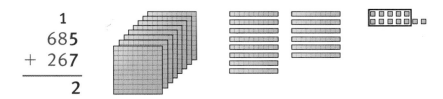

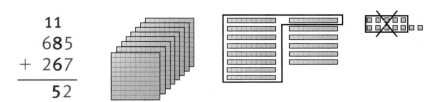

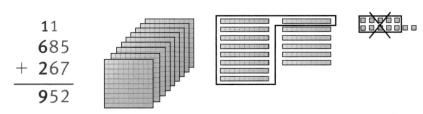

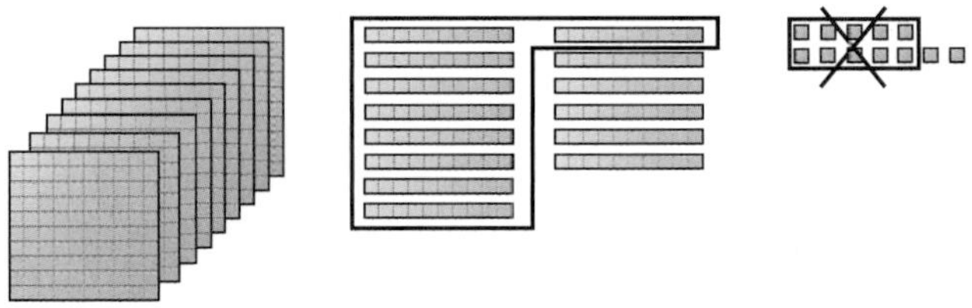

Addition Laws

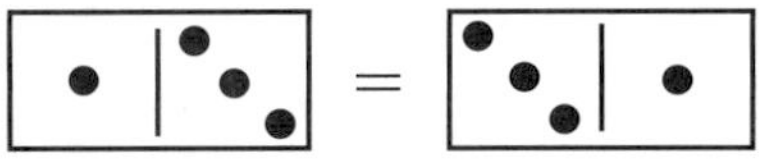

Commutative Law of Addition

The order of two numbers does not affect their sum. For example, the sum of $1 + 3$ is the same as the sum of $3 + 1$.

Associative Law of Addition

When adding three numbers, it does not matter whether the first pair or the last pair is added first.

$5 + 4 + 3 = (5 + 4) + 3 = 5 + (4 + 3)$

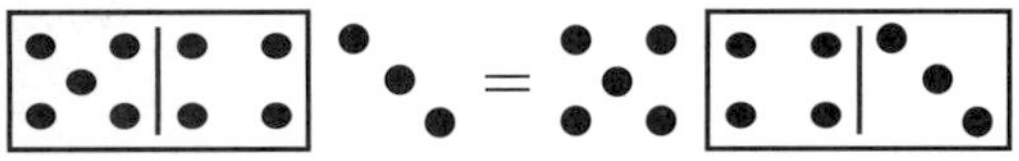

$9 + 3$ $\quad$ $5 + 7$

Additive Identity

Adding a number to 0 gives that number.

$6 + 0 = 6$

Additive Inverse

Adding a positive number and a negative number with the same absolute value (distance from 0) gives 0.

$4 + (-4) = 0$.

Subtraction

One Way to Subtract

365
− 178

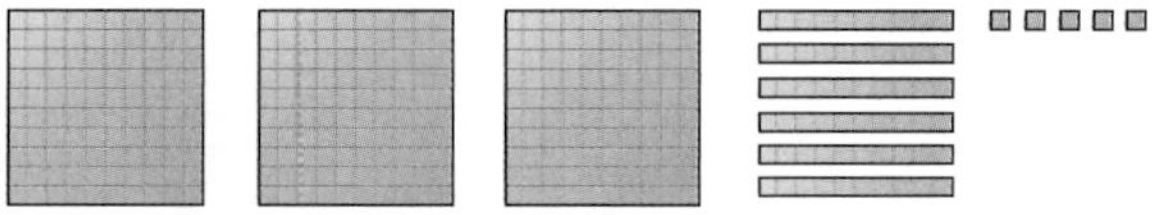

Start at the right because it is easier.

There are not enough ones to subtract 8, so rename 6 tens as 5 tens and 10 ones.

5 15
365
− 178

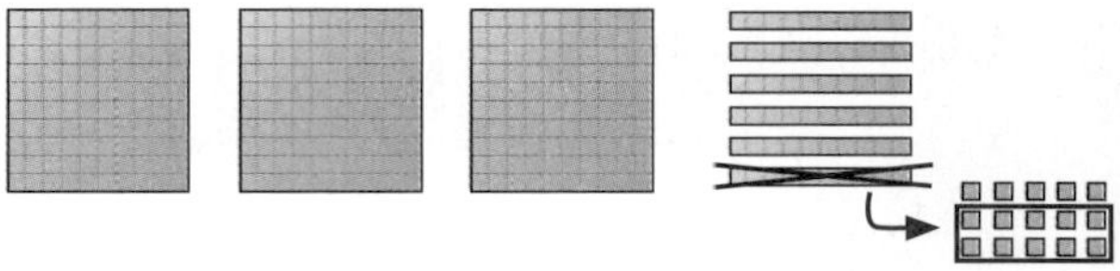

Subtract ones.

5 15
365
− 178
7

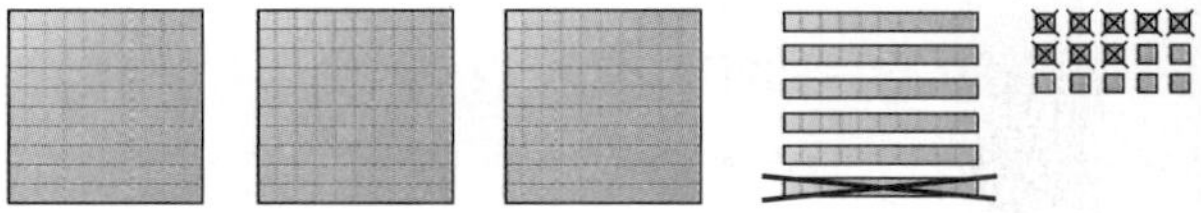

There are not enough tens to subtract 7, so rename 3 hundreds as 2 hundreds and 10 tens.
Subtract tens.

2 15 15
365
− 178
87

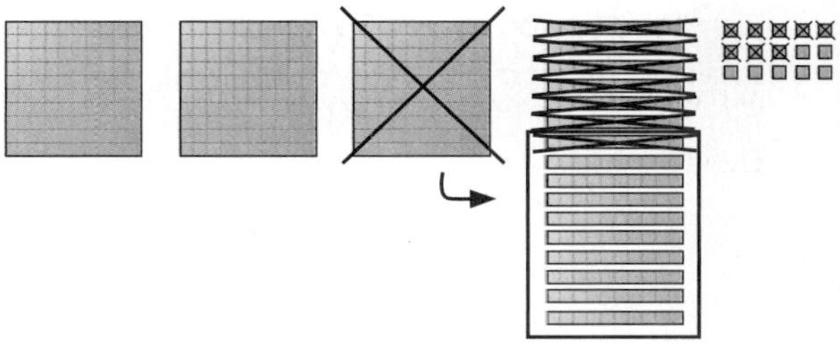

Subtract hundreds.

2 15 15
365
− 178
187

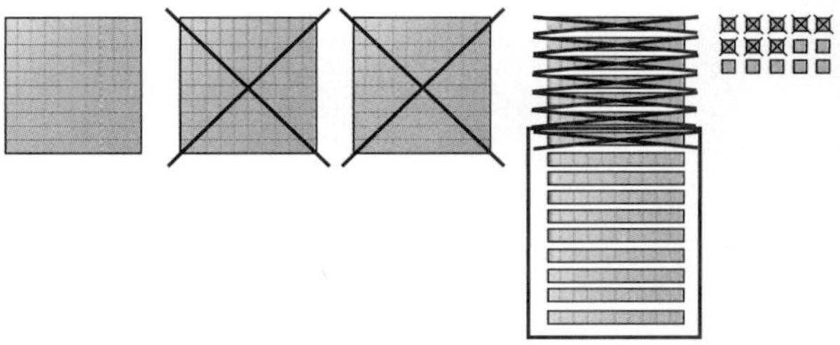

Multiplication Table

You can use the Multiplication Table to find basic facts.

×	0	1	2	3	4	5	6	7	8	9	10	11	12
0	0	0	0	0	0	0	0	0	0	0	0	0	0
1	0	1	2	3	4	5	6	7	8	9	10	11	12
2	0	2	4	6	8	10	12	14	16	18	20	22	24
3	0	3	6	9	12	15	18	21	24	27	30	33	36
4	0	4	8	12	16	20	24	28	32	36	40	44	48
5	0	5	10	15	20	25	30	35	40	45	50	55	60
6	0	6	12	18	24	30	36	42	48	54	60	66	72
7	0	7	14	21	28	35	42	49	56	63	70	77	84
8	0	8	16	24	32	40	48	56	64	72	80	88	96
9	0	9	18	27	36	45	54	63	72	81	90	99	108
10	0	10	20	30	40	50	60	70	80	90	100	110	120
11	0	11	22	33	44	55	66	77	88	99	110	121	132
12	0	12	24	36	48	60	72	84	96	108	120	132	144

Multiplication Facts

Fact Helper Strategies

To multiply by:

10 Write a "0" after the number.
9 Subtract the number from 10 times the number.
0 The answer is 0.
1 The answer is the number.
2 Add the number to itself.
5 Multiply half the number by 10 if it is even. If the number is odd, multiply half of the next smaller number by 10 and add 5.
4 Double the number, and then double that answer.
3 Add the number to its double.
8 Double 4 times the number, or subtract the number from 9 times the number.
6 Double 3 times the number.
7 If you've learned all the other facts and can remember that $7 \times 7 = 49$, you know all the multiples of 7.

Fact Families

Fact families show how multiplication and division are related.

$2 \times 3 = 6$	$6 \div 2 = 3$
$3 \times 2 = 6$	$6 \div 3 = 2$

Multiplication

Think of multiplication as finding many areas.

	100	100	100	10	10	10	10	6
10								
10								
10	$300 \times 50 = 15,000$			$40 \times 50 = 2,000$				
10								
10								
2	$300 \times 2 = 600$			$40 \times 2 = 80$				

$6 \times 2 = 12$

$6 \times 50 = 300$

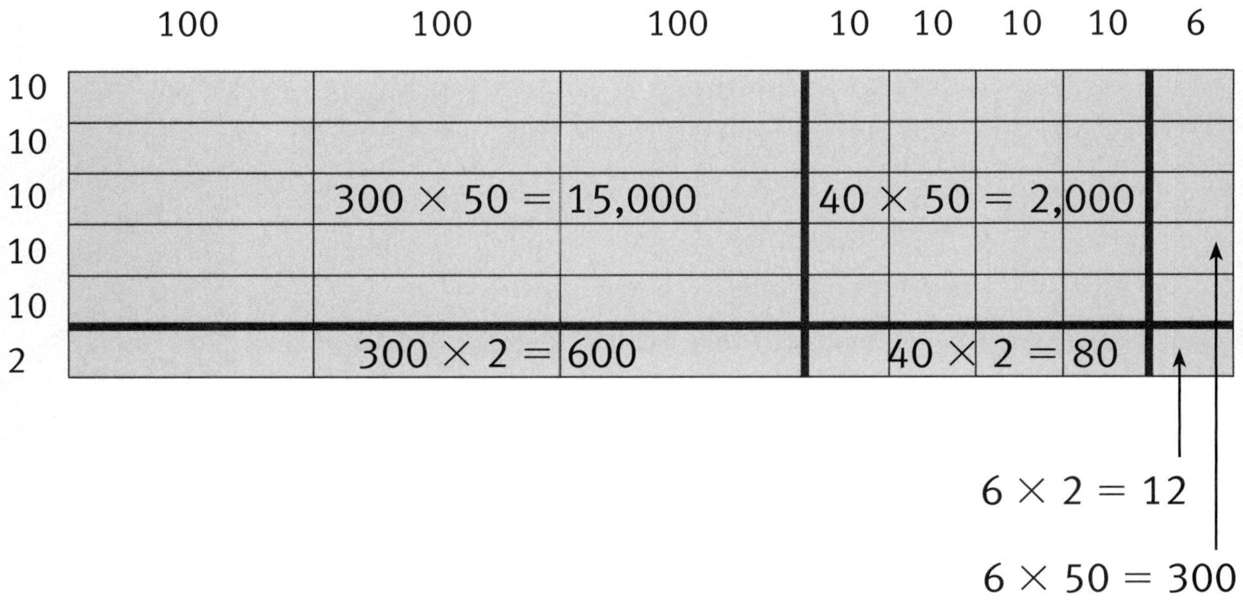

Partial Products

Multiplying using partial products may help you keep track of place values. Starting with the rightmost column, multiply each position in the top number by the ones-column digit, then the tens-column digit, and so on. Then add the partial products to find the final product. You could start with any column, but it is easier if you start on the right.

$$
\begin{array}{r}
346 \\
\times\ 52 \\
\hline
\end{array}
$$

$2 \times 6 = 12$	12
$2 \times 40 = 80$	80
$2 \times 300 = 600$	600
$50 \times 6 = 300$	300
$50 \times 40 = 2,000$	2000
$50 \times 300 = 15,000$	+ 15000
Add partial products.	17992

A Shorter Way to Multiply

Beginning at the rightmost column, find the product. Write the ones digit of the product below the line in the ones column, and write the tens digit at the top of the tens column. Then repeat this process for each digit of the second factor.

$$\begin{array}{r} 346 \\ \times \quad 52 \\ \hline \end{array}$$

Multiply 2 times the ones. $6 \times 2 = 12$
12 ones = 1 ten and 2 ones

Multiply 2 times 4 tens, and add the carried ten.
$(2 \times 4) + 1 = 9$

$$\begin{array}{r} ^{1}\;\; \\ 346 \\ \times \quad 52 \\ \hline 2 \end{array} \qquad \begin{array}{r} ^{1}\;\; \\ 346 \\ \times \quad 52 \\ \hline 92 \end{array}$$

Multiply 2 times 3 hundreds. $2 \times 3 = 6$

$$\begin{array}{r} ^{1}\;\; \\ 346 \\ \times \quad 52 \\ \hline 692 \end{array}$$

Multiply 5 tens times 6 ones. $5 \times 6 = 30$
30 tens = 3 hundreds and 0 tens

Multiply 5 tens times 4 tens, and add the carried hundreds. $(5 \times 4) + 3 = 23$
23 = 2 thousands and 3 hundreds

$$\begin{array}{r} ^{3}\;\;\; \\ 346 \\ \times \quad 52 \\ \hline 692 \\ 00\; \end{array} \qquad \begin{array}{r} ^{2\,3}\;\;\; \\ 346 \\ \times \quad 52 \\ \hline 692 \\ 300 \end{array}$$

Multiply 5 tens times 3 hundreds, and add the carried thousands. $(5 \times 3) + 2 = 17$
17 thousands = 1 ten thousand and 7 thousands

$$\begin{array}{r} ^{2\,3}\;\;\; \\ 346 \\ \times \quad 52 \\ \hline 692 \\ 17300 \end{array}$$

Add partial products.

$$\begin{array}{r} ^{2\,3}\;\;\; \\ 346 \\ \times \quad 52 \\ \hline 692 \\ +\; 17300 \\ \hline 17992 \end{array}$$

Division

One Way to Divide

$5\overline{)423}$

Five does not divide into 4, but it will divide into 42 eight times.

$$\begin{array}{r} 8 \\ 5\overline{)423} \\ 40 \end{array}$$

Subtract 40 from 42.

$$\begin{array}{r} 8 \\ 5\overline{)423} \\ -\,40 \\ \hline 2 \end{array}$$

Bring down the next digit, 3.

$$\begin{array}{r} 8 \\ 5\overline{)423} \\ -\,40 \\ \hline 23 \end{array}$$

Five divides into 23 four times.

$$\begin{array}{r} 84 \\ 5\overline{)423} \\ -\,40 \\ \hline 23 \\ 20 \end{array}$$

Subtract 20 from 23.

$$\begin{array}{r} 84 \\ 5\overline{)423} \\ -\,40 \\ \hline 23 \\ -\,20 \\ \hline 3 \end{array}$$

$423 \div 5 = 84$ R3

Divisibility Patterns

Divisibility by 2

An even number is a number divisible by 2. We can recognize even numbers because their last digit must also be divisible by 2 (the last digit must be 0, 2, 4, 6, or 8). For example, 78,950 has a 0 as its last digit; therefore, it's divisible by 2.

Divisibility by 3

A number is divisible by 3 if the sum of its digits is divisible by 3. The number 492,603 has a digit sum of 24. Twenty-four is divisible by 3; therefore, 492,603 is divisible by 3.

Divisibility by 5

We can recognize a number that is divisible by 5 because its last digit must be either a 0 or a 5. The number 47,825 has a 5 as its last digit; therefore, it's divisible by 5.

Divisibility by 11

A two-digit number is divisible by 11 if the two digits are equal to each other. Take 33, for example: $3 = 3$, so 33 is divisible by 11. There are patterns for divisibility by 11 for numbers greater than 100. Can you find them?

Geometric Figures

Plane Figures

Circle A circle is composed of all points in a plane the same distance from the center.

Polygon A polygon is a closed figure with sides that are all line segments.

Angles Angles are measured based on the amount of turn they represent. A quarter turn is a right angle. Angles of less than a quarter turn are acute angles. Angles of more than a quarter turn but less than half a turn are obtuse angles.

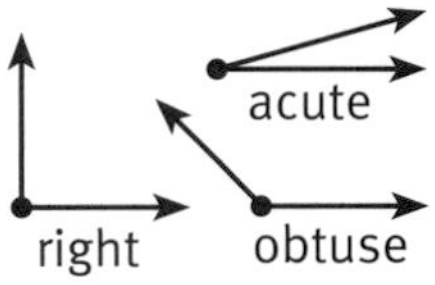

Triangle A triangle is a polygon with three sides.

Polygons

Rectangle A rectangle has four sides with opposite pairs of sides of equal length and four right angles.

Square A square is a quadrilateral with four equal sides and four right angles.

Rhombus A rhombus is a quadrilateral with four equal sides.

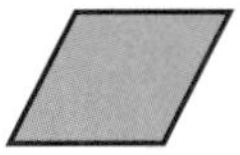

Trapezoid A trapezoid is a quadrilateral with two sides parallel.

Pentagon A pentagon is a polygon with five sides.
Hexagon A hexagon is a polygon with six sides.

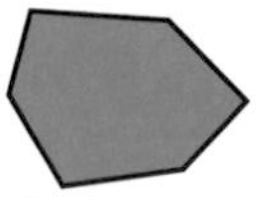

hexagon

pentagon

Space Figures

Cube A cube is a space figure with six square faces.
Sphere A sphere is a space figure composed of all points in space the same distance from its center.
Cone A cone is a space figure made by connecting every point on a circle or other plane figure to a point not on the figure.
Cylinder A cylinder is a space figure with two parallel bases (usually circles).
Polyhedron A polyhedron is a closed space figure whose faces are polygons.

cube

sphere

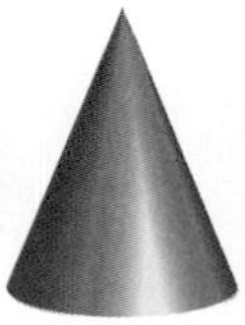

cone

cylinder

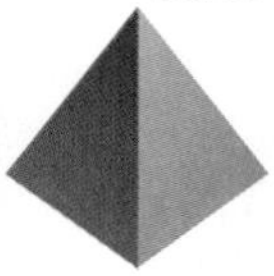

polyhedron

Measurements

Decimal and Metric Prefixes

1000 = thousand = *kilo-*
100 = hundred = *hecto-*
10 = ten = *deca-*
0.10 = tenth = *deci-*
0.01 = hundredth = *centi-*
0.001 = thousandth = *milli-*

The basic units in the metric system are *meter, gram,* and *liter.*

Measuring Length

Metric	Equivalency
1 millimeter (mm)	1mm: -
1 centimeter (cm)	10 millimeters
1 decimeter (dm)	10 centimeters
1 meter (m)	100 centimeters
1 dekameter (dam)	10 meters
1 hectometer (hm)	100 meters
1 kilometer (km)	1,000 meters

Customary	Equivalency
1 inch (in.)	1 inch: ————
1 foot (ft)	12 inches
1 yard (yd)	3 feet
1 mile (mi)	5,280 feet 1,760 yards

Measuring Temperature

Celsius		Fahrenheit
0	Water Freezes	32
100	Water Boils	212

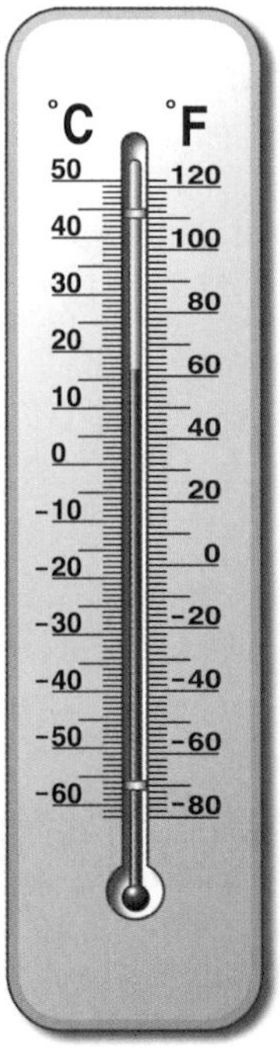

Measuring Weight (Mass)

Metric	Equivalent
1 gram (g)	a dollar bill weighs about 1 gram
1 dekagram (dag)	10 grams
1 hectogram (hg)	100 grams
1 kilogram (kg)	1,000 grams
1 metric ton (t)	1,000 kilograms

Customary	Equivalent
1 ounce (oz)	11 pennies weigh about 1 ounce
1 pound (lb)	16 ounces
1 ton	2,000 pounds

Measuring Capacity

Metric	Equivalent
1 milliliter (mL)	an eyedropper holds about 1 milliliter
1 centiliter (cL)	0.01 liter
1 deciliter (dL)	0.1 liter
1 liter (L)	1,000 milliliters
1 dekaliter (daL)	10 liters
1 hectoliter (hL)	100 liters
1 kiloliter (kL)	1,000 liters

Customary	Equivalent
1 fluid ounce (fl oz)	approximately the volume of 1 ounce of water
1 cup (c)	8 fluid ounces
1 pint (pt)	2 cups
1 quart (qt)	2 pints
1 gallon (gal)	4 quarts

Time

Months of the Year

Month	Number of Days
January	31
February	28, except in leap year every four years when there are 29
March	31
April	30
May	31
June	30
July	31
August	31
September	30
October	31
November	30
December	31

Equivalents of Time

60 seconds	1 minute
60 minutes	1 hour
24 hours (the time it takes Earth to rotate)	1 day
7 days 168 hours	1 week
12 months $52\frac{1}{7}$ weeks 365.25 days (the time it takes Earth to revolve around the sun)	1 year

A.M. (ante meridiem; before midday) means between midnight and noon

P.M. (post meridiem; after midday) means between noon and midnight

Military or 24-Hour Time Equivalents

1:00	1 A.M.	7:00	7 A.M.	13:00	1 P.M.	19:00	7 P.M.
2:00	2 A.M.	8:00	8 A.M.	14:00	2 P.M.	20:00	8 P.M.
3:00	3 A.M.	9:00	9 A.M.	15:00	3 P.M.	21:00	9 P.M.
4:00	4 A.M.	10:00	10 A.M.	16:00	4 P.M.	22:00	10 P.M.
5:00	5 A.M.	11:00	11 A.M.	17:00	5 P.M.	23:00	11 P.M.
6:00	6 A.M.	12:00	12 Noon	18:00	6 P.M.	24:00	12 Midnight

A.D. or C.E. means the common era, after the year 0

B.C. or B.C.E. means before the common era, before the year 0

Frequency Tables

A frequency table shows tally marks and how often each kind of data occurs in a set of data.

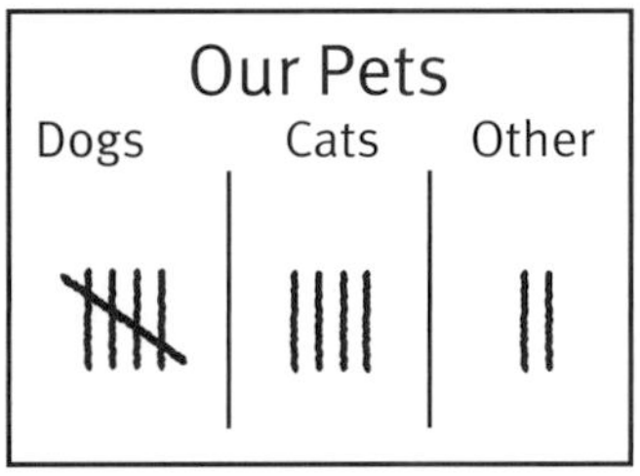

Tally Marks

Tally marks are used to keep count.

Tallies of Five

Tally marks represent 5 when four tallies are combined with one diagonal mark.

Graphs

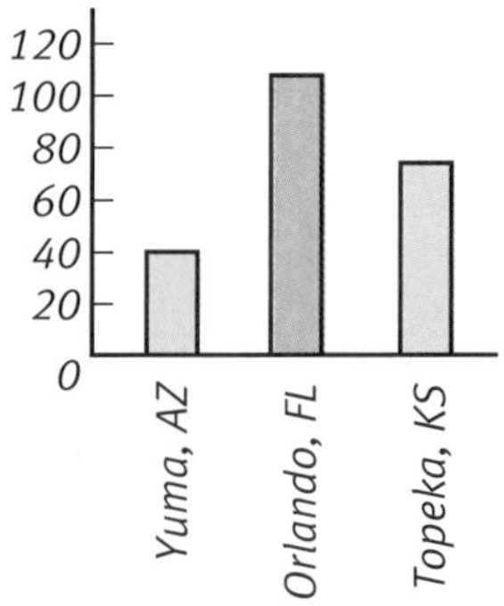

Bar Graph

A bar graph is a graph with bars of lengths that represent amounts.

Circle Graph

A circle graph has sectors that represent different categories.

Line Graph

A line graph connects points to show change over time.

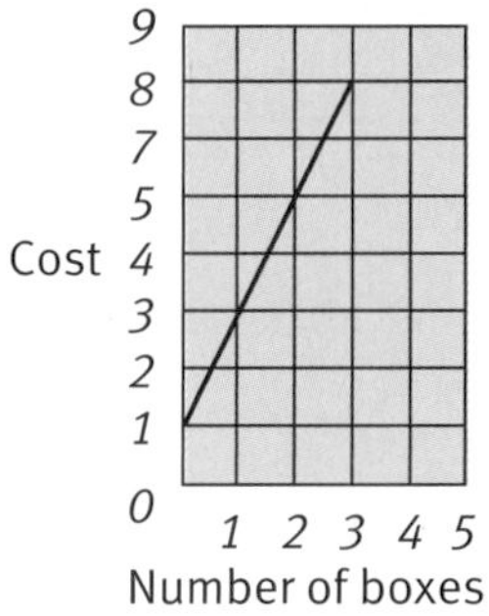

Fractions, Decimals, and Percentages

Fractions, decimals, and percentages are called *rational numbers* because they can be written as ratios. Whole numbers, counting numbers, integers, fractions, decimals, improper fractions, and mixed numbers are all examples of rational numbers.

Percentages are special ratios that compare a number to 100.

A ratio is the comparison of two quantities by division, such as a fraction.

Ratios are commonly used to relate one number to another. Ratios have no labels. There are three major representations of ratios: 3 out of 4, 3:4, and $\frac{3}{4}$. Probabilities are represented most often by ratios.

The ratio of blue to red dots can be written $\frac{2}{5}$.
The ratio of blue dots to the total number of dots is $\frac{2}{7}$.

A number line helps you think about rational numbers. You can see whole numbers, negative numbers, and fractions as belonging to the same system.

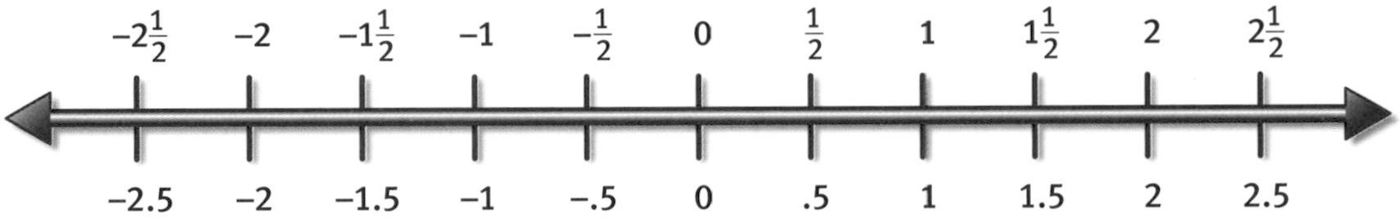

Benchmark for Fractions, Decimals, and Percentages

Fractions, decimals, and percentages can all represent the same rational number or part of a whole.

$1 = 1.0 = 100\%$

$\frac{3}{4} = 0.75 = 75\%$

$\frac{1}{2} = 0.5 = 50\%$

$\frac{1}{4} = 0.25 = 25\%$

$\frac{1}{8} = 0.125 = 12.5\%$

3 — *numerator*
4 — *denominator*

Algebraic Functions

A function pairs a number (the input) with a second number (the output).
A function table lists the pairs of numbers.

If a girl is 3 years older than her brother, you can say:

Brother's age + 3 = Sister's age

No matter how old they are, the sister will always be three years older than her brother.

$\rightarrow (+3) \rightarrow$

in	out
1	4
2	5
3	6
4	7
5	8

A **function machine** shows the input, output, and rule for a function. A **function rule** tells how the input of a function is related to the output of a function.

Composite functions involve more than one step in the function rule.

$$x \rightarrow (\times 3) \rightarrow n \rightarrow (+3) \rightarrow y$$

Linear functions create a straight line when graphed.

An **equation** is a mathematical statement showing that one quantity or expression is equal to another quantity or expression. These are the sentences of mathematical language.

Math Symbols

$+$	Plus Add	$7 + 3 = 10$
$-$	Minus Subtract	$10 - 3 = 7$
$\times$ or * on the computer	Times Multiply	$3 \times 2 = 6$
$\div$, $\overline{)\quad}$, or / on the computer	Divided by	$6 \div 2 = 3$
$=$	Is equal to	$4 + 2 = 6$
¢	Cents	39¢
$	Dollars	$1.00
°F	Degrees Fahrenheit	100°F
°C	Degrees Celsius	25°C
$>$	Greater than	$47 > 39$
$<$	Less than	$2 + 6 < 10$
4^3 ← exponent ↑ base	Exponents are used as a shorthand notation to show repeated multiplication.	$4^3 = 4 \times 4 \times 4 = 64$
$\angle$	Angle	$\angle ABC$
Δ	Triangle	ΔJKL
$\cong$	Is congruent to	$\angle ABC \cong \angle DEF$
$\backsim$	Is similar to	$\Delta JKL \backsim \Delta ABC$

Glossary

A

acute angle **\ə kūt'** *n.* an angle which measures between 0° and 90°

These are acute angles:

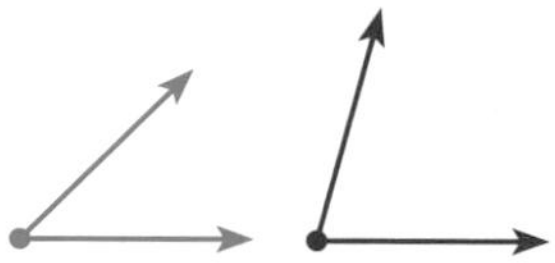

addend **\ad' end** *n.* any number or quantity that is to be added to another; for example:

```
 35 —— addend     7 + 8 = 15 —sum
+48 —— addend     |     └──── addend
 83 —— sum        └────────── addend
```

A.M. (ante meridiem) *abbr.* before noon; the time from midnight to noon

angle **\ang'gəl** *n.* the figure formed by two rays extending from the same point

approximate **\ə prok' sə māt'** *v.* to come near or close. **\ə prok' sə mit** *adj.* nearly correct or exact

approximation **\ə prok' sə mā' shən** *n.* something that is nearly correct, as an estimated amount

area **\âr' ē ə** *n.* the measure of the interior, or inside, of a figure; the area of this rectangle is 6 square centimeters:

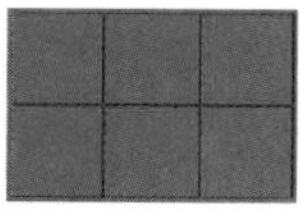

array **\ə rā'** *n.* a group of objects arranged in an orderly way in rows and columns

associative\ə sō"shē ā'tiv *adj.* a law stating that the sum or product of two or more quantities will be the same regardless of the way in which they are grouped

axes (of a graph) **\ak' sēs** *n.* the two zero lines of a graph that give the coordinates of points

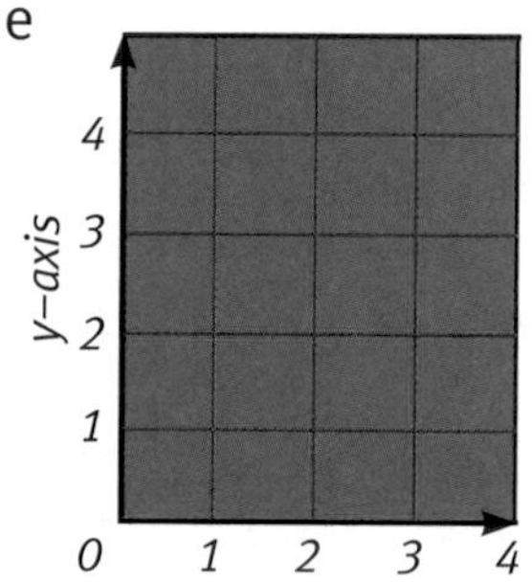

B

bar graph **\bär** *n.* a graph that uses bars (rectangles) to represent data

benchmark **\bench märk** *n.* something that serves as a standard or reference by which something else can be measured or compared

C

capacity **\kə pas' i tē** *n.* the amount (of anything) a container can hold

center **\sen 'tər** *n.* a point within a circle equally distant from every point on the circle

centimeter **\sen" tə mē'\ tər** *n.* a unit of length equal to one-hundredth of a meter; The prefix *centi-* means "one hundredth."

circle **\sûr' kəl** *n.* a continuous, closed curved line, every point of which is equally distant from the center

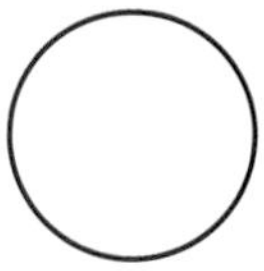

Commutative Law of Multiplication *n.* the order of factors does not affect the product when multiplying; generally, for any numbers a and b, $a \times b = b \times a$

congruent **\kən grü' ənt** *adj.* figures that are the same size and same shape; that is, they fit perfectly when placed on top of one another

coordinates **\kō ôr" də nits** *n.* a pair of numbers that gives the location of a point on a graph; also called an ordered pair of numbers. In the figure shown, for example, the coordinates of point A are (2, 3). The *x*–coordinate is 2 and the *y*–coordinate is 3.

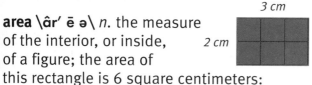

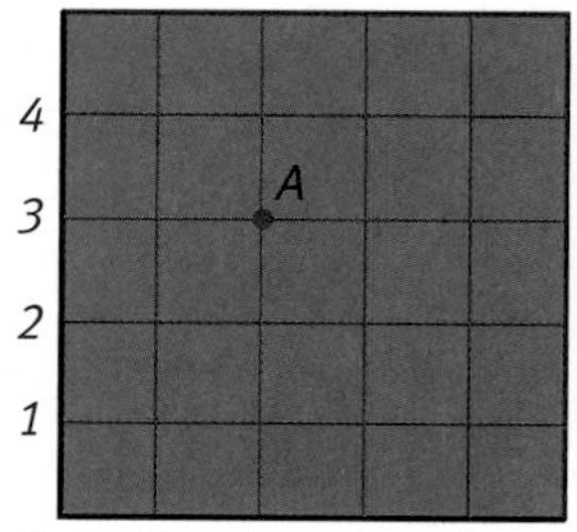

cube **\kūb** *n.* a solid figure with six equal, square sides

cubic units *n.* units that are used to measure volume

cup **\kup** *n.* a customary measure of capacity equal to 16 fluid ounces

cylinder **\sil′ ən dər** *n.* a solid geometric figure bounded by two equal, parallel circles and a curved surface that is formed by a straight line moving parallel to itself with its ends always on the circumferences of the circles

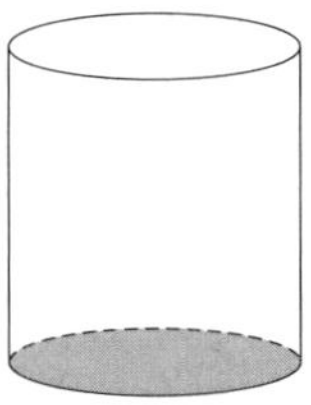

D

data **\dā′ tə, dat′ ə** *pl. n.* information from which conclusions can be drawn; facts and figures

decimal point *n.* a dot used in separating the ones digit from the tenths digit

decimeter **\de sə** *n.* a metric measure of length equal to one-tenth of a meter

degree **\di grē** *n.* a unit of measurement for angles or temperature

denominator **\di nom′ ə nā′ tər** *n.* a number below the line in a fraction that indicates the number of equal parts into which the whole is divided

diameter **\dī am′ i tər** *n.* a straight line passing through the center of a circle or sphere, from one side to the other

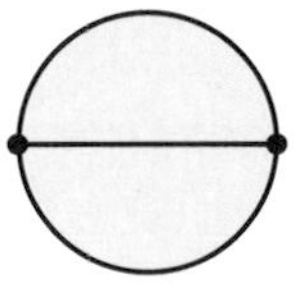

difference **\dif′ rəns** *n.* remainder left after subtracting one quantity from another
For example:

43 — minuend
− 16 — subtrahend
27 — difference

10 − 7 = 3 — difference
7 — subtrahend
10 — minuend

digit **\dij′ it** *n.* any of the ten Arabic numerals from 0 through 9

Distributive Law *n.* a law stating that the product of multiplication is the same when the operation is performed on a whole set as when it is performed on the individual members of the set: $4 \times (2 + 5) = 4 \times 2 + 4 \times 5$

dividend **\div′ i dend** *n.* the number that is to be divided; for example:

6 ÷ 3 = 2 — quotient
3 — divisor
6 — dividend

divisor — 8)347 — dividend
43 — quotient
− 32
27
− 24
3

division **\di vizh' ən** *n.* the act of separating into parts or pieces; in mathematics, the process of dividing two numbers to show how many times one number contains the other number

divisor **\di vī′ zər** *n.* the number the dividend is to be divided by

double **\dub′ əl** *n.* to make a number twice as great by adding the number to itself (multiplying by 2)

E

edge **\ej** *n.* a line or place where an object or area begins or ends; extreme or outermost border; a line segment where two faces meet or a planar area begins or ends

Glossary

elapsed \i lapst' *n.* the amount of time that has passed

equation \i kwā' zhən *n.* a mathematical statement showing that one quantity or expression is equal to another quantity or expression

equilateral \ē' kwə lat'ər əl *adj.* having all sides equal in length

equivalent \i kwiv' ə lənt *adj.* having the same value

equivalent fractions \i kwiv' ə lənt *n.* fractions that name the same rational number

estimate \n., es' tə mit; v., es' tə māt' *n.* a judgment or opinion, as of the value, quality, extent, size, or cost of something. *v.* to form a judgment or opinion (based on available information) about the extent or size of something; calculate

even number *n.* a number that can be divided exactly by two

exponent \ek spō' nənt *n.* a numeral or symbol placed at the upper right side of another numeral or symbol to indicate the number of times it is to be used as a factor

F

face \fās *n.* a plane figure that serves as one side of a space figure

fact family \fakt fam'ə lē *n.* a group of number sentences that uses the same numbers to relate addition and subtraction

factor \fak' tər *n.* numbers you multiply to get a product; for example:
3 (multiplier) × 5 (multiplicand) = 15 (product)

foot \fu̇t *n.* a customary measure of length equal to 12 inches

fraction \frak' shən *n.* a quantity expressing the division of one number by a second number, written as two numerals separated by a line

frequency \frē' kwen sē *n.* the number of times something happens

function \fungk' shən *n.* a relationship that pairs every element of one set with an element of a second set; for example, a relationship that pairs any number with another number

function machine *n.* a machine (sometimes imaginary) that does the same thing to every number that is put into it

G

gallon \ga' lən *n.* a customary measure of capacity equal to 4 quarts

graph \graf *n.* a diagram showing the relationship between two or more sets of data

greatest common factor *n.* the greatest factor shared by a pair of numbers

grid \grid *n.* a pattern of intersecting lines that divides a map or table into small squares

H

halfway \haf' wā *n.* in the middle

heptagon \hep' tə gon' *n.* a plane figure having seven sides and seven angles

hexagon \hek' sə gon' *n.* a plane figure having six sides and six angles

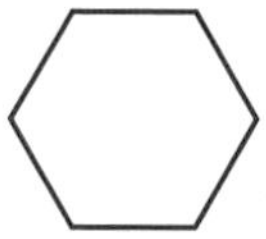

hour \au(ə)r *n.* a measure of time equal to 60 minutes

hundredth **\hun′ dridth** *n.* one of a hundred equal parts; $\frac{1}{100}$

hypotenuse **\hī pot′ ə nūs′** *n.* the side of a right triangle opposite the right angle

I

improper fraction *n.* a fraction whose numerator is greater than, or equal to, its denominator

inequality **\in′ i kwol′ i tē** *n.* mathematical statement showing that two numbers are not equal or that one number is greater than or less than another number

integer **\in′ ti jər** *n.* any positive or negative whole number or zero

intersecting lines
n. lines that meet and cross each other

inverse **\in′ vərs** *n.* opposite in order

isosceles **\ī säs′ lēz** *adj.* having two equal sides. These are isosceles triangles:

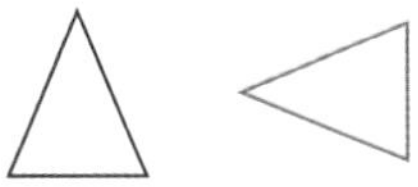

K

kilo– **\kē′ lo; kil′ ō** *prefix* one thousand

kilometer **\ki lom′ i tər, kil′ ə mē′ tər** *n.* a unit of length in the metric system equal to 1,000 meters

L

least common multiple *n.* the smallest multiple of a pair of numbers

length **\lengkth** *n.* describes how long something is

line **\līn** *n.* a straight path that extends infinitely in opposite directions, thought of as having length but no thickness

line graph *n.* a graph that represents data as ordered pairs connected with a line

line of symmetry *n.* a line on which a figure can be folded into two or more congruent parts

line plot *n.* a data graph showing frequency on a number line

line segment *n.* a part of a line with two endpoints

M

mean **\mēn** *n.* the typical or usual amount, which is found by dividing the sum of two or more quantities by the number of quantities

median **\mē′ dē ən** *n.* the middle number in a set of data

metric system *n.* a decimal system of measurement that uses the meter as the fundamental unit of length

milliliter **\mil′ ə lē′ tər** *n.* a metric measure of capacity equal to one thousandth of a liter

millimeter **\mil′ ə mē′ tər** *n.* a metric measure of length equal to one thousandth of a meter

minuend **\min′ ū end′** *n.* the number from which another is to be subtracted

minute **\min′ it** *n.* a measure of time equal to 60 seconds

mixed number *n.* a number consisting of a whole number and a fraction

mode **\mōd** *n.* the number appearing most frequently in a set of data

Glossary

multiple \mul′ tə pəl *n.* a number that is some whole number times another number; for example, 12 is a multiple of 2 because $2 \times 6 = 12$

multiplicand \mul tə pli kand′ *n.* a number multiplied by another number, the multiplier

For example:

```
  5  ——— multiplicand
× 3  ——— multiplier
 15  ——— product
```

```
3 × 5 = 15 —product
|   |_______ multiplicand
|___________ multiplier
```

multiplier \mul′ tə plī ər *n.* a factor of a product

multiply \mul′ tə plī′ *v.* to find the product of a number that is repeatedly added to itself $(4 + 4 + 4 + 4 = 4 \times 4 = 16)$

N

negative \ne′gə tiv *n.* less than zero

net \net *n.* a pattern used to create a space figure

number line *n.* a line of infinite extent whose points correspond to the real numbers according to their distance in a positive or negative direction from a point arbitrarily taken as zero

numeral\nü′ mər əl *n.* a symbol that represents a number, such as 7 or VII

numerator \nü′ mə rā′ tər *n.* the part of a fraction written above the line; the numerator tells how many parts are being referred to

O

obtuse angle *n.* an angle that is greater than 90°

These are obtuse angles:

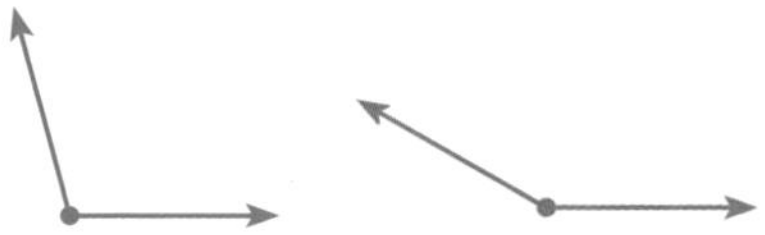

octagon \ok′ tə gon′ *n.* a polygon having eight sides and eight angles

odd number *n.* a whole number that cannot be divided into two equal whole numbers

ordered pair *n.* a set of numbers that describes the location of a point on a graph; an example is (3, 4)

outcome \out′ kum *n.* a result or consequence

outlier\out′ līər *n.* a number that is far off from all other numbers in a data set

P

parallel lines *n.* lines that are the same distance apart and that go in the same direction and never meet

parallelogram \par′ ə lel′ ə gram′ *n.* a quadrilateral that has two pairs of parallel sides

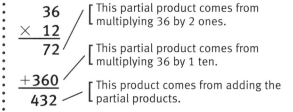

parentheses \pə ren′ thə sēz *n.* curved marks ( ) used to enclose symbols or numbers to indicate which expression to evaluate first

partial product *n.* the product that comes from multiplying the multiplicand by one of the digits of the multiplier: for example:

```
   36
×  12
   72   [This partial product comes from multiplying 36 by 2 ones.
 +360   [This partial product comes from multiplying 36 by 1 ten.
  432   [This product comes from adding the partial products.
```

pattern \pat′ ərn *n.* an arrangement or design of colors, shapes, or lines

pentagon \pen′ tə gon′ *n.* a polygon with five line segments as sides

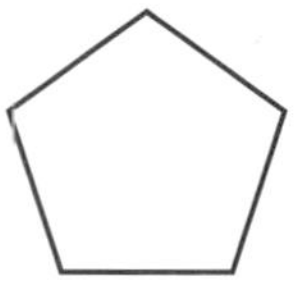

percent \pər sent′ *n.* a fraction with a denominator of 100; the number of parts in every hundred

perimeter \pə rim′ i tər *n.* the length of the path around a figure

perpendicular lines *n.* lines that intersect at right angles

pictograph \pik′ tə graf *n.* a graph that uses pictures or symbols to represent data

pint\pīnt′ *n.* a customary measure of capacity equal to 2 cups

place value *n.* the value of a digit determined by its position within a number

plane \plān *n.* a flat surface wholly containing every line connecting any two points on it

plane figure *n.* a figure having only height and width

P.M. (post meridiem) *abbr.* after noon; the time from noon to midnight

point\point *n.* something having position but no length, width, or height

polygon \pä′ lē gän′ *n.* a closed plane figure with three or more line segments as sides

polyhedron \pä′ lē hē′ drən *n.* a space figure that has only flat faces, which are polygons

pound\paůnd *n.* a customary measure of weight equal to 16 ounces

prism \priz′ əm *n.* a solid having two congruent and parallel faces, and whose other faces are parallelograms

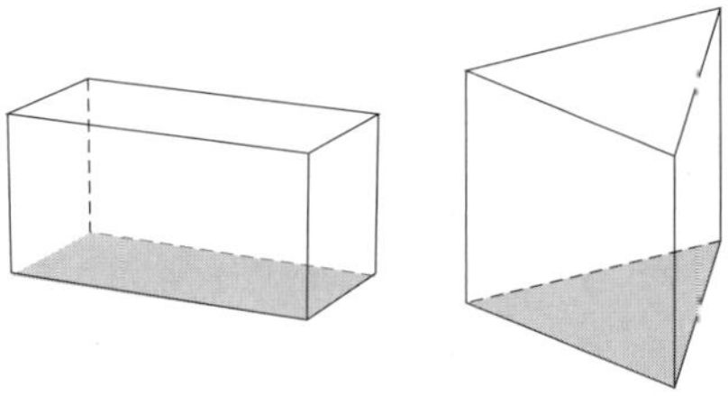

prisms

probability \prob′ ə bil′ i tē *n.* how likely it is for something to happen

product \prod′ əkt *n.* the result of multiplying two (or more) numbers together

profit \prof′ it *n.* the amount remaining after all the costs of a business have been paid

pyramid \pir′ ə mid′ *n.* a solid figure having a polygon for a base and triangular sides intersecting at a point

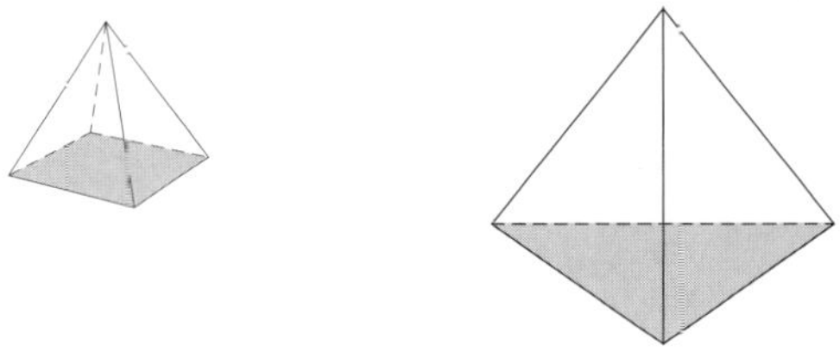

Q

quadrilateral \kwod′ rə lat′ ər əl *n.* a polygon with four sides and four angles

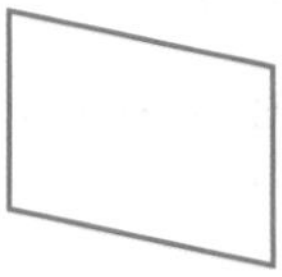

quart\kwort *n.* a customary measure of capacity equal to 2 pints

quarter\kwôr′ tər *n.* one-fourth of an hour; fifteen minutes

quotient \kwō′ shənt *n.* the answer to a division problem

R

radius \rā′ dē əs *n.* a line segment going from the center to the outside of a circle or sphere

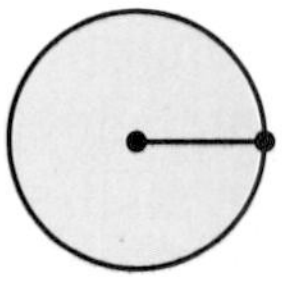

Glossary

range \rānj\ *n.* the difference between the greatest and least numbers in a set of data

ray \rā\ *n.* a set of points that has one endpoint and extends forever in one direction

rectangle \rek′ tang′ gəl\ *n.* a parallelogram having four right angles

reflection \ri flek′ shən\ *n.* a change in the location of a figure when it is flipped over a line

regroup \rē grüp\ *v.* to rename a number to make adding and subtracting easier

$$\begin{array}{r} {\scriptstyle 1\ 15} \\ \not{2}\not{5} \\ -\ 17 \\ \hline 8 \end{array}$$

(To subtract in the ones column, 2 tens and 5 is regrouped as 1 ten and 15.)

regular polygon *n.* a polygon with sides of equal length

relation signs *n.* the three basic relation signs are > (greater than), < (less than), and = (equal to)

remainder \ri mān′ dər\ *n.* the number left over when a set of objects is shared equally or separated into equal groups. For example, when you divide 25 by 4, the quotient is 6 with a remainder of 1

$$\begin{array}{r} 6\ \text{R1} \\ 4\overline{)25} \\ -\ 24 \\ \hline 1 \end{array}$$

rhombus \räm′ bəs\ *n.* a parallelogram whose sides are all the same length

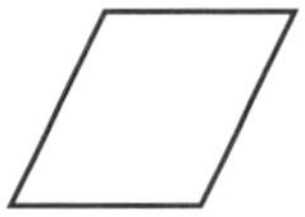

right angle *n.* an angle measuring 90°

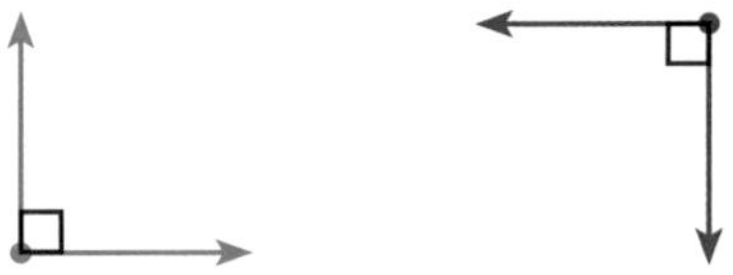

right triangle *n.* a triangle with one right angle

rotation \rō tā′ shən\ *n.* a change in the location of a figure when it is turned in a circle around a point

rounding \round ing\ *v.* changing a number to another number that is easier to work with and that is close enough for the purpose

S

sample \sam′ pəl\ *n.* a smaller set of data that belongs to a larger set of data and reflects the characteristics of members in a larger set

scale \skāl\ *n.* a series of marks made along a line at regularly spaced intervals; used in measuring

scatter plot *n.* a graph that represents data as ordered pairs

segment \seg′ mənt\ *n.* a part of a line with two endpoints

set \set\ *n.* a collection of numbers, points, objects, or other things that are grouped together

similar \sim′ ə lər\ *adj.* figures that have the same shape, but that differ in size

sphere \sfîr\ *n.* a round three-dimensional figure having all the points at an equal distance from the center

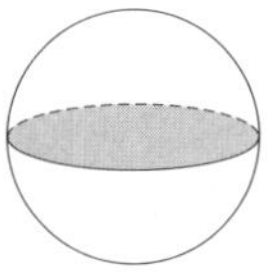

square \skwâr\ *n.* a plane figure having four sides of equal length and four right angles

standard \stan′ dərd\ *adj.* widely accepted and used as a model

stem-and-leaf plot *n.* a data graph showing data from least to greatest using the digits from the greatest place value to group the data

subtrahend \sub′ trə hend\ *n.* the number that is to be subtracted from another

sum \sum\ *n.* a result obtained from addition

surface area *n.* the sum of the areas of the faces of a space figure

symmetry \sim′ i trē\ *n.* having the same size and shape across a dividing line

T

table \tā′ bəl\ *n.* graphic display of information

tally \tal′ ē\ *n.* a series of marks to keep a record of data

tenth \tenth\ *n.* one of ten equal parts

term \tûrm\ *n.* a number or other symbol that is connected by addition or subtraction to another term

translation \tranz la′ shən\ *n.* a change in the location of a figure when it slides without being turned

trapezoid \trap′ ə zoid′\ *n.* quadrilateral with exactly one pair of parallel lines

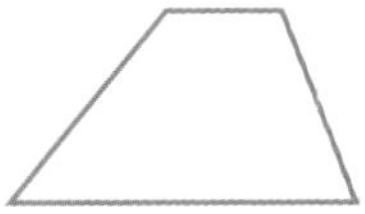

tree chart *n.* a display of data that shows possible combinations where the trunk represents the first set of choices and the branches represent the second, third, and so on set of choices

triangle \trī′ ang gəl′\ *n.* a plane figure with three sides and three angles

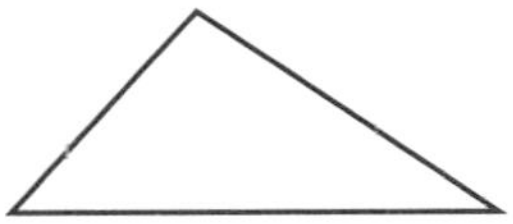

U

unit cost *n.* the cost of one out of a number of goods or services

upper and lower bounds *n.* numbers that an answer must be less than or greater than

V

variable \vâr′ ē ə bəl\ *n.* a symbol representing a quantity that can have any of a set of values

variability \vâr′ ē ə bil ity\ *n.* the likelihood that something will change

vertex \ver′ teks\ *n.* 1. the point of intersection of two rays 2. the point of intersection of three edges of a space figure

volume \vol′ ūm\ *n.* the amount of space anything fills

W

weight \wāt\ describes how much something weighs

withdrawal \with drô′ əl\ *n.* the act of taking away or removing

whole number *n.* a number that tells how many complete things there are

Y

yard \yärd\ *n.* a customary measure of length equal to 3 feet

Z

zero \zîr′ ō\ *n.* the number that leaves any number unchanged when it is added to it

Index

Index

G

H

I

J

K

L

M

Index

N

O

P

Q

R

S

Index

Photo Credits

Cover © Morgan Cain & Associates; **i** © Pete Stone/CORBIS; **ii** © David Madison/Getty Images, Inc.; **iv** © Dave King/Getty Images, Inc.; **v** © PhotoDisc/Getty Images, Inc.; **vi** © age fotostock/SuperStock; **vii** © PhotoDisc/Getty Images, Inc.; **ix** © Kit Houghton/CORBIS; **x** © Kevin Miller/Getty Images, Inc.; **xi** © Robert Landau/CORBIS; **xii** © Alex Mares-Manton/Getty Images, Inc.; **2** © David Young-Wolff/Photo Edit; **4** © Digital Vision/Getty Images, Inc.; **6** (b) © Pete Stone/CORBIS; **6** (tr) © Royalty-Free/CORBIS; **8** © Matt Meadows; **9** © PhotoDisc/Getty Images, Inc.; **10** © Peter Adams/Getty Images, Inc.; **11** © Geoff Dann/Getty Images, Inc.; **19** © Bob Daemmrich/Photo Edit; **21** © Comstock Images/Alamy; **22** © Brand X Pictures/Getty Images, Inc.; **24** (t) © PhotoDisc/Getty Images, Inc.; **24** (b) © Henry Westheim Photography/Alamy; **40** © Martin Barraud/Getty Images, Inc.; **43** © Royalty-Free/CORBIS; **45, 46** © Matt Meadows; **51** © Kayte M. Deioma/Photo Edit; **53** © Matt Meadows; **54** © Stockdisc/Getty Images, Inc.; **57** (l) © PhotoDisc/Getty Images, Inc.; **57** (r) © Brand X Pictures; **64** © Kenna Love/Getty Images, Inc.; **65** © Digital Vision/Getty Images, Inc.; **67** © David Madison/Getty Images, Inc.; **68, 69** © Tony Hopewell/Getty Images, Inc.; **71, 72** © PhotoDisc/Getty Images, Inc.; **74** © Bettmann/CORBIS; **75** © Lee Lockwood/Time Life Pictures/Getty Images; **76** (tr) © PhotoDisc/Getty Images, Inc.; **76** (cr) © Angelo Cavalli/Getty Images, Inc.; **77** (b) © Jeremy Horner/CORBIS; **77** (tr) © Erich Lessing/Art Resource, NY; **80** (b) © Matt Meadows; **81** (tr) © Comstock Images/Getty Images, Inc.; **96** © Rudi Von Briel/Photo Edit; **98, 104** © PhotoDisc/Getty Images, Inc.; **106** (tr, 2, 4, 7) © Matt Meadows; **106** (3, 6) © PhotoDisc/Getty Images, Inc.; **106** (4) © Royalty Free/CORBIS; **107** © PhotoDisc/Getty Images, Inc.; **108** (tr, 5) © Matt Meadows; **108** (1, 2, 3) © PhotoDisc/Getty Image, Inc.; **108** (4) © Ken Cavanagh; **117** © PhotoDisc/Getty Images, Inc.; **120** © David Young-Wolff/Photo Edit; **121** (l) © PhotoDisc/Getty Images, Inc.; **121** (r) © F. Damm/zefa/CORBIS; **122** © Royalty-Free/CORBIS; **123** © David Young-Wolff/Getty Images, Inc; **126** © PhotoDisc/Getty Images, Inc.; **138** © T. Ozonas/Masterfile; **140** (t to b) © Ken Cavanagh; **140** (2) © Matt Meadows; **140** (3) © Dave King/Getty Images, Inc; **140** (4) © PhotoDisc/Getty Images, Inc..; **141** (t to b, 2) © Matt Meadows; **141** (3) © Brand X Pictures/Getty Images, Inc..; **143** © Matt Meadows; **147** (l) © Matt Meadows; **147** (r) © Comstock Images/Alamy; **147** (c) © Ken Cavanagh/The McGraw-Hill Companies Inc; **150** (b) © Matt Meadows; **152, 154** © PhotoDisc/Getty Images, Inc.; **168** © PhotoDisc/Getty Images, Inc.; **174** © Gary S. Chapman/Getty Images, Inc.; **176, 177, 178** © PhotoDisc/Getty Images, Inc.; **179, 180** © Royalty-Free/CORBIS; **181** © PhotoDisc/Getty Images, Inc.; **181** © Royalty-Free/CORBIS; **188** (tl) © Brand X Pictures/Getty Images, Inc.; **188** (br) © PhotoDisc/Getty Images, Inc.; **189** © PhotoDisc/Getty Images, Inc.; **190** © Royalty-Free/CORBIS; **192** © Brand X Pictures; **193** (t) © PhotoDisc/Getty Images, Inc.; **193** (cr, bl, br) © Phillip Colla/oceanlight.com; **194, 195** © PhotoDisc/Getty Images, Inc.; **196** © Matt Meadows; **197** © PhotoDisc/Getty Images, Inc.; **198** © Matt Meadows; **214** © age fotostock/SuperStock; **216** © Eyewire/Getty Images, Inc.; **217** © PhotoDisc/Getty Images, Inc.; **230** © Gabe Palmer/CORBIS; **232** (tr) © Brand X Pictures/Getty Images, Inc.; **232** (cr) © PhotoDisc/Getty Images, Inc.; **232** (br) © Eyewire/Getty Images, Inc.; **233** © PhotoDisc/Getty Images, Inc.; **248** © Jim Cummins/Getty Images, Inc.; **250** © Matt Meadows; **251** (t) © Matt Meadows; **251** (b) © Davidson Madison/Getty Images, Inc.; **252** © Brand X Pictures/Getty Images, Inc.; **254** © Ariel Skelley/CORBIS; **257** © Ryan McVay/Getty Images, Inc.; **258** (t) © Judith Haeusler/Getty Images, Inc.; **258** (b) © Matt Meadows; **264, 265** © PhotoDisc/Getty Images, Inc; **266** © Carl Schneider/Getty Images, Inc.; **267** (t) © Markus Cuff/CORBIS; **267** (b) © Stockdisc/Getty Images, Inc.; **270** © PhotoDisc/Getty Images, Inc.; **272** © Tom Stewart/CORBIS; **273** © Gabe Palmer/zefa/CORBIS; **274** (tr) © Gabe Palmer/CORBIS; **274** © Matt Meadows; **276** © PhotoDisc/Getty Images, Inc.; **281** © LWA-Dann Tardif/CORBIS; **284** © Royalty-Free/CORBIS; **287** © Amanda Hall/Getty Images, Inc.; **287** © Taxi/Getty Images, Inc.; **292, 294, 298, 299** © Matt Meadows; **300** © Ken Cavanagh; **301** (t) © PhotoDisc/Getty Images, Inc.; **301** (b) © Matt Meadows; **302** © Royalty-Free/CORBIS; **306** © Matt Meadows; **308** © PhotoDisc/Getty Images, Inc.; **309** (br) © PhotoDisc/Getty Images, Inc.; **314** © Matt Meadows; **319** © Michael T. Sedam/CORBIS; **342** © Tony Freeman/Photo Edit; **344** © Matt Meadows; **345** © PhotoDisc/Getty Images, Inc.; **346** © Brand X Pictures/Getty Images, Inc.; **347** © PhotoDisc/Getty Images, Inc.; **348** © SuperStock/age fotostock; **349** © Ken Cavanagh/The McGraw-Hill Companies, Inc.; **350** (l) © Matt Meadows; **350** (r) © PhotoDisc/Getty Images, Inc.; **351** (t to b) © Kit Houghton/CORBIS; **351** (2) © Dave King/Getty Images, Inc.; **351** (3) © Stephen Ogilvy/The McGraw-Hill Companies, Inc.; **351** (4, 6) © PhotoDisc/Getty Images, Inc.; **351** (5) © Royalty-Free/CORBIS; **356** © Matt Meadows; **357** (b) © Bob Elsdale/Getty Images, Inc.; **357** (tr, cr, br) © PhotoDisc/Getty Images, Inc.; **357** (cl) © Brand X Pictures/Getty Images, Inc.; **358** (tl, bl, br) © PhotoDisc/Getty Images, Inc.; **358** (tr, cr) © Matt Meadows; **359** (tl) © PhotoDisc/Getty Images, Inc.; **359** (tr, br) © Matt Meadows; **359** (bl) © Morton & White; **360** (tl) © Royalty-Free/CORBIS; **360** (tr) © Matt Meadows; **360** (cr) © Frithjof Hirdes/zefa/CORBIS; **360** (bl) © PhotoDisc/Getty Images, Inc.; **360** (br) © Comstock Images/Alamy; **361** (tl) © Seth Wenig/Reuters/CORBIS; **361** (tr) © Royalty-Free/CORBIS; **361** (cl) © Michael N. Paras/CORBIS; **361** (cr) © Matt Meadows; **361** (bl) © Robert Holmes/CORBIS; **361** (br) © Ken Karp/The McGraw-Hill Companies, Inc.; **362** © PhotoDisc/Getty Images, Inc.; **363** © Felix Clouzot/Getty Images, Inc.; **365** © PhotoDisc/Getty Images, Inc.; **380** © Bill Ross/CORBIS; **382** © Matt Meadows; **383** © PhotoDisc/Getty Images, Inc.; **384** (r) © PhotoDisc/Getty Images, Inc.; **385** (r) © PhotoDisc/Getty Images, Inc.; **385** (t) © Matt Meadows; **387** (t) © PhotoDisc/Getty Images, Inc.; **387** (b) © Darrell Gulin/Getty Images, Inc.; **388, 389** © PhotoDisc/Getty Images, Inc.; **390** (t) © Stockdisc/Getty Images, Inc.; **390** (b) © Thinkstock/Getty Images, Inc.; **391** © Rubberball Productions/Getty Images, Inc.; **398, 399** © Stockdisc/Getty Images, Inc.; **400** © Royalty-Free/CORBIS; **401** © David Noton/Getty Images, Inc.; **402** (b) © Stockdisc/Getty Images, Inc.; **402** (tr) © Royalty-Free/CORBIS; **403** © Streeter Lecka/Getty Images, Inc.; **404** © PhotoDisc/Getty Images, Inc.; **405** (t) © Rubberball Productions/Getty Images, Inc.; **405** (b) © Matt Meadows; **406** © David Young-Wolff/Photo Edit; **422** © Robert Landau/CORBIS; **424** © PhotoDisc/Getty Images, Inc.; **425** © Ryan McVay/Getty Images, Inc.; **426** © PhotoDisc/Getty Images, Inc.; **432** © Emma Lee/Life File/Getty Images, Inc.; **436** © Diego Lezama Orezzoli/CORBIS; **450** © Matt Meadows; **452** © Morgan Art Foundation Limited/Art Resource, NY; **457** © David Madison/Getty Images, Inc.; **465** © Matt Meadows; **480** © Angelo Cavalli/Getty Images, Inc.; **481** © Alex Mares-Manton/Getty Images, Inc.; **482** © PhotoDisc/Getty Images, Inc.; **487** © APA/Getty Images; **488** © Brand X Pictures/Getty Images, Inc.; **495** © Matt Meadows; **497** © Royalty-Free/CORBIS; **498** © Lew Robertson/Getty Images, Inc.; **507** © Matt Meadows; **510** © PhotoDisc/Getty Images, Inc.